THE ARCHITECT'S STUDIO COMPANION

RULES OF THUMB FOR PRELIMINARY DESIGN

Fourth Edition

Edward Allen and Joseph Iano

BICENTENNIAL
1807
WILEY
2007
BICENTENNIAL

John Wiley & Sons, Inc.

DISCLAIMER

The information in this book has been interpreted from sources that include building codes, industry standards, manufacturers' literature, engineering reference works, and personal contacts with many individuals. It is presented in good faith, but although the authors and the publisher have made every reasonable effort to make this book accurate and authoritative, they do not warrant, and assume no liability for, its accuracy or completeness or its fitness for any particular purpose. The user should note especially that this is a book of first approximations, information that is not intended to be used for final design of any building or structure. It is the responsibility of users to apply their professional knowledge in the use of information contained in this book, to consult original sources for more detailed information, and to seek expert advice as needed, especially in the later stages of the process of designing a building.

For general information about our other products and services, please contact our Customer Care Department within the United States at (800) 762-2974, outside the United States at (317) 572-3993 or fax (317) 572-4002.

Wiley also publishes its books in a variety of electronic formats. Some content that appears in print may not be available in electronic books. For more information about Wiley products, visit our web site at www.wiley.com.

Library of Congress Cataloging-in-Publication Data:

ISBN-13: 978-0-471-73622-6(cloth)
ISBN-10: 0-471-73622-8 (cloth)

Printed in the United States of America

10 9 8 7 6 5 4 3 2 1

CONTENTS

ACKNOWLEDGMENTS

The authors would like to acknowledge the many individuals who have contributed to the making of this book:

At John Wiley & Sons, Joseph Iano would especially like to thank Paul Drougas, Acquisitions Editor, for his unflagging support through every stage of the writing and production of this fourth edition. During production, Lauren LaFrance, Assistant Developmental Editor; Donna Conte, Senior Production Editor; Raheli Millman, assistant to Paul Drougas; and Helen Greenberg, copyeditor, each played invaluable parts. Amanda Miller, Associate Publisher, deserves special mention for the support she has provided to both authors through many years and many projects. Both authors also would like to express their everlasting thanks to Judith R. Joseph and Claire Thompson, editors during the publication of this book's first edition, and Karin Kincheloe, designer, for their special roles in bringing this book from its original concept to first publication.

The preparation of this fourth edition was aided by the valuable comments and suggestions of reviewers Elliot Dudnick of the University of Illinois at Chicago, Dan Faoro of Lawrence Technological University, Ralph Hammann of the University of Arizona, James Edwin Mitchell of Drexel University, Kevin Nute of the University of Oregon, Mahesh Senagala of the University of Texas at San Antonio, Sandy Stannard of California Polytechnic State University San Luis Obispo, Bruce E. Moore of Drury University, and Diane Armpriest of the University of Idaho. Previous editions of this book benefited from the review and comments of David Glasser of Temple University, Roger N. Goldstein of Goody, Clancy Associates, Jack Kremers of Kent State University, Sandra Davis Lakeman of California Polytechnic University, Alan Levy of the University of Pennsylvania, John Reynolds of the University of Oregon, Donald Prowler of the University of Pennsylvania, and Marc Shiler of the University of Southern California. Joseph Iano also would like to thank David Lipe for his assistance with the preparation of the manuscript for this fourth edition.

Many more professionals graciously have offered to share their expertise with the authors during the formative stages of this book's technical content. Professor Carl Bovill of the University of Maryland strongly influenced this book's underlying philosophy. Professor Stephen Vamosi of the University of Cincinnati contributed expertise in mechanical and electrical systems, as did Robert Heryford, P.E., and Peter S. Watt, P.E., of R.G. Vanderweil Associates, and Marvin Mass of Cosentini Associates. Richard J. Farley of the University of Pennsylvania and Daniel Schodek of Harvard University gave valuable advice on structural matters. Joel Loveland of the University of Washington provided much helpful advice in the development of daylighting design guidelines. Additional contributions were made by Harvey Bryan, Mark Dooling, Jerry Hicks, Douglas Mahone, and Peter Stone.

Joseph Iano finally would like to express his gratitude to Lesley, Allen, Paul, and Ethan, for all their support and patience, and to Edward Allen, for the knowledge and friendship he has shared over many years. Edward Allen thanks Mary M. Allen and expresses his extreme gratitude to Joseph Iano for his expertise, imagination, and friendship.

HOW TO USE THIS BOOK

This book is your desktop technical advisor for the earliest stages of building design. It reduces complex engineering and building code information to simple formal and spatial approximations that are readily incorporated into design explorations. If you are not familiar with this book, below is a recommended pathway for completing the preliminary design of your building.

For more detailed guidance on how to use the information in this book, see the full example beginning on page 455. Alternatively, information in this book may be accessed in any sequence that fits your particular needs or approach to designing buildings. To jump to any major topic in this book, use the quick index that appears on the inside cover. From within any particular section, you may also follow the many cross references to related information in other parts. In the end, we hope this becomes your personalized handbook, an essential reference for your way of creating buildings.

Step 1: Determine your building code and occupancy. Starting on page 5, determine what model building code to use for your project and what Occupancy Groups apply to the planned activities within your building. These pieces of information are your key to unlocking information throughout other sections of this book.

Step 2: Find what types of construction are permitted for your project. Based on the information determined in Step 1, consult the Height and Area Tables that begin on page 350 to determine what code-defined Construction Types are permitted for a building of your size and use.

Step 3: Complete a preliminary structural design. Review possible structural systems for your project, beginning on page 22, and consider approaches to the overall configuration of such systems, beginning on page 37. Once you have settled on a system for further study, you can complete a preliminary structural layout and assign approximate sizes to the system's major elements using information beginning on page 53.

Step 4: Consider using daylighting. Use the information beginning on page 146 to study the potential benefits and formal implications of using daylight illumination in your project.

Step 5: Plan for mechanical and electrical systems. Use the information beginning on page 166 for large buildings, or on page 223 for small buildings, to consider heating and cooling systems that meet the needs of your project. Once a viable system has been selected, use the information in the following sections to allocate spaces within your building for its HVAC, electrical, plumbing, and other systems.

Step 6: Determine building code requirements for egress and accessibility. Use the information that begins on page 253 to lay out the necessary components of your building's exiting system. If needed, incorporate provisions for accessibility as well.

Step 7: Add accommodations for parking. If provision for parking is a requirement of your project, use the information beginning on page 315 to evaluate both surface and structured parking options.

THE ARCHITECT'S
STUDIO COMPANION

DESIGNING WITH BUILDING CODES

1
DESIGNING WITH BUILDING CODES

This section will help you determine which model building code to apply to the project you are designing and, within that code, to which Occupancy Groups your project belongs. You will need to know these two facts to have full access to the information throughout this book.

BUILDING CODES AND ZONING ORDINANCES

A designer works under complex legal constraints that exert a powerful influence on the form a building may take. Local zoning ordinances control building uses, heights, areas, distances from property lines, and on-site parking capacities. Building codes enacted at the local, county, state, or provincial level regulate everything from building heights and areas to the types of interior finish materials that may be used. Further constraints are often imposed by local fire districts, by state regulations pertaining to particular uses, and by national regulations governing equal access to public facilities and housing.

Zoning laws and use-specific codes are most often promulgated at the local or state level and do not lend themselves to simple generalization from one jurisdiction to the next. For this reason, this book does not attempt to address these requirements, and the designer should consult local regulations for guidance in these areas. On the other hand, although building codes are also enacted at local levels, the vast majority of North American building codes are derived from just a few nationally recognized "model codes." The use of model codes as the basis for the majority of local building codes results in sufficient standardization that these regulations can be simplified and generalized in a meaningful way. Thus, preliminary

guidelines can be provided for incorporating building code requirements into your project.

This book provides building code information based on two model building codes: the International Code Council's *International Building Code,* and the National Research Council of Canada, Institute for Research in Construction's *National Building Code of Canada.* These two model codes form the basis for the vast majority of building codes enacted by jurisdictions throughout the United States and Canada. This book condenses, from these two model codes, the provisions that have the most direct and important effects on building form: height and area limitations, beginning on page 349, and requirements for the design of egress systems, starting on page 251. Code requirements having to do with the detailed design of structural and mechanical components of buildings are reflected here indirectly through the preliminary sizing charts for structural elements (pages 53–143) and the rules of thumb for providing space for mechanical and electrical systems (pages 165–249).

To make use of the information provided in this book, start by selecting the model code appropriate to your project: for projects in the United States, the International Building Code, and for projects in Canada, The National Building

Code of Canada. Next, consult the appropriate code-specific index that follows to ascertain the Occupancy Group or Groups for the building you are designing. These two pieces of information—model code and occupancy—are the keys that will unlock code-related information throughout other sections of this book.

The building code information provided in the following pages is intended for preliminary purposes. The extent to which this information may accurately reflect the code and other regulations with which any particular project must comply will differ from one locale to another: In some instances, a jurisdiction may adopt one of the model codes included in this book almost verbatim. In many cases, you will find that your project's locale has adopted one of these model codes, but with amendments or alterations to its requirements. And occasionally, you may encounter a jurisdiction that has written its own code or based its regulations on a model not addressed in this book. For these reasons, before becoming too deeply immersed in your design, be sure exactly which codes and regulations govern your project and verify that the information you use fully and accurately reflects the legal requirements that apply, whether that information comes from this book or from other sources.

WHICH BUILDING CODE TO CONSULT

If your project is in the United States, use the International Building Code, starting on this page, as the basis for determining preliminary code requirements for your project. If your project is in Canada, use the National Building Code of Canada, starting on page 13. For more information about model building codes and their applicability to your project, see page 5.

OCCUPANCY CLASSIFICATION

Buildings, or portions of buildings, are classified by the activities for which they are used, termed *Occupancy Groups.* These classifications reflect the relative life-safe-ty hazard associated with the activities and occupant characteristics. In general, buildings intended for larger numbers of occupants, for public use, and for inherently hazardous activities are afforded greater levels of protection than those planned for smaller groups, private uses, or nonhazardous activities. Use the following two tables to determine which occupancy groups most appropriately describe your project.

If your building contains multiple uses, determine the occupancy classification for each part. Later in this book, you will find more information on how to apply the various code requirements to such mixed-use facilities; if you would like to learn more about mixed-use buildings right now, turn to pages 352–355.

GENERAL DESCRIPTION OF OCCUPANCY GROUPS

The following table describes each Occupancy Group according to the classifications of the International Building Code.

Occupancy	General Description
A ASSEMBLY	Assembly occupancies include social, recreational, entertainment, and civic gatherings of 50 or more persons. Assembly occupancy includes five subgroups:
	A-1: This group includes theaters for the viewing of motion pictures, dramatic arts, and performances, usually with fixed seating.
	A-2: This group includes food and drink establishments.
	A-3: This group includes recreational, amusement, and worship uses not specifically falling under other Assembly groups, including, for example, galleries, auditoriums, churches, community halls, courtrooms, dance halls, gymnasiums, lecture halls, libraries, museums, passenger station waiting areas, and the like.
	A-4: This group includes indoor sports arenas with spectator seating.
	A-5: This group includes outdoor sports arenas.
	Gathering spaces less than 750 sq ft (70 m^2) in area or accommodating fewer than 50 persons are treated as Group B, Business occupancies or, when located within other occupancies, as part of the surrounding occupancy. Assembly spaces located within Group E, Educational facilities are treated as part of the Group E occupancy.
B BUSINESS	Business occupancies include office, professional, and service activities, and storage of related records and accounts. Business occupancy also includes education facilities past the 12th grade, but does not include retail or wholesale sales, which are classified as Group M Mercantile.

(continued)

OCCUPANCY GROUPS: INTERNATIONAL BUILDING CODE

Occupancy	General Description
E EDUCATIONAL	Educational occupancies include schools for grades K through 12 and day care facilities for children older than 2½ years of age with 6 or more occupants. Assembly areas within Group E facilities are treated as part of the Group E occupancy. Day care for not more than 100 children 2½ years of age or less may also be classified as a Group E occupancy when each day care room is located on the level of exit discharge and has an exit door opening directly to the exterior.
	Educational facilities above the 12th grade are classified as Group B Business. Educational rooms and auditoriums within religious facilities are considered part of that facility's overall classification, usually Group A-3 Assembly. Day care facilities with 5 or fewer occupants are classified as Group R-3 Residential.
F FACTORY	Factory occupancies include manufacturing and industrial processes, except those considered highly hazardous, which are classified as Group H, Hazardous. Factory occupancy has two subgroups:
	F-1: This group includes manufacturing and industrial processes using materials of moderate flammability, such as those involving aircraft, appliances, automobiles, machinery, electronics, plastics, printing, and woodworking.
	F-2: This group includes manufacturing and industrial processes using nonflammable materials, such as those involving nonalcoholic beverages, brick and masonry, ceramics, glass, gypsum, ice, and metal fabrication.
HAZARDOUS	Hazardous occupancies include manufacturing, processing, or storage of materials with a high potential for health or physical safety hazard. Hazardous use classifications are specific and detailed about the amounts and types of explosive, flammable, corrosive, or toxic materials involved. If you are considering the design of such a facility, you should consult the building code from the very outset of the project to verify requirements.
	Hazardous occupancy has four subgroups:
	H-1: This group includes processes involving significant quantities of materials that are at risk of explosion or are otherwise chemically highly unstable, for example, dynamite.
	H-2: This group includes processes involving significant quantities of materials that can act as accelerants in a fire, for example, flammable gasses or combustible dust.
	H-3: This group includes processes involving significant quantities of materials that readily support combustion or that otherwise present a physical hazard to occupants, such as combustible solids, consumer fireworks, or oxidizing chemicals.
	H-4: This group includes processes involving significant quantities of materials that do not present a special fire hazard but are corrosive or highly toxic.
	H-5: This group includes particular industrial facilities, such as semiconductor fabrication plants or similar research and development facilities, which use significant quantities of certain hazardous materials in their manufacturing processes.
INSTITUTIONAL	Institutional occupancies include facilities where occupants cannot fully care for themselves, including residential care, day care, assisted living, health care, and correctional facilities. Institutional occupancies are divided into four subgroups:
	I-1: This group includes 24-hour residential care facilities for 17 or more occupants, in which occupants are capable of responding to an emergency without physical assistance from facility staff. A facility such as this with 5 or fewer occupants may be classified as Group R-3 Residential or, with between 6 and 16 occupants, Group R-4.
	I-2: This group includes 24-hour medical, psychiatric, and custodial care facilities with 6 or more occupants, in which occupants are not capable of self-preservation in an emergency. A facility such as this with 5 or fewer occupants may be classified as Group R-3 Residential. Group I-2 also includes 24-hour care for 6 or more infants 2½ years of age or less.
	I-3: This group includes facilities whose occupants are under restraint, detention, or security, including prisons, correctional centers, and the like.

Occupancy	General Description

I-4: This group includes custodial day care (care on less than a 24-hour basis) for 6 or more occupants of any age. Day care for fewer than 6 persons is classified as Group R-3 Residential. Day care for children older than 2½ years may also be categorized as Group E Educational. In some cases, day care for up to 100 children 2½ years of age or less may be classified as Group E; see E Educational in this table for more information. Day care for able-bodied adults who are capable of responding to emergencies without assistance should be classified as A-3 Assembly.

M MERCANTILE — Mercantile occupancies include the display and sale of retail and wholesale merchandise and the related stocking of such goods.

R RESIDENTIAL — Residential occupancies include facilities where people live and sleep when not in a supervised setting that would be classified as an Institutional occupancy. Residential occupancies are subdivided into four subgroups:

R-1: This group includes residential facilities where occupants are transient, such as hotels, motels, and transient boarding houses. Resident stays of 30 days or less are generally considered transient.

R-2: This group includes residential facilities where occupants are primarily permanent, such as apartment houses, nontransient boarding houses, convents, dormitories, nontransient hotels and motels, timeshare properties, and similar facilities.

R-3: This group includes residential facilities not classified as other Group I Institutional or R Residential occupancies, including one- and two-family residences, and care facilities (both 24-hour and day) for not more than 5 occupants of any age. Congregate living facilities, in which up to 16 residents share bathroom and/or kitchen facilities, may also be classified as Group R-3.

R-4: This group includes residential care or assisted living facilities for between 6 and 16 occupants above the age of 2½ years. (For 24-hour care of children 2½ years or less in age, see Groups R-3 and I-2 .)

Detached one- and two-family dwellings and townhouses, not more than 3 stories in height, must comply with the International Code Council's *International Residential Code,* a separate model code written specifically for these building types. Where the activities described above in Occupancy Groups R-3 or R-4 are housed in a single-family residence, these buildings may in many cases be constructed to the requirements of this code. For more information on the application of the International Residential Code, see page 414.

S STORAGE — This group includes storage not classified as H, Hazardous, and is divided into two subgroups:

S-1: This group includes storage of moderate-hazard items such as books and paper, furniture, grain, lumber, tires, and other materials, as well as motor vehicle repair facilities.

S-2: This group includes parking garages and the storage of goods considered low hazard and nonflammable.

U UTILITY AND MISCELLANEOUS — This group includes agricultural buildings and other miscellaneous uses such as aircraft hangers, barns, carports, private garages, greenhouses, livestock shelters, retaining walls, sheds, stables, tanks, towers, and the like.

OCCUPANCY GROUPS: INTERNATIONAL BUILDING CODE

INDEX OF OCCUPANCIES

You may use the following index of uses to determine the Occupancy Group classification for your project. If the specific use for your project is not listed, choose the most similar use based on comparisons of the number and density of occupants, nature of the activity, and any associated fire- or life-safety risks.

WHERE DO I GO FROM HERE?

Once you have determined the building code Occupancy Group classifications for your project, you can use this information throughout the other sections of this book. If you are unsure of where to go next, see page ix, How to Use This Book, for suggestions on how to proceed.

Building Use	Occupancy
Agricultural buildings, barns, livestock shelters	U
Aircraft hangers	S-1
Aircraft hangers, accessory to one- or two-family residences	U
Airport traffic control towers	B
Alcohol and drug centers, 24-hour, 17 or more persons	I-1
Amusement arcades	A-3
Amusement park structures	A-5
Animal hospitals, kennels, pounds	B
Apartment houses	R-2
Art galleries	A-3
Assisted living	See Institutional and Residential Care Occupancies, page 12.
Auditoriums	A-3
Auditoriums part of Group E Educational facilities	E
Banks	B
Banquet halls	A-2
Barber and beauty shops	B
Barns	U
Bleachers, outdoors	A-5
Boarding houses, not transient	R-2
Boarding houses, transient	R-1
Bowling alleys	A-3
Business offices	B
Car washes	B
Carports	U

Building Use	Occupancy
Child care	See Institutional and Residential Care Occupancies, page 12.
Churches	See Places of worship
Civic administration	B
Clinic, outpatient	B
Community halls	A-3
Concert halls	A-2
Congregate care facilities, 24-hour, 17 or more persons	I-1
Convalescent facilities, 24-hour, 17 or more persons	I-1
Convents	R-2
Correctional centers	I-3
Courtrooms	A-3
Dance halls	A-3
Day care	See Institutional and Residential Care Occupancies, p.12.
Department stores	M
Detention centers	I-3
Detoxification facilities, 24-hour	I-2
Doctors' offices	B
Drug stores	M
Dry Boat Storage	S-2
Dry Cleaning and laundries	B
Educational occupancies above the 12th grade	B
Educational occupancies K through 12	E
Educational rooms in religious facilities	Same as the main occupancy, usually A-3
Electronic data processing	B
Exhibition halls	A-3

OCCUPANCY GROUPS: INTERNATIONAL BUILDING CODE

Building Use	Occupancy
Factories	F-1 or F-2, depending on hazard
Fences, more than 6 ft (2 m) high	U
Fire and police stations	B
Fraternities, sororities	R-2
Funeral parlors	A-3
Grandstands, outdoors	A-5
Greenhouses	U
Group homes	See Institutional and Residential Care Occupancies, page 12.
Gymnasiums	A-3
Halfway houses, 17 or more persons	I-1
Hazardous materials processing and storage	H-1 through H-5; consult the code for more information
Hospitals	I-2
Hotels	R-1
Jails	I-3
Laboratories, testing and research	B
Lecture halls	A-3
Libraries	A-3
Markets	M
Medical care, 24-hour, with 5 or fewer persons	R-3
Medical care, 24-hour, with 6 or more persons	I-2
Monasteries	R-2
Mosques	See Places of worship
Motels	R-1
Motion picture theaters	A-1
Motor vehicle repair	S-1
Motor vehicle service stations	M
Motor vehicle showrooms	B
Museums	A-3
Night clubs	A-2
Nursing homes	I-2
Offices	B
Outpatient facilities	B
Parking garages, public, open or closed	S-2
Parking garages, private	U
Passenger station waiting areas	A-3

Building Use	Occupancy
Places of worship, including public areas, gathering spaces, and educational rooms	A-3
Places of worship, business areas	B
Pool and billiard halls	A-3
Post offices	B
Prisons	I-3
Professional services	B
Radio and television stations, without audience facilities	B
Radio and television studios, admitting an audience	A-1
Reformatories	I-3
Rehabilitation facilities	See Institutional and Residential Care Occupancies, page 12.
Religious facilities	See Places of worship
Residential care	See Institutional and Residential Care Occupancies, page 12.
Restaurants	A-2
Retail or wholesale stores	M
Retaining walls	U
Sales rooms	M
Sheds	U
Skating rinks with spectator seating, indoor	A-4
Sports arenas, indoor	A-4
Stadiums, outdoors	A-5
Storage	S-1 or S-2, depending on hazard
Swimming pools, indoor, with spectator seating	A-4
Swimming pools, indoor, without spectator seating	A-3
Tanks	U
Taverns and bars	A-2
Telephone exchanges	B
Tennis courts, indoors, with spectator seating	A-4
Tennis courts, indoors, without spectator seating	A-3
Theaters	A-1
Towers	U
Training centers (nonacademic)	B

Institutional and Residential Care Occupancies

In the International Building Code, day care and residential care facilities are assigned to Occupancy Groups based on the ages of the individuals under care, the number of occupants, the duration of the care, and the extent to which occupants can fend for themselves in the event of a building emergency. Use the following table to determine the most appropriate Occupancy Group for such uses. Other related classifications, not listed in the table, include the following:

■ Child care within places of worship during religious functions is classified with the main occupancy, usually Group A-3.

■ Day care for able-bodied adults who are capable of responding to emergencies without assistance is classified as Group A-3.

■ Day care for not more than 100 children 2½ years of age or less may optionally be classified as Group E when each day care room is located on the level of exit discharge and has an exit door opening directly to the exterior.

■ Doctors' offices, outpatient clinics, and similar facilities are classified Group B.

■ Hospitals, nursing homes, detoxification facilities, and other 24-hour care facilities where residents require physical assistance in the case of a building emergency are classified as Group I-2.

OCCUPANCY GROUP

Age of Occupants	Day Care (less than 24-hour)		24-Hour Care		
	1–5 occupants	6 or more occupants	1–5 occupants	6–16 occupants	17 or more occupants
2½ years or less	R-3	I-4	R-3	I-2	I-2
Above 2½ years	R-3	I-4	R-3	R-4	I-1

WHICH BUILDING CODE TO CONSULT

If your project is in Canada, use the National Building Code of Canada, starting on this page, as the basis for determining preliminary code requirements for your project. If your project is in the United States, use the International Building Code, starting on page 7. (For more information about model building codes and their applicability to your project, see page 5.)

OCCUPANCY CLASSIFICATION

Buildings, or portions of buildings, are classified by the activities for which they are used, termed *Occupancy Groups*. These classifications reflect the relative life-safety hazard associated with the activities and occupant characteristics. In general, buildings intended for larger numbers of occupants, for public use, and for inherently hazardous activities are afforded greater levels of protection than those planned for smaller groups, private uses, or nonhazardous activities. Use the following two tables to determine what Occupancy Group classifications most appropriately describe your project.

If your building contains multiple uses, determine the occupancy for each part. Later in this book you will find more detailed information on how to apply the various code requirements to such mixed-use facilities; if you would like to learn more about mixed-use buildings right now, turn to page 355.

GENERAL DESCRIPTION OF OCCUPANCIES

The following table describes each Occupancy Group according to the classifications of the National Building Code of Canada.

Occupancy	General Description
A ASSEMBLY	Assembly occupancies include social, recreational, and civic gatherings. Assembly occupancy includes four subdivisions:
	A-1: This division includes facilities for the production and viewing of the performing arts.
	A-2: This division includes recreational, amusement, and worship uses not specifically falling under other Assembly groups, including, for example, auditoriums, churches, community halls, courtrooms, dance halls, gymnasiums, lecture halls, libraries, museums, passenger stations and depots, nonresidential schools and colleges, and the like.
	A-3: This division includes indoor arena-type facilities.
	A-4: This division includes outdoor gathering facilities.
B CARE OR DETENTION	Care or Detention occupancies include facilities where occupants cannot fully care for themselves, including residential care, assisted living, health care, and correctional facilities. Care or Detention occupancy includes two subdivisions:
	B-1: This division includes facilities where occupants are under restraint or are rendered incapable of self-preservation by facility security systems.
	B-2: This division includes facilities where occupants have cognitive or physical limitations requiring special care.
	Convalescent homes and children's custodial homes with not more than 10 occupants living in a single housekeeping unit are classified as C Residential.
C RESIDENTIAL	Residential occupancies include all kinds of residential uses not classified as Care or Detention, such as apartments, boarding houses, residential colleges and schools, hotels, single-family houses, and the like.
D BUSINESS AND PERSONAL SERVICES	Business and Personal Services occupancies include office, professional, and service activities, but do not include retail or wholesale sales, which are classified as E Mercantile.
E MERCANTILE	Mercantile occupancies include the display and sale of retail and wholesale merchandise and the related stocking of such goods.
F INDUSTRIAL	Industrial occupancies include manufacturing and industrial processes. Industrial occupancy includes three subdivisions:
	F-1: This group includes high-hazard manufacturing processes.
	F-2: This group includes medium-hazard manufacturing processes and materials.
	F-3: This division includes low-hazard manufacturing processes and materials.

INDEX OF OCCUPANCIES

You may also use the following index of uses to determine the Occupancy classification for your project. If the specific use for your project is not listed, choose the most similar use based on comparisons of the number and density of occupants, nature of the activity, and any associated fire- or life-safety risks.

WHERE DO I GO FROM HERE?

Once you have determined the building code Occupancy Group classifications for your project, you can use this information throughout the other sections of this book. If you are unsure of where to go next, see page ix, How to Use This Book, for suggestions on how to proceed.

Building Use	Occupancy
Aircraft hangars	F-2
Amusement park structures	A-4
Apartments	C
Arenas	A-3
Art galleries	A-2
Auditoriums	A-2
Banks	D
Barber and hairdressing shops	D
Beauty parlors	D
Beverage establishments	A-2
Bleachers, outdoors	A-4
Boarding houses	C
Bowling alleys	A-2
Children's custodial homes	B-2, except as noted below
Children's custodial homes, with not more than 10 ambulatory persons living in a dwelling unit as a single housekeeping unit	C
Churches, places of worship	A-2
Clubs, nonresidential	A-2
Clubs, residential	C
Cold-storage plants	F-2
Colleges, nonresidential	A-2
Colleges, residential	C
Community halls	A-2
Convalescent homes	B-2, except as noted below
Convalescent homes, with not more than 10 ambulatory persons living in a dwelling unit as a single housekeeping unit	C
Convents, residential	C

Building Use	Occupancy
Courtrooms	A-2
Creameries	F-3
Dance halls	A-2
Dental offices	D
Department stores	E
Distilleries	F-1
Dormitories	C
Dry cleaning establishments, self-service	D
Dry cleaning plants	F-1
Electrical substations	F-2
Exhibition halls, mercantile	E
Exhibition halls, other than mercantile	A-2
Factories	F-1, F-2, or F-3, depending on hazard
Farm buildings	Must conform to the National Farm Building Code, not covered in this publication
Freight depots	F-2
Garages, including open-air parking	F-3
Grain elevators	F-1
Grandstands, outdoors	A-4
Gymnasiums	A-2
Helicopter rooftop landing areas	F-2
Hospitals	B-2
Hotels	C
Houses	C
Infirmaries	B-2
Jails	B-1
Laboratories	F-2 or F-3, depending on hazard

Building Use	Occupancy
Laundries, self-service	D
Lecture halls	A-2
Libraries	A-2
Lodging houses	C
Manufacturing or processing plants for chemicals, paint, varnish, lacquer, rubber, waste paper	F-1
Markets	E
Medical offices	D
Mills for cereal, feed, grain	F-1
Monasteries	C
Motels	C
Motion picture theaters	A-1
Museums	A-2
Nursing homes	B-2
Offices	D
Opera houses	A-1
Orphanages	B-2
Passenger stations and depots	A-2
Penitentiaries	B-1
Police stations, with detention quarters	B-1
Police stations, with detention quarters, not more than 1 story in height or 600 m² (6460 ft²) in area	B-2
Police stations, without detention quarters	D
Power plants	F-3
Prisons	B-1
Psychiatric hospitals, with detention quarters	B-1
Psychiatric hospitals, without detention quarters	B-2
Radio stations	D
Recreational piers	A-2

Building Use	Occupancy
Reformatories, with detention quarters	B-1
Reformatories, without detention quarters	B-2
Restaurants	A-2
Reviewing stands, outdoors	A-4
Rinks, indoors	A-3
Sanatoriums, without detention quarters	B-2
Schools and colleges, nonresidential	A-2
Schools and colleges, residential	C
Service stations	F-2
Shops	E
Spray painting operations	F-1
Stadiums	A-4
Storage	F-1, F-2, or F-3, depending on hazard
Stores	E
Supermarkets	E
Swimming pools, indoors, with or without spectator seating	A-3
Television studios, admitting a viewing audience	A-1
Television studios, not admitting a viewing audience	F-2
Theaters, including experimental theaters	A-1
Tool and appliance rental and service establishments, small	D
Undertaking premises	A-2
Warehouses	F-1, F-2, or F-3, depending on hazard
Woodworking factories	F-2
Workshops	F-2 or F-3, depending on hazard

DESIGNING WITH BUILDING CODES

15

DESIGNING THE STRUCTURE

1
SELECTING THE STRUCTURAL SYSTEM

This section will help you select a structural system for the preliminary design of your building.

BUILDING CODE CRITERIA FOR THE SELECTION OF STRUCTURAL SYSTEMS

When choosing a structural system for a building, you must first determine the range of systems permitted by the building code in effect for your project. Each of the model codes requires you to do this by first determining the Occupancy Groups into which your building falls. Then you must consult numerous detailed provisions of the code that prescribe the maximum height and floor area to which a building may be built, based on its Occupancy and a range of code-defined Construction Types. To streamline this laborious process, simplified tables of area and height limitations for each model code are provided in this book. To use these tables, proceed as follows:

■ If you have not already done so, first determine which model code applies to your building and the Occupancy Groups into which it falls (pages 7–15).

■ Refer to the Height and Areas Tables, beginning on page 349, and locate the one or more tables that apply to your building.

■ Based on the size of the building required for your project, read from the Height and Area Tables the allowable Construction Types.

■ To learn more about each acceptable Construction Type, see pages 360–368.

Knowing what Construction Types are permitted for your project will help you in making preliminary selections of structural systems on the pages that follow in this section.

DESIGN CRITERIA FOR THE SELECTION
OF STRUCTURAL SYSTEMS

If you wish to create a building with a highly irregular form:

Choose systems with simple floor and roof framing that are fabricated mostly on-site, such as

Sitecast concrete using any slab system without beams or ribs (pages 113–129)
Light gauge steel framing (pages 94–97)
Platform frame (pages 56–63)
Masonry construction with either concrete slab or wood light floor framing (pages 77–91)

If you wish to leave the structure exposed while retaining a high fire-resistance rating:

Choose structural systems that are inherently resistant to fire and heat, including

All concrete systems (although ribbed systems may require added thickness in the ribs or slab, or applied fireproofing) (pages 113–141)
Heavy timber frame (pages 64–75)
Mill construction (pages 77–91)

Structural steel is highly susceptible to loss of strength in a fire and usually must be protected with a fire-resistive finishing system. For further information on the fire resistance of various structural systems and uses for which they are permitted, see pages 360–368.

If you wish to allow column placements that deviate from a regular grid:

Use systems that do not include beams or joists in the floor and roof structure, such as

Sitecast concrete two-way flat plate or flat slab (pages 124–127)
Metal space frame

If you wish to minimize floor thickness to reduce total building height or to reduce floor spandrel depth on the building facade:

The thinnest floor systems are concrete slabs without ribs, preferably prestressed, such as

Sitecast concrete two-way flat plate or flat slab, especially when posttensioned (pages 124–127)
Precast prestressed hollow core or solid slab (pages 138–139)
Posttensioned one-way solid slab (pages 120–121)

If you wish to minimize the area occupied by columns or bearing walls:

Consider long-span structural systems, such as

Heavy wood trusses (pages 72–73)
Glue laminated wood beams (pages 70–71)
Glue laminated wood arches (pages 74–75)
Conventional steel frame (pages 98–105)
Open-web steel joists (pages 106–107)
Single-story rigid steel frame (pages 108–109)
Steel trusses (pages 110–111)
Sitecast concrete one-way joist or waffle slab, particularly when posttensioned (pages 122–123, 128–129)
Precast concrete single or double tees (pages 140–141)

You may also wish to consider other long-span systems, such as specially fabricated steel beams, suspended systems, arches, vaults, and shells.

DESIGN CRITERIA FOR THE SELECTION
OF STRUCTURAL SYSTEMS

If you wish to allow for changes to the building over time:

Consider short-span one-way systems that permit easy structural modification, such as

Light gauge or conventional steel frame (pages 93–111)
Any wood system, including those incorporating masonry construction (pages 55–91)
Sitecast concrete one-way solid slab or one-way joist construction, excluding posttensioned (pages 120–123)
Precast concrete solid or hollow core slab (pages 138–139)

If you wish to permit construction under adverse weather conditions:

Select a system that does not depend on on-site chemical processes (such as the curing of concrete or mortar) and that can be erected quickly, such as

Any steel system (pages 93–111)
Any wood system (pages 55–75)
Precast concrete systems, particularly those that minimize the use of sitecast concrete toppings and grouting (pages 131–141)

If you wish to minimize off-site fabrication time:

Consider systems in which the building is constructed on-site from easily formed, relatively unprocessed materials, such as

Any sitecast concrete system (pages 113–129)
Light gauge steel framing (pages 94–97)
Platform frame (pages 56–63)
Any masonry system (pages 77–91)

If you wish to minimize on-site erection time:

Consider systems using highly preprocessed, prefabricated, or modular components, such as

Single-story rigid steel frame (pages 108–109)
Conventional steel frame, particularly with hinge connections (pages 98–107)
Any precast concrete system (pages 131–141)
Heavy timber frame (pages 64–75)

If you wish to minimize construction time for a one- or two-story building:

Consider systems that are lightweight and easy to form, or prefabricated and easy to assemble, such as

Any steel system (pages 93–111)
Heavy timber frame (pages 64–75)
Platform frame (pages 56–63)

DESIGN CRITERIA FOR THE SELECTION
OF STRUCTURAL SYSTEMS

If you wish to minimize construction time for a 4- to 20-story building:	Choose from the following systems
	
	    Precast concrete (pages 131–141)
	    Conventional steel frame (pages 98–107)
	
	Once the structural components for either of the above systems are pre-fabricated, on-site erection proceeds quickly.
	
	    Any sitecast concrete system (pages 113–129)
	
	The absence of lead time for the prefabrication of components in these systems allows construction of the building to begin on-site at the earliest time.

If you wish to minimize construction time for a building 30 stories or more in height:	Choose a system that is strong, lightweight, prefabricated, and easy to assemble Steel frame (pages 98–105) Systems of precast and sitecast concrete are economical alternatives to steel frame construction in some regions. The structural design of high-rise buildings is a specialized task, and the necessary consultants should be sought out as early as possible in the design process.

If you wish to minimize the need for diagonal bracing or shear walls:	Choose a system that is capable of economically forming rigid joints, such as
	
	    Any sitecast concrete system, particularly those with beams or deepened slabs around the columns (pages 113–129)
	    Steel frame with welded rigid connections (pages 98–105)
	    Single-story rigid steel frame (pages 108–109)
	
	When depending on a rigid frame for lateral stiffness, the sizes of the framing members often must be increased to resist the added bending stresses produced in such systems.

If you wish to minimize the dead load on the building foundation:	Consider lightweight or short-span systems, such as
	
	    Any steel system (pages 93–111)
	    Any wood system (pages 55–75)

If you wish to minimize structural distress due to unstable foundation conditions:	Frame systems without rigid joints are recommended, such as
	
	    Steel frame, with bolted connections (pages 98–107)
	    Heavy timber frame (pages 64–69)
	    Precast concrete systems (pages 131–141)
	    Platform framing (pages 56–63)
	
	Welded steel frames, masonry bearing walls, and sitecast concrete frames are particularly to be avoided.

DESIGN CRITERIA FOR THE SELECTION
OF STRUCTURAL SYSTEMS

If you wish to minimize the number of separate trades and contracts required to complete the building:	Consider systems that incorporate many of the functions of a complete wall system in one operation, such as
	Masonry construction, including Mill or Ordinary construction (pages 77–91)
	Precast concrete loadbearing wall panel systems (pages 134–135)
If you wish to provide concealed spaces within the structure itself for ducts, pipes, wires, and other building mechanical systems:	Consider systems that naturally provide convenient hollow spaces, such as
	Truss and open-web joist systems (pages 63–63, 70–71, 106–107, 110–111)
	Light gauge steel framing (pages 94–97)
	Platform frame (pages 56–63)
	Light gauge steel framing and platform frame construction are often applied as finish or infill systems in combination with other types of building structures to provide such spaces. For more information on the integration of building services and the structural system, see pages 196–215 and 228–247.

DESIGN CRITERIA: SUMMARY CHART

GIVE SPECIAL CONSIDERATION TO THE SYSTEMS INDICATED IF YOU WISH TO:	WOOD AND MASONRY				STEEL			
	Platform Frame (Pages 55–63)	Timber Frame (Pages 55, 64–75)	Ordinary Construction (Pages 77–91)	Mill Construction (Pages 77–91)	Light Gauge Steel Framing (Pages 93–97)	Single-Story Rigid Steel Frame (Pages 93, 108–109)	Steel Frame—Hinged Connections (Pages 93, 98–107)	Steel Frame—Rigid Connections (Pages 93, 98–107)
Create a highly irregular building form	●		●		●			
Expose the structure while retaining a high fire-resistance rating		●		●				
Allow column placements that deviate from a regular grid								
Minimize floor thickness								
Minimize the area occupied by columns or bearing walls						●	●	●
Allow for changes in the building over time	●	●	●	●	●		●	●
Permit construction under adverse weather conditions	●	●			●	●	●	●
Minimize off-site fabrication time	●		●	●	●			
Minimize on-site erection time		●				●	●	●
Minimize construction time for a one- or two-story building	●	●			●	●	●	●
Minimize construction time for a 4- to 20-story building							●	●
Minimize construction time for a building 30 stories or more in height							●	●
Avoid the need for diagonal bracing or shear walls						●		●
Minimize the dead load on a foundation	●	●			●	●	●	●
Minimize structural distress due to unstable foundation conditions	●	●					●	
Minimize the number of separate trades needed to complete a building			●	●				
Provide concealed spaces for ducts, pipes, etc.	●		●		●			

DESIGN CRITERIA: SUMMARY CHART

	SITECAST CONCRETE										PRECAST CONCRETE			
	Pages 113, 120–121	Pages 113, 120–121	Pages 113, 122–123	Pages 113, 122–123	Pages 113, 124–125	Pages 113, 124–125	Pages 113, 126–127	Pages 113, 126–127	Pages 113, 128–129	Pages 113, 128–129	Pages 131, 138–139	Pages 131, 138–139	Pages 131, 140–141	Pages 131, 140–141
	One-Way Solid Slab	Posttensioned One-Way Solid Slab	One-Way Joist	Posttensioned One-Way Joist	Two-Way Flat Plate	Posttensioned Two-Way Flat Plate	Two-Way Flat Slab	Posttensioned Two-Way Flat Slab	Waffle Slab	Posttensioned Waffle Slab	Solid Slab	Hollow Core Slab	Double Tee	Single Tee
	●	●			●	●	●	●						
	●	●	●	●	●	●	●	●	●	●	●	●	●	●
					●	●	●	●						
		●			●	●	●	●			●	●		
			●	●					●	●			●	●
	●	●									●	●		
											●	●	●	●
	●	●	●	●	●	●	●	●	●	●				
											●	●	●	●
	●	●	●	●	●	●	●	●	●	●	●	●	●	●
	●	●	●	●	●	●	●	●	●	●				
											●	●	●	●

PRACTICAL SPAN RANGES FOR STRUCTURAL SYSTEMS

This chart gives practical ranges for various structural systems. Greater or lesser spans may be possible in some circumstances. Page references are included where a system is covered in greater detail elsewhere in this book.

STRUCTURAL SYSTEM		Pages	Span Range
WOOD	Joists	58–59	
	Decking	66–67	
	Solid Beams	68–69	
	Rafter Pairs	59–60	
	Light Floor Trusses	62–63	
	Light Roof Trusses	62–63	
	Glue Laminated Beams	70–71	
	Heavy Trusses	72–73	
	Glue Laminated Arches	74–75	
	Domes		
BRICK & CONCRETE MASONRY	Lintels	82–83	
		90–91	
	Arches	85	
STEEL	Corrugated Decking	102–103	
	Light Gauge Joists	96–97	
	Beams	104–105	
	Open-Web Joists	106–107	
	Single-Story Rigid Frame	108–109	
	Heavy Trusses	110–111	
	Arches and Vaults		
	Space Frame		
	Domes		
	Cable-Stayed		
	Suspension		
SITECAST CONCRETE	One-Way Slabs	120–121	
	Two-Way Slabs	124–127	
	One-Way Joists	122–123	
	Waffle Slab	128–129	
	Beams	118–119	
	Folded Plates and Shells		
	Domes		
	Arches		
PRECAST CONCRETE	Slabs	138–139	
	Beams	136–137	
	Double Tees	140–141	
	Single Tees	140–141	
PNEUMATIC	Air Inflated		
	Air Supported		

Span Range scale: 10' / 3 m, 20' / 6 m, 30' / 9 m, 50' / 15 m, 100' / 30 m, 200' / 60 m, 300' / 90 m, 500' / 150 m

LIVE LOAD RANGES FOR BUILDING OCCUPANCIES

LIVE LOAD RANGES FOR BUILDING OCCUPANCIES

OCCUPANCY	Light Loads	Medium Loads		Heavy Loads	Very Heavy Loads
	20 psf / 1.0 kPa	60 psf / 2.9 kPa	100 psf / 4.8 kPa	150 psf / 7.2 kPa	250 psf / 12.0 kPa
Assembly Areas		Fixed seats	Movable seats		
			Stage areas		
Building Corridors	Private		Public		
Garages		Passenger cars		Trucks and buses	
Hospitals	Private rooms	Operating rooms			
		Laboratories			
Hotels and Multifamily Housing	Private rooms		Public rooms		
Libraries		Reading rooms		Stacks	
Manufacturing				Light	Heavy
Office Buildings	Offices		Lobbies		
One- and Two-Family Dwellings	Attics Bedrooms	Living spaces			
Outdoor Areas				Pedestrian	Vehicular
Roof Loads	No snow	Moderate snow	Heavy snow	Extreme snow	
Storage Areas			Pedestrian	Light	Heavy
Schools	Classrooms	Assembly	Shops		
Stores			Retail	Wholesale	
Miscellaneous Public Facilities	Penal institutions	Bowling alleys	Gymnasium Dance halls	Armories	
	Cell blocks	Poolrooms	Dining rooms Restaurants Stadiums Skating rinks	Drill rooms	

30

LIVE LOAD RANGES FOR STRUCTURAL SYSTEMS

LIVE LOAD RANGES FOR STRUCTURAL SYSTEMS

STRUCTURAL SYSTEM		Pages	Light Loads	Medium Loads	Heavy Loads	Very Heavy Loads
WOOD	Platform Frame	56–63	▬▬▬▬	▬▬▬▬		
	Timber Frame	64–75	▬▬▬▬	▬▬▬▬	▬▬▬▬	
MASONRY	Ordinary Construction	77–91	▬▬▬▬	▬▬▬▬		
	Mill Construction	77–91		▬▬▬▬	▬▬▬▬	
STEEL	Light Gauge Steel Framing	94–97	▬▬▬▬	▬▬▬▬		
	Single-Story Rigid Steel Frame	108–109	▬▬▬▬	▬▬▬▬	(Roof loads only)	
	Conventional Steel Frame	98–107		▬▬▬▬	▬▬▬▬	
SITECAST CONCRETE	One-Way Solid Slab	120–121	▬▬▬▬	▬▬▬▬	▬▬▬▬	
	One-Way Beam and Slab	120–121			▬▬▬▬	▬▬▬▬
	One-Way Joists	122–123		▬▬▬▬	▬▬▬▬	
	Two-Way Flat Plate	124–125	▬▬▬▬	▬▬▬▬		
	Two-Way Flat Slab	126–127		▬▬▬▬	▬▬▬▬	▬▬▬▬
	Waffle Slab	128–129		▬▬▬▬	▬▬▬▬	▬▬▬▬
	Two-Way Beam and Slab	124–125			▬▬▬▬	▬▬▬▬
PRECAST CONCRETE	Solid Slab	138–139	▬▬▬▬	▬▬▬▬	▬▬▬▬	
	Hollow Core Slab	138–139	▬▬▬▬	▬▬▬▬	▬▬▬▬	
	Double Tee	140–141		▬▬▬▬	▬▬▬▬	▬▬▬▬
	Single Tee	140–141		▬▬▬▬	▬▬▬▬	▬▬▬▬

Use the charts on these two pages to identify appropriate structural systems based on the activities planned within the building. Read the chart on the facing page first to determine the approximate live load range associated with the expected building use. Once a load range has been determined, consult the chart on this page to select systems that are recommended within that range. Roof loads are also covered to aid in the selection of roof structural systems.

If a building will have multiple uses, read from the chart for the higher load range. Or, if the different uses will be physically separate within the building, the load ranges for each use may be applied to the appropriate areas.

SOME TYPICAL CHOICES OF STRUCTURAL SYSTEMS FOR DIFFERENT BUILDING TYPES

Use the chart on these two facing pages to identify common structural systems used for various building types.

BUILDING TYPE	Platform Frame (Pages 55–63)	Heavy Timber (Pages 55, 64–69)	Glue Laminated Beams (Pages 55, 72–73)	Trusses—Heavy (Pages 55, 72–73)	Glue Laminated Arches (Pages 55, 70–71)	Brick Masonry Columns and Walls (Pages 77–81)	Concrete Masonry Columns and Walls (Pages 77, 86–89)	Steel Lightweight Framing (Pages 93–97)	Beams and Girders (Pages 93, 104–105)	Open-Web Joists (Pages 93, 106–107)	Single-Story Rigid Frame (Pages 93, 108–109)	Trusses (Pages 93, 110–111)	Long-span Cables, Arches, Space Frames, Domes
						WOOD AND MASONRY			STEEL				
Arenas									●	●		●	●
Concert halls									●			●	
Hospitals, laboratories						●	●		●	●		●	
Industrial & warehouse buildings		●	●	●	●	●	●		●	●	●	●	
Institutional, small to medium size	●		●			●	●	●	●	●			
Institutional, large									●	●		●	
Libraries									●				
Office buildings, small to medium size	●		●				●	●	●	●			
Parking garages									●				
Places of worship	●	●	●		●	●	●	●	●	●	●		
Residential, one- and two-family	●	●				●	●	●					
Residential, small to medium size	●					●	●	●					
Residential, large						●	●		●				
Schools			●			●	●		●	●			
Shopping malls						●	●		●	●			
Tall buildings									●		●		
Theaters			●			●	●		●	●	●	●	

SOME TYPICAL CHOICES OF STRUCTURAL SYSTEMS FOR DIFFERENT BUILDING TYPES

SITECAST CONCRETE						PRECAST CONCRETE		
Pages 113, 118–119	Pages 113, 120-121	Pages 113, 122–123	Pages 113, 124–125	Pages 113, 126–127	Pages 113, 128-129	Pages 131, 136–137	Pages 131, 138–139	Pages 131, 140-141
Beams & Girders	One-Way Solid Slab	One-Way Joists	Two-Way Flat Plate	Two-Way Flat Slab	Waffle Slab	Beams and Girders	Solid and Hollow Core Slab	Single and Double Tee
●								
●	●			●	●			
●	●			●		●	●	
●	●			●		●	●	●
●	●		●				●	
●	●	●	●	●		●	●	●
●	●			●				
●	●		●	●			●	
●	●	●		●		●	●	●
●	●		●				●	
●	●		●				●	
●	●	●		●	●	●	●	
●			●	●	●	●	●	
●			●			●	●	
●	●	●	●			●		

2 CONFIGURING THE STRUCTURAL SYSTEM

This section will aid you in making a preliminary layout of the structural system of a building.

LATERAL STABILITY AND STRUCTURAL SYSTEMS

STABILIZING ELEMENTS

All buildings must be designed to resist lateral forces such as wind and earthquake. Three basic structural configurations may be used, either singly or in combination: the shear wall, the braced frame, and the rigid frame. The choice of the lateral force resisting system and the location of its elements will have a fundamental influence on the form of the building and the arrangement of its interior space.

Shear Walls

Shear walls are solid walls constructed to resist the application of lateral forces. They can be made of almost any structural material and can range in size from small sections of panel-sheathed stud walls in residential buildings to massive steel and concrete core structures in the tallest buildings. In comparison to the other systems described on this page, shear walls are especially stiff, making them a good choice wherever a relatively compact arrangement of stabilizing elements is desired. Shear walls must be mostly solid, with limited if any openings through the wall. To minimize interference with floor plan arrangements, shear walls are often incorporated into the building core, stair towers, or other vertical structures within the building. Shear walls can also be part of the exterior wall, although in this location they may impact users' access to daylight and exterior views.

Braced Frames

Braced frames are composed of open, triangulated frameworks, most often constructed of steel or wood. In terms of strength per weight, they are the most efficient lateral force-stabilizing system. Like shear walls, braced frames are often incorporated into the building core or other vertical structures. They can also be part of exterior wall systems, where, in comparison to shear walls, their greater degree of openness results in less of an impact on daylight access and views.

Rigid Frames

Rigid frames depend on extra-stiff connections in the structural framework to resist the effects of lateral forces. The rigid joints required in this system are most easily constructed in steel, though at added cost in comparison to other systems, or in sitecast concrete, where they are formed as a natural part of concrete's internal reinforcing. Rigid joints may also be constructed in precast concrete, though with greater difficulty. The absence of solid panels or diagonal bracing makes this system attractive where the greatest flexibility in plan configuration is desired. However, rigid frame is the most structurally inefficient of the lateral force-resisting systems. It is most suitable for low or broad structures requiring relatively modest resistance. In taller buildings, it may be used in combination with another system. In addition, rigid frame also places greater stresses on the structural framework, and as a result, columns and beams may be heavier, and column spacing may be less than in a structure relying on some other lateral force-resisting system.

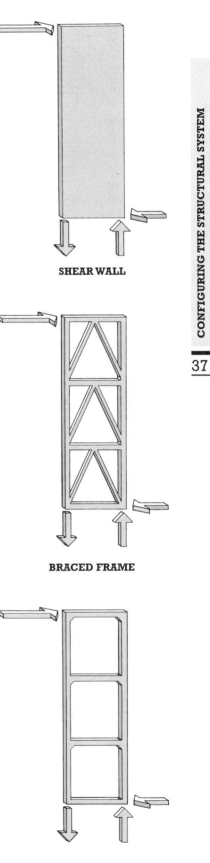

SHEAR WALL

BRACED FRAME

RIGID FRAME

CONFIGURING STABILIZING ELEMENTS

The arrangement of shear walls, diagonal braces, or rigid frames in a structure is crucial to their effectiveness in resisting lateral forces acting on the building. As illustrated in the adjacent schematic floor plans, these elements may be placed within the interior of the building or at the perimeter, and they may be combined in a variety of ways. However, they must be arranged so as to resist lateral forces acting from all directions. This is usually accomplished by aligning one set of stabilizing elements along each of the two perpendicular plan axes of the building. Stabilizing elements must also be arranged in as balanced a fashion as possible in relation to the mass of the building. Unbalanced arrangements result in the displacement of the center of resistance of the building away from its center of mass. Such a condition may lead to difficult-to-control building movements under lateral load conditions.

In general, lateral force-resisting elements are heaviest and most extensive at the base of a building, where the accumulated forces are greatest, and diminish in weight and extent as they approach the top of the building. In addition, considerations of lateral stability become increasingly important as the height of the building increases. The configuration of stabilizing elements is discussed in more detail on the following pages.

38

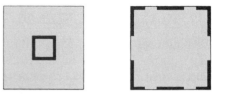

Stabilizing elements may be placed within the interior or at the perimeter of a building.

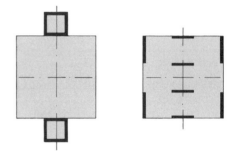

Stabilizing elements should be arranged in a balanced fashion.

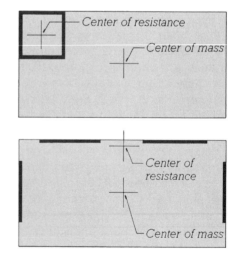

Unbalanced arrangements of stabilizing elements result in the displacement of the center of resistance of the building away from its center of mass. Such arrangements should be avoided.

LATERAL STABILITY AND STRUCTURAL SYSTEMS

This chart indicates the methods of resisting lateral forces most appropriate to each structural system. More detailed information on the individual systems can be found on the pages noted in the chart.

STRUCTURAL SYSTEM		Pages	Rigid Frame	Semi-Rigid Joints w/Supplemental Braced Frame or Shear Wall	Braced Frame	Shear Wall
WOOD	Platform Frame	56–63			● Let-in bracing	● Panel sheathing
	Timber Frame	64–75	● Glue Laminated		● Timber bracing	● Diagonal or panel sheathing
MASONRY	Ordinary Construction	77–91				● Masonry walls
	Mill Construction	77–91				● Masonry walls
STEEL	Light Gauge Steel Framing	94–97			● Strap bracing	● Panel sheathing
	Single-Story Rigid Steel Frame	108–109	● Parallel to frames only		● Perpendicular to frames	
	Conventional Steel Frame	98–107	● Requires welded connections	●	●	● Sitecast concrete
SITECAST CONCRETE	One-Way Solid Slab	120–121	○ May require added structure	●		
	One-Way Beam and Slab	120–121	●	●		
	One-Way Joist	122–123	●	●		
	Two-Way Flat Plate	124–125	○ May require added structure	●		
	Two-Way Flat Slab	126–127	○ May require added structure	●		
	Waffle Slab	128–129	●	●		
	Two-Way Beam and Slab	124–125	●	●		
PRECAST CONCRETE	Solid Slab	138–139	○		○ Uncommon	●
	Hollow Core Slab	138–139	○		○ Uncommon	●
	Double Tee	140–141	○		○ Uncommon	●
	Single Tee	140–141	○		○ Uncommon	●

● Recommended
○ Possible in some circumstances

WALL AND SLAB SYSTEMS

VERTICAL LOAD RESISTING ELEMENTS

Wall and slab systems are composed of loadbearing walls spanned by horizontal slabs. The placement of walls in this system is restricted by their role as structural elements, as they must be located to support the loads from slabs and walls above. Due to the significant presence of the walls in the plan of the building, the use of a wall and slab system generally implies a close correspondence between the structural module and the planning of building functions. In addition, economic considerations usually dictate that the arrangement of walls be as uniform as possible, making this system particularly attractive for building types that require regular arrangements of uniformly sized spaces, such as apartments, schools, and hotels.

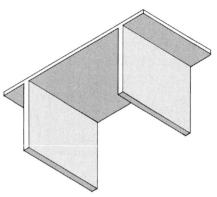

WALL AND SLAB SYSTEMS
(shown from below)

LATERAL LOAD-RESISTING ELEMENTS

The regularly placed structural walls used in this system are well suited to act as shear walls for lateral stability. They may be used alone or combined with rigid frames or braced frames, for instance, where structural walls run in only one direction in a building.

When used alone, shear walls must be arranged to resist lateral forces in all directions, such as in some variation of a complete or partial box form. Shear walls should always be placed as symmetrically as possible in the building plan, particularly in taller buildings. The sizes and spacing of openings in shear walls may need to be restricted as well.

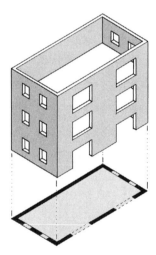

Shear walls may be arranged in a box form to resist lateral forces from all directions.

SYSTEMS WELL SUITED TO WALL AND SLAB FRAMING

Bearing walls of any type may be used to create wall and slab structural systems. See the following sections for more information:

Systems	Pages
Wood Stud Walls	56–57
Brick Masonry Walls	80–81
Concrete Block Walls	86–87
Lightweight Steel Stud Walls	94–95
Sitecast Concrete Walls	116–117
Precast Concrete Wall Panels	134–135

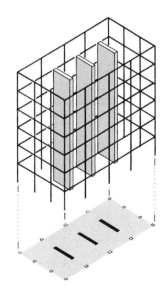

When combined with other stabilizing mechanisms, shear walls may be arranged so as to resist forces in only one direction of a building.

WALL AND SLAB SYSTEMS

WALL AND SLAB SYSTEM LAYOUTS

The distance between walls is equal to the span of the slab. Walls can be any length but are required wherever slabs are supported. Where necessary, openings in walls can be made by including beams over such openings to carry loads from above. In multistory buildings, the locations of bearing walls should coincide from floor to floor. However, where it is desirable to omit bearing walls from a lower floor, it may be possible to design the wall above as a deep beam supported at its ends only.

Wall and slab systems can be combined with column systems to permit greater open areas in a plan. Wherever possible, keep walls in locations that are most desirable for lateral load resistance.

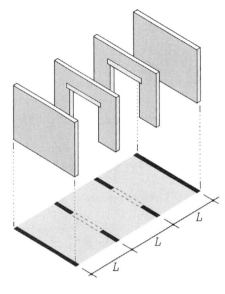

In wall and slab systems, the distance between walls is equal to the span of the slab. Openings in walls may be made when beams are added to carry loads from above.

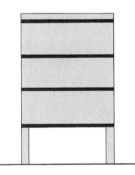

Bearing walls may act as deep beams to span across openings below, as shown in this schematic cross section.

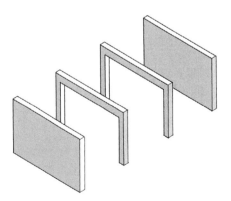

Bearing wall and column systems may be combined for more flexibility in plan layouts.

COLUMN AND BEAM SYSTEMS

VERTICAL LOAD-RESISTING ELEMENTS

Column and beam systems are composed of vertical columns, horizontally spanning girders and beams, and a slab spanning between the beams. The columns in this system have less impact than loadbearing walls on the planning of spaces within a building. Where the sizes of interior spaces of a building do not correspond with a structural module or are irregular in shape or size, where maximum open space is desired, or where a high degree of flexibility in the use of space over time is desired, column and beam systems are a good choice. Compared to column and slab systems, column and beam systems are also practical over a greater range of spans and bay proportions.

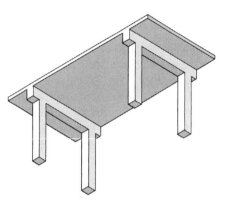

COLUMN AND BEAM SYSTEMS
(shown from below)

LATERAL LOAD-RESISTING ELEMENTS

Column and beam systems of steel frame or sitecast concrete construction are well suited to rigid frame action. When used in this way, rigid joints are required at some or all column to beam connections. In sitecast concrete, rigid joints are produced as a normal feature of the system. In steel, rigid connections are generally more expensive to construct. Rigid joints are difficult to construct and are rarely used in precast concrete. Because no added braces or walls are required, rigid frame systems are often preferred for their minimal interference with the plan of a building. However, the use of rigid frames generally restricts column placements to regular, orthogonal layouts, and often requires deeper beams and more closely spaced and larger columns than would otherwise be required with either braced frame or shear walls. Rigid frames are normally not well suited for structures with unusually long spans or tall columns.

When braced frames or shear walls are used for lateral stability, columns and beams may be joined with simpler, hinged connections, such as the bolted connections normally used in steel and timber structures or the flexible welded connections used in precast concrete. The stabilizing braces or walls may be located within the interior of the building or at the perimeter, but they must be placed so as to resist lateral forces in all directions. Building cores or stair towers housing vertical circulation or other systems often can be easily designed to incorporate such elements, thus eliminating their intrusion into the remainder of the building floor plan. When located at the perimeter of the structure, these elements may influence the design of the building facade.

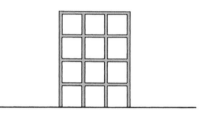

Rigid frame structures require no additional bracing or shear walls, as shown in this elevation and plan.

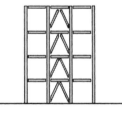

The locations of braced frames or shear walls must be considered in relation to the elevation and plan of the building.

42

COLUMN AND BEAM SYSTEMS

SYSTEMS WELL SUITED TO COLUMN AND BEAM FRAMING

Information on column and beam systems may be found in the following sections:

Systems	Pages
Wood Beams	68–71
Steel Beams and Girders	104–105
Sitecast Concrete Beams and Girders	118–119
Precast Concrete Beams and Girders	136–137

COLUMN AND BEAM SYSTEM LAYOUTS

Columns are located on the lines of the beams above. Although column spacings may vary within the limits of the spanning capacity of the beams, for reasons of economy, columns are typically restricted to some regular gridded arrangement.

Various combinations of beams and slabs are possible. Beams can span in one direction only, with slabs spanning perpendicular to them. With this arrangement, column spacing in one direction is equal to the span of the beams; in the other direction, it is equal to the span of the slabs.

More flexibility in the location of columns can be achieved with beams spanning in both directions. Deeper beams, termed *girders*, span the columns. The girders, in turn, support shallower secondary beams, spanning perpendicular to them. Finally, the distance between the secondary beams is spanned by the slab. Column spacings with such beam and girder arrangements are limited only by the spanning capacity of the beams in either direction. The choice of the direction of the span of the girders and beams in such a structure can be influenced by a variety of factors, including the particular structural systems involved, the relative structural efficiency of either arrangement, the lateral stability requirements for the overall structure, and the integration of the floor structure with other building systems such as electrical wiring in the slab or ducts and piping running beneath the floor framing. These considerations are covered in more detail in the sections of this book covering specific structural or mechanical systems.

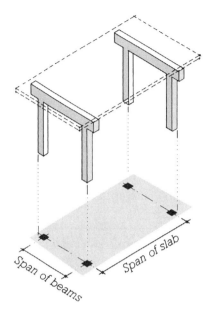

In column and beam systems, columns are located on beam lines.

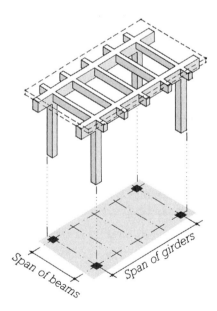

Beams span both directions in beam and girder systems.

COLUMN AND SLAB SYSTEMS

VERTICAL LOAD RESISTING ELEMENTS

Column and slab systems are composed of vertical columns directly supporting horizontally spanning slabs without intermediary beams. As with column and beam systems, the reliance on columns for vertical load support permits greater independence between the building plan and the structural system. The absence of beams in column and slab systems may permit even greater flexibility in column placements than with column and beam systems, because columns are not restricted to beam lines. Column and slab systems may also be attractive economically due to the simplification of construction techniques and the reduction in total floor depths that they make possible.

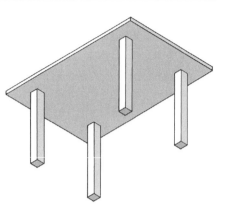

COLUMN AND SLAB SYSTEMS
(shown from below)

LATERAL LOAD-RESISTING ELEMENTS

Rigid frame action is possible in column and slab systems, although its effectiveness depends on the depth of the slab, particularly in the areas close to the columns. Where large lateral forces are expected with systems with shallow slabs, a deepening of the slab or the addition of structural beams between columns may be required to achieve sufficient lateral resistance.

Shear walls or braced frames may also be used to develop lateral resistance in column and slab systems. These elements may be used either as the sole means of lateral bracing, or as enhancements to the rigid frame action of the system. They may be located within the interior of the building or at the perimeter, but they must be placed so as to resist lateral forces in all directions. The locations of interior elements must be coordinated with the building plan. Building cores housing vertical circulation or other systems can often be easily designed to incorporate such elements, thus eliminating their intrusion from the remainder of the floor plan. When located at the perimeter of the structure, shear walls or braces may influence the design of the building facade.

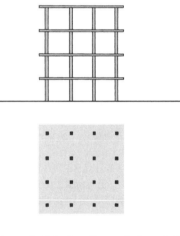

As shown in this elevation and plan, rigid frame action is possible with column and slab systems, although its effectiveness may be limited.

SYSTEMS WELL SUITED TO COLUMN AND SLAB FRAMING

Conventional structural systems that are configured as column and slab systems are metal space frame, or sitecast concrete systems, including two-way flat plate, two-way flat slab, and either one-way joist or waffle slab construction (when these two systems are used with shallow beams that do not extend below the surface of the ribs). For further information, see the following sections:

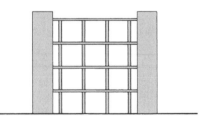

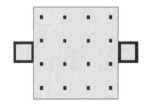

Shear walls are frequently used with column and slab systems. In this elevation and plan, the shear walls are shown incorporated into a pair of vertical cores.

COLUMN AND SLAB SYSTEMS

COLUMN AND SLAB SYSTEM LAYOUTS

Column spacing in either direction is equal to the span of the slab. For maximum economy and structural efficiency, column bays should be approximately square in proportion, and column displacements from regular lines should be minimized. However, column layouts are more flexible in column and slab systems because columns are not restricted to beam lines. Variations in column placements, changes in bay sizes, and irregular plan shapes may be more easily accommodated than in other framing systems.

STRUCTURAL LIMITATIONS OF COLUMN AND SLAB SYSTEMS

The absence of beams in sitecast concrete flat plate and flat slab construction imposes some limits on the structural performance of these systems. The relatively shallow depth of the joint between the columns and slabs can restrict their load-carrying capacity and limit their resistance to lateral forces. Though the addition of beams to these systems adds substantially to construction costs, it may be a practical alternative where longer spans are required, very heavy loads must be carried, or additional lateral resistance is needed and the use of shear walls or braced frames is undesirable. Such configurations are covered in more detail in the sections describing these structural systems.

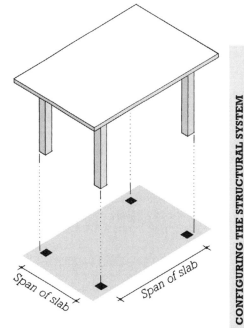

In column and slab systems, the span of the slab is equal to the column spacing in either direction.

The absence of beams in column and slab systems may facilitate irregular column layouts or plan shapes.

HIGH-RISE STRUCTURAL CONFIGURATIONS

THE DESIGN OF HIGH-RISE STRUCTURES

As a building's height increases, the design of its structural system becomes increasingly specialized. Factors that may influence the form and configuration of a tall building structure include the large cumulative effect of vertical loads, site-specific wind, earthquake, soils, and foundation conditions, the regional availability and costs of various construction systems, unique requirements of the building program, and even the particular expertise of the structural consultant. The information on the following pages will help you to understand the structural options available for your building in relation to some of these considerations. However, it cannot fully address them all. For this reason, the design of high-rise structures should also include the participation of the structural designer from the earliest phases of design.

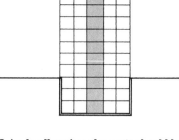

Major loadbearing elements should be continuous vertically to the foundations of the building.

VERTICAL LOAD–RESISTING SYSTEMS

The vertical load-resisting systems for high-rise buildings are essentially the same as those for low-rise structures described on previous pages. In the tallest buildings, column and beam systems predominate due to their efficient use of space, structural versatility, and ease of construction. Because of the large gravity loads associated with taller structures, special care should be taken that major structural elements are not interrupted vertically. To the greatest extent possible, building core structures, columns, and other loadbearing elements should extend continuously to the foundation, and should avoid offsets from floor to floor or other vertical discontinuities.

Nevertheless, conditions may arise in which loadbearing elements cannot have direct and continuous paths to the building's foundation: In some cases, it is structurally advantageous to redistribute vertical loads outward toward the corners of a building to increase the building's resistance to overturning; public spaces such as auditoriums, lobbies, or atria, located in the lower floors of a building, may require large column-free areas that interrupt the paths of structural elements from above; or other variations in program requirements or building massing may necessitate less dramatic but still significant shifts in the arrangement of structural elements. In such cases, where only minor changes in load paths are required, columns may be subtly sloped or shifted between floors. Where more significant redistributions of load are required, transfer beams or heavy, long-span truss structures may be used. In the most extreme cases, a building's primary structural system may be significantly adjusted or redesigned so as to better meet the structural and programmatic requirements of the project.

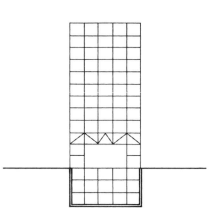

Transfer beams or trusses may be used to interrupt vertical loadbearing elements where necessary.

HIGH-RISE STRUCTURAL CONFIGURATIONS

LATERAL LOAD-RESISTING SYSTEMS

Increasing the height of a building increases especially its sensitivity to both wind and earthquake forces. The taller the building, the more these forces will dominate the design of the structure, and the more the influence of these forces on building form should be considered during preliminary design. The following guidelines are particularly important in the design of high-rise buildings, especially for those in areas of high seismic activity.

As building height increases, expect the lateral support system to increase in prominence within the design: Its structural elements may become heavier, lateral force-resisting structures (shear walls, braced frames, and rigid frames) may be more closely spaced or may increase in horizontal extent, and the choice of lateral support systems and their configuration may become more limited.

Designs that are asymmetric in plan, that are unbalanced in their massing, or that have irregular arrangements of stabilizing elements become increasingly problematic in taller buildings. Under the influence of lateral loads, these conditions can lead to difficult-to-control building motions or excessive stresses in structural elements. These conditions should be avoided to the maximum extent possible.

Where large buildings are composed of discrete masses, each part can be expected to move differently under the conditions associated with lateral loads. The leg of an L-shaped building, the stem of a T-shaped building, a tower offset to one corner of a wider base, or other such irregular arrangements are prone to interacting in adverse ways under dynamic conditions. Where such elements occur, each independent mass should be designed as a separate structure, with substantial joints between the abutting masses that can safely absorb differential movements between them.

Buildings of inherently unstable massing or form should be avoided. Large or irregular openings in floor plates are detrimental, especially those constituting 50% or more of the overall floor area. Discontinuities in the stiffness of a structure at different levels should be avoided. For example, an open space with long horizontal spans at the base of a tall building can produce excessive flexibility or weakness at that level. If such a "soft story" cannot be avoided, extra care to provide adequate vertical and lateral support at that level may be required.

Tall buildings may interact with winds in unpredictable ways. Where buildings are irregular in their exterior form, or are located on sites with the potential for unpredictable wind effects, special studies of the building's response to that location's unique wind pressures and fluctuations may be required.

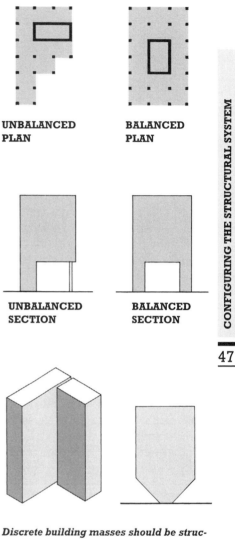

UNBALANCED PLAN   **BALANCED PLAN**

UNBALANCED SECTION   **BALANCED SECTION**

Discrete building masses should be structurally independent. Inherently unstable building masses should be avoided.

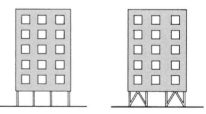

Discontinuities in the stiffness of structures at different levels should be avoided, or additional stabilizing elements may be required.

HIGH-RISE STRUCTURAL CONFIGURATIONS

The design of high-rise structures is dominated by the requirement to resist lateral forces. As building height increases, the three basic systems of lateral force resistance—the shear wall, braced frame, and rigid frame— may be uniquely configured for use in such structures. The following tall building configurations are presented in order of suitability for structures of increasing height. The adjacent diagrams illustrate schematically in both plan and section each of the configurations described.

CONVENTIONAL CONFIGURATIONS

The conventional arrangements of stabilizing elements used in low-rise buildings may be extended for use in buildings up to as many as 20 to 25 stories in height. The same considerations that apply to low-rise buildings apply to taller buildings as well: Stabilizing elements should be arranged so as to resist lateral forces along all major axes of the building. These elements should be arranged in a balanced manner either within the building or at the perimeter. And such elements must be integrated with the building plan or elevation.

Shear walls and braced frames are the stabilizing elements most commonly used in buildings of this height, due to their structural efficiency. They may be used either separately or in combination. The use of rigid frame systems as the sole means of achieving lateral stability may be feasible in buildings up to 15–20 stories in height in areas of low seismic activity or perhaps 10–15 stories in areas of greater seismicity. However, even where feasible, rigid frame structures may be a less attractive option due to the greater difficulty of their fabrication and the increased size of the beams and columns they require. More commonly in buildings of this height, rigid frame systems are used in combination with either shear walls or braced frames to enhance the lateral resistance of the structure as a whole.

CORE STRUCTURES

Core structures constitute the system most commonly used to stabilize all but the tallest buildings. In these structures, stabilizing elements are integrated into the vertical cores that house circulation and mechanical systems in tall buildings. One of the principal advantages of core structures is that with the placement of the resisting elements in the building core, interference with the surrounding usable space in the building is minimized. In concrete construction, core walls already intended to enclose these other building systems can easily be designed to also act as shear walls, in many cases with no increase in size. In steel construction, core structures are usually designed as braced frames.

A single core servicing an entire building should be located at the center of the building. In buildings with more than one core, the cores should be located symmetrically in the building plan so as to provide balanced resistance under lateral loads from any direction. Cores typically comprise approximately 20%–25% of the total floor area of a high-rise building. They should be formed as closed elements, approximately square or cylindrical, with openings into the core kept to a minimum.

Simple core structures can be used in buildings as high as 35 to 40 stories. Core structures can also be enhanced structurally with the addition of bracing in the form of "hat" trusses. Hat trusses involve the perimeter columns of the building in resisting lateral loads, thus improving the overall performance of the building. Such trusses may influence the design of

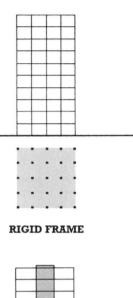

RIGID FRAME

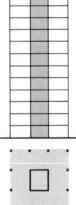

RIGID CORE

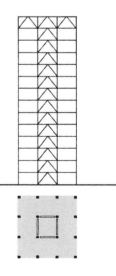

BRACED CORE WITH HAT TRUSS

HIGH-RISE STRUCTURAL CONFIGURATIONS

the building facade or the location of mechanical floors. Columns at the perimeter of the building may also increase in size with these systems. These core-interactive structures are suitable for buildings up to approximately 60 stories in height.

For further information on the design of building cores to accommodate mechanical and circulation systems, see pages 196–210.

TUBE STRUCTURES

The tallest buildings are currently most often designed as tube structures. In this system stabilizing elements are located at the perimeter of the structure, leaving the layout of the interior of the building virtually unrestricted by considerations of lateral stability. Either braced frame or rigid frame elements, constructed from either steel or concrete, may be used. Simple tube structures and their variations are generally most suitable for buildings approximately 55 stories or greater in height.

The use of rigid frame tubes may affect the size and spacing of framing elements at the perimeter of the building. Beams may need to be deeper and columns may need to be larger and more closely spaced than would otherwise be required. When building in steel, the welded joints required in this system may be more costly to construct, although construction systems have been developed that allow the off-site fabrication of these joints, minimizing this disadvantage.

Braced frame tubes are one of the most structurally efficient lateral load-resisting configurations. When built in steel, these structures also rely on more easily constructed bolted connections. The diagonal braces that are an integral part of this system often have a significant impact on the appearance of the building facade.

The performance of rigid frame tube structures may be enhanced with the addition of belt trusses located at the perimeter of the structure. These trusses may be located at various levels in the structure, and like hat trusses, they may influence the location of mechanical floors and overall facade design.

Variations on the tube structure are also possible. "Tube-in-tube" structures, in which perimeter tubes interact with rigid cores, may be designed for enhanced structural performance. Or, "bundled tube" structures permit greater variation in the massing of a structure and can enhance the overall performance of the structure as well.

PRACTICAL LIMITS ON THE HEIGHT OF TALL BUILDINGS

At the time of this writing, the tallest completed building in the world is Taiwan's 101–story Taipei 101. Its official height, including the building's tower, is 1667 ft (508 m). The height of the roof, excluding the tower, is 1475 ft (450 m). Other tall buildings under construction or currently on the boards are reported to have heights in the range of 1550 to 2310 ft (474 to 705 m), with as many as 160 floors. When considering the width of tall buildings, those with a slenderness ratio of 5 or more (ratio of height to least plan dimension at the base of the building) should be considered increasingly challenging from the point of view of ensuring lateral stability. The practical limit for tall building slenderness appears to be on the order of 10:1 (excluding specialized tower structures and the like).

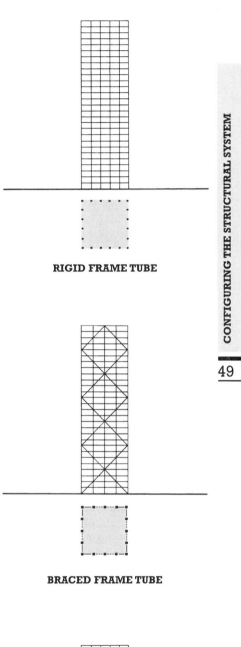

RIGID FRAME TUBE

BRACED FRAME TUBE

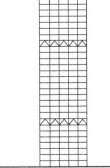

RIGID FRAME TUBE WITH BELT TRUSSES

SPECIAL CONSIDERATIONS IN THE DESIGN OF TALL STRUCTURES

Steel Structural Systems

Structural steel is well suited to the construction of tall buildings. The light weight of steel in relation to its strength results in a building of the least possible mass, thereby reducing the amount of structure and foundation required to support the weight of the building itself. This characteristic also results in columns and other structural elements of least size, minimizing their consumption of space within the building that could otherwise be productively used by its occupants or reserved for other building systems.

Structural steel also has particular advantages for buildings located in areas of high seismic activity. A lower-mass structure experiences lower forces during an earthquake. In addition, the high ductility of steel (its ability to resist repeated high levels of stress without failure) allows for the design of a structure capable of resisting extreme loads and dissipating the large quantities of dynamic energy imparted into it during sustained earthquake shaking. Designing a building frame that takes full advantage of these characteristics results in a structure that is flexible, resilient, and capable of safely withstanding severe seismic events.

Concrete Structural Systems

In comparison to structural steel, concrete is a more massive and less ductile material. For these reasons, it has traditionally been considered at a disadvantage for the design of tall buildings. Especially when the effects of earthquake loads are considered, the higher mass of concrete implies higher forces acting on the structure. This material's lesser ductility also makes it less capable of absorbing the dynamic energy imparted into it during sustained earthquake loading. However, in recent years, higher-strength concretes have been developed, and a better understanding has been gained of the design of steel reinforcing to develop ductility within a concrete structure. With these developments, concrete's disadvantages in comparison to steel have been minimized, and it remains a viable choice as a structural material for even very tall buildings. In fact, as of this writing, the world's tallest building currently on the drawings boards is purportedly being designed as an all-concrete structure.

Concrete's unique characteristics can also be advantageous. Concrete is tough and resistant to impact, and unlike steel, it does not require a separate covering to protect it from the heat of building fires. Because concrete structures typically undergo smaller deflections than ones constructed of structural steel, the detailing of connections to nonstructural elements such as cladding and partitions may be simplified, and the performance of these elements under severe load conditions may be less problematic. The superior stiffness of concrete shear walls is especially well suited to structures where there is a desire to keep the stabilizing elements as compact as possible, and to very slender structures where there is insufficient depth to make effective use of alternative stabilizing systems. Even in areas of high seismicity, the greater stiffness of concrete structures may be especially well suited to building sites where ground movements associated with earthquakes are such that the shorter period of vibration of a stiffer structure is advantageous.

Concrete is also frequently used together with steel in ways that exploit the attributes of both materials simultaneously. For example, composite columns made of steel box shapes filled with high-strength concrete can achieve very high load capacity. Such composite columns form a primary structural element in the world's currently tallest building, the Taipei 101: At the base of this building, each of eight so-called "super columns" measures almost 8×10 ft (2.4×3.0 m) in cross section. Even in building structures nominally described as steel, concrete core structures and floor systems commonly play critical roles as well.

Active Mechanisms for Resisting Lateral Forces

A building structure's response to the effects of wind or earthquake can also be enhanced with devices designed to moderate the movements imparted into it by these loads. *Dampers* are shock-absorber-like devices. They may be incorporated into the building frame, where they can moderate building deflections during high lateral loading as well as increase the structure's energy-absorbing capacity, or they may be combined with a system of *base isolators* at the foundation level of the building. In the latter case, the base isolators allow a degree of separation between the building structure and the ground upon which it rests. In the event of an earthquake, a significant portion of the ground motions that occur is never transmitted into the building structure at all. Meanwhile, the dampers act to prevent the structure from drifting beyond the physical limits of the isolation system. In severe earthquake zones, base isolation and damper systems accommodating displacements of up to 30 in. (760 mm) may be used.

Tuned mass dampers may be used to control deflection or "side sway" in tall buildings. These are heavy masses, suspended within the building structure, usually near its top, and connected to it by an array of dampers similar to those discussed above. As wind forces act to deflect the structure sideways, the inertia of the suspended mass resists these movements and reduces the magnitude of the sideways deflection. The rates at which the structure accelerates as it periodically reverses its sway can also be reduced, an important consideration for occupant comfort. More recently, water tanks with specially configured internal chambers and baffles have been designed to work in a similar manner.

By enhancing the performance of the passive lateral force-resisting systems discussed previously, active devices may help to reduce the physical extent of these other systems or the size of the elements of which they are composed. When considering base isolation systems, the designer should also make allowance for the displacements that are to be expected between the building and the adjacent ground. Utility lines will require flexible connections where they enter the foundation. Connections to perimeter site structures, such as stairs, plazas, sidewalks, and adjacent buildings, must also be able to accommodate the significant differential movements that this system allows.

CONFIGURING THE STRUCTURAL SYSTEM

51

3
SIZING THE STRUCTURAL SYSTEM

This section will assist you in assigning approximate sizes to structural elements. Additional information on designing and building with each structural system is also provided.

WOOD STRUCTURAL SYSTEMS

Wood construction typically takes one of two distinct forms: Wood Light Frame Construction uses relatively thin, closely spaced members to form walls, floors, and roofs in a system called Platform Frame Construction. Heavy Timber Construction uses larger members configured as a post and beam system. Both of these systems are fully treated in this section.

Either Wood Light Frame or Heavy Timber Construction can be combined with masonry construction for increased fire resistance and load capacity. These systems are more fully described under Masonry Structural Systems, beginning on page 77.

PLATFORM FRAME CONSTRUCTION

Platform Frame Construction is an economical and flexible building system. It is used extensively for single-family and multifamily housing, as well as for low-rise apartment buildings and small commercial structures.

Because this system is largely fabricated on-site and the individual framing members are small, it is also well suited for use where unusual layouts or irregular forms are desired. Where economy is a primary concern, the use of a 2- or 4-ft (600- or 1200-mm) modular plan dimension is recommended. Platform Frame Construction easily and unobtrusively incorporates mechanical systems and other building services.

Platform framing is a wall and slab system. Lateral bracing may be supplied either by shear wall or braced frame action of the load-bearing walls. Information on the components of Platform Frame Construction can be found on pages 56–63.

HEAVY TIMBER CONSTRUCTION

Heavy Timber Construction is characterized by high fire resistance (it has a higher fire rating than unprotected steel), high load capacity, and the unique aesthetic qualities of the exposed wood frame. The framing members for Heavy Timber Construction may be either solid wood or glue laminated. Heavy timber frames are used for low-rise commercial and industrial buildings and in residential construction. Because the framing members are typically prefabricated, on-site erection times can be rapid with this system. However, the larger sizes of the framing members make this system less suitable than platform framing for structures that are highly irregular in form or layout. Mechanical and electrical systems are also often less easily concealed in this system.

As in platform framing, economy of construction may be maximized with the use of a 2- or 4-ft (600- or 1200-m) design module when planning a timber frame structure.

Timber frames may be stabilized laterally by the shear resistance of the walls or panels used to enclose the frame, or with diagonal bracing. The masonry bearing walls of Ordinary or Mill Construction are also well suited to acting as shear walls. Information on the components of Heavy Timber Construction can be found on pages 64–75.

WOOD STUD WALLS—CONVENTIONAL CONSTRUCTION

Use the diagram below to select a wood stud size and spacing for conventional low-rise light wood frame residences and buildings. For wood stud walls designed for a wider variety of loading and span conditions, use the charts on the opposite page.

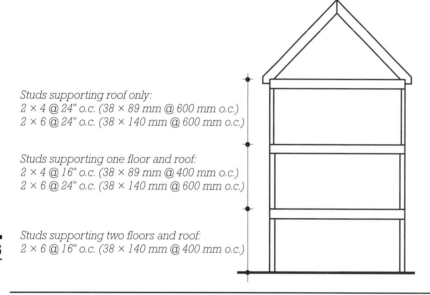

Studs supporting roof only:
2 × 4 @ 24" o.c. (38 × 89 mm @ 600 mm o.c.)
2 × 6 @ 24" o.c. (38 × 140 mm @ 600 mm o.c.)

Studs supporting one floor and roof:
2 × 4 @ 16" o.c. (38 × 89 mm @ 400 mm o.c.)
2 × 6 @ 24" o.c. (38 × 140 mm @ 600 mm o.c.)

Studs supporting two floors and roof:
2 × 6 @ 16" o.c. (38 × 140 mm @ 400 mm o.c.)

ACTUAL SIZES OF WALL STUDS

Nominal Size	Actual Size
2×4	1½" × 3½" (38 × 89 mm)
2×6	1½" × 5½" (38 × 140 mm)
2×8	1½" × 7¼" (38 × 184 mm)

WOOD STRENGTH

When reading the charts on the opposite page, examples of strong woods include Select Structural grades of Douglas Fir, Larch, Hemlock, or Southern Pine. Examples of average strength woods include No. 2 grades of Hem-Fir or Spruce-Pine-Fir. For other species and grade combinations of intermediate strength, you may interpolate between the results charted for these two groups.

SPACING OF WALL STUDS

Wall studs are most commonly spaced at 16 or 24 in. (400 or 600 mm) on center. A 12-in. (300-mm) spacing may also be used where greater loads must be supported. Studs should always be spaced within a 4-ft (1200-mm) module in order to coordinate with the standard width of various sheathing and wallboard products that are commonly used with this type of construction.

FIRE-RESISTANCE RATINGS FOR WOOD STUDS

Wood stud walls may be used in Ordinary Construction and Wood Light Frame Construction. They may qualify for a 1-hour fire rating when covered on both sides with ⅝-in. (16-mm) Type X gypsum wallboard or its equivalent.

WOOD STUD WALLS

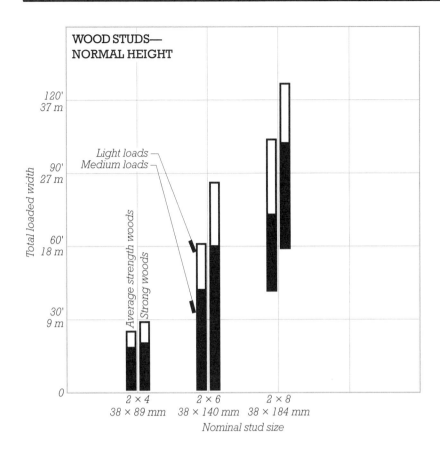

WOOD STUDS—NORMAL HEIGHT

Total loaded width

120'
37 m

90'
27 m

60'
18 m

30'
9 m

0

Light loads
Medium loads

Average strength woods
Strong woods

2 × 4
38 × 89 mm

2 × 6
38 × 140 mm

2 × 8
38 × 184 mm

Nominal stud size

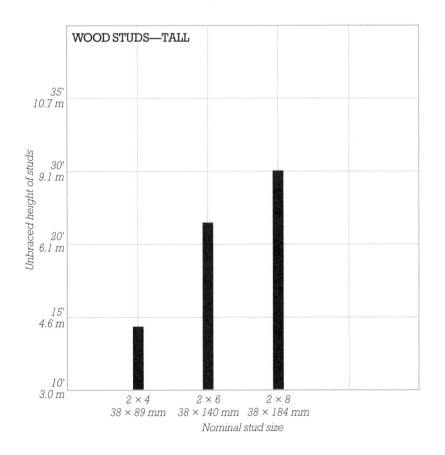

WOOD STUDS—TALL

Unbraced height of studs

35'
10.7 m

30'
9.1 m

20'
6.1 m

15'
4.6 m

10'
3.0 m

2 × 4
38 × 89 mm

2 × 6
38 × 140 mm

2 × 8
38 × 184 mm

Nominal stud size

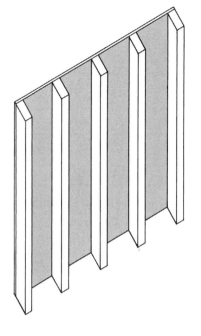

The top chart is for loadbearing wood stud walls up to 10 ft (3.0 m) in height. For each nominal stud size, read from the right-hand bar for strong woods or from the left-hand bar for average-strength woods. Read in the top open areas for light loads or the lower solid areas for medium loads. *Total loaded width* is the tributary width of one floor multiplied by the number of floors and roof above the wall.

For stud walls taller than 10 ft (3.0 m), read from both charts on this page, using the larger size indicated by either chart. *Unbraced height of studs* is the vertical distance between floors or other supports that brace the studs laterally against buckling.

■ On the lower chart, for strong woods, light loads, and close stud spacing, read toward the top in the indicated areas. For average-strength woods, heavy loads, and greater stud spacing, read toward the bottom.

■ Wall height may be increased with the addition of intermediate bracing perpendicular to the wall plane.

ACTUAL SIZES OF FLOOR JOISTS

Nominal Size	Actual Size	
2 × 6	1½" × 5½"	(38 × 140 mm)
2 × 8	1½" × 7¼"	(38 × 184 mm)
2 × 10	1½" × 9¼"	(38 × 235 mm)
2 × 12	1½" × 11¼"	(38 × 286 mm)

TOTAL FINISHED FLOOR THICKNESS

To estimate total finished floor thickness, add 2 in. (50 mm) to the actual joist size for finish ceiling, subflooring, and finish flooring.

BEAMS SUPPORTING FLOOR FRAMING

Wood Beams

For sizing wood beams, see the chart on page 69. To determine clearance under a wood beam, assume that the top of the beam is level with the top of the floor joists.

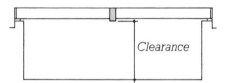

JOISTS WITH WOOD FLOOR BEAM

Steel Beams

Beam Size	Approximate Depth of Beam		Span of Beam	
W8	8"	(203 mm)	8'–13'	(2.4–4.0 m)
W10	10"	(254 mm)	10'–16'	(3.0–4.9 m)
W12	12"	(305 mm)	12'–18'	(3.7–5.5 m)

For lightly loaded beams, use the longer spans indicated. For heavily loaded beams, use the shorter spans. To determine clearance under a steel beam, assume that the top of the beam is level with the top of the foundation wall.

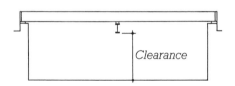

JOISTS WITH STEEL FLOOR BEAM

FIRE-RESISTANCE RATINGS FOR WOOD LIGHT FRAME JOISTS

Wood floor joists may be used in Ordinary Construction and Wood Light Frame Construction. Wood Light Frame floors with nominal 1-in. (19-mm) subflooring and finish flooring can have a 1-hour fire-resistance rating when the underside of the framing is finished with ⅝-in. (16-mm) Type X gypsum board or its equivalent.

WOOD FLOOR JOISTS

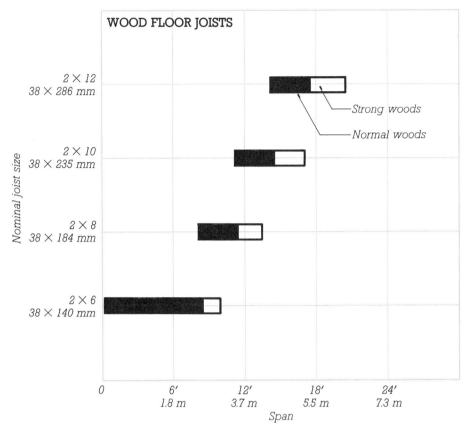

WOOD FLOOR JOISTS

Nominal joist size

2 × 12
38 × 286 mm

2 × 10
38 × 235 mm

2 × 8
38 × 184 mm

2 × 6
38 × 140 mm

Strong woods

Normal woods

0   6'
1.8 m   12'
3.7 m   18'
5.5 m   24'
7.3 m

Span

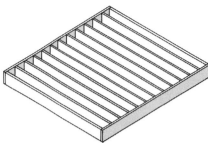

The top chart is for wood floor joists with residential floor loads. For larger loads, increase the indicated joist size by one size (plus 2 in., or 50 mm). For ceiling joists supporting only residential attic loads, decrease the indicated joist size by one size (less 2 in., or 50 mm).

■ Strong woods include Douglas Fir, Larch, Southern Pine, and Oak.

■ For 12-in. (300-mm) joist spacings, increase allowable spans 1 to 2 ft (0.3 to 0.6 m). For 24-in. (600-mm) joist spacings, decrease allowable spans 1 to 2 ft (0.3 to 0.6 m).

■ Most often wood floor joists are spaced 16 in. (400 mm) center-to-center. Spacings of 12 and 24 in. (300 and 600 mm) are also used. In all cases, members should fall on a 4-ft. (1200-mm) module to coordinate with the standard width of various panel products that are used as an integral part of this system.

■ The bottom table is for wood I-joists. Consisting of top and bottom flanges of solid wood or laminated veneer lumber and webs of plywood or oriented strand board, these manufactured framing components can span further than conventional solid wood joists. Spans shown in the table are for normal residential floor loads.

WOOD I-JOIST SPANS

I-Joist Depth	I-Joist Spacing O. C.			
	24" (610 mm)	19.2" (488 mm)	16" (406 mm)	12" (305 mm)
16" (406 mm)	21'-5" (6.5 m)	23'-2" (7.1 m)	24'-8" (7.5 m)	27'-1" (8.3 m)
14" (356 mm)	19'-4" (5.9 m)	20'-11" (6.4 m)	22'-3" (6.8 m)	24'-6" (7.5 m)
11⅞" (295 mm)	15'-10" (4.8 m)	17'-1" (5.2 m)	18'-2" (5.5 m)	20'-0" (6.1 m)
9½" (241 mm)	13'-4" (4.1 m)	14'-5" (4.4 m)	15'-4" (4.7 m)	16'-10" (51 m)

WOOD ROOF RAFTERS

ACTUAL SIZES OF ROOF RAFTERS

Nominal Size	Actual Size	
2×4	1½" × 3½"	(38 × 89 mm)
2×6	1½" × 5½"	(38 × 140 mm)
2×8	1½" × 7¼"	(38 × 184 mm)
2×10	1½" × 9¼"	(38 × 235 mm)

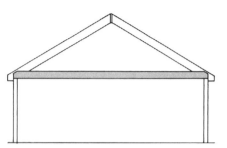

RAFTERS WITH RAFTER TIES

TIES OR BEAMS
SUPPORTING ROOF RAFTERS

Rafter ties connecting rafters at their bases may be sized either as floor joists, if they are intended to support habitable space, or as ceiling joists, if they are supporting attic loads only. See the chart on the facing page.

Structural ridge beams can eliminate the need for ties at the base of the rafters. See page 69 for sizing wood beams.

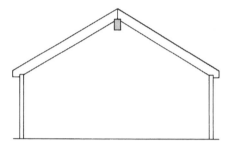

RAFTERS WITH RIDGE BEAM

FIRE-RESISTANCE RATINGS FOR WOOD LIGHT FRAME RAFTERS

Wood roof rafters may be used in Ordinary Construction and Wood Light Frame Construction. Wood Light Frame roofs can have a 1-hour fire-resistance rating when the underside of the framing is finished with ⅝-in. (16-mm) Type X gypsum board or its equivalent.

WOOD ROOF RAFTERS

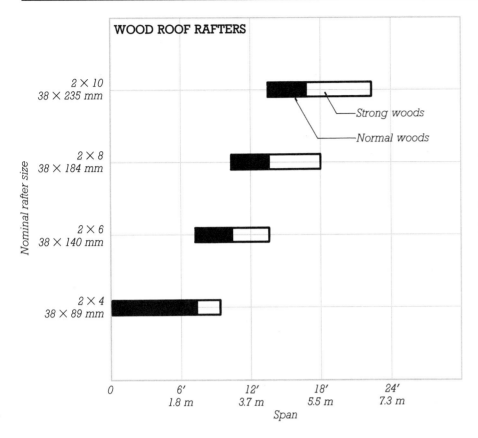

WOOD ROOF RAFTERS

Nominal rafter size

2 × 10
38 × 235 mm

— Strong woods

— Normal woods

2 × 8
38 × 184 mm

2 × 6
38 × 140 mm

2 × 4
38 × 89 mm

| 0 | 6'
1.8 m | 12'
3.7 m | 18'
5.5 m | 24'
7.3 m |

Span

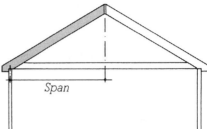

Span

This chart is for wood rafters with a pitch of at least 3:12 and no finish ceiling attached to the underside of the rafters.

■ For rafters with lower slopes (including flat roofs) or with attached finish ceilings, reduce allowable spans by 1 to 2 ft (0.3 to 0.6 m).

■ For unusually heavy roof loads, increase rafter size by one size (plus 2 in., or 50 mm).

■ Strong woods include Douglas Fir, Larch, Southern Pine, and Oak.

■ Most often wood roof rafters are spaced 16 in. (400 mm) center-to-center. Spacings of 12 and 24 in. (300 and 600 mm) are also used. In all cases members should fall on a 4-ft. (1200-mm) module to coordinate with the standard width of various panel products that are used as an integral part of this system.

WOOD FLOOR AND ROOF TRUSSES—LIGHT

Light wood floor and roof trusses are commonly used in place of conventional wood joists and rafters in Platform Frame Construction. These prefabricated elements permit quicker erection in the field, greater clear spans, simplified framing due to the lack of interior loadbearing walls, and easier running of electrical and mechanical services due to the open spaces within the trusses.

FIRE-RESISTANCE RATINGS
FOR LIGHT WOOD TRUSSES

Lightwood trusses may be used in Ordinary Construction and Wood Light Frame Construction. They can have a 1-hour fire-resistance rating when covered with nominal 1-in. (19-mm) subflooring and finish flooring and when the underside of the framing is finished with ⅝-in. (16-mm) Type X gypsum board or its equivalent.

WOOD FLOOR AND ROOF TRUSSES—LIGHT

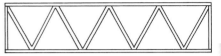

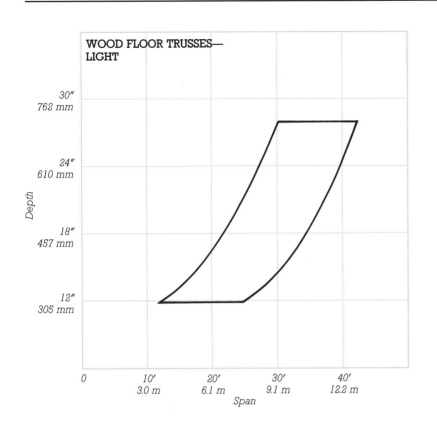

WOOD FLOOR TRUSSES—
LIGHT

Depth

30″ / 762 mm
24″ / 610 mm
18″ / 457 mm
12″ / 305 mm

0
10′ / 3.0 m
20′ / 6.1 m
30′ / 9.1 m
40′ / 12.2 m

Span

The top chart is for wood floor trusses constructed from light members (up to 6 in., or 140 mm, deep). For heavy loads, read toward the left in the indicated area. For light loads, read toward the right. For preliminary design, use depths in even 2-in. (50-mm) increments. The sizes available may vary with the manufacturer.

■ Typical truss spacing is 16 to 48 in. (400 to 1200 mm).

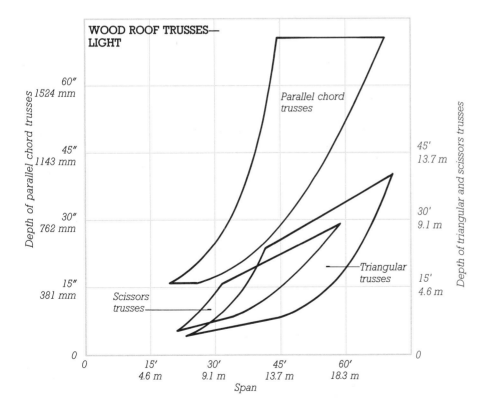

WOOD ROOF TRUSSES—
LIGHT

Depth of parallel chord trusses

60″ / 1524 mm
45″ / 1143 mm
30″ / 762 mm
15″ / 381 mm
0

Parallel chord trusses

Triangular trusses

Scissors trusses

Depth of triangular and scissors trusses

45′ / 13.7 m
30′ / 9.1 m
15′ / 4.6 m
0

0
15′ / 4.6 m
30′ / 9.1 m
45′ / 13.7 m
60′ / 18.3 m

Span

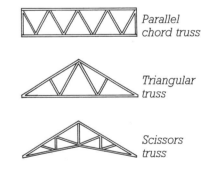

Parallel chord truss

Triangular truss

Scissors truss

The bottom chart is for wood roof trusses constructed from light members (up to 6 in., or 140 mm, deep). Read depths of parallel chord trusses from the left-hand scale and depths of other trusses from the right-hand scale. For heavy loads, read toward the left in the indicated area. For light loads, read toward the right. Triangular or scissors trusses are commonly available with top chord slopes in whole number pitches from 2:12 to 7:12. Available sizes may vary with the manufacturer.

■ Typical truss spacing is 16 to 48 in. (400 to 1200 mm).

WOOD STRENGTH

When reading the charts on the opposite page, examples of strong woods include Select Structural grades of Douglas Fir, Larch, Hemlock, or Southern Pine. Examples of average-strength woods include No. 2 grades of Hem-Fir or Spruce-Pine-Fir. For other species and grade combinations of intermediate strength, you may interpolate between the results charted for these two groups.

FIRE-RESISTANCE RATINGS FOR WOOD COLUMNS

Wood columns may be used in any Combustible Construction type. To qualify as components of Heavy Timber Construction, wood columns supporting floor loads must have a nominal size of at least 8 × 8 in. (191 × 191 mm). Columns supporting roof and ceiling loads only may be as small as 6 × 8 in. (140 × 191 mm). Columns of lesser dimensions may be used in Ordinary and Wood Light Frame Construction.

WOOD COLUMNS

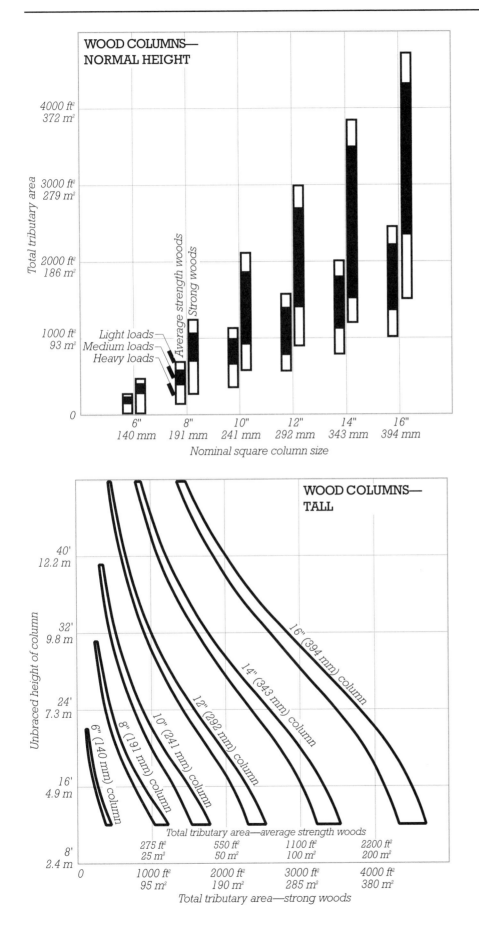

**WOOD COLUMNS—
NORMAL HEIGHT**

Total tributary area

- 4000 ft² / 372 m²
- 3000 ft² / 279 m²
- 2000 ft² / 186 m²
- 1000 ft² / 93 m²
- 0

Average strength woods
Strong woods

Light loads
Medium loads
Heavy loads

Nominal square column size

| 6" / 140 mm | 8" / 191 mm | 10" / 241 mm | 12" / 292 mm | 14" / 343 mm | 16" / 394 mm |

**WOOD COLUMNS—
TALL**

Unbraced height of column

- 40' / 12.2 m
- 32' / 9.8 m
- 24' / 7.3 m
- 16' / 4.9 m
- 8' / 2.4 m

6" (140 mm) column
8" (191 mm) column
10" (241 mm) column
12" (292 mm) column
14" (343 mm) column
16" (394 mm) column

Total tributary area—average strength woods

| 275 ft² / 25 m² | 550 ft² / 50 m² | 1100 ft² / 100 m² | 2200 ft² / 200 m² |

Total tributary area—strong woods

| 0 | 1000 ft² / 95 m² | 2000 ft² / 190 m² | 3000 ft² / 285 m² | 4000 ft² / 380 m² |

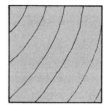

The top chart is for solid wood columns up to 12 ft (3.7 m) in height. For each column size, read from the right-hand bar for strong woods or from the left-hand bar for average-strength woods. Read in the top open area for light loads, the middle solid area for medium loads, or the lower open area for heavy loads. *Total tributary area* is the summed area of the roof and all floors supported by the column.

■ For rectangular columns, select a column of area equal to the square size indicated.

■ Actual column size is ½ in. less than nominal English unit sizes. Metric equivalents are actual size.

For columns taller than 12 ft (3.7), read from both charts on this page, using the larger column size indicated by either chart. *Unbraced height of column* is the vertical distance between floors or other supports that brace the column laterally against buckling.

■ On the lower chart, read *Total tributary area* from the lower scale for strong woods, or from the upper scale for average-strength woods. Read toward the right within the indicated curves for light loads and toward the left for medium loads. For heavy loads, read the total tributary area for light loads and then divide by half.

■ For rectangular columns, read the lower chart using the smallest dimension of the column.

FIRE-RESISTANCE RATINGS FOR WOOD DECKING

Wood decking may be used in any Combustible Construction type. To qualify for Heavy Timber Construction as defined by the building codes, wood floor decking must be at least 3 in. (64 mm) in nominal thickness, with minimum 1-in. nominal (19-mm) wood finish flooring laid over it at right angles. Roof decking for Heavy Timber construction must be at least 2 in. (38 mm) in nominal thickness. Decking of lesser thickness may be used in Ordinary Construction and Wood Light Frame Construction.

WOOD DECKING

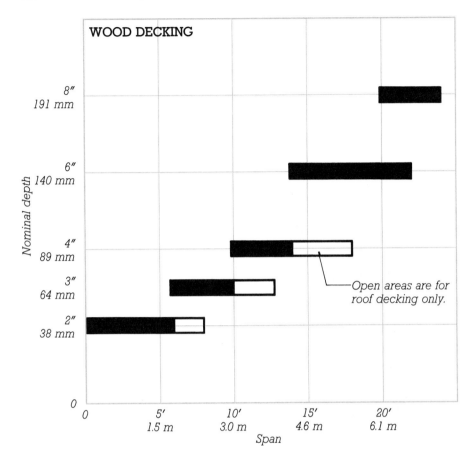

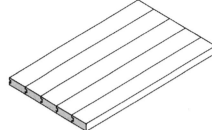

This chart is for solid or laminated wood decking. For light loads or strong woods, read toward the right in the indicated areas. For large loads or normal woods, read toward the left.

■ Strong woods include Douglas Fir, Larch, Southern Pine, and Oak.

■ Decking comes in various nominal widths, 6 and 8 in. (150 and 200 mm) being the most common. Actual depth is ½ in. (13 mm) less than nominal.

■ Allow approximately ¾ in. (19 mm) for the depth of finish flooring.

WOOD BEAMS

SIZES OF SOLID WOOD BEAMS

Nominal Depth	Actual Depth
4"	3½" (89 mm)
6"	5½" (140 mm)
8", 10", 12"	¾" (19 mm) less than nominal for beam widths of 2", 3", and 4", and
	½" (13 mm) less than nominal for beam widths greater than 4"
14" or greater	½" (13 mm) less than nominal

The actual widths of solid beams are ½ in. (13 mm) less than nominal.

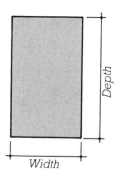

FRAMING FOR HEAVY TIMBER CONSTRUCTION

A heavy timber framing system that uses both beams and girders allows for a great range of bay sizes and proportions. The beam spacing is determined by the allowable span of the floor or roof decking as tabulated on page 67. For preliminary design, limit beam and girder spans to a maximum of 20 ft (6 m) for solid wood, or 24 ft (7.3 m) for laminated wood.

FIRE-RESISTANCE RATINGS FOR WOOD BEAMS

Wood beams may be used in any Combustible Construction type. To qualify for Heavy Timber Construction, minimum size requirements for wood beams vary slightly between the model building codes. For preliminary purposes, wood beams supporting floors should be no smaller than nominal 6 × 10 (140 × 241 mm actual size), and those supporting roofs only, no smaller than 4 × 6 (89 × 140 mm). Beams of lesser dimensions may be used in Ordinary and Wood Light Frame Construction. For more information on the minimum size requirements for wood beams used in Heavy Timber Construction in both model codes, see pages 366–367.

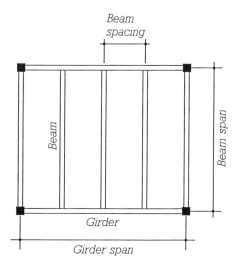

HEAVY TIMBER FLOOR FRAMING

WOOD BEAMS

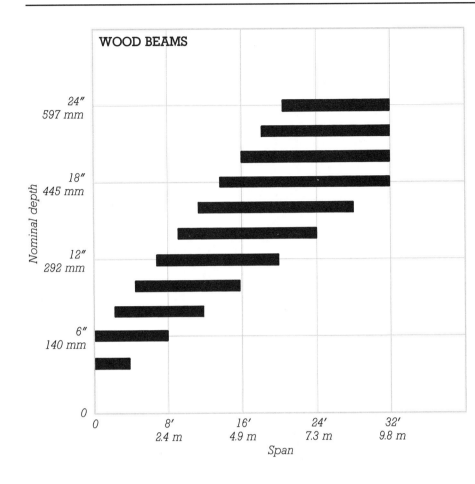

SOLID BEAM

BUILT-UP BEAM

This chart is for solid or built-up beams as shown. For girders, or for beams carrying large loads, read toward the left in the indicated areas. For light loads or strong woods, read toward the right.

■ Strong woods include Douglas Fir, Larch, Southern Pine, and Oak.

■ Practical widths for solid beams range from one-fourth of the depth of the beam to equal to the depth of the beam.

■ A girder should be at least 2 in. (50 mm) deeper than the beams it supports.

GLUE LAMINATED WOOD BEAMS

SIZES OF GLUE LAMINATED BEAMS

Glue laminated beams are specified by their actual size. Depths must be a multiple of 1½ in. (38 mm), the thickness of one lamination.

Width	Depth	
3⅛" (79 mm)	3"–24"	(76–610 mm)
5⅛" (130 mm)	4½"–36"	(114–914 mm)
6¾" (171 mm)	6"–48"	(152–1219 mm)
8¾" (222 mm)	9"–63"	(229–1600 mm)
10¾" (273 mm)	10½"–75"	(267–1905 mm)

CONTINUOUS SPAN GLUE LAMINATED BEAMS

For maximum efficiency, glue laminated beams may be configured with continuous spans. For such configurations, read toward the right in the indicated area on the chart on the facing page. Practical spans for continuous span beam systems range from 25 to 65 ft (7.5 to 20.0 m).

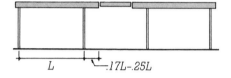

CONTINUOUS SPAN GLUE LAMINATED BEAMS

FIRE-RESISTANCE RATINGS FOR GLUE LAMINATED WOOD BEAMS

Glue laminated wood beams may be used in any Combustible Construction type. To qualify for Heavy Timber Construction, minimum size requirements for glue laminated wood beams vary with each model building code. For preliminary purposes, beams supporting floors should be no smaller than 5 × 10½ in. (127 × 267 mm) actual size, and those supporting roofs only, no smaller than 3 × 6⅞ in. (76 × 175 mm). Beams of lesser dimensions may be used in Ordinary and Wood Light Frame Construction. For more information on the minimum size requirements for wood beams used in Heavy Timber Construction in both model codes, see pages 366–367.

GLUE LAMINATED WOOD BEAMS

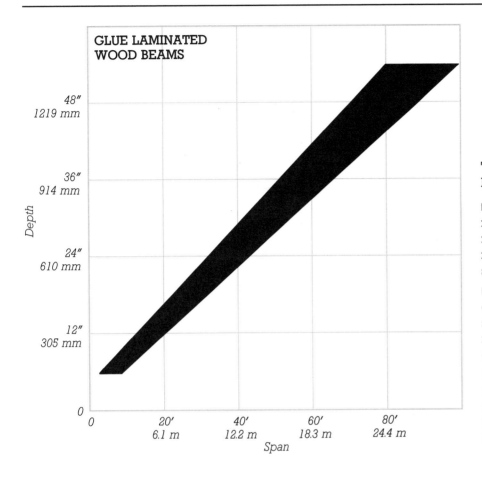

This chart is for glue laminated beams.

■ Normal spacings for glue laminated beams range from 4 ft (1.2 m) for small beams supporting decking to 24 ft (7.3 m) for larger beams supporting joists or purlins.

■ Typical widths for glue laminated beams are one-fourth to one-seventh of the depth, rounded to the nearest standard width, as shown on the facing page.

■ For girders, read depths from the extreme left-hand edge of the indicated area. A girder should be at least 1½ in. (38 mm) deeper than the beams it supports.

SPACING OF HEAVY WOOD ROOF TRUSSES

Roof trusses spaced no greater than 4 to 8 ft (1.2 to 2.4 m) require no additional joists or purlins. The maximum practical spacing of trusses with joists or purlins is approximately 20 ft (6.1 m).

FIRE-RESISTANCE RATINGS FOR HEAVY WOOD TRUSSES

Heavy wood trusses may be used in any Combustible Construction type. To qualify for Heavy Timber Construction, minimum size requirements for wood trusses vary slightly between the model building codes. For preliminary purposes, trusses supporting floors should be made of members no smaller than nominal 8 × 8 (191 × 191 mm actual size), and those supporting roofs only, of members no smaller than 4 × 6 (89 × 140 mm). Trusses made of members of lesser dimensions may be used in Ordinary and Wood Light Frame Construction. For more information on the minimum size requirements for wood trusses used in Heavy Timber Construction in both model codes, see pages 366–367.

WOOD TRUSSES — HEAVY

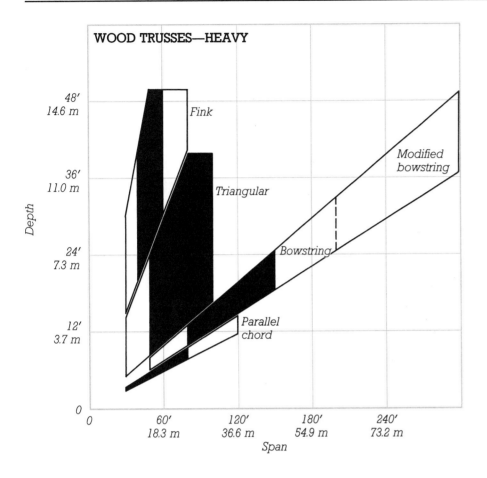

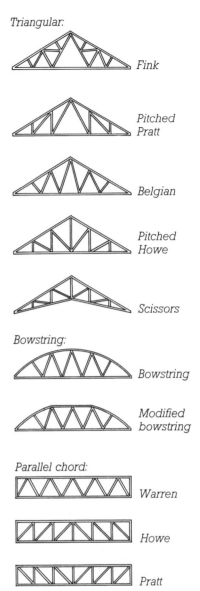

This chart is for wood trusses constructed from heavy members (a minimum of 4 × 6 in., or 89 × 140 mm, in nominal size).

■ The most economical span ranges for each truss type are indicated with the solid tone.

GLUE LAMINATED WOOD ARCHES

DIMENSIONS FOR POINTED ARCHES

LOW- TO MEDIUM-PITCH ARCHES (3:12 TO 8:12)

Wall Height	Thickness of Arch	Depth of Base	Depth of Crown
10'–18' (3.0–5.5 m)	3⅛", 5⅛", 6¾" (79, 130, 171 mm)	7½"–18" for short spans (191–457 mm) 8"–30" for medium spans (203–762 mm) 8½"–35" for long spans (216–889 mm)	7½"–27" (191–686 mm)

HIGH-PITCH ARCHES (10:12 TO 16:12)

Wall Height	Thickness of Arch	Depth of Base	Depth of Crown
8'–12' (2.4–3.7 m)	5⅛" (130 mm)	7½" for short spans (191 mm) 7¾" for medium spans (197 mm) 9½"–10" for long spans (241–254 mm)	7¾"–24½" (197–622 mm)

FIRE-RESISTANCE RATINGS FOR GLUE LAMINATED ARCHES

Glue laminated wood arches may be used in any Combustible Construction type. To qualify for Heavy Timber Construction, minimum size requirements for such arches vary slightly between the model building codes. For preliminary purposes, arches supporting floors should be no smaller than 6¾ × 8¼ in. (171 × 210 mm) actual size, and those supporting roofs only, no smaller than 5 × 8¼ in. (127 × 210 mm). Arches of lesser dimensions may be used in Ordinary and Wood Light Frame Construction. For more information on the minimum size requirements for glue laminated wood arches used in Heavy Timber Construction in both model codes, see pages 366–367.

GLUE LAMINATED WOOD ARCHES

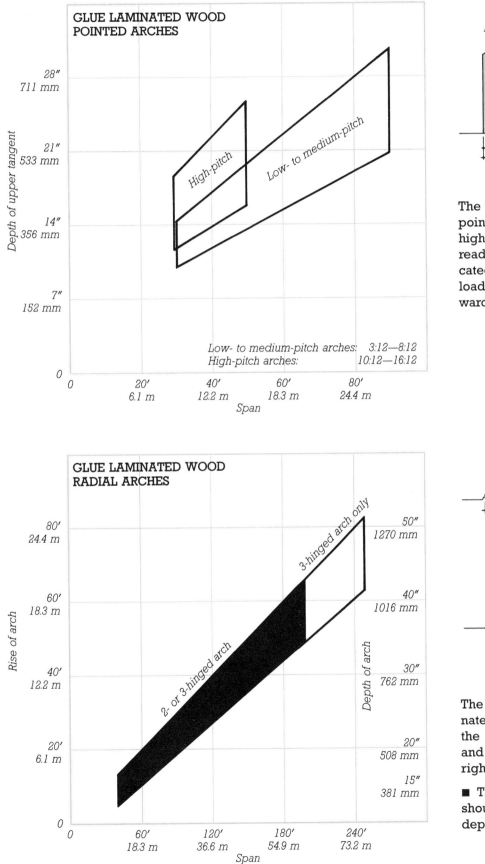

GLUE LAMINATED WOOD
POINTED ARCHES

Depth of upper tangent

28″
711 mm

21″
533 mm

14″
356 mm

7″
152 mm

0

High-pitch

Low- to medium-pitch

Low- to medium-pitch arches: 3:12—8:12
High-pitch arches: 10:12—16:12

Span

0   20′   40′   60′   80′
     6.1 m   12.2 m   18.3 m   24.4 m

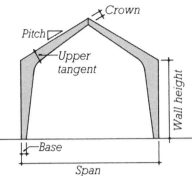

Crown

Pitch

Upper
tangent

Wall height

Base

Span

The top chart is for glue laminated
pointed arches. For low pitches,
high loads, and high side walls,
read toward the top in the indicated areas. For high pitches, low
loads, and low side walls, read toward the bottom.

GLUE LAMINATED WOOD
RADIAL ARCHES

Rise of arch

80′
24.4 m

60′
18.3 m

40′
12.2 m

20′
6.1 m

0

3-hinged arch only

2- or 3-hinged arch

Depth of arch

50″
1270 mm

40″
1016 mm

30″
762 mm

20″
508 mm

15″
381 mm

Span

0   60′   120′   180′   240′
     18.3 m   36.6 m   54.9 m   73.2 m

Depth

Rise

Span

2-HINGE RADIAL ARCH

3-HINGE RADIAL ARCH

The bottom chart is for glue laminated radial arches. Read the rise of
the arch from the left-hand scale
and the depth of the arch from the
right-hand scale.

■ The thickness of a radial arch
should be at least one-fifth of its
depth.

MASONRY STRUCTURAL SYSTEMS

Masonry construction rarely forms a complete building system by itself. Nonbearing masonry walls can be combined with other structural systems either in the form of infill between framing elements or as a veneer applied over wall or frame systems. Loadbearing masonry walls and columns can be combined with various spanning elements to form complete structural systems.

Masonry walls may be constructed in a great variety of ways. Use the following guidelines for preliminary design: Single-wythe walls are generally limited to nonbearing applications or as a veneer over other wall systems. Cavity wall construction is a preferred choice for exterior walls because of its greater resistance to water penetration and improved thermal performance. Concrete block construction is generally more economical than brick because of the reduced labor of laying the larger units and the lower material costs. Loadbearing masonry walls and columns must be steel reinforced in all but the smallest structures.

Since masonry construction takes place on-site and utilizes elements of small size, it is well suited for use in the construction of buildings of irregular form. Modular dimensions should be used, however, to minimize the need for partial units in construction. Use a module of one-half the nominal length of a masonry unit in plan, and the height of one brick or block course in elevation.

MASONRY AND WOOD CONSTRUCTION

Masonry can form the exterior (and sometimes interior) loadbearing walls for either Wood Light Frame Construction or Heavy Timber Construction, systems traditionally named Ordinary Construction and Mill Construction, respectively. Both of these systems have higher fire-resistance ratings than all-wood construction and are permitted for use in larger and taller buildings. For more information on the fire resistance of these systems and the building types for which their use is permitted, see pages 366–367. For sizing the wood elements of Ordinary or Heavy Timber Construction, see the appropriate pages under Wood Structural Systems beginning on page 55.

MASONRY AND STEEL CONSTRUCTION

Open-web joists are the steel spanning elements most commonly used with loadbearing masonry construction because of the relatively small concentrated loads produced by these lightweight, closely spaced elements. Where steel beams and girders bear upon masonry walls, pilasters may be required at points of support. For economy and strength, interior columns in such systems are typically structural steel rather than masonry. See pages 93–111 for information on steel construction.

MASONRY AND CONCRETE CONSTRUCTION

The sitecast and precast concrete spanning elements most commonly used with loadbearing masonry walls are shorter span slabs without ribs or beams. These systems are often highly economical due to the minimal floor depths associated with these spanning elements, the absence of any requirement for added fire-resistive finishes, and the acoustical and energy performance of these high-mass materials. See pages 113–129 for information on sitecast concrete construction and pages 131–141 for information on precast concrete construction.

BRICK MASONRY COLUMNS

MASONRY STRENGTH

The strength and cost of brick masonry construction increase as stronger materials (including brick, steel reinforcing, and mortar) are used in its construction. When reading the top chart on the facing page, begin by assuming low-strength masonry and read from the lower set of bars. If the wall sizes yielded by this result are impractically large, then consider using higher-strength masonry, reading from the upper set of bars, or interpolating between the two sets.

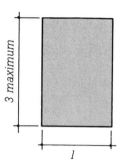

RECTANGULAR COLUMNS

BRICK MASONRY COLUMN SIZES

For lightly loaded structures, the minimum size for reinforced brick masonry columns is 8 in. (200 mm) nominally on each side. For other conditions, use columns 12 in. (300 mm) square or larger. For rectangular columns, the wider side should be no more than three times the width of the more narrow side. For pilasters (columns part of walls), the wider side should not exceed four times the width of the shorter side. For maximum economy, size brick masonry columns in increments of 4 in. (100 mm).

FIRE-RESISTANCE RATINGS FOR BRICK MASONRY COLUMNS

Brick masonry construction may be used in both Combustible and Noncombustible Construction. The fire resistance of brick masonry construction varies with the type of brick unit. For preliminary design, assume that a 1-hour fire-resistance rating can be achieved with an 8-in. (200-mm) square column and a 2-hour or greater rating with a 12-in. (300-mm) column.

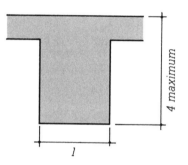

RECTANGULAR PILASTERS

BRICK MASONRY COLUMNS

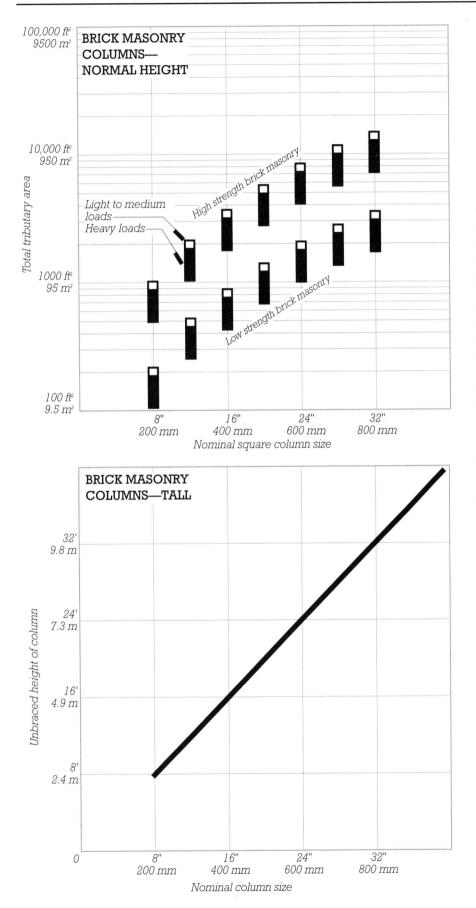

BRICK MASONRY COLUMNS— NORMAL HEIGHT

Total tributary area

100,000 ft² / 9500 m²
10,000 ft² / 950 m²
1000 ft² / 95 m²
100 ft² / 9.5 m²

Light to medium loads
Heavy loads

High strength brick masonry
Low strength brick masonry

8" / 200 mm   16" / 400 mm   24" / 600 mm   32" / 800 mm

Nominal square column size

BRICK MASONRY COLUMNS—TALL

Unbraced height of column

32' / 9.8 m
24' / 7.3 m
16' / 4.9 m
8' / 2.4 m

0   8" / 200 mm   16" / 400 mm   24" / 600 mm   32" / 800 mm

Nominal column size

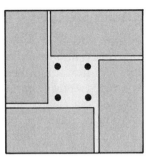

The top chart is for reinforced brick masonry columns up to 12 ft (3.7 m) tall between floors. For high compressive strength masonry, read from the upper set of bars. For low strength masonry, read from the lower set. For light to medium loads, read in the upper open areas of each bar; for heavy loads, read in the lower solid areas. *Total tributary area* is the summed area of the roof and all floors supported by the column.

■ For rectangular columns, select a column of area equal to the square size indicated.

■ Actual column size is ⅜ in. (10 mm) less than nominal size.

For columns taller than 12 ft (3.7 m), read from both charts on this page, using the larger size indicated by either chart. *Unbraced height of column* is the vertical distance between floors or other supports that brace the column laterally against buckling.

■ For rectangular columns, read the chart's nominal column size using the lesser dimension of the column.

MASONRY STRENGTH

The strength and cost of brick masonry construction increase as stronger materials (including brick, steel reinforcing, and mortar) are used in its construction. When reading the top chart on the facing page, begin by assuming low-strength masonry and read from the lower set of curves. If the wall sizes yielded by this result are impractically large, then consider using higher-strength masonry, reading from the upper set of curves or interpolating between the two sets.

MINIMUM WIDTHS OF WALLS

Reinforced brick masonry walls 6 in. (150 mm) wide should be used for one-story structures only. Use walls 8 in. (200 mm) or wider for multistory structures.

MAXIMUM UNBRACED LENGTH OF WALL

Use the bottom chart on the facing page to determine the maximum permissible unbraced length of wall in plan in addition to its maximum permissible height. Masonry walls should be braced by crosswalls spaced at distances not exceeding those indicated on the chart. If the proposed crosswall spacing in your design is too great, either thicken the wall or add pilasters at intermediate spacing (see pages 78–79 for sizing of pilasters).

DESIGNING WITH MASONRY BEARING WALLS

Reinforced brick masonry walls may be used in structures up to approximately 20 stories in height. In high-rise structures, the cellular arrangements of the bearing wall structure make this system best suited to apartment buildings, hotels, dormitories, and other residential occupancies which require relatively small, repetitively arranged spaces.

For structures up to approximately 6 stories in height, interior crosswalls and corridor walls should be sufficient to provide the needed lateral bracing for the structure. This permits exterior walls to remain relatively open in design. At greater heights, lateral stability requirements increasingly dictate a more complete cellular configuration of walls. In this case, the sizes of openings in the exterior walls will become increasingly restricted.

Loadbearing walls should be aligned consistently from floor to floor and should be continuous from the roof to the building foundation. Where it is desirable to create a larger space on a lower floor, it may be possible to design one or more of the walls above to act as deep beams spanning between columns. Such wall beams may span as much as 20 to 30 ft (6 to 9 m).

FIRE-RESISTANCE RATINGS FOR BRICK MASONRY WALLS

Brick masonry construction may be used in both Combustible and Noncombustible Construction. The fire resistance of brick masonry construction varies with the type of brick unit. For preliminary design, assume that a 2- to 3-hour fire-resistance rating can be achieved with a 6-in. (150-mm)-wide wall, and a 4-hour rating with an 8-in. (200-mm) wall.

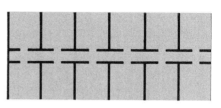

LOW-RISE BEARING WALL CONFIGURATION (*shown in plan*)

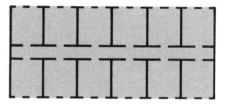

HIGH-RISE BEARING WALL CONFIGURATION (*shown in plan*)

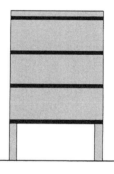

Bearing walls may act as deep beams to span across openings below, as shown in this schematic cross section.

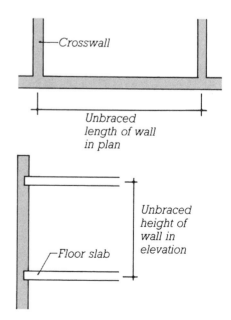

UNBRACED HEIGHT OR LENGTH OF MASONRY WALLS

BRICK MASONRY WALLS

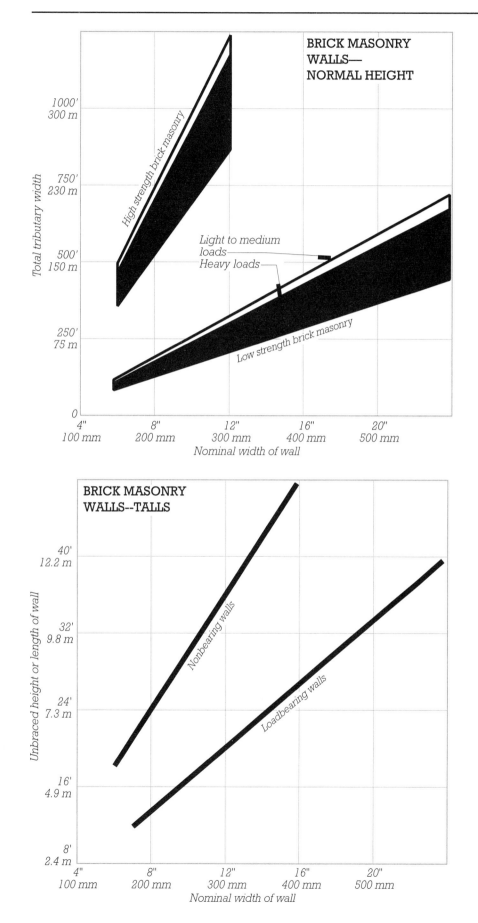

BRICK MASONRY WALLS— NORMAL HEIGHT

Total tributary width

1000'
300 m

750'
230 m

500'
150 m

250'
75 m

0

High strength brick masonry

Light to medium loads
Heavy loads

Low strength brick masonry

4" 100 mm | 8" 200 mm | 12" 300 mm | 16" 400 mm | 20" 500 mm

Nominal width of wall

BRICK MASONRY WALLS--TALLS

Unbraced height or length of wall

40'
12.2 m

32'
9.8 m

24'
7.3 m

16'
4.9 m

8'
2.4 m

Nonbearing walls

Loadbearing walls

4" 100 mm | 8" 200 mm | 12" 300 mm | 16" 400 mm | 20" 500 mm

Nominal width of wall

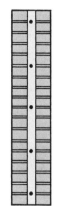

The top chart is for reinforced brick masonry walls up to 12 ft (3.7 m) tall between floors. For high compressive strength masonry, read from the upper set of curves. For low strength masonry, read from the lower set. For light loads, read in the upper open areas of each curve; for medium to heavy loads, read in the lower solid areas. *Total tributary width* is one-half the span of one floor supported by the wall multiplied by the number of floors and the roof above.

■ For cavity walls, use only the net width of the structural wythe when reading the charts on this page.

■ Actual width of a wall is ⅜ in. (10 mm) less than the nominal size.

For walls greater than 12 ft (3.7 m) in height or in unbraced length, read from both charts on this page, using the larger size indicated by either chart. Read along the *Loadbearing walls* curve for walls bearing gravity loads or wind loads. Read along the *Nonloadbearing walls* curve for interior nonloadbearing partitions. *Unbraced height of wall* is the vertical distance between floors. *Unbraced length of wall* is the horizontal distance between crosswalls or pilasters. See the facing page for more information on the maximum unbraced length of the wall.

BRICK MASONRY LINTELS

STEEL ANGLE LINTELS

The chart below is for steel angle lintels carrying wall loads only. Heavier structural shapes, such as channels or wide flange sections combined with plates, may be used where longer spans or greater load capacities are required.

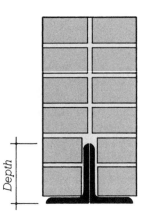

Depth of Angle	Maximum Span
3" (76 mm)	5' (1.5 m)
4" (102 mm)	6' (1.8 m)
5" (127 mm)	7' (2.1 m)
6" (152 mm)	8' (2.4 m)

FIRE-RESISTANCE RATINGS FOR BRICK MASONRY LINTELS

Brick masonry lintels may be used in both Combustible and Noncombustible Construction. Lintels not less than 8 in. (200 mm) in nominal dimension may be assumed to have a fire-resistance rating of 3 hours.

BRICK MASONRY LINTELS

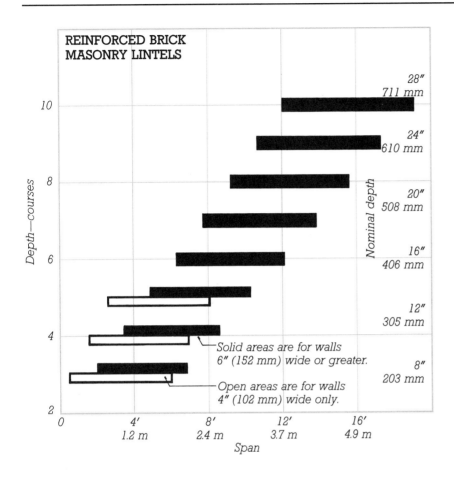

REINFORCED BRICK
MASONRY LINTELS

Depth—courses (y-axis): 2, 4, 6, 8, 10

Nominal depth (right axis):
- 28″ / 711 mm
- 24″ / 610 mm
- 20″ / 508 mm
- 16″ / 406 mm
- 12″ / 305 mm
- 8″ / 203 mm

Span (x-axis): 0, 4′ (1.2 m), 8′ (2.4 m), 12′ (3.7 m), 16′ (4.9 m)

Solid areas are for walls 6″ (152 mm) wide or greater.

Open areas are for walls 4″ (102 mm) wide only.

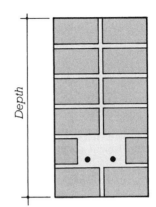

Depth

This chart is for steel reinforced brick masonry lintels. For lintels carrying only wall loads, read toward the right in the indicated areas. For additional superimposed loads, such as floor loads, read toward the left. For most applications, lintel depths of 4 to 7 courses are sufficient.

■ Depths for this chart are based on modular brick coursing: 3 courses = 8 in. (200 mm). For other sizes, read depths in inches from the right-hand scale and round up to a whole course height.

■ Actual depth is the thickness of one mortar joint less than the nominal depth (approximately ½ in., or 13 mm).

BRICK MASONRY ARCHES

MINOR BRICK ARCHES

The following rules apply to arches with spans of up to 6 to 8 ft (1.8 to 2.4 m): Almost any shape of arch will work at these spans, particularly when the arch is embedded in a wall. Depths of arches typically range from 4 to 16 in. (100 to 400 mm). Thicknesses of minor arches should be at least 4 to 8 in. (100 to 200 mm). Concentrated loads bearing directly on minor brick arches, especially jack arches, should be avoided. The thrusts produced by any arch must be resisted at its supports. This resistance can be provided by buttressing from an adjacent arch or an adjacent mass of masonry, or by an arch tie.

Segmental arches are most efficient when the rise of the arch is between 0.08 and 0.15 times the span of the arch. Apply the following rules for jack arches:

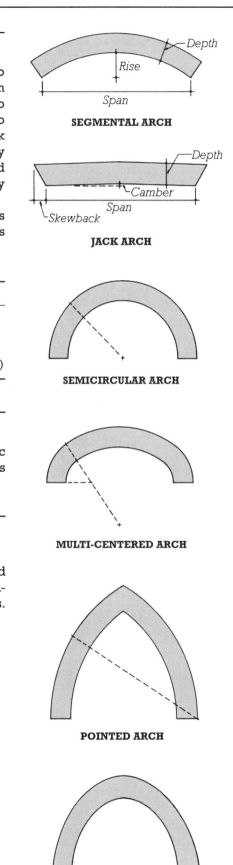

SEGMENTAL ARCH

JACK ARCH

SEMICIRCULAR ARCH

MULTI-CENTERED ARCH

POINTED ARCH

PARABOLIC ARCH

Camber	Depth	Skewback
⅛" per foot of span (1:100)	8" (200 mm) minimum	½" per foot of span for every 4" of arch depth (40 mm per meter of span for every 100 mm of arch depth)

MAJOR BRICK ARCHES

Major brick arches can span to approximately 250 ft (75 m). Parabolic shapes are recommended for long span arches. The most efficient rise is approximately 0.20 to 0.25 times the span of the arch.

FIRE-RESISTANCE RATINGS FOR BRICK MASONRY ARCHES

Brick masonry arches may be used in both Combustible and Noncombustible Construction. Arches not less than 8 in. (200 mm) in nominal dimension may be assumed to have a fire-resistance rating of 3 hours.

CONCRETE BLOCK COLUMNS

MASONRY STRENGTH

The strength and cost of concrete masonry construction increase as stronger materials (including concrete units, steel reinforcing, and mortar) are used in its construction. When reading the top chart on the facing page, begin by assuming low strength masonry and read from the lower set of bars. If the column sizes yielded by this result are impractically large, then consider using higher strength masonry, reading from the upper set of bars or interpolating between the two sets.

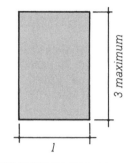

RECTANGULAR COLUMNS

CONCRETE BLOCK COLUMN SIZES

For lightly loaded structures, the minimum size for reinforced concrete masonry columns is 8 in. (200 mm). For other conditions, use columns 12 in. (300 mm) square or larger. For rectangular columns, the wider side should be no more than three times the width of the more narrow side. For pilasters (columns part of walls), the wider side should not exceed four times the width of the shorter side. For maximum economy, size concrete block columns in increments of 4 in. (100 mm).

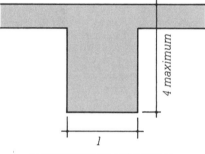

RECTANGULAR PILASTERS

86 FIRE-RESISTANCE RATINGS FOR CONCRETE MASONRY COLUMNS

Concrete masonry may be used in Combustible and Noncombustible Construction. The fire resistance of concrete masonry construction varies with the type of concrete units. For preliminary design, concrete columns with a least dimension of 8 in. (200 mm) may be assumed to have a fire-resistance rating of 1 hour, and those with least dimensions of 10 in. (250 mm), 12 in (300 mm), and 14 in (350 mm) to have fire-resistance ratings of 2, 3, and 4 hours, respectively.

CONCRETE BLOCK COLUMNS

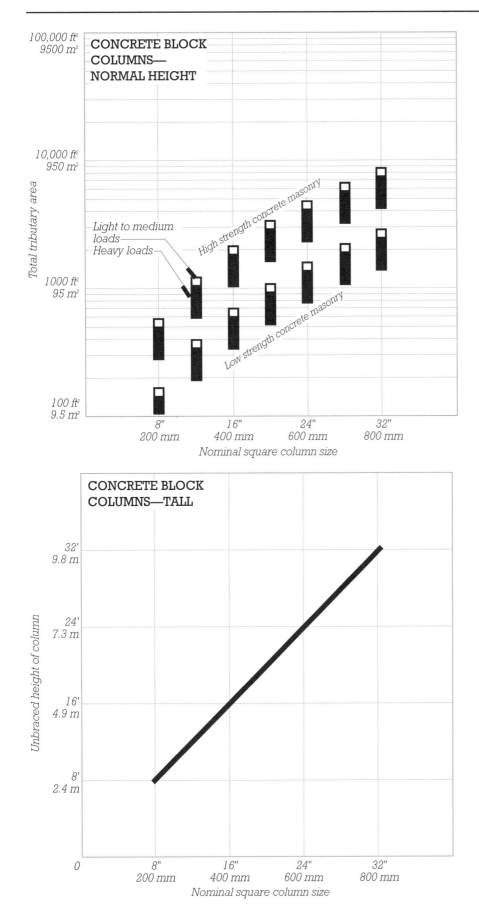

CONCRETE BLOCK COLUMNS— NORMAL HEIGHT

Total tributary area

- 100,000 ft² / 9500 m²
- 10,000 ft² / 950 m²
- 1000 ft² / 95 m²
- 100 ft² / 9.5 m²

Light to medium loads
Heavy loads

High strength concrete masonry
Low strength concrete masonry

Nominal square column size: 8" / 200 mm, 16" / 400 mm, 24" / 600 mm, 32" / 800 mm

CONCRETE BLOCK COLUMNS—TALL

Unbraced height of column

- 32' / 9.8 m
- 24' / 7.3 m
- 16' / 4.9 m
- 8' / 2.4 m
- 0

Nominal square column size: 8" / 200 mm, 16" / 400 mm, 24" / 600 mm, 32" / 800 mm

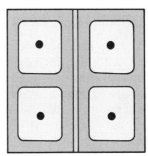

The top chart is for concrete masonry columns up to 12 ft (3.7 m) tall between floors. For high compressive strength masonry, read from the upper set of bars. For low strength masonry, read from the lower set. For light to medium loads, read in the upper open areas of each bar; for heavy loads, read in the lower solid areas. *Total tributary area* is the summed area of the roof and all floors supported by the column.

- For rectangular columns, select a column of area equal to the square size indicated.

- Actual column size is $\frac{3}{8}$ in. (10 mm) less than nominal size.

For columns taller than 12 ft (3.7 m), read from both charts on this page, using the larger size indicated by either chart. *Unbraced height of column* is the vertical distance between floors or other supports that brace the column laterally against buckling.

- For rectangular columns, read *Square column size* using the lesser dimension of the column.

CONCRETE BLOCK WALLS

MASONRY STRENGTH

The strength and cost of concrete masonry construction increase as stronger materials (including concrete block, steel reinforcing, and mortar) are used in its construction. When reading the top chart on the facing page, begin by assuming low strength masonry and read from the lower set of bars. If the wall sizes yielded by this result are impractically large, then consider using higher strength masonry, reading from the upper set of bars, or interpolate between the two sets.

CAVITY WALLS

For cavity walls, use only the nominal width of the structural wythe when reading the charts on the facing page.

MINIMUM WIDTHS OF WALL

For most construction, 8 in. (200 mm) is the minimum practical width for reinforced concrete masonry walls. Though walls 6 in. (150 mm) wide are feasible, they are difficult to construct and only suitable for the support of light loads. The minimum width for unreinforced masonry walls is 8 in. (200 mm) for the support of light loads, otherwise, 12 in. (300 mm). The use of unreinforced masonry construction in modern buildings is rare due to this system's lack of resistance to seismic forces. For more information on the design of loadbearing masonry structures, see Designing with Masonry Bearing Walls on page 80.

MAXIMUM UNBRACED LENGTH OF WALL

Use the bottom chart on the facing page to determine the maximum permissible unbraced length of wall in plan in addition to its maximum permissible height. Masonry walls should be braced by crosswalls spaced at distances not exceeding those indicated on the chart. If the proposed crosswall spacing in your design is too great, either thicken the wall or add pilasters at intermediate spacing (see pages 86–87 for sizing of pilasters).

FIRE-RESISTANCE RATINGS FOR CONCRETE MASONRY WALLS

Concrete masonry construction may be used in both Combustible and Noncombustible Construction. The fire resistance of concrete masonry construction varies with the type of masonry unit. For preliminary design, assume that a 1-hour fire-resistance rating can be achieved with concrete masonry walls 4 in. (100 mm) wide and that ratings of 2 to 4 hours can be achieved with walls 6–8 in. (150–200 mm) wide.

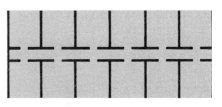

LOW-RISE BEARING WALL CONFIGURATION (shown in plan)

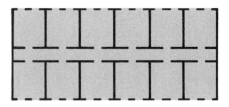

HIGH-RISE BEARING WALL CONFIGURATION (shown in plan)

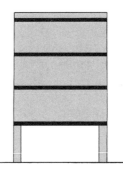

Bearing walls may act as deep beams to span across openings below, as shown in this schematic cross section.

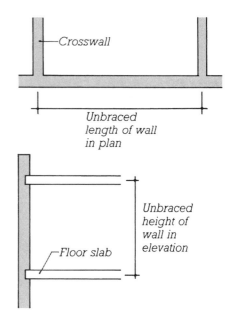

UNBRACED HEIGHT OR LENGTH OF MASONRY WALLS

CONCRETE BLOCK WALLS

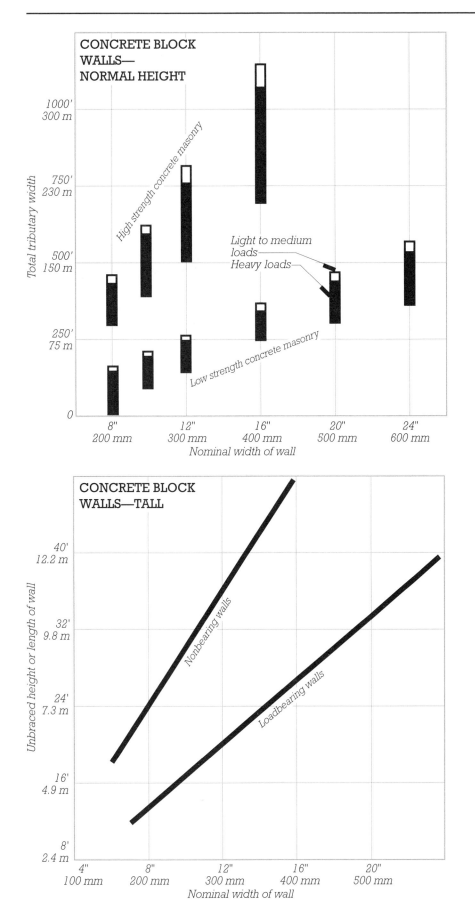

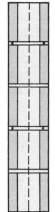

The top chart is for reinforced brick masonry walls up to 12 ft (3.7 m) tall between floors. For high compressive strength masonry, read from the upper set of bars. For low strength masonry, read from the lower set. For light loads, read in the upper open areas of each bar; for medium to heavy loads, read in the lower solid areas. *Total tributary width* is one-half the span of one floor supported by the wall multiplied by the number of floors and roof above.

■ For unreinforced masonry walls, increase the indicated width of the wall thickness by 25%.

■ Actual width of the wall is ³⁄₈ in. (10 mm) less than nominal size.

For walls greater than 12 ft (3.7 m) in height or unbraced length, read from both charts on this page, using the larger size indicated by either chart. Read along the solid line for the appropriate wall type. *Unbraced height of wall* is the vertical distance between floors. *Unbraced length of wall* is the horizontal distance between crosswalls or pilasters. See the facing page for more information on the maximum unbraced length of the wall.

CONCRETE BLOCK LINTELS

PRECAST CONCRETE AND STRUCTURAL STEEL LINTELS

Precast concrete lintels that are 8 in. (200 mm) deep can span up to approximately 8 ft (2.4 m). Lintels 16 in. (400 mm) deep can span up to approximately 16 ft (4.9 m).

Lintels made of combinations of steel angles can span up to approximately 8 ft (2.4 m). Greater spans are possible with heavier structural steel shapes, such as channels or wide flange sections combined with plates.

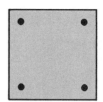

PRECAST CONCRETE LINTELS

FIRE-RESISTANCE RATINGS FOR CONCRETE BLOCK LINTELS

Concrete masonry lintels may be used in both Combustible and Noncombustible Construction. The fire resistance of concrete masonry construction varies with the composition and design of the masonry units themselves. For preliminary design, concrete masonry lintels not less than 8 in. (200 mm) in nominal dimension may be assumed to have a fire-resistance rating of 3 hours.

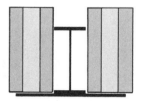

STRUCTURAL STEEL LINTELS

CONCRETE BLOCK LINTELS

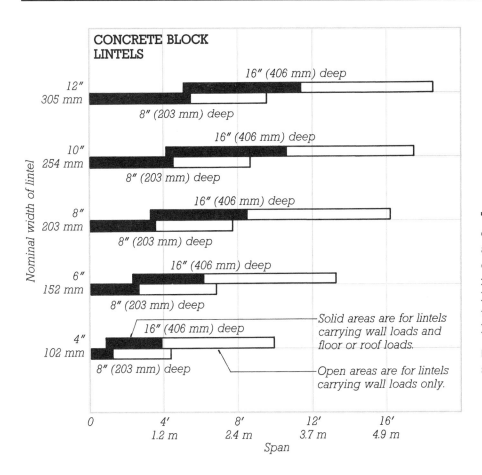

CONCRETE BLOCK LINTELS

Nominal width of lintel

12″ 305 mm
16″ (406 mm) deep
8″ (203 mm) deep

10″ 254 mm
16″ (406 mm) deep
8″ (203 mm) deep

8″ 203 mm
16″ (406 mm) deep
8″ (203 mm) deep

6″ 152 mm
16″ (406 mm) deep
8″ (203 mm) deep

4″ 102 mm
16″ (406 mm) deep
8″ (203 mm) deep

Solid areas are for lintels carrying wall loads and floor or roof loads.

Open areas are for lintels carrying wall loads only.

| 0 | 4′ 1.2 m | 8′ 2.4 m | 12′ 3.7 m | 16′ 4.9 m |

Span

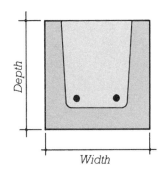

Depth

Width

This chart is for steel reinforced concrete block lintels. Open areas are for lintels carrying wall loads only. Solid areas are for lintels carrying wall loads and floor or roof loads. For light loads, read toward the right in the indicated areas. For heavy loads, read toward the left.

■ Actual sizes are equal to nominal size less ⅜ in. (10 mm).

STEEL STRUCTURAL SYSTEMS

Steel elements are of two basic types: *Structural steel* shapes are formed into their final shapes by hot-rolling. This method produces such common elements as wide flange sections, angles, channels, bars, and plates. *Lightweight steel* members are cold-formed from thin sheets or rods. Such elements include roof and floor decking and a variety of light framing members such as channels, studs, and joists.

STRUCTURAL STEEL FRAMING

Conventional hot-rolled structural steel is a versatile material that has applications ranging from single-story structures to the tallest buildings. The extent of prefabrication normally used with structural steel results in a system that is precise and quickly erected.

Structural steel elements are normally configured as a post and beam frame, with other materials or systems added to make a complete building. The slab system most commonly used with structural steel framing is a sitecast concrete slab poured over corrugated steel decking. Other sitecast or precast concrete systems are also used. Steel frames can support a great variety of cladding systems, with curtain walls of steel, aluminum, glass, masonry, and stone being the most common.

Due to steel's rapid loss of the strength at elevated temperatures, special measures must be taken in most circumstances to protect the structural elements in a steel frame from the heat of fire. The required fire-resistive assemblies or coatings may have a significant impact on the architectural use of structural steel. See pages 362–366 for more information on the requirements for fire protection of structural steel.

LIGHTWEIGHT STEEL FRAMING

Lightweight steel framing finds applications in low-rise structures where the light weight and ease of assembly of these elements are advantages. Many of the details of this system and the sizes of the structural elements are similar to those used in Wood Light Frame Construction, a system lightweight steel framing often competes with. However, the noncombustibility of steel allows this system to be used in building types where wood construction is not permitted. (See pages 362–366 for more information on building types permitted using lightweight steel framing.) The small size of the individual structural elements and the reliance on on-site fabrication and erection also make this system a good choice where buildings of irregular or unusual form are desired.

SIZING THE STRUCTURAL SYSTEM

93

SIZE, WEIGHT, AND SPACING OF LIGHTWEIGHT STEEL STUDS

The charts on the facing page list the most commonly available sizes of lightweight steel studs. Other sizes may be available from some manufacturers. Studs typically vary in width from 1⅜ to 2½ in. (35 to 64 mm). For preliminary purposes, a width of 2 in. (51 mm) may be assumed.

The load-carrying capacity of lightweight steel studs varies with the strength and thickness of the steel material from which the studs are made. When reading the charts on the facing page, the highest values indicated for loaded width or stud height in each stud size represent studs manufactured from thicker, higher strength metal. Lower values represent studs manufactured from thinner, lower strength material.

The capacity of steel stud systems also depends on the spacing of the studs. Studs should always be spaced on a 4-ft (1200-mm) module to coordinate with standard wall panel widths. The most common spacings are 12, 16, and 24 in. (300, 400, and 600 mm) on center. When reading the charts on the facing page, the highest values shown for each stud size represent framing systems with studs spaced at 12 in. (300 mm). Lower values represent systems with studs spaced at 16 or 24 in. (400 or 600 mm).

FIRE-RESISTANCE RATINGS FOR STEEL STUD FRAMING

94

Lightweight steel stud construction may be used in both Combustible and Noncombustible Construction. To achieve a 1-hour fire-resistance rating, framing may be covered with rated gypsum wallboard or plaster materials in thicknesses ranging from ½ to 1 inch (12 to 25 mm). Fire-resistance ratings of up to 4 hours can be achieved with finishes ranging in thickness from 2 to 3 in. (50 to 75 mm). Even where no fire-resistance rating is required, stud framing typically must be covered with some form of wallboard or panel material to stabilize its relatively slender members against buckling.

STEEL LIGHTWEIGHT WALL STUDS

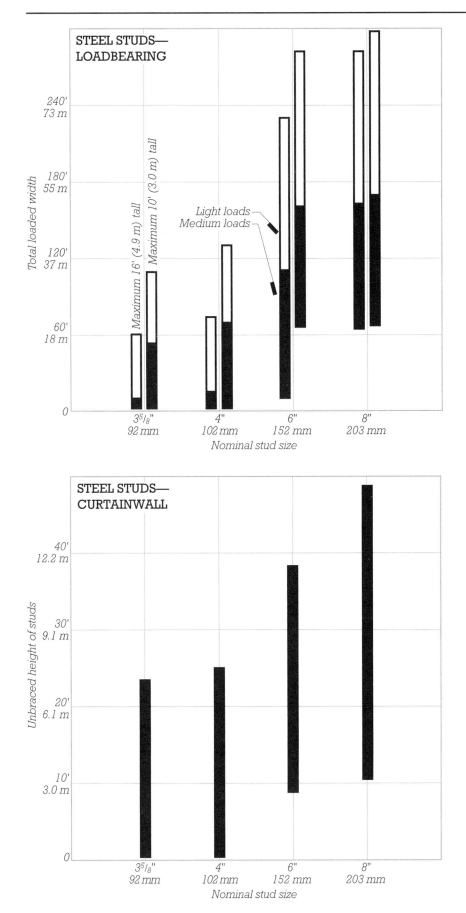

STEEL STUDS— LOADBEARING

Total loaded width

240' / 73 m
180' / 55 m
120' / 37 m
60' / 18 m
0

Maximum 16' (4.9 m) tall

Maximum 10' (3.0 m) tall

Light loads
Medium loads

3⅝" / 92 mm   4" / 102 mm   6" / 152 mm   8" / 203 mm

Nominal stud size

STEEL STUDS— CURTAINWALL

Unbraced height of studs

40' / 12.2 m
30' / 9.1 m
20' / 6.1 m
10' / 3.0 m
0

3⅝" / 92 mm   4" / 102 mm   6" / 152 mm   8" / 203 mm

Nominal stud size

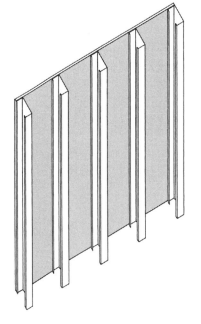

The top chart is for loadbearing lightweight steel stud walls. For walls up to 10 ft (3.0 m) high, read from the taller right-hand bars. For walls up to 16 ft (4.9 m) high, read from the left-hand bars. For light loads, read in the open areas of each bar. For medium loads, read in the solid areas. *Total loaded width* is the tributary width of one floor multiplied by the number of floors and roof above the wall.

■ Actual stud depth is equal to the nominal size.

The lower chart is for curtainwall studs—studs resisting wind but not gravity loads. For light wind loads and for cladding systems such as glass or metal that are relatively tolerant of deflection, read toward the top in the indicated areas. For heavy wind loads and for claddings of stone, clay masonry, or other materials requiring stiffer support, read toward the bottom. *Unbraced height of studs* is the vertical distance between floors or other supports that brace the studs against buckling.

■ Stud height may be increased with the addition of intermediate bracing perpendicular to the wall plane.

FIRE-RESISTANCE RATINGS FOR LIGHTWEIGHT STEEL

Lightweight steel floor joists may be used in both Combustible and Noncombustible Construction. Fire-resistance ratings of 1 to 2 hours may be achieved with ceilings of gypsum board or plaster in thicknesses ranging from 1 to 2 in. (25 to 50 mm).

STEEL LIGHTWEIGHT FLOOR JOISTS

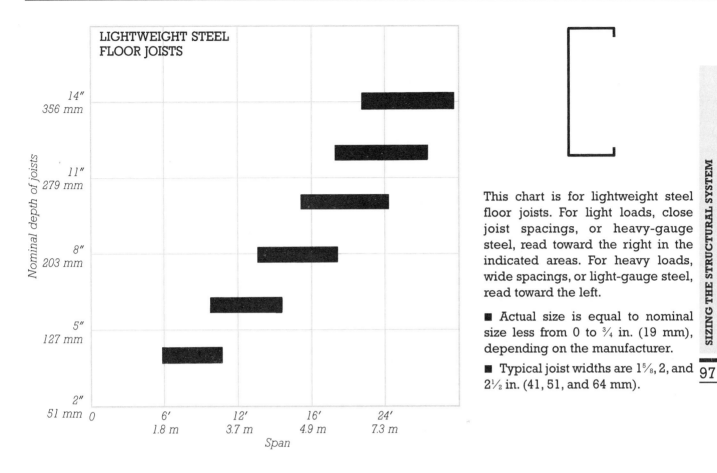

This chart is for lightweight steel floor joists. For light loads, close joist spacings, or heavy-gauge steel, read toward the right in the indicated areas. For heavy loads, wide spacings, or light-gauge steel, read toward the left.

■ Actual size is equal to nominal size less from 0 to ¾ in. (19 mm), depending on the manufacturer.

■ Typical joist widths are 1⅝, 2, and 2½ in. (41, 51, and 64 mm).

STRUCTURAL STEEL COLUMNS

COLUMN LAYOUT

Columns at the perimeter of a building should be oriented with their flanges facing outward to facilitate the attachment of cladding to the building's structural frame. Elsewhere, columns should be oriented with their webs parallel to the axis on which the building is most vulnerable to lateral forces so that the columns may make their maximum contribution to resisting these forces. For example, in buildings with rectangular footprints, the weaker axis is most frequently parallel to the shorter sides of the structure.

FINISH DIMENSIONS OF STEEL COLUMNS

In most cases, structural steel columns are not exposed in the completed construction, and their overall finish dimensions must be increased from those shown in the charts on the facing page to account for the application of fireproofing and finishes. The added thickness depends on the materials involved, the degree of fire resistance required, and the weight of the steel section itself (heavier sections require less added fire protection than lighter ones). For common conditions, an allowance of 1 to 4 in. (25 to 100 mm) per side of column should be sufficient for preliminary sizing. When applying these allowances to the actual column sizes, remember to double them to account for materials applied to opposite sides of the column (2 to 8 in., or 50 to 200 mm, total). As a more costly alternative, in cases where fire protection is required but there is a desire for steel to remain exposed, thin paint-like intumescent coatings may be applied to the steel. Under normal conditions, these coatings add only negligibly to the size of the column. Under fire conditions, they expand to form an insulating layer that protects the steel from the heat of the fire.

Depending on how individual sections of column are connected, an additional allowance of 1 to 2 inches (25 to 50 mm) per side may be required, added to the deeper dimension of the column, to account for splice plates and fasteners where column joints occur. Where required, these connections typically are located several feet above the floor level.

FIRE-RESISTANCE RATINGS FOR STRUCTURAL STEEL COLUMNS

Exposed structural steel columns may be used in both Unprotected Noncombustible and Unprotected Combustible Construction. For Protected Construction types, fire-resistance ratings of up to 4 hours are easily achieved with any number of conventional fireproofing materials in thicknesses of as little as 1 to 4 in. (25 to 100 mm). As an alternative, intumescent coatings, as described above, can provide up to 3 hours of fire resistance.

STRUCTURAL STEEL COLUMNS

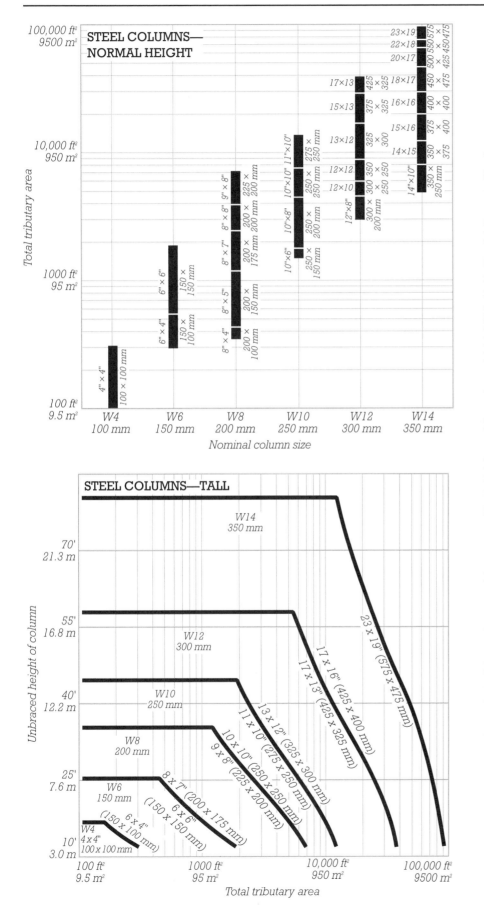

The top chart is for steel wide flange section columns up to 12 ft (3.7 m) tall between floors. *Total tributary area* is the summed area of the roof and all floors supported by the column.

■ For medium loads, read directly from the chart. For light loads, reduce the total tributary area supported by the column by 10% before reading the chart; for heavy loads increase the area supported by 15%.

■ Actual column sizes are shown to the sides of the bars. Not all available sizes are shown. Consult a steel handbook for additional options.

■ For columns located at the perimeter of a building or part of a rigid frame system, select one nominal size larger than least nominal size indicated by this chart.

■ W14 sections are the largest standard rolled sizes commonly available for use as columns. Larger built-up sections capable of carrying greater loads may be shop-fabricated.

For columns taller than 12 ft (3.7 m), read from both charts on this page, using the larger column size indicated by either. *Unbraced height of column* is the vertical distance between floors or other supports that brace the column laterally against buckling.

■ Actual column sizes are shown alongside the nominal shape curves. Intermediate sizes between those shown may be interpolated.

■ Minimum column size will be larger for heavily loaded columns or columns that are part of rigid frame systems.

STRUCTURAL HOLLOW STEEL SECTIONS

Standard shapes for structural hollow steel sections (HSS) include square tubes, rectangular tubes, and round pipes. Compared to wide flange sections, tubes and pipes are more resistant to buckling forces, making them good choices for columns and compressive struts in all types of steel systems. They are employed as columns in long-span steel structures for their greater efficiency, and because they are available in lighter weights than other standard shapes, they are frequently used in one- or two-story steel structures as well. Tube and pipe sections are popular choices for use in the fabrication of steel trusses and space frames, and their high torsional resistance makes them excellent choices for single post supports such as for signs or platforms.

The simple profiles and clean appearance of hollow steel sectons and pipes also make them popular for use where the steel may remain visible in the finished structure, or for structures exposed to the weather where the absence of moisture- and dirt-trapping profiles and ease of maintenance are desirable characteristics. Tubes and pipes are generally available in whole-inch (25-mm) sizes up to 6 or 8 in. (152 or 203 mm) and in even-inch (51-mm) increments up to 12 to 16 in. (305 to 406 mm).

FINISH DIMENSIONS OF HOLLOW STEEL SECTION COLUMNS

Where finishes are applied to hollow steel section columns, the added thickness depends on the materials involved, the degree of fire resistance required, and the weight of the steel section itself (heavier sections require less added fire protection than lighter ones). For preliminary sizing, an allowance of 1 to 4 in. (25 to 100 mm) per side of column should be sufficient (a total of 2 to 8 in. or 50 to 200 mm, accounting for both sides of the column). In cases where fire protection is required but there is a desire for steel to remain exposed, more costly, paint-like intumescent coatings may be applied to the steel. Under fire conditions, these normally thin coatings expand to form an insulating layer that protects the steel from the heat of the fire.

FIRE-RESISTANCE RATINGS FOR HOLLOW STEEL SECTION COLUMNS

Exposed hollow steel section columns may be used in both Unprotected Noncombustible and Unprotected Combustible Construction. For Protected Construction Types, fire-resistance ratings of up to 3 hours for very light sections and 4 hours for heavier ones are achievable with any number of conventional fireproofing materials applied in thicknesses of 2 to 4 in. (100 to 200 mm) per side. Fire-resistance ratings of up to 3 hours can also be achieved with intumescent coatings, as described above, or with specially designed hollow section columns filled with concrete.

STRUCTURAL STEEL TUBE COLUMNS

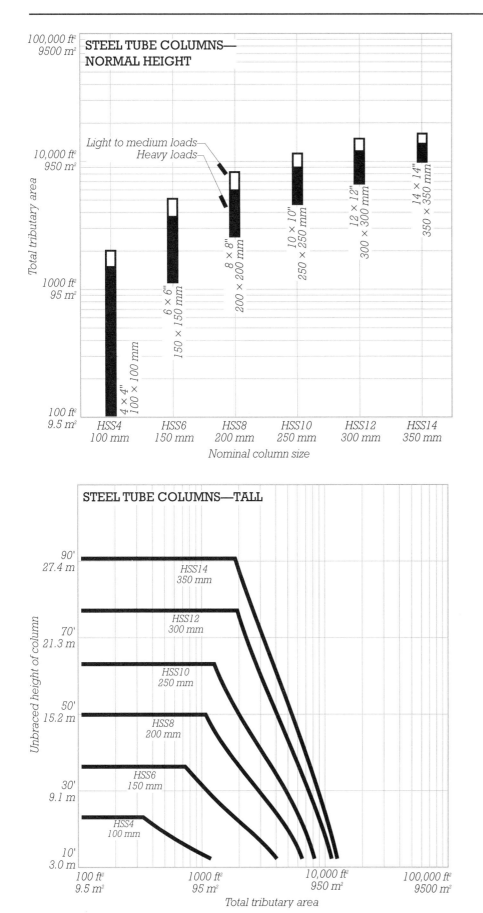

STEEL TUBE COLUMNS—NORMAL HEIGHT

Total tributary area (vertical axis): 100,000 ft² / 9500 m², 10,000 ft² / 950 m², 1000 ft² / 95 m², 100 ft² / 9.5 m²

Light to medium loads
Heavy loads

4 × 4" / 100 × 100 mm
6 × 6" / 150 × 150 mm
8 × 8" / 200 × 200 mm
10 × 10" / 250 × 250 mm
12 × 12" / 300 × 300 mm
14 × 14" / 350 × 350 mm

Nominal column size (horizontal axis): HSS4 / 100 mm, HSS6 / 150 mm, HSS8 / 200 mm, HSS10 / 250 mm, HSS12 / 300 mm, HSS14 / 350 mm

STEEL TUBE COLUMNS—TALL

Unbraced height of column (vertical axis): 90' / 27.4 m, 70' / 21.3 m, 50' / 15.2 m, 30' / 9.1 m, 10' / 3.0 m

HSS14 350 mm
HSS12 300 mm
HSS10 250 mm
HSS8 200 mm
HSS6 150 mm
HSS4 100 mm

Total tributary area (horizontal axis): 100 ft² / 9.5 m², 1000 ft² / 95 m², 10,000 ft² / 950 m², 100,000 ft² / 9500 m²

The top chart is for hollow steel section columns up to 12 ft (3.7 m) tall between floors. Read in the top open areas for light and medium loads. Read in the lower solid areas for heavy loads. *Total tributary area* is the summed area of the roof and all floors supported by the column.

■ Actual column size is equal to nominal size.

■ For columns located at the perimeter of a building, or ones that are part of a rigid frame system, select one nominal size larger than size indicated by this chart.

For columns taller than 12 ft (3.7 m), read from both charts on this page, using the larger column size indicated by either. *Unbraced height of column* is the vertical distance between floors or other supports that brace the column laterally against buckling.

■ Minimum column size will be larger for heavily loaded columns or columns that are part of rigid frame systems.

STEEL FLOOR DECKING

Corrugated steel floor decking with a sitecast concrete topping is the slab system most commonly used over structural steel framing. Typical span ranges for steel floor decking when used with structural steel framing are 6 to 15 ft (1.8 to 4.6 m). Longer spans or shallower depths than those indicated on the chart on the facing page may be possible, although increased construction costs may result from the need for additional temporary shoring of the decking during erection.

CELLULAR FLOOR DECKING

The use of cellular decking to provide protected spaces within the floor slab for the running of electrical and communications wiring may influence the overall framing plan for the building. The layout of such a distribution system can determine the direction in which the decking cells will run in various areas of the building plan. The orientation of the beams or joists carrying the decking will be determined from this in turn, as in all cases these elements must run perpendicular to the cells in the decking. See page 213 for additional information on the planning of such systems. When reading from the chart for cellular decking on the facing page, read toward the bottom in the indicated area.

STEEL ROOF DECKING

Steel roof decking may have a sitecast concrete or gypsum topping or may be covered directly with a variety of board or roofing products. A common and economical configuration for roof decking is $1\frac{1}{2}$–in. (38-mm) decking spanning up to approximately 8 ft (2.4 m). Many proprietary metal roof decking systems, with a wide variety of performance characteristics, are also available. For information on such systems, consult individual manufacturers.

FIRE-RESISTANCE RATINGS FOR STEEL DECKING

Steel roof and floor decking may be used in both Combustible and Noncombustible Construction. The fire resistance of roof or floor decking with a concrete topping varies with the configuration of the decking and the thickness of the topping. Though resistance ratings of as high as 3 hours may be possible, for preliminary design, assume that decking must be protected with applied fireproofing or an appropriately fire-resistive ceiling to achieve ratings of more than 1 hour.

STEEL FLOOR AND ROOF DECKING

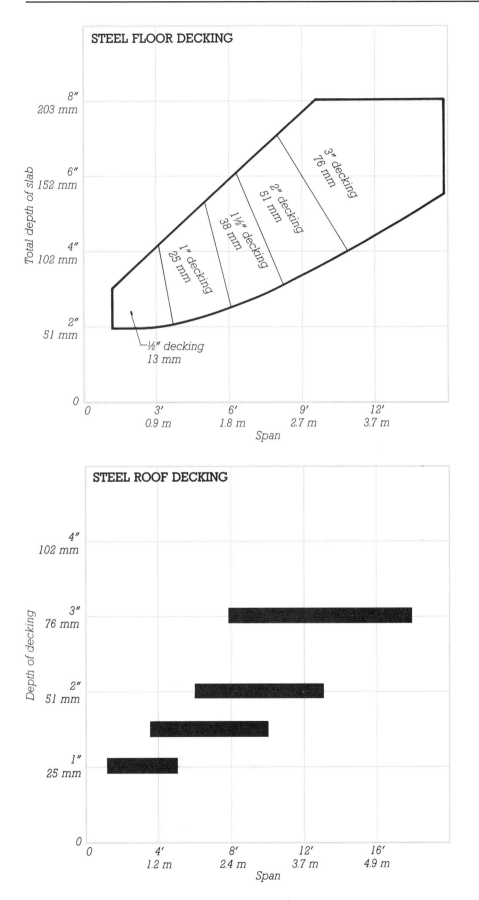

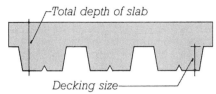

The top chart is for corrugated or cellular steel floor decking with concrete slab topping. For light loads, read toward the bottom in the indicated areas. For heavy loads, read toward the top.

■ *Total depth of slab* is the depth of the decking and the concrete topping. Approximate sizes for the steel decking alone are shown within the chart.

■ Deeper deck sections with spans of up to approximately 25 ft (7.6 m) may be available from some manufacturers.

The bottom chart is for corrugated steel roof decking. For light loads, read toward the right in the indicated areas. For heavy loads, read toward the left.

■ Deeper deck sections with spans of up to approximately 25 ft (7.6 m) may be available from some manufacturers.

STRUCTURAL STEEL BEAMS AND GIRDERS

Structural steel is a versatile building material. While it can be used in a great variety of ways, consider the following guidelines for what is most economical in common practice.

FLOOR AND ROOF FRAMING

The most economical span range for conventional steel floor and roof framing is 25 to 40 ft (8 to 12 m). Individual column bays should be approximately 1,000 sq ft (95 m²) in area and rectangular in shape, with the long side 1.25 to 1.5 times as long as the shorter side. Above spans of approximately 40 ft (12 m), consider open-web steel joists for their lighter weight and greater economy (see pages 106–107).

The spacing between individual beams depends on the applied loads and the decking system. Spacings from 6 to 15 ft (1.8 to 4.6 m) are common with corrugated steel and concrete slab decking. Spacings up to approximately 8 ft (2.4 m) are typical for roof decking systems.

BEAM AND GIRDER CONFIGURATION

The orientation of beams and girders in a floor or roof framing system may depend on a variety of factors. In relation to the building at large, it may be advantageous to run girders parallel to the building's shorter axis, the direction most susceptible to lateral forces. In this way, these stronger members can contribute additional lateral resistance to the building through rigid frame action.

Within individual column bays, it is usually more economical to run girders in the shorter direction of a rectangular bay, allowing the lighter beams to span the longer distance. However, when cellular decking is used as part of a wiring system, beam and girder directions may be set so that the wire conduits within the decking run in preferred directions as required by communications or power distribution plans (see page 213).

COMPOSITE BEAMS

In composite construction, shear studs are added to the top of the floor beams. This causes the concrete deck and steel framing to act as a unified structural element and results in reduced beam depths. Composite construction can be more economical, particularly at longer spans. However, a thicker concrete deck may be required. In some cases, "partial" composite design, where fewer studs are used and less than full composite action is achieved, proves to be the most economical solution.

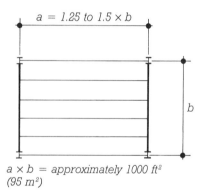

For economical framing of steel bays, the lighter beams should span 1.25 to 1.5 times the span of the heavier girders. Bay area should equal approximately 1000 ft² (95 m²).

STRUCTURAL STEEL BEAMS AND GIRDERS

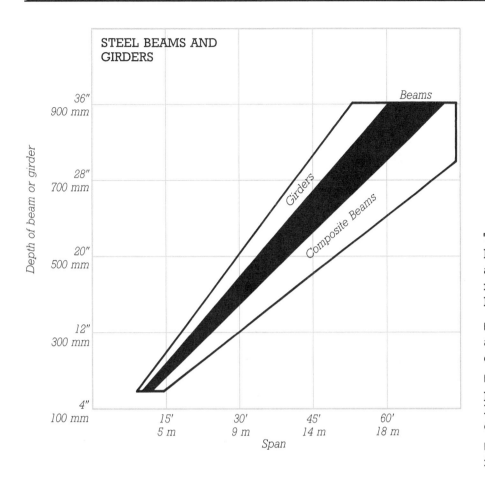

STEEL BEAMS AND GIRDERS

Depth of beam or girder

36" / 900 mm
28" / 700 mm
20" / 500 mm
12" / 300 mm
4" / 100 mm

Beams
Girders
Composite Beams

15' / 5 m
30' / 9 m
45' / 14 m
60' / 18 m

Span

This chart is for steel wide flange beams and girders. For average and light loads, read toward the right in the indicated areas. For heavy loads, read toward the left.

■ For beams acting as girders or as composite beams, read in the open areas indicated.

■ Beams or girders also acting as part of a rigid frame for lateral stability may be deeper than indicated by this chart.

■ Standard depths of shapes come in 2-in. (50-mm) increments up to 18 in. deep (450 mm), and in 3-in. (75-mm) increments for larger sizes.

■ Typical widths of beams and girders range from approximately one-third to one-half the depth of the member. Heavy sections used for heavy loads or to conserve depth may be wider.

■ Depths of up to 36 in. (914 mm) are available as standard rolled sections. Deeper beams capable of longer spans may be shop fabricated.

FIRE-RESISTANCE RATINGS FOR STEEL BEAMS AND GIRDERS

Steel beams and girders may be used in both Combustible and Noncombustible Construction. Fire-resistance ratings of as high as 4 hours are achievable with applied fireproofing or an appropriately fire-resistive ceiling. Some building codes also allow reduced fire protection or exposed steel for roof structures that are 15 to 25 ft (4.6 to 7.6 m) or more above the floor.

OPEN-WEB JOIST FRAMING

The light weight of open-web steel joists makes them an economical alternative to conventional structural steel members for spans greater than 30 to 40 ft (9 to 12 m). Where significant concentrated loads exist, open-web joists may need to be supplemented with additional structural members.

Girders used with open-web joists may be joist girders (a heavier version of an open-web joist) or conventional structural steel members. For greater loads and spans, heavy steel trusses may also be used. For rectangular bays, the joists usually span the longer direction. (See pages 104–105 for structural steel beams and girders and pages 110–111 for heavy steel trusses.)

A variety of proprietary composite systems are also available. Such systems are particularly effective at overcoming the excessive flexibility sometimes encountered with long-span joist systems.

FIRE-RESISTANCE RATINGS
FOR OPEN-WEB STEEL JOISTS

Open-web steel joists may be used in both Combustible and Noncombustible Construction. Fire-resistance ratings of as high as 3 hours are achievable with applied fireproofing or an appropriately fire-resistive ceiling. The fire-resistive ceiling is used more commonly due to the difficulty of applying fireproofing directly to the complex surfaces of an open-web joist. Some building codes also permit reduced fire protection or exposed steel for roof structures that are 15 to 25 ft (4.6 to 7.6 m) or more above the floor.

OPEN-WEB STEEL JOISTS

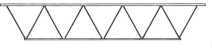

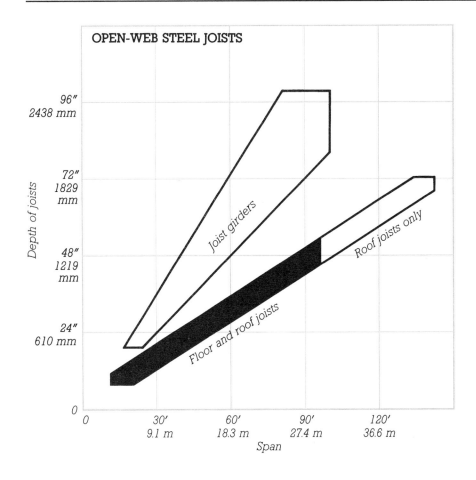

This chart is for open-web steel joists and joist girders for floors and roofs. For light loads or close joist spacings, read toward the right in the indicated areas. For heavy loads or large joist spacings, read toward the left.

■ Joist spacings range from 2 to 10 ft (0.6 to 3.0 m) or more, depending on the floor loads and the decking system applied over the joists.

■ Joists generally come in depths of 8 to 32 in. in 2-in. increments (from 203 to 813 mm in 51-mm increments) and from 32 to 72 in. in 4-in. increments (from 813 to 1829 mm in 102-mm increments). Availability of sizes varies with the manufacturer.

■ Joist girders come in depths of 20 to 96 in. in 4-in. increments (from 508 to 2438 mm in 102-mm increments).

SINGLE-STORY RIGID STEEL FRAMES

RELATED DIMENSIONS FOR SINGLE-STORY RIGID STEEL FRAMES

For the span ranges indicated on the chart on the facing page, the following dimensions may be used:

Wall Height	Depth at Base	Roof Pitch
8'–30' (2.4–9.1 m)	7"–21" (178–533 mm)	1:12–4:12

Typical spacing of frames is 20 or 25 ft (6.1 or 7.6 m). For variations on the rigid frame system, or for sizes outside the range of those shown in the chart, consult with individual manufacturers.

FIRE-RESISTANCE RATINGS FOR SINGLE-STORY RIGID STEEL FRAMES

Single-story rigid steel frames may be used in both Combustible and Noncombustible Construction. Fire-resistance ratings of as high as 4 hours are achievable with applied fireproofing. Some building codes also allow reduced fire protection or exposed steel for roof structures that are 15 to 25 ft (4.6 to 7.6 m) or more above the floor.

SINGLE-STORY RIGID STEEL FRAMES

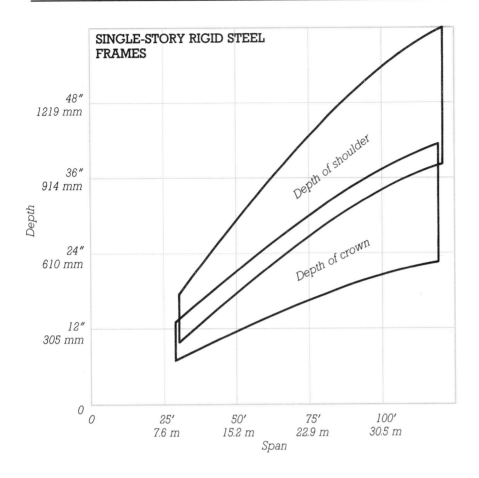

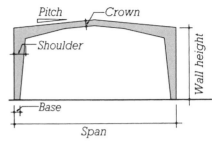

This chart is for single-story rigid steel frame structures. For heavy loads, read toward the top in the indicated areas. For light loads, read toward the bottom.

■ Spans as great as 200 ft (61.0 m) or more may be available from some manufacturers. Greater spans are also available with the use of intermediate columns.

STRUCTURAL STEEL TRUSSES

ECONOMICAL SPAN RANGES FOR PARALLEL CHORD TRUSSES

Parallel chord trusses are most economical for spans up to 120 to 140 ft (35 to 45 m) due to the increased difficulty of shipping elements greater than 12 ft (3.7 m) deep. Triangular and bowstring trusses can be shipped at slightly greater depths. Trusses spanning 300 ft (90 m) or more may be fabricated on-site.

FIRE-RESISTANCE RATINGS FOR STEEL TRUSSES

Structural steel trusses may be used in both Combustible and Noncombustible Construction. Fire-resistance ratings of as high as 4 hours are achievable with applied fireproofing or an appropriately fire-resistive ceiling. Some building codes also allow reduced fire protection or exposed steel for roof structures that are 15 to 25 ft (4.6 to 7.6 m) or more above the floor.

STRUCTURAL STEEL TRUSSES

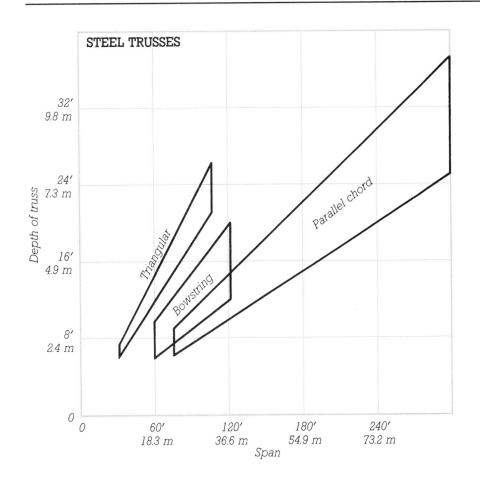

STEEL TRUSSES

Depth of truss

32'
9.8 m

24'
7.3 m

16'
4.9 m

8'
2.4 m

0

Triangular

Bowstring

Parallel chord

0   60'   120'   180'   240'
     18.3 m   36.6 m   54.9 m   73.2 m
                    Span

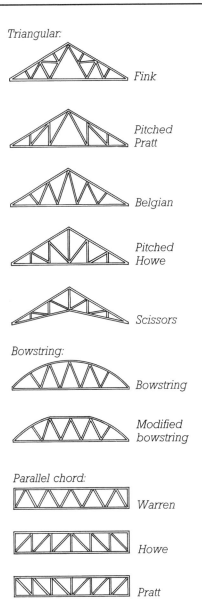

Triangular:

Fink

Pitched Pratt

Belgian

Pitched Howe

Scissors

Bowstring:

Bowstring

Modified bowstring

Parallel chord:

Warren

Howe

Pratt

This chart is for steel trusses fabricated from structural steel members. Because these trusses are custom designed and fabricated, a great variety of shapes and configurations is possible.

SITECAST CONCRETE STRUCTURAL SYSTEMS

The choice of sitecast concrete framing systems is most often dictated by the required structural spans or spacing of columns and by the expected magnitude of in-service loads. The following systems are listed in order of increasing span and load capacity. Those listed in bold type are also generally the most economical within their span range.

- One-Way Solid Slab
- **Two-Way Flat Plate**
- **Two-Way Flat Slab**
- **One-Way Joist**
- Waffle Slab
- One-Way Beam and Slab
- Two-Way Beam and Slab

For lightly loaded, short span conditions, choose a system from near the top of the list. For longer spans or heavier loads, choose systems lower down. Where cost is a primary consideration, preference should be given to those systems listed in bold type.

POSTTENSIONING

The span ranges of sitecast concrete systems can be increased by the use of posttensioned reinforcing. Charts for the sizing of posttensioned systems are included in this section. Posttensioning also reduces the depth of spanning members and may be desirable where floor-to-floor heights must be kept to a minimum. The extensive use of posttensioning in a concrete structure may limit the ease with which such a structure can be modified in the future, since penetrations in slabs and beams must not interrupt the continuity of the reinforcing or surrounding concrete. This may make posttensioning an undesirable choice for buildings where significant change in program or structure must be anticipated.

ARCHITECTURAL SITE-CAST CONCRETE CONSTRUCTION

The inherent fire-resistive qualities of concrete construction allow concrete systems to remain wholly or partially exposed in a finished building. The process by which concrete is formed on-site and its monolithic and plastic qualities as a finished product also give this material unique architectural potential. For these reasons, the choice of a concrete framing system may have significant architectural implications that should be considered early in the design process. Factors to consider include the added cost and difficulty of achieving acceptable levels of finish quality and dimensional accuracy with exposed concrete, the ease of integrating building mechanical and electrical services into the exposed structure, and the potential aesthetic qualities of the various construction elements and systems.

SITECAST CONCRETE COLUMNS

CONCRETE STRENGTH AND COLUMN SIZE

The top chart on the facing page is based on 4000 psi (25 MPa) concrete with reinforcing appropriate for buildings of low to moderate height. For taller buildings or longer-span systems, the larger column sizes indicated may become uneconomical due to the increasing quantity and weight of materials required, as well as the greater encroachment on usable floor area. In these circumstances, higher strength concrete and greater amounts of reinforcing can be used to maintain columns of more practical size. To adjust the column size in the top chart on the facing page for variations in concrete strength, use the factors in the table to the right.

MINIMUM COLUMN SIZES

Square concrete columns should not be less than 10 in. (250 mm) on each side. Rectangular columns should not be less than 8 x 10 in. (200 x 250 mm), with the wider side never more than three times the width of the shorter side. Round columns should not be less than 12 in. (150 mm) in diameter.

For columns used with any of the two-way slab systems listed in the table to the right, see the pages indicated for additional limits on minimum column size in relation to the depth of the slab.

ECONOMICAL CONCRETE COLUMN DESIGN

Column sizes should change as little as possible throughout a building. Where loads vary, column size can be held constant while its load capacity is varied by adjusting the strength of the concrete mix or the amount of steel reinforcing. For example, in multistory buildings, column sizes should not vary between floors. Rather, higher strength concrete or greater quantities of reinforcing are used in lower story columns to compensate for the larger loads on those columns. Where size variations cannot be avoided, changing only one dimension of a column at a time, in multiples of 2-in. (50-mm) increments, is preferred.

Column placements should be as uniformly spaced as possible. Irregular column placements prevent the use of the most economical forming methods. Rectangular or square columns should conform to standard orthogonal alignments. Deviations from the normal complicate formwork where the column and the slab meet. See the diagrams to the right.

FIRE-RESISTANCE RATINGS FOR SITECAST CONCRETE COLUMNS

Sitecast concrete columns may be used in both Combustible and Noncombustible Construction. The fire resistance of sitecast concrete varies with its ingredients and density. For preliminary design, you may assume that a 1-hour fire-resistance rating can be achieved with columns not less than 8 in. (200 mm) on a side. Fire-resistance ratings of 2, 3, and 4 hours can be achieved with columns 10 in. (250 mm), 12 in. (300 mm), and 14 in. (350 mm) in minimum dimension, respectively.

114

Concrete Strength		Multiply Column Size by
6000 psi	(40 MPa)	0.80
8000 psi	(48 MPa)	0.70
12,000 psi	(85 MPa)	0.60
16,000 psi	(110 MPa)	0.50

Systems	Pages
Sitecast Concrete Two-Way Flat Plate	124–125
Sitecast Concrete Two-Way Flat Slab	126–127
Sitecast Concrete Waffle Slab	128–129

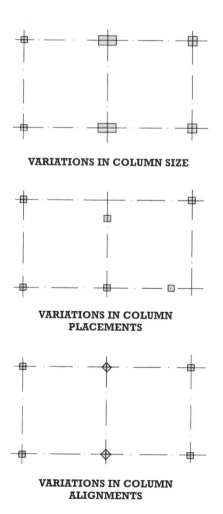

VARIATIONS IN COLUMN SIZE

VARIATIONS IN COLUMN PLACEMENTS

VARIATIONS IN COLUMN ALIGNMENTS

SITECAST CONCRETE COLUMNS

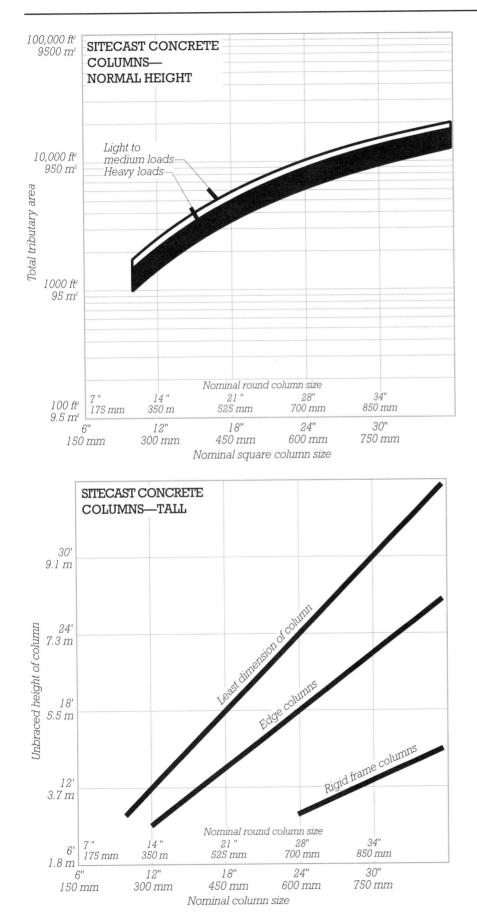

SITECAST CONCRETE COLUMNS—NORMAL HEIGHT

Total tributary area

- Light to medium loads
- Heavy loads

100,000 ft² / 9500 m²
10,000 ft² / 950 m²
1000 ft² / 95 m²
100 ft² / 9.5 m²

Nominal round column size
7" / 175 mm   14" / 350 m   21" / 525 mm   28" / 700 mm   34" / 850 mm

6" / 150 mm   12" / 300 mm   18" / 450 mm   24" / 600 mm   30" / 750 mm

Nominal square column size

SITECAST CONCRETE COLUMNS—TALL

Unbraced height of column

30' / 9.1 m
24' / 7.3 m
18' / 5.5 m
12' / 3.7 m
6' / 1.8 m

Least dimension of column

Edge columns

Rigid frame columns

Nominal round column size
7" / 175 mm   14" / 350 m   21" / 525 mm   28" / 700 mm   34" / 850 mm

6" / 150 mm   12" / 300 mm   18" / 450 mm   24" / 600 mm   30" / 750 mm

Nominal column size

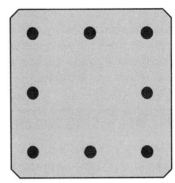

The top chart is for sitecast concrete columns with a clear height of up to 10 ft (3.0 m). Clear height is the distance from the top of the slab below the column to the underside of the slab or beam above. For light to medium loaded columns, read in the upper open area of the curve. For heavily loaded columns, read in the lower solid area. *Total tributary area* is the summed area of the roof and all floors supported by the column.

■ For rectangular columns, select a column of area equal to the square size indicated.

■ Actual column size is equal to nominal size.

For columns with a clear height greater than 10 ft (3.0 m), read from both charts on this page, using the larger size indicated by either. First, read along the line labeled Least dimension of column to determine the smallest permitted size. Columns subject to high bending forces are further restricted as follows: For those part of a rigid frame lateral force resisting system, the column's minimum size in the direction to which it is subject to bending is indicated by the line labeled *Rigid frame columns*. For columns located close to the edge of the slab it supports (within one-quarter of a span or less), the column's minimum size perpendicular to the slab edge is indicated by the line labeled *Edge columns*.

SITECAST CONCRETE WALLS

Sitecast concrete bearing walls may be used as the primary loadbearing element in a structural system or may be an integrated part of many other systems. Some of the most common uses for concrete walls include construction below grade, building structural cores, and shear walls in steel or concrete frame construction.

CONCRETE STRENGTH AND WIDTH OF WALL

The top chart on the facing page is based on 4000 psi (25 MPa) concrete with reinforcing levels appropriate for buildings of low to moderate height. For taller buildings or longer-span systems, the wider wall sizes indicated may become uneconomical due to the increasing quantity and weight of materials required, as well as the greater encroachment on usable floor area. In these circumstances, higher strength concrete can be used to maintain wall sizes that are more practical. To adjust the width of walls in the top chart on the facing page for variations in concrete strength, use the factors in the table to the right.

Column Strength	Multiply Concrete Size by
6000 psi (40 MPa)	0.80
8000 psi (55 MPa)	0.65
12,000 psi (85 MPa)	0.45
16,000 psi (100 MPa)	0.35

DESIGN OF SITECAST CONCRETE WALLS

Nonloadbearing walls may be as thin as 4 in. (100 mm). Loadbearing sitecast concrete walls 6 in. (150 mm) wide should be used for light loads and one-story structures only. Loadbearing walls 8 in. (200 mm) wide are suitable for low-rise structures and light to medium loads. For taller structures and heavy loads, use concrete walls 10 in. (250 mm) or wider. Vary wall thickness as little as possible. Where necessary, changes in thickness should be in 2- or 4-in. (50- or 100-mm) increments.

Loadbearing wall locations should be consistent from floor to floor and continuous to the building foundation. Where it is desirable to omit bearing walls on a lower floor, an economical alternative may be to design the wall above to act as a deep beam spanning between columns at each end. The space between columns may then remain open. Such wall beams may economically span up to 20 to 30 ft (6 to 9 m).

Sitecast concrete walls are frequently used as shear walls to help stabilize buildings against wind and seismic forces. The guidelines for minimum widths of walls provided on these two facing pages should normally result in walls with sufficient capacity to also act as shear walls where required. In addition, conventional concrete shear walls should be proportioned so that their total height, from foundation to top of wall, is no more than four times the length of the wall. For more information on designing building lateral stability systems, see pages 37–38.

Bearing walls may act as deep beams to span across openings below.

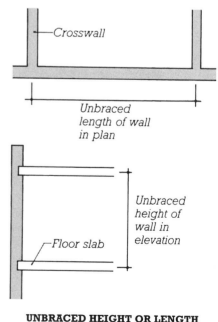

UNBRACED HEIGHT OR LENGTH OF CONCRETE WALLS

FIRE-RESISTANCE RATINGS FOR SITECAST CONCRETE WALLS

Sitecast concrete walls may be used in both Combustible and Noncombustible Construction. The fire resistance of sitecast concrete varies with the type of concrete ingredients. For preliminary design purposes, assume that a 1-hour fire-resistance rating can be achieved with a wall 4 in. (100 mm) in width. Fire-resistance ratings of 2, 3, and 4 hours can be achieved with walls 5 in. (125 mm), 6 in. (150 mm), and 7 in. (175 mm) in width, respectively.

SITECAST CONCRETE WALLS

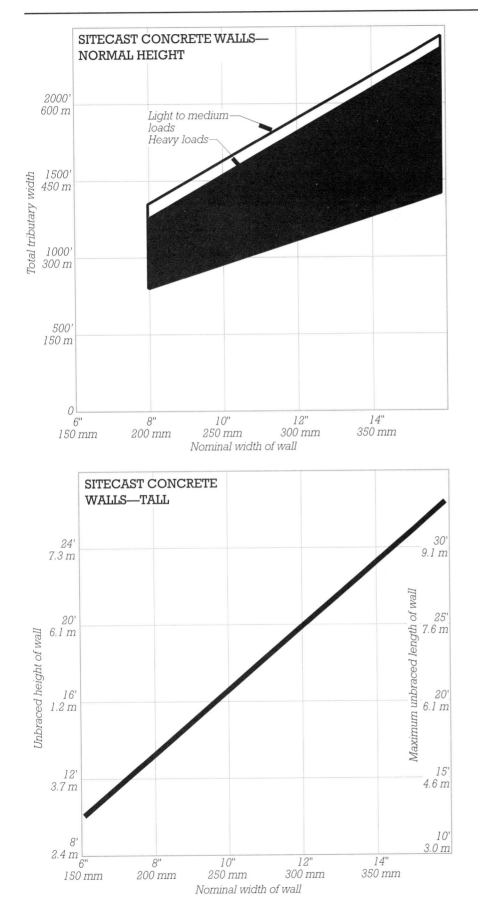

SITECAST CONCRETE WALLS— NORMAL HEIGHT

Total tributary width

2000'
600 m

Light to medium loads
Heavy loads

1500'
450 m

1000'
300 m

500'
150 m

0

6"   8"   10"   12"   14"
150 mm   200 mm   250 mm   300 mm   350 mm

Nominal width of wall

SITECAST CONCRETE WALLS—TALL

Unbraced height of wall

24'
7.3 m

20'
6.1 m

16'
1.2 m

12'
3.7 m

8'
2.4 m

Maximum unbraced length of wall

30'
9.1 m

25'
7.6 m

20'
6.1 m

15'
4.6 m

10'
3.0 m

6"   8"   10"   12"   14"
150 mm   200 mm   250 mm   300 mm   350 mm

Nominal width of wall

The top chart is for sitecast concrete walls up to 10 ft (3.0 m) tall between floors. For light loads, read in the upper open area of the curve. For medium to heavy loads, read in the lower solid area. *Total tributary width* is one-half the span of one floor supported by the wall multiplied by the number of floors and roof above.

■ Actual width of wall is equal to nominal width.

For walls greater than 10 ft (3.0 m) in height, read from both charts on this page, using the larger size indicated by either chart. *Unbraced height of wall* is the vertical distance between floors or other supports that brace the wall laterally against buckling along the wall's vertical axis.

Use the lower chart to also check the *Maximum unbraced length of wall,* the maximum permissible length of the wall between crosswalls, pilasters, or other elements bracing the wall along its horizontal axis. (See the diagrams on the facing page.) Starting with the wall's nominal width, read up to the curve and then across to the scale on the right-hand side of the chart to determine the wall's maximum length between supports.

ECONOMICAL BEAM DESIGN

Vary the sizes of beams throughout the building as little as possible. Size the beam with the longest span, using the chart on the facing page. Beams with shorter spans can often be the same size with reduced reinforcement.

Use beam widths equal to or greater than the widths of the columns supporting them.

In some systems, an economical alternative to conventionally sized beams and girders is wide, shallow beams called either *slab bands* (for solid slab construction) or *joist bands* (for one-way joist construction). Savings in floor-to-floor heights are possible with the reduced beam depths, and formwork costs are reduced. The depth of the slab itself may be reduced as well, since with the broader beams, the span of the slab between beams is lessened. See pages 120–121 for slab bands and pages 122–123 for joist bands.

FIRE-RESISTANCE RATINGS FOR
SITECAST CONCRETE BEAMS AND GIRDERS

Sitecast concrete beams and girders may be used in both Combustible and Noncombustible Construction. Fire-resistance ratings for concrete beams and girders vary with the type and density of concrete used, as well as with the proximity of the steel reinforcing to the surface of the beam. Use the following guidelines for preliminary design:

Concrete beams and girders with a minimum width of 9.5 in. (241 mm) may have a fire-resistance rating of up to 4 hours.

SITECAST CONCRETE BEAMS AND GIRDERS

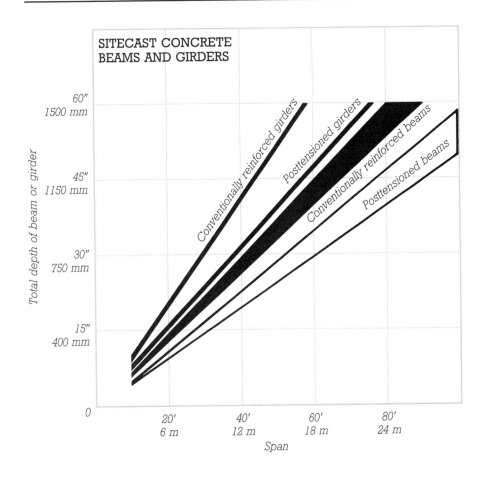

SITECAST CONCRETE BEAMS AND GIRDERS

Total depth of beam or girder

60″ / 1500 mm
45″ / 1150 mm
30″ / 750 mm
15″ / 400 mm
0

20′ / 6 m 40′ / 12 m 60′ / 18 m 80′ / 24 m

Span

Conventionally reinforced girders
Posttensioned girders
Conventionally reinforced beams
Posttensioned beams

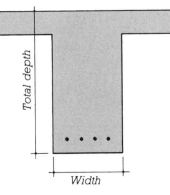

Total depth

Width

This chart is for sitecast concrete beams and girders, either conventionally reinforced or posttensioned. For lightly to moderately loaded beams, read toward the right in the indicated areas. For heavy loads or simple spans, read toward the left.

■ For girders, read on the lines indicated.

■ Size beam depths in even 2-in. (50-mm) increments.

■ *Total depth of beam or girder* is measured from the bottom of the beam to the top of the slab.

■ Normal beam widths range from one-third to one-half of the beam depth. Use beam widths in multiples of 2 or 3 in. (50 or 75 mm).

SITECAST CONCRETE ONE-WAY SOLID SLAB

One-way solid slab construction supported by bearing walls is the least expensive sitecast concrete framing system for short spans and light loads. It is a popular concrete system for multiple dwelling building types such as apartments or hotels, where the regular spacing of bearing walls is easily coordinated with the layout of the small, uniformly arranged rooms typical of these buildings.

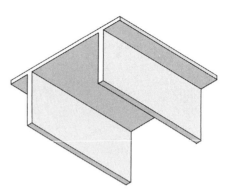

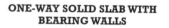

ONE-WAY SOLID SLAB WITH BEARING WALLS

ONE-WAY BEAM AND SLAB SYSTEMS

The addition of beams and girders to one-way solid slab construction can increase the load capacity and span range of the system and eliminate the need for regularly spaced walls in the building plan. The increased complexity of a beam and girder system, however, makes this one of the most expensive of all sitecast concrete systems to construct. One-way beam and slab construction is usually economical only where long spans or high loads must be accommodated, such as with industrial uses or in areas of high seismic risk.

Slab bands can be an economical alternative to conventional deeper beams when beams are used. Savings in floor-to-floor heights are possible with the reduced beam depths, and formwork costs are reduced. The depth of the slab itself may be reduced as well, since with the broader beams, the span of the slab between the beams is lessened.

Maximum repetition of standard sizes increases the economy of slab and beam systems. Wherever possible, beam depths should be sized for the longest spans, and then the same depths should be used throughout. Beam widths and spacings, slab depths, and column sizes and spacings should also vary as little as possible within the structure.

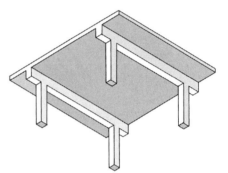

ONE-WAY SOLID SLAB WITH BEAMS

FIRE-RESISTANCE RATINGS FOR ONE-WAY SOLID SLAB CONSTRUCTION

Sitecast concrete one-way solid slabs may be used in both Combustible and Noncombustible Construction. Fire-resistance ratings for concrete construction vary with the type and density of concrete used. Use the following guidelines for preliminary design:

To achieve a 3-hour fire-resistance rating, a solid slab must be at least 6.5 in. (165 mm) thick. For a 2-hour rating, the minimum thickness is 5 in. (127 mm), for 1½ hours, 4.5 in. (114 mm), and for 1 hour, 3.5 in. (89 mm).

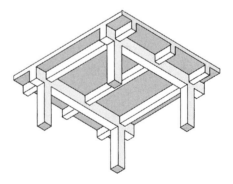

ONE-WAY SOLID SLAB WITH BEAMS AND GIRDERS

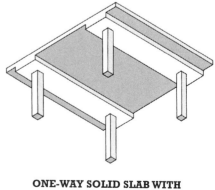

ONE-WAY SOLID SLAB WITH SLAB BANDS

SITECAST CONCRETE ONE-WAY SOLID SLAB

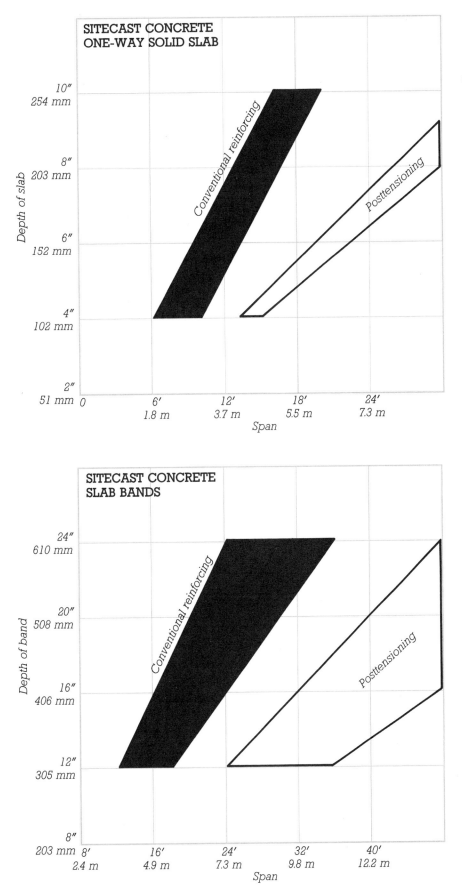

SITECAST CONCRETE ONE-WAY SOLID SLAB

Depth of slab — Conventional reinforcing — Posttensioning

10″ / 254 mm
8″ / 203 mm
6″ / 152 mm
4″ / 102 mm
2″ / 51 mm

0 — 6′ / 1.8 m — 12′ / 3.7 m — 18′ / 5.5 m — 24′ / 7.3 m

Span

SITECAST CONCRETE SLAB BANDS

Depth of band — Conventional reinforcing — Posttensioning

24″ / 610 mm
20″ / 508 mm
16″ / 406 mm
12″ / 305 mm
8″ / 203 mm

8′ / 2.4 m — 16′ / 4.9 m — 24′ / 7.3 m — 32′ / 9.8 m — 40′ / 12.2 m

Span

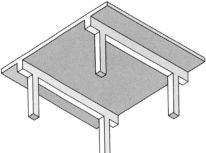

The top chart is for sitecast concrete one-way solid slab construction, either conventionally reinforced or posttensioned. For light to medium loads, read toward the right in the indicated areas. For heavy loads, read toward the left.

■ Size slab depth up to the nearest ½ in. (10 mm).

■ For the sizing of concrete beams, see pages 118–119.

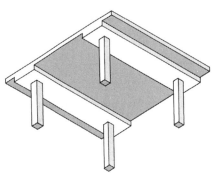

The bottom chart is for concrete slab bands—deep, wide beams that can be used with one-way solid slab construction. For light loads, read toward the right in the indicated areas. For heavy loads, read toward the left.

■ Size beam depths to the nearest inch (25 mm) and widths to the nearest foot (300 mm).

■ Typical widths for slab bands range from one-sixth to one-third of the span of the slab between the beams. For slab bands that are relatively deep or that span short distances, choose a narrow width. For those that are relatively shallow or that span long distances, choose a wide width.

SITECAST CONCRETE ONE-WAY JOISTS

One-way joist construction is an economical system for heavy loads or relatively long spans. This system is also sometimes desirable for the distinctive appearance of the underside of the slab, which may be left exposed in finished construction.

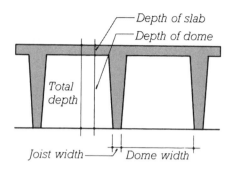

ONE-WAY JOISTS

JOIST LAYOUT

The spacing of joists depends on the widths of the pans and the joists. Standard pan widths are 20 and 30 in. (508 and 762 mm). Joists typically range in width from 5 to 9 in. (127 to 229 mm). A 6-in. (152-mm)-wide joist may be assumed for preliminary purposes.

In medium- and light-load applications, alternate joists may be omitted for greater economy. This system, called *wide module* or *skip joist* construction, is economical for spans of up to approximately 40 ft (12 m). In some instances, joist spacing may be increased to as much as 9 ft (2.7 m).

In long-span or heavy-load applications, joists may be broadened 2 to 2½ in. (50 to 65 mm) over the last 3 ft (1 m) toward their ends for increased capacity.

For joist spans of greater than 20 ft (6.1 m), distribution ribs running perpendicular to the joists are required. These ribs are 4 in. (102 mm) wide and the same depth as the joists. For longer spans, allow a maximum of 15 ft (4.6 m) between evenly spaced lines of ribs.

The economy of this system depends on the maximum repetition of standard forms and sizes. Depths, thicknesses, and spacings should vary as little as possible.

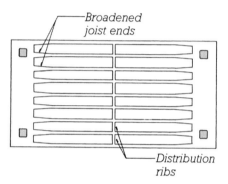

Joist bands usually run the shorter direction in rectangular bays.

JOIST BANDS

The use of joist bands the same depth as the joists is a highly economical alternative to conventional deeper beams. This system reduces building height, speeds construction, and simplifies the installation of building utilities. In some instances, it may even prove economical to use a joist system deeper than otherwise necessary in order to match the required depth of the joist bands.

With rectangular column bays and normal to heavy loads, joist bands should usually run in the shorter direction.

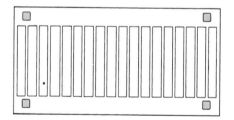

With light loads, it may be more economical to run joist bands in the long direction in a rectangular bay.

FIRE-RESISTANCE RATINGS FOR ONE-WAY JOIST CONSTRUCTION

Sitecast concrete one-way joists may be used in both Combustible and Noncombustible Construction. Fire-resistance ratings for concrete construction vary with the type and density of concrete used. Use the following guidelines for preliminary design:

A slab that is 3 in. (76 mm) deep between joists has a fire-resistance rating of 0 to 1½ hours. A 4½-in. (114-mm) deep slab provides 1½ to 3 hours of fire protection. For higher fire-resistance ratings, the slab thickness may be increased, fireproofing materials may be applied to the underside of the joists and slab, or an appropriately fire-resistive ceiling may be used.

SITECAST CONCRETE ONE-WAY JOISTS

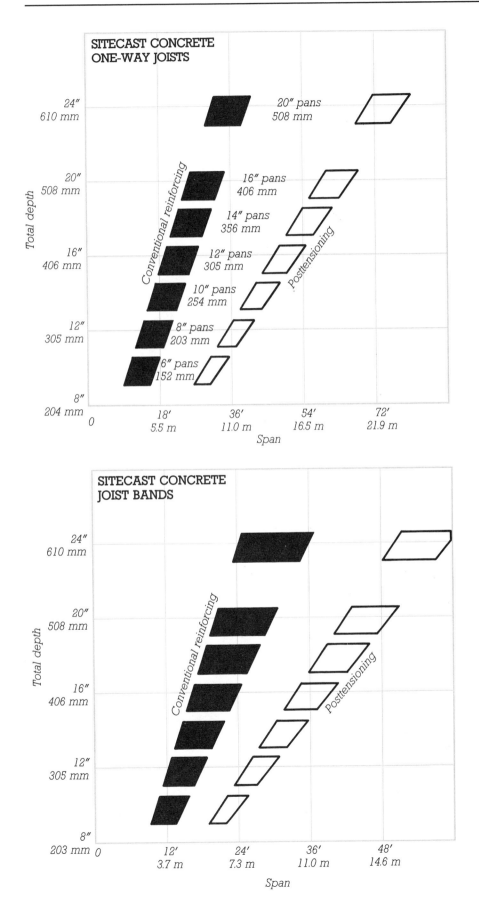

SITECAST CONCRETE ONE-WAY JOISTS

Total depth

24" / 610 mm	
20" / 508 mm	
16" / 406 mm	
12" / 305 mm	
8" / 204 mm	

Conventional reinforcing

Posttensioning

20" pans / 508 mm
16" pans / 406 mm
14" pans / 356 mm
12" pans / 305 mm
10" pans / 254 mm
8" pans / 203 mm
6" pans / 152 mm

Span: 0 | 18' / 5.5 m | 36' / 11.0 m | 54' / 16.5 m | 72' / 21.9 m

SITECAST CONCRETE JOIST BANDS

Total depth

24" / 610 mm	
20" / 508 mm	
16" / 406 mm	
12" / 305 mm	
8" / 203 mm	

Conventional reinforcing

Posttensioning

Span: 0 | 12' / 3.7 m | 24' / 7.3 m | 36' / 11.0 m | 48' / 14.6 m

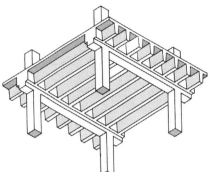

The top chart is for sitecast concrete one-way joist construction, either conventionally reinforced or posttensioned. For light loads, read toward the right in the indicated areas. For heavy loads, read toward the left.

■ *Total depth* is measured from the bottom of the joist to the top of the slab. (See the diagram on the facing page.) Depths are indicated on the chart for slabs of 3 to 4½ in. (76 to 114 mm) deep with standard pan sizes. The choice of the slab depth usually depends on the required fire-resistance rating for the system.

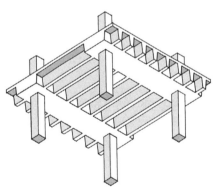

The bottom chart is for concrete joist bands—deep, wide beams used with the one-way joist system. For light loads, read toward the right in the indicated areas. For heavy loads, read toward the left.

■ For economy of formwork, use a joist band of the same depth as the joists.

■ Typical widths for joist bands range from 1 to 6 ft (0.3 to 1.8 m).

SITECAST CONCRETE TWO-WAY FLAT PLATE

Two-way flat plate construction is one of the most economical concrete framing systems. This system can span farther than one-way slabs, and the plain form of the slab makes it simple to construct and easy to finish. This system is commonly used in apartment and hotel construction, where it is well suited to the moderate live loads, it is economical to construct, and the flexibility of its column placements permits greater ease of unit planning and layout.

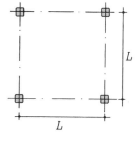

SQUARE BAYS

COLUMN LAYOUTS FOR FLAT PLATE CONSTRUCTION

For maximum economy and efficiency of the two-way structural system, the following guidelines on column placement should be followed whenever possible:

Column bays are most efficient when square or close to square. When rectangular bays are used, the sides of the bays should differ in length by a ratio of no more than 2:1.

Individual columns may be offset by as much as one-tenth of the span from regular column lines. (Columns on floors above and below an offset column must also be equally offset to maintain a vertical alignment of columns.)

Successive span lengths should not differ by more than one-third of the longer span. Slabs should also span over at least three bays in each direction.

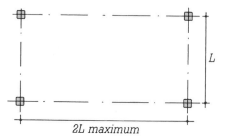

RECTANGULAR BAYS

TWO-WAY SLAB AND BEAM CONSTRUCTION

Two-way slab and beam construction uses beams to support the slab between columns. The high construction costs of this system make it economical only for long spans and heavy loads, such as in heavy industrial applications, or where high resistance to lateral forces is required. For preliminary sizing of slab depths, read from the area for posttensioned construction in the chart on the facing page.

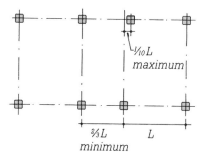

COLUMN OFFSETS AND BAY SIZE VARIATIONS

FIRE-RESISTANCE RATINGS FOR TWO-WAY FLAT PLATE CONSTRUCTION

Sitecast concrete two-way flat plate construction may be used in both Combustible and Noncombustible Construction. Fire-resistance ratings for concrete construction vary with the type and density of concrete used. Use the following guidelines for preliminary design:

To achieve a 3-hour fire-resistance rating, the slab must be at least 6.5 in. (165 mm) thick. For a 2-hour rating, the minimum thickness is 5 in. (127 mm), for 1½ hours, 4.5 in. (114 mm), and for 1 hour, 3.5 in. (89 mm).

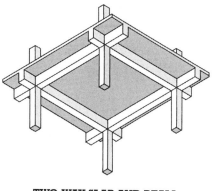

TWO-WAY SLAB AND BEAM CONSTRUCTION

SITECAST CONCRETE TWO-WAY FLAT PLATE

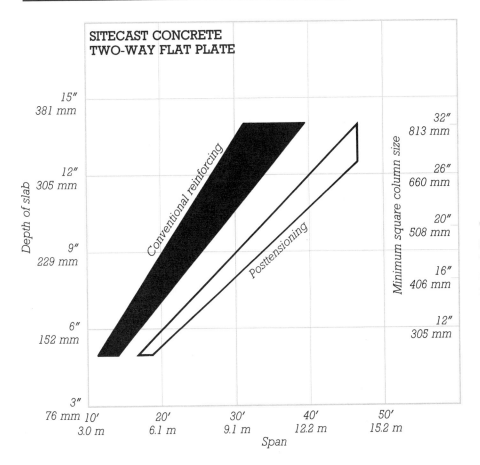

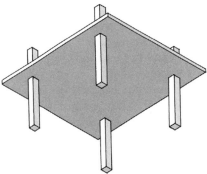

This chart is for sitecast concrete flat plate construction, either conventionally reinforced or posttensioned. For medium to light loads, read toward the right in the indicated areas. For heavy loads, read toward the left.

■ For rectangular column bays, use the span of the longer of the two sides of the bay in reading from this chart.

■ Size slab depth to the nearest ½ in. (10 mm).

COLUMN SIZES FOR FLAT PLATE CONSTRUCTION

The shallow depth of the junction between the slab and the column in flat plate construction restricts the minimum column size in this system. The right-hand scale on the chart above provides minimum square column sizes for various slab thicknesses. The required minimum column sizes for this system also depend on the applied loads on the structure. For light loads, reduce the indicated column size by 2 in. (50 mm). For heavy loads, increase the column size by 2 to 4 in. (50 to 100 mm).

■ For rectangular columns, use a column whose area is equal to that of the square column indicated. For round columns, use a column diameter one-third greater than the square column size indicated. Column sizes may also need to be increased at the edges of a slab.

■ For columns in multistory buildings, or for columns over 12 ft (3.7 m) tall, column size should also be checked using the charts on pages 114–115.

■ If smaller column sizes are desired, consider two-way flat slab construction as an alternative construction system. See pages 124–125.

SITECAST CONCRETE TWO-WAY FLAT SLAB

The two-way flat slab system is distinguished from flat plate construction by the strengthening of the column-to-slab junction, usually in the form of drop panels and/or column caps. Flat slab construction is an economical alternative to flat plate construction for heavier loads and longer spans. It also has increased resistance to lateral forces and often requires smaller columns than flat plate construction. However, the drop panels and column caps used in this system result in increased construction costs and greater overall floor depths than with flat plate construction.

DROP PANELS, COLUMN CAPS, AND SHEARHEADS

All flat slab construction requires some form of strengthening at the column-to-slab junction. Most commonly this is accomplished with the addition of drop panels, a deepening of the slab in the column region.

There are a number of alternatives to the exclusive use of drop panels in flat slab construction. Column caps, a widening of the columns toward their tops, may be used in place of drop panels where the loads on the slab are light, or in conjunction with drop panels where loads are very high. Where all such formed elements are considered undesirable, special arrangements of steel reinforcing in the slab, termed *shearheads*, may be an acceptable alternative to these methods.

The minimum size for drop panels is a width of one-third the span of the slab and a total depth of one and one-fourth times the depth of the slab. For heavy loads, panels may increase in width and depth.

For maximum economy, keep all drop panels the same dimensions throughout the building. The difference in depth between the slab and the drop panels should be equal to a standard lumber dimension. The edges of drop panels should be a minimum of 16 ft 6 in. (5.0 m) apart to utilize standard 16-ft (4.9-m) lumber in the formwork.

When column caps are used, their overall width should be eight to ten times the slab depth. Column caps are commonly either tapered or rectangular in profile, but should be approximately half as deep as their width at the top.

The addition of beams to flat slab construction can increase the load capacity and span range of the system, though with increased costs.

FIRE-RESISTANCE RATINGS
FOR TWO-WAY FLAT SLAB CONSTRUCTION

Sitecast concrete two-way flat plate construction may be used in both Combustible and Noncombustible Construction. Fire-resistance ratings for concrete construction vary with the type and density of concrete used. Use the following guidelines for preliminary design:

To achieve a 3-hour fire-resistance rating, the slab must be at least 6.5 in. (165 mm) thick. For a 2-hour rating, the minimum thickness is 5 in. (127 mm), for 1½ hours, 4.5 in. (114 mm), and for 1 hour, 3.5 in. (89 mm).

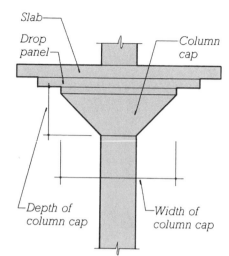

DROP PANELS AND COLUMN CAPS

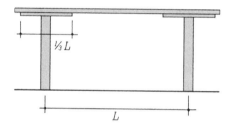

DROP PANEL WIDTH

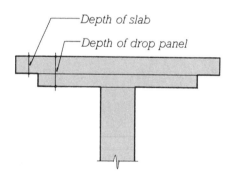

DROP PANEL DEPTH

SITECAST CONCRETE TWO-WAY FLAT SLAB

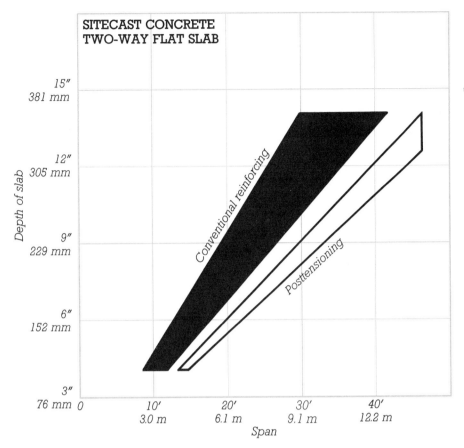

This chart is for concrete two-way flat slab construction, either conventionally reinforced or posttensioned. For light loads, read toward the right in the indicated areas. For heavy loads, read toward the left.

■ For rectangular column bays, use the span of the longer of the two sides of the bay in reading from this chart.

■ Size slab depth to the nearest ½ in. (10 mm).

COLUMN SIZES AND LAYOUTS FOR FLAT SLAB CONSTRUCTION

For light to moderate loads, use a minimum square column size of 12 in. (300 mm) for preliminary design. For heavier loads, larger columns or the addition of column caps may be required. Column size may be increased by 4 to 12 in. (100 to 300 mm) for extremely heavy loads.

For rectangular columns, use a column whose area is equal to that of the recommended square column size. For round columns, use a column diameter one-third greater than the recommended square column size. Column sizes may also need to be increased in multistory buildings or for columns taller than 12 ft (3.7 m). See pages 114–115 for checking column sizes for these conditions.

For maximum economy and efficiency of the two-way structural system, column layouts for flat slab construction should adhere to the same guidelines as those described for flat plate construction. Column bays should be approximately square, and column offsets from regular lines should be minimized. See page 124 for a complete discussion of these guidelines.

SITECAST CONCRETE WAFFLE SLAB

The waffle slab (or two-way joist) system is best suited for long span or heavy load conditions. This system is often desirable for the distinctive appearance of the underside of the slab, which may be left exposed in finished construction.

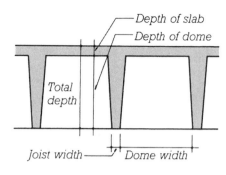

WAFFLE SLAB

RIB LAYOUT FOR WAFFLE SLAB CONSTRUCTION

Standard 19-in (483-mm) domes are used with ribs that are 5 in. (127 mm) wide to create a 24-in. (610-mm) module. Domes of 30 in. (762 mm) are used with 6-in. (152-mm) ribs to create a 36-in. (914-mm) module. Standard domes are also available for 4- and 5-ft (1.2- and 1.5-m) modules, and other square or rectangular sizes can be specially ordered.

Solid heads must be created over all columns by omitting domes in the vicinity of each column and pouring the slab flush with the bottom of the ribs. The number of domes omitted varies, increasing with longer spans and heavier loads. In some cases, solid strips may extend continuously between columns in both directions.

The economy of this system depends on the maximum repetition of standard forms and sizes. Depths, thicknesses, and spacings should vary as little as possible.

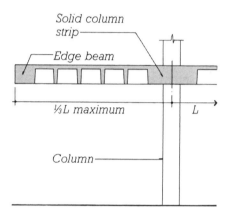

EDGE BEAMS AND CANTILEVERS

EDGE CONDITIONS

When the slab ends flush with the edge columns, the area between the outermost rib and the slab edge is filled solid to create an edge beam. The slab may also cantilever beyond the columns by as much as one-third of a full span. In this case, both an edge beam and a solid strip running between the edge columns may be required.

FIRE-RESISTANCE RATINGS FOR WAFFLE SLAB CONSTRUCTION

Sitecast concrete waffle slabs may be used in both Combustible and Noncombustible Construction. Fire-resistance ratings for concrete construction vary with the type and density of concrete used. Use the following guidelines for preliminary design:

A 3-in. (76-mm) slab thickness between ribs gives a fire-resistance rating of 0 to 1 hour. A 3½-in. (89-mm) thickness gives 1 hour, a 4½-in. (114-mm) thickness gives 1½ hours, and a 5-in. (127-mm) thickness gives 2 hours. For higher fire-resistance ratings, the slab thickness may be increased further, fireproofing materials may be applied to the underside of the ribs and slab, or an appropriately fire-resistive ceiling may be used.

SITECAST CONCRETE WAFFLE SLAB

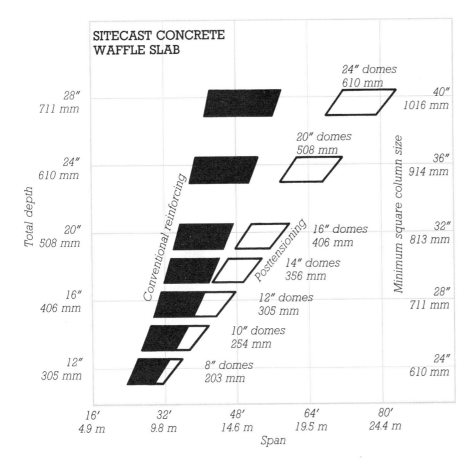

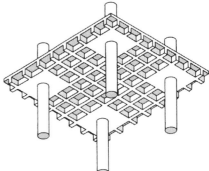

This chart is for concrete waffle slab construction, either conventionally reinforced or posttensioned. For light loads, read toward the right in the indicated areas. For heavy loads, read toward the left.

■ For rectangular bays, use the average of the spans of the two sides of the bay when reading from this chart.

■ *Total depth* is the sum of the depth of the ribs and the slab. (See the diagram on the facing page.) Depths are indicated on the chart for slabs from 3 to 4½ in. (76 to 114 mm) deep with standard pan sizes. The choice of the slab depth usually depends on the required fire-resistance rating for the system. See the facing page for fire-resistance information.

COLUMN SIZES AND LAYOUTS FOR WAFFLE SLAB CONSTRUCTION

In waffle slab construction, minimum column size is dependent on the overall thickness of the slab. The right-hand scale on the chart above provides minimum square column sizes for various slab thicknesses. For light loads, reduce the indicated column size by 2 to 4 in. (50 to 100 mm). For heavy loads, increase the indicated column size by 4 to 12 in. (100 to 300 mm).

For rectangular columns, use a column whose area is equal to that of the square column indicated. For round columns, use a column diameter one-third greater than the square column size indicated.

For columns in multistory buildings or for columns over 12 ft (3.7 m) tall, column size should also be checked using the charts on pages 114-115.

For maximum economy and efficiency of the two-way structural system, column layouts for waffle slab construction should adhere to the same guidelines as those described for flat plate construction. Column bays should be approximately square, and column offsets from regular lines should be minimized. See page 124 for a complete discussion of these guidelines.

PRECAST CONCRETE STRUCTURAL SYSTEMS

Precast prestressed concrete framing systems are characterized by reduced depths and deflections for spanning members, faster construction, and increased quality and durability of the concrete itself as compared to conventional sitecast concrete. Where future changes to a structure are anticipated, precast concrete may be a preferred choice due to the ease with which individual elements in the system may be removed or replaced. The difficulty of fabricating rigid joints in these systems leads to a greater reliance on shear walls or cross bracing to achieve lateral stability than in sitecast concrete structures, and makes them potentially more sensitive to vibrations produced by heavy machinery or other sources. Precast concrete spanning elements are also often used in combination with other site-fabricated vertical systems such as sitecast concrete, masonry, or steel.

SELECTING A PRECAST CONCRETE FRAMING SYSTEM

The initial choice of a framing system should be based on the desired spanning capacity or column spacing of the system and the magnitude of the expected loads on the structure. The following precast concrete systems are listed in order of increasing spans, load capacity, and cost:

- Solid Flat Slab
- Hollow Core Slab
- Double Tee
- Single Tee

For short spans and light loads, select a system from the top of the list. For longer spans and heavier loads, systems toward the bottom of the list are required.

As with sitecast concrete, the inherent fire-resistive qualities of precast concrete construction allow these systems to remain wholly or partially exposed in the finished building. For this reason, the choice of a concrete framing system often has significant architectural implications that should be considered early in the design process. These include, for example, the ease of integration of building services into the structural system, the possible use of the underside of the structural slab as a finish ceiling, and the aesthetic qualities of the system.

LAYING OUT A PRECAST CONCRETE SYSTEM

The economy of precast concrete construction depends on the maximum repetition of standard elements and sizes. Use the following guidelines for preliminary layout of a precast concrete structure to ensure maximum economy:

- In the direction of the span of the deck members, use a modular dimension of 1 ft (0.3 m). If a wall panel has been selected, use the width of the panel as the modular dimension.
- In the direction transverse to the span of the deck members, use a module of 8 ft (2.4 m). If a deck member has been selected, use the width of the member as the modular dimension.
- Floor-to-floor heights need not be designed to any particular module, though the maximum repetition of the dimension chosen is desirable. Where precast wall panels are used, floor-to-floor heights should be coordinated with the height of the wall panel.

- Restrictions due to shipping and handling of members usually limit span lengths to 60 to 80 ft (18 to 24 m) maximum. Further transportation restrictions on depths of elements usually limit bay widths to between 24 and 40 ft (7 and 12 m) where girders are used.

In general, any design features that require unique structural elements, excessive variations in the sizes of elements, alterations in structural configuration, or deviation from the standard dimensions of the system should be avoided. Where the maximum flexibility of layout with precast concrete elements is desired, solid flat slabs or hollow core slabs may be preferred for their shorter spans and the greater ease with which they may be sawn after casting to conform to irregular conditions.

PROJECT SIZE

The economy of precast concrete construction also depends on the size of the construction project. The following figures are approximate minimum quantities for which the production of precast concrete elements may be economical:

- 10,000 sq ft (1000 m²) of architectural wall panels, or
- 15,000 sq ft (1500 m²) of deck or slab members, or
- 1000 linear feet (300 m) of girders, columns, or pilings.

PRECAST CONCRETE COLUMNS

Precast concrete columns are most commonly combined with precast beams in a post and beam configuration. Unlike sitecast concrete, where rigid or semirigid joints between columns and beams are easily made, in precast concrete framing systems such joints are difficult to construct. For this reason, precast concrete framing systems most often rely on shear walls or braced framing for resistance to lateral forces.

Precast concrete columns are usually provided with conventional reinforcing. Prestressing may also be used to reduce stresses on the columns during transportation and handling or to improve a column's resistance to anticipated bending forces in service.

**PRECAST CONCRETE COLUMN
WITH TWO CORBELS**

STANDARD SIZES AND SHAPES FOR PRECAST CONCRETE COLUMNS

Precast concrete columns are most commonly available in square profile in the sizes indicated on the charts on the facing page. Rectangular shapes can also be produced, although availability may vary with suppliers. For larger projects (requiring 1000 linear ft, or 300 m, or more of columns), economies of scale may make practical a greater range of sizes and configurations.

Columns of up to approximately 60 ft (18 m) in length can be transported easily. Columns of up to approximately 100 ft (30 m) in length may be shipped with special transportation arrangements.

For ease of casting, columns with corbels should be limited to corbels on two opposite sides or, at most, three sides.

Like all precast concrete elements, precast columns should be as consistent and regular as possible in dimensions and layout in order to achieve maximum economy.

CONCRETE STRENGTH AND COLUMN SIZE

The top chart on the facing page is based on 5000 psi (35 MPa) concrete. Higher strength concrete may also be used to reduce the required column size. To adjust the column sizes indicated in the top chart for variations in concrete strength, use the factors in the table to the right.

Concrete Strength		Multiply Column Size by
6000 psi	(40MPa)	0.90
7000 psi	(50 MPa)	0.85
8,000 psi	(55 MPa)	0.80
10,000 psi	(70 MPa)	0.70

FIRE-RESISTANCE RATINGS FOR PRECAST CONCRETE COLUMNS

Precast concrete columns may be used in both Combustible and Noncombustible Construction. The fire resistance of precast concrete varies with its ingredients and density. For preliminary design, you may assume that a 2-hour fire-resistance rating can be achieved with columns not less than 10 in. (250 mm) on a side. Fire-resistance ratings of 3 and 4 hours can be achieved with columns 12 in. (300 mm) and 14 in. (350 mm) in the minimum dimension, respectively.

PRECAST CONCRETE COLUMNS

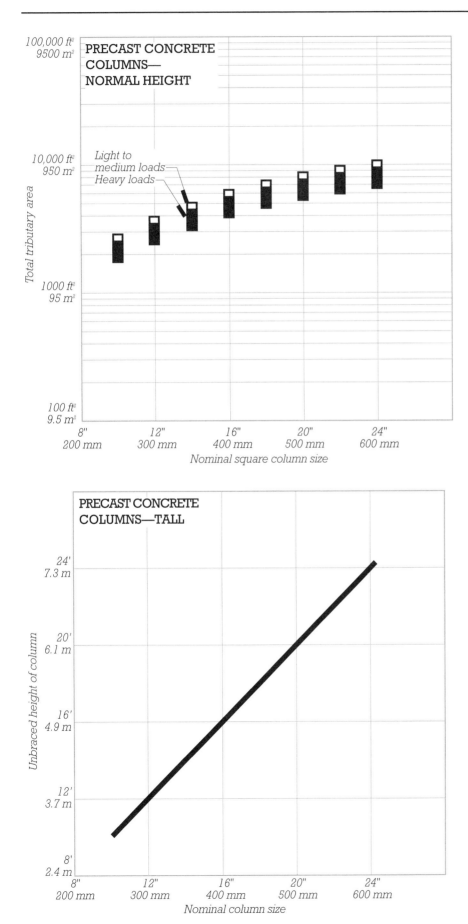

PRECAST CONCRETE COLUMNS— NORMAL HEIGHT

Total tributary area

100,000 ft²
9500 m²

10,000 ft²
950 m²

Light to medium loads
Heavy loads

1000 ft²
95 m²

100 ft²
9.5 m²

8"
200 mm

12"
300 mm

16"
400 mm

20"
500 mm

24"
600 mm

Nominal square column size

PRECAST CONCRETE COLUMNS—TALL

Unbraced height of column

24'
7.3 m

20'
6.1 m

16'
4.9 m

12'
3.7 m

8'
2.4 m

8"
200 mm

12"
300 mm

16"
400 mm

20"
500 mm

24"
600 mm

Nominal column size

The top chart is for precast concrete columns up to 12 ft (3.7 m) tall between floors. For light to medium loads, read in the upper open areas of each bar. For high loads, read in the lower solid areas. *Total tributary area* is the summed area of the roof and all floors supported by the column.

■ For rectangular columns, select a column of area equal to the square size indicated.

■ Actual column size is equal to nominal size.

For columns taller than 12 ft (3.7 m), read from both charts on this page, using the larger size indicated by either chart. *Unbraced height of column* is the vertical distance between floors or other supports that brace the column laterally against buckling.

■ For rectangular columns, read the chart's nominal column size using the least dimension of the column.

PRECAST CONCRETE WALL PANELS

There is great variety in precast concrete wall panel types and applications. Panels may be prestressed or conventionally reinforced; they may be loadbearing or nonbearing; they may or may not contribute to the lateral stability of a building; they may be flat, ribbed, or more intricately shaped; and they may be solid, hollow, or a sandwich of concrete with an insulating core. Precast concrete wall panels may be used in conjunction with a precast concrete framing system or with other framing systems, such as steel or concrete.

PANEL TYPES

Flat panels may be one to two stories high. Ribbed panels may be up to four stories high.

Wall panels may also be formed in a great variety of original shapes. The design of such panels depends on specialized knowledge of precasting methods. When the use of such panels is planned, the necessary consultants should be sought out early in the design process. For the preliminary sizing of these panels, use the chart for ribbed panels on the facing page. Loadbearing wall panels such as these may be used in buildings up to approximately 16 to 20 stories in height.

Panels with openings usually may not be prestressed. Panels without openings may be prestressed to reduce thickness or to limit stresses in the panels during transportation and handling.

SIZES OF PRECAST CONCRETE WALL PANELS

Solid panels are commonly available in thicknesses of $3\frac{1}{2}$ to 10 in. (89 to 254 mm). Sandwich or hollow core panels range in thickness from $5\frac{1}{2}$ to 12 in. (140 to 305 mm). Ribbed wall panels are commonly available in thicknesses of 12 to 24 in. (305 to 610 mm).

For preliminary design, assume an 8-ft (2.4-m) width for all panel types. With special provisions, panels in widths of up to approximately 14 ft (4.3 m) may be transported without excessive economic penalty.

FIRE-RESISTANCE RATINGS FOR
PRECAST CONCRETE WALL PANELS

Precast concrete wall panels may be used in both Combustible and Noncombustible Construction. Fire-resistance ratings will vary with the density of concrete used in the panel and, in sandwich panels, with the type of core insulation as well. The following guidelines may be used for preliminary design:

Panels must be at least 6.5 in. (165 mm) thick to achieve a fire-resistance rating of 4 hours. A 3-hour rating is achieved at a thickness of 6 in. (152 mm), a 2-hour rating at 5 in. (127 mm), and a 1-hour rating at 3.5 in. (89 mm).

PRECAST CONCRETE WALL PANELS

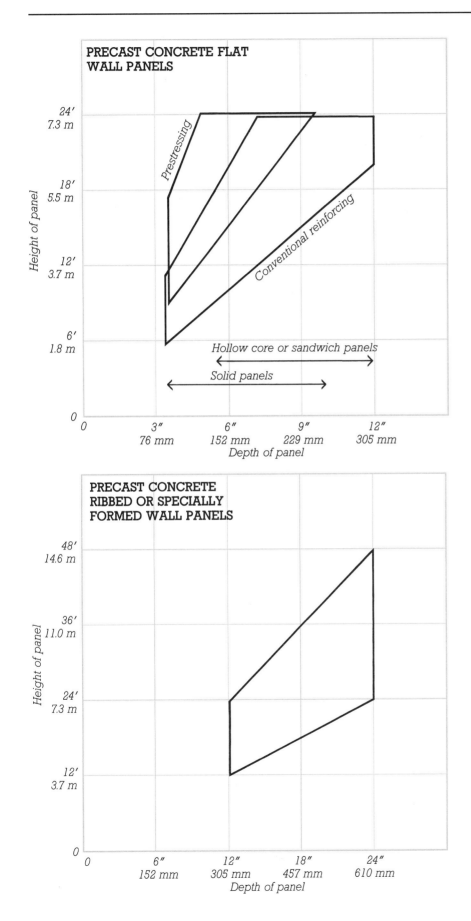

PRECAST CONCRETE FLAT WALL PANELS

Height of panel

24' 7.3 m

18' 5.5 m

12' 3.7 m

6' 1.8 m

0

Prestressing

Conventional reinforcing

Hollow core or sandwich panels

Solid panels

0   3" 76 mm   6" 152 mm   9" 229 mm   12" 305 mm

Depth of panel

PRECAST CONCRETE RIBBED OR SPECIALLY FORMED WALL PANELS

Height of panel

48' 14.6 m

36' 11.0 m

24' 7.3 m

12' 3.7 m

0

0   6" 152 mm   12" 305 mm   18" 457 mm   24" 610 mm

Depth of panel

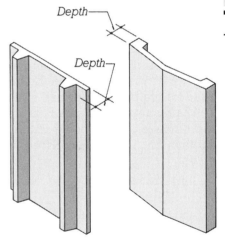

Depth

Depth

The top chart is for flat precast concrete wall panels, either prestressed or conventionally reinforced. For nonbearing panels, read toward the left in the indicated areas. For loadbearing panels, read toward the right.

The bottom chart is for precast concrete wall panels formed with ribs, stems, or other stiffening features. For nonbearing or prestressed panels, read toward the left in the indicated area. For loadbearing panels, conventionally reinforced panels, or panels with integral window openings, read toward the right.

■ *Depth of panel* is the total depth of the panel and any stiffening features.

■ For the preliminary design of spandrel panels, use the distance between columns for the height indicated on either chart.

PRECAST CONCRETE BEAMS AND GIRDERS

Precast prestressed concrete girders are commonly used to carry all varieties of precast concrete decking elements between columns or bearing walls. They can be used in any building type where precast concrete construction is to be considered.

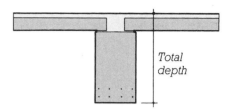

RECTANGULAR BEAM WITH SOLID OR HOLLOW CORE SLABS

TOTAL DEPTH OF FLOOR SYSTEMS

Rectangular beams are commonly used with solid or hollow core slabs resting on top of the beam. Total floor depth at the beam is the sum of the depths of the slab (and topping, if any) and the beam.

Inverted T- and L-beams are commonly used with double and single tees. When erected, the top of the tees should be level with or slightly above the top of the beam. When the tees rest directly on the beam ledge, the total floor depth at the beam is the depth of the tee (and topping, if any) plus the depth of the ledge. Deeper tees may have their ends notched or "dapped" so as to rest lower on the beam. The use of dapped tees may result in total floor depths of as little as the depth of the tee itself plus any topping.

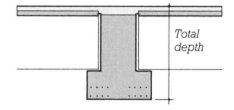

INVERTED T-BEAM WITH SINGLE OR DOUBLE TEES

FIRE-RESISTANCE RATINGS FOR PRECAST BEAMS AND GIRDERS

Precast concrete beams and girders can be used in both Combustible and Noncombustible Construction. Fire-resistance ratings will vary with the density of concrete used in the beams. The following guidelines may be used for preliminary design:

A prestressed concrete beam not smaller than 9.5 in. (241 mm) in width has a fire-resistance rating of 3 hours. For a 2-hour rating, the minimum width is 7 in. (178 mm), and for 1 hour, 4 in. (102 mm).

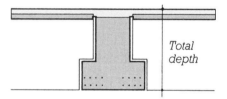

INVERTED T-BEAM WITH DAPPED TEES

PRECAST CONCRETE BEAMS AND GIRDERS

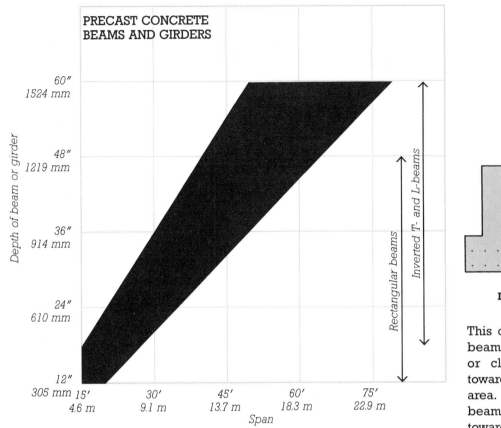

PRECAST CONCRETE
BEAMS AND GIRDERS

Depth of beam or girder

60″ / 1524 mm
48″ / 1219 mm
36″ / 914 mm
24″ / 610 mm
12″ / 305 mm

15′ / 4.6 m
30′ / 9.1 m
45′ / 13.7 m
60′ / 18.3 m
75′ / 22.9 m

Span

Rectangular beams

Inverted T- and L-beams

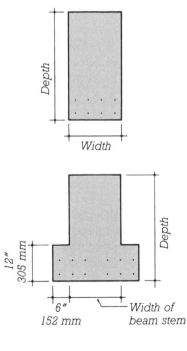

RECTANGULAR BEAM

INVERTED T- AND L-BEAMS

This chart is for precast concrete beams and girders. For light loads or close beam spacings, read toward the right in the indicated area. For heavy loads and large beam spacings, or for girders, read toward the left.

COMMON SIZES OF PRECAST CONCRETE BEAMS AND GIRDERS

Rectangular beams commonly range in depth from 18 to 48 in. (450 to 1200 mm). Widths range from 12 to 36 in. (300 to 900 mm).

Inverted T- and L-beams commonly range in depth from 18 to 60 in. (450 to 1500 mm), although sections deeper than 48 in. (1200 mm) may be subject to shipping or handling restrictions. Widths of the beam stem (not including the ledges) range from 12 to 30 in. (300 to 750 mm).

Standard dimensions for beam ledges are 6 in. (150 mm) wide and 12 in. (300 mm) deep.

Beam sizes typically vary in increments of 2 or 4 in. (50 or 100 mm). Availability of sizes varies with suppliers.

Depth

Width

12″ / 305 mm

Depth

6″ / 152 mm

Width of beam stem

PRECAST CONCRETE SLABS

Precast prestressed concrete solid and hollow core slabs are commonly used in hotels, multifamily dwellings, commercial structures, hospitals, schools, and parking structures.

CONCRETE TOPPING ON PRECAST SLABS

Sitecast concrete topping is often applied over precast concrete slabs to increase the structural capacity of the slab, to increase the fire resistance of the floor system, to allow the integration of electrical and communications services into the floor, or to provide a more level and smoother floor surface in preparation for subsequent finishing. In buildings such as hotels, housing, and some parking structures, where these requirements may not exist, the use of untopped slabs may be an acceptable and economical system choice.

SPECIAL SYSTEMS

Both solid and hollow core slabs may be combined with other spanning elements to create several variations of floor systems referred to as *spread systems*. These systems can provide increased economy and may allow greater flexibility in the choice of building module.

- Either slab type may be used as a secondary element spanning transversely between longer spanning single tees, double tees, or channels.

- Hollow core slabs can be spread from 2 to 3 ft (0.6 to 0.9 m), with corrugated steel decking spanning between the slabs. This system is usually topped. Where many floor penetrations are expected, this is an especially attractive system due to the ease of creating openings through the steel decking.

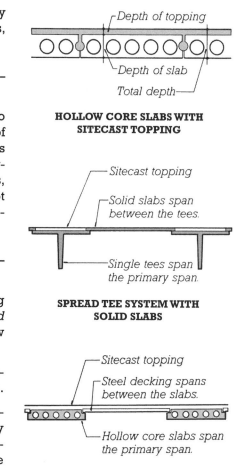

HOLLOW CORE SLABS WITH SITECAST TOPPING

SPREAD TEE SYSTEM WITH SOLID SLABS

HOLLOW CORE SLAB SPREAD SYSTEM

FIRE-RESISTANCE RATINGS FOR SOLID FLAT SLABS AND HOLLOW CORE SLABS

Precast concrete slabs can be used in both Combustible and Noncombustible Construction. Fire-resistance ratings will vary with the density of concrete used in the slabs and the topping. Use the following guidelines for preliminary design:

Solid slab floors must be at least 5.5 in. (140 mm) thick to have a fire resistance rating of 3 hours. For a 2-hour rating, the required thickness is 4.5 in. (115 mm). A 1½-hour rating requires a minimum thickness of 4 in. (100 mm) and a 1-hour rating, 3.5 in. (90 mm). These thicknesses include the depth of any topping.

Hollow core slabs at least 8 in. (200 mm) deep achieve a fire-resistance rating of 2 hours without a concrete topping. With the addition of a 2-in. (50-mm) topping, the rating rises to 3 hours.

PRECAST CONCRETE SLABS

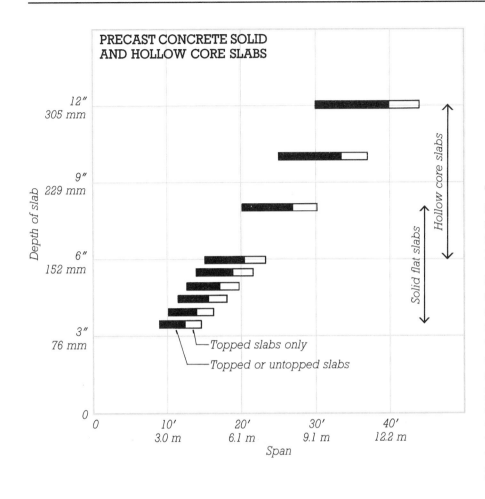

PRECAST CONCRETE SOLID
AND HOLLOW CORE SLABS

Depth of slab

12″
305 mm

9″
229 mm

6″
152 mm

3″
76 mm

0

Hollow core slabs

Solid flat slabs

Topped slabs only

Topped or untopped slabs

0   10′   20′   30′   40′
       3.0 m   6.1 m   9.1 m   12.2 m

Span

SOLID FLAT SLAB

HOLLOW CORE SLAB

SIZING THE STRUCTURAL SYSTEM

This chart is for precast concrete solid flat slabs and hollow core slabs. For light loads, read toward the right in the indicated areas. For heavy loads, read toward the left.

■ The open areas indicated on the chart are for slabs with an added sitecast concrete topping only. The solid areas are for either topped or untopped slabs. The depths indicated on the chart are for the slabs alone, without any additional topping. Where a topping is used, add 2 in. (50 mm) to the indicated depths for preliminary design. See the facing page for further information on the use of concrete toppings.

139

COMMON SIZES OF SOLID AND HOLLOW CORE SLABS

Solid flat slabs come in depths of 3½ to 8 in. (90 to 200 mm). For depths of 6 in. (150 mm) and above, however, hollow core slabs are usually more economical. Typical widths are 8 to 12 ft (2.4 to 3.7 m).

Hollow core slabs come in depths of 6 to 12 in. (150 to 300 mm). Typical widths are 2 ft, 3 ft 4 in., 4 ft, and 8 ft (0.6, 1.0, 1.2, and 2.4 m). Availability of sizes varies with suppliers.

PRECAST CONCRETE SINGLE AND DOUBLE TEES

Precast prestressed single and double tees can span farther than precast slabs and are commonly used in such building types as commercial structures, schools, and parking garages.

SPREAD TEE SYSTEMS

Single and double tees may be combined with other spanning elements to create framing systems referred to as *spread systems.* In these systems, the tees are erected with spaces between. These gaps are then bridged with precast solid or hollow core slabs, or with sitecast concrete that is poured as part of the topping. These systems can increase the economy of long-span structures and may allow greater flexibility in the choice of building module.

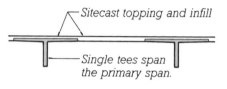

SPREAD TEE SYSTEM WITH SITECAST CONCRETE TOPPING AND INFILL

FIRE-RESISTANCE RATINGS FOR SINGLE AND DOUBLE TEES

Precast concrete single and double tees may be used in both Combustible and Noncombustible Construction. Fire resistance will vary with the density of concrete used in the slabs and topping. Use the following guidelines for preliminary design:

For a fire-resistance rating of 3 hours, single and double tees require applied fire-protection materials or an appropriately fire-resistive ceiling. For ratings of 2 hours and less, protection may be achieved by regulating the thickness of the concrete topping: 3.5 in. (90 mm) for 2 hours, 3.0 in. (75 mm) for 1½ hours, and 2.0 in. (50 mm) for 1 hour.

PRECAST CONCRETE SINGLE AND DOUBLE TEES

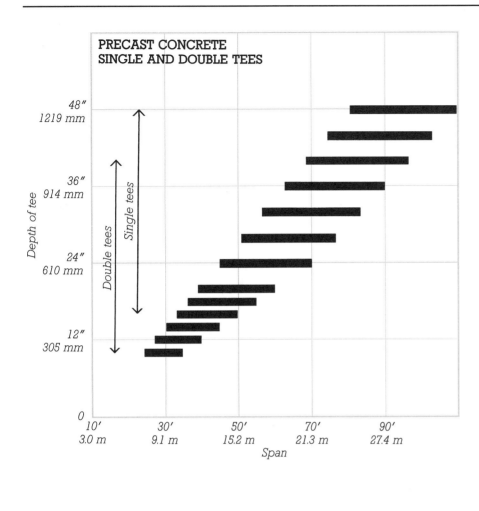

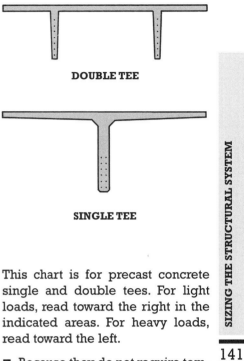

DOUBLE TEE

SINGLE TEE

141

This chart is for precast concrete single and double tees. For light loads, read toward the right in the indicated areas. For heavy loads, read toward the left.

■ Because they do not require temporary support against tipping, double tees are easier and more economical to erect than single tees. Their use is preferred wherever possible.

■ Double tees are most commonly used with a concrete topping. For preliminary purposes, add 2 in. (50 mm) to the depths indicated on the chart. Roof slabs and deep single tees may not need to be topped.

COMMON SIZES OF PRECAST SINGLE AND DOUBLE TEES

Double tees come in widths of 4, 8, 10, and 12 ft (1.2, 2.4, 3.0, and 3.7 m). Common depths are 10 to 40 in. (250 to 1000 mm). Single tees come in widths of 6, 8, 10, and 12 ft (1.8, 2.4, 3.0, and 3.7 m). Common depths are 16 to 48 in. (400 to 1200 mm). Tees longer than 60 to 80 ft (18 to 24 m) may be less economical because of increased transportation and handling costs. Availability of sizes varies with suppliers.

SECTION
3

DESIGNING WITH DAYLIGHT

1
DESIGN CRITERIA FOR DAYLIGHTING SYSTEMS

This chapter will help you evaluate the suitability of daylight illumination to your project and, if you choose to proceed with daylighting design, to select appropriate daylighting strategies.

DESIGN WITH DAYLIGHT

Daylighting is the use of natural light to illuminate the interior of a building. Daylight can provide high-quality, color-balanced lighting. It can reduce a building's energy consumption, contribute to the conservation of natural resources and the protection of the environment, improve the aesthetic quality of the workplace, provide a psychological connection to nature and the outdoors, and increase business productivity. There are many factors that influence the potential for daylighting design on a project. Location, climate, building form, program, and the perceived value of daylighting by the building's owners and its occupants can all play a role. When buildings are designed for daylight illumination, the architectural impact is significant. Massing, orientation, structural configuration, layout of interior elements and spaces, and choice of materials are all influenced by daylighting considerations. For these reasons, day-

lighting should be addressed at the earliest stages of design, when the opportunities for successfully incorporating effective strategies into a project are greatest. The information in the following pages will help you evaluate the potential of daylighting for your project, and, if you choose to pursue this option, provide preliminary design guidelines for developing a building that effectively utilizes natural daylight for illumination.

A quality luminous environment requires adequate levels of illumination; it requires light that is well distributed to prevent excessive contrast, brightness, and glare; and it requires light that is reliably available. Sources of daylight include both the sun and the surrounding, clear or clouded, luminous sky. Direct sunlight is too intense to be allowed to fall directly on tasks or within the visual field. It must be diffused, reflected, or moderated in some way. Furthermore, direct sunlight is not necessarily the most reli-

able source of daylight. The sun's position in the sky changes constantly, causing the quality of its light to vary with orientation, time of day, and season. At any time, the sun may be obscured by cloud cover, geographic features, or nearby man-made structures. For these reasons, the simplest way to incorporate daylighting into most projects is to rely on indirect sky light as the primary source of illumination and, where sunlight is present, to ensure that it does not directly intrude into the task area. This is the daylighting approach emphasized in the following pages.

Designs utilizing direct sunlight as the primary source of illumination are also feasible, particularly in areas with prevailing clear skies. The information provided here is relevant to such projects as well. However, the behavior of such systems is more complex, and their design will require more sophisticated analysis and modeling techniques than provided here.

SKY COVER

The map on this page indicates average clear and covered (cloudy) sky conditions within the continental United States. Conditions are characterized as *predominantly clear, moderate,* or *heavily covered,* corresponding to an average annual sky cover of less than 50%, from 50% to 70%, or greater than 70%, respectively. Only in areas indicated as predominantly clear — mainly the Southwest and parts of Florida — are clear skies prevalent on average more than half of all daylight hours. In the remaining areas — most of the continental United States — covered or partially covered sky conditions predominate more than half of the time. Though not shown on this map, the heavily populated regions of Canada are also within moderate or heavily covered areas as well.

In predominantly clear areas, direct sun is most prevalent and daylight conditions are most constant. In these areas, the levels of available daylight are consistently highest. Consequently, in using the sizing charts shown toward the end of this chapter for projects falling within predominantly clear areas, you should read low in the recommended lighting level ranges because of the higher available light levels. In areas characterized as moderate, sky conditions are more variable. In using the sizing charts for projects falling within moderate sky cover areas, you should read near the middle of the recommended lighting level ranges. In heavily covered areas, cloudy skies predominate, and average daylight availability is lowest. When using the sizing charts for these projects, you should read near the top of the recommended lighting level ranges. Because local sky conditions can vary from regional averages, this information should be supplemented with local data wherever possible.

Regardless of sky cover conditions, control of direct sunlight is always an important consideration. To prevent unacceptable levels of glare and contrast, sunlight should always be prevented from falling directly within the visual field of task areas.

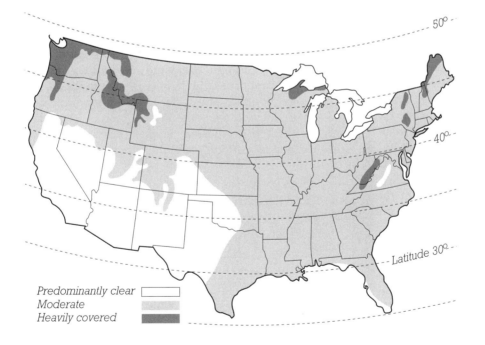

Predominantly clear
Moderate
Heavily covered

SKY COVER CONDITIONS

THE PATH OF THE SUN

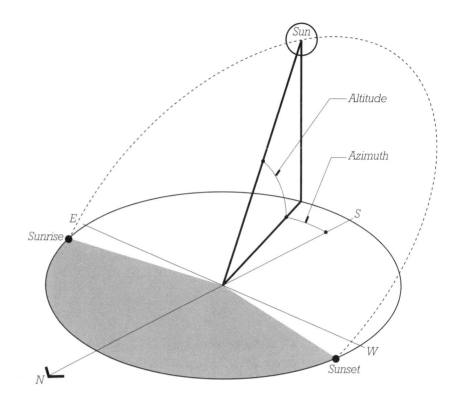

The sun moves over and around a building during the course of each day. Successful daylighting design requires that the building occupants receive acceptable levels of consistent, quality illumination throughout this cycle. The chart below provides information about the path of the sun for various latitudes and different times of the year, information that is important to understanding the impact of the sun on a building. To find the approximate latitude for a project located in the continental United States, use the latitude indications on the Sky Cover Conditions map on the previous page. For other locations, consult comparable sources of information. As an example, Savannah, Georgia, lies approximately at 32° North latitude. At the summer solstice, June 21, the sun rises at an azimuth of 115° (measured from the South axis), and at solar noon, reaches an altitude of 81° (measured from the horizon). The length of the day from sunrise to sunset is approximately 14 hours.

The path of the sun also varies over the course of the year, the magnitude of this variation increasing with greater distance from the equator. For example, at 24° North latitude, from summer solstice to winter solstice, the length of the day varies by 4 hours and the sun's rising or setting position moves on the horizon 47°. In comparison, at 52° North latitude, the length of the day varies by 8 hours, and the sun's rising or setting position moves 120°. In addition, at 24° North latitude, at the winter solstice, the sun rises to 42° above the horizon at noon. At 52° North, it rises only 16° above the horizon at its highest point.

Use the information in this table to chart the approximate path of the sun around your building. As you continue on the following pages, this information will help you to determine a favorable building orientation and opening configuration in order to maximize daylight access and limit exposure to unwanted direct sunlight. In particular, pay special attention to times of the day and year when the sun is low in the sky. These times present the most difficult problems for sunlight control. Attention to building orientation, configuration of daylight openings, and the anticipated hours of building occupancy should all be considered relative to these low-angle sun conditions.

Latitude	Hours of Daylight (sunrise to sunset)	Altitude of Noon Sun	Azimuth of Rising or Setting Sun
24° North			
Summer Solstice	14 hours	90°	115°
Winter Solstice	10 hours	42°	68°
32° North			
Summer Solstice	14 hours	81°	115°
Winter Solstice	10 hours	36°	62°
40° North			
Summer Solstice	14 hours	74°	120°
Winter Solstice	9 hours	28°	60°
48° North			
Summer Solstice	15 hours	66°	125°
Winter Solstice	8 hours	20°	55°
52° North			
Summer Solstice	16 hours	62°	130°
Winter Solstice	8 hours	16°	50°

SKY DOME OBSTRUCTION

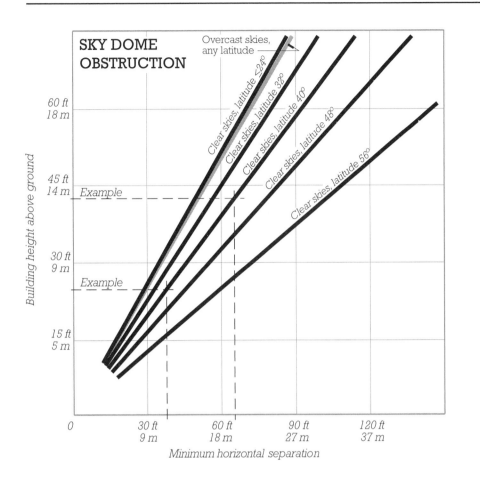

SKY DOME OBSTRUCTION

Building height above ground

Overcast skies, any latitude

Clear skies, latitude <24°
Clear skies, latitude 32°
Clear skies, latitude 40°
Clear skies, latitude 48°
Clear skies, latitude 56°

60 ft / 18 m
45 ft / 14 m — Example
30 ft / 9 m
Example
15 ft / 5 m

0 | 30 ft / 9 m | 60 ft / 18 m | 90 ft / 27 m | 120 ft / 37 m

Minimum horizontal separation

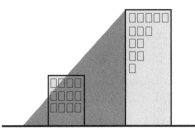

This chart is for determining daylight obstruction between buildings.

■ To ensure full access to daylight for your building, read the chart using the height of adjacent buildings or structures. Locate your building so that it is at least as far away from each of these structures as indicated on the chart.

■ To ensure that your building does not obstruct access to daylight for adjacent structures, read the chart using the height of your building and locate your building at least as far away from the adjacent structures as indicated.

■ For buildings in predominantly covered sky conditions at any latitude, read the chart along the sloped line for overcast skies. For buildings located in predominantly clear sky areas, read the chart along the sloped line for the latitude of the project or interpolate between lines for other latitudes. For buildings located in moderate sky cover areas, read along the line for overcast skies to find the optimum building separation under worst case conditions, or read along the appropriate line for clear skies to determine building separation under more favorable clear sky conditions. To determine sky conditions and the latitude of a project located in the continental United States, consult the Sky Cover Conditions map on page 147. For other project locations, use comparable sources of information.

Daylighting design requires a building to have line-of-sight access to sufficient sky area for adequate daylight exposure. The chart above can be used in two ways: first, to determine the extent to which surrounding structures may obstruct your building's access to daylight, and second, to determine the extent to which your building obstructs surrounding structures' access to daylight.

For example, assume a project location at 40° North latitude, with clear sky conditions, a neighboring building 24 ft (7 m) tall, and a planned height of 42 ft (13 m) for your building. To ensure that your building has full access to daylight, read the chart using the adjacent building's height of 24 ft (7 m) to determine that there should be at least 37 ft (11 m) between the two structures. To ensure that the adjacent building's daylight is not obstructed by your project, read the chart using your building's height of 42 ft (13 m) to determine that there should be at least 65 ft (20 m) between the two structures. To protect access to daylight for both buildings, use the larger of the two answers, in this case, 65 ft (20 m).

BUILDING SITING AND SHAPE

Daylighting design is intimately related to building form. This section provides guidelines for the siting, massing, and internal configuration of a building to provide the greatest opportunities for successful daylighting.

BUILDING SIZE

Strategies for daylighting differ with building size. For small buildings, the ratio of exterior skin area to enclosed volume is relatively large. This means that residences and small-scale nonresidential buildings generally have ample opportunities to locate occupied areas in close proximity to daylight sources such as windows and rooftop openings. In small buildings, the main challenge for the designer is to control the quality of the daylight, distributing it effectively and avoiding excessive contrast or brightness. On the other hand, in large buildings, the ratio of exterior envelope area to enclosed space is less, and providing adequate levels of daylight to interior areas becomes a design challenge with significant formal implications. Both the shape of the building and its interior configuration are critical to a successful daylighting scheme.

ORIENTATION

Daylight openings should be oriented to allow the control of direct sunlight while providing access to sources of daylight that are consistent in quality and provide high levels of illumination. In the Northern Hemisphere, these conditions are best met in a south orientation, where for the largest part of the day, the sun remains high in the sky and the surrounding sky provides high levels of manageable daylight. Northern exposure is also favorable, providing consistent daylight, though at illumination levels lower than from a southern exposure. The most difficult orientations for daylight openings are toward those portions of the sky in which the sun is low in its daily path, generally toward the east and west, though precise orientation varies with location and time of year. These exposures should be avoided or, if used, studied carefully, as the quality of the daylight is highly variable and the control of direct sunlight problematic. Thus, buildings elongated in the east–west direction, and plan configurations that otherwise maximize exposure to the north and south sky while shielding exposure to the east and west, will generally provide the most favorable daylighting opportunities. In some cases, strategically located adjacent structures may also play a role in shielding a building from unfavorable exposure to the sun when it is low in the sky.

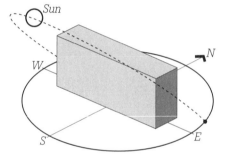

BUILDING ORIENTATION

BUILDING SITING AND SHAPE

BUILDING SHAPE

In large multistory buildings, daylighting is most often provided through windows in exterior walls. Daylighting such as this is termed *sidelighting,* and its effectiveness is limited by the depth to which it can penetrate horizontally into the building's interior. For example, in a typical office building, daylighting can provide full illumination to task areas no farther than 12 to 15 ft (3.5 to 4.5 m) from exterior wall openings and can provide partial illumination to areas no farther than 24 to 30 ft (7.5 to 9 m) from the exterior. Thus, to maximize effective daylighting in a commercial office building, work areas should be located, to the greatest extent possible, no more than 30 ft (9 m) from exterior walls with daylight access. Consider, for example, a double-loaded corridor plan. Total building depth in the north–south direction should not exceed approximately 70 ft (21 m), allowing 30 ft (9 m) for work areas on either side of a 10- ft (3-m)-wide central corridor. In general, narrow or elongated plans, L- or U-shaped plans, and courtyard or atrium buildings provide greater access to daylight than more compact arrangements.

Where occupied areas occur directly below roofs, daylighting may also be provided through overhead skylights or other types of roof openings, devices collectively referred to as *toplighting.* Large single-story buildings, such as industrial factory buildings, are well suited to toplighting configurations, as are the topmost floors of many multistory buildings. Opportunities for toplighting can be increased with building sections that step or are otherwise configured to create increased roof area. Considering sidelighting and toplighting together, daylighting design generally benefits from elongated or articulated building massing that increases the building perimeter and thereby increases opportunities for daylight access to the interior.

BUILDING DESIGN DEVELOPMENT

As a design progresses and the building configuration continues to develop, the impact of daylighting should be investigated in more detail and with more attention to specific local conditions. For example, a building not oriented on the cardinal points of the compass may interact with early morning and late afternoon sun in ways that require more detailed investigation. Local topography and climatic conditions may affect access to daylight at various times of the day or year. Adjacent structures may reflect light or obscure the sky in ways that positively or negatively affect a project. Patterns of use within a building may also favor certain orientations or times of day. For example, an elementary school building in which classrooms are unoccupied after 3 P.M. may be more tolerant of western exposure than a commercial office space habitually occupied until later in the day. As the project design develops, more detailed analysis, daylighting modeling, and the advice of daylighting experts should all be used.

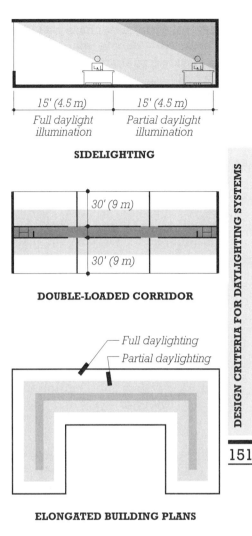

15' (4.5 m) — *Full daylight illumination*   *15' (4.5 m)* — *Partial daylight illumination*

SIDELIGHTING

30' (9 m)

30' (9 m)

DOUBLE-LOADED CORRIDOR

— *Full daylighting*
— *Partial daylighting*

ELONGATED BUILDING PLANS

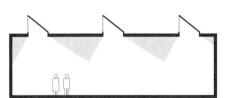

TOPLIGHTING

BUILDING INTERIOR CONFIGURATION

Not all activities within a building necessarily benefit equally from daylighting, and an analysis of the daylighting needs of the various components of the program can help guide decisions regarding where each component may be located. For example, vertical circulation, bathrooms, and storage gain little if any benefit from daylighting and can be located in portions of the floor plate that daylight cannot reach. Or such functions can be grouped on the east and west ends of a building, acting as shields against these problematic exposures.

A critical factor in daylighting design is the treatment of ceiling height, especially close to the exterior. Considering the section diagram on this page, the exterior wall can be divided into three distinct zones. The portion of the wall below 30 in. (760 mm), roughly the level of a typical work surface, makes no significant contribution to daylighting. Openings in the middle portion of the wall, up to approximately 7 ft (2.1 m), provide daylighting in areas closest to the opening and offer exterior views. To maximize the effectiveness of daylight illumination deeper in the space, the window opening must extend above 7 ft (2.1 m), necessitating a ceiling as high as possible and the avoidance of spandrel beams or other elements close to the perimeter that can obscure this portion of the wall opening. This criterion places significant constraints on the planning of structural and mechanical building systems, such as the location of deep beams or HVAC ductwork, and must be considered in the earliest stages of design if it is to be achieved. (For

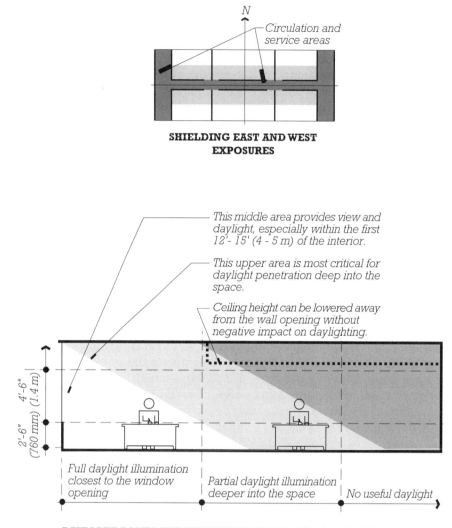

SHIELDING EAST AND WEST EXPOSURES

This middle area provides view and daylight, especially within the first 12'- 15' (4 - 5 m) of the interior.

This upper area is most critical for daylight penetration deep into the space.

Ceiling height can be lowered away from the wall opening without negative impact on daylighting.

Full daylight illumination closest to the window opening

Partial daylight illumination deeper into the space

No useful daylight

DAYLIGHT ZONES AND THE WINDOW WALL (Thanks to Joel Loveland, University of Washington Department of Architecture and Seattle Lighting Design Lab for the concept of this diagram.)

more detailed information about window opening height and daylight horizontal penetration, see pages 157–159.)

For a task area to benefit significantly from daylight illumination, a source of daylight, such as a window, skylight, or a surface off which daylight is reflected, must be directly in line of sight with that task area. Partitions, structural elements, mechanical and electrical system components, furnishings, and other elements that extend above the lower third of the space should be arranged to minimize their potential to obstruct daylight sources. See page 158 for more information about configuring interior elements for optimal daylighting.

DAYLIGHTING AND ENERGY CONSERVATION

SMALL BUILDINGS

Small building energy consumption tends to be driven primarily by heating and cooling loads associated with thermal exchange through the building's exterior skin. Thus, in cold climates, energy consumption is dominated by the need to replace heat lost through the walls and roof during the cold months. In warmer regions, energy consumption is driven by the removal of heat gained through the exterior envelope during the warm months. Daylighting design can contribute to the reduction of energy consumption in both of these circumstances.

In cold climates, south-facing sidelighting can provide daylight illumination as well as solar heat gain for energy savings. Where sunlight is admitted into the structure as a source of heat, internal shading, diffusing, or reflecting devices should be used to protect visual task areas from direct sun or excessive brightness or contrast. To control heat gain during warmer months, external overhangs or other shading devices can be used to exclude direct sun from the interior during these periods. For more information on solar heating strategies for small buildings, see pages 242–243.

Daylight illumination can also contribute to reduced cooling loads in warm climates. Indirect light from the north sky or from well-shaded southern exposures is an excellent source of illumination with low heat content. Direct sunlight can be reflected off exterior surfaces before it is admitted into a structure, thereby leaving a significant portion of its heat content outside the building. And, as explained in more detail in the next section, even direct sunlight can be an energy-efficient source of illumination when it is properly controlled and efficiently distributed within the interior.

LARGE BUILDINGS

In large buildings, energy consumption is most often dominated by internally generated heat loads, rather than by exterior climate conditions or characteristics of the building skin. The removal of heat generated by occupants, lighting, and equipment is often the most significant factor in the overall energy performance of a large building.

In conditions such as these, daylighting can contribute significantly to energy savings. Natural daylight illumination is free. Wherever daylighting can replace an electric light source, electric energy consumption is reduced directly. In addition, because well-designed daylight illumination generates less heat than common sources of artificial illumination, daylighting can lessen a building's internal heat load, further reducing energy consumption. The following chart tabulates the *efficacy* of daylight and several forms of electric lighting—that is, the amount of useful light in relation to the heat produced (measured in lumens per watt). The higher the efficacy, the more energy-efficient the light source. Note that daylighting compares favorably to all common types of electric lighting.

For daylight to achieve its potential for high efficacy, it must be well utilized within the building. Direct sunlight that causes excessive heat gain, or daylighting that in any way creates an unsatisfactory visual environment, will not reduce the use of electric light or save energy. However, when well designed and implemented, natural daylighting offers significant opportunities for savings in large building energy consumption.

Light Source Efficacy, Measured in Lumens/Watt[a]	
Natural daylighting	90–150 lm/W
Incandescent electric lighting	15–25 lm/W
Fluorescent electric lighting	55–90 lm/W
Metal halide electric lighting	80–100 lm/W

[a]Higher values represent higher efficiency.

■■■

2
CONFIGURING AND SIZING DAYLIGHTING SYSTEMS

This chapter will help you lay out the components of a daylighting system and estimate the size of daylight openings to provide the required levels of interior illumination for a project.

Different tasks require different levels of illumination. The nature of a task, the need for accuracy and efficiency, and the visual acuity of the occupants are all contributing factors. For example, navigating the lobby of a commercial office building requires minimal attention to detail and is not a task with unusual demands for speed or accuracy. Consequently, relatively low ambient lighting levels are acceptable. On the other hand, an accountant, much of whose day is spent reading and transcribing densely formatted, low-contrast financial statements and ledgers, and whose efficiency and accuracy of work are critical, requires significantly higher levels of task illumination. Follow the steps below to determine recommended lighting levels for a project and to estimate the size and quantity of daylight sources for your building.

Step 1: Choose a Lighting Level Category

From the chart above, make a preliminary choice of lighting level by selecting the category that most closely matches the activity that takes place in the given space.

Step 2: Adjust Your Choice

Each lighting level category represents a range of illumination levels suitable for the tasks described. On the charts on the following pages, each category is shown as a band, representing the range of values. When reading from charts, you may read higher or lower in the appropriate band, depending on the following factors:

Higher light levels are recommended in areas with occupants primarily of age 55 years or older, in areas with predominantly dark, nonreflective surroundings or task backgrounds, and in areas where

General Space Illumination

Category A—Public spaces, dark spaces	Nighttime corridors and lobbies, waiting rooms, bedrooms
Category B—Simple orientation	Dance halls, dining halls, transportation terminal concourses, residential living spaces
Category C—Occasional visual tasks	Daytime corridors and lobbies, reception areas, auditoriums, banks, worship spaces

Task Illumination

Category D—Visual tasks of high contrast or large size	Conference rooms, office work with high-contrast tasks, factory simple assembly, residential kitchens
Category E—Visual tasks of medium contrast or small size	Drafting of high-contrast work, classrooms, offices, clerical tasks, factory work of low contrast or moderately difficult assembly
Category F—Visual tasks of low contrast or very small size	Drafting of low-contrast work, laboratories, factory work with difficult assembly

tasks are carried out that require an unusually high degree of speed and accuracy. If two or more of these factors apply, read *high* in the lighting level category bands in the following charts. Conversely, lower light levels are recommended in areas with occupants primarily under the age of 40, in areas with light-colored, highly reflective surroundings or task backgrounds, and in areas where tasks are carried out that do not demand unusual speed or accuracy. If two or more of these factors apply, read *low* in the lighting level category bands in the following charts.

AMBIENT SPACE AND TASK ILLUMINATION

The table above lists recommended lighting levels for both general space illumination and task illumi-

nation, with task illumination requiring higher light levels because of the greater visual demands associated with these activities. For projects for which full reliance on daylighting is not achievable or desired, a strategy that may be considered is to provide ambient space illumination with daylighting and supplement this with electric lighting for task illumination. Thus, for example, where a typical office space may require Category E task illumination levels at the worker's desk, Category C illumination levels should be adequate for movement around these areas. In this case, daylighting design can be based on Category C illumination levels and task lighting at the desk can be provided from electric sources.

156

SIDELIGHTING

With the exception of large single-story structures, sidelighting through windows and clerestories is the predominant means of providing daylight illumination in buildings.

The intensity of sidelighting is highest near the opening and diminishes with increasing distance from the opening. The depth to which sidelighting can provide illumination within a building is largely dependent on the height of the opening. Under typical conditions, sidelighting can provide effective illumination for depths up to approximately $2\frac{1}{2}$ times the height of the opening above the plane of the work surface. For example, in an office with 9-ft (2.7-m)-high windows and 30-in. (760-mm)-high desks, the top of the window is $6\frac{1}{2}$ ft (2.0 m) above the work plane, and daylight should be able to provide full illumination up to a depth of approximately 16 ft (5 m) (6.5 ft $\times$ 2.5 = 16.25 ft). For more detailed information on the depth of sidelighting penetration for various illumination levels and opening heights, see page 159.

In designing with sidelighting, attention must be given to maximizing its reach deep into the structure, as well as minimizing excessive brightness close to the wall openings. A variety of techniques are possible. *Light shelves* create more evenly distributed illumination levels throughout a space. Though light shelves may reflect some light deeper into the interior, their primary benefit comes from reducing brightness levels close to the window. By reducing the highest illumination levels, more uniform lighting is achieved overall, giving the impression of an improved lighting environment. Light shelves can also prevent direct sunlight from falling directly within the work area.

Exterior overhangs may be solid or louvered. Extending a solid overhang beyond the building wall is essentially the same as increasing the depth of the room, and illumination is reduced comparably. If light levels are adequate, this can be an effective way to block direct sun as well as reduce excessive brightness close to the window. Louvered overhangs, if designed with attention to prevailing sun angles, can block direct sunlight selectively while admitting indirect light.

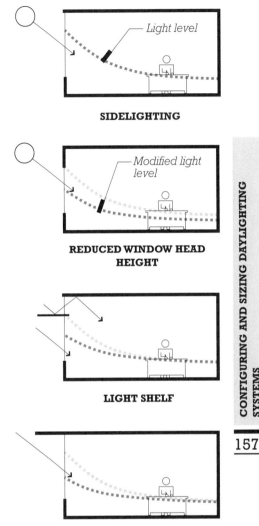

Light level

SIDELIGHTING

Modified light level

REDUCED WINDOW HEAD HEIGHT

LIGHT SHELF

EXTERIOR OVERHANG

Reflective sills can increase the depth to which light penetrates within the space. However, care must be taken to avoid creating excessive glare for occupants close to the opening.

Secondary sources of daylight that are located at some distance from a primary wall opening, such as rear windows or skylights, can be used to increase light levels deep within a space, thereby creating more uniform lighting, as well as reducing strong shadowing and contrast.

Obstructions to daylight within the space should be prevented. Wherever possible, elements that can block daylight, particularly those high up in the space, should be located as far from wall openings as possible. Where a plan includes both open plan areas and enclosed space, the open plan areas should be placed closest to the wall openings and the enclosed spaces should be located so as to minimize the obstruction of daylight. Where enclosed spaces must be located close to wall openings, consider transparent or translucent enclosing materials to allow daylight to penetrate beyond these areas. Opaque elements, such as partitions or ceiling beams, can assist in daylight distribution when oriented perpendicular to wall openings. Particularly when such elements are light-colored and located close to such openings, they can both reflect daylight more deeply into the space and reduce contrast levels close to the opening.

158

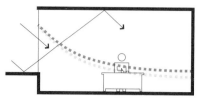

REFLECTIVE SILL

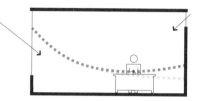

SECONDARY DAYLIGHT SOURCE

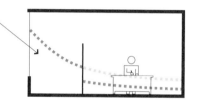

DAYLIGHT OBSTRUCTIONS

SIZING SIDELIGHTING

Use the charts on the opposite page to estimate the required size of wall openings for natural daylighting. Both charts assume that window bottoms are no higher than 30 in. (760 mm) above the floor, window glazing is clear, and walls and ceilings are white or light-colored. If these conditions are not met, daylighting effectiveness may be reduced.

For example, reading the top chart, a window extending 9 ft (2.7 m) above the floor will provide full daylighting for normal office tasks up to a horizontal distance of approximately 16 ft (4.9 m) from the window. Daylighting supplemented with electric lighting can be provided up to 29 ft (8.8 m) away.

As a second example, reading the bottom chart, a 6000 sq ft (560 m²) business office area is to be illuminated with daylight from adjacent windows. Using the table on page 156, we select Category E, visual tasks of medium contrast and size, as the appropriate lighting level. Reading the chart, we determine that 6000 sq ft (560 m²) of floor area requires between 1000 and 2000 sq ft (93 and 186 m²) of window area for full daylighting. Or, if electric task lighting is to be provided, general area illumination meeting Category C criteria can be provided with windows 200 to 400 sq ft (19 to 37 m²) in area. (This scenario is not illustrated on the chart.)

SIDELIGHTING

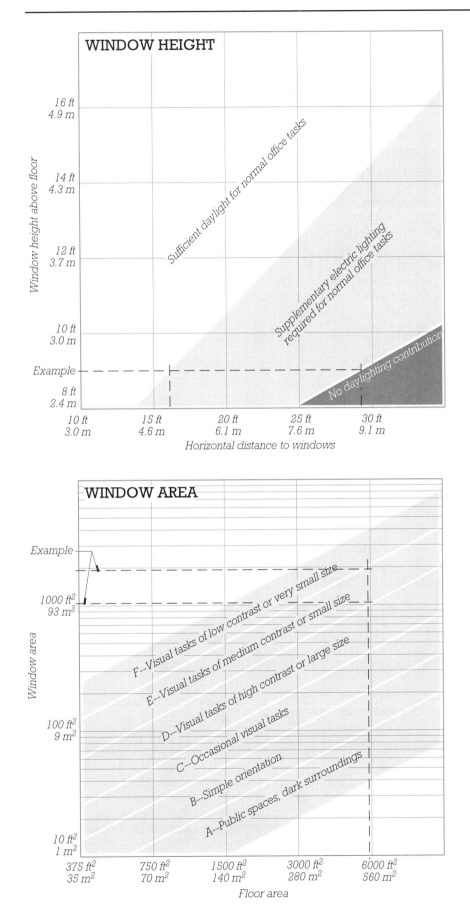

WINDOW HEIGHT

Window height above floor

16 ft / 4.9 m
14 ft / 4.3 m
12 ft / 3.7 m
10 ft / 3.0 m
Example
8 ft / 2.4 m

Sufficient daylight for normal office tasks

Supplementary electric lighting required for normal office tasks

No daylighting contribution

10 ft / 3.0 m — 15 ft / 4.6 m — 20 ft / 6.1 m — 25 ft / 7.6 m — 30 ft / 9.1 m

Horizontal distance to windows

WINDOW AREA

Window area

Example

1000 ft² / 93 m²
100 ft² / 9 m²
10 ft² / 1 m²

F--Visual tasks of low contrast or very small size
E--Visual tasks of medium contrast or small size
D--Visual tasks of high contrast or large size
C--Occasional visual tasks
B--Simple orientation
A--Public spaces, dark surroundings

375 ft² / 35 m² — 750 ft² / 70 m² — 1500 ft² / 140 m² — 3000 ft² / 280 m² — 6000 ft² / 560 m²

Floor area

Horizontal distance

Height

Use the top chart to determine the minimum wall opening height for adequate horizontal daylight penetration for normal office tasks.

■ To ensure even light distribution throughout a space, window openings should be at least half as wide as the length of the wall in which they are located. For more detailed help in estimating required window area, see the chart below.

Use the bottom chart to determine the total wall opening area necessary for full daylighting of various tasks occupying a given floor area. To determine the most appropriate illumination category for the space under consideration, see page 156. For floor areas larger than those tabulated on the chart, read the chart using a smaller area and then multiply the result proportionally.

■ For buildings in predominantly clear sky areas, read low in the ranges indicated on the chart. For buildings in heavily covered sky areas, read high in the indicated ranges. See page 147 to determine sky cover conditions for your project's location.

Toplighting is most effectively employed in large single-story structures and in the topmost floors of multistory buildings.

Toplighting can be provided either by *skylights,* with horizontal or low-sloped glazing, or by *roof monitors,* with vertical or steeply sloped glazing. Because of variation in the brightness of the sky from horizon to directly overhead, illumination levels from skylights are roughly three times greater than those associated with windows of the same opening area. Illumination is highest directly below a skylight opening and diminishes with increasing horizontal distance. With roof monitors, which admit daylight from the side, highest illumination levels tend to to be offset to the side opposite the monitor glazing. The intensity of illumination from roof monitors varies with their orientation. In the Northern Hemisphere, south-facing monitors provide illumination levels approximately equal to those of skylights of the same glazing area. Monitors facing other directions provide approximately one-half the illumination of a skylight of the same area.

Spaced toplighting with multiple sources can minimize extremes in illumination levels. Sources of toplighting should be spaced no more than one to two times the height of the openings above the floor in order to provide acceptably uniform levels of illumination within the space.

In predominantly overcast areas, toplighting with clear glazing and no other means of sunlight control may be acceptable. In most areas, toplighting should be oriented away from the sun, or control devices should be used to prevent sunlight from passing unimpeded to the task area. *Interior reflectors,* exterior louvers, translucent light-diffusing materials, and deep

160

openings with reflective sides can all be effective in this regard. When these devices are placed on the interior, they may also be helpful in distributing daylight farther from the opening and creating more even illumination within the space. Devices located exterior to the opening can exclude solar heat from the interior and may be helpful in areas where high heat gain is particularly a concern.

Combined sidelighting and toplighting can be used to distribute daylighting deeper into the interior than is possible with sidelighting alone. To avoid excessive variation in illumination levels, spacing of daylight sources should not exceed the recommendations in the adjacent diagram.

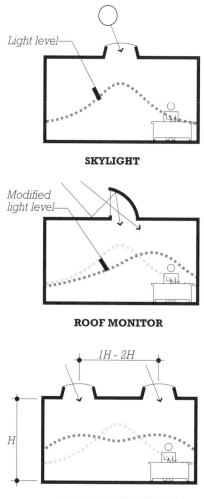

SKYLIGHT

ROOF MONITOR

SPACED TOPLIGHTING

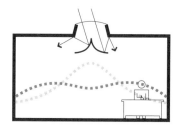

INTERIOR REFLECTORS

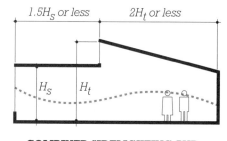

COMBINED SIDELIGHTING AND TOPLIGHTING

SIZING TOPLIGHTING

Use the charts on the facing page to estimate the required area of roof openings for natural daylighting.

For example, reading the top chart, with a floor-to-ceiling height of 15 ft (4.5 m), small skylights should be spaced horizontally no more than 15 ft (4.5 m) center-to-center, roof monitors should be spaced no more than 22 ft (7 m), and large skylights no more than 30 ft (9 m).

As a second example, reading the bottom chart, a 1000-sq-ft (93-m²) hotel lobby area is to be illuminated with north-facing roof monitors. Using the table on page 156, we select Category C, simple orientation, as the appropriate lighting level. Reading the chart, we determine that 1000 sq ft (93 m²) of floor area requires between 10 and 20 sq ft (0.9 and 1.9 m²) of skylight area for full daylighting. Doubling the result for a north-facing monitor, our final answer is 20 to 40 sq ft (1.9 to 3.7 m²) of glass area.

TOPLIGHTING

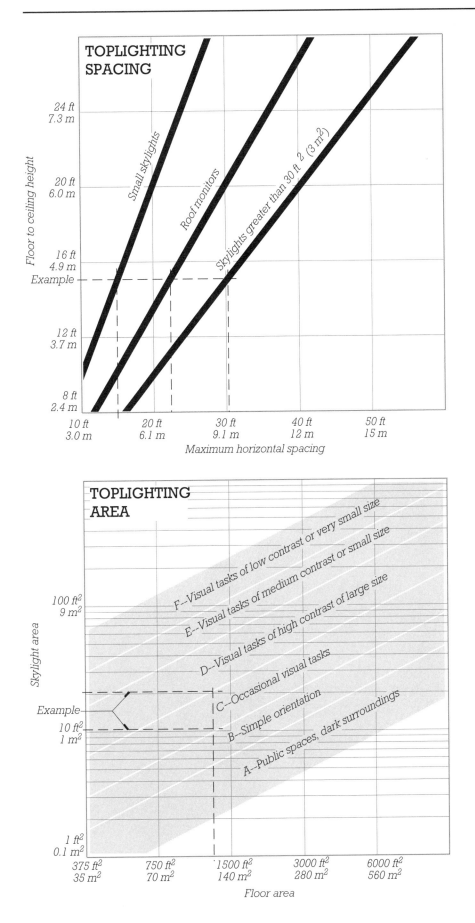

TOPLIGHTING SPACING

Floor to ceiling height

24 ft / 7.3 m
20 ft / 6.0 m
16 ft / 4.9 m
Example
12 ft / 3.7 m
8 ft / 2.4 m

Small skylights

Roof monitors

Skylights greater than 30 ft² (3 m²)

10 ft / 3.0 m — 20 ft / 6.1 m — 30 ft / 9.1 m — 40 ft / 12 m — 50 ft / 15 m

Maximum horizontal spacing

TOPLIGHTING AREA

Skylight area

100 ft² / 9 m²
Example
10 ft² / 1 m²
1 ft² / 0.1 m²

F--Visual tasks of low contrast or very small size
E--Visual tasks of medium contrast or small size
D--Visual tasks of high contrast of large size
C--Occasional visual tasks
B--Simple orientation
A--Public spaces, dark surroundings

375 ft² / 35 m² — 750 ft² / 70 m² — 1500 ft² / 140 m² — 3000 ft² / 280 m² — 6000 ft² / 560 m²

Floor area

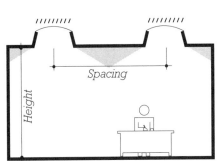

Spacing

Height

Use the top chart to determine maximum horizontal spacing for skylights and roof monitors so as to maintain acceptably even lighting levels throughout a space.

Use the bottom chart to determine the skylight or roof monitor opening area necessary for daylighting various tasks over a given floor area. To determine the most appropriate illumination category for the space under consideration, see the table on page 156. For floor areas larger than those tabulated on the chart, read the chart using a smaller area and then multiply the result proportionally.

■ For skylights and south-facing roof monitors, read directly from the chart. For roof monitors facing other than south, use twice the indicated area.

■ For buildings in predominantly clear sky areas, read low in the ranges indicated on the chart. For buildings in heavily covered sky areas, read high in the indicated ranges. See page 147 to determine sky cover conditions for the project's location.

SECTION

4

DESIGNING SPACES FOR MECHANICAL AND ELECTRICAL SERVICES

163

■■■■

1
SELECTING HEATING AND COOLING SYSTEMS FOR LARGE BUILDINGS

This chapter will help you select a heating and cooling system for the preliminary design of a large building.

If you wish to minimize, the first cost of the heating and cooling system:	Choose the simplest possible all-air system:
	
	    Single duct, constant air volume (pages 176–177)
	
	or choose a system that involves no ductwork or piping:
	
	    Through-the-wall and packaged terminal units (page 184)

If you wish to minimize operating cost:	Choose systems that convert fuel to heating and cooling energy with maximum efficiency:
	
	    Variable air volume (pages 174–175)
	    Single duct, constant air volume (pages 176–177)
	    Hydronic convectors (pages 182–183)
	
	or choose a system that uses ambient heat from the surrounding environment:
	
	    Closed-loop heat pump system (page 181)

If you wish to maximize control of air quality and air velocity:	Choose one of the all-air heating systems:
	
	    Variable air volume (VAV) (pages 174–175)
	    VAV reheat (page 175)
	    VAV induction (page 175)
	    Dual-duct VAV (page 175)
	    Single duct, constant air volume (pages 176–177)
	    Multizone (page 177)

If you wish to maximize individual control over temperature in a number of rooms or zones:	Choose a system that can react separately to a number of thermostats:
	
	    Variable air volume (VAV) (pages 174–175)
	    VAV reheat (page 175)
	    VAV induction (page 175)
	    Dual-duct VAV (page 175)
	    Constant air volume reheat (page 177)
	    Multizone (page 177)
	    Air-water induction (pages 178–179)
	    Fan-coil terminals (page 180)
	    Through-the-wall and packaged terminal units (page 184)

If you wish to minimize system noise:	Choose a system that operates at low air velocities and whose moving parts are distant from the occupied spaces, such as:
	
	    Any all-air system other than an induction system (pages 174–177)
	    Hydronic convectors (pages 182–183)

DESIGN CRITERIA FOR THE SELECTION OF HEATING AND COOLING SYSTEMS FOR LARGE BUILDINGS

If you wish to minimize the visual obtrusiveness of the heating and cooling system:	Choose a system that has minimal hardware in the occupied spaces of the building, such as: Any all-air system (pages 174–177)

If you wish to minimize the floor space used for the mechanical system or the floor-to-floor height of the building:	Choose a local system that has no ductwork or piping, such as:
	    Through-the-wall and packaged terminal units (page 184)
	or a system that minimizes the size of the ductwork or piping, such as:
	    Induction systems (pages 175, 178–179)
	    Hydronic convectors (pages 182–183)

If you wish to minimize maintenance requirements of the heating and cooling system:	Choose systems that are very simple and have few moving parts in the occupied spaces of the building:
	    Variable air volume (pages 174–175)
	    Single duct, constant air volume (pages 176–177)
	    Hydronic convectors (pages 182–183)

If you wish to avoid having a chimney in the building:	Choose systems that are electrically powered:
	    Electric boilers (pages 174–183)
	    Through-the-wall and packaged terminal units (page 184)
	    Closed-loop heat pumps (page 181)

If you wish to maximize the speed of construction:	Choose systems that can be installed by a single trade, such as: Through-the-wall and packaged terminal units (page 184)

HEATING AND COOLING SYSTEMS FOR LARGE BUILDINGS: SUMMARY CHART

GIVE SPECIAL CONSIDERATION TO THE SYSTEMS INDICATED IF YOU WISH TO:	Variable Air Volume (VAV) (page 174)	VAV Reheat (page 175)	VAV Induction (page 175)	Dual-Duct VAV (page 175)	Single-Duct, Constant Air Volume (CAV) (page 176)
Minimize first cost					●
Minimize operating cost	●				●
Maximize control of air velocity and air quality	●	●		○	●
Maximize individual control over temperature	●	●	○	○	
Minimize system noise	●	●		○	●
Minimize visual obtrusiveness	●	●	○	○	●
Maximize flexibility of rental space	●	●	○	○	●
Minimize floor space used for the heating and cooling systems			○		
Minimize floor-to-floor height			○		
Minimize system maintenance	●				●
Avoid having a chimney					
Maximize the speed of construction					

● Frequently used.
○ Infrequently used.
[a] System for heating only.

HEATING AND COOLING SYSTEMS FOR LARGE BUILDINGS: SUMMARY CHART

CAV Reheat (page 177)	Multizone (page 177)	Air-Water Induction (page 178)	Fan-Coil Terminals (page 180)	Closed-Loop Heat Pumps (page 181)	Hydronic Convectors[a] (page 182)	Packaged Terminal Units or Through-the-Wall Units (page 184)
						●
				●	●	
○	○					
○	○	○	●	●		●
○	○				●	
○	○				●	
○	○	○	●		●	●
		○	●	●	●	●
		○	●	●	●	●
					●	
						●
						●

SOME TYPICAL CHOICES OF HEATING AND COOLING SYSTEMS FOR LARGE BUILDINGS

OCCUPANCY	Variable Air Volume (VAV) (page 174)	VAV Reheat (page 175)	VAV Induction (page 175)	Dual-Duct VAV (page 175)	Single Duct, Constant Air Volume (CAV) (page 176)
Apartments					
Arenas, Exhibition Halls	●[a]				●[a]
Auditoriums, Theater	●[a]				●[a]
Factories	●[a]	●			●[a]
Hospitals	●	●		●	
Hotels, Motels, Dormitories	●				
Laboratories	●	●		●	●
Libraries	●				
Nursing Homes	●				
Offices	●[a]		●		
Places of Worship	●				●
Schools	●[a]	●			
Shopping Centers	●[a]				
Stores	●[a]				

● Frequently used.
○ Infrequently used.
[a] Sometimes installed as packaged systems.
[b] System for heating only.

SOME TYPICAL CHOICES OF HEATING AND COOLING SYSTEMS FOR LARGE BUILDINGS

CAV Reheat (page 177)	Multizone (page 177)	Air-Water Induction (page 178)	Fan-Coil Terminals (page 180)	Closed-Loop Heat Pumps (page 181)	Hydronic Convectors[b] (page 182)	Packaged Terminal Units or Through-the-Wall Units (page 184)
			●	●	●	●
			●			
	●[a]					
	●[a]	○	●		●	
●	●	○	●			
		○	●	●		●
●						
	●					
			●			●
	●[a]	○			●	
	●				●	
			●			
	●[a]					
	●[a]					

ZONING A BUILDING FOR HEATING AND COOLING

Before attempting to select a heating and cooling system, rough out a zoning scheme for the building, establishing separately controlled zones so that thermal comfort can be achieved throughout a building despite conditions that differ between one space and another. Sometimes a zone should be no larger than a single room (a classroom, a hotel room). Sometimes a number of spaces with similar thermal requirements can be grouped into a larger zone (a group of offices that are occupied during the day but not at night; a group of galleries in a museum). Sometimes rooms must be put in separate zones because they have differing requirements for air quality or temperature (locker rooms in a gymnasium complex, cast dressing rooms in a theater). Sometimes different zones must be established to deal effectively with different rates of internal generation of heat (a kitchen in a restaurant or dining hall, a computer room in a school, a metal casting area in an industrial building).

Buildings in which solar heat gain through windows is a major component of the cooling load need to be zoned according to the various window orientations of the rooms. In commercial buildings where each tenant will be billed separately for heating and cooling costs, each tenant space will constitute a separate zone. A large business or mercantile building might be divided into several large zones of approximately equal size to fit the capacities of the fans and ductwork or the capacities of packaged air conditioning systems. A multiuse building may incorporate parking, retail shops, lobbies, offices, and

apartments, each requiring a different type of heating and cooling system.

The zoning of a building is significant in the early stages of design because it may suggest a choice of heating and cooling system: Room-by-room zoning suggests an all-water fan-coil system or packaged terminal units for an apartment building, for example, meaning that the building does not have to be designed to accommodate major ductwork. Zoning may also have an impact on where the major equipment spaces are placed. It often makes sense to put major equipment on the "seam" between two zones. An example of this might be placing the major heating and cooling equipment on the second or third floor of a multiuse downtown building, above retail and lobby spaces and below multiple floors of office space.

CENTRAL SYSTEMS VERSUS LOCAL SYSTEMS

In a *central system,* heat is supplied to a building or extracted from it by large equipment situated in one or several large mechanical spaces. Air or water is heated or cooled in these spaces and distributed to the inhabited areas of the building by ductwork or piping to maintain comfortable temperatures.

In a *local system,* independent, self-contained pieces of heating and cooling equipment are situated throughout the building, one or more in each room.

Central systems are generally quieter and more energy efficient than local systems and offer better control of indoor air quality. Central equipment tends to last longer than local equipment and is more convenient to service. Local systems occupy less space in a building

than central systems because they do not require central mechanical spaces, ductwork, or piping. They are often more economical to buy and install. They can be advantageous in buildings that have many small spaces requiring individual temperature control.

Pages 174–183 describe alternative choices of central heating and cooling systems for large buildings. Local systems are described on page 184.

FUELS

Heating and cooling equipment in large buildings may be powered by oil, gas, electricity, steam, or hot water. In central areas of many large cities, utility-generated pipeline steam is available. In some large complexes of buildings, such as university campuses, steam or hot water is furnished to each structure, along with chilled water for cooling, via underground pipelines from a single central boiler/chiller plant. Steam and hot water, where available, are ideal energy sources for heating and cooling, because no chimney is needed and the necessary heat exchange equipment for steam or hot water is more compact than the fuel-burning boilers that would otherwise be required. Electricity is also an ideal energy source, because it is clean, it is distributed through compact lines, and electrical equipment tends to be quieter and smaller than fuel-burning equipment. In most geographic areas, however, electricity converted directly into heat is a very costly fuel compared to oil or gas. Gas burns cleanly and requires no on-site storage of fuel. In areas where it is more economical than gas, fuel oil is favored despite its need for on-site storage tanks.

172

MEANS OF DISTRIBUTION

The distribution of heating and cooling energy in central systems involves the circulation of air or water or both to the inhabited spaces.

■ In *all-air systems,* central fans circulate conditioned air to and from the spaces through long runs of ductwork.

■ In *air and water systems,* air is ducted to each space. Heated water and chilled water are also piped to each space, where they are used to modify the temperature of the circulated air at each outlet to meet local demands. Air and water systems circulate less air than all-air systems, which makes them somewhat more compact and easier to house in a building.

■ In *all-water systems,* air is circulated locally rather than from a central source, so ductwork is eliminated. Only heated water and chilled water are furnished to each space. The water piping is much smaller

than equivalent ductwork, making all-water systems the most compact of all.

All-air systems offer excellent control of interior air quality. The central air-handling equipment can be designed for precise control of fresh air, filtration, humidification, dehumidification, heating, and cooling. When the outdoor air is cool, an all-air system can switch to an economizer cycle, in which it cools the building by circulating a maximum amount of outdoor air. All-air systems concentrate maintenance activities in unoccupied areas of the building because there are no water pipes, condensate drains, valves, fans, or filters outside the mechanical equipment rooms.

Air-and-water and all-water systems, besides saving space, can offer better individual control of temperature in the occupied spaces than some all-air systems, but they are inherently more complicated, and much of the maintenance activity must be carried out in the occupied spaces.

SELECTING HEATING AND COOLING SYSTEMS FOR LARGE BUILDINGS

The next few pages summarize the choices of heating and cooling systems for large buildings. To determine the space required by any system, look first at the list of major components that is included with each system description. The dimensions of any components that are unique to the system are given immediately following this list. Components that are common to more than one system may be sized using the charts on pages 216–219.

CENTRAL ALL-AIR SYSTEMS: SINGLE DUCT, VARIABLE AIR VOLUME (VAV)

Description

Air is conditioned (mixed with a percentage of outdoor air, filtered, heated or cooled, and humidified or dehumidified) at a central source. Supply and return fans circulate the conditioned air through ducts to the occupied spaces of the building. At each zone, a thermostat controls room temperature by regulating the volume of air that is discharged through the diffusers in the zone.

Typical Applications

VAV is the most versatile and most widely used system for heating and cooling large buildings.

Advantages

This system offers a high degree of local temperature control at moderate cost. It is economical to operate and virtually self-balancing.

Disadvantages

VAV is limited in the range of heating or cooling demand that may be accommodated within a single system. When one area of a building needs heating while another needs cooling, a VAV system cannot serve both areas without help from a secondary system (see Variations, following).

Major Components

Boilers and chimney, chilled water plant, cooling tower, fan room, outdoor fresh air and exhaust louvers, vertical supply and return ducts,

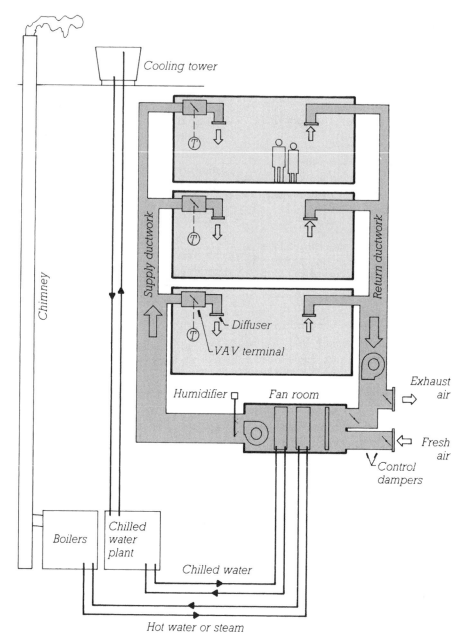

SINGLE DUCT, VARIABLE AIR VOLUME (VAV)

CENTRAL ALL-AIR SYSTEMS: SINGLE DUCT, VARIABLE AIR VOLUME (VAV)

horizontal supply and return ducts, a VAV control box for each zone, supply diffusers, return grilles. (For an illustration of typical diffusers and grilles, see page 215.)

Alternately, in buildings of moderate size, a *packaged system* may be used in place of all components other than ducts, VAV control boxes, diffusers, and grilles. A *single-packaged system,* incorporating all central components in a single metal box, may be installed on the roof or outside an exterior wall, or a *split-packaged system* may be installed, with a compressor and condensing unit in an outdoor box and an air handling unit in an indoor box. Multiple packaged systems are often used to serve buildings that are large in horizontal extent. For more detailed information on packaged units, see pages 192–193.

Sizing the Components

The VAV control box is usually concealed above a suspended ceiling. It is approximately 8 to 11 in. (200 to 280 mm) high for zones up to 1500 sq ft (150 m^2) in area and up to 18 in. (460 mm) high for zones up to 7000 sq ft (700 m^2). Its horizontal dimensions vary with its capacity, up to a maximum length of about 5 ft (1.5 m). To size the other components of a VAV system, use the charts on pages 216–219.

Variations

1. In buildings with large areas of windows, VAV is often combined with a second system around the perimeter of the building to deal with the large differences in heating and cooling demand between interior and perimeter rooms. The second system is most commonly either an induction system (see variation 3, following) or hydronic convectors (see pages 182–183).

2. A single duct *variable air volume reheat system* is identical to the basic VAV system up to the point at which the air enters the local ductwork for each zone. In a reheat system, the air then passes through a reheat coil before it is distributed to the local diffusers. The reheat coil may be either an electric resistance coil or a pipe coil that carries hot water circulated from the boiler room. A local thermostat controls the flow of water or electricity through the reheat coil, allowing for close individual control of room temperature. This variation can overcome the inability of VAV systems to cope with a wide range of heating and cooling demands. VAV reheat systems are more energy-efficient than constant air volume reheat systems (page 177) because in the VAV systems the reheat coil is not activated unless the VAV system is incapable of meeting the local requirement for temperature control, and a much smaller amount of tempered air is circulated.

3. In the *variable air volume induction system,* a smaller volume of conditioned air is circulated through small high-velocity ducts from a central source. Each outlet is designed so that the air discharging from the duct continually pulls air from the room into the outlet, mixes it with air from the duct, and discharges the mixture into the room. This variation is used where limited space is available for ducts. It is also used to maintain a sufficient level of air movement in spaces that do not have a high demand for heating or cooling.

4. In a *dual duct variable air volume system,* paired side-by-side ducts carry both heated and cooled air to each zone in the building. At each zone, the two airstreams are proportioned and mixed under thermostatic control to achieve the desired room temperature. This variation gives excellent local temperature control, but it requires an expensive and space-consuming dual system of ductwork, and it is not energy-efficient.

CENTRAL ALL-AIR SYSTEMS: SINGLE DUCT, CONSTANT AIR VOLUME (CAV)

Description

Air is conditioned (mixed with a percentage of outdoor air, filtered, heated or cooled, and humidified or dehumidified) at a central source. Supply and return fans circulate the air through ducts to the occupied spaces of the building. A master thermostat controls the central heating and cooling coils to regulate the temperature of the building.

Typical Applications

Spaces that have large open areas, few windows, and uniform loads, such as lobbies, department stores, theaters, auditoriums, and exhibition halls.

Advantages

This system offers a high degree of control of air quality. It is comparatively simple and easy to maintain.

Disadvantages

The entire area served by the system is a single zone, with no possibility for individual temperature control.

Major Components

Boilers and chimney, chilled water plant, cooling tower, fan room, outdoor fresh air and exhaust louvers, vertical supply and return ducts, horizontal supply and return ducts, supply diffusers, and return grilles. (For an illustration of typical diffusers and grilles, see page 215.)

Alternately, in buildings of moderate size, a *packaged system* may be used in place of all components other than ducts, diffusers, and grilles. A *single-packaged system,* incorporating all central components in a single metal box, may be installed on the roof or outside an exterior wall, or a *split-packaged system* may be installed, with a compressor and a condensing unit in an outdoor box and an air

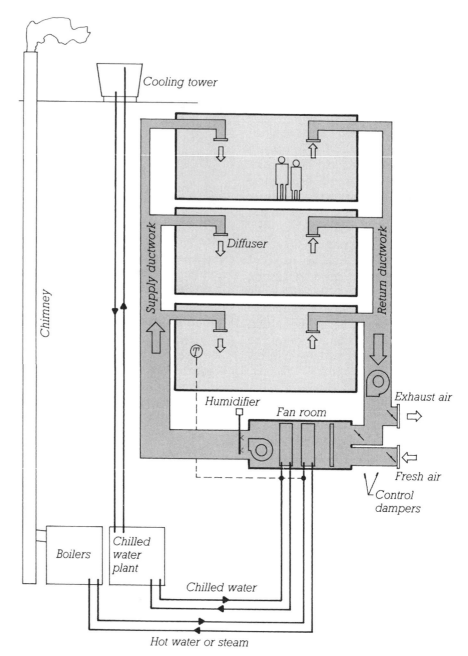

SINGLE DUCT, CONSTANT AIR VOLUME (CAV)

handling unit in an indoor box. Multiple packaged systems are often used to serve buildings that are large in horizontal extent. For more detailed information on packaged units, see pages 192–193.

Sizing the Components

For the dimensions of these components, see the charts on pages 216–219.

CENTRAL ALL-AIR SYSTEMS: SINGLE DUCT, CONSTANT AIR VOLUME (CAV)

Variations

1. A *furnace* is an indoor unit that incorporates a source of heat and an air circulating fan into a single metal box. The source of heat may be a gas burner, an oil burner, an electric resistance coil, or a heat pump coil. Cooling coils may also be incorporated if desired. The capacity of furnaces is limited to such an extent that they are used mostly in single-family houses and other very small buildings; multiple furnaces are sometimes used to heat and cool somewhat larger buildings. For a more extended discussion of furnaces, see pages 229–231.

2. A single duct, *constant air volume reheat system* is identical to the CAV system first described up to the point at which the air enters the local ductwork for each zone. In reheat systems, the air then passes through a reheat coil. The reheat coil may carry hot water or steam piped from the boiler room, or it may be an electric resistance coil. A local thermostat controls the temperature of the reheat coil, allowing for close individual control of room temperature. Reheat systems are typically used in situations requiring precise temperature control and constant airflow, such as laboratories, hospital operating rooms, or specialized industrial processes. Because constant air volume reheat systems are inherently wasteful of energy, first cooling air and then heating it, they are not often specified for new buildings.

3. In the *multizone system,* several ducts from a central fan serve several zones. In one type of multizone system, dampers blend hot and cold air at the fan to send air into each duct at the temperature requested by the thermostat in that zone. In another type (the one illustrated here), reheat coils in the fan room regulate the temperature of the air supplied to each zone. Multizone systems require a large amount of space for ductwork in the vicinity of the fan, so they are generally restricted to a small number of zones with short runs of ductwork. Packaged multizone units are available.

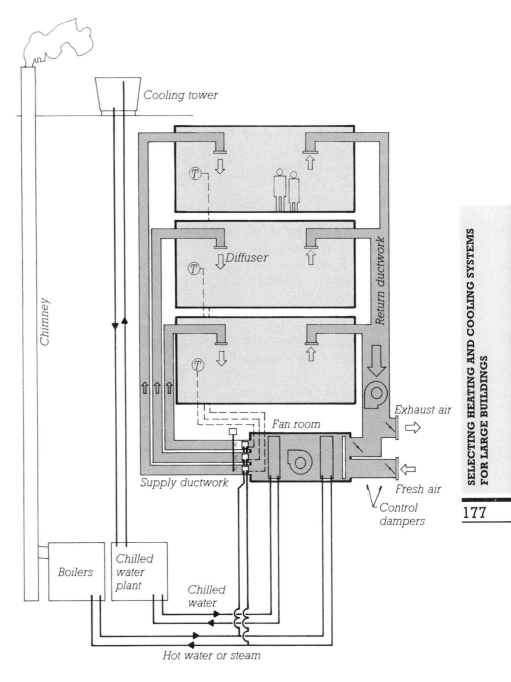

MULTIZONE SYSTEM

CENTRAL AIR AND WATER SYSTEMS: AIR-WATER INDUCTION SYSTEM

Description

Fresh air is heated or cooled, filtered, and humidified or dehumidified at a central source and circulated in small high-velocity ducts to the occupied spaces of the building. Each outlet is designed so that the air discharging from the duct (called *primary air*) draws a much larger volume of room air through a filter. The mixture of primary air and room air passes over a coil that is either heated or cooled by *secondary water* piped from the boiler room and chilled water plant. The primary air (about 15% to 25% of the total airflow through the outlet) and the heated or cooled room air that has been induced into the outlet (75% to 85% of the total airflow) are mixed and discharged into the room. A local thermostat controls water flow through the coil to regulate the temperature of the air. Condensate that drips from the chilled water coil is caught in a pan and removed through a system of drainage piping (not shown in the accompanying diagram).

Typical Applications

Exterior spaces of buildings with a wide range of heating and cooling loads where close control of humidity is not required, especially office buildings.

Advantages

This system offers good local temperature control. Space requirements for ductwork and fans are less than those for all-air systems. There are no fans in the occupied spaces.

178

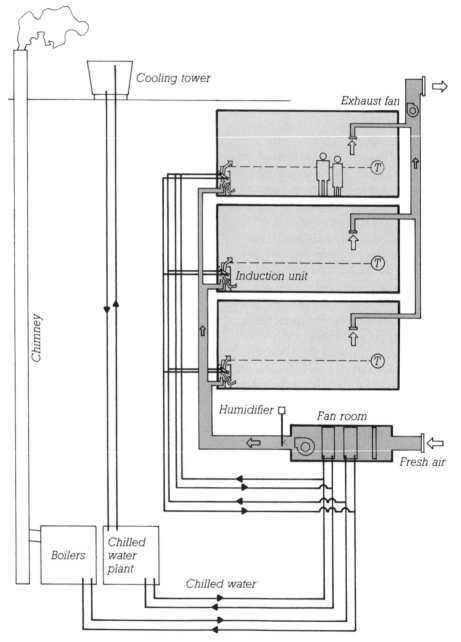

AIR-WATER INDUCTION SYSTEM

CENTRAL AIR AND WATER SYSTEMS:
AIR-WATER INDUCTION SYSTEM

Disadvantages

This is a relatively complicated system to design, install, maintain, and manage. It tends to be noisy, and it is very inefficient in its use of energy. Humidity cannot be closely controlled. It is rarely designed or specified today.

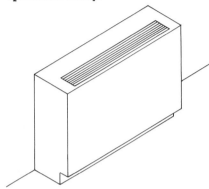

AIR-WATER INDUCTION UNIT

Major Components

Boilers and chimney, chilled water plant, cooling tower, fan room, outdoor fresh air and exhaust louvers, vertical supply and return ducts, horizontal supply and return ducts, vertical supply and return piping, horizontal supply and return piping, condensate drainage piping, air-water induction units. The water piping to each unit may consist of two, three, or four pipes, depending on whether a single coil is used for both heating and cooling or separate coils are provided for each. An additional pipe is required for condensate drainage.

Sizing the Components

Induction units are usually sized to fit beneath a window. Heights range from 25 to 28 in. (635 to 710 mm), depths from 9 to 12 in. (230 to 305 mm), and lengths from 30 to 84 in. (760 to 2130 mm). For the dimensions of the other components of the system, see the charts on pages 216–219.

Variations

Fan-coil units with primary air supply are similar to induction units, but use a fan to blow air through the coils instead of relying on the induction action of the primary airstream to circulate air from the room. The advantage of the fan-coil unit is that it can continue to circulate air even when the primary air is turned off. The primary air can be supplied through either the fan-coil unit or a separate diffuser.

Description

Hot and/or chilled water are piped to fan-coil terminals. At each terminal, a fan draws a mixture of room air and outdoor air through a filter and blows it across a coil of heated or chilled water and then back into the room. A thermostat controls the flow of hot and chilled water to the coils to control the room temperature. Condensate that drips from the chilled water coil is caught in a pan and removed through a system of drainage piping (not shown in this diagram). In most installations, the additional volume of air brought from the outdoors is used to pressurize the building to prevent infiltration or is exhausted through toilet exhaust vents.

Typical Applications

Buildings with many zones, all located on exterior walls, such as schools, hotels, motels, apartments, and office buildings.

Advantages

No fan rooms or ductwork spaces are required in the building. The temperature of each space is individually controlled.

Disadvantages

Humidity cannot be closely controlled. This system requires considerable maintenance, most of which must take place in the occupied space of the building.

Major Components

Boilers and chimney, chilled water plant, cooling tower, vertical supply and return piping, horizontal supply and return piping, condensate drainage piping, fan-coil terminals, outside air grilles.

Sizing the Components

Fan-coil terminals are usually sized to fit beneath a window. Heights range from 25 to 28 in. (635 to 710 mm), depths from 9 to 12 in. (230 to 305 mm), and lengths from 30 to 84 in. (760 to 2130 mm). For the dimensions of the other components of the system, see the chart on pages 216-217.

Variations

Fan-coil terminals are also manufactured in a horizontal ceiling-hung configuration and in a tall, slender configuration for mounting in vertical chases.

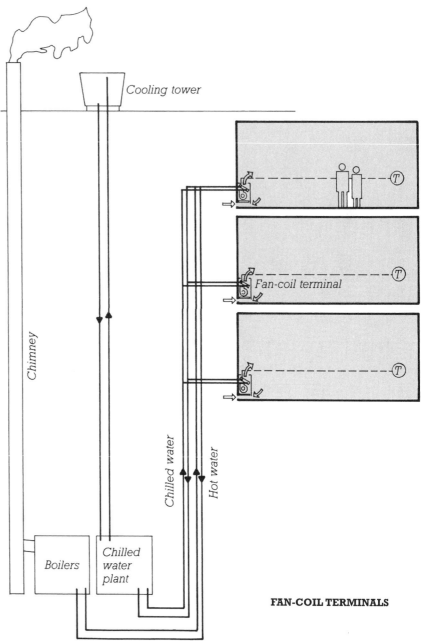

FAN-COIL TERMINALS

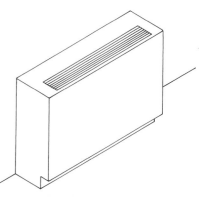

FAN-COIL TERMINAL

CENTRAL ALL-WATER SYSTEMS: CLOSED-LOOP HEAT PUMPS

Description

A water-to-air heat pump unit in each space provides heating, cooling, and fresh air. The water source for all the heat pumps in the building circulates in a closed loop of piping. Control valves allow the water source to circulate through a cooling tower in the summer and a boiler in the winter, and to bypass both the boiler and the cooling tower in spring and fall and at any other time when the heating and cooling needs of the various rooms in the building balance one another.

Typical Applications

Hotels containing chronically overheated areas (kitchens, laundry, assembly rooms, restaurants).

Advantages

This is an efficient system in which heat extracted from chronically overheated areas can be used to heat underheated areas (e.g., guest rooms).

Disadvantages

This is an expensive system to install, and careful economic analysis is needed to determine if the high installation costs can be balanced by energy savings. The heat pumps require that much of the routine maintenance take place in the occupied spaces.

Major Components

Heat pump units, boiler room, cooling tower.

Sizing the Components

The heat pumps may be located above a dropped ceiling over the bathroom and dressing areas in hotel rooms or below windows. A typical under-window heat pump unit is approximately 30 in. (760 mm) high, 12 in. (305 mm) deep, and 60 in. (1525 mm) long. An above-ceiling unit has approximately the same dimensions, with the 12-in. (305-mm) dimension vertical. For the dimensions of the other components of the system, see the chart on pages 216–217.

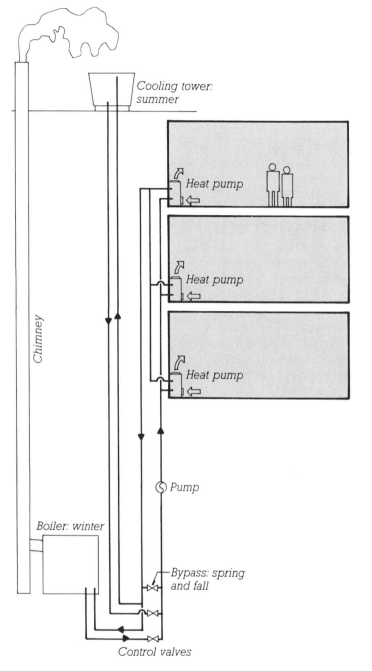

CLOSED-LOOP HEAT PUMPS

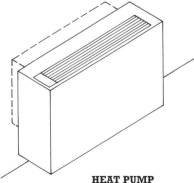

HEAT PUMP

CENTRAL ALL-WATER SYSTEMS: HYDRONIC CONVECTORS

Description

Hot water from the boiler room is circulated through fin-tube convectors, which are horizontal pipes with closely spaced vertical fins, usually mounted in a simple metal enclosure with an air inlet opening below and outlet louvers above. The heated fins, working by convection, draw cool room air into the enclosure from below, heat it, and discharge it out the top.

Typical Applications

Hydronic convectors are used alone in buildings where cooling is not required and where ventilation may be accomplished by opening windows or through a supplemental ventilation system. They are also used as a supplemental source of heat in combination with other heating and cooling systems.

Advantages

This is an economical system to install and operate. It provides excellent comfort during the heating season. Convectors are available in configurations ranging from continuous horizontal strips to cabinet units, either recessed or surface-mounted. Local control of temperature is possible through thermostatically controlled zone pumps or zone valves, through self-contained, thermostatically controlled valves at each convector or, in some types of convectors, through manually controlled dampers.

182

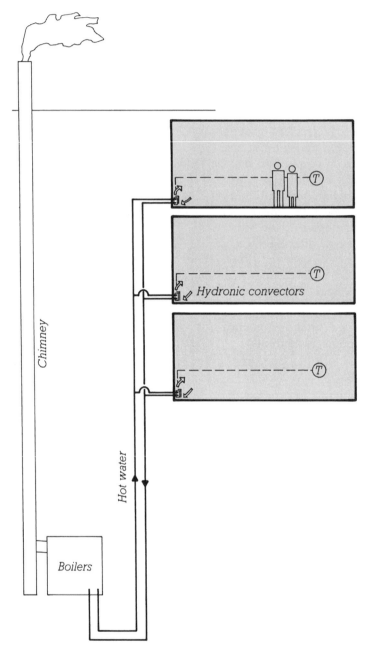

HYDRONIC CONVECTORS

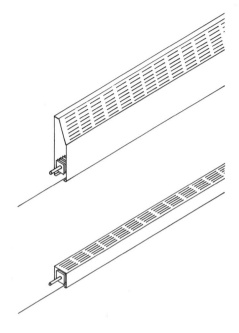

HYDRONIC FIN-TUBE CONVECTORS

Disadvantages

This is a system for heating only. Cooling, humidity control, and ventilation must be provided by separate means.

Major Components

Boilers and chimney, vertical supply and return piping, horizontal supply and return piping, convectors.

Sizing the Components

Hydronic convectors usually run continuously around the perimeter of a building. Each contains one or sometimes two continuous fin-tubes. The sheet metal enclosures for the fin-tubes are available in a variety of configurations: The smallest is about 5 in. (127 mm) square in cross section and should be mounted at least 4 in. (100 mm) above the floor. Enclosures up to 28 in. (710 mm) high and 6 in. (152 mm) deep are often used for improved thermal performance. The top of the enclosure contains small louvers and may be sloping or flat. For the dimensions of the other components of a hydronic heating system, see the chart on pages 216–217.

Variations

1. Hydronic heating is useful in buildings down to the scale of single-family residences. See pages 232–233.

2. In spaces where insufficient perimeter is available for convectors or where the presence of convectors is undesirable, fan-forced unit heaters may be used. These are housed in metal cabinets that may be recessed in a wall, mounted on the surface of a wall, or suspended from the ceiling structure. Each heater contains a hot-water coil fed from the boiler room and an electric fan to circulate air across the coil. Unit heaters are very compact in relation to their heating capacity as compared to convectors.

LOCAL SYSTEMS: PACKAGED TERMINAL UNITS AND THROUGH-THE-WALL UNITS

Description

One or several through-the-wall units or packaged terminal units are mounted on the exterior wall of each room. Within each unit, an electric-powered compressor and evaporator coil provide cooling capability. Heating is supplied either by electric resistance coils or by utilizing the compressor in a reversible cycle as a heat pump. A fan draws indoor air through a filter, adds a portion of outdoor air, passes the air across the cooling and heating coils, and blows it back into the room. Another fan circulates outdoor air independently through the unit to cool the condensing coils (and, in a heat pump cycle, to furnish heat to the evaporator coils). A control thermostat is built into each unit.

There are several alternative types of equipment that fit into this category. *Packaged terminal units* are contained primarily in an indoor metal cabinet that fits beneath a window; they are connected to outdoor air with a wall box and an outdoor grille. *Through-the-wall* units are contained in a rectangular metal box that is mounted directly in an opening in the exterior wall of the building. A variation of the through-the-wall unit is the familiar *window-mounted unit,* used only for low-cost retrofitting of existing buildings. The only service distribution to any of these types of units is an electric cable or conduit.

Typical Applications

Apartments, dormitories, motels, hotels, office buildings, schools, nursing homes.

Advantages

Units are readily available and easily installed. Initial costs are often lower than those for central systems. Each room has individual control of temperature. No building space is utilized for central equipment, ductwork, or piping. Operating costs may be lower than those for central systems in buildings in which not all spaces need to be heated or cooled all the time, such as motels.

Disadvantages

Maintenance costs are high and equipment life is relatively short. Maintenance must be carried out in the occupied spaces. The equipment is often noisy and inefficient. Air distribution can be uneven. Wintertime humidification is not possible. Operating costs are high in areas with very cold winters and costly electricity. Through-the-wall and window-mounted units can be unsightly.

Major Components

Packaged terminal units or through-the-wall units. Typical dimensions of these units are given in the table above.

TYPICAL DIMENSIONS OF PACKAGED TERMINAL UNITS AND THROUGH-THE-WALL UNITS

	Width	Depth	Height
Packaged terminal units	43" (1100 mm)	14"–20" (360–510 mm)	16" (410 mm)
Through-the-wall units	24–26" (610–660 mm)	17"–30" (430–760 mm)	16"–18" (410–460 mm)

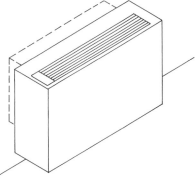

PACKAGED TERMINAL UNIT

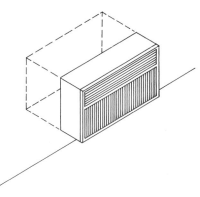

THROUGH-THE-WALL UNIT

■■■■

2
CONFIGURING AND SIZING MECHANICAL AND ELECTRICAL SERVICES FOR LARGE BUILDINGS

This chapter will help you lay out the necessary spaces for mechanical and electrical equipment in a preliminary design for a large building.

The major equipment spaces for a large building are discussed in alphabetical order on the pages that follow.

BOILER ROOM AND CHIMNEY

The boiler room produces hot water or, less commonly, steam to heat the building and to heat domestic water. Sometimes steam is also used to power absorption chilling equipment. A boiler room for a large building normally contains at least two boilers so that one may be in service even if the other is being cleaned or repaired. All boilers are connected to a single chimney. The boiler room may be placed anywhere in a building; common locations are a basement, a mechanical room on grade, a mechanical floor, or the roof. It should be on an outside wall because it needs an intake grille for combustion air and a door or removable panel to allow for removal and replacement of boilers. Because of the noise and heat it gives off, a boiler room should be placed below or adjacent to areas such as loading docks and lobbies that will not be adversely affected. It is helpful to locate the boiler room next to the chilled water plant; the two facilities are often combined in a single room. Hot water supply and return pipes run from the boilers through vertical shafts to reach the other floors of the building.

Boilers and their associated equipment create very heavy floor loadings that need to be taken into account when designing the supporting structure.

Boilers may be fueled by gas, electricity, or oil. Electric boilers, which generally are economical only in areas where electricity costs are very low, eliminate the need for combustion air inlets and a chimney. Generally, a 2-week supply of fuel for an oil-fired boiler is stored in tanks in or near the building. The filler pipes must be accessible to oil delivery vehicles. These tanks are usually buried next to the building if space permits. If the tanks are inside the building, they must be installed in a naturally ventilated room that is designed so that it can contain the full contents of a tank and keep the contents from escaping into the building if the tank should leak. A basement location on an outside wall is preferred. Oil for a boiler on an upper floor of a building is pumped up a shaft through a pipe from the tanks below.

An approximate floor area for a boiler room may be determined using the chart on pages 216–217. In larger buildings, a long, narrow room is usually preferable to a square one. The ceiling height of a boiler room varies from a minimum of 12 ft (3.66 m) for a building of moderate size to a maximum of 16 ft (4.88 m) for a large building.

The size of the chimney that is associated with fuel-burning boilers varies with the type of fuel, the height of the chimney, the type of draft (natural, forced, or induced) that is employed, and other factors. For preliminary design purposes, allow a floor area of 2 ft × 2 ft (610 mm square) for a chimney in a very small building, and 6 ft × 6 ft (1.83 m square) in a very large building, interpolating between these extremes for buildings of other sizes. Keep in mind that the chimney runs through every floor of the building above the boiler room.

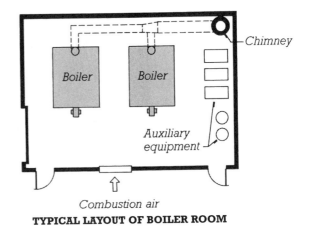

TYPICAL LAYOUT OF BOILER ROOM

MAJOR EQUIPMENT SPACES FOR LARGE BUILDINGS

CHILLED WATER PLANT

The chilled water plant produces cold water (usually 42° to 45°F, or 5° to 6°C) that is used for cooling the building. The chillers are fueled by electricity, gas, or steam. The chillers give off heat, noise, and vibration, and should not be located near spaces they will adversely affect. They may be placed anywhere in the building from basement to roof, but they are heavy and require deeper-than-normal structural members for support. An outside wall location is desirable to allow for the necessary ventilation and maintenance access. Ideally, the chilled water plant should be adjacent to the boiler room; the two are often housed in the same room in a building of moderate size. Chilled water supply and return pipes run from the chilled water pumps to the fan rooms or terminals that they serve. Condenser water supply and return pipes run between the chillers and the cooling towers.

An approximate floor area for a chilled water plant may be determined using the chart on pages 216–217. In larger buildings a long, narrow room is usually preferable to a square one. The ceiling height of a chilled water plant varies from a minimum of 12 ft (3.66 m) for a building of moderate size to a maximum of 16 ft (4.88 m) for a very large building.

COOLING TOWERS

Cooling towers extract heat from the water that is used to cool the condenser coils of the chilled water plant. In effect, the cooling towers are the mechanism by which the heat removed from a building by the air conditioning system is dissipated into the atmosphere. Most cooling towers are "wet," meaning that the hot water from the condensers splashes down through the tower, giving off heat by evaporation and convection to a stream of air that is forced through the tower by fans. The cooled water is collected in a pan at the bottom of the tower and circulated back to the chillers.

The size and number of cooling towers are related to the cooling requirements of the building. Cooling towers may be located on the ground if they are at least 100 ft (30 m) from any building or parking lot to avoid property damage and unhealthful conditions from the splash, fog, and microorganisms given off by the towers. An alternate location is the roof of the building, but because of the noise and vibration they generate, the towers should be isolated acoustically from the frame of the building, and noise-sensitive areas such as auditoriums and meeting rooms should not be located directly below them. Rooftop cooling towers must be located well away from windows and fresh air louvers.

A preliminary estimate of the roof or ground area occupied by cooling towers may be obtained from the chart on pages 216–217. Cooling towers range between 13 and 40 ft (4 and 12 m) in height; the height for a given building can be estimated by interpolating between these two extremes. The towers usually have a 4-ft (1.2-m) crawlspace beneath. For free airflow, they should be located one full width apart and at least 10 to 15 ft (3 to 5 m) from any screen wall or parapet wall unless the wall has very large louvers at the base to allow for intake air.

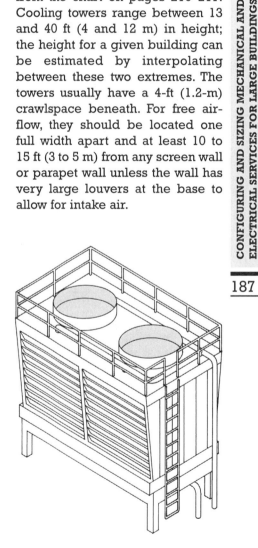

COOLING TOWER

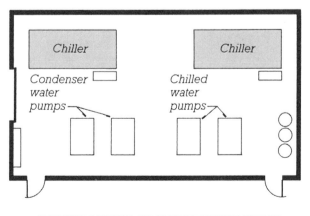

TYPICAL LAYOUT OF CHILLED WATER PLANT

Chiller

Chiller

Condenser water pumps

Chilled water pumps

ELECTRICAL SERVICE ENTRANCE, TRANSFORMERS, SWITCHGEAR, AND EMERGENCY POWER SUPPLY

Every building has an electrical transformer or transformers, a meter or meters, and a panel or switchgear that distributes the power to the interior wiring that services the building. The locations and sizes of these elements vary considerably, depending on the size and purpose of the building, the type of electric service provided by the local utility, the standards and practices of the utility company, the preferences of the building owner, the judgment of the electrical engineer, and local electrical codes.

For reasons of efficiency, electric utilities transmit electricity at high voltages. Transformers reduce this to lower voltages that can be utilized directly in the building—typically 120/208 volts or 115/230 volts in wall and floor receptacles, and up to 480/277 volts in some types of machinery and lighting fixtures. A commercial building of up to 25,000 sq ft (2500 m²) or a residential building of up to twice this size will most often buy its electricity at these lower voltages. For buildings in this size range, the transformer is provided by the utility company and may be mounted overhead on a transmission pole, on the ground (especially where transmission lines are underground), or, in some dense urban situations, in a nearby building or underground vault. A meter or meters belonging to the utility company are installed on or in the building where the service wires enter, and distribution within is usually by means of panels of circuit breakers that are located in an adjacent utility space or a small electrical closet.

Owners of larger buildings sometimes prefer to buy electricity at these lower voltages, but they can obtain energy more economically by providing their own transformers and purchasing electricity at the higher transmission voltage. One typical pattern is to bring electricity to the building at 13,800 volts and then to step down to 480/277 volts with a large primary transformer or transformers at the service entrance. The 277-volt electricity is used directly in many types of commercial and industrial lighting, and at 480 volts, electricity can be distributed efficiently to electrical closets in various parts of the building. Each electrical closet houses one or more small secondary transformers to step down from 480 volts to the lower voltages needed for convenience receptacles and machinery.

Primary transformers may be located either outside or inside the building. Where space is available, an outdoor transformer mounted on a ground-level concrete pad is preferred to an indoor transformer, because it is less expensive, cools better, is easier to service, transmits less noise to the building, and is safer against fire. Some common dimensions of pad-mounted transformers are shown in the upper table on the facing page. A trans-

former of this type does not need to be fenced except for visual concealment, in which case there must be a clear space of 4 ft (1.2 m) all around the pad for ventilation and servicing. The pad should be within 30 ft (9 m) of a service road and requires a clear service lane 6 ft (1.83 m) wide between the transformer and the road. Multiple outdoor transformers are often used to serve larger buildings and are usually placed at intervals around the perimeter of the building to supply electricity as close as possible to its point of final use.

In a dense urban situation, or where the building owner finds outdoor placement objectionable, the primary transformer or transformers must be located within the building. Oil-filled transformers of the type the utility company provides for large buildings must be placed in a transformer vault, which is a fire-rated enclosure with two exits. In a few large cities, it is customary to place the transformer vault under the sidewalk, covered with metal gratings for ventilation. Dry-type transformers of the kind usually bought by owners of small and medium-sized buildings do not need a vault; they may be placed in the main electric room. The transformer vault or main electric room is often placed in the basement or on the ground floor but may be located on higher floors. Primary transformers are very heavy and require a heavier, deeper supporting structure than the rest of the building.

In buildings with dry-type transformers, the switchgear, consisting of disconnect switches, secondary switches, fuses, and circuit breakers, may be housed in the same enclosure with the transformers in a configuration known as a *unit substation*. In large buildings with oil-filled transformers, the switchgear is located in a room adjacent to the transformer vault.

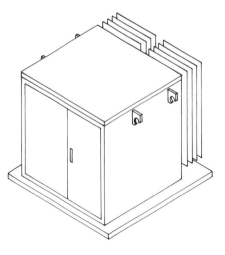

PAD-MOUNTED TRANSFORMER

MAJOR EQUIPMENT SPACES FOR LARGE BUILDINGS

Transformers and switchgear must be ventilated because they give off large quantities of heat. It is best to locate them against an outside wall so that high and low convective ventilation openings can be provided. If this is not possible, ventilation can be accomplished by ductwork and fans connected to outdoor air louvers. Access panels or doors must be provided for servicing and replacing switchgear and transformers. Some examples of sizes of transformer vaults and switchgear rooms are given in the lower table on this page.

Note also that where a high priority is placed on maintaining a continuous supply of electrical power, power may be brought to the building from two or more independent electric substations. In this way, a failure at any single substation will not interrupt power to the building.

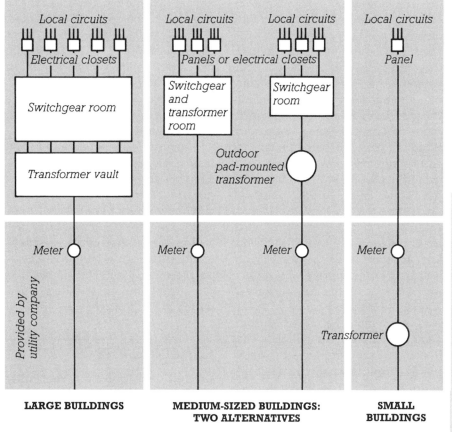

LARGE BUILDINGS

MEDIUM-SIZED BUILDINGS:
TWO ALTERNATIVES

SMALL
BUILDINGS

TYPICAL DIMENSIONS OF PAD-MOUNTED TRANSFORMERS

Floor Area of Commercial Building in ft² (m²)	Number of Residential Units	Pad Size in in. (m)
18,000 (1,700)	50	52 × 44 (1.3 × 1.2)
60,000 (5,700)	160	52 × 50 (1.3 × 1.3)
180,000 (17,000)	—	96 × 96 (2.4 × 2.4)

TYPICAL SIZES OF TRANSFORMER VAULTS AND SWITCHGEAR ROOMS

Floor Area of Commercial Building in ft² (m²)	Floor Area of Residential Building in ft² (m²)	Size of Combined Room for Transformers and Switch gear in ft (m)	Size of Transformer Vault in ft (m)	Size of Switchgear Room in ft (m)
150,000 (15,000)	300,000 (30,000)	30 × 30 × 11 (9.14 × 9.14 × 2.44)		
100,000 (10,000)	200,000 (20,000)		20 × 20 × 11 (6.0 × 6.0 × 3.35)	30 × 20 × 11 (9.0 × 6.0 × 3.35)
300,000 (30,000)	600,000 (60,000)		20 × 40 × 11 (6.0 × 12.0 × 3.35)	30 × 40 × 11 (9.0 × 12.0 × 3.35)
1,000,000 (100,000)	2,000,000 (200,000)		20 × 80 × 11 (6.0 × 24.0 × 3.35)	30 × 80 × 11 (9.0 × 24.0 × 3.35)

MAJOR EQUIPMENT SPACES FOR LARGE BUILDINGS

In many buildings an emergency generator is required to furnish electricity during power outages. The emergency generator is driven by an engine fueled with propane gas or diesel oil. This engine needs large quantities of air for combustion and cooling, and it gives off exhaust gases, noise, and vibration. The best location for the emergency power supply is on the ground outside the building, near the switchgear room. Engine-generator sets in prefabricated weather-resistant housings are available for this purpose. The next best location is on the roof of the building; alternatively, the emergency power supply may be placed inside the building on an exterior wall, as remote as possible from occupied areas of the building. The housing or room for an emergency power supply is usually 12 ft (3.66 m) wide. A length of 18 ft (5.5 m) will accommodate an emergency power supply for an average commercial building of up to 150,000 sq ft (14,000 m^2); 22-ft (6.7-m) length will accommodate the supply for a building of up to 400,000 sq ft (37,000 m^2). Where a building owner requires emergency power for other than life-safety loads, these space requirements can grow very rapidly.

There is a loss of power for a period of up to 10 seconds between the time a power interruption occurs and the time the emergency generator takes over. This is usually acceptable, but in some buildings with specialized medical equipment, computers, communications equipment, certain types of lighting, or an extraordinary need for security, an uninterruptible power supply (UPS) is needed to keep electricity flowing during the brief transition from utility electricity to that generated on-site. Where a UPS is needed, it requires, in addition to the emergency power supply, a room for batteries and an adjacent room for specialized circuit break-ers and electronic controls. These should be located close to the area that utilizes the UPS power. A typical computer room of 10,000 sq ft (1000 m^2) requires an outside-ventilated battery room of 500 sq ft (47 m^2), and a room of 200 sq ft (19 m^2) for electronic equipment. Both of these rooms require air conditioning.

Several large conductors run from the transformers to the switchgear and from the switchgear to the vertical and horizontal distribution components that feed electrical closets throughout the building. For information on vertical distribution and electrical closets, see page 199. For information on horizontal distribution, see pages 211–215.

EXHAUST FANS

Exhaust fans draw air constantly from toilet rooms, locker rooms, bathrooms, janitor closets, storage rooms, corridors, and kitchens and deliver it to the outdoors to keep the air fresh in these spaces. Exhaust fans are also used to evacuate air from laboratory fume hoods and many industrial processes. The fans are usually housed in small mushroom ventilators on the roof and are connected to the spaces they serve by ducts that run through the vertical shafts in the cores of the building. It is extremely difficult to generalize about the sizes of exhaust ducts and fans; they tend not to be extremely large, so it is usually sufficient to allow a small amount of shaft space and roof space that can later be adjusted in consultation with the mechanical engineer.

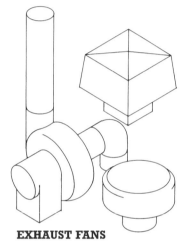

EXHAUST FANS

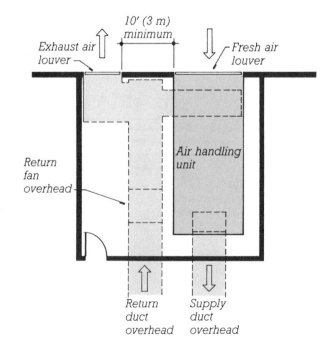

TYPICAL LAYOUT OF FAN ROOM

10' (3 m) minimum

Exhaust air louver

Fresh air louver

Return fan overhead

Air handling unit

Return duct overhead

Supply duct overhead

MAJOR EQUIPMENT SPACES FOR LARGE BUILDINGS

FAN ROOMS AND OUTDOOR AIR LOUVERS

In an all-air system, an air handling unit in a fan room circulates air through a filter and thermostatically controlled hot water and chilled water coils to condition it. The conditioned air is ducted to the occupied spaces of the building. A return fan draws air from the occupied spaces into return grilles and back to the fan room through return ducts. Just before it passes through the heating and cooling coils again, a portion of the air is diverted by a damper and exhausted through a louver to the outdoors. An equal portion of fresh air is drawn in through another outdoor louver and added to the stream of return air.

Fan rooms may be located anywhere in the building; they are supplied with hot and chilled water through insulated pipes from the boiler room and chilled water plant. A floor plan of a typical fan room is shown on the facing page. If only a single fan room is used, it may be placed in the basement, on the ground floor, on the roof, or on any intermediate floor, as close to the vertical distribution shafts as possible. It is convenient to locate this room near an outside wall, but if an outside wall location is not possible, ducts to the outdoors are used to convey fresh air and exhaust air to and from the fan. These ducts may run horizontally, above a ceiling, or vertically, in a shaft.

The maximum vertical "reach" of a fan room is approximately 25 stories up and/or down; more typically, fan rooms are located so none needs to circulate air more than 11 to 13 stories in each direction.

Multiple fans distributed throughout the building are often desirable because they allow the building to be zoned for better local control, and they reduce the total volume of ductwork in the building. It can be advantageous to

FAN ROOM IN BASEMENT

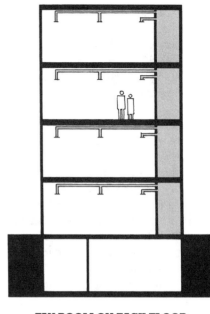

FAN ROOM ON EACH FLOOR

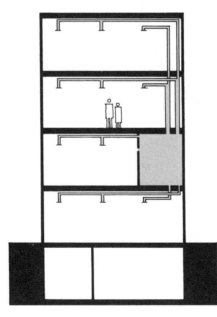

FAN ROOM ON INTERMEDIATE FLOOR

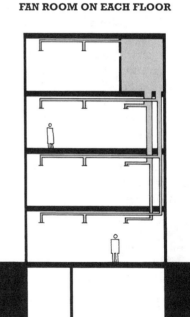

FAN ROOM AT TOP OF BUILDING

have a separate fan room for each floor of a building, because this saves floor space by eliminating most or all of the vertical runs of ductwork. Separate fan rooms are used in buildings that bill tenants individually for heating and cooling costs. Again, it is preferable to locate each fan room at the perimeter of the building.

Fan room equipment is often heavy enough to require stronger structural support than the surrounding areas of the building. Noise-sensitive areas such as meeting rooms and auditoriums should not be located adjacent to fan rooms, which produce vibration and noise.

The fresh air and exhaust air louvers associated with a fan room are noisy and create local winds. They need to be located a short distance apart, usually at least 10 ft (3 m), on the exterior wall, so that the outgoing and incoming air will not mix. Louvers for small pieces of equipment such as fan-coil units are very small. With careful design work, they can be integrated unobtrusively into the fabric of the wall. Louvers for larger pieces of equipment grow progressively larger with the floor area each serves. They are large and conspicuous for central fans serving a number of floors and require special attention on the part of the architect.

Use the graph on pages 218–219 to determine the approximate sizes of outdoor louvers for preliminary design purposes. The same graph gives information on sizing fan rooms as a function of floor area served. Using this graph, one may quickly evaluate a number of schemes for air distribution, using one fan room or many, to determine the effect of each scheme on the space planning and exterior appearance of the building.

LOADING DOCK AND ASSOCIATED SPACES

Every large building needs at least a single loading dock and freight room for receiving and sending mail and major shipments, moving tenant furniture in and out, removing rubbish, and facilitating the servicing of mechanical and electrical equipment. The dock needs to be situated so that trucks may back up to it easily without obstructing traffic on the street. The freight room inside the dock area should open directly to the rubbish compactor and the freight elevators, and should be connected to the major mechanical equipment

spaces and the mail room. It is often appropriate to locate the oil filler pipes next to the truck ramp that leads to the loading dock. If possible, the access doors to the major equipment spaces should also open to the dock or ramp area. For dimensional information on truck ramps and loading docks, consult *Architectural Graphic Standards.*

PACKAGED CENTRAL HEATING AND COOLING EQUIPMENT

Packaged central heating and cooling equipment comes in two different configurations:

■ *Single-packaged* heating and cooling equipment combines the functions of a boiler room and chimney, a chilled water plant, and a fan room into a compact, rectangular, weatherproof unit that is specified, purchased, and installed as a single piece of equipment. The supply and return ducts from the building are connected through the roof or the wall of the building to the fan inside the packaged unit.

■ *Split-packaged* units are furnished in two parts, an outdoor package that incorporates the compressor and condensing coils, and an indoor package that contains the cooling and heating coils and

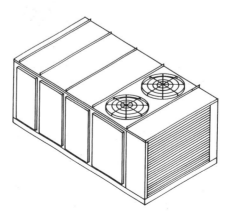

SPLIT-PACKAGED UNIT

the circulating fan. The two packages are connected by insulated refrigerant tubing and control wiring. Split-packaged units cost slightly more than single-packaged units, but they are slightly more energy efficient because none of their ductwork is located outside the insulated shell of the building.

Packaged units, whether single or split, are fueled entirely by electricity or by a combination of electricity and gas. Packaged equipment is simple for the designer to select and specify and is easy to purchase and install because it is supplied as off-the-shelf units that need only external connections to fuel, electricity, control wiring, and air ducts.

Packaged units are available in single-zone and multizone configurations in a variety of sizes to serve a wide range of demands for cooling and heating. They can be purchased as variable air volume or constant air volume (VAV or CAV) systems (see pages 174–177).

Single-packaged units are generally located either on the roof or on a concrete pad alongside the building. If alongside, the supply and return ducts are connected to the end of the unit and pass through the side wall of the building before branching out to the spaces inside. In a rooftop installation, the ducts pass through the bottom of the unit and into the building. The ducts from single-packaged units can serve low multistory buildings through vertical shafts that connect to above-ceiling branch ducts on each floor. Rooftop units may be placed at intervals to serve a building of any horizontal extent. The same is true of units located alongside the building, although the depth of the building is somewhat restricted by the maximum practical reach of the ducts. Using the chart on pages 218–219, you may select a combination of

MAJOR EQUIPMENT SPACES FOR LARGE BUILDINGS

unit size and numbers of units to serve any desired size and shape of building. For buildings taller than four or five stories, or large buildings where only one central plant may be installed, conventional central equipment assembled from components must be used because of the relatively limited capacity range of packaged units.

The table below will help to determine preliminary sizes for split-packaged equipment. The inside package may be obtained as a horizontal unit that hangs from the roof structure, or as a vertical unit that stands on the floor. The outside package may be located on the roof or on a concrete pad next to the building.

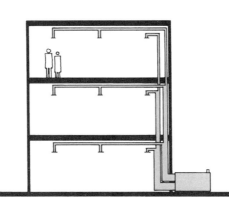 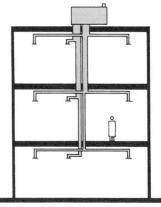

THROUGH-THE-WALL SINGLE-PACKAGED UNIT **ROOFTOP SINGLE-PACKAGED UNIT**

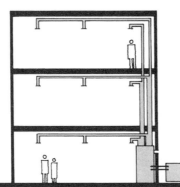

SPLIT-PACKAGED UNITS

TYPICAL DIMENSIONS OF SPLIT-PACKAGED COMPONENTS

Cooling Capacity In Tons (mcal/sec)		10 (35)	20 (70)	30 (106)	40 (141)	50 (176)
Outdoor Unit	Length	6'–4" (1.93 m)	12'–11" (3.94 m)	12'–11" (3.94 m)	12'–11" (3.94 m)	12'–11" (3.94 m)
	Width	3'–8" (1.12 m)	4'–0" (1.22 m)	4'–10" (1.47 m)	7'–1" (2.16 m)	7'–1" (2.16 m)
	Height	3'–4" (1.02 m)	2'–4" (0.71 m)	3'–2" (0.97 m)	4'–9" (1.45 m)	5'–8" (1.73 m)
Indoor Ceiling-Suspended Unit	Length	8'–3" (2.51 m)	7'–10" (2.39 m)	9'–0" (2.74 m)	9'–8" (2.95 m)	9'–8" (2.95 m)
	Width	5'–3" (1.60 m)	6'–8" (2.03 m)	7'–10" (2.39 m)	10'–7" (3.23 m)	10'–7" (3.23 m)
	Height	2'–2" (0.66 m)	2'–6" (0.76")	3'–0" (0.91")	3'–10" (1.17 m)	3'–10" (1.17 m)
Indoor Floor-Mounted Unit	Length	5'–3" (1.60 m)	6'–8" (2.03 m)	7'–10" (2.39 m)	10'–7" (3.23 m)	10'–7" (3.23 m)
	Width	2'–2" (0.66 m)	2'–6" (0.76 m)	3'–0" (0.91 m)	3'–10" (1.17 m)	3'–10" (1.17 m)
	Height	8'–3" (2.51 m)	7'–10" (2.39 m)	9'–0" (2.74 m)	9'–8" (2.95 m)	9'–8" (2.95 m)

Use the chart on pages 216–217 to estimate the required cooling capacity.

SEWAGE EJECTOR PIT

If the lowest level of a building lies below the level of the sewer or septic tank, sewage is collected in an underfloor pit and pumped up to the sewer. The pumps do not necessarily occupy floor space, because they are usually contained within the pit, but the pit must lie beneath unobstructed floor space so that it can be inspected and serviced through a removable cover.

TELECOMMUNICATIONS ROOM

A central room for telephone and data systems should be located in the basement or on the ground floor as close to the telecommunications service entrance as possible. Where telecommunications distribution closets are stacked on

floors above, this room should be located directly below these closets as well. Equipment needs in this room will vary, depending on the particular systems to be installed, and are also likely to vary significantly over time. For this reason, this room, and all other components of the telecommunications distribution system in the building, should be configured with ease of access and maximum flexibility in mind. For preliminary design purposes, the service entrance room should be no smaller than 60 sq ft (6 m^2), and may be 400 sq ft (40 m^2) in size or larger for a large commercial office building. The room should be free of plumbing, steam or other piping, and should be in a separate cooling zone to allow independent temperature control. From this room, telecommunications wiring extends to distribution closets on each floor (see page 199).

WASTE COMPACTOR

A waste compactor is necessary in most large buildings. It may be coupled with a container system to facilitate the trucking of the compacted rubbish.

The compactor is often served by a vertical refuse chute from the upper floors of the building. The chute must be placed in a fire-rated enclosure and must be provided with an automatic sprinkler head above the top opening. Some codes also require the provision of a 2-hour enclosed chute room outside the chute opening at each floor. Inside diameters of chutes range from 15 to 30 in. (380 to 760 mm), with 24 in. (610 mm) being a typical dimension.

The waste compactor should be located directly beneath the refuse chute and adjacent to the loading dock. The size and shape

MAJOR EQUIPMENT SPACES FOR LARGE BUILDINGS

of the compactor itself vary widely with the manufacturer and the capacity of the unit. A compactor room of 60 sq ft (5.6 m^2) is sufficient for a small apartment building. A larger building will require 150 to 200 sq ft (14.0 to 18.6 m^2), and industrial waste compacting facilities can be much larger.

WATER PUMPS

Where the water service enters the building, a room is required to house the water meter and the sprinkler and standpipe valves. In a building taller than three or four stories, a suction tank and a pair of water pumps are needed to boost the water pressure in the domestic water system. A similar pair of pumps are required for a sprinkler system. A chiller for drinking water and a heat exchanger to heat domestic hot water are often located in the same area. The table below will assist in determining the necessary floor areas for water pumps.

In a few large cities, local codes require the provision of a large gravity tank on the roof of the building to furnish a reserve of water in case of fire. In most areas, however, the pumps alone are sufficient.

WORKROOMS, CONTROL ROOMS, AND OFFICES

Operating and maintenance personnel in large buildings need space in which to work. Offices should be provided for operating engineers and maintenance supervisors. A room is required to house the control console for a large-building heating and cooling system. Lockers and workrooms are needed for mechanics, plumbers, electricians, and custodial workers. Storage facilities should be provided near the loading dock and service elevator for tools, spare parts, and custodial equipment and supplies.

SPACE REQUIREMENTS FOR WATER PUMPS

Domestic Water Pumps	
Area Served	**Room Dimensions**
Up to 200,000 ft^2 (Up to 18,600 m^2)	8' × 12' (2.44 × 3.66 m)
200,000 to 1,000,000 ft^2 (18,600 to 93,000 m^2)	16' × 12' (4.88 × 3.66 m)

Fire Pumps (assuming sprinklers)	
Area Served	**Room Dimensions**
Up to 100,000 ft^2 (Up to 9300 m^2)	8' × 12' (2.44 × 3.66 m)
100,000 to 200,000 ft^2 (9300 to 18,600 m^2)	20' × 12' (6.1 × 3.66 m)
1,000,000 ft^2 (93,000 m^2)	30' × 24' (9.15 × 7.32 m)

PLANNING SERVICE CORES

Spaces for the vertical distribution of mechanical and electrical services in a large building need to be planned simultaneously with other building elements that are vertically continuous or that tend to occur in stacks—principally the structural columns, bearing walls, shear walls, and wind bracing; exit stairways; elevators and elevator lobbies; and rooms with plumbing: toilet rooms, bathrooms, kitchens, and janitor closets. These elements tend to coalesce into one or more core areas where the vertically continuous elements are concentrated into efficient, neatly packaged blocks of floor space, leaving most of each floor open for maximum flexibility of layout.

Different types of buildings call for different sorts of core arrangements. In high-rise office buildings, where a maximum amount of unobstructed, rentable area is the major criterion for floor layout, a single central core is almost universal. In low-rise commercial and institutional buildings, horizontal distances are often great enough that a single core would be inefficient, and vertical elements are divided into several cores of varied internal composition. These are likely to be located asymmetrically in response to particular requirements relating to the servicing and circulation patterns of the building. In a dormitory, apartment building, or hotel, a common pattern of vertical services features slender shafts sandwiched between the units. Shafts next to the interior corridor carry the plumbing for the bathrooms and kitchens that back up to them. If the heating and cooling equipment for the units is located over the bathrooms and kitchens, the hot and chilled water piping and ductwork may share these same shafts. If the heating and cooling are done

196

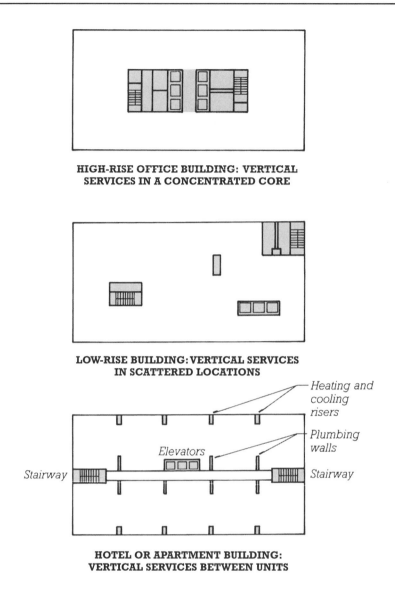

HIGH-RISE OFFICE BUILDING: VERTICAL SERVICES IN A CONCENTRATED CORE

LOW-RISE BUILDING: VERTICAL SERVICES IN SCATTERED LOCATIONS

Heating and cooling risers

Plumbing walls

Elevators

Stairway   Stairway

HOTEL OR APARTMENT BUILDING: VERTICAL SERVICES BETWEEN UNITS

along the outside walls, another set of shafts may be created between units around the perimeter of the building to serve this equipment.

Vertical distribution shafts need to connect directly with the major equipment spaces that feed them and the horizontal distribution lines they serve. The boiler room, chilled water plant, central fan room, exhaust fans, water pumps, sewage ejector, waste compactor, and cooling towers need to cluster closely around the vertical distribution shafts. The electric and telecommu-

nications switchgear should not be far away. The electrical and telecommunications closets must stack up along the wiring shafts at each floor. The toilet rooms, bathrooms, kitchens, and janitor closets must back up to plumbing walls. Horizontal supply and return ducts need to join easily with the vertical ducts in the shafts, and horizontal piping for hot and chilled water distribution must branch off conveniently from the riser pipes.

VERTICAL DISTRIBUTION OF SERVICES FOR LARGE BUILDINGS

LOCATING THE CORES IN THE BUILDING

A centrally located core leaves the daylit perimeter area of the building open for use. It also works efficiently with a scheme that distributes services horizontally from one set of shafts, because it minimizes duct and pipe sizes. The central location can be undesirable, however, because it interrupts the open space of the floor. A core at one edge of the building does not have this problem, but it may not be able to incorporate exit stairways that are separated widely enough (see page 255), and it obstructs a portion of the daylit perimeter. Either of these core locations connects well to major equipment at the ground, the roof, and any intermediate mechanical floors.

A core located in a corner, on the other hand, is undesirable because horizontal distribution lines from the core are long, exit stairways are too close together, and connections to major equipment are congested. Two or more corner cores used in combination can overcome some of these problems.

Multiple cores often work well, particularly in broad, low-rise buildings. Exit stairways can be widely separated and connected to a simple, clear system of corridors and elevators. Vertical risers for mechanical services can be located where they work best, minimizing the congestion of ducts and pipes at points of connection to horizontal networks.

Core locations may also be dictated in part by the structural scheme that provides lateral stability to the building. A large, centrally located core or two symmetrically placed cores can furnish ideal locations for wind bracing. A core at the edge of the building or a detached core cannot house all the wind bracing for the building because it is located asymmetrically with respect to one of the principal axes of the building (see pages 37–39). Scattered cores and corner cores may not be large enough to develop the required depth of wind trusses.

The chart below summarizes some of the advantages and disadvantages of different options for core placement.

CHARACTERISTICS OF CORE PLACEMENTS

1 = Best   5 = Worst

	Edge	Detached	Central	Two	Corners	Scattered
Flexibility of typical rental areas	2	1	3	4	2	5
Perimeter for rental areas	4	3	1	1	5	2
Ground floor high-rent area	3	1	3	4	2	5
Typical distance of travel from core	4	5	2	1	3	3
Clarity of circulation	3	4	2	1	3	5
Daylight and view for core spaces	2	1	5	5	1	4
Service connections at roof	3	4	2	1	5	3
Service connections at ground	3	4	2	1	5	3
Suitability for lateral bracing	4	5	1	1	2	3

This table is adapted by permission of John Wiley & Sons, Inc., from Benjamin Stein, John S. Reynolds, and William J. McGuinness, *Mechanical and Electrical Equipment for Buildings,* 7th ed., copyright© 1986, by John Wiley & Sons, Inc.

PLANNING THE INTERNAL ARRANGEMENT OF THE CORES

The ratio of the total floor area of the core or cores of a building to the floor area served varies widely from one building to the next. The average total area of the cores in 40- to 70-story New York City office buildings, including the stairways, toilets, elevators, and elevator lobbies, is approximately 27% of the open area of each floor served by the core. This ratio runs as high as 38% in some older buildings but is around 20% to 24% in office towers of recent design. At the other extreme, the total core area of a three-story suburban office building is likely to be about 7% of the floor area served, because there are few elevators, much less lobby space for elevators, and much smaller shafts for mechanical and electrical services.

These percentages also vary with the relative requirements for mechanical and electrical services; they can be higher in a hospital or laboratory and are much lower in a hotel or apartment building. Core area is directly related to the type of heating and cooling system used: The percentages quoted in the preceding paragraph apply to buildings with all-air systems. Buildings with air-and-water and all-water systems require somewhat less shaft space.

A building with a fan room on each floor will need very little core area for ductwork, but the fan room is likely to occupy at least as much floor space as the vertical ductwork it eliminates.

The structural scheme of a building can also have a direct effect on core area. Of the total core area of a tall office building, about 12% is usually occupied by columns, bracing, walls, and partitions. This percentage is lower for lower buildings and can be very low in buildings whose core areas contain no columns or lateral bracing.

The most critical elements of the core, those that should be located first in at least a tentative way, are the columns and bracing, the exit stairways, and the elevators and elevator lobbies. Next should come the plumbing walls and the shafts for ductwork. For help in laying out the structural elements, see pages 37–51. Details of the location and configuration of exit stairways are given on pages 260–264. Pages 207–209 give advice on the number, size, and layout of elevator shafts and lobbies. Plumbing walls are illustrated on page 201, and ductwork shafts can be sized using the chart on pages 218–219.

The chimney is another element for which there may be little flexibility of location. Usually the chimney exits from a corner of the boiler room. It may be sloped at an angle not less than 60° to the horizontal to bring it to a more convenient position in the core. For help sizing chimneys, refer to page 186.

TOTAL SHAFT AREA

The total open area of all the mechanical and electrical shafts in a tall office building is normally equal to about 4% of the area served on each floor, and can be estimated at about half this amount for a low-rise building. This should be divided into at least two separate shafts to relieve the congestion that would otherwise occur where the vertical and horizontal distribution networks connect. It is especially effective to provide separate shafts for supply and return ducts because it is often possible to use a separate return shaft as a plenum, a shaft that is itself the duct. Separate supply and return shafts also minimize conflict in the bulky ductwork connections and crossovers. For maximum utility, the horizontal proportions of each shaft should lie in the range of 1:2 to 1:4. To allow sufficient space for connections to horizontal distribution networks at each floor, no shaft should adjoin stair towers or elevator shafts on more than one long side and one short side. Most shafts must be enclosed within 1- to 2-hour fire-resistance rated walls—see pages 360–363 for more information.

ELECTRICAL AND TELECOMMUNICATIONS CLOSETS

Electrical and telecommunications closets must be accessible from public areas of the floor, must be stacked above one another, must include wiring shafts, and must be kept free of plumbing, steam, and other types of wiring. Typical sizes and configurations for electrical closets are illustrated in the accompanying diagrams. In an office building, major electrical closets should be located in such a way that no point on a floor lies more than 125 ft (40 m) away. If this is difficult to arrange, satellite closets served by cables from the major closets may be used to feed electricity to the more distant areas. In smaller buildings or buildings other than offices, satellite-size closets may serve in place of major closets.

At least one telecommunications distribution closet should be provided for every floor and for every 10,000 sq ft (930 m²) of area served. For commercial office space, telecommunications closets should measure 10 × 12 ft (3.0 × 3.7 m) internally. For less data-intensive occupancies, closets as small as 4 × 7 ft (1.2 × 2.1 m) may be acceptable. Separate cooling zones should be provided to permit independent temperature control of these areas.

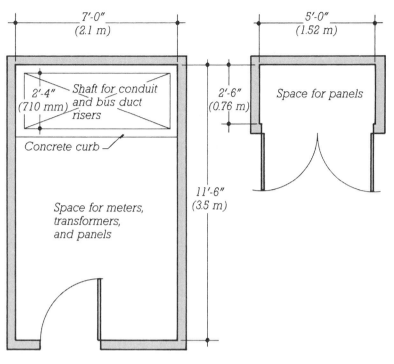

MAJOR ELECTRICAL CLOSET

SMALL OR SATELLITE ELECTRICAL CLOSET

FAN ROOMS

Local fan rooms, if their fresh air and exhaust air connections are provided by means of duct risers, should be placed against shafts. If local fan rooms need only hot and chilled water from central equipment, it is better to put them against outside walls, so that they can exchange air directly with the outdoors, and to serve them with water via horizontal piping from the core. (Alternatively, centrally located local fan rooms can be connected to fresh air and exhaust louvers by horizontal ducts.) If fan rooms on an outside wall are stacked above one another, of course, it is usually possible to provide an immediately adjacent shaft, separate from the main core, for the water riser piping. See pages 190–192 and 218–219 for information on planning fan rooms.

MAIL FACILITIES

Vertical gravity chutes for mail deposit are often provided in multistory buildings. The chute occupies an area of about 5 × 15 in. (125 × 375 mm) in plan and terminates in a receiving box in the base of the building.

Vertical mail conveyors are sometimes provided for delivery of mail in a large multistory office building. The mailroom at the base of the conveyor should be adjacent to the loading dock and can be sized at about $\frac{2}{10}$ of 1% of the area it serves. The walls around the conveyor shaft itself will vary in plan from 4 ft × 4 ft 6 in. (1220 × 1370 mm) to 7 ft 3 in. × 8 ft 6 in. (2210 × 2590 mm) inside dimensions, depending on the system's capacity and manufacturer. The conveyor should discharge into a service mailroom of at least 6 × 7 ft

(1830 × 2135 mm) on each floor. A 1- or 2-hour fire enclosure is required around the conveyor shaft.

PIPE RISERS FOR HEATING AND COOLING

The insulated pipes that conduct heated and chilled water to and from the spaces in a building require considerable space. In a tall apartment building or hotel, a clear shaft of 12 × 48 in. (300 × 1200 mm) is generally sufficient to serve two stacks of units. This may be sandwiched between units at the perimeter of the building or located adjacent to the central corridor, depending on where the heating and cooling equipment is located in the units.

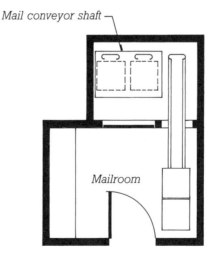

Mail conveyor shaft

Mailroom

PLUMBING WALLS, JANITOR CLOSETS, AND TOILET ROOMS

Fixtures in bathrooms, toilet rooms, shower rooms, kitchens, laundries, and other areas with plumbing should back up to plumbing walls. A plumbing wall has an internal cavity large enough to house the supply, waste, and vent piping necessary to serve the fixtures. Plumbing walls should be stacked vertically from the bottom of the building to the top. It is possible to offset plumbing walls a few feet from one floor to the next, but the horizontal offsets are expensive and cause maintenance headaches. A typical plumbing wall arrangement, complete with janitor closet, is illustrated and dimensioned on the diagram to the right. The given widths are adequate for floor-mounted fixtures. If wall-hung fixtures are used, a 24-in. (600-mm) dimension is needed to accommodate the fixture carriers.

Fixture requirements for toilet rooms are established by plumbing codes and vary widely from one code to the next. Requirements for the model plumbing codes included in this book are reproduced on the following pages. The designer must also keep in mind the general requirement that toilet rooms be usable by disabled persons. For detailed layout dimensions of toilet rooms and accessible facilities, consult *Architectural Graphic Standards* and the appropriate references listed in this book's bibliography.

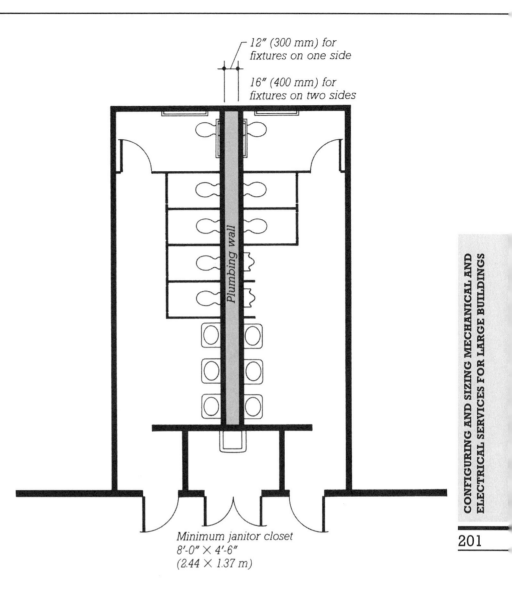

12" (300 mm) for fixtures on one side

16" (400 mm) for fixtures on two sides

Plumbing wall

Minimum janitor closet
8'-0" × 4'-6"
(2.44 × 1.37 m)

Minimum Toilet Fixture Requirements in the International Building Code

Consult the table on the facing page to determine the minimum number of toilet fixtures required based on the type of occupancy and number of occupants served. See pages 7–12 for more information on determining the Occupancy Groups for your building, and page 281 for determining occupant load. For occupancy types not listed in the table, select the most comparable Group in terms of patterns of use and occupant density.

When determining fixture requirements, the following should also be considered:

■ Under most circumstances, separate toilet facilities are required for each sex. Separate facilities are not required for private facilities, for areas where the total occupant load is 15 or less, for employee facilities where 15 or fewer persons are employed, and for Mercantile occupancies with 50 or fewer occupants.

■ For male toilet facilities, urinals may be substituted for not more than two-thirds of the required water closets.

■ In most circumstances, required toilet facilities for public and employee use must be located within one story above or below and within a 500-ft (152-m) travel distance of the space served. Facilities may in most cases be shared between employees and the public.

■ Employee toilet facilities in occupancies other than Assembly and Mercantile must be located within the employee work area.

■ In covered malls, toilet facilities may be located within individual stores or centrally located. The travel distance to public facilities may not exceed 300 ft (91 m) measured from the main entrance to any store or tenant space.

■ In I-2, I-3, and I-4 Institutional occupancies, employee and visitor toilet facilities must be separate from resident facilities.

■ Group R-2 and R-3 residential dwelling units must be provided with at least one kitchen sink per dwelling unit. In multifamily apartment houses or attached one- or two-family dwellings, at least one automatic clothes washer connection is required for every 20 dwelling units.

■ Required toilet room facilities must be free of charge.

■ At least one service sink for maintenance personnel should be provided per floor or use area.

Accessible Toilet Facilities in the International Building Code

In buildings required to provide access for disabled persons, accessible routes must be provided to toilet and bathing facilities, and each facility must have at least one accessible fixture of each type. In toilet rooms with partitioned water closet compartments, at least one such compartment must be wheelchair accessible. Where six or more compartments are provided, one additional compartment must be at least 36 in. (914 mm) in width, must have an outward-swinging door, and must be equipped with grab bars. In accessible buildings at least one-half of the required drinking fountains, but no fewer than one per floor, must be accessible.

In Group A Assembly and Group M Mercantile occupancies, unisex toilet rooms that provide private access to facilities for disabled individuals and their assistants are required wherever an aggregate of six or more male and female water closets are required. In recreational facilities where separate-sex bathing facilities with more than one set of fixtures in each bathing room are provided, at least one accessible unisex bathing room is also required.

Accessible unisex toilet or bathing rooms should have only one set of each fixture type. They must be located on accessible routes, not more than one story above or below other separate-sex toilet rooms, with a maximum travel distance along the accessible route of 500 ft (152 m) from those rooms. The fixtures provided in accessible unisex toilet rooms may be counted toward the overall fixture requirements of the space.

VERTICAL DISTRIBUTION OF SERVICES FOR LARGE BUILDINGS

Occupancy	Water Closets	Lavatories	Drinking Fountains	Bathrooms/ Showers
A: Assembly				
A-1: Theaters and halls with fixed seating	Male: 1 per 125 Female: 1 per 65	1 per 200	1 per 500	None
A-2: Nightclubs, taverns, dance halls	1 per 40	1 per 75	1 per 500	None
A-2: Restaurants, food courts	1 per 75	1 per 200	1 per 500	None
A-3: Auditoriums without fixed seating, galleries, museums, gymnasiums, etc.	Male: 1 per 125 Female: 1 per 65	1 per 200	1 per 500	None
A-3: Places of worship	Male: 1 per 150 Female: 1 per 75	1 per 200	1 per 1000	None
A-3: Passenger terminals and transportation facilities	1 per 500	1 per 750	1 per 1000	None
A-4 and A-5: Indoor and outdoor arenas with up to 1500 seats	Male: 1 per 75 Female: 1 per 40	Male: 1 per 200 Female: 1 per 150	1 per 1000	None
A-4 and A-5: Indoor and outdoor arenas with more than 1500 seats	As above for the first 1500 seats, then as follows for the remainder:		1 per 1000	None
	Male: 1 per 120 Female: 1 per 60	Male: 1 per 200 Female: 1 per 150		
B: Business	First 50 occupants: 1 per 25 Remaining occupants: 1 per 50	First 80 occupants: 1 per 40 Remaining occupants: 1 per 80	1 per 100	None
E: Educational	1 per 50	1 per 50	1 per 100	None
F: Factory	1 per 100	1 per 100	1 per 400	Emergency showers and eyewash stations may be required
I: Institutional				
I-1: Residential care	1 per 10	1 per 10	1 per 100	1 per 8
I-2: Medical and custodial care (residents only)	1 per room	1 per room	1 per 100	1 per 15
	Two patient rooms may share one toilet room with direct access from each room			
I-3: Prisons (residents only)	1 per cell	1 per cell	1 per 100	1 per 15
I-3: Reformatories, detention centers, correctional centers (residents only)	1 per 15	1 per 15	1 per 100	1 per 15
I-4: Adult and child day care (residents only)	1 per 15	1 per 15	1 per 100	None
I-2, I-3, and I-4: Employee toilet facilities	1 per 25	1 per 35	1 per 1000	None
I-2, I-3, and I-4: Visitor toilet facilities	1 per 75	1 per 100	1 per 500	None
M: Mercantile	1 per 500	1 per 750	1 per 1000	None
R: Residential				
R-1: Hotels and motels	1 per guestroom	1 per guestroom	None	1 per guestroom
R-2: Dormitories, fraternities, sorority houses, boarding houses	1 per 10	1 per 10	1 per 100	1 per 8
R-2: Multifamily housing	1 per dwelling unit	1 per dwelling unit	None	1 per dwelling unit
R-3: One- and two-family dwellings	1 per dwelling unit	1 per dwelling unit	None	1 per dwelling unit
R-4: Assisted living	1 per 10	1 per 10	1 per 100	1 per 8
S: Storage	1 per 100	1 per 100	1 per 1000	Emergency showers and eyewash stations may be required

This table was compiled from information contained in the International Building Code 2006. It does not represent an official interpretation by the organization that issues this code.

Minimum Toilet Fixture Requirements in the National Building Code of Canada

Consult the table on the facing page to determine the minimum number of toilet fixtures required for projects located in Canada based on the type of occupancy and number of occupants served. See pages 13–15 for more information on determining the Occupancy Groups for your building, and page 281 for determining occupant load.

In determining fixture requirements, the following should also be considered:

■ Under most circumstances, separate toilet facilities are required for each sex. Separate facilities are not required for the following occupancies with an occupant load of 10 or less: Assembly, Residential, Business and Personal Services, Mercantile, and Industrial.

■ Fixture requirements should be based on the assumption of equal numbers of male and female occupants, unless an unequal distribution of the sexes in the occupant population can be demonstrated with reasonable accuracy.

■ For male toilet facilities, urinals may be substituted for not more than two-thirds of the required water closets. Where only two water closets are required, a urinal may be substituted for one closet.

■ For Business and Personal Service Occupancy Groups with a floor area of more than 600 m² (6460 sq ft), toilet facilities must be available to the public.

Accessible Toilet Facilities in the National Building Code of Canada

Most buildings must provide at least one accessible, barrier-free washroom. All washrooms on floors requiring barrier-free access must themselves be barrier-free, except that barrier-free washrooms are not required:

■ Within a residential occupancy suite

■ Where other barrier-free facilities are located on the same floor area and within a path of travel of 45 m (148 ft)

■ Within Occupancy Groups Business and Personal Services, Merchantile, and Industrial, individual suites less than 500 m² (5380 sq ft) in area that are separated from the rest of the building and to which no barrier-free access is provided

In Assembly occupancies with shower facilities, at least one shower stall must be barrier-free.

Special barrier-free, single-fixture, unisex washrooms may be provided as an alternative to the barrier-free washroom requirements above. When such special washrooms are provided, the occupant load used to calculate fixture requirements for the general public may be reduced by 10 persons in Assembly, Business and Personal Services, Mercantile, or Industrial occupancies, as well as in primary schools, day care facilities, places of worship, and undertaking premises.

VERTICAL DISTRIBUTION OF SERVICES FOR LARGE BUILDINGS

Occupancy	Number of Occupants of Each Sex	Number of Water Closets for Each Sex	Number of Lavatories
A: Assembly			
Assembly spaces, except those listed below	1–25	Male: 1; Female: 1	At least 1, and not less than 1 per every 2 water closets
	26–50	Male: 1; Female: 3	
	51–75	Male: 2; Female: 3	
	76–100	Male: 2; Female: 4	
	101–125	Male: 3; Female: 5	
	126–150	Male: 3; Female: 6	
	151–175	Male: 4; Female: 7	
	176–200	Male: 4; Female: 8	
	201–250	Male: 5; Female: 9	
	251–300	Male: 5; Female: 10	
	301–350	Male: 6; Female: 11	
	351–400	Male: 6; Female: 12	
	Over 400	Male: 7 plus 1 for each additional increment of 200 occupants over 400 Female: 13 plus 1 for each additional increment of 100 occupants over 400	
Primary schools and day care centers	Any number	Male: 1 per 30 Female: 1 per 25	Same as above
Places of worship, undertaking premises	Any number	1 per 50	Same as above
B: Care and Detention	Any number	Based on the specific needs of the occupants, determined on a case-by-case basis	Same as above
C: Residential			
Except dwelling units	Any number	1 per 10	Same as above
Dwelling units	Any number	1 per unit	Same as above
D: Business and Personal Services	1–25	1	Same as above
	25–50	2	
	Over 50	3 plus 1 for each additional increment of 50 occupants over 50	
E: Mercantile	Any number	Male: 1 per 300 Female: 1 per 150	Same as above
F: Industrial	1–10	1	Same as above
	11–25	2	
	26–50	3	
	51–75	4	
	76–100	5	
	Over 100	6 plus 1 for each additional increment of 100 occupants over 100	

This table was compiled from information contained in the National Building Code of Canada 2005. It does not represent an official interpretation by the organization that issues this code.

STANDPIPES

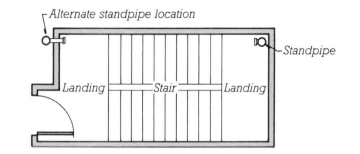

A standpipe is a large-diameter steel water pipe extending vertically through a building, with fire hose connections at every floor. There are two types of standpipes: A *wet standpipe* is continually filled with water and is fitted with hoses for emergency use by building occupants. A *dry standpipe* contains no water and is reserved for use by firefighters. In case of fire, the firefighters supply water to the dry standpipe by connecting pumper trucks to a Y-shaped Siamese connection on the front of the building at street level, and they carry their own hoses into the building to connect to the standpipe.

Standpipe requirements in the building codes are fairly complex. A safe initial assumption is that there is a dry standpipe in a corner of every exit stairway enclosure or in the vestibule of a smokeproof stair enclosure. Some fire departments prefer that the dry standpipes be located on the landings between floors, where each hose connection can serve two floors. It should also be assumed that wet standpipes and fire hose cabinets will be located in such a way that every point on a floor lies within reach of a 30-ft (9-m) stream from the end of a 100-ft (30-m) hose. A typical recessed wall cabinet for a wet standpipe hose and a fire extinguisher is 2 ft 9 in. (840 mm) wide,

9 in. (230 mm) deep, and 2 ft 9 in. (840 mm) high.

Under some codes, a wet standpipe may also serve as the riser to supply water to an automatic sprinkler system, but usually a separate sprinkler riser is required. The horizontal piping for the sprinkler system branches from the standpipe at each floor and, if it is concealed, runs just above the ceiling. An assembly of

valves and alarm fittings must be furnished at the point where the sprinkler system joins the domestic water system, usually in the same room with the domestic water pumps. Two Siamese fittings are required in readily accessible locations on the outside of the building to allow the fire department to attach hoses from pumper trucks to the dry standpipe and to the sprinkler riser.

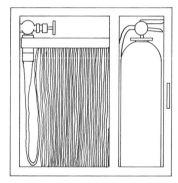

HOSE CABINET

SIAMESE FITTING

206

DESIGNING ELEVATORS AND ELEVATOR LOBBIES

The tables to the right can be used to arrive at an approximate number of elevators and appropriate sizes for the cars. In very tall buildings, the number of shafts can be reduced by as much as one-third with schemes of express and local elevators or advanced control sytems.

Walking distance from the elevator lobby to any room should not exceed 150 ft (45 in). In many buildings, elevators also must be sized to comply with building code requirements for accommodating persons with disabilities or emergency aid personnel with medical stretchers. For more information, see page 267 for the International Building Code and page 271 for the National Building Code of Canada.

Laying Out Banks of Elevators

Elevators serving the same zone of the building should be arranged in a single bank so that waiting persons can keep all the doors in sight at one time. A bank of three in a row is the largest that is desirable; four in a row is acceptable. Banks of elevators serving different zones of the building may open on opposite walls of the same elevator lobby or onto separate lobbies. The minimum width of an elevator lobby serving a single bank of elevators is 8 ft (2.45 m); for a lobby with banks of elevators on both sides, the minimum width is 10 ft (3 m).

Building codes in some circumstances require elevator lobbies to be separated from adjacent floor areas to reduce the risk of smoke from a building fire spreading from floor to floor through elevator shafts. In the International Building Code, where elevators open into rated exit access corridors, there must usually be a rated separation between the lobby and the corridor. For infor-

APPROXIMATE NUMBERS OF ELEVATOR SHAFTS

Use	Number of Shafts	Capacity of Elevator
Apartment Buildings	1 per 75 units, plus 1 service elevator for 300 units or more in a high-rise building	2000 to 2500 lb (900 to 1140 kg)
Hotels	1 per 75 rooms, plus 1 service elevator for up to 100 rooms and 1 service elevator for each additional 200 rooms	2500 to 3000 lb (1140 kg to 1360 kg)
Office Buildings	1 per 35,000 sq ft (3250 m²) of area served, plus 1 service elevator per 265,000 sq ft (24,600 m²) of area served	2500 to 3500 lb (1360 to 1590 kg)

ELEVATOR DIMENSIONS

Use	Capacity	Inside Car Dimensions	Inside Shaft Dimensions (width × depth)
Apartments, Hotels, Office Buildings, Stores	2000 lb (900 kg) 2500 lb (1140 kg)	5'-8" × 4'-3" (1727 × 1295 mm) 6'-8" × 4'-3" (2032 × 1295 mm)	6'-7" × 7'-4" (2006 × 2235 mm) 8'-4" × 6'-8" (2540 × 2032 mm)
Office Buildings, Hotels, Stores	3000 lb (1360 kg)	6'-8" × 4'-9" (2032 × 1448 mm)	8'-4" × 7'-5" (2540 × 2261 mm)
Office Buildings, Stores	3500 lb (1590 kg)	6'-8" × 5'-5" (2032 × 1651 mm)	8'-4" × 8'-1" (2540 × 2464 mm)
Hospitals, Nursing Homes	6000 lb (2730 kg)	5'-9" × 10'-0" (1750 × 3050 mm)	8'-2" × 11'-9" (2490 × 3580 mm)
Freight, Service	4000 to 6000 lb (1820 to 2730 kg)	8'-4" × 10'-0" (2540 × 3050 mm)	10'-10" × 10'-8" (3300 × 3250 mm)

mation on corridor rating requirements in this code, see page 257. In the National Building Code of Canada, elevators designated for firefighter access in high buildings must be separated from adjacent spaces and corridors. For more information on such firefighter access requirements, see page 278.

Elevator shafts are noisy and should not be located next to occupied space, especially in hotels and residential buildings.

Elevator cars ordinarily have doors on one side only. Cars with doors on opposing sides are available; this necessitates a shaft that is slightly wider than normal, to allow the counterweights to be placed next to the side of the car.

Freight and service elevators should open to separate service rooms or workrooms. Mailrooms, receiving rooms, and maintenance and housekeeping facilities should relate closely to service elevators.

See the following page for information on elevator types, penthouses, pits, and machine rooms.

ELEVATOR TYPES, PENTHOUSES, PITS, AND MACHINE ROOMS

Choice of elevator type is most commonly based on the height of floors to be served. For vertical travel distances up to 40–60 ft (12–18 m), hydraulic elevators are typically the most economical. With this elevator type, a hydraulic piston is located either in a drilled well at the bottom of the shaft or within the shaft itself. A machine room approximately 45 sq ft (4.2 m²) in area is required, connected to the elevator shaft by hydraulic lines and electrical control wiring. Its preferred location is adjacent to the elevator shaft on the lowest level served by the elevator. However, the machine room is also noisy and should not be located close to acoustically sensitive areas. When necessary, it may be located on other levels or at a greater distance from the shaft. The inside top of the elevator shaft itself must extend 13 –14 ft (3.9 – 4.25 m) above the uppermost floor level served; frequently this results in the shaft construction projecting at least several feet above adjacent roof areas. When referring to the Elevator Dimensions table on the previous page, inside shaft dimensions should be increased by 6 in. (150 mm) in width and reduced by 12 in. (300 mm) in depth from those listed to account for differences in the lifting machinery of this elevator type.

At greater heights, electric traction elevators are required. In its most common form, this type of elevator has its hoisting machinery located in a penthouse machine room above the top of the elevator shaft. This room's inside dimensions must be approximately 9 ft (2.7 m) high, as wide as the shaft itself, and 16–18 ft (5–5.5 m) long. It is located exactly over the top of the elevator shaft, extending

208

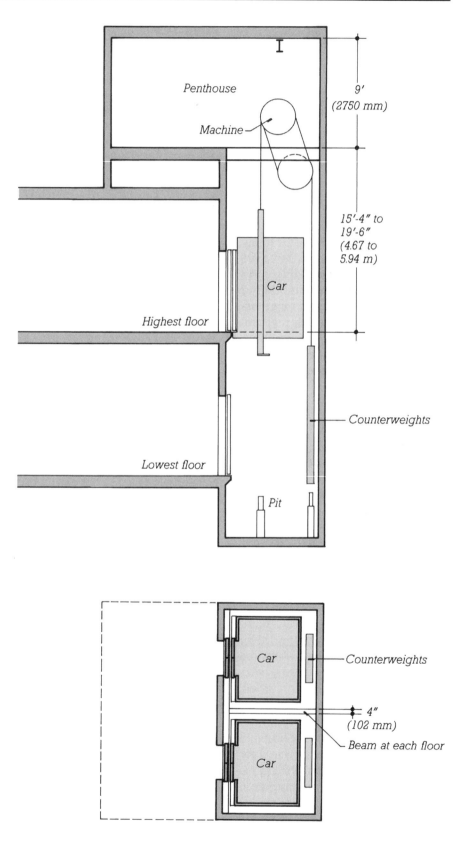

VERTICAL DISTRIBUTION OF SERVICES FOR LARGE BUILDINGS

beyond the shaft on the side above the elevator doors. Below the elevator machine room, the inside top of the elevator shaft itself must extend from 15 to 20 ft (4.5 to 6.1 m) above the uppermost level served. For this reason, the penthouse must frequently be raised above the adjacent roof surface, making it a significant presence on the building rooftop.

Another option for serving vertical distances from 50 to 300 ft (15 to 90 m) is an electric traction elevator using relatively new, compact hoisting machinery. With this type, the machinery can be located either entirely within the elevator shaft or within a machine room of significantly smaller dimensions than is possible with traditional electric systems. Sometimes referred to as *machine room-less,* these elevators are available in capacities of up to 4000 lb (1800 kg) for passenger service and 5000 lb (2300 kg) for hospital service or freight. For preliminary inside shaft dimensions, use the sizes listed in the Elevator Dimensions table on

page 207. Where the hoisting machinery is entirely within the elevator shaft, a separate control room is required, ranging from 25 to 90 sq ft (2.5 to 8 m²) in area depending on the number and capacity of elevators in operation. Depending on the manufacturer's requirements, it may be possible to locate this room as far as 100 ft (30 m) from the elevator shaft. In other configurations, both the hoisting machinery and controls may be located in a room above the elevator shaft or in a room approximately 5 ft (1.5 m) deep directly adjacent to the shaft on the topmost level served by the elevator. The minimum height required from the uppermost floor level served to the inside top of the shaft varies significantly among configurations available; consult manufacturers' technical literature for more information.

Every elevator shaft must terminate with a pit at the bottom. For electric traction elevators, the inside depth of the pit below the lowest floor level served varies from approximately 5 to 13 ft (1.5 to 4 m),

depending on the speed and capacity of the elevator—the bigger and faster the elevator, the deeper the pit. Hydraulic elevators normally require a pit 4 ft (1.2 m) deep.

ESCALATORS

Escalators are useful in situations where large numbers of people wish to circulate among a small number of floors on a more or less continual basis. An escalator cannot be counted as a means of egress. The structural and mechanical necessities of an escalator are contained in the integral box that lies beneath the moving stairway. Structural support is required only at the two ends of the unit. Some basic dimensional information on escalators is tabulated below.

	32" Escalator	48" Escalator
A	3'-9" (1145 mm)	5'-1" (1550 mm)
B	3'-7" (1090 mm)	4'-11" (1500 mm)

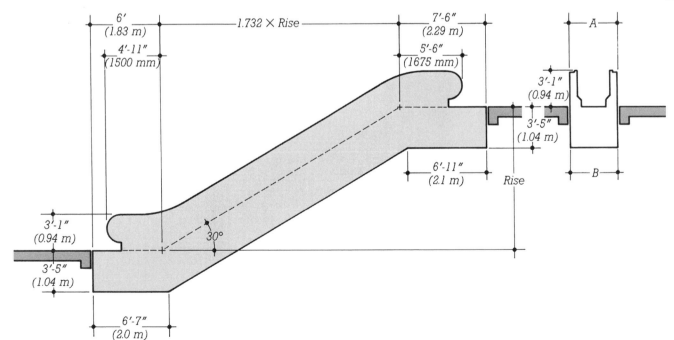

A CHECKLIST OF CORE COMPONENTS

The following is an alphabetical listing of components that are often incorporated into the cores of a building. For more information on any component, follow the accompanying page reference.

Chimneys (page 186)

Drinking fountains and water coolers (page 202)

Electrical closets (page 199)

Elevators (page 207)

Dumbwaiters and vertical conveyors

Elevator lobbies

Freight elevators and freight rooms

Passenger elevators

Service elevators and service lobbies

Escalators (page 209)

Fan rooms (page 191)

Fire hose and fire extinguishers cabinets (page 206)

Janitor closets (page 201)

Kitchens

Mail facilities (page 200)

Mail chutes

Mail conveyors

Mailrooms

Plumbing walls (including waste and vent pipes) (page 201)

Refuse facilities (page 194)

Refuse chute

Refuse room

Shafts (pages 196–201)

Domestic water piping:

Chilled drinking water supply and return piping

Domestic cold water supply and return piping

Domestic hot water supply and return piping

Liquid soap supply piping to toilet rooms

Supply riser to rooftop gravity tank

Electrical and communications shafts:

Electrical wires or bus bars

First communications wiring: Alarms, smoke and heat detectors, firefighter communications

Telephone, telex, local area networks, cable television, community antenna, etc.

Heating and cooling shafts:

Control wiring

Ducts (page 218)

Exhaust ducts from toilets, baths, janitor closets, shower rooms, locker rooms, storage rooms, kitchens, corridors, fume hoods, laboratory areas, workshop areas, industrial processes (page 190)

Fire exhaust and pressurization ducts

Outdoor air and exhaust air ducts to local fan rooms

Supply ducts (page 218)

Return ducts (page 218)

Piping

Air piping for controls

Chilled water supply and return

Condenser water supply and return between chilled water plant and cooling towers

Fuel oil piping

Gas piping

Hot water and/or steam supply and return

Piping, miscellaneous: Compressed air, vacuum, deionized water, distilled water, fuel gas, medical gases, scientific gases, industrial gases

Piping, plumbing waste and vent (page 201)

Piping, storm drainage risers from roofs and balconies

Sprinkler riser (page 206)

Stairways (pages 260–264)

Standpipes, fire (page 206)

Structure (pages 17–141)

Beams and girders, including special support around shafts and under heavy equipment

Bracing

Columns

Shear walls

Telecommunications closets (page 199)

Toilet rooms (pages 201–205)

HORIZONTAL DISTRIBUTION OF SERVICES FOR LARGE BUILDINGS

The horizontal distribution system for mechanical and electrical services in a large building should be planned simultaneously with the structural frame and the interior finish systems, because the three are strongly interrelated. The floor-to-floor height of a building is determined in part by the vertical dimension needed at each story for horizontal runs of ductwork and piping. The selection of finish ceiling, partition, and floor systems is often based in part on their ability to contain the necessary electrical and mechanical services and to adjust to future changes in these services. All these strategies involve close cooperation among the architect and the structural and mechanical engineers.

CONNECTING HORIZONTAL AND VERTICAL DISTRIBUTION LINES

Horizontal mechanical and electrical lines must be fed by vertical lines through smooth, functional connections. Plumbing waste lines, which must be sloped to drain by gravity, have top priority in the planning of horizontal service lines; if they are confined to vertical plumbing walls, they will not interfere with other services. Sprinkler heads, which have next highest priority in the layout of horizontal services, are served from the fire standpipe by horizontal piping that seldom exceeds 4 in. (100 mm) in outside diameter. The spacing of the heads is coordinated with the placement of walls and partitions; the maximum coverage per head is about 200 sq ft (18.6 m²) in light-hazard buildings such as churches, schools, hospitals, office buildings, museums, apartment houses, hotels, theaters, and auditoriums. Coverage in industrial and storage buildings ranges from 130 to 90 sq ft (12.1 to 8.4 m²) per head, depending on the substances handled in the building.

Air conditioning ducts, the next priority, branch out from a local fan room or from vertical ducts in supply and return shafts. Return ducts are often very short and confined to the interior areas of the building. Supply ducts extend from the main ducts through VAV or mixing boxes, then through low-velocity secondary ducts to air diffusers throughout the occupied area of the floor, with special emphasis on the perimeter, which may be on an independent, separately zoned set of ducts. Diffusers are generally required at the rate of four to seven diffusers per 1000 sq ft (100 m²). For some typical diffuser designs, see the illustration on page 215.

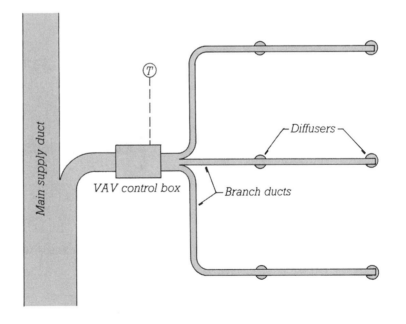

PLAN OF VAV DUCTING

GROUPED HORIZONTAL DISTRIBUTION

Sometimes the major runs of ductwork, piping, and wiring can be grouped in the ceiling area above the central corridor of each floor of a building, leaving the ceilings of the surrounding rooms essentially "clean." This works especially well in hotels, dormitories, and apartment buildings that rely on above-ceiling all-water or electric equipment in the area adjacent to the corridor for heating, cooling, and ventilating. A low corridor ceiling is readily accepted in exchange for high, unobstructed space in the occupied rooms, where the structure may be left exposed as the finish ceiling, saving cost and floor-to-floor height. If the building has a two-way flat plate or hollow core precast slab floor structure, the overall thickness of the ceiling–floor structure can be reduced to as little as 8 in. (200 mm). Conduits containing wiring for the lighting fixtures may be cast into the floor slabs or exposed on the surface of the ceilings. Wiring to wall outlets is easily accommodated in permanently located partitions.

212

FLOORWIDE HORIZONTAL DISTRIBUTION

In broad expanses of floor space, particularly where all electrical and communications services must be available at any point in the area, an entire horizontal layer of space is reserved on each story for mechanical and electrical equipment. This layer may be beneath a raised access floor just above the structural floor. It may also lie within the structural floor, or just beneath the floor, above a suspended ceiling. Sometimes combinations of these locations are used.

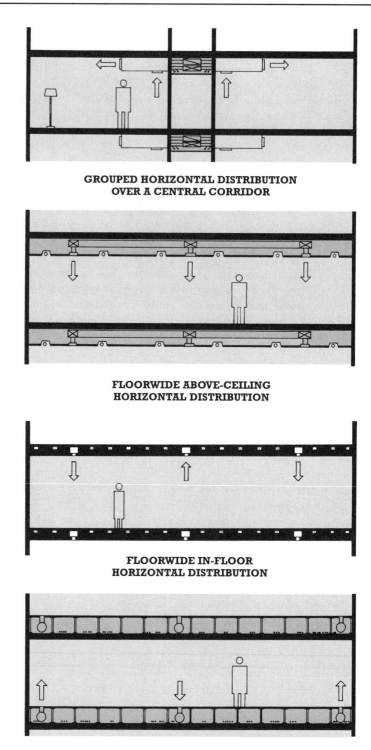

**GROUPED HORIZONTAL DISTRIBUTION
OVER A CENTRAL CORRIDOR**

**FLOORWIDE ABOVE-CEILING
HORIZONTAL DISTRIBUTION**

**FLOORWIDE IN-FLOOR
HORIZONTAL DISTRIBUTION**

**FLOORWIDE RAISED ACCESS FLOOR
HORIZONTAL DISTRIBUTION**

HORIZONTAL DISTRIBUTION OF SERVICES FOR LARGE BUILDINGS

Distribution above a Suspended Ceiling

Above a ceiling, wiring is run in conduits or cable trays attached to the structure above. Lighting fixtures are served directly from this horizontal wiring. Outlets on the floor below may be served by electrified partitions or power poles. Outlets on the floor above may be fed via poke-through fixtures that are cut through the structural floor. Poke-through fixtures can be added or removed at any time during the life of the building; their major disadvantage is that electrical work being done for the convenience of a tenant on one floor is done at the inconvenience of the tenant on the floor below.

Distribution within the Structural Floor

Electrical and communications wiring may be embedded in the floor slab in conventional conduits. For greater flexibility in buildings where patterns of use are likely to change over time, systems of cellular steel decking over steel framing, or cellular raceways cast into a topping over concrete slabs, may be selected. These provide a tree-like structure: The trunk is a wiring trench that runs from the electrical closet to the outside wall of the building, and the branches are the hollow cells that run in the perpendicular direction. Electrical and communications wires and outlets can be added, removed, or changed at any time during the life of the building. Cellular steel decking can affect the layout of the beams and girders in a steel-framed building: For optimum distribution of wiring, the cells in the decking generally run parallel to the wall of the core, and for structural reasons the cells must run perpendicular to the beams. This requires close coordination among the architect and the electrical and structural engineers.

Distribution above the Structural Floor

A raised access floor system allows maximum flexibility in running services because it can accommodate piping, ductwork, and wiring with equal ease. It is especially useful in industrial or office areas where large numbers of computers or computer terminals are used and where frequent wiring changes are likely. It is also valuable in retrofitting old buildings for modern services. Though floors can be raised to any desired height above the structural deck, heights of 4 to 8 in. (100 to 200 mm) are most common. Less costly, lower-profile systems, ranging from 2½ to 3 in. (65 to 75 mm) in height, are also available.

Undercarpet flat wiring may be used instead of a raised access floor in buildings with moderate needs for future wiring changes. Flat wiring does not increase the overall height of the building as raised access floors usually do, but it does not offer the unlimited capacity and complete freedom of wire location of the raised floors. Flat wiring is used in both new buildings and retrofit work.

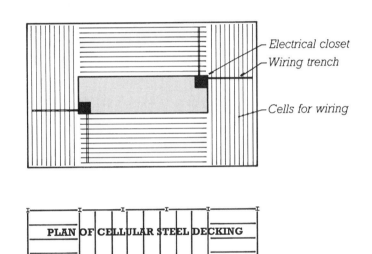

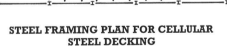

STEEL FRAMING PLAN FOR CELLULAR STEEL DECKING

DESIGNING THE CEILING/FLOOR PLENUM SPACE

An above-ceiling location is ordinarily best for ductwork, which is often too large and bulky to fit above or within the structural floor, The wiring and ductwork must share the above-ceiling plenum space with lighting fixtures and sprinkler piping. This requires careful planning. Generally the lowest stratum, about 8 in. (200 mm) thick, is reserved for the sprinkler piping and lighting fixtures. Lighting fixture selection plays an important role in determining the thickness of this stratum, because some types of lighting fixtures require more space than others. The ducts, which are usually 8 to 10 in. (200 to 250 mm) deep, run between this layer and the beams and girders. Adding about 2 in. (50 mm) for the thickness of a suspended ceiling, we see that a minimum height of about 18 in. (460 mm), and preferably 20 in. (500 mm), must be added to the thickness of the floor structure and fireproofing in a typical building to allow for mechanical and electrical services. A larger dimension is often called for, depending on the requirements of the combination of systems that is chosen.

As an example, let us assume that a steel-framed building has a maximum girder depth of 27 in. (690 mm) and a 4-in. (100-mm) floor slab, for a total floor structure height of 31 in. (790 mm). Adding 20 in. (510 mm) for ceiling and services, we arrive at an overall ceiling-to-floor height of 51 in. (1300 mm) that must

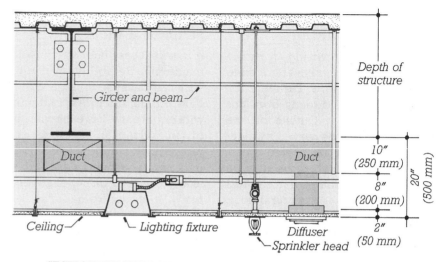

SECTION THROUGH CEILING/FLOOR ASSEMBLY

be added to the desired room height to give the floor-to-floor height of the building. If fireproofing must be added to the girders, this dimension will increase by a couple of inches (50 mm or so).

There is tremendous economic pressure to reduce this height to a practical minimum in a tall building. A few inches saved per floor adds up to an enormous saving in the cost of structure, core components, and cladding. Sometimes it is possible to arrange the framing so that ductwork never passes beneath a girder. If the ductwork must cross the girders, the designers should explore such options as shallower ducts, running the ducts through holes cut in the webs of the girders, or reducing the depth of the girders by using a heavier steel shape. In the average tall office building, the height of the ceiling-floor assembly is about 46 in. (1170 mm).

In some medical, research, and industrial buildings, the underfloor services are unusually complex, bulky, and subject to change. In these cases, the layer above the ceiling and below the floor structure is expanded to a height that allows workers to walk freely in it, and the ceiling is strengthened into a structure that can support their weight. This arrangement, called an *interstitial ceiling*, allows workers to maintain and change the services without disrupting the occupied spaces above or below.

With all its service penetrations — lighting fixtures, air diffusers and grilles, sprinkler heads, smoke detectors, intercom speakers — a ceiling can take on a visually chaotic appearance. It is advisable to compose the relationships of these penetrations carefully on a reflected ceiling plan.

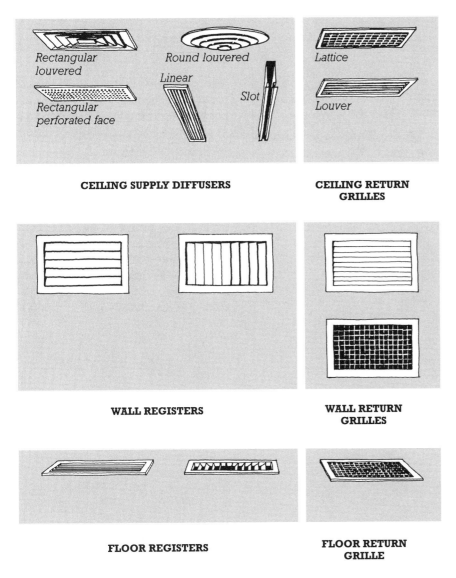

Rectangular louvered

Rectangular perforated face

Round louvered

Linear

Slot

CEILING SUPPLY DIFFUSERS

Lattice

Louver

CEILING RETURN GRILLES

WALL REGISTERS

WALL RETURN GRILLES

FLOOR REGISTERS

FLOOR RETURN GRILLE

TYPICAL GRILLE AND DIFFUSER DESIGNS

EXPOSED VERSUS CONCEALED SERVICES

In many buildings, the designer has a choice between exposing the mechanical and electrical services and concealing them above a suspended ceiling. Exposed services are the rule in warehouses and industrial buildings. In other types of buildings, exposed pipes and ducts can have an attractive sculptural complexity. They are easy to reach for maintenance and revision. They make sense in many large, open buildings (athletic arenas, exhibition halls), as well as in certain other kinds of buildings in which partitions are not often changed and a frank, functional appearance is appropriate (schools, art galleries, pubs and restaurants, avant-garde stores). There are some disadvantages: Exposed services that must look good are more expensive to design and install, and usually the cost of painting them must be added to the bill. They also need to be cleaned from time to time. Although exposed services are readily accessible for changes, any changes must be made with care, and a painter has to follow after the mechanics who do the work. For these reasons, it is usually cheaper to install a suspended ceiling than to omit one.

CONFIGURING AND SIZING MECHANICAL AND ELECTRICAL SERVICES FOR LARGE BUILDINGS

215

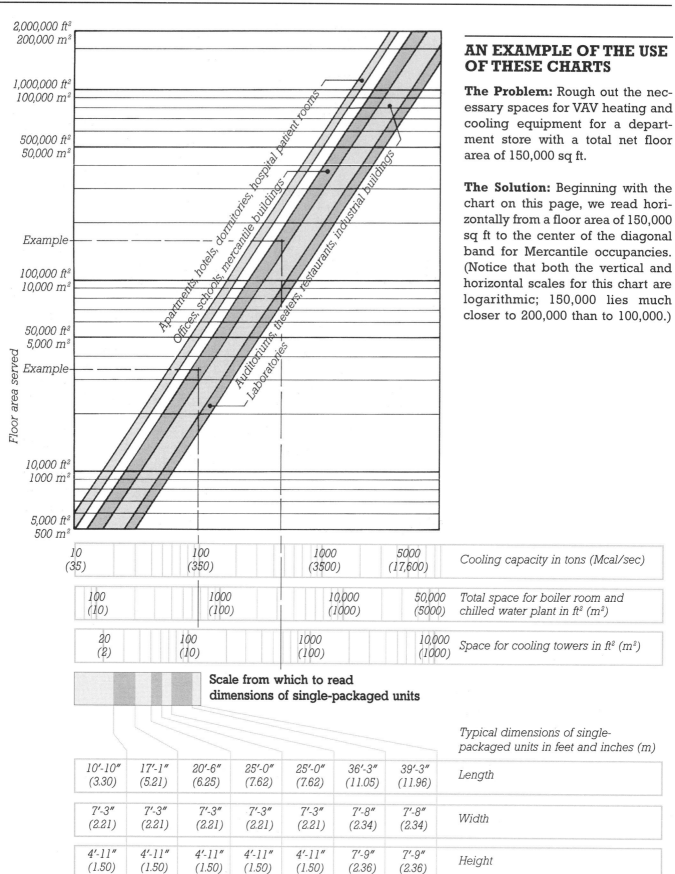

AN EXAMPLE OF THE USE OF THESE CHARTS

The Problem: Rough out the necessary spaces for VAV heating and cooling equipment for a department store with a total net floor area of 150,000 sq ft.

The Solution: Beginning with the chart on this page, we read horizontally from a floor area of 150,000 sq ft to the center of the diagonal band for Mercantile occupancies. (Notice that both the vertical and horizontal scales for this chart are logarithmic; 150,000 lies much closer to 200,000 than to 100,000.)

				Cooling capacity in tons (Mcal/sec)
10 (35)	100 (350)	1000 (3500)	5000 (17,600)	

				Total space for boiler room and chilled water plant in ft² (m²)
100 (10)	1000 (100)	10,000 (1000)	50,000 (5000)	

				Space for cooling towers in ft² (m²)
20 (2)	100 (10)	1000 (100)	10,000 (1000)	

Scale from which to read dimensions of single-packaged units

Typical dimensions of single-packaged units in feet and inches (m)

10'-10" (3.30)	17'-1" (5.21)	20'-6" (6.25)	25'-0" (7.62)	25'-0" (7.62)	36'-3" (11.05)	39'-3" (11.96)	Length
7'-3" (2.21)	7'-3" (2.21)	7'-3" (2.21)	7'-3" (2.21)	7'-3" (2.21)	7'-8" (2.34)	7'-8" (2.34)	Width
4'-11" (1.50)	4'-11" (1.50)	4'-11" (1.50)	4'-11" (1.50)	4'-11" (1.50)	7'-9" (2.36)	7'-9" (2.36)	Height

SIZING SPACES FOR MAJOR HEATING AND COOLING EQUIPMENT

Reading down, we find that the required cooling capacity for this building is approximately 450 tons, requiring a chilled water plant and boiler room that together will occupy an area of approximately 3200 sq ft. Cooling towers will occupy about 560 sq ft on the roof or alongside the building. The width of the diagonal band from which we have read gives us a range of 400 to 520 tons for the cooling requirement, so we know that these space requirements may grow somewhat smaller or larger as the system is designed in detail.

These values assume a central plant for heating and cooling. Could rooftop single-packaged units be used instead? We see at the bottom of the chart that no single-packaged unit is large enough to handle the entire load. Starting from the largest available packaged unit and reading up, we intersect the diagonal band and read to the left to find that the unit could serve about 33,000 sq ft of this building. Five such units could be distributed about the roof to furnish heating and air conditioning for the entire building, each serving about 30,000 sq ft. Each would need a capacity of about 90 tons and would measure 39 ft 3 in. long, 7 ft 8 in. wide, and 7 ft 9 in. high. A larger number of smaller units could also be used.

For more detailed information on boiler rooms, see page 186. Chilled water plants and cooling towers are explained on page 187 and single packaged units on page 192.

Move to the following page to continue this example.

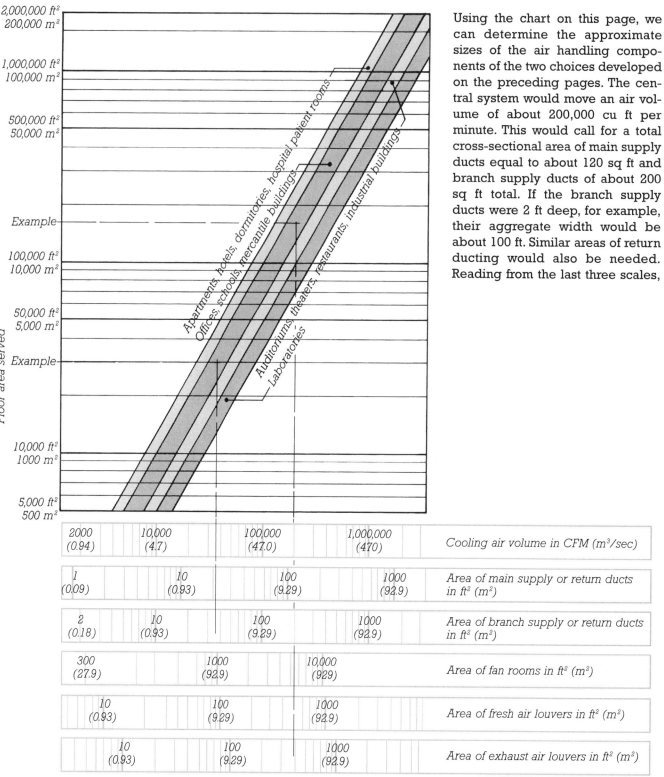

Using the chart on this page, we can determine the approximate sizes of the air handling components of the two choices developed on the preceding pages. The central system would move an air volume of about 200,000 cu ft per minute. This would call for a total cross-sectional area of main supply ducts equal to about 120 sq ft and branch supply ducts of about 200 sq ft total. If the branch supply ducts were 2 ft deep, for example, their aggregate width would be about 100 ft. Similar areas of return ducting would also be needed. Reading from the last three scales,

2000 (0.94)	10,000 (4.7)	100,000 (47.0)	1,000,000 (470)	Cooling air volume in CFM (m³/sec)
1 (0.09)	10 (0.93)	100 (9.29)	1000 (92.9)	Area of main supply or return ducts in ft² (m²)
2 (0.18)	10 (0.93)	100 (9.29)	1000 (92.9)	Area of branch supply or return ducts in ft² (m²)
300 (27.9)	1000 (92.9)	10,000 (929)		Area of fan rooms in ft² (m²)
10 (0.93)	100 (9.29)	1000 (92.9)		Area of fresh air louvers in ft² (m²)
10 (0.93)	100 (9.29)	1000 (92.9)		Area of exhaust air louvers in ft² (m²)

we further determine that fan rooms totaling about 5200 sq ft are needed, served by fresh air louvers adding up to about 500 sq ft in area and exhaust air louvers totaling nearly 400 sq ft. The location and distribution of this louver area on the outside surfaces of the building are of obvious architectural importance.

Each of the rooftop single-packaged units would need about 21 sq ft of main duct for supply air and the same for return, with a total area of 35 sq ft for branch ducts. Fans and louvers are incorporated into the units and do not need to be provided separately.

For further information on fan rooms and louvers, see page 191.

CONFIGURING AND SIZING MECHANICAL AND
ELECTRICAL SERVICES FOR LARGE BUILDINGS

219

3
MECHANICAL AND ELECTRICAL SYSTEMS FOR SMALL BUILDINGS

This chapter will help you select a heating and cooling system for the preliminary design of a small building. It also summarizes typical plumbing and electrical systems for small buildings.

DESIGNING SPACES FOR MECHANICAL AND ELECTRICAL SERVICES FOR SMALL BUILDINGS

Small buildings are defined for purposes of this section as those that use residential-scale mechanical and electrical systems. This category includes small educational, commercial, retail, industrial, and institutional buildings as well as houses, rowhouses, and small apartment buildings.

Heating and cooling loads in small buildings are usually dominated by heat gains and losses through the skin of the building. In many small buildings, mechanical fresh air ventilation is not an issue because of the low density of occupancy and the ability of operable windows and normal air leakage through the skin of the building to provide adequate ventilation. Most of the distribution lines for the mechanical and electrical systems in small buildings can be concealed within the hollow cavities that are a normal part of the floor, wall, and ceiling structures. A basement, crawlspace, or attic is often available as a location for the major mechanical equipment and larger horizontal distribution lines. There is an enormous variety of heating and cooling systems from which the designer may choose. This section summarizes the choices of heating and cooling systems and the typical plumbing and electrical systems. Approximate dimensions of the components of the various systems are also given.

DESIGN CRITERIA FOR THE SELECTION OF HEATING AND COOLING SYSTEMS FOR SMALL BUILDINGS

Decide first if the building needs a heating system only or both heating and cooling:	Some systems are capable of heating only, such as: Hydronic heating (pages 232–233) Solar heating (pages 234, 242–243) Electric convectors and heaters (pages 237–238) Radiant panel heating (page 239) Wall furnace and direct-vent space heaters (page 240) Heating stoves (page 241) Some systems are capable of both heating and cooling the building, such as: Forced air (pages 229–231) Heat pump (pages 184, 230–231) Packaged terminal units or through-the-wall units (page 236) Single-packaged and split-packaged systems (pages 192–193)
If you wish to minimize the first cost of the system:	Choose systems that do not require the installation of extensive piping or ductwork, such as: Evaporative cooler (page 235) Packaged terminal units or through-the-wall units (page 236) Electric convectors or fan-forced heaters (pages 237–238) Wall furnace and direct-vent space heaters (page 240) Heating stoves (page 241)
If you wish to minimize operating costs in cold climates:	Choose systems that burn fossil fuels efficiently, systems that utilize solar heat, or systems that burn locally available, low-cost fuels, such as: Forced air (pages 229–231) Hydronic heating (pages 232–233) Active and passive solar (pages 234, 242–243) Heating stoves (page 241)
If you wish to minimize operating costs in moderate climates:	Choose systems that utilize ambient energy sources, such as: Heat pump systems (pages 184, 230–231) Solar heating systems (pages 234, 242–243) Heating stoves (page 241) Evaporative cooler (page 235)
If you wish to maximize control of air quality and air velocity for maximum comfort:	Choose a system that filters and moves the air mechanically, namely: Forced air (pages 229–231)
If you wish to maximize individual control over temperature:	Choose systems that offer separate thermostats in a number of rooms or zones, such as: Hydronic heating (pages 232–233) Packaged terminal units or through-the-wall units (page 236) Electric convectors or fan-forced heaters (pages 237–238)

DESIGN CRITERIA FOR THE SELECTION OF HEATING AND COOLING SYSTEMS FOR SMALL BUILDINGS

If you wish to minimize the noise created by the heating and cooling system:	Choose systems in which motors, pumps, and fans are distant from the occupied space, such as: Forced air (pages 229–231) Hydronic heating (pages 232–233) Electric convectors and radiant heating (pages 237–239) Passive solar heating (pages 242–243)
If you wish to minimize the visual obtrusiveness of the heating and cooling system:	Choose systems that place as little hardware as possible in the occupied spaces, such as: Forced air (pages 229–231) Radiant heating (page 239)
If you wish to maximize the inhabitants' enjoyment of the changing weather and seasons:	Choose systems that change prominently with the seasons, such as: Passive solar heating (pages 242–243) Heating stoves (page 241)
If you wish to minimize the amount of floor space occupied by heating and cooling equipment:	Choose systems that do not occupy floorspace, such as: Evaporative cooler (page 235) Packaged terminal units or through-the-wall units (page 236) Electric fan-forced heaters (page 238) Electric radiant heating (page 239) Wall furnace and direct-vent space heaters (page 240) Passive solar heating (pages 242–243)
If you wish to minimize system maintenance:	Choose systems with few or no moving parts, such as: Forced air (pages 229–231) Hydronic heating (pages 232–233) Electric convectors (page 237) Electric radiant heating (page 239) Wall furnace and direct-vent space heaters (page 240) Passive solar heating (pages 242–243)
If you wish to avoid having a chimney in the building:	Choose systems that do not burn fuel in the building, such as: Heat pump furnace (pages 230–231) Single-packaged and split-packaged systems (pages 192–193) Packaged terminal units or through-the-wall units (page 236) All types of electric heat (pages 229-230, 237–239) With some fuel-burning systems, high-efficiency furnaces may be available that can be ventilated through a wall and do not require a chimney. Consult manufacturers' literature for more detailed information.
If you wish to maximize the speed of construction:	Choose systems that involve as few components and as few trades as possible, such as: Packaged terminal and through-the-wall units (page 236) All types of electric heat (pages 237–239)

GIVE SPECIAL CONSIDERATION TO THE SYSTEMS INDICATED IF YOU WISH TO:	Forced Air (page 229)	Heat Pump Furnace (page 230)	Hydronic Heating[a] (page 232)	Active Solar Heating[a] (page 234)	Evaporative Cooler[b] (page 235)
Combine heating and cooling in one system	●	●			
Minimize first cost					●
Minimize operating costs in very cold climates	●		●	●	
Minimize operating costs in moderate climates		●		●	●
Maximize control of air velocity and air quality	●	●			
Maximize individual control over temperature			●		
Minimize system noise	●	●	●	●	
Minimize visual obtrusiveness	●	●			
Maximize enjoyment of the seasons					
Minimize floor space used for the mechanical system					●
Minimize system maintenance	●				
Avoid having a chimney		●			
Maximize the speed of construction					

[a]System for heating only.
[b]System for cooling only.

226

HEATING AND COOLING SYSTEMS FOR SMALL BUILDINGS: SUMMARY CHART

Packaged Terminal Units or Through-the-Wall Units (page 236)	Electric Baseboard Convectors[a] (page 237)	Electric Fan-Forced Unit Heaters[a] (page 238)	Radiant Heating[a] (page 239)	Wall Furnace and Direct-Vent Space Heaters[a] (page 240)	Heating Stoves[a] (page 241)	Passive Solar Heating[a] (page 242)
●						
●	●	●		●	●	
					●	●
				●	●	●
●	●	●				
	●		●			●
			●			
					●	●
●	●	●	●	●		●
	●	●	●	●		●
●	●	●	●			
●	●	●		●		

CENTRAL SYSTEMS VERSUS LOCAL SYSTEMS

In a *central system,* heat is supplied to a building or extracted from it by equipment situated in a mechanical space—a furnace or a boiler in a basement, for example. Air or water is heated or cooled in this space and distributed to the inhabited areas of the building by ductwork or piping to maintain comfortable temperatures. In a *local system,* independent, self-contained pieces of heating and cooling equipment are situated throughout the building, one or more in each room. Central systems are generally quieter and more energy-efficient than local systems and offer better control of indoor air quality. Central equipment tends to last longer than local equipment and is easier to service. Local systems occupy less space in a building than central systems because they do not require a central mechanical space, ductwork, or piping. They are often more economical to buy and install. They can be advantageous in buildings that have many small spaces requiring individual temperature control.

Pages 229–234 describe central heating and cooling systems for small buildings, and pages 235–243 describe local systems.

FUELS

Heating equipment in small buildings may be fueled by oil, pipeline gas, liquid propane gas, kerosene, electricity, sunlight, or solid fuels—coal or wood. Cooling equipment is almost always powered by electricity. In functional respects electricity is the ideal fuel: It is clean, it is distributed through small wires, no chimney is needed, and electrical heating and cooling equipment is compact and often lower in first cost than equivalent fossil-fuel-burning equipment. In most geographic areas, however, electricity is a very costly fuel compared to oil or gas. Gas and oil are usually the fuels of choice for small buildings. Sunlight, wood, and coal are generally less convenient energy sources than electricity, gas, and oil. They are appropriate in particular buildings where owner preferences and building occupancy patterns permit or encourage their use.

On-site storage requirements for the various fuels are summarized in the table below.

TYPICAL DIMENSIONS OF FUEL STORAGE COMPONENTS

Component	Width	Depth	Height
Coal storage, minimum, 1 ton (1 tonne)	4'-0" (1.2 m)	4'-0" (1.2 m)	4'-0" (1.2 m)
Firewood storage, minimum, ½ cord	4'-0" (1.2 m)	4'-0" (1.2 m)	4'-0" (1.2 m)
Liquid propane tanks, upright cylinders	16" (410 mm) diameter		60" (1525 mm)
Liquid propane tank, horizontal	41" (1040 mm) diameter, 16'-3" (5.0 m) long		

There are many sizes of propane tanks, of which these are two of the most common. Upright cylinders are located outdoors, usually against the wall of the building, often in pairs. They may not be closer than 36" (915 mm) to a door or a basement window. The horizontal tank must be at least 25' (7.6 m) from the building or a property line and may be buried if desired.

Oil or kerosene storage tank, 275 gal (1000 l)	27" (685 mm)	60" (1525 mm)	54" (1375 mm)

For greater capacity, multiple tanks may be installed inside the building, or a larger tank may be buried just outside the foundation.

FORCED AIR HEATING AND COOLING

Description

A furnace heats air with a gas flame, an oil flame, or electric resistance coils. The heated air is circulated through the inhabited space by a fan and a system of ductwork. With an upflow furnace, the horizontal ducts are located above the furnace at the ceiling of the floor on which the furnace is located. With a downflow furnace, the ducts are located beneath the furnace in the crawlspace or floor slab. A third type, the horizontal furnace, is designed to fit in a low attic or under-floor crawlspace.

Cooling capability may be added to the furnace by installing evaporator coils in the main supply ductwork adjacent to the furnace. An outdoor compressor and condensing unit supplies cold refrigerant to the evaporator coils through small-diameter insulated tubing.

Typical Applications

Forced air heating and air conditioning is the most versatile and most widely used system for heating and cooling small buildings. Multiple furnaces may be installed to establish multiple zones of control and to heat and cool buildings of up to 10,000 sq ft (1000 m^2) and more.

Advantages

A forced air system can incorporate every type of humidification, dehumidification, air filtration, and cooling equipment. If properly designed, installed, and maintained, it is quiet and fuel efficient and distributes heat evenly.

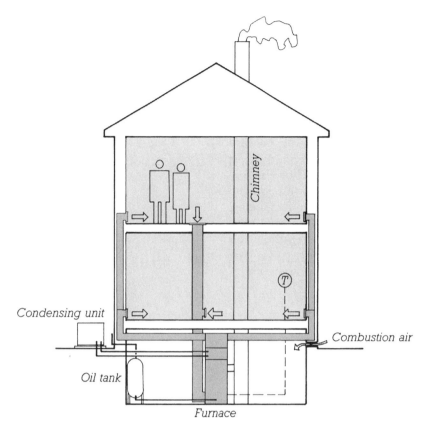

Condensing unit

Combustion air

Oil tank

Furnace

UPFLOW FURNACE

Disadvantages

Multiple zones of control are relatively difficult to create and can be wasteful of energy.

Major Components

Furnace, fuel storage, chimney, ductwork, and, if cooling capability is included, an outdoor condensing unit. Some high-efficiency gas furnaces may be vented through the wall and do not require a chimney. Typical dimensions for these components are summarized in the table on the facing page. For dimensions of fuel storage components, see page 228.

Variations

1. A heat pump furnace uses a reversible refrigeration cycle to create and circulate either heated or cooled air as required: An outdoor heat pump unit either extracts heat from the outdoor air and releases it through coils in the furnace or extracts heat from the coils in the furnace and releases it to the outdoor air, depending on whether heating or cooling is required. A heat pump furnace is generally economical to operate in moderate climates, but when outdoor temperatures fall well below freezing, the heat pump cycle becomes inefficient and is turned off automatically.

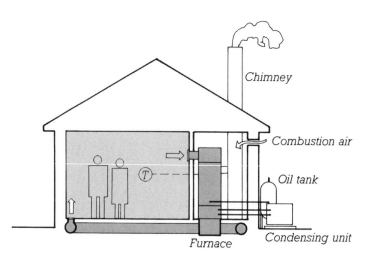

DOWNFLOW FURNACE ON SLAB

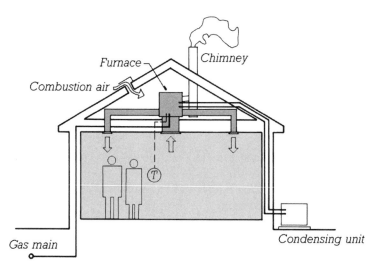

HORIZONTAL FURNACE IN ATTIC

FORCED AIR HEATING AND COOLING

Electric resistance coils are then activated to generate heat, which raises operating costs dramatically. For this reason, heat pumps are not usually used in severe climates unless they use water or earth as a heat source rather than air. Heat pump furnaces are available in vertical upflow, vertical downflow, and horizontal configurations and are similar in dimension to other furnaces.

2. A multifuel furnace is designed to burn solid fuel (wood or coal) as well as a backup fuel (gas or oil). It is larger and more expensive than a single-fuel furnace.

3. A packaged system, either single-packaged or split-packaged, is often used to heat and cool small commercial, industrial, and institutional buildings. For information on packaged systems, see pages 192–193.

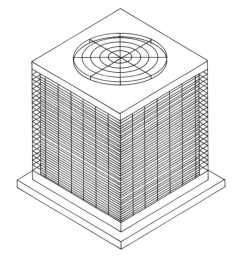

CONDENSING UNIT

TYPICAL DIMENSIONS OF COMPONENTS OF FORCED AIR HEATING SYSTEMS

Component	Width	Depth	Height
Chimney, masonry	20" (510 mm)	20" (510 mm)	a
Chimney, metal	10" (255-mm) diameter		a
Condensing unit, outdoor			
Small	24" (610 mm)	24" (610 mm)	24" (610 mm)
Large	40" (1015 mm)	50" (1270 mm)	33" (840 mm)
Ducts, sheet metal			
Main horizontal supply and return ducts, each	24" (610 mm)		12" (305 mm)
Supply risers, typical (notice that these are made to fit between wall studs)	10" (255 mm) 12" (305 mm) 7" oval (175 mm	3.25" (83 mm) 3.25" (83 mm) oval)	
Return risers (these are usually fewer in number than the supply risers and require special wall framing provisions)	8" (200 mm)	14" (360 mm)	

For duct insulation, add 1" (25 mm) all around. Insulation is recommended on heating ducts and is mandatory on cooling ducts that run through non-air-conditioned space.

Fuel storage—see page 228

	Width	Depth	Height
Furnaces, including adjacent primary ductwork			
Horizontal furnace	24" (610 mm)	84" (1170 mm)	28" (710 mm)
Upright furnace, upflow or downflow	24" (610 mm)	30" (760 mm)	84" (1170 mm)
Multifuel furnace, upright, upflow	48" (1220 mm)	60" (1525 mm)	84" (1170 mm)

A working space 3' (900 mm) square is required on the side of the furnace adjacent to the burner. Furnaces have varying requirements for installation clearances to combustible materials; some need only an inch or two.

---

[a]Under most codes, a chimney must extend at least 3' (900 mm) above the highest point where it passes through the roof and at least 2' (600 mm) above any roof surface within a horizontal distance of 10' (3 m).

HYDRONIC (FORCED HOT WATER) HEATING

Description

A flame or electric resistance coil heats water in a boiler. Small pumps circulate the hot water through fin-tube convectors, which are horizontal pipes with closely spaced vertical fins, mounted in a simple metal enclosure with inlet louvers below and outlet louvers above. The heated fins, working by convection, draw cool room air into the enclosure from below, heat it, and discharge it out the top. Instead of fin-tube convectors, especially where space is tight, fan-coil units, either surface-mounted or wall-recessed, may be used. The fan in a fan-coil unit blows room air past a hot water coil to heat it.

Typical Applications

Hydronic heating is a premium-quality heating system for any type of building.

Advantages

Hydronic heating is quiet if properly installed and maintained. It gives excellent heat distribution and is easily zoned for room-by-room control by adding thermostatically controlled zone valves or zone pumps at the boiler. The boilers for small-building systems are very compact. Some gas or electric boilers are so small that they can be mounted on a wall.

Disadvantages

Cooling, air filtration, and humidification, if desired, must be accomplished with independent systems, which raises the overall system cost. The convectors occupy considerable wall perimeter and can interfere with furniture placement.

Major Components

Boiler, chimney, fuel storage, expansion tank, circulator pumps, zone valves, convector or fan-coil units. Some high-efficiency gas boilers may be vented through a wall and do not require a chimney.

232

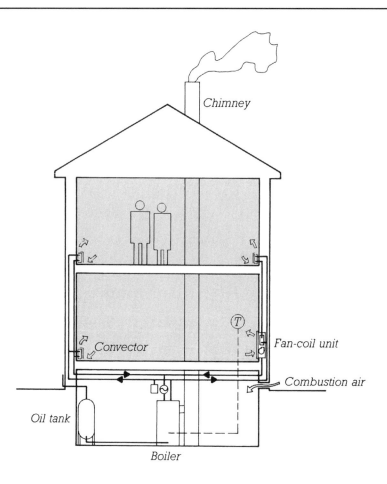

Chimney

Convector

Fan-coil unit

Combustion air

Oil tank

Boiler

HYDRONIC (FORCED HOT WATER) HEATING

Typical dimensions for these components are summarized in the table to the right. For dimensions of fuel storage components, see page 228.

Variations

1. A *multifuel boiler* is designed to burn both solid fuel (coal or wood) and a backup fuel (gas or oil). It is larger and more expensive than a single-fuel boiler.

2. Radiant heating panels in ceilings or floors may be warmed with hot water from a hydronic boiler (see page 239).

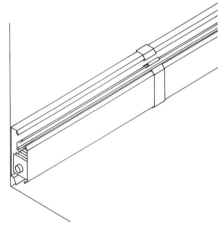

HYDRONIC CONVECTOR

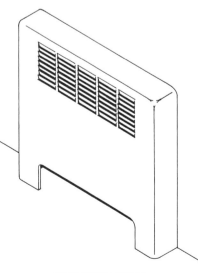

FAN-COIL UNIT

TYPICAL DIMENSIONS OF COMPONENTS OF A HYDRONIC HEATING SYSTEM

Component	Width	Depth	Height
Chimney, masonry	20" (510 mm)	20" (510 mm)	a
Chimney, metal	10" (250-mm) diameter		a
Boiler, hydronic, with expansion tank, valves, and pumps (add 10" or 250 mm on two adjacent sides for piping)			
Upright	25" (635 mm)	25" (635 mm)	84" (2135 mm)
Wall-mounted, gas or electric	30" (760 mm)	24" (610 mm)	84" (2135 mm)
Solid fuel or combination fuel	36" (900 mm)	60" (1530 mm)	84" (2135 mm)

A boiler requires a working space 3' (910 mm) square on the side adjacent to the burner. Required clearances to combustible surfaces vary, depending on the design of the boiler; for some boilers, they may be as little as an inch or two.

Component	Width	Depth	Height
Convector, baseboard	3" (75 mm)	7.5" (190 mm)	
Fan-coil units			
Recessed or surface-mounted	24" (610 mm)	4" (100 mm)	30" (760 mm)
Toespace heater	21" (535 mm)	18" (460 mm)	4" (100 mm)

[a]Under most codes, a chimney must extend at least 3' (900 mm) above the highest point where it passes through the roof and at least 2' (600 mm) above any roof surface within a horizontal distance of 10' (3 m).

ACTIVE SOLAR SPACE HEATING

Description

Outdoor south-facing collector panels, usually mounted on the roof of the building, are heated by sunlight. A pump or fan circulates liquid or air to withdraw the heat from the panels and store it in a tank of liquid or a bin of rocks or phase-change salts. This storage is usually located in the basement or a mechanical equipment room. A fan circulates indoor air through a heat exchanger coil filled with the warm storage liquid, or through the rock bin, and distributes the heated air to the inhabited space of the building through a system of ductwork.

Typical Applications

Active solar heating is feasible in buildings that are exposed to sunlight throughout the day in climates with a high percentage of sunny weather during the winter.

Advantages

Solar heating has zero fuel cost and does not pollute the air.

Disadvantages

The initial cost of active solar heating systems tends to be so high that they are uneconomical at present fuel prices. The collector surfaces become a very prominent and often dominating part of the architecture of the building. A full backup heating system (such as forced air or hydronic heating) is required to heat the building during extended sunless periods. Cooling must be done by a separate system.

Major Components

Solar collector panels, heat storage tank or bin, ductwork for air collectors or piping for water collectors, heat exchanger, and building heating ductwork. Typical dimensions for these components are summarized in the table to the right. For dimensions of fuel storage components, see page 228.

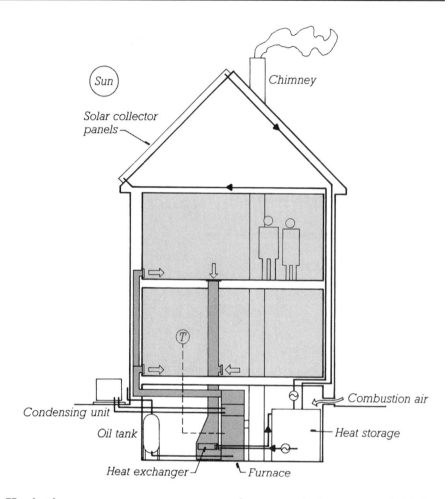

Variations

A heat pump may be added to the system to draw heat from the storage medium at relatively low temperatures and distribute it to the occupied spaces at higher temperatures. This provides a higher degree of comfort and increases the efficiency of the solar collectors.

TYPICAL DIMENSIONS OF ACTIVE SOLAR HEATING COMPONENTS

Component	Width	Depth	Height
For dimensions of the backup furnace, chimney, fuel storage, and ductwork, see pages 228 and 231.			
Collector panels, average residence	24' (7.3 m)	6" (150 mm)	20' (6 m)
Collector panels should face within 20° of true south and should be sloped at an angle to the ground equal to or up to 15° more than the latitude of the site.			
Heat exchanger with ductwork	30" (760 mm)	30" (760 mm)	30" (760 mm)
Heat storage			
Rock bed	minimum of 600 ft³ (17 m³)		
Water storage tank	8' (2.4 m) diameter		7' (2.1 m)

EVAPORATIVE COOLER

Description

A fan blows air through a wetted pad. Water evaporates from the pad into the air, cooling the air by extracting from it the latent heat of vaporization. The fan circulates the cooled air through the building. The metal cabinet in which the pad and fan are located is usually located on the roof or adjacent to the building.

Typical Applications

The cooling of buildings in which humidity control is not critical in hot, dry climates.

Advantages

Cooling costs are low.

Disadvantages

The humidity inside the building is difficult to control and may become excessive. The system is inefficient in humid climates. A separate system is required for heating the building.

Major Components

Evaporative cooling unit, ductwork. Typical dimensions for these components are summarized in the accompanying table.

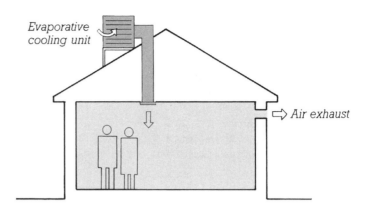

Evaporative cooling unit

Air exhaust

TYPICAL DIMENSIONS OF EVAPORATIVE COOLING SYSTEM COMPONENTS

Component	Width	Depth	Height
Evaporative cooler, average	36" (915 mm)	36" (915 mm)	36" (915 mm)
Duct	18" (460 mm)	18" (460 mm)	

Packaged terminal units and through-the-wall units are used extensively in small buildings as well as large. See page 184 for more detailed information on these systems.

Small split-packaged units are also available for use in small buildings.

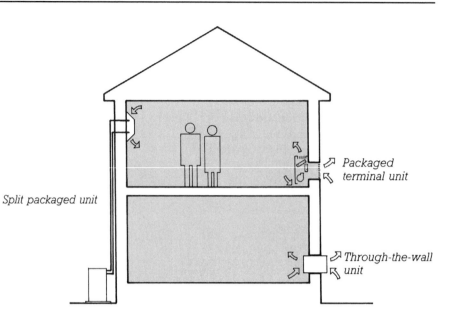

Split packaged unit

Packaged terminal unit

Through-the-wall unit

ELECTRIC BASEBOARD CONVECTORS

Description

Electric resistance wires in sheet metal enclosures are installed around the perimeter of the room at the junction of the floor and the wall. Room air circulates through slots in the enclosures by means of convection and is heated by the resistance wires.

Typical Applications

Heating systems in buildings of any type, especially where electric rates are low.

Advantages

Electric baseboard convectors are quiet and distribute heat evenly. Each room has individual temperature control. Installation costs are low. No chimney is required.

Disadvantages

The baseboard convectors occupy considerable wall perimeter and can interfere with furniture placement. There is no means of controlling humidity or air quality. Electricity is an expensive fuel in most areas. A separate system is required for cooling.

Major Components

Electric baseboard convector units. A typical convector is 3 in. (75 mm) deep and 7.5 in. (190 mm) high and extends for some feet along a wall.

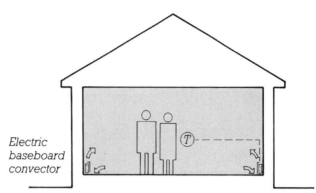

Electric baseboard convector

ELECTRIC FAN-FORCED UNIT HEATERS

Description

Fan-forced electric unit heaters are compact units inside which a fan draws in room air and heats it by passing it over electric resistance wires before blowing it back into the room.

Typical Applications

Any room or building that requires electric heating from small sources.

Advantages

They are economical to buy and install, and they do not interfere with furniture placement as much as baseboard convectors. Each room has individual temperature control. No chimney is required.

Disadvantages

Heat distribution in the room can be uneven, and the fans become noisy unless they are maintained regularly. There is no means of controlling humidity or air quality. Electricity is an expensive fuel in most areas. Separate systems are required for humidification and cooling.

Major Components

Electric fan-forced unit heaters. Typical dimensions for these components are summarized in the table to the right.

Variations

Fan-forced unit heaters are available for wall mounting in recessed or surface-mounted configurations. Toespace heaters are designed for use in the low, restricted space under kitchen cabinets or shelves. Recessed floor units lie beneath a simple floor register. Industrial unit heaters are mounted in rectangular metal cabinets that are designed to be suspended from the roof or ceiling structure.

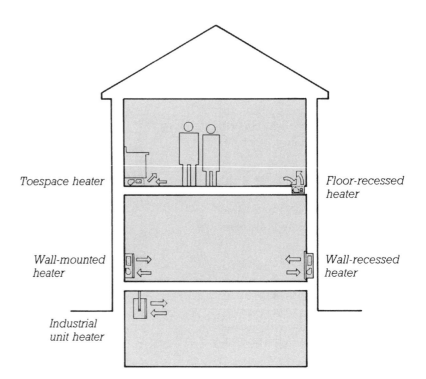

Toespace heater

Floor-recessed heater

Wall-mounted heater

Wall-recessed heater

Industrial unit heater

TYPICAL DIMENSIONS OF EVAPORATIVE COOLING SYSTEM COMPONENTS

Component	Width	Depth	Height
Floor-recessed heater	16" (400 mm)	8" (200 mm)	8" (200 mm)
Industrial unit heater	16" (400 mm)	12" (300 mm)	16" (400 mm)
Toespace heater	24" (610 mm)	12" (300 mm)	4" (100 mm)
Wall-recessed or wall surface-mounted heater	16" (400 mm)	4" (100 mm)	20" (510 mm)

ELECTRIC RADIANT HEATING

Description

Electric resistance heating wires are embedded in the ceiling or floor. The warm surface radiates heat directly to the body and also warms the air in the room.

Typical Applications

Residences, nursing homes.

Advantages

Heating is even and comfortable. No heating equipment is visible in the room.

Disadvantages

The system is slow to react to changing needs for heat. Tables and desktops beneath a radiant ceiling cast cold "shadows" on the legs and feet. Carpeting and furniture reduce the effectiveness of radiant floor panels. Cooling and humidity control must be provided by a separate system. Electricity is an expensive fuel in most areas.

Major Components

Resistance wires, resistance mats, or prefabricated, electrified ceiling panels.

Variations

Ceiling or floor radiant panels may be heated by hot water coils fed from a hydronic boiler.

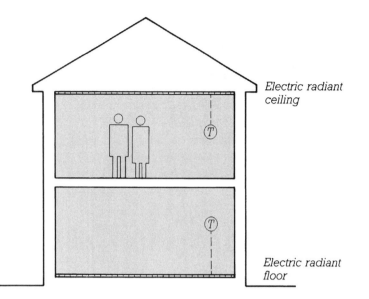

Electric radiant ceiling

Electric radiant floor

WALL FURNACE AND DIRECT-VENT SPACE HEATERS

Description

A wall furnace is a tall, wall-recessed or surface-mounted heating unit in which air flows from the room and circulates by convection past metal heat exchange surfaces warmed by a gas flame. Most wall furnaces can heat the spaces on both sides of the wall. Sometimes a short run of ductwork can be added to circulate heat to a third room.

Direct-vent space heaters are a newer generation of self-contained heating units. Inside air is fan-forced over a sealed burner unit. The unit draws exterior air for combustion and may be fueled by kerosene, natural gas, or propane. In comparison to the wall furnace, direct-vent space heaters are smaller in size, have greater fuel efficiency, provide improved heat distribution, and offer more choices of fuel source. These units are usually surface-mounted on the inside of an exterior wall, or vent pipes may be extended 10 to 15 ft (3 to 4.5 m) horizontally or vertically to permit more choice in heater location.

Typical Applications

Low-cost dwellings, offices, and motels in mild climates.

Advantages

Both systems are inexpensive to buy and install. Direct-vent space heaters are also highly fuel efficient.

Disadvantages

They require vent pipes to the outdoors, they distribute heat unevenly, and they are unattractive visually. Cooling and humidity control must be provided by separate systems.

Major Components

For wall furnaces, gas meter and service entrance or propane tank and regulator, gas piping, wall fur-

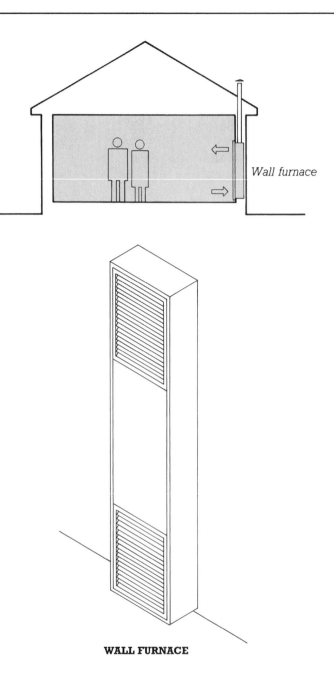

Wall furnace

WALL FURNACE

nace, vent pipes through the wall or to the roof. A typical wall furnace is 14 in. wide, 12 in. deep, and 84 in. high (360 × 305 × 2135 mm). The vent pipe to the roof is typically a 4-in. (100-mm) oval that may be concealed between the studs in a wall.

For direct-vent space heaters, the fuel supply may consist of gas service entrance and meter, propane tank and regulator, or kerosene tank. Kerosene may be

gravity-fed, or if the heater is above the level of the tank, a lift pump may be used. Heater unit dimensions are 16–38 in. wide, 9–16 in. deep, and 21–28 in. high (405–965 mm × 230–450 mm × 535–710 mm). Dual concentric vent pipes that provide both fresh air intake and combustion exhaust may be extended through exterior wall or roof, and range in size from 2 to 3 in. (50 to 75 mm) in outside diameter.

HEATING STOVES

Description

Heating stoves are small appliances that sit conspicuously within each room they heat. They burn wood, coal, gas, oil, or kerosene, and transmit heat to the room and its occupants by a combination of convection and radiation.

Typical Applications

Residential, industrial, and commercial buildings, especially in areas where firewood or coal is inexpensive and readily available. Wood- and coal-burning stoves are frequently used as supplementary sources of heat in centrally heated houses.

Advantages

Wood and coal are cheap fuels in many areas, and the experience of tending a stove and basking in its warmth can be aesthetically satisfying. Some stoves are visually attractive.

Disadvantages

Heating stoves use a surprisingly large amount of floor space and require chimneys. Most stoves are hot enough to burn the skin. They do not distribute heat evenly. Solid fuel stoves require constant tending and are difficult to control precisely. Solid fuel and ashes generate considerable dirt within the building. A stove becomes a fire hazard unless it and its chimney are conscientiously maintained and operated. Most solid-fuel stoves pollute the air through incomplete combustion.

Major Components

Chimney, stove and stovepipe, floor protection, wall protection, fuel storage, ash storage for solid-fuel stoves. Typical dimensions for these components are summarized in the table to the right. For dimensions of fuel storage components, see page 228.

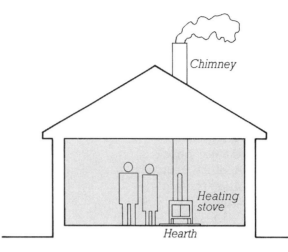

TYPICAL DIMENSIONS OF HEATING STOVES

Component	Width	Depth	Height
Ash storage	Covered metal bucket 14" (360 mm) in diameter		
Chimney, masonry			
One stove	20" (510 mm)	20" (510 mm)	a
Two stoves	20" (510 mm)	28" (710 mm)	a
Chimney, metal	10" (254-mm) diameter		
Fuel storage: see page 228			
Stove			
Gas-fired	38" (965 mm)	13" (330 mm)	40" (1015 mm)
Oil-fired	32" (815 mm)	30" (760 mm)	40" (1015 mm)
Wood-fired	Varies widely, up to the dimensions shown for gas-fired and oil-fired stoves		
Stovepipe, uninsulated, typical	7" (180 mm) diameter		
Stovepipe, insulated, typical	9" (230 mm) diameter		

Heating stoves typically require a clearance of 36" (914 mm) to combustible or plaster surfaces. They also require a noncombustible hearth that extends 12" (305 mm) to each side and to the back of the stove and 18" (460 mm) to the front. Some stoves are shielded to allow them to be as close as 12" to combustible surfaces to the back and sides. An uninsulated metal stovepipe may not come closer than 18" (460 mm) to the ceiling. Insulated pipes are usually designed for a 2" (51-mm) clearance to combustible materials.

---

[a]Under most codes, a chimney must extend at least 3' (900 mm) above the highest point where it passes through the roof and at least 2' (600 mm) above any roof surface within a horizontal distance of 10' (3 m).

PASSIVE SOLAR HEATING

Description

The interior space of the building acts as a solar collector, receiving sunlight directly through large south-facing windows and storing excess heat in concrete, masonry, or containers of water or phase-change salts. During sunless periods, as the room temperature drops below the temperature of the heat storage materials, the stored heat is released into the interior air.

Typical Applications

Dwellings, schools, offices, industrial buildings.

Advantages

Passive solar heating has zero fuel cost, does not pollute the air, requires little or no maintenance, and can be aesthetically satisfying.

Disadvantages

Construction cost is high for passive solar heating schemes, and a full backup heating system must be provided to heat the building during long sunless periods. Relatively large swings in interior temperature must be expected. Most passive solar systems require the occupants of the building to perform daily control duties such as opening and closing insulating shutters or curtains. The architecture of solar-heated buildings is strongly influenced by the need to orient and configure the building for optimum solar collection. Cooling and humidity control must be accomplished with separate systems.

Variations

1. In *direct gain passive solar heating,* sunlight enters south-facing windows and warms the interior directly. Roof overhangs or louvers are configured to block out high summer sun. Internal mass (masonry, concrete, large containers of water, or small containers of phase-

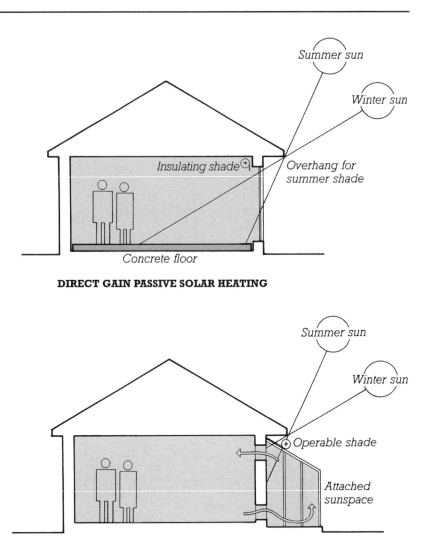

DIRECT GAIN PASSIVE SOLAR HEATING

ATTACHED SUNSPACE PASSIVE SOLAR HEATING

change salts) must be provided, preferably in direct sunlight, to absorb excess heat. Insulating closures are needed to cover the glass during sunless periods. This is a simple, enjoyable way of bringing heat into a building, one that puts the occupants into a very intimate relationship with the seasons and the weather. However, the direct sunlight causes visual glare, and it fades and deteriorates interior materials. Heat loss through the large glass areas during nights and cloudy days is considerable. Temperature control is often unsatisfactory.

2. In *attached sunspace passive solar heating,* an intermittently occupied greenhouse or glassy

atrium attached to the building collects solar heat by direct gain. Heated air is "borrowed" by the adjacent, fully inhabited spaces of the building by means of convection or small circulating fans. Undesirable glare and fading are largely or wholly confined to the sunspace. The sunspace can be closed off during sunless periods and allowed to grow cold. The extreme range of temperatures that occurs in the sunspace allows it to be inhabited only during limited periods and prevents plant growth unless additional temperature control mechanisms are provided.

3. *Fan-forced rock bed solar heating* is a hybrid of passive and active

PASSIVE SOLAR HEATING

systems. Sunlight is brought directly into the inhabited space of the building. When the interior air becomes heated above the comfort level, a thermostat actuates a fan that draws the overheated air through a large container of stones, where the excess heat is absorbed. During sunless periods, the fan is actuated again to warm the room air by passing it through the heated stones. Compared to direct gain solar heating, a fan-forced rock bed system gives better control of temperature and does not require the presence of massive materials within the inhabited spaces. The rock bed is large and expensive to construct. Glare and fading are problems unless the system is coupled with an attached sunspace.

4. *Trombe wall passive solar heating* features a massive wall made of masonry, concrete, or containers of water. This wall is located immediately inside the windows that receive sunlight. The interior of the building is warmed by the heat that is conducted through the Trombe wall, by allowing room air to convect between the wall and the glass, or both. Compared to direct gain solar heating, a Trombe wall system blocks most or all direct sunlight from the inhabited space, preventing glare and fading. The wall occupies considerable space, however, and obstructs desirable visual contact between the inhabitants and the sun. The room temperature is difficult to control. An insulating closure is needed to reduce heat losses through the glass during sunless periods.

Typical dimensions of passive solar components are summarized in the table to the right. A backup heating system must also be provided; the backup system may be selected from the other heating systems described in this section.

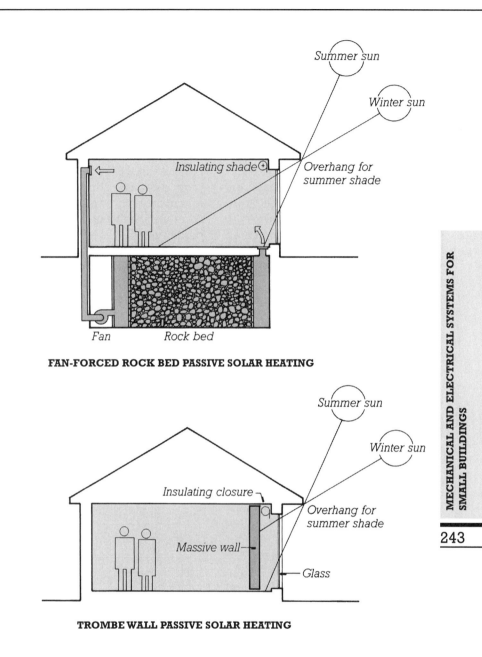

FAN-FORCED ROCK BED PASSIVE SOLAR HEATING

TROMBE WALL PASSIVE SOLAR HEATING

TYPICAL DIMENSIONS OF PASSIVE SOLAR HEATING COMPONENTS

Component

South-facing windows for passive solar heating for an average house should total at least 150 ft² (14 m²) in area.

If the floor is used for thermal storage, it should be made of masonry or concrete at least 4" (100 mm) thick.

An attached sunspace should have a minimum floor area of 10' × 12' (3 × 3.7 m). A rock bed should have a minimum volume of 600 ft³ (17 m³).

A Trombe wall is typically 12" (300 mm) thick and as tall as the adjacent windows. There is usually a space of a foot or two between the glass and the wall.

WATER SUPPLY

Water from a municipal main reaches the building via an underground service pipe and a water meter. In warm climates, the meter may be outside the building, but in cold climates, it must be installed in a heated space, usually the basement or the mechanical equipment room. In many areas a tiny electronic readout, connected by wires to the inside water meter, is mounted on the outside of the building so that the meter reader does not need to enter the building.

From the water meter, domestic cold water flows directly to the fixtures by means of small-diameter copper or plastic pipes. If the water is "hard" (contains a heavy concentration of calcium ions), a water softener may be installed to remove these ions from the water that goes to the domestic water heater. The water heater uses a gas flame, an oil flame, solar-heated liquid, or electric resistance heating to warm the water to a preset temperature at which it is held in an insulated tank for subsequent use. A tree of hot water piping parallels the cold water piping as it branches to the various fixtures in the building. Supply piping should be kept out of exterior walls of buildings in cold climates to prevent wintertime freezeups.

If water is obtained from a private well, it is lifted from the well and pressurized by a pump. If the well is deep, the pump is usually placed at the bottom of the well. If the well is shallow (less than 20 to 25 ft, or 6 to 8 m), the pump may be located inside the building. In either case, the pump pushes the water into a pressure tank, from which it flows on demand into the hot and cold water piping. The pressure tank may be located inside the well, or in the basement or mechanical equipment room of the building.

WASTE PIPING AND SEWAGE DISPOSAL

Sewage flows from each fixture through a trap into waste pipes that drain by gravity. To ensure that the traps do not siphon dry and to maintain constant atmospheric pressure in the waste piping, a vent pipe is attached to the waste system near each trap. The vent pipes rise through the building until they penetrate the roof, where they are left open to the air. The vent pipes may be gathered together into a single pipe in the attic of the building to minimize the number of roof penetrations. A horizontal run of vent can be used to move a plumbing vent to a less prominent rooftop location.

The waste piping descends through the building, gathering waste from all the fixtures, until it reaches the ground, the crawl space, or the basement. If it lies above the sewer or the private dis-

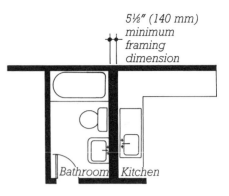

5½" (140 mm) minimum framing dimension

Bathroom   Kitchen

posal system at this point, it turns to an almost horizontal orientation, sloping toward its outlet (the sewer main or the septic tank) at a pitch of at least 1 in 100. If it lies below the elevation of its outlet at this point, an automatically operated underground ejector pump must be installed to lift the sewage and empty it into the outlet.

Waste and vent piping is larger in diameter than supply piping and requires careful planning to fit

TYPICAL DIMENSIONS OF PLUMBING COMPONENTS

Component	Width	Depth	Height
Gas meter and piping	18" (460 mm)	12" (305 mm)	24" (610 mm)

Sewage disposal, private

The size and configuration of private sewage disposal systems vary widely, depending on soil conditions, topography, local laws, and the required capacity of the system. As a starting point, allow an area of level or nearly level ground 40' × 80' (12 × 25 m), with its short side against the building. No part of this area may be closer than 100' (30 m) to a well, pond, lake, stream, or river.

Water heater			
Gas-fired	20" (510-mm) diameter		60" (1525 mm)
Electric	24" (610-mm) diameter		53" (1350 mm)
Water meter and piping	20" (510 mm)	24" (305 mm)	10" (255 mm)
Water pressure tank for a pump that is located in a well	20" (510-mm) diameter		64" (1625 mm)
Water pump and pressure tank for a shallow well	36" (915 mm)	20" (510 mm)	64" (1625 mm)
Water softener	18" (460-mm) diameter		42" (1070 mm)

244

PLUMBING SYSTEMS FOR SMALL BUILDINGS

gracefully and efficiently into a building. Bathrooms and toilet rooms should be stacked to avoid horizontal displacements of the waste and vent stacks. For maximum economy, fixtures should be aligned along thickened plumbing walls, and rooms containing fixtures should be clustered back-to-back around the plumbing walls. The major horizontal runs of waste piping should be located in a crawlspace, beneath a slab, or just inside the perimeter of a basement. Some typical wood framing details for plumbing walls are shown in the diagram to the right.

Private sewage disposal systems vary considerably in configuration and size, depending chiefly on soil conditions and local health regulations. The most common type includes a septic tank, usually 1000 to 1500 gal (4000 to 6000 l) in capacity, in which the sewage is digested by anaerobic action. Effluent from the septic tank flows by gravity to a disposal field of open-jointed pipe laid below ground in a bed of crushed stone. In nearly all areas of North America, private sewage disposal systems may be designed only by a registered sanitary engineer. The engineer's design is based on soil tests that in some municipalities may be performed only during those limited periods of the year when the soil is saturated, and a building permit will not be issued until a permit has been granted for the construction of the disposal system. This often delays the start of a construction project for many months.

Typical dimensions of plumbing components are summarized in the table on the facing page.

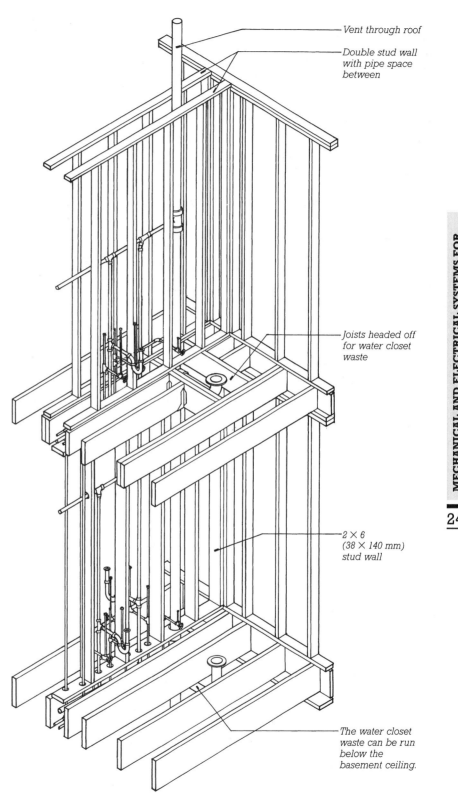

Vent through roof

Double stud wall with pipe space between

Joists headed off for water closet waste

2 × 6 (38 × 140 mm) stud wall

The water closet waste can be run below the basement ceiling.

FRAMING DETAILS FOR PLUMBING WALLS

PLUMBING SYSTEMS FOR SMALL BUILDINGS

GAS SERVICE

Natural gas is distributed to buildings through mains located beneath the street. Each building is served by an underground pipe that surfaces at a gas meter and pressure regulator next to or just inside the building. From this service entrance, the gas is piped through the building to the various appliances—furnaces, boilers, water heaters, clothes dryers, fireplaces, barbecues, kitchen ranges, and industrial equipment.

Where there are no gas mains, liquid propane gas can be delivered by tanker truck to pressurized tanks outside the building. The gas flows from the tanks through a pressure regulator and evaporator into the building's gas piping system.

Gas piping is small in diameter and is made up of threaded black iron pipe and fittings. It does not usually require special consideration in the design of the building, but space does need to be provided, usually at the basement ceiling or in the crawlspace or slab, for long horizontal runs of gas piping. For dimensions of gas meters in a small building, see the table on page 244. For dimensions of liquid propane storage tanks, see the table on page 228.

SPRINKLER SYSTEMS IN SMALL BUILDINGS

In most small buildings, sprinkler protection, when it is required, can be provided at a maximum rate of one sprinkler head per 144 sq ft (13.4 m^2) of floor area. The average coverage per sprinkler head will be somewhat less than this because of the problems of fitting sprinkler layouts to rooms of varying sizes and shapes. The horizontal piping to the sprinklers is small in diameter and must run below the roof insulation in cold climates, either above a suspended ceiling or just on top of the ceiling material and between the joists. Vertical risers must be installed on the warm side of the wall insulation or in interior partitions. A small assembly of valves and alarm fittings must be furnished at the point where the sprinkler system joins the domestic water system, and a Siamese fitting is required for many installations. If the available water supply is inadequate to feed the sprinkler system, a backup water supply has to be furnished in the form of a gravity tank, an air-pressurized tank, or a reservoir and pump, any of which is custom designed for the given situation.

ELECTRICAL AND COMMUNICATIONS WIRING FOR SMALL BUILDINGS

Electrical, telephone, and cable television services reach the building via either overhead or underground wires, depending on the practices of the local utilities. Overhead wires at the street may be converted to an underground service to the building by running the service wires down the face of the pole to the required depth and then laterally to the building.

An electric meter is mounted at eye level in an accessible location on the outside surface of the building. Wires from an overhead service arrive at the building high above the meter and descend to it in a large cable or a metal conduit mounted on the exterior wall surface. Wires from an underground service are brought up to the meter in a conduit. A cable or conduit from the meter enters the building at the basement or main floor level and connects to the main electric panel, which should be as close to the meter as possible.

From the main panel, wiring fans out to branch panels and individual circuits. Exposed wiring or wiring in masonry or concrete must be placed in metal or plastic conduits. In frame buildings, most wiring is done with flexible plastic-sheathed cable that is routed through the cavities of the frame. In a very small building, all the branch circuits connect directly to the main panel. In a larger building, especially one with multiple tenant spaces, most circuits connect to branch panels scattered at convenient points around the building. The branch panels, in turn, are connected by cables or conduits to the main panel.

Panel locations need to be worked out fairly early in the building design process. In small framed buildings, the designer seldom needs to be concerned about providing space for the wires and cables, unless the construction system features exposed framing members and decking. In this case, conduit routes for the wiring must be carefully planned to avoid visual chaos.

Wiring systems for telephone service, cable television, computer local area networks, centralized entertainment systems, security systems, fire alarms, intercoms, antennas, and so on generally have minimal impact on the planning of a small building in the early stages of design. At their simplest, such systems may not require any dedicated space, or may require only small, wall-mounted panels that can share space in general purpose closets, basements, or mechanical equipment rooms. As systems increase in complexity, dedicated wiring closets may be necessary. Such closets should be centrally located to best accommodate the star topology of most such systems and to minimize the length of individual cable runs. For example, a central stair may offer closet space at its lowest level as well as easy cable access up through the center of the building—at each floor or ceiling level cables can then branch out to reach their final destinations. Closets must be located so that cable lengths do not exceed their maximum limits for reliable performance. For example, with the most common type of local area network cabling, referred to as *unshielded twisted pair* or *Category 5 cabling*, individual cables should not exceed approximately 285 ft (85 m) in length. To avoid electrical interference from other systems, communications closets should be separated from electrical service entrance cables, service panels, lightning protection, and mechanical equipment by at least 6 ft (1.8 m).

Typical dimensions of components of electrical systems in small buildings are summarized in the table below.

TYPICAL DIMENSIONS OF COMPONENTS OF ELECTRICAL SYSTEMS

Component	Width	Depth	Height
Electric meter	12" (305 mm)	9" (230 mm)	15" (380 mm)
Main panel	14" (360 mm)	4" (100 mm)	27" (685 mm)
Branch panel	14" (360 mm)	4" (100 mm)	20" (685 mm)

SECTION

5

DESIGNING FOR EGRESS AND ACCESSIBILITY

■■■■■

1
CONFIGURING THE EGRESS SYSTEM AND PROVIDING ACCESSIBLE ROUTES

This chapter will assist you in laying out doors, corridors, stairways, exit discharges, and accessible routes for a preliminary building design in accordance with the egress requirements of the model building codes.

COMPONENTS OF THE EGRESS SYSTEM

The function of a building egress system is to conduct the occupants of the building to a safe place in case of a fire or other emergency. In most instances, that safe place is a public way or other large, open space at ground level. For the occupants of the upper floors of a tall building, or for people who are incapacitated or physically restrained, the safe place may be a fire-protected area of refuge within the building itself.

Although the model building codes differ in their approaches to sizing the components of an egress system, their requirements for the configuration of egress systems are similar and are summarized together in this section. (For the sizing of components of the egress system, see pages 283–287 for the International Building Code and pages 289–293 for the National Building Code of Canada.)

A building egress system has three components:

1. The *exit access* begins at any occupied point in the building and continues up to the portion of the egress system termed the exit. The exit access may include pathways within a room, aisles between fixed seating, hallways, corridors, ramps, open stairways, and other such spaces.

2. The *exit* is the protected portion of the egress system leading to the building exterior. Most commonly, it is an enclosed stairway that conducts occupants from multiple floors of a building to a door opening to the outside. It may also

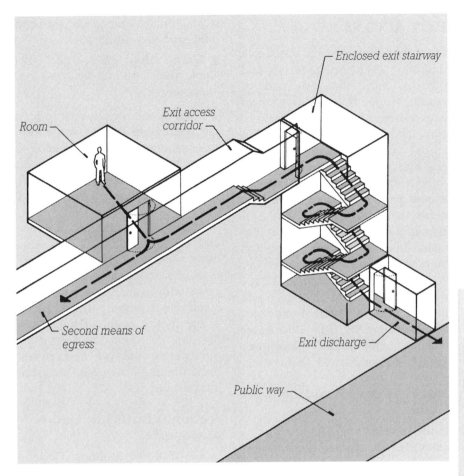

Room

Exit access corridor

Enclosed exit stairway

Second means of egress

Exit discharge

Public way

include enclosed passageways connecting exit stairs to exterior doors. Or from a ground floor room, the exit may consist solely of a door opening from that room directly to the outside.

3. The *exit discharge* is the exterior portion of the means of egress leading to the public way or other place of safety.

These three components of an egress system are discussed in greater detail on the pages that follow. Also included are simplified standards for the preliminary design of these components, condensed from the model building codes treated in this book.

The standards summarized here apply to new buildings. For existing buildings, certain of the standards are more permissive; consult the appropriate building code for details.

EXIT ACCESS PATHS

Every occupied room or space in a building must have at least one and possibly more than one path of egress, depending on its type of occupancy and the number of occupants within that space. In both model codes, whenever more than one exit access is required from a room or space, each individual exit access path may count toward no more than one-half of the total egress capacity required for that space. In other words, egress paths must be sized so that the loss of any single path will not reduce the remaining capacity of all other paths to less than one-half of the total required capacity. (For information on sizing components of the egress system, see pages 281–293.)

International Building Code

In the International Building Code, examples of spaces requiring at least two exit access ways leading to two independent exits include the following:

■ Group A, B, E, F, M, and U Occupancies with an occupant load exceeding 49

■ Group S Occupancies with an occupant load exceeding 29

■ Group R and I Occupancies with an occupant load exceeding 10

■ Day care occupancies with an occupant load exceeding 10

■ Mall tenant spaces with an occupant load exceeding 49

■ Group H-1, H-2, and H-3 Occupancies with an occupant load exceeding 3

Any space requires three ways out leading to three independent exits whenever its occupant load exceeds 500 and four ways out leading to four independent exits when its occupant load exceeds 1000.

Group I-2 Institutional Medical and Custodial Care Occupancies have special exit access requirements reflecting the needs of occupants who in many cases may be incapable of moving themselves to safety in the event of a building fire. See the code for details. For emergency escape and rescue requirements for residential occupancies, see page 277.

National Building Code of Canada

In the National Building Code of Canada, examples of spaces requiring two ways out include:

■ Spaces with an occupant load exceeding 60

■ Rooms with area exceeding limits ranging from 100 to 300 m^2 (1076 to 3229 sq ft), depending on the type of occupancy and the presence of a sprinkler system

■ Rooms with High-Hazard Occupancy exceeding 15 m^2 (2420 sq ft) in area

Because occupants in Care or Detention Occupancies may not have ready access to conventional exits, floor areas in these occupancies are required to be divided by fire separations into at least two separate areas, none larger in area than 1000 m^2 (93 sq ft).

Individual dwelling units within Residential Occupancies must have two means of egress, except where a single exit door leads directly to the exterior not more than 1.5 m (5 ft) above grade, the exit door is within one story of every floor level within the unit, and the uppermost floor of the unit opens to an exterior balcony that is not more than 6 m (20 ft) above grade.

EGRESS THROUGH ADJACENT SPACES

In their most conventional configuration, exit access pathways are expected to proceed from rooms to corridors and then to exits. The International Building Code in most circumstances also permits exit access pathways to flow through intermediate spaces to which the originating space is functionally related. However, once an exit access path reaches a corridor, it must proceed directly to an exit stair or other exit component and cannot reenter other spaces.

THE EXIT ACCESS

DISTANCE BETWEEN EXITS

Wherever access to more than one exit is required, these exits must be sufficiently remote from one another to minimize the possibility that a fire or other emergency condition could simultaneously render both exits unsafe or inaccessible.

In the International Building Code, where a room, space, or whole floor requires more than one way out, at least two of the ways out must be separated by a distance equal to not less than one-half the diagonal measure of the room, space, or floor. Where the building is sprinklered, the distance may be reduced to one-third the diagonal measure of the space. Normally, these distances are taken as straight-line measurements. However, when exits off a floor are interconnected by a 1-hour rated corridor, the distance between the two exits is measured along the path of travel in the corridor rather than in a straight line (see the diagram on this page).

In the National Building Code of Canada, the straight-line distance between exits off a floor normally cannot be less than one-half the diagonal measure of the floor and not less than 9 m (30 ft). Where the exits are interconnected by a corridor, the separation between them is measured along the path of travel of the corridor, rather than in a straight line, and need not exceed 9 m (30 ft). A minimum distance between exits need not be provided where the floor is divided by a fire separation into two major portions, each containing one of the exits.

MAXIMUM TRAVEL DISTANCE TO THE EXIT

Travel distance is the distance from any occupied point in a building to the nearest exit stairway or other exit component. Both model build-

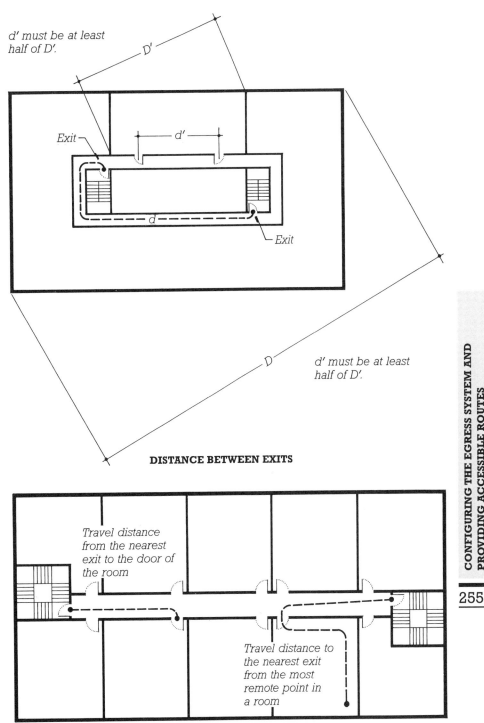

d′ must be at least half of D′.

Exit

d′

d

Exit

d′ must be at least half of D′.

DISTANCE BETWEEN EXITS

Travel distance from the nearest exit to the door of the room

Travel distance to the nearest exit from the most remote point in a room

TRAVEL DISTANCE

ing codes limit travel distance so that in the event of a building emergency, the amount of time that an occupant may be exposed to smoke from fire or another hazardous condition is limited before reaching the more fully protected exit portion of the egress system. Maximum permitted travel distances, limited according to Occupancy Group, are listed on page 284 for the International Building Code and page 290 for the National Building Code of Canada.

Travel distance is always measured along the actual path an occupant must take to reach the exit portion of the egress system. For example, where a room or space can reasonably be expected to be furnished with tables, desks, or arrayed seating, or where other obstacles may prevent a direct line of travel from some parts of the room to its way out, travel distance should be measured along paths that realistically reflect the expected conditions. Travel within exit stairways and other exit components is normally not included in travel distance calculations, except as noted below.

In the International Building Code, travel distance is always measured from the most remote point on a floor to the nearest enclosed exit. While travel within enclosed exits is not included in travel distance calculations, travel along open stairways or other unenclosed exit components is included. Furthermore, when open stairways are included in travel distance calculations, the path of travel along the stair is measured parallel to the plane of the stair, not in horizontal plan projection.

In the National Building Code of Canada, travel distance is also measured from the most remote occupied point to the nearest exit. However, travel distance from rooms or suites separated from the remainder of the floor, and opening onto a corridor or exterior passageway, may be measured from the door of the space opening onto the corridor or passageway, rather than from the most remote point within the space.

TRAVEL LIMITATIONS WITHIN THE EXIT ACCESS

The International Building Code restricts the maximum length of the *common path of egress travel* within the exit access portion of the egress system as well. This is the length of travel starting anywhere in the building and continuing to a point at which two independent means of egress become available to the building occupant. For example, in a room with just one doorway leading to a corridor, where the corridor provides egress in two separate directions, the length of the common path of egress travel would be the travel distance within the room to the doorway. (See the diagram on this page.) Common path of egress travel limitations for the International Building Code are summarized on page 284.

In the National Building Code of Canada, where a room or space is permitted only one means of egress, the travel distance from any point in the space to its egress doorway cannot exceed 25 m (82 ft) when sprinklered or the following when unsprinklered:

■ Group A Assembly, E Mercantile, F-3 Low-Hazard Industrial Occupancies, and Group C Residential Occupancy excluding individual dwelling units: 15 m (49 ft)

■ Group D Business and Personal Services Occupancy: 25 m (82 ft)

■ Group F-2 Medium Hazard Industrial Occupancy: 10 m (33 ft)

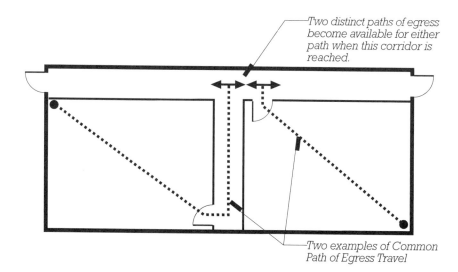

Two distinct paths of egress become available for either path when this corridor is reached.

Two examples of Common Path of Egress Travel

INTERNATIONAL BUILDING CODE COMMON PATH OF EGRESS TRAVEL

THE EXIT ACCESS

CORRIDORS

Corridors are dedicated exit access components that connect a floor's occupied spaces to its exits. In the event of the need to evacuate a building, corridors must provide safe, efficient passage to those exits: Corridors must be sufficiently wide to accommodate the number of occupants that may need to pass through them efficiently in the event of an emergency; corridors must lead to exits that are not so distant as to result in occupants' excessive exposure to smoke or other hazardous conditions that may occur during an emergency; corridors must be easy to navigate, without lengthy dead ends that could trap occupants who are unfamiliar with the building or who are disoriented by low-visibility conditions; depending on the type of occupancy, number of occupants, and presence of sprinklers, corridors may require rated wall and ceiling assemblies to provide occupants added protection from smoke and fire as they move toward exits.

International Building Code

In the International Building Code, enclosures for exit access corridors must be constructed with at least a 1-hour fire-resistance rating, except as follows:

■ For Group A, B, E, F M, S, and U Occupancies, unrated enclosures are permitted for corridors serving 30 or fewer occupants in unsprinklered buildings and for all corridors in sprinklered buildings.

■ For Group R Occupancies, unrated enclosures are permitted for any corridor serving 10 or few occupants, and ½-hour rated enclosures are permitted for corridors serving more than 10 occupants within sprinklered buildings.

■ Unrated corridor enclosures are permitted in all Group I-2 and I-4 occupancies, as well as in certain subdivided residential areas within Group I-3 Occupancies.

■ For Group H-4 and H-5 Occupancies, unrated corridor enclosures are permitted for any corridor with an occupant load of 30 or less.

■ Corridors in Group E Occupancies may be unrated where each classroom has at least one door opening directly to grade and each assembly space has at least 50% of its egress opening directly to grade.

■ Corridors within Group R Occupancy individual dwelling or sleeping units may be unrated.

■ Within Group B Occupancies with an occupant load of not more than 49, corridor enclosures may be unrated.

National Building Code of Canada

In the National Building Code of Canada, exit access corridors in buildings of 1- or 2-Hour Construction must be enclosed with 1-hour fire-resistance-rated walls and floor/ceiling assemblies. In buildings of ¾-Hour or Unprotected Construction, corridor enclosures may be ¾-hour rated. In other than Group B Care or Detention and Group C Residential Occupancies, corridor enclosures may be unrated when the floor is sprinklered throughout and the maximum travel distance on the floor to the nearest exit is no greater than 45 m (148 ft).

Corridor sizing information can be found on page 285 for the International Building Code and page 291 for the National Building Code of Canada.

EXTERIOR CORRIDORS

Exit access ways may include open balconies on the exterior of a building. Such balconies should be designed to prevent the accumulation of ice and snow in cold climates. In the International Building Code, a balcony leading to only one exit stair must be separated from interior spaces by rated walls and protected door and window openings with fire ratings equal to those required for corridors. Where balconies have two ways off, adjacent walls, windows, and doors are not required to be fire rated, provided that from any point on the balcony, a fire burning through any one door or window cannot simultaneously block an occupant's access to both ways off the balcony.

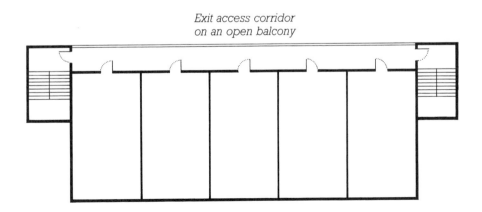

*Exit access corridor
on an open balcony*

DEAD-END CORRIDORS

Dead-end pockets in exit access corridors are undesirable, but they are tolerated for most building occupancies within the length restrictions listed for each model code on pages 285 and 291.

DOORS

The International Building Code requires all doors serving an occupant load of 50 or more, or serving any Group H Hazardous occupancy, to swing in the direction of egress travel. The National Building Code of Canada requires all doors serving exits, all doors serving Group F-1, High-Hazard Occupancies, and all exit access doors serving an occupant load greater than 60, to swing in the direction of egress travel.

Ideally, doors should be arranged so that their swing does not obstruct the required width of an aisle, corridor, stair landing, or stair. Building codes typically permit some obstruction, however: Up to one-half of the required width can be obstructed during the swing of the door, and when the door is fully open, it may project as much as 7 in. (178 mm) into the required width.

Even when locked, doors along an exit path must be easily openable in the direction of egress travel.

In the International Building Code, doors opening into corridors with rated enclosures must be themselves 20-minute fire-resist-

ance rated. In the National Building Code of Canada, doors opening into corridors with rated enclosures must be 45-minute rated. Where there is no corridor enclosure fire-resistance rating requirement, doors opening into the corridor may be unrated as well.

Information on sizing of egress doorways may be found on page 285 for the International Building Code and page 291 for the National Building Code of Canada.

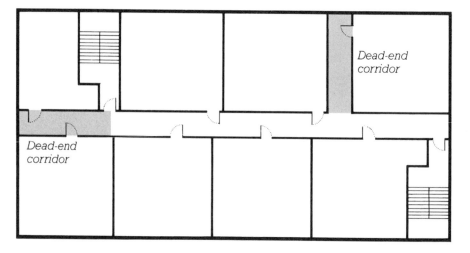

Dead-end corridor

Dead-end corridor

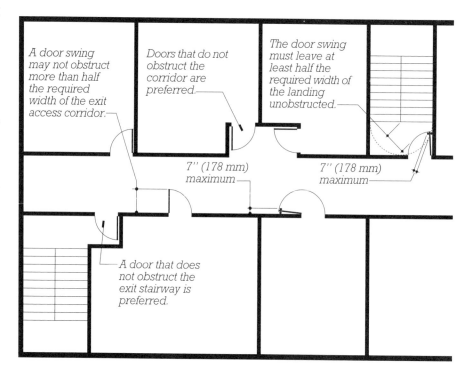

A door swing may not obstruct more than half the required width of the exit access corridor.

Doors that do not obstruct the corridor are preferred.

The door swing must leave at least half the required width of the landing unobstructed.

7" (178 mm) maximum

7" (178 mm) maximum

A door that does not obstruct the exit stairway is preferred.

OTHER EXIT ACCESS REQUIREMENTS

The model building codes also contain detailed provisions relating to illumination and emergency illumination of exit access facilities, marking of exit paths, combustibility of finish materials in exit access corridors, alarm systems, door hardware, and other safety concerns. Consult the appropriate building code for details.

THE EXIT

EXITS

The exit is that portion of the means of egress between the exit access and the exterior of the building. In general, exit components are required to provide a greater degree of protection from the heat and smoke of a building fire than that required of the exit access. In both model codes, each floor of a building usually must have at least two independent exits. Whenever more than one exit is required, each may only count toward up to one-half of the total egress capacity required. In other words, the capacity of each exit must be sized so that the loss of any single exit will not reduce the remaining capacity of all other exits to less than one-half of the total required. Exit requirements unique to each model building code follow below. For information on sizing components of the egress system, see pages 283–287 for the International Building Code and pages 289–293 for the National Building Code of Canada.

International Building Code

For most buildings, each floor with 500 or fewer occupants must have at least two independent exits. Floors with between 501 and 1000 occupants must have at least three such exits, and floors with more than 1000 occupants must have at least four. Certain buildings of limited size and occupancy may have only one exit per floor:

■ Single-story buildings of Occupancy Groups A, B, E, F, M, and U having not more than 49 occupants and a travel distance not exceeding 75 ft (23 m). In a Group B Occupancy building, fully sprinklered, the maximum travel distance may be increased to 100 ft (30 m).

■ Single-story buildings of Occupancy Groups H-2 and H-3 having not more than three occupants and a maximum travel distance of 25 ft (8 m).

■ Single-story buildings of Occupancy Groups H-4, H-5, I, and R, or any day care occupancy, having not more than 10 occupants and a maximum travel distance of 75 ft (23 m).

■ Single-story buildings of Occupancy Group S having not more than 29 occupants and a maximum travel distance of 75 ft (23 m).

■ One- or two-story buildings of Occupancy Groups B, F, M, and S with not more than 30 occupants and a travel distance of 75 ft (23 m).

■ One- or two-story buildings of Occupancy R-2 with not more than four dwelling units per floor and a maximum travel distance of 50 ft (15 m). When fully sprinklered, such buildings may be up to four stories in height.

■ All Occupancy Group R-3 buildings.

National Building Code of Canada

Most buildings must have at least two independent exits per floor. Floors of one- or two-story buildings may have one exit if they have not more than 60 occupants and do not exceed the floor area and travel distance limits in the table below. In the case of Group B Care or Detention or Group C Residential Occupancies (other than dwelling units), such exits must open directly to the exterior, without enclosed stairways, not more than 1.5 m (5 ft) above the adjacent ground level.

NATIONAL BUILDING CODE OF CANADA

Single-Exit Occupancies	Unsprinklered		Sprinklered	
	Maximum Floor Area	Maximum Travel Distance	Maximum Floor Area	Maximum Travel Distance
A: Assembly	150 m^2 (1615 ft^2)	15 m (49 ft)	200 m^2 (2150 ft^2)	25 m (82 ft)
B: Care or Detention	75 m^2 (805 ft^2)	10 m (33 ft)	100 m^2 (1075 ft^2)	25 m (82 ft)
C: Residential	100 m^2 (1075 ft^2)	15 m (49 ft)	150 m^2 (1615 ft^2)	25 m (82 ft)
D: Business and Personal Services	200 m^2 (2150 ft^2)	25 m (82 ft)	300 m^2 (3330 ft^2)	25 m (82 ft)
E: Mercantile	150 m2 (1615 ft^2)	15 m (49 ft)	200 m^2 (2150 ft^2)	25 m (82 ft)
F-2: Industrial	150 m^2 (1615 ft^2)	10 m (33 ft)	200 m^2 (2150 ft^2)	25 m (82 ft)
F-3: Industrial	200 m^2 (2150 ft^2)	15 m (49 ft)	300 m^2 (3330 ft^2)	25 m (82 ft)
Interstitial Floor Service Spaces	200 m^2 (2150 ft^2)	25 m (82 ft)	200 m^2 (2150 ft^2)	25 m (82 ft)
Rooftop Enclosures	200 m^2 (2150 ft^2)	Not applicable	200 m^2 (2150 ft^2)	Not applicable
Occupied Rooftop Areas	2 exits required if occupant load is greater than 60			

THE EXIT

DIRECT EXIT

The simplest exit is a door opening directly from an interior room or space to the exterior, as it might from an exhibition hall, theater, gymnasium, or classroom. Exit doors of this type do not need to have a fire-resistance rating.

EXIT STAIRWAYS

The International Building Code requires stairways serving four stories or more to be enclosed within 2-hour fire-resistance rated construction and 1½-hour self-closing doors opening into the stairway. Enclosures of stairways serving fewer than four floors may be of 1-hour rated construction, with 1-hour self-closing doors. Exit enclosure doors opening to the exterior are not required to be rated. Exit enclosures are not required for:

■ Stairways within dwelling units

■ Stairways not part of the required means of egress

■ Exit stairways in open parking garage structures or open arenas

■ In other than Occupancy Groups H and I, exit stairways serving only one adjacent floor and providing not more than 50% of a floor's required egress capacity, or exit stairways (providing up to 100% of the required exit capacity) serving only the first and second floors of a building, where the building is fully sprinklered, there are at least two exits from both floors, and these floors are not open to any other floors in the building

The National Building Code of Canada requires the construction of an exit enclosure to match the construction of the floor above that on which the enclosure is located (or below, if there is no floor above), but to be not more than a 2-hour and not less than a ¾-hour enclosure. Doors opening into the stairway must be self-closing, and in 2-hour enclosures must be 1½-hour rated; in

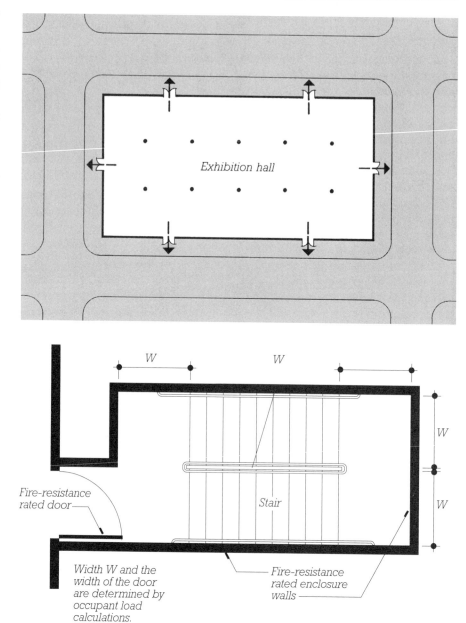

Exhibition hall

W   W   W   W

Fire-resistance rated door

Width W and the width of the door are determined by occupant load calculations.

Stair

Fire-resistance rated enclosure walls

1½-hour enclosures, 1-hour rated; and in 1-hour or ¾-hour enclosures, ¾-hour rated.

The International Building Code requires doors in exit enclosures serving an occupant load of 50 or more to swing in the direction of egress travel. The National Building Code of Canada requires all doors in exit enclosures to swing in the direction of egress travel.

Stairway and landing widths are determined in accordance with the occupant load they serve. See pages 283–287 for the International

Building Code and pages 289–293 for the National Building Code of Canada. Dimensions and typical designs for stairways and stair enclosures are provided on pages 299–309.

In general, escalators and elevators may not serve as required exits. However, both the International Building Code and the National Building Code of Canada permit elevators in a smokeproof shaft to serve as a means of egress for disabled persons. For more information, see Accessible Means of Egress on pages 267–268.

THE EXIT

SMOKEPROOF ENCLOSURES

The model building codes require exit stair enclosures in tall buildings to be designed as smokeproof enclosures to provide a higher level of protection to occupants exiting the building during a fire emergency. In the International Building Code, these requirements generally apply to buildings with occupied floors over 75 ft (23 m) above the lowest level of fire department access, as well as to buildings with significant underground occupancy. The National Building Code of Canada has similar requirements, most commonly applicable to buildings with occupied floors more than 18 to 36 m (59 to 188 ft) above grade, depending on the type of occupancy. For more detailed descriptions of the specific building types to which these requirements apply, see Highrise and Underground Buildings, page 277, for the International Building Code, and High Buildings, page 278 for the National Building Code of Canada.

Specific design requirements for smokeproof enclosures are detailed, and vary with the particular code and building circumstances. The adjacent diagrams summarize the most common requirements. See the applicable code for more information.

There are two ways to make a smokeproof enclosure, as illustrated in the diagrams: natural ventilation and mechanical ventilation. In fully sprinklered buildings, a smokeproof enclosure may also be created by means of mechanical pressurization without the need for the vestibule that is shown in the bottom drawing. A mechanical ventilating system must be backed up with a standby power supply so that it will continue operating if the main source of power is interrupted during a fire.

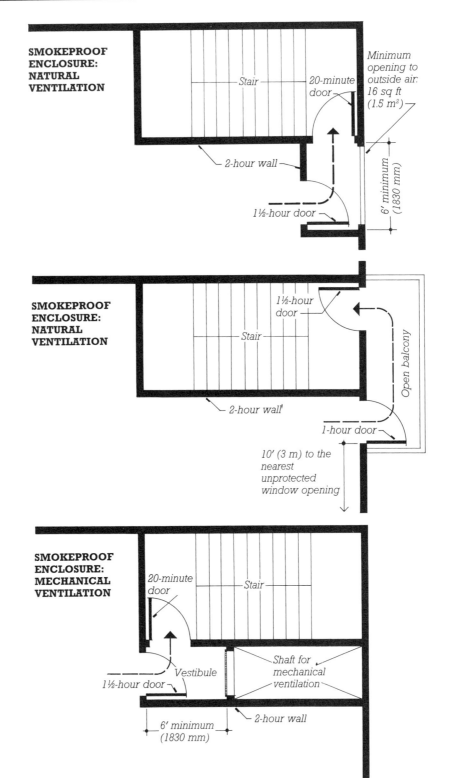

THE EXIT

A stairway in a smokeproof enclosure must discharge directly into a public way, an outdoor space having direct access to a public way, or an enclosed exit passageway with no other openings. It may not discharge through a vestibule or lobby at the exit discharge level.

OUTSIDE STAIRWAYS AND FIRE ESCAPES

Outside stairways may be used as exits. An outside stairway must be constructed with solid treads (as distinct from the open metal gratings used for treads of outside fire escapes). It must be built to the same fire-resistive requirements as an interior stair, including separation from the interior of the building by walls and openings with fire-resistance ratings as specified for interior stairs. Outside stairways must be protected against the accumulation of standing water, and must be roofed in snowy climates to prevent accumulation of snow.

A traditional metal fire escape is not permitted as an exit except as a second exit on existing buildings where it is impractical to construct a stair to current standards. Escape slides, rope ladders, escalators, and elevators cannot be counted as required exits. Fixed ladders are permitted as required exits only in certain situations in mechanical rooms and industrial occupancies where a very limited number of able-bodied workers are served by the ladder, and then the ladder may serve only as a second means of egress from the space.

THE EXIT

HORIZONTAL EXITS

A horizontal exit is passage through a fire-resistant wall to an area of refuge on the same level in the same building or in an adjacent building. A horizontal exit may be designed to function for travel in one direction only, as in the case of a building that has one exit stairway and a horizontal exit to an adjoining building that has two or more exit stairways. In this case, the corridors and lobbies of the adjoining building serve as the area of refuge. A horizontal exit may also be designed to function for travel in both directions, as shown on the drawing to the right. Here the corridor on the left side of the building serves as an area of refuge for the occupants of the right side of the building, and vice versa.

The wall of a horizontal exit must have a fire-resistance rating ranging from 2 to 4 hours, depending on the occupancies involved. For preliminary purposes, a 2-hour rated wall, with 1½ hour rated doors, may be assumed. Penetrations in the wall for pipes or conduits must be tightly sealed, and exit doors must be self-closing and tight-fitting to prevent the passage of smoke.

The doors should swing in the direction of exit. If the area on each side of the wall serves reciprocally as an area of refuge for the area on the other side, the doors should be furnished in oppositely swinging pairs so that at least one door will swing in the direction of exit travel for a person approaching from either side. In sizing the doors for occupant load, only doors swinging in the direction of egress may be counted.

Horizontal exits are advantageous in tall buildings, because they allow a person to escape the danger of a fire much more quickly than a stairway to the ground. They

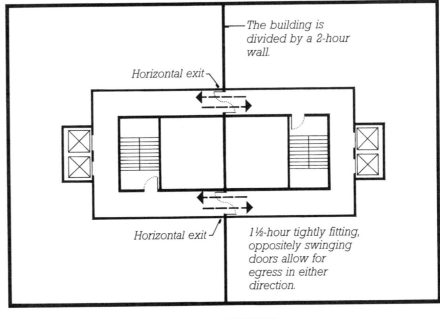

The building is divided by a 2-hour wall.

Horizontal exit

Horizontal exit

1½-hour tightly fitting, oppositely swinging doors allow for egress in either direction.

HORIZONTAL EXITS

are also useful in hospitals, because they allow patients to be moved to safety while still in their beds. In general, horizontal exits may provide up to half of the required exit capacity of a story or a building. Each area of refuge on either side of a horizontal exit must be large enough to accommodate all the occupants from both sides of the exit. Each area of refuge must also meet all exit requirements and have sufficient exit capacity for its original occupants, but need not be designed with exit capacity for added occupants.

In the International Building Code, areas of refuge may consist of corridors, lobbies, and other publicly accessible areas. They also may include private areas when these areas are controlled by the same tenant that controls the space from which occupants are exiting. However, spaces controlled by separate tenants may not be used as horizontal exit areas of refuge. In this model code, the area of refuge occupant capacity is cal-

culated for most occupancies at the rate of 3 sq ft (0.28 m^2) per person. In Group I-3 Institutional, Restrained Care occupancies, 6 sq ft (0.56 m^2) per person is required. In Group I-2 Institutional, Medical Care occupancies, 15 sq ft (1.4 m^2) per ambulatory occupant is required, and 30 sq ft (2.8 m^2) per nonambulatory occupant. The International Building Code allows horizontal exits in Institutional, Medical Care Group I-2 occupancies to provide up to two-thirds of the required exit capacity of a floor or a building, and in Institutional, Restrained Group I-3 occupancies to provide up to 100% of the required exit capacity. In addition, at least one of the exits from the area of refuge must lead directly to the exterior or into an exit enclosure.

The National Building Code of Canada requires area of refuge occupant capacity to be calculated at the rate of 0.5 m^2 (5.4 sq ft) per person, with the exception of 1.5 m^2 (16 sq ft) per wheelchair occupant and 2.5 m^2 (27 sq ft) per bedridden occupant.

EXIT PASSAGEWAYS

An exit passageway is a horizontal means of exit travel that is protected from fire in the same manner as an enclosed exit stair. An exit passageway has several uses: It may be used to preserve the continuity of enclosure for an exit stair whose location shifts laterally as it descends through the building. It may be used to eliminate excessive travel distance to an exit. And it may be used as part of an exit discharge to connect an enclosed stair to an exterior door.

The widths of passages, doors, landings, and stairs used as exits must be determined in accordance with values given by the model codes, as shown on pages 283–287 and 289–293. For detailed design requirements concerning illumination, emergency illumination, marking, finish materials, and hardware of exits, consult the appropriate building code.

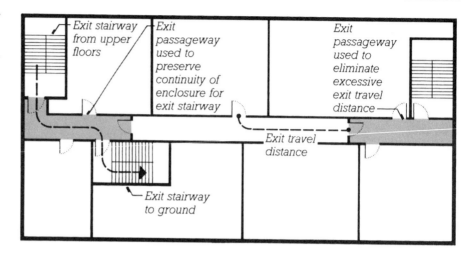

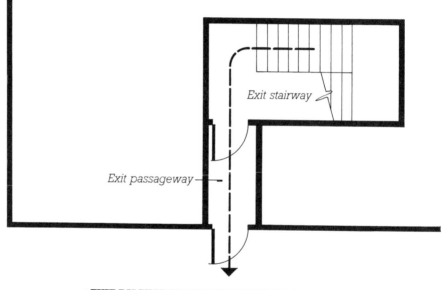

EXIT DISCHARGE THROUGH AN EXIT PASSAGEWAY

THE EXIT DISCHARGE

The exit discharge is the portion of means of egress between the exit and a public way. It may include various exterior elements such as pathways, balconies, stairways, ramps, and courts. In the International Building Code, where access to a public way cannot be provided, the exit discharge may alternatively lead to a dispersal area on the same property located at least 50 ft (15 m) from the building and providing at least 5 sq ft (0.28 m^2) of space per person.

Lobbies and Vestibules

Both model codes permit exits to discharge through lobby areas when certain conditions are met. The International Building Code permits up to 50% of the required egress capacity to discharge through a lobby, provided that the pathway through the lobby is readily visible and identifiable from the point of discharge from the exit, that the entire story at the lobby level is sprinklered, and that the fire-resistance rating of the floor construction at the lobby level is at least equal to that required for an exit enclosure. The National Building Code of Canada permits no more than one exit through a lobby, provided that the path of travel through it does not exceed 15 m (49 ft), that the lobby does not directly serve abutting residential or industrial occupancies, and that the lobby and all areas not separated from it are sprinklered.

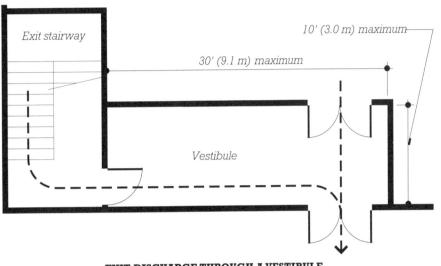

EXIT DISCHARGE THROUGH A VESTIBULE

The International Building Code also permits exits with up to 50% of the required egress capacity to discharge through an enclosed vestibule, whose maximum dimensions are shown to the right. The vestibule must serve only as a means of egress, it must be separated from other spaces by at least the equivalent of a ¾-hour rated partition, and the fire-resistance rating of the vestibule floor construction must be at least equal to that required for an exit enclosure.

Revolving Doors

Revolving doors are also permitted as exit discharge components, provided they are constructed so as to allow free passage in a panic situation by collapsing under pressure into a book-fold position. The International Building Code limits revolving doors to a capacity of 50 persons per door and, in total, to no more than half the required exit capacity of a building. There must be a swinging door in the same wall and within 10 ft (3 m) of the revolving door, and revolving doors may not be located within 10 ft (3 m) of the foot or top of a stair or escalator. The National Building code of Canada limits the exit capacity of each revolving door to 45 persons and permits revolving doors to serve as egress for ground-floor occupants only. Swinging doors must be located adjacent to revolving doors, and revolving doors must not be located at the foot of a stairway.

ACCESSIBLE ROUTES

The goal of accessibility legislation in the both the United States and Canada is to provide people with physical disabilities full access to nearly all types of buildings, including, for example, government buildings, schools, houses of worship, retail establishments, places of business, public and private transportation facilities, bars, restaurants, hotels, housing, places of entertainment and culture, recreational facilities, and places of work. Buildings and their surroundings must provide continuous, unobstructed routes by which physically disabled persons can park their vehicles or disembark from public transportation, approach the building, enter, reach virtually any point in the building, and gain access to the same amenities and activities available to others, such as retail counters, ticket windows, drinking fountains, toilet and washroom fixtures, public telephones, and spectator seating. This section summarizes accessibility requirements of the two model building codes as they affect the form and organization of buildings. It does not address all technical requirements or occupant circumstances addressed by these codes, or the requirements of other accessibility regulations such as those enacted at provincial, state, or national levels. Be sure to consult the building code and other regulations applicable to your project as your building design progresses.

THE INTERNATIONAL BUILDING CODE

In the International Building Code, most buildings and spaces are required to be made accessible for persons with physical disabilities. Exceptions include the following:

■ Detached one- and two-family dwellings

■ Most Occupancy Group U Utility and Miscellaneous buildings

■ Occupancy Group R-1 Residential hotel and motel buildings when owner-occupied and containing not more than five sleeping units

■ Certain common-use portions of detention and correctional facilities

■ Single-occupant structures accessed primarily by underground tunnels or overhead walkways such as tool booths

■ Equipment spaces, services spaces, and nonoccupiable limited access spaces

In addition, accessibility requirements for employee work areas are generally limited to common use circulation paths such that persons with disabilities can enter and exit the work area. See the code for details.

Where a building is required to be accessible, its main entrance and not less than 60% of all its public entrances must be accessible, accessible routes must lead to each portion of the building, and at least one entrance to each accessible tenant space must be accessible. If only one accessible route is provided within a building, it may not pass through kitchens, storage rooms, restrooms, or other such ancillary spaces. However, in dwelling units, a single accessible route may pass through a kitchen or storage room. In multilevel buildings, an accessible route must connect each level, including mezzanines, except:

■ Floors above and below accessible levels, not more than 3000 sq ft (280 m2) in area, unless such floors contain offices of health care providers, passenger transportation facilities, or Occupancy Group M Mercantile tenant spaces

■ Levels in Occupancy Group A Assembly, I Institutional, R Residential, and S Storage occupancies containing no areas themselves required to be accessible

■ In two-story buildings, a single story with an occupant load of five or less and not containing public spaces

Key dimensional criteria in the design of accessible routes include the following:

■ Corridors, passages, and doorways without doors must be at least 36-in. (915-mm) wide. Projections not more than 24 in. (610 mm) in length may reduce passage width to not less than 32 in. (815 mm).

266

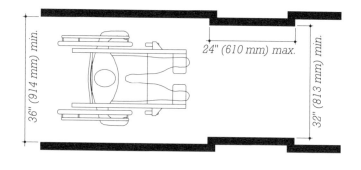

36" (914 mm) min.   *24" (610 mm) max.*   *32" (813 mm) min.*

INTERNATIONAL BUILDING CODE ACCESSIBLE CORRIDOR

■ Walking surfaces, except for ramps, may not be sloped greater than 1:20.

■ Doorway openings must have a minimum 32-in. (815-mm) clear width.

■ Latchside clearance for manually operated doors varies from 12 in. (305 mm) to 42 in. (1065 mm), depending on the manner in which the door is approached. When approaching straight toward a door opening toward the approach side, 18 in. (445 mm) is required.

■ The minimum diameter of a wheelchair turning circle is 60 in. (1525 mm).

■ Ramps may not slope greater than 1:12, must have a minimum clear width of 36 in. (915 mm) between handrails, and may not rise more than 30 in. (760 mm) between landings. Landings must be not less than 60 in. (1525 mm) in length.

Elevator car minimum clear inside dimensions vary with the size and position of the elevator car door:

■ With a 36-in. (915-mm) clear door opening, in any location: 60 in. (1525 mm) wide by 60 in. (1525 mm) deep, or 54 in. (1370 mm) wide by 80 in. (2030 mm) deep

■ With a 36-in. (915-mm) clear door opening, offset to one side: 68 in. (1725 mm) wide by 51 in. (1295 mm) deep

■ With a 42-in. (1065-mm) clear door opening, centered: 80 in. (2030 mm) wide by 51 in. (1295 mm) deep

Though not strictly speaking a requirement for accessible access, where one or more elevators are provided in a building with floors four or more stories above or below grade-level access, the International Building Code also requires that at least one elevator serving all stories be large enough

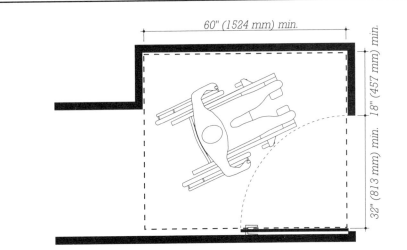

INTERNATIONAL BUILDING CODE EXAMPLE OF ACCESSIBLE DOORWAY AND APPROACH

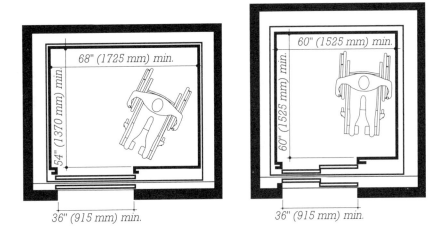

INTERNATIONAL BUILDING CODE AND NATIONAL BUILDING CODE OF CANADA EXAMPLE OF ACCESSIBLE ELEVATORS

to accommodate a medical stretcher 24 in. (610 mm) wide and 84 in. (2134 mm) long and its attendants. The code does not specify minimum car dimensions that satisfy this requirement. For preliminary design purposes, the following may be considered one example of acceptable minimum size:

■ With 42 in. (1065 mm) clear door opening, offset to one side: 80 in. (2032 mm) deep by 54 in. (1372 mm) wide

Accessible Means of Egress

Wherever spaces are required to be accessible, at least one accessible means of egress must also be provided. Where two or more means of egress are required from any space or floor, there must be at least two accessible means of egress. Such accessible means of egress may include level accessible routes, accessible ramps, horizontal exits, areas of refuge, and appropriately designed stairways or elevators. In buildings with accessible floors four or more stories above or below a level of exit discharge, at least one accessible means of egress must consist of an elevator with a secure power supply in a smokeproof shaft. Alternatively, in a fully sprinklered building,

ACCESSIBLE ROUTES

floors above the level of exit discharge may be served by horizontal exits instead of an elevator. (See page 263 for more information about horizontal exits.) In certain limited circumstances, platform lifts are also permitted to form part of an accessible means of egress.

Where elevators are used to provide an accessible means of egress, they must themselves be accessed from either an area of refuge (see below) or a horizontal exit. However, this requirement does not apply to parking garages. Most buildings with accessible floors also rely on enclosed or unenclosed stairways as part of the required egress for disabled occupants. Such stairs must meet the following requirements:

Where the building is not sprinklered, the stairway must be at least 48 in. (1219 mm) in clear dimension between the handrails, meaning that the overall width of the stair must be approximately 56 in. (1400 mm). Except in unenclosed stairways serving fully sprinklered buildings, an area of refuge must be provided within or adjacent to the stairway on each accessible level of the building, or the stairway must be accessed from a horizontal exit. (Areas of refuge are not required for parking garage exit stairways.)

An *area of refuge* is a place where people who are unable to use stairs may safely await assistance during an emergency evacuation. The area of refuge must have direct access to the stairway. It must be clearly identified with visual and tactile signage within the enclosure, protected from smoke and fire, provided with instructions for use, and provided with two-way electronic communications with the primary entry point of the building. A wheelchair space 30 × 48 in. (760 × 1220 mm) must be provided for each 200 occupants or portion thereof on each floor, with a mini-

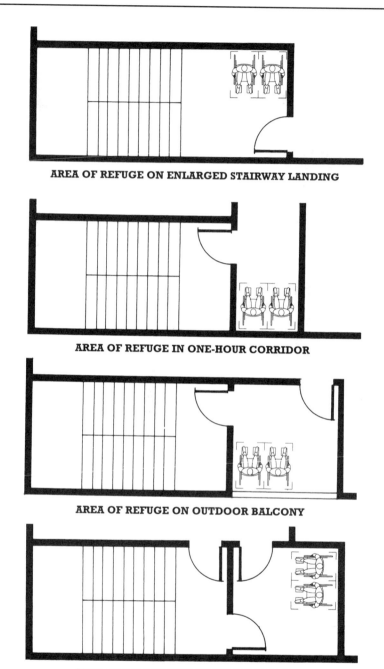

AREA OF REFUGE ON ENLARGED STAIRWAY LANDING

AREA OF REFUGE IN ONE-HOUR CORRIDOR

AREA OF REFUGE ON OUTDOOR BALCONY

AREA OF REFUGE IN STAIRWAY VESTIBULE

mum provision of two such spaces for each area of refuge.

There are many ways to create an area of refuge. It may be a landing in a smokeproof enclosure. It may be on an outdoor balcony leading to a stairway in a smokeproof enclosure. It may be adjacent to a stairway in a corridor enclosed with 1-hour fire resistive walls or in a vestibule with the same degree of

fire protection. It may be in an elevator lobby if the lobby and the adjacent shafts are pressurized as smokeproof enclosures. And an area of refuge may be created by a horizontal exit, as explained on page 263. In each of these cases, the wheelchair spaces may not encroach on the required width of the egress path.

ACCESSIBLE ROUTES

Accessible Dwelling and Sleeping Units

In the International Building Code, accessibility requirements for sleeping and dwelling units apply to some extent to most residential occupancies, including:

- Hotels and motels
- Apartment buildings and condominiums
- Nursing homes and assisted living facilities
- Boarding houses, and residential hotels and motels
- Hospices and homeless shelters
- Corporate housing, dormitories, and migrant worker housing
- Seasonal vacation units and timeshare units
- Residential structures comprised of four or more dwelling or sleeping units

Where accessibility requirements apply, dwelling or sleeping units may be required to achieve one of three levels of accessibility. *Accessible units* are the most fully accessible. For example, these units must meet all clear space and maneuverability requirements for wheelchair navigation and provide fully accessible fixtures and equipment. *Type A* units must meet the same wheelchair clear space and maneuverability requirements as Accessible units. But other elements, such as special height work surfaces and toilet room grab bars, are not required in this unit type as long as provision is made for their installation at a later date. *Type B* units provide the lowest level of accessibility. Wheelchair maneuverability requirements are less stringent, and some parts of units (for example, sunken living rooms or mezzanine-level bedrooms) need not be accessible.

Accessible Units. For Accessible unit requirements, see the table on this page. For Occupancy

Occupancy	Minimum Number of Accessible Units
Group I-1 supervised residential facilities	4%, but never less than 1
Group I-2 nursing homes	50%, but never less than 1
Group I-2 hospitals and rehabilitation facilities	10%, but never less than 1
Group I-2 hospitals and rehabilitation facilities when specializing in the treatment of patients with impaired mobility	100%
Group I-3 detention and security facilities	2%, but never less than 1
Group R-1 hotels and motels, and Group R-2 boarding houses, dormitories, fraternity houses, sorority houses, and any other facilities constructed with federal government funding	
With from 1 to 25 units total	1
With from 26 to 50 units total	2
With from 51 to 75 units total	4
With from 76 to 100 units total	5
With from 101 to 150 units total	7
With from 151 to 200 units total	8
With more than 200 units total	Approximately 3%; see the code for exact numbers
Group R-2 apartment houses and condominiums constructed without federal goverment funding, monasteries, and convents	None (see Type A unit requirements in the text)
Group R-3 one- and two-family residences, and townhouses	None
Group R-4 assisted living facilities	1

Group R-1, requirements should be based on the total number of sleeping or dwelling units on a site, even when these units are contained in multiple detached buildings.

Type A Units. Group R-2 Residential buildings not required to provide Accessible units are subject to Type A unit requirements. This includes apartment houses constructed without federal government funding, monasteries, and convents. When they contain more than 20 dwelling or sleeping units, at least 2% but never less than 1 unit in these building types must be Type A.

Type B Units. In the following occupancy type buildings, where

one building or multiple attached buildings contain four or more dwelling or sleeping units combined, all such units that are not Accessible or Type A must meet the requirements of at least Type B units: Groups I-1, I-2, R-2, R-3, and R-4. This requirement also applies to Group R-1 hotels and motels to the extent that units in these buildings are occupied as permanent or semipermanent residences rather than as transitory accommodations. For example, where rooms in a hotel or motel are conventionally let out to overnight or short-term guests, Type B unit requirements do not apply. However, where such units may be used for extended-stay housing or as seasonal vacation units, they are considered occupied as residences, and compliance with Type B unit requirements is required. Any sleeping accommodation occupied continuously for more than 30 days should be considered occupied as a residence. In addition, accommodations occupied for shorter periods may at times fall into this category when the nature of the occupancy, terms of payment, amenities provided, and other such factors are considered.

Where residential buildings do not have elevator service to all floors, or where site impracticality limits accessibility, reductions in the number of required Type A or B units may be permitted. See the code for details.

Additional Accessibility Information

Other aspects of design for the physically disabled are addressed elsewhere in this book: For accessible wheelchair space requirements in assembly seating areas, see page 276, for accessibility requirements for toilet and bathing facilities, see pages 202–204, and for accessible parking requirements, see pages 318–319.

BARRIER-FREE DESIGN IN THE NATIONAL BUILDING CODE OF CANADA

The National Building Code of Canada requires all buildings to be barrier-free except:

■ Single-family residences, including detached and semidetached houses, triplexes, townhouses, row houses, and boarding houses

■ Buildings with Group F-1 High-Hazard Industrial as their principal occupancy

■ Buildings not intended to be occupied daily or full-time, such as

automatic telephone exchanges, pump houses, and electrical substations

In some cases, barrier-free access may not be required in all parts of Group F-2 or F-3 Industrial Occupancies where such areas contain greater than normal risks to occupants due to the storage of hazardous materials or the nature of hazardous processes that take place.

Where a building is required to be barrier-free, its principal entrance, and not less than one-half of all its pedestrian entrances, must be barrier-free. Where barrier-free access is required, barrier-free paths of travel must be provided throughout entrance stories and other normally occupied floor areas served by passenger elevators or other accessible means. Where escalators provide public access to multiple levels, alternative barrier-free means of access must be provided. Barrier-free paths of travel to the following locations are not required:

■ Building service areas, crawlspaces, attics, rooftops

■ Floor levels not served by a passenger elevator, passenger-elevating device, escalator, or moving walk

■ Mezzanines not served by passenger elevators or other accessible means

■ Portions of fixed-seating floor areas within assembly occupancies not part of the path of travel to designated wheelchair spaces

■ Portions of residential occupancy suites not at the entrance level

■ Portions of floor areas not at the same level as the entrance level, provided that similar accessible amenities are provided at the entrance level

Key dimensional criteria in the design of barrier-free routes include the following:

■ Corridors, passages, and doorways without doors must be at least 920 mm (36¼ in.) wide. Barrier-free paths longer than 30 m (98 ft) must provide a passing/turning space not less than 1500 mm (59 in.) square at intervals not exceeding 30 m (98 ft).

■ Walking surfaces, except for ramps, may not be sloped greater than 1:20.

■ Doorway openings must have a minimum 800-mm (31½-in.) clear width.

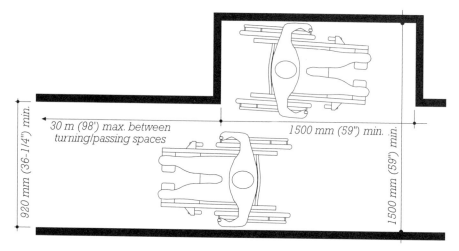

NATIONAL BUILDING CODE OF CANADA BARRIER-FREE CORRIDOR

920 mm (36-1/4") min.

30 m (98') max. between turning/passing spaces

1500 mm (59") min.

1500 mm (59") min.

ACCESSIBLE ROUTES

■ Latchside clearance for manually operated doors is 600 mm (24 in.) for doors swinging toward the approach side and 300 mm (12 in.) for doors swinging away from the approach side.

■ The minimum diameter of a wheelchair turning circle is 1500 mm (59 in.).

■ Ramps may not slope greater than 1:12, and must have a minimum clear width of 870 mm (34¼ in.) between handrails and a maximum horizontal distance of 9 m (29 ft 6in.) between landings. Landings must be not less than 1500 mm (59 in.) square.

Elevator car minimum clear inside dimensions are identical to the requirements of the International Building Code and are repeated here for convenience. Minimum size requirements vary with the size and position of the elevator car door (see illustrations page 267):

■ With a 915-mm (36-in.) clear door opening in any location: 1525 mm (60 in.) deep by 1525 mm (60 in.) wide or 2030 mm (80 in.) deep by 1370 mm (54 in.) wide

■ With a 915-mm (36-in.) clear door opening, offset to one side: 1295 mm (51 in.) deep by 1725 mm (68 in.) wide

■ With a 1065-mm (42-in.) clear door opening, centered: 1295 mm (51 in.) deep by 2030 mm (80 in.) wide

Though not strictly speaking a requirement for barrier-free access, where one or more elevators are provided in a building, the National Building Code of Canada also requires that at least one elevator serving all stories be large

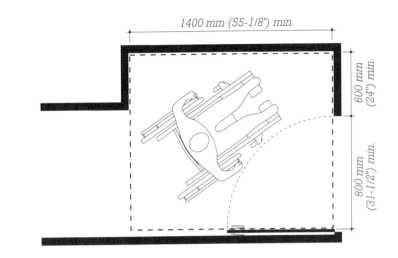

1400 mm (55-1/8") min.

600 mm (24") min.

800 mm (31-1/2") min.

NATIONAL BUILDING CODE OF CANADA EXAMPLE OF BARRIER-FREE DOORWAY AND APPROACH

enough to accommodate a medical stretcher 610 mm (24 in.) wide and 2010 mm (79 in.) long and its attendants. The code does not specify minimum car dimensions that satisfy this requirement, but does provide the following examples of recommended minimum sizes:

■ With a 1067-mm (42-in.) clear door opening, offset to one side: 2032 mm (80 in.) wide by 1295 mm (51 in.) deep

■ With a 915-mm (36-in.) clear door opening in any location: 1295 mm (51 in.) wide by 2032 mm (80 in.) deep

Barrier-Free Egress

In the National Building Code of Canada, every accessible floor above or below the ground entrance level that is not sprinklered throughout must include provisions for the temporary refuge of disabled occupants. This may be provided by elevator service meeting the requirements for firefighter use. Elevator entrances must be protected by vestibules on

each floor separating the entrances from surrounding floor areas. If the building is four or more stories in height, the elevator must be provided with smoke protection as well. Alternatively, such floors may be divided into at least two separate areas by fire separation walls, providing protected areas for the disabled while awaiting rescue assistance. Exits leading to grade, or to ramps that themselves lead to grade, are also acceptable. In residential occupancies, exterior balconies may also be used to provide the required refuge areas.

Additional Information on Barrier-Free Design

Other aspects of barrier-free design are addressed elsewhere in this book: For wheelchair space requirements in assembly seating areas, see page 276, for accessibility requirements for toilet and bathing facilities, see pages 202–204, and for accessible parking requirements, see pages 318–319.

EGRESS FROM AUDITORIUMS, CONCERT HALLS, AND THEATERS

Assembly rooms, with their intense concentration of occupants, require special egress provisions. Two traditional fixed seating arrangements are possible: In *conventional seating*, the length of seating rows is more limited, and a network of broad aisles is laid out to conduct the audience to a relatively small number of exits. In *continental seating*, longer rows of seating are permitted. Rows must be spaced farther apart, and more exit doors must be provided. See the illustrations on this page diagramming these two approaches. The International Building Code and the National Building Code of Canada permit both approaches to assembly seating although in a single, consolidated set of egress requirements applicable to both. Specific requirements for the two model codes are tabulated on the following pages.

INTERNATIONAL BUILDING CODE ASSEMBLY EGRESS REQUIREMENTS

For Assembly Occupancies serving more than 300 occupants, the International Building Code requires that the main exit of the building provide capacity for at least half of the total building occupant load. Each individual level having an occupant load greater than 300 must provide access both to the main exit, and to alternative exits with an aggregate capacity equal to at least one-half the required exit capacity for that level. For buildings without a main exit, or with multiple main exits, exits should be distributed around the building. See the code for additional requirements.

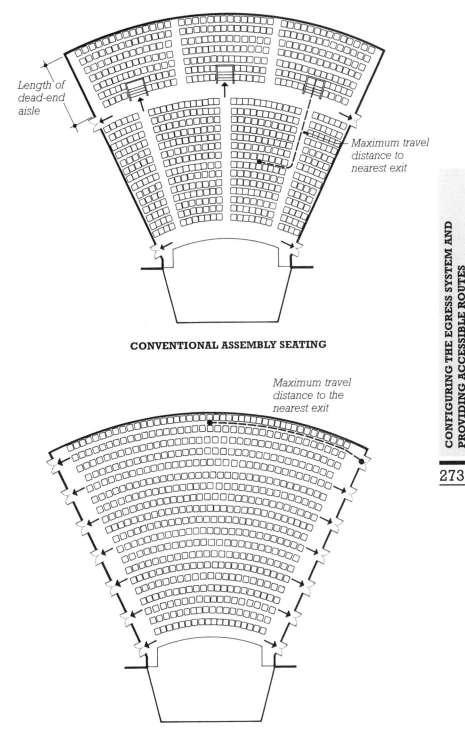

CONVENTIONAL ASSEMBLY SEATING

Length of dead-end aisle

Maximum travel distance to nearest exit

Maximum travel distance to the nearest exit

CONTINENTAL ASSEMBLY SEATING

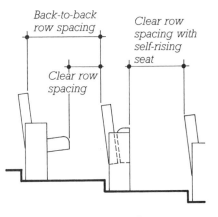

Back-to-back row spacing

Clear row spacing with self-rising seat

Clear row spacing

ROW SPACING

	Seating	Aisles
International Building Code	For a row with egress at both ends: Maximum row length: 100 seats Minimum clear row spacing: 12" (305 mm) plus 0.3" (7.6 mm) for every seat above 14 For a row with egress at one end only: Maximum length: 20 ft (6 m) Minimum clear row spacing: 12" (305 mm) plus 0.6" (15.3 mm) for every seat above 7 In all cases, clear row spacing need never exceed 22" (559 mm).	Aisle width: Minimum: 30" (762 mm) for aisles serving not more then 14 seats; 36" (914 mm) for aisles serving seating on one side, or not more than 50 seats on two sides; 42" (1067 mm) for aisles serving more than 50 seats on two sides For occupant load: Not less than 0.2" (5.1 mm) per person for aisles sloped not more than 1:12, or 0.22" (5.6 mm) per person for aisles with greater slopes Aisles providing egress at only one end may vary in width; aisles with egress at both ends must be uniform in width. Longest dead end aisle: 20' (6 m), unless seats served by a dead-end aisle are within no more than 24 seats of another aisle and minimum clear row spacing is as required for rows with egress on one end only Cross-aisle width: Same as for aisles, sized for combined capacity of converging aisles Maximum slope of aisle: 1:8
	With special smoke control provisions, the International Building Code permits reductions in seating row width, aisle width, and travel distance requirements, particularly for spaces with larger occupant loads. Consult the code for details.	
National Building Code of Canada	Continental seating: Maximum row length: 100 seats, with exit doorways provided at the end of each row, each doorway serving not more than three rows Minimum clear row spacing: 400 mm (15.8") Conventional seating: Maximum row length: 7 seats with backs, or 20 seats without backs between any seat and an aisle Minimum clear row spacing: 400 mm	Aisle width: Minimum: For continental seating, 1100 mm (43.3"); for conventional seating, 1100 mm (43.3") for seating on both sides, 900 mm (35.4") for seating on one side, 750 mm (29.5") for any aisle serving not more than 60 seats For occupant load: Add to the minimum 25 mm (1") for each meter (39.4") of length from the most remote point in the aisle. Aisles providing egress at only one end may vary in width; aisles with egress at both ends must be uniform in width. Longest dead end aisle: 6 m (19'-8") Cross-aisle width: Equal to the width of the widest aisle served, plus 50% of width of remaining aisles served Maximum slope of aisle: 1:8

EGRESS REQUIREMENTS FOR ASSEMBLY SEATING

Aisle Stairs And Handrails

Minimum tread depth: 11" (279 mm)

Maximum riser height: 8" (203 mm); up to 9" (229 mm) permitted where necessitated by slope of adjacent seating

Minimum riser height: 4" (102 mm)

Stair width:

Minimum: 36" (914 mm) for stairs serving seating on one side or not more than 50 seats on two sides, or 48" (1219 mm) for stairs serving more than 50 seats on two sides.

For occupant load: Not less 0.3" (7.6 mm) per person for stairs with risers not greater than 7" (178 mm); add an additional 0.005" (0.13 mm) per person for each additional 0.1" (2.5 mm) of riser height; where egress requires stair descent and no handrail is within 30" (762 mm) to either side, add an additional 0.005" (0.13 mm) per person

Handrails:

Required: All stairs; ramped aisles serving seats on not more than one side and sloped more than 1:15 (ramped aisles not sloped more than 1:8 serving seats on two sides do not require handrails)

Handrails subdividing stairs or aisles serving seats on both sides may be discontinuous to allow aisle access; the minimum space between the handrail and adjacent seating is 23" (574 mm).

Travel Distance Limits
For an explanation of these distance limits, see pages 255–266.

Maximum travel distance to an exit:

Unsprinklered: 200' (61 m)

Sprinklered: 250' (76 m)

In open air seating: 400' (122 m) to the exterior, or unlimited in Type I or II Construction

Common path of egress travel:

Areas serving not more than 50 occupants: 75' (23 m)

Other areas: 30' (9 m)

Minimum tread depth: 230 mm (9.1")

Maximum riser height: 200 mm (7.9")

Minimum riser height: 110 mm (4.3")

Stair width: See page 291.

Handrails: No special requirements

Maximum travel distance to an exit:

Unsprinklered and sprinklered: 45 m (148')

WHEELCHAIR SEATING CAPACITY

In Assembly spaces, accommodations for a minimum amount of wheelchair seating must be provided according to the adjacent table. Additionally, the International Building Code requires that wheelchair spaces within luxury suites or boxes be allocated within individual suites, and across all suites, according to the same rates. For example, a luxury box with 4 seats requires at least one wheelchair space, a box with 40 seats requires two such spaces, and 10 boxes of 3 seats each (30 seats total) require at least two wheelchair spaces among them.

Code	Total Capacity	Wheelchair Places
International Building Code	4–25	1
	26–50	2
	51–100	3
	101–300	5
	301–500	6
	501–5000	6, plus 1 additional for each 150 seats or portion thereof
	5001 and over	36, plus 1 additional for each 200 seats or portion thereof
National Building Code of Canada	2–100	2
	101–200	3
	201–300	4
	301–400	5
	401–500	6
	501–900	7
	901–1300	8
	1301–1700	9
	1701 and over	9, plus 1 additional for each 400 seats or portion thereof

SIZE AND ARRANGEMENT OF WHEELCHAIR SEATING PLACES

The International Building Code requires wheelchair spaces to be at least 36 in. (914 mm) wide for single-chair spaces and at least 33 in. (838 mm) wide each for multiple adjacent spaces. At least one fixed seat for a companion must be provided beside each required wheelchair space. Wheelchair spaces must be an integral part of the space seating plan. They must be separated into not less than the number of distinct locations indicated in the table on this page, and these locations must be dispersed to provide a variety of viewing angles and distances, and offer access to multiple seating levels and varying amenities.

The National Building Code of Canada requires wheelchair spaces to be at least 900 mm (35.4 in.) wide, and if entered from the front or rear, at least 1220 mm (48 in.) deep, or if entered from the side, at least 1525 mm (60 in.) deep. Wheelchair spaces should be arranged so that at least two such spaces are located side by side; they should not infringe on any other egress path or width requirements, and they should be distributed so as to provide a choice of viewing location and a clear view of the event taking place.

Code	Total Capacity	Minimum Number of Separate Wheelchair Locations
International Building Code	Up to 150	1
	151–500	2
	501–1000	3
	1001–5000	3, plus 1 additional for each 1000 seats or portion thereof over 1001
	5001 and over	7, plus 1 additional for each 2000 or portion thereof over 5001

MISCELLANEOUS EGRESS REQUIREMENTS

INTERNATIONAL BUILDING CODE

Emergency Exterior Door or Window Egress

In Occupancies R and I-1, basements and each sleeping room below the fourth story must have an exterior door or window for emergency escape and rescue. Escape windows must have a sill height of not more than 44 in. (1118 mm), minimum clear opening dimensions of 24 in. (610 mm) high by 20 in. (508 mm) wide, and a minimum clear opening area of at least 5.7 sq ft (0.53 m²). Emergency escape windows or doors are not required for:

■ Fully sprinklered buildings other than Group R-3 Occupancies

■ Occupancy R-3 bedrooms, where the door from the bedroom opens to a fire-rated corridor with access to two remote exits in opposite directions

■ Basements with a ceiling height of less than 80 in. (2030 mm), or with no habitable space and less than 200 sq ft (18.6m²) in area.

■ Buildings over 75 ft (23 m) tall conforming to the code requirements for high-rise buildings

Emergency escape windows and doors may also open onto interior atrium balconies, provided that the balcony leads to an exit and that the dwelling unit has a second independent means of egress that does not pass through the atrium.

High-Rise and Underground Buildings

Buildings with occupied floors more than 75 ft (23 m) above grade must have exits designed as smokeproof enclosures. This requirement does not apply to open parking garages, airport traffic control towers, outdoor sports arenas, and some unusually tall, low- and medium-hazard industrial buildings. See page 261 for more information about the design of such systems. For additional construction type requirements for high-rise buildings, see page 361.

Smokeproof stair enclosures are also required for buildings with occupied floors more than 30 ft (9 m) below grade, as is a smoke control system for the entire underground portion of the structure. Buildings with floors more than 60 ft (18 m) below grade must have each floor, up to the highest level of exit discharge, divided into at least two compartments with a 1-hour separation between. Where elevators are provided, each compartment must have direct access to an elevator. Or, where one elevator serves multiple compartments, a lobby with a 1-hour separation from each compartment must be provided. These requirements do not apply to fully sprinklered enclosed garages below grade, below-grade portions of stadiums, arenas, and similar facilities, underground fixed-guideway transit systems, below-grade one- and two-family dwellings in fully sprinklered buildings, and buildings in which only the lowest story is more than 30 ft (9 m) below grade and that story is no more than 1500 sq ft (139 m²) in area, with an occupant load of less than 10.

See the code for additional special requirements for high-rise and underground buildings.

NATIONAL BUILDING CODE OF CANADA

Emergency Bedroom Door or Window Egress

In buildings three stories or less in height and not greater than 900 m² (9700 sq ft) in area, dwelling units and other residential suites that are not sprinklered must have a window or door that opens directly to the exterior. Such doors and windows must be operable from the inside without the need of keys, special tools, or special knowledge. Windows must not require the removal of sashes or hardware. The unobstructed area of such openings must not be less than 0.35 m² (3.8 sq ft), with a least dimension of 380 mm (15 in.) in either height or width.

Firefighter Access

On unsprinklered floors less than 25 m (82 ft) above grade, firefighter access must be provided by at least one unobstructed window or access panel, minimum dimensions 1100 mm (43 in.) high by 550 mm (22 in.) wide with a sill height not greater than 900 mm (35 in.), for each 15 m (49 ft) of wall required to face the street. Access panels above the first floor must allow operation from both the inside and outside, or must be glazed with plain glass. Unsprinklered basements greater than 25 m (82 ft) in either horizontal dimension must provide firefighter access in the form of an exit stair connected directly to the outdoors, or a window or access panel as described

above. In buildings more than three stories in height with a roof slope less than 1:4, rooftop access must be provided from the floor immediately below either by a stairway or by a fixed ladder and roof hatch.

High Buildings

The National Building Code of Canada defines high buildings as any of the following:

- Buildings containing Occupancy Groups A Assembly, D Business and Personal Services, E Mercantile, or F Industrial, with a story greater than 36 m (118 ft) above grade

- Buildings containing Occupancy Groups A Assembly, D Business and Personal Services, E Mercantile, or F Industrial, with a story greater than 18 m (59 ft) above grade where the total occupant load on any story above the first story, divided by 1.8, exceeds 300 times the width in meters of all exit stairs serving that story

- Buildings with Group B Care or Detention Occupancy on a story greater than 18 m (59 ft) above grade

- Buildings with Group B-2, Care or Detention Occupancy, with occupants having cognitive or physical limitations, on the fourth or higher story

- Buildings with Group C Residential Occupancy on a story greater than 18 m (59 ft) above grade

In high buildings, at least one elevator must be provided for firefighter access. This elevator must be located within 15 m (49 ft) of firefighter access to the building,

have a usable platform area of not less than 2.2 m² (24 sq ft), and be protected by an unoccupied ¾-hour vestibule or an unoccupied 1-hour corridor enclosure at each floor. Elevator access must be provided to all floors above grade, by a single elevator, or with not more than one change of elevators.

Special smoke control systems are also required in high buildings to prevent the spread of smoke between floors, within exit stair enclosures, and between connected buildings, summarized as follows:

- Exit stairway shafts serving floors above and below the lowest level of exit discharge must either be entirely separate, or must have internal separations between the stair portions serving floors above and below this level. Additionally, stairway enclosures must be provided with smoke control systems designed to maintain these enclosures free of smoke. For information on smokeproof exit stair enclosures, see page 261.

- Elevator shafts serving floors above and below the lowest level of exit discharge must similarly be either entirely separate or, at each floor below the lowest level of exit discharge, a vestibule must separate the elevator from surrounding corridors and spaces.

- Connected buildings must be separated by fire walls. Where openings are provided, they must be protected with vestibule separations with either naturally vented openings or mechanical pressurization to control the passage of smoke.

2
SIZING
THE
EGRESS
SYSTEM

This chapter presents simplified data for use in sizing egress components under the model building codes.

HOW TO SIZE THE EGRESS SYSTEM

The various parts of a building's egress system must be sized to accommodate the number of occupants and types of activities within the building so that in the event of an emergency, occupants can safely and efficiently exit the building or move to protected locations. The information you need to complete the design of your building's egress system can be found in the tables and charts beginning on page 283 for the International Building Code and page 289 for the National Building Code of Canada. The following text explains how to apply this information to your project.

DETERMINING OCCUPANT LOADS

Begin with the Occupant Loads table on either page 283 or 289, depending on your model code, to determine the number of occupants the various parts of your egress system must serve. For each distinct activity within your building, find the most closely matching use listed in the table, and then read the floor area per occupant for that use. Divide the area in your building available for this activity by this figure to determine the number of occupants, or occupant load, for that area. The following additional information should be taken into consideration when determining occupant loads:

In both model codes, the occupant load for any space is determined by the larger of two calculations: either the number of persons dictated by the code-prescribed occupant densities (as explained in the previous paragraph) or the actual number of persons for whom the space is intended. For example, consider an open office space 3000 sq ft in area with workstations planned for 35 workers. According to the International Building Code (page 283), the prescribed occupant density for a business use is 100 sq ft per person, and the minimum occupant load for this space is therefore 30. However, since the workstations within the space have been designed to accommodate 35 persons, this second, larger number should be used for determining the capacity of the egress from this area.

Spaces are not always designed for a single purpose. Where a space is intended for more than one activity, the greatest occupant load determined for any of the activities should be used as the basis for sizing the egress system. Where a space designed for one activity could possibly be changed to some other use in the future, one that generates a higher occupant load, it may be appropriate to design the current egress system for such a future use, since enlarging egress system components at a later date is unlikely to be easily accomplished.

Within any floor of a building, occupant loads are cumulative. For example, in a room with a single doorway leading to a corridor, the doorway must be sized to accommodate the number of occupants in that room. However, where one room discharges into a second room that then opens to a corridor, the door opening to the corridor must be sized to accommodate the combined occupant load of both rooms. Likewise, corridors must be sized to accommodate the number of occupants from all spaces that discharge through them. And doorways into exit stairways and the stairways themselves must each be sized to accommodate their apportioned share of all the occupants of a floor.

Occupant loads from multiple floors are normally not cumulative. Thus, within an exit stairway, the width of the stairway and its discharge to the exterior are sized for the number of occupants from the single largest floor served, but not for the total number of all occupants on all floors served by the stair. However, where egress paths from floors above and below converge at an intermediate level within a stairway, stairway width from that point on must be based on the sum of the converging occupant loads. Mezzanine occupants are also normally treated as a converging occupant load. Where a mezzanine discharges through the floor below, egress components serving that floor are sized for the combined occupant load of the floor and the mezzanine. In the National Building Code of Canada, where occupant loads converge from mezzanines or theater balconies, a space providing temporary holding capacity for occupants can in some cases be used as an alternative to providing sufficient exit capacity for converging occupant loads; see the code for details.

EGRESS SYSTEM CRITERIA ACCORDING TO OCCUPANCY GROUP

The next step is to refer to the Egress System Criteria table on either page 284 or 290. For each building Occupancy Group classification, information such as maximum travel distance, minimum width of corridors and stairs, permitted length of dead-end corridors, and other criteria can be found. (If you have not already done so, turn to pages 7–15 to determine the Occupancy Groups for your building.) If your building is single-occupancy, the requirements for that Occupancy Group apply throughout. If your building is mixed occupancy, the requirements for each Occupancy Group should be applied to the portion of the building in which that Occupancy Group resides. Where criteria in this table vary with the number of occupants served, use the occupant loads you calculated in the previous step to determine the appropriate requirements.

HOW TO SIZE THE EGRESS SYSTEM

CALCULATING EGRESS SYSTEM CAPACITY

As the final step, calculations are performed to check the width of each door, corridor, ramp, and stairway in the egress system to ensure that these components have sufficient capacity for the number of occupants they must serve. Minimum widths based on occupant load are determined using the Egress Component Widths table (page 286 or 293). For example, in the International Building Code, the minimum clear width for a doorway providing egress for 250 occupants in a sprinklered business use area would be calculated as follows:

250 person × 0.15" per person = 37.5", rounded up to 38 in.

Taking into account the geometry of an opened door and its frame, not less than a nominal 40-in. wide doorway should be provided. Similar calculations should be performed for each component in the egress system. As a shortcut to performing these calculations, the Egress Width Calculator chart, on page 287 or 292, can be used to determine these numbers graphically.

Note that the widths calculated in this step should be applied to egress components only when they exceed the minimums listed in the Egress System Criteria table. For example, consider again a doorway serving a business use area in a sprinklered building, this time serving an occupant load of 60. According to the Egress Component Widths table, 0.15 in. of width is required per occupant, or in this case, not less than 9 in. total (60 × 0.15 in. = 9.0 in.). However, since the Egress System Criteria table lists a minimum doorway width of 32 in., this larger figure should be used. More detailed examples of calculating required widths of egress components using either model code are included on page 286 or 292.

In determining the widths of egress components, the following should also be considered: Means of egress capacity may not diminish in the direction of egress travel. For example, an exit stairway providing egress for 50 occupants may not lead to an exit passageway with a capacity of only 40 occupants. Likewise, a stairway providing an egress capacity of 50 persons exiting from the fourth floor of a building must maintain at least that capacity all the way to the ground-level exit discharge, even if lower floors require a capacity of only 40 persons each.

Where a space or floor requires more than one independent means of egress, the required egress capacity may be distributed among the various egress ways provided. However, individual means of egress must be sized such that the elimination of any single one will not render the remaining capacity less than 50% of the total required. In other words, where a space or floor requires two or more means of egress, no one can be counted toward more than half of the total required capacity. For example, consider an assembly hall with an occupant load of 600 persons, and three means of egress, where the main entrance provides a capacity of 400 persons and the two remaining exits provide a capacity of 100 persons each. Even though a total egress capacity of 600 has been provided, elimination of the main entrance would leave a remaining capacity of only 200 persons. Since 200 is less than half of 600, this is not a permitted arrangement. One solution to this problem would be to increase the size of just one of the smaller exits to a capacity of 200 persons. In this way, the elimination of any single exit still preserves an egress capacity of 300 or more.

INTERNATIONAL BUILDING CODE

OCCUPANT LOADS

Use	Floor Area per Occupant
Accessory storage area	300 ft² (28 m²) gross
Agricultural buildings	300 ft² (28 m²) gross
Aircraft hangers	500 ft² (46 m²) gross
Airport terminal baggage claim	20 ft² (1.86 m²) gross
Airport terminal baggage handling	300 ft² (28 m²) gross
Airport terminal concourses	100 ft² (9.3 m²) gross
Airport terminal waiting areas	15 ft² (1.4 m²) gross
Assembly occupancy, gaming floors	11 ft² (1.0 m²) gross
Assembly occupancy, concentrated seating (chairs only, not fixed)	7 ft² (0.65 m²) net
Assembly occupancy, standing space	5 ft² (0.46 m²) net
Assembly occupancy, unconcentrated seating (tables, chairs, stages, platforms)	15 ft² (1.4 m²) net. For booth seating without dividing arms, use 18" (457-mm) width per occupant.
Bowling centers	7 ft² (0.65 m²) net, plus 5 occupants per lane
Business areas	100 ft² (9.3 m²) gross
Courtrooms, other than fixed seating	40 ft² (3.7 m²) net
Day care areas	35 ft² (3.3 m²) net
Educational occupancy, classroom areas	20 ft² (1.86 m²) net
Educational occupancy, shops and vocational areas	50 ft² (4.65 m²) net
Exercise areas	50 ft² (4.65 m²) gross
Factories, industrial areas	100 ft² (9.3 m²) gross
Hazardous Occupancies: Groups H-1, H-2, H-3, H-4	100 ft² (9.3 m²) gross
Hazardous Occupancies: Groups H-5 fabrication and manufacturing areas	200 ft² (18.6 m²) gross
Institutional occupancy, sleeping areas	120 ft² (11.2 m²) gross
Institutional occupancy, inpatient treatment areas	240 ft² (22.3 m²) gross
Institutional occupancy, outpatient treatment areas	100 ft² (9.3 m²) gross
Kitchens, commercial	200 ft² (18.6 m²) gross
Libraries, reading rooms	50 ft² (4.65 m²) net
Libraries, stack areas	100 ft² (9.3 m²) gross
Locker rooms	50 ft² (4.65 m²) gross
Mechanical equipment rooms	300 ft² (28 m²) gross
Mercantile occupancy, areas other than listed below	60 ft² (5.6 m²) gross
Mercantile occupancy, basement and grade floor levels	30 ft² (2.8 m²) gross
Mercantile occupancy, enclosed shopping malls	Consult the code
Mercantile occupancy, storage, stock, and shipping areas	300 ft² (28 m²) gross
Parking garages	200 ft² (19 m²) gross
Residential occupancy, dormitories	50 ft² (4.65 m²) gross
Residential occupancy, general	200 ft2 (19 m2) gross
Skating rinks and swimming pools, rink and pool area	50 ft² (4.65 m²) gross
Skating rinks and swimming pools, decks	15 ft² (1.4 m²) gross
Storage	300 ft² (28 m²) gross
Warehouses	500 ft² (46 m²) gross

EGRESS SYSTEM CRITERIA

Occupancy Group (see pages 7–12)	Maximum Travel Distance (see page 255)		Maximum Common Path of Egress Travel (see page 256)	Largest Room or Area That May Have Only One Means of Egress (see page 254)
	Unsprinklered	Sprinklered		
A: Assembly	200' (61 m) 400' (122 m) for open-air seating of combustible construction or unlimited distance of noncombustible construction	250' (76 m)	30' (9 m) for assembly seating more than 50 occupants 75' (23 m) for others	49 occupants
B: Business	200' (61 m)	300' (91 m)	75' (23 m) unsprinklered 100' (30 m) sprinklered or for unsprinklered tenant spaces with occupant load of 30 or less	49 occupants
E: Educational	200' (61 m)	250' (76 m)	75' (23 m)	49 occupants
F-1: Factory, Moderate Hazard	200' (61 m)	200' (76 m) 400' (122 m) for single-story buildings with automatic heat and smoke ventilation systems	75' (23 m)	49 occupants
F-2: Factory, Low Hazard	300' (91 m)	400' (122 m)	75' (23 m) unsprinklered 100' (30 m) sprinklered	49 occupants
H-1, H-2, H-3: Hazardous	Not Permitted	H-1: 75' (23 m) H-2: 100' (30 m) H-3: 150' (46 m)	25' (8 m)	3 occupants
H-4, H-5: Hazardous	Not Permitted	H-4: 175' (53 m) H-5: 200' (61 m)	75' (23 m)	10 occupants
I-1: Institutional, Residential Care	Not Permitted	250' (76 m)	75' (23 m)	10 occupants
I-2: Institutional, Custodial Care	Not Permitted	200' (61 m)	75' (23 m)	1000 ft² (93 m²) for sleeping rooms or suites; 2500 ft² (232 m²) other areas
I-3 Institutional, Detention and Security	Not Permitted	200' (61 m)	100' (30 m)	10 occupants
I-4: Institutional, Day Care	Not Permitted	200' (61 m)	75' (23 m)	10 occupants
M: Mercantile	200' (61 m)	250' (76 m)	75' (23 m)	49 occupants
M: Mercantile, Covered malls	Not Permitted	200' (61 m) from within tenant space to common circulation 200' (61 m) from within common circulation to an exit	75' (23 m)	49 occupants
R-1: Hotels and Motels	Not Permitted	250' (76 m)	75' (23 m)	10 occupants
R-2: Residential, Multifamily	Not Permitted	250' (76 m)	75' (23 m) unsprinklered 125' (38 m) sprinklered	10 occupants
R-3: Residential, One- and Two-Family, except below	Not Permitted	250' (76 m) 200' (61 m) with NFPA 13D sprinkler system	75' (23 m)	10 occupants
Detached, 3-story maximum, one- and two-family dwellings and townhouses	Not Applicable	Not Applicable	Not Applicable	Not Applicable
R-4: Residential, Assisted Living	Not Permitted	250' (76 m)	75' (23 m)	10 occupants
S-1: Storage, Moderate Hazard	200' (61 m)	250' (76 m) 400' (122 m) for single-story buildings with automatic heat and smoke ventilation systems	75' (23 m) unsprinklered 100' (30 m) sprinklered or for unsprinklered tenant spaces with occupant load of 30 or less	29 occupants
S-2: Storage, Low Hazard, and Parking Garages	300' (91 m)	400' (122 m)	Same as above	29 occupants
U: Utility, and Private Garages	300' (91 m)	400' (122 m)	Same as above	49 occupants

ᵃMinimum corridor width for access to electrical, mechanical, or plumbing systems is 24" (610 mm).

Minimum Length of Dead-End Corridor (see page 258)	See also minimum width requirements for occupant load served, pages 282–283. For minimum dimensions of accessible routes, see pages 266–268.			Additional Requirements
	Door Width	Minimum Clear Corridor Width[a]	Minimum Stair Width	
20' (6 m)	Min: 32" (813 mm) net clear Max: 48" (1220 mm) nominal	44" (1118 mm) serving more than 49 occupants 36" (914 mm) serving 49 or fewer	44" (1118 mm) serving more than 49 occupants 36" (914 mm) serving 49 or fewer	For special egress requirements in assembly seating areas, see pages 273–275.
20' (6 m) unsprinklered 50' (15 m) sprinklered	Same as above	Same as above	Same as above	
20' (6 m)	Same as above	Same as above; 72" (1829 mm) for 100 or more occupants	Same as above	
20' (6 m) unsprinklered 50' (15 m) sprinklered	Same as above	44" (1118 mm) serving more than 49 occupants 36" (914 mm) serving 49 or fewer	Same as above	
20' (6 m) unsprinklered 50' (15 m) sprinklered	Same as above	Same as above	Same as above	
4' (1.2 m) –20' (6 m)	Same as above	Same as above	Same as above	Consult the code for special egress requirements
4' (1.2 m) –20' (6 m)	Same as above	Same as above	Same as above	Consult the code for special egress requirements
20' (6 m)	Same as above	Same as above, and 72" (1829 mm) where occupants are incapacitated	Same as above	Emergency door or window egress from sleeping areas required—see page 277.
20' (6 m)	Min: 32" (813 mm) net clear; 41.5" (1054 mm) where beds must be moved Max: 48" (1220 mm) nominal	Same as I-1 above 96" (2438 mm) where beds must be moved	Same as above	Each floor must be subdivided by at least one smokeproof wall with horizontal exits.
20' (6 m) 50' (15 m) under some conditions— consult the code	Min: 32" (813 mm) net clear; 28" (711 mm) for resident sleeping rooms Max: 48" (1220 mm) nominal	44" (1118 mm) serving more than 49 occupants 36" (914 mm) serving 49 or fewer	Same as above	Same as above
20' (6 m)	Min: 32" (813mm) net clear Max: 48" (1220 mm) nominal	Same as above	Same as above	
20' (6 m)	Same as above	Same as above	Same as above	
20' (6 m) No limit for mall spaces not longer than twice their width	Same as above	20' (6 m) for mall space 66" (1676 mm) for corridors	66" (1676 mm)	See the code for additional egress requirements.
20' (6 m)	Same as above	44" (1118 mm) serving more than 49 occupants 36" (914 mm) serving 49 or fewer, or within dwelling units	44" (1118 mm) serving more than 49 occupants 36" (914 mm) serving 49 or fewer	Emergency door or window egress from sleeping areas required—see page 272.
20' (6 m)	Same as above	Same as above	Same as above	Same as above
20' (6 m)	Same as above	Same as above	Same as above	Same as above
Not applicable	Nominal 36" (914 mm) at required exits Max: 48" (1220 mm) nominal	36" (914 mm)	36" (914 mm)	Same as above
20' (6 m)	Min: 32" (813 mm) net clear Max: 48" (1220 mm) nominal	44" (1118 mm) serving more than 49 occupants 36" (914 mm) serving 49 or fewer, or within dwelling units	44" (1118 mm) serving more than 49 occupants 36" (914 mm) serving 49 or fewer	Same as above
20' (6 m)	Same as above	44" (1118 mm) serving more than 49 occupants 36" (914 mm) serving 49 or fewer	Same as above	
20' (6 m)	Same as above	Same as above	Same as above	Open parking garage exit stairways may be open
20' (6 m)	Same as above	Same as above	Same as above	

DETERMINING WIDTHS OF EGRESS COMPONENTS

An Example of the Use of this Chart

The Problem: Design an exit for a department store basement, sprinklered, dimensions 105 × 292.55 ft.

The Solution: From the index on page 10, we find that a department store belongs to Occupancy Group M, Mercantile. Multiplying the two dimensions of the building, we arrive at a gross floor area of 30,720 sq ft. From the table on page 283, we see that for purposes of designing the exits we must allocate 30 sq ft per occupant, to arrive at an occupant load of 1024 for this floor. Assume that our design provides four exits, which is the minimum number required according to the information provided on page 259. Dividing 1024 occupants by 4 exits gives an occupant load per exit of 256.

From the table on this page, we find that for Occupancy Group M, we must provide 0.15 in. of width per occupant in corridors and doorways and 0.2 in. per occupant in stairways. Moving to the chart on the facing page, we read horizontally from 256 occupants to the 0.15-in. line and then downward to find that a width of 38 in. is required for the corridor. We must round this up to the 44-in. minimum width indicated on page 285. Extending this line farther downward, we select either two 3-ft doors, a single 4-ft door, or a pair of 3-ft doors without center mullion.

Reading horizontally from 256 occupants to the 0.2-in. line, then downward, we arrive at a required stair width of 52 in. (For stair design charts, see pages 299–309.)

EGRESS COMPONENT WIDTHS

Occupancy Group (see pages 7–12)	Doorways, Corridors, Ramps, and Other Components		Stairs	
	Unsprinklered	Sprinklered[a]	Unsprinklered	Sprinklered[a]
H-1, H-2, H-3, and H-4: Hazardous	Normally Not Permitted. 0.4" (10 mm) under special circumstances	0.2" (5 mm)	Normally Not Permitted. 0.7" (18 mm) under special circumstances	0.3" (8 mm)
I-2	Not Permitted	0.2" (5 mm)	Not Permitted	0.3" (8 mm)
All other occupancies	0.2" (5 mm)	0.15" (4 mm)	0.3" (8 mm)	0.2" (5 mm)

[a]For commercial and residential class NFPA 13R sprinkler systems, use the "Sprinklered" column. For NPFA 13D systems, use the "Unsprinklered" column.

EGRESS WIDTH CALCULATOR

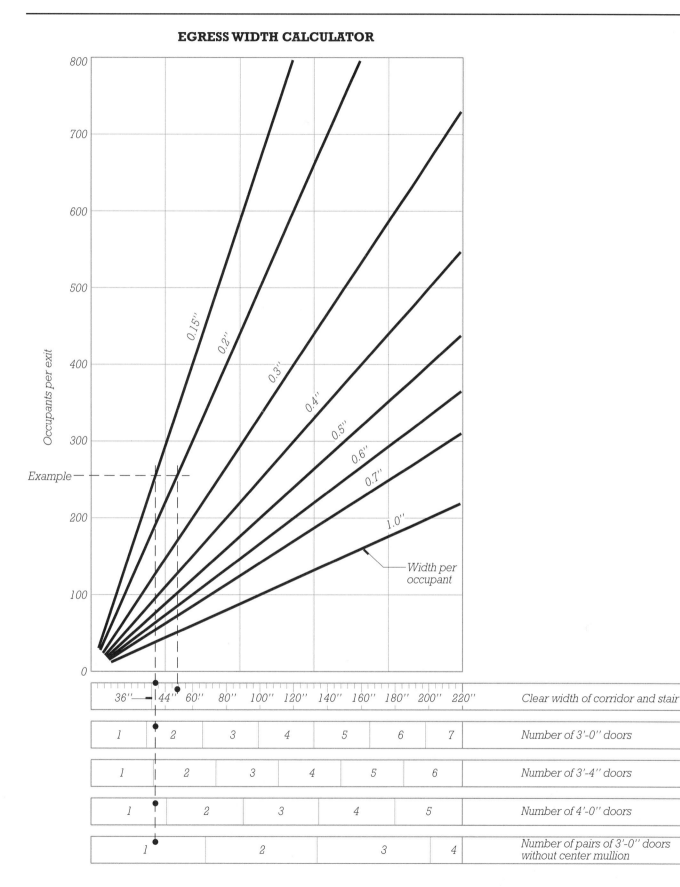

Occupants per exit

Example

0.15"
0.2"
0.3"
0.4"
0.5"
0.6"
0.7"
1.0"

Width per occupant

36" — 44" 60" 80" 100" 120" 140" 160" 180" 200" 220"   Clear width of corridor and stair

| 1 | 2 | 3 | 4 | 5 | 6 | 7 | Number of 3'-0" doors |

| 1 | 2 | 3 | 4 | 5 | 6 | Number of 3'-4" doors |

| 1 | 2 | 3 | 4 | 5 | Number of 4'-0" doors |

| 1 | 2 | 3 | 4 | Number of pairs of 3'-0" doors without center mullion |

SIZING THE EGRESS SYSTEM

287

NATIONAL BUILDING CODE OF CANADA

OCCUPANT LOADS

Occupancy	Use	Floor Area per Occupant
A: Assembly	Space with fixed seats	Actual number of seats
	Space with nonfixed seats, performance stages	0.75 m² (8.1 ft²)
	Space with nonfixed seats and tables	0.95 m² (10 ft²)
	Standing space	0.40 m² (4.3 ft²)
	Bowling alleys, pool and billiard rooms, school shops and vocational rooms	9.30 m² (100 ft²)
	Classrooms, reading or writing rooms, lounges	1.85 m² (20 ft²)
	Dining, beverage, and cafeteria spaces	1.20 m² (13 ft²)
	Laboratories in schools	4.60 m² (50 ft²)
	Stadiums and grandstands	0.60 m² (6.5 ft²)
B: Care or Detention	Treatment and sleeping room areas	10.00 m² (107 ft²)
	Detention quarters	11.60 m² (125 ft²)
C: Residential	Dwelling units	2 persons per sleeping room
	Dormitories	4.60 m² (50 ft²)
D: Business and Personal Services	Personal services shops	4.60 m² (50 ft²)
	Offices	9.30 m² (100 ft²)
E: Mercantile	Basements and first stories	3.70 m² (40 ft²)
	Second stories having a principal entrance from a pedestrian thoroughfare or a parking area	3.70 m² (40 ft²)
	Other stories	5.60 m² (60 ft²)
F: Industrial	Manufacturing or processing rooms	4.60 m² (50 ft²)
	Storage garages (parking), aircraft hangers	46.00 m² (495 ft²)
	Storage spaces (warehouses)	28.00 m² (300 ft²)
Other Uses	Cleaning and repair goods	4.60 m² (50 ft²)
	Kitchens	9.30 m² (100 ft²)
	Public corridors intended for occupancies in addition to pedestrian travel	3.70 m² (40 ft²)
	Storage	46.00 m² (495 ft²)

SIZING THE EGRESS SYSTEM

289

EGRESS SYSTEM CRITERIA

Occupancy (see pages 13–15)	Maximum Travel Distance from Most Remote Point to Nearest Exit Enclosure[a] (See page 255)		Largest Room or Suite That May Have Only One Door (See page 254)	
	Unsprinklered	Sprinklered	Unsprinklered	Sprinklered
A-1: Assembly, Performing Arts	30 m (98 ft)	45 m (148 ft)	Not permitted	Maximum occupancy of 60 persons, 200 m² (2153 ft²) maximum area, and 25 m (82 ft) travel distance within the space
A-2: Assembly, General	30 m (98 ft)	45 m (148 ft)	Maximum occupancy of 60 persons, 150 m² (1615 ft²) maximum area, and 5 m (49 ft) travel distance within the space	Same as above
A-3: Assembly, Arenas	30 m (98 ft)	45 m (148 ft)	Same as above	Same as above
A-4: Assembly, Outdoors	45 m (148 ft) to the ground, an exit, an opening to a passage-way leading from the seating area, or a portal, vomitory or other opening in the seating deck structure.	Not Applicable	Same as above	Same as above
B-1: Care or Detention, Restrained	30 m (98 ft)	45 m (148 ft)	Not permitted	Maximum occupancy of 60 persons, 100 m² (1076 ft²) maximum area, and 25 m (82 ft) travel distance within the space
B-2: Care or Detention, Cognitively or Physically Limited	30 m (98 ft)	45 m (148 ft)	Not permitted	Sleeping rooms same as above, other spaces 200 m² (2153 ft²) maximum area
C: Residential	30 m (98 ft)	45 m (148 ft)	Maximum occupancy of 60 persons, 100 m² (1076 ft²) maximum area, and 15 m (49 ft) travel distance within the space	Maximum occupancy of 60 persons, 150 m² (1615 ft²) maximum area, and 25 m (82 ft) travel distance within the space.
D: Business or Personal Services	40 m (131 ft)	45 m (148 ft)	Maximum occupancy of 60 persons, 200 m² (2153 ft²) maximum area, and 25 m (82 ft) travel distance within the space	Maximum occupancy of 60 persons, 300 m² (3229 ft²) maximum area, and 25 m (82 ft) travel distance within the space
E: Mercantile	30 m (98 ft)	45 m (148 ft)	Maximum occupancy of 60 persons, 150 m² (1615 ft²) maximum area, and 15 m (49 ft) travel distance within the space	Maximum occupancy of 60 persons, 200 m² (2153 ft²) maximum area, and 25 m (82 ft) travel distance within the space
F-1: Industrial, High-Hazard	25 m (82 ft)	25 m (82 ft)	Maximum occupancy of 60 persons, and 15 m² (161 ft²) maximum area	Maximum occupancy of 60 persons, and 15 m² (161 ft²) maximum area
F-2: Industrial, Medium-Hazard	30 m (98 ft)	45 m (148 ft)	Maximum occupancy of 60 persons, 150 m² (1615 ft²) maximum area, and 10 m (33 ft) travel distance within the space	Maximum occupancy of 60 persons, and 200 m² (2153 ft²) maximum area, and 25 m (82 ft) travel distance within the space
F-3: Industrial, Low-Hazard	30 m (98 ft)	45 m (148 ft)	Maximum occupancy of 60 persons, 200 m² (2153 ft²) maximum area, and 15 m (49 ft) travel distance within the space	Maximum occupancy of 60 persons, and 300 m² (3229 ft²) maximum area, and 25 m (82 ft) travel distance within the space
F-3: Open-Air Garages	60 m (197 ft)	60 m (197 ft)	Not Applicable	Not Applicable

Maximum Length of Dead-End Corridor (see page 258)	See also minimum width requirements for occupant load served on pages 282–289. See also accessible routes on pages 270-271.			Additional Requirements
	Minimum Clear Corridor Width	Minimum Net Clear Egress Door Width	Minimum Stair Width	
6 m (20 ft)	1100 mm (43 in)	800 mm (31 in)	1100 mm (43 in) for a stair serving more than two stories above grade or more than one story below grade, 900 mm (35 in) otherwise	See detailed requirements for row spacings, aisles, and exits on pages 273–275.
6 m (20 ft)	1100 mm (43 in)	800 mm (31 in) opening into or within a corridor, 790 mm (31 in) at exits	Same as above	Same as above
6 m (20 ft)	1100 mm (43 in)	Same as above	Same as above	Same as above
6 m (20 ft)	1100 mm (43 in)	Same as above	Same as above	A tier or balcony with occupant load of 1001 to 4000 persons requires at least three exits, an occupant load of more than 4000 requires at least four exits. See the code for aisle and bleacher requirements.
6 m (20 ft), for corridors serving the public or patients' sleeping rooms permitted only if these areas have a second separate means of egress	1100 mm (43 in), 2400 mm (94 in) for patients in bed	Same as above, except 1050 mm (41 in) for patients in beds	Same as above, except 1650 mm (65 in) for patients in bed	
Same as above	Same as above	Same as above	Same as above	
6 m (20 ft)	1100 mm (43 in)	800 mm (31 in)	1100 mm (43 in) for a stair serving more than three stories above grade or more than one story below grade, 900 mm (35 in) otherwise	At least one stairway between each two floors within a dwelling unit must have a minimum width of 860 mm (34 in).
6 m (20 ft)	1100 mm (43 in)	Same as above	Same as above	
6 m (20 ft)	1100 mm (43 in)	Same as above	Same as above	
6 m (20 ft)	1100 mm (43 in)	Same as above	Same as above	[a]If a room is enclosed with at least a ¾-hour fire separation in nonsprinklered buildings or a nonrated separation in sprinklered buildings, and opens into a corridor or exterior passageway, travel distance may be measured from the door of the room. In fully sprinklered buildings, floor areas served by a public corridor not less than 9 m (30 ft) wide and 4 m (13 ft) tall may have a maximum travel distance of up to 105 m (344 ft).
6 m (20 ft)	1100 mm (43 in)	Same as above	Same as above	
6 m (20 ft)	1100 mm (43 in)	Same as above	Same as above	
6 m (20 ft)	1100 mm (43 in)	Same as above	Same as above	

SIZING THE EGRESS SYSTEM

291

EGRESS WIDTH CALCULATOR

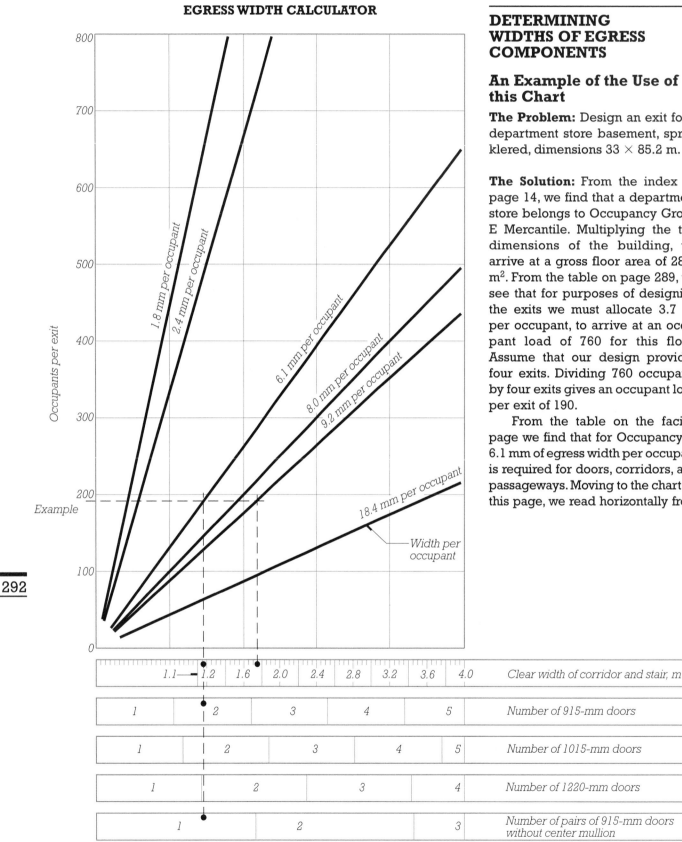

DETERMINING WIDTHS OF EGRESS COMPONENTS

An Example of the Use of this Chart

The Problem: Design an exit for a department store basement, sprinklered, dimensions 33 × 85.2 m.

The Solution: From the index on page 14, we find that a department store belongs to Occupancy Group E Mercantile. Multiplying the two dimensions of the building, we arrive at a gross floor area of 2812 m². From the table on page 289, we see that for purposes of designing the exits we must allocate 3.7 m² per occupant, to arrive at an occupant load of 760 for this floor. Assume that our design provides four exits. Dividing 760 occupants by four exits gives an occupant load per exit of 190.

From the table on the facing page we find that for Occupancy E, 6.1 mm of egress width per occupant is required for doors, corridors, and passageways. Moving to the chart on this page, we read horizontally from

190 occupants to the 6.1-mm line, then downward, to find that a corridor width of 1160 mm is required. Extending this line farther downward, we select either two 915-mm doors or one pair of 915-mm doors without a center mullion. To find the required width for our egress stair, we read downward from the 9.2-mm line, finding that a width of 1750 mm is required for the steepest possible stair. (For stair design tables, see pages 299–309.)

EGRESS COMPONENT WIDTHS

Occupancy Group (see pages 13–15)	Width per Occupant		
	Doors, Corridors, Ramps Not More Than 1:8 Slope	Stairs with Rise Not More Than 180 mm (7") and Run Not Less Than 280 mm (11")	Stairs with Rise More Than 180 mm (7") and Run Less Than 280 mm (11"); Ramps with Slope Greater Than 1:8
A: Assembly C: Residential D: Business and Personal Services E: Mercantile F: Industrial	6.1 mm (0.24")	8 mm (0.31")	9.2 mm (0.36")
A-4: Stadiums and Grandstands	2.4 mm (0.09") for exit stairs 1.8 mm (0.07") for aisles, ramps, passageways, exits, and stairs other than exit stairs		
B: Care or Detention	18.4 mm (0.72")	18.4 mm (0.72")	18.4 mm (0.72")

SIZING THE EGRESS SYSTEM

3
STAIRWAY
AND
RAMP
DESIGN

This chapter will help you design stairways and ramps in accordance with the model building codes.

STAIRWAY AND RAMP PROPORTIONS

Stair Proportions	Stairs, Nonresidential				Residential Stairs[a]	
	Maximum Riser Height	Minimum Riser Height	Minimum Tread Run	Maximum Vertical Distance Between Landings	Maximum Riser Height	Minimum Tread Run
International Building Code	7" (178 mm)	4" (102 mm)	11" (279 mm)	12' (3658 mm)	7.75" (197 mm)	10" (254 mm)
National Building Code of Canada	180 mm (7.1")	125 mm (4.9")	280 mm (11.0")	3.7 m (12'-2"), except 2.4 m (7'-10") in Group B-2 Occupancy	200 mm (7.9")	235 mm (9.25")
Small Buildings[b]	200 mm (7.9")	125 mm (4.9")	230 mm (9.1")	Same as above		
Minimum Number of Risers	3, except no minimum within dwelling unit and Group A-2 Occupancies used for the serving of food and beverages when the stair is not less than 900 mm (35.4") wide					

[a]In the International Building Code, Residential Stairs includes stairs in Group R-3 occupancies, within dwelling units in Group R-2 occupancies, and in Group U occupancies accessory to R-3 occupancies. In the National Building Code of Canada, Residential Stairs includes stairs within dwelling units and exterior stairs serving individual dwelling units.

[b]Small Buildings includes buildings three stories or less in height, not exceeding 600 m² (6460 ft²) in area, and classified as Group C, D, E, F-2, or F-3 Occupancies.

Ramp Proportions	Maximum Ramp Slope	Minimum Ramp Width	Maximum Distance Between Landings
International Building Code	1:12 for ramps part of means of egress or on accessible routes 1:8 for other ramps	36" (914 mm) clear width between sides of ramp, or handrails if any	30" (762 mm) rise
Other Landing Requirements	Landings are required at points of turning, ramp entrances and exits, and door openings onto ramps. Landings must be at least as wide as the ramp. The minimum length for a ramp part of an accessible route is 60" (1525 mm), for a ramp not part of an accessible route, 48" (1219 mm), and within Group R-2 and R-3 individual dwelling units, 36" (914 mm).		
National Building Code of Canada	1:12 for barrier-free ramps 1:10 for Assembly, Care or Detention, or Residential occupancies 1:6 for Mercantile or Industrial occupancies 1:8 for other interior ramps 1:10 for other exterior ramps	870 mm (34.25") between handrails for barrier-free ramps	9 m (29'-6") run
Other Landing Requirements	Where a doorway or stairway opens onto the side of a ramp, a landing extending a minimum of 300 mm (11.8") beyond either side of the opening is required. Where a doorway or stairway opens onto the end of a ramp, a landing extending along the ramp for at least 900 mm (35.4") is required. In addition, barrier-free ramps require landings with a minimum size of 1500 mm (59") square at the top and bottom of the ramp, and landings at least 1200 mm (47.25") long and at least as wide as the ramp at abrupt changes in direction.		

CURVED AND SPIRAL STAIRS

	MAY A CURVED STAIR SERVE AS A REQUIRED EXIT?	Dimensional Restrictions
International Building Code, except residential occupancies listed below	Yes	The smaller radius of the stair must be at least twice the width of the stairway. Risers may not exceed 7" (178 mm) in height. Winder treads may not be less than 11" (279 mm) deep measured 12" (305 mm) from the narrow end and not less than 10" (254 mm) at the most narrow point.
International Building Code, Group R-3 occupancies, and individual dwelling units within Group R-2 occupancies	Yes	Risers may not exceed 7.75" (178 mm) in height. Winder treads may not be less than 10" (254 mm) deep measured 12" (305 mm) from the narrow end and not less than 6" (152 mm) at the most narrow point.
National Building Code of Canada	Yes	The smaller radius of the stair must be at least twice the width of the stairway. Treads and risers must conform to the dimensions shown on page 296, measured 230 mm (9.1") from the narrow end of the tread. Minimum tread depth at the narrow end is 240 mm (9.4"), not including nosings. Curved stairs not serving as an exit may have a minimum average tread depth of not less than 200 mm (7.9") and a minimum depth of 150 mm (5.9") at the narrow end.

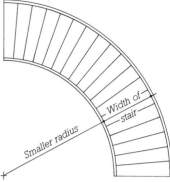

	MAY A SPIRAL STAIR SERVE AS A REQUIRED EXIT?	Dimensional Restrictions
International Building Code	A spiral stair may serve as a required exit only within a dwelling unit or from a space not more than 250 ft^2 (23 m^2) in area and serving not more than five occupants.	The tread may not measure less than 7.5" (191 mm) at a distance of 12" (305 mm) from the narrow end. The riser height may not exceed 9.5" (241 mm). The clear width of the stair must be at least 26" (660 mm), and the minimum headroom must be 78" (1981 mm).
National Building Code of Canada	No	For spiral stairs not required as an exit, the tread may not measure less than 150 mm (5.9") in depth at any point and must average at least 200 mm (7.9") in depth. Riser height must be no greater than 180 mm (7.1") and no less than 125 mm (4.9").

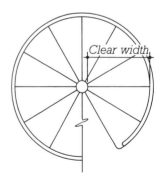

WINDING STAIRS

	MAY WINDERS BE USED IN A REQUIRED EXIT STAIRWAY?	Dimensional Restrictions
International Building Code, other than within dwelling units	No	Risers may not exceed 7" (178 mm) in height. Winder treads may not be less than 11" (279 mm) deep measured 12" (305 mm) from the narrow end and not less than 10" (254 mm) at the most narrow point.
International Building Code, Group R-3 Occupancies, within dwelling units in Group R-2 Occupancies, and in Group U Occupancies accessory to R-3 Occupancies	Winders may be used in a required exit stairway only within individual dwelling units.	Risers may not exceed 7.75" (178 mm) in height. Winder treads may not be less than 10" (254 mm) deep measured 12" (305 mm) from the narrow end and not less than 6" (152 mm) at the most narrow point.
National Building Code of Canada	Only stairs within dwelling units may have winders.	Winders may converge to a point. They may be arrayed only at angles of 30°, 45°, or 60°, and the total angle of all winders may not exceed 90°.

Winders

EXIT STAIRWAY DESIGN TABLES

The tables that follow allow you to make a rapid preliminary design for an exit stairway. After selecting the desired stairway configuration, consult an accompanying table to find the required interior dimensions and the tread and riser proportions of a stairway that corresponds to the stair width and floor-to-floor height for which you are designing.

The stairway lengths for the English-unit tables are based on a maximum 7-in. (178-mm) riser and 11-in. (279-mm) tread, conforming to the requirements of the International Building Code. Stairway lengths for the metric tables are based on a maximum 180-mm (7.1-in.) riser and a 280-mm (11-in.) tread, conforming to the requirements of the National Building Code of Canada for buildings not classified as small or residential. See page 296 for more information on stairway proportions.

The "Overall Inside Length of Stair Enclosure" figures represent an absolute minimum configuration. Handrail extension requirements may dictate either that the door be recessed into an alcove that falls outside this length or that the length of the stair enclosure be increased, in order to satisfy the limitations on obstruction of the width of the landing by the open door. The minimum overall inside width for a stair enclosure is twice the required width of the stair itself, but construction of the stair may be facilitated by increasing this dimension by several inches. Under both the International Building Code and the National Building Code of Canada, the required stairway width is measured from the inside of the stairway or guards, and handrails may project into the required width of the stair for the purposes of computing its occupancy.

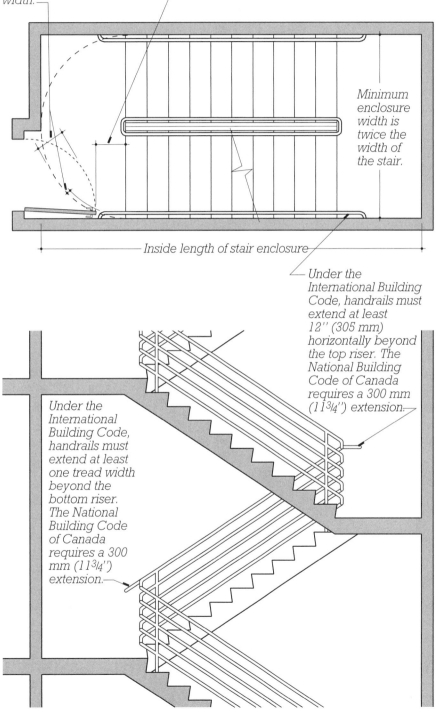

Under the International Building Code, the door swing must leave at least half the required width of the landing unobstructed, and when fully open the door must not project more than 7" (178 mm) into the required egress width.

Under the National Building Code of Canada, no riser may be located within 300 mm (11¾") of the leading edge of an exit door throughout its swing.

Minimum enclosure width is twice the width of the stair.

Inside length of stair enclosure

Under the International Building Code, handrails must extend at least 12" (305 mm) horizontally beyond the top riser. The National Building Code of Canada requires a 300 mm (11¾") extension.

Under the International Building Code, handrails must extend at least one tread width beyond the bottom riser. The National Building Code of Canada requires a 300 mm (11¾") extension.

EXIT STAIRWAY DESIGN TABLES

ONE-FLIGHT STAIR: ENGLISH UNITS

Floor-to-Floor Height (ft-in.)	Number of Risers	Riser Height (in.)	Tread Depth (in.)	Overall Inside Length of Stair Enclosure (ft-in.)				
				36" Width	44" Width	56" Width	66" Width	88" Width
1-8	3	6.67	11	7-10	9-2	11-2	12-10	16-6
2-0	4	6.00	11	8-9	10-1	12-1	13-9	17-5
2-4	4	7.00	11	8-9	10-1	12-1	13-9	17-5
2-8	5	6.40	11	9-8	11-0	13-0	14-8	18-4
3-0	6	6.00	11	10-7	11-11	13-11	15-7	19-3
3-4	6	6.67	11	10-7	11-11	13-11	15-7	19-3
3-8	7	6.29	11	11-6	12-10	14-10	16-6	20-2
4-0	7	6.86	11	11-6	12-10	14-10	16-6	20-2
4-4	8	6.50	11	12-5	13-9	15-9	17-5	21-1
4-8	8	7.00	11	12-5	13-9	15-9	17-5	21-1
5-0	9	6.67	11	13-4	14-8	16-8	18-4	22-0
5-4	10	6.40	11	14-3	15-7	17-7	19-3	22-11
5-8	10	6.80	11	14-3	15-7	17-7	19-3	22-11
6-0	11	6.55	11	15-2	16-6	18-6	20-2	23-10
6-4	11	6.91	11	15-2	16-6	18-6	20-2	23-10
6-8	12	6.67	11	16-1	17-5	19-5	21-1	24-9
7-0	12	7.00	11	16-1	17-5	19-5	21-1	24-9
7-4	13	6.77	11	17-0	18-4	20-4	22-0	25-8
7-8	14	6.57	11	17-11	19-3	21-3	22-0	26-7
8-0	14	6.86	11	17-11	19-3	21-3	22-11	26-7
8-4	15	6.67	11	18-10	20-2	22-2	23-10	27-6
8-8	15	6.93	11	18-10	20-2	22-2	23-10	27-6
9-0	16	6.75	11	19-9	21-1	23-1	24-9	28-5
9-4	16	7.00	11	19-9	21-1	23-1	24-9	28-5
9-8	17	6.82	11	20-8	22-0	24-0	25-8	29-4
10-0	18	6.67	11	21-7	22-11	24-11	26-7	30-3
10-4	18	6.89	11	21-7	22-11	24-11	26-7	30-3
10-8	19	6.74	11	22-6	23-10	25-10	27-6	31-2
11-0	19	6.95	11	22-6	23-10	25-10	27-6	31-2
11-4	20	6.80	11	23-5	24-9	26-9	28-5	32-1
11-8	20	7.00	11	23-5	24-9	26-9	28-5	32-1
12-0	21	6.86	11	24-4	25-8	27-8	29-4	33-0

Stairway widths may be determined rapidly by using the tables and graphs on pages 286-287 and 292-293.

EXIT STAIRWAY DESIGN TABLES

ONE-FLIGHT STAIR: METRIC UNITS (280-MM TREAD, 180-MM RISER)

Floor-to-Floor Height (m)	Number of Risers	Riser Height (mm)	Tread Depth (mm)	Overall Inside Length of Stair Enclosure (m)				
				900-mm Width	1100-mm Width	1400-mm Width	1650-mm Width	2200-mm Width
0.5	3	167	280	2.36	2.76	3.36	3.86	4.96
0.6	4	150	280	2.64	3.04	3.64	4.14	5.24
0.7	4	175	280	2.64	3.04	3.64	4.14	5.24
0.8	5	160	280	2.92	3.32	3.92	4.42	5.52
0.9	5	180	280	2.92	3.32	3.92	4.42	5.52
1.0	6	167	280	3.20	3.60	4.20	4.70	5.80
1.1	7	158	280	3.48	3.88	4.48	4.98	6.08
1.2	7	172	280	3.48	3.88	4.48	4.98	6.08
1.3	8	163	280	3.76	4.16	4.76	5.26	6.36
1.4	8	175	280	3.76	4.16	4.76	5.26	6.36
1.5	9	167	280	4.04	4.44	5.04	5.54	6.64
1.6	9	178	280	4.04	4.44	5.04	5.54	6.64
1.7	10	170	280	4.32	4.72	5.32	5.82	6.92
1.8	10	180	280	4.32	4.72	5.32	5.82	6.92
1.9	11	173	280	4.60	5.00	5.60	6.10	7.20
2.0	12	167	280	4.88	5.28	5.88	6.38	7.48
2.1	12	175	280	4.88	5.28	5.88	6.38	7.48
2.2	13	170	280	5.16	5.56	6.16	6.66	7.76
2.3	13	177	280	5.16	5.56	6.16	6.66	7.76
2.4	14	172	280	5.44	5.84	6.44	6.94	8.04
2.5	14	179	280	5.44	5.84	6.44	6.94	8.04
2.6	15	174	280	5.72	6.12	6.72	7.22	8.32
2.7	15	180	280	5.72	6.12	6.72	7.22	8.32
2.8	16	175	280	6.00	6.40	7.00	7.50	8.60
2.9	17	171	280	6.28	6.68	7.28	7.78	8.88
3.0	17	177	280	6.28	6.68	7.28	7.78	8.88
3.1	18	173	280	6.56	6.96	7.56	8.06	9.16
3.2	18	178	280	6.56	6.96	7.56	8.06	9.16
3.3	19	174	280	6.84	7.24	7.84	8.34	9.44
3.4	19	179	280	6.84	7.24	7.84	8.34	9.44
3.5	20	175	280	7.12	7.52	8.12	8.62	9.72
3.6	20	180	280	7.12	7.52	8.12	8.62	9.72
3.7	21	177	280	7.40	7.80	8.40	8.90	10.00

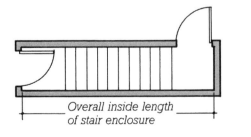

Overall inside length of stair enclosure

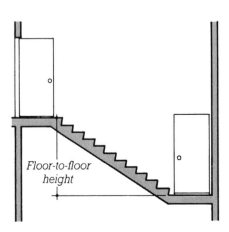

Floor-to-floor height

EXIT STAIRWAY DESIGN TABLES

TWO-FLIGHT STAIR: ENGLISH UNITS

Floor-to-Floor Height (ft-in.)	Number of Risers	Riser Height (in.)	Tread Depth (in.)	Overall Inside Length of Stair Enclosure (ft-in.)				
				36" Width	44" Width	56" Width	66" Width	88" Width
7-8[a]	14	6.57	11	11-6	12-10	14-10	16-6	20-2
8-0[a]	14	6.86	11	11-6	12-10	14-10	16-6	20-2
8-4	15	6.67	11	12-5	13-9	15-9	17-5	21-1
8-8	15	6.93	11	12-5	13-9	15-9	17-5	21-1
9-0	16	6.75	11	12-5	13-9	15-9	17-5	21-1
9-4	16	7.00	11	12-5	13-9	15-9	17-5	21-1
9-8	17	6.82	11	13-4	14-8	16-8	18-4	22-0
10-0	18	6.67	11	13-4	14-8	16-8	18-4	22-0
10-4	18	6.89	11	13-4	14-8	16-8	18-4	22-0
10-8	19	6.74	11	14-3	15-7	17-7	19-3	22-11
11-0	19	6.95	11	14-3	15-7	17-7	19-3	22-11
11-4	20	6.80	11	14-3	15-7	17-7	19-3	22-11
11-8	20	7.00	11	14-3	15-7	17-7	19-3	22-11
12-0	21	6.86	11	15-2	16-6	18-6	20-2	23-10
12-4	22	6.73	11	15-2	16-6	18-6	20-2	23-10
12-8	22	6.91	11	15-2	16-6	18-6	20-2	23-10
13-0	23	6.78	11	16-1	17-5	19-5	21-1	24-9
13-4	23	6.96	11	16-1	17-5	19-5	21-1	24-9
13-8	24	6.83	11	16-1	17-5	19-5	21-1	24-9
14-0	24	7.00	11	16-1	17-5	19-5	21-1	24-9
14-4	25	6.88	11	17-0	18-4	20-4	22-0	25-8
14-8	26	6.77	11	17-0	18-4	20-4	22-0	25-8
15-0	26	6.92	11	17-0	18-4	20-4	22-0	25-8
16-0	28	6.86	11	17-11	19-3	21-3	22-11	26-7
17-0	30	6.80	11	18-10	20-2	22-2	23-10	27-6
18-0	31	6.97	11	19-9	21-1	23-1	24-9	28-5
19-0	33	6.91	11	20-8	22-0	24-0	25-8	29-4
20-0	35	6.86	11	21-7	22-11	24-11	26-7	30-3
21-0	36	7.00	11	21-7	22-11	24-11	26-7	30-3
22-0	38	6.95	11	22-6	23-10	25-10	27-6	31-2
23-0	40	6.90	11	23-5	24-9	26-9	28-5	32-1
24-0	42	6.86	11	24-4	25-8	27-8	29-4	33-0

[a]The headroom in these stairs may be deficient, depending on the detailing of the stair structure.

Stairway widths may be determined rapidly by using the tables and graphs on pages 286–287 and 292–293.

EXIT STAIRWAY DESIGN TABLES

TWO-FLIGHT STAIR: METRIC UNITS (280-MM TREAD, MAXIMUM 180-MM RISER)

Floor-to-Floor Height (m)	Number of Risers	Riser Height (mm)	Tread Depth (mm)	Overall Inside Length of Stair Enclosure (m)				
				900-mm Width	1100-mm Width	1400-mm Width	1650-mm Width	2200-mm Width
2.3	13	177	280	3.48	3.88	4.48	4.98	6.08
2.4	14	172	280	3.48	3.88	4.48	4.98	6.08
2.5	14	179	280	3.48	3.88	4.48	4.98	6.08
2.6	15	174	280	3.76	4.16	4.76	5.26	6.36
2.7	15	180	280	3.76	4.16	4.76	5.26	6.36
2.8	16	175	280	3.76	4.16	4.76	5.26	6.36
2.9	17	171	280	4.04	4.44	5.04	5.54	6.64
3.0	17	177	280	4.04	4.44	5.04	5.54	6.64
3.1	18	173	280	4.04	4.44	5.04	5.54	6.64
3.2	18	178	280	4.04	4.44	5.04	5.54	6.64
3.3	19	174	280	4.32	4.72	5.32	5.82	6.92
3.4	19	179	280	4.32	4.72	5.32	5.82	6.92
3.5	20	175	280	4.32	4.72	5.32	5.82	6.92
3.6	20	180	280	4.32	4.72	5.32	5.82	6.92
3.7	21	177	280	4.60	5.00	5.60	6.10	7.20
3.8	22	173	280	4.60	5.00	5.60	6.10	7.20
3.9	22	178	280	4.60	5.00	5.60	6.10	7.20
4.0	23	174	280	4.88	5.28	5.88	6.38	7.48
4.1	23	179	280	4.88	5.28	5.88	6.38	7.48
4.2	24	175	280	4.88	5.28	5.88	6.38	7.48
4.3	24	180	280	4.88	5.28	5.88	6.38	7.48
4.4	25	176	280	5.16	5.56	6.16	6.66	7.76
4.5	25	180	280	5.16	5.56	6.16	6.66	7.76
4.8	27	178	280	5.44	5.84	6.44	6.94	8.04
5.1	29	176	280	5.72	6.12	6.72	7.22	8.32
5.4	30	180	280	5.72	6.12	6.72	7.22	8.32
5.7	32	179	280	6.00	6.40	7.00	7.50	8.60
6.0	34	177	280	6.28	6.68	7.28	7.78	8.88
6.3	35	180	280	6.56	6.96	7.56	8.06	9.16
6.6	37	179	280	6.84	7.24	7.84	8.34	9.44
6.9	39	177	280	7.12	7.52	8.12	8.62	9.72
7.2	40	180	280	7.12	7.52	8.12	8.62	9.72
7.4	42	177	280	7.40	7.80	8.40	8.90	100

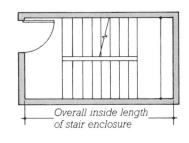

Overall inside length of stair enclosure

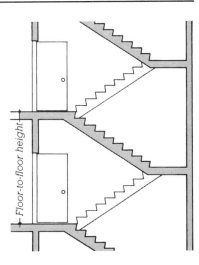

Floor-to-floor height

EXIT STAIRWAY DESIGN TABLES

THREE-FLIGHT STAIR: ENGLISH UNITS

Floor-to-Floor Height (ft-in.)	Number of Risers	Riser Height (in.)	Tread Depth (in.)	Overall Inside Length of Stair Enclosure (ft-in.)				
				36" Width	44" Width	56" Width	66" Width	88" Width
12-0	21	6.86	11	11-6	12-10	14-10	16-6	20-2
12-4	22	6.73	11	12-5	13-9	15-9	17-5	21-1
12-8	22	6.91	11	12-5	13-9	15-9	17-5	21-1
13-0	23	6.78	11	12-5	13-9	15-9	17-5	21-1
13-4	23	6.96	11	12-5	13-9	15-9	17-5	21-1
13-8	24	6.83	11	12-5	13-9	15-9	17-5	21-1
14-0	24	7.00	11	12-5	13-9	15-9	17-5	21-1
14-4	25	6.88	11	13-4	14-8	16-8	18-4	22-0
14-8	26	6.77	11	13-4	14-8	16-8	18-4	22-0
15-0	26	6.92	11	13-4	14-8	16-8	18-4	22-0
16-0	28	6.86	11	14-3	15-7	17-7	19-3	22-11
17-0	30	6.80	11	14-3	15-7	17-7	19-3	22-11
18-0	31	6.97	11	15-2	16-6	18-6	20-2	23-10
19-0	33	6.91	11	15-2	16-6	18-6	20-2	23-10
20-0	35	6.86	11	16-1	17-5	19-5	21-1	24-9
21-0	36	7.00	11	16-1	17-5	19-5	21-1	24-9
22-0	38	6.95	11	17-0	18-4	20-4	22-0	25-8
23-0	40	6.90	11	17-11	19-3	21-3	22-11	26-7
24-0	42	6.86	11	17-11	19-3	21-3	22-11	26-7

Stairway widths may be determined rapidly by using the tables and graphs on pages 286–287 and 292–293.

EXIT STAIRWAY DESIGN TABLES

THREE-FLIGHT STAIR: METRIC UNITS (280-MM TREAD, MAXIMUM 180-MM RISER)

Floor-to-Floor Height (m)	Number of Risers	Riser Height (mm)	Tread Depth (mm)	Overall Inside Length of Stair Enclosure (m)				
				900-mm Width	1100-mm Width	1400-mm Width	1650-mm Width	2200-mm Width
3.6	20	180	280	3.48	3.88	4.48	4.98	6.08
3.7	21	177	280	3.48	3.88	4.48	4.98	6.08
3.8	22	173	280	3.76	4.16	4.76	5.26	6.36
3.9	22	178	280	3.76	4.16	4.76	5.26	6.36
4.0	23	174	280	3.76	4.16	4.76	5.26	6.36
4.1	23	179	280	3.76	4.16	4.76	5.26	6.36
4.2	24	175	280	3.76	4.16	4.76	5.26	6.36
4.3	24	180	280	3.76	4.16	4.76	5.26	6.36
4.4	25	176	280	4.04	4.44	5.04	5.54	6.64
4.5	25	180	280	4.04	4.44	5.04	5.54	6.64
4.8	27	178	280	4.04	4.44	5.04	5.54	6.64
5.1	29	176	280	4.32	4.72	5.32	5.82	6.92
5.4	30	180	280	4.32	4.72	5.32	5.82	6.92
5.7	32	179	280	4.60	5.00	5.60	6.10	7.20
6.0	34	177	280	4.88	5.28	5.88	6.38	7.48
6.3	35	180	280	4.88	5.28	5.88	6.38	7.48
6.6	37	179	280	5.16	5.56	6.16	6.66	7.76
6.9	39	177	280	5.16	5.56	6.16	6.66	7.76
7.2	40	180	280	5.44	5.84	6.44	6.94	8.04
7.4	42	177	280	5.44	5.84	6.44	6.94	8.04

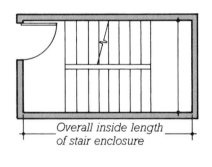

Overall inside length of stair enclosure

THREE-FLIGHT STAIR

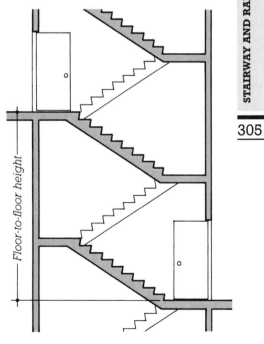

Floor-to-floor height

EXIT STAIRWAY DESIGN TABLES

FOUR-FLIGHT STAIR: ENGLISH UNITS

Floor-to-Floor Height (ft-in.)	Number of Risers	Riser Height (in.)	Tread Depth (in.)	Overall Inside Length of Stair Enclosure (ft-in.)				
				36" Width	44" Width	56" Width	66" Width	88" Width
16-0	28	6.86	11	11-6	12-10	14-10	16-6	20-2
17-0	30	6.80	11	12-5	13-9	15-9	17-5	21-1
18-0	31	6.97	11	12-5	13-9	15-9	17-5	21-1
19-0	33	6.91	11	13-4	14-8	16-8	18-4	22-0
20-0	35	6.86	11	13-4	14-8	16-8	18-4	22-0
21-0	36	7.00	11	13-4	14-8	16-8	18-4	22-0
22-0	38	6.95	11	14-3	15-7	17-7	19-3	22-11
23-0	40	6.90	11	14-3	15-7	17-7	19-3	22-11
24-0	42	6.86	11	15-2	16-6	18-6	20-2	23-10

Stairway widths may be determined rapidly by using the tables and graphs on pages 286–287 and 292–293.

EXIT STAIRWAY DESIGN TABLES

FOUR-FLIGHT STAIR: METRIC UNITS (280-MM TREAD, MAXIMUM 180-MM RISER)

Floor-to-Floor Height (m)	Number of Risers	Riser Height (mm)	Tread Depth (mm)	Overall Inside Length of Stair Enclosure (m)				
				900-mm Width	1100-mm Width	1400-mm Width	1650-mm Width	2200-mm Width
4.8	27	178	280	3.48	3.88	4.48	4.98	6.08
5.1	29	176	280	3.76	4.16	4.76	5.26	6.36
5.4	30	180	280	3.76	4.16	4.76	5.26	6.36
5.7	32	179	280	3.76	4.16	4.76	5.26	6.36
6.0	34	177	280	4.04	4.44	5.04	5.54	6.64
6.3	35	180	280	4.04	4.44	5.04	5.54	6.64
6.6	37	179	280	4.32	4.72	5.32	5.82	6.92
6.9	39	177	280	4.32	4.72	5.32	5.82	6.92
7.2	40	180	280	4.32	4.72	5.32	5.82	6.92
7.4	42	177	280	4.60	5.00	5.60	6.10	7.20

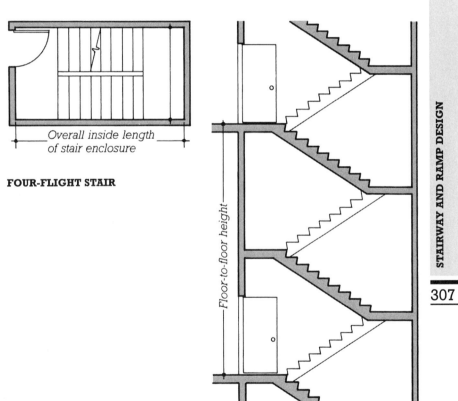

Overall inside length of stair enclosure

FOUR-FLIGHT STAIR

Floor-to-floor height

EXIT STAIRWAY DESIGN TABLES

DOUGHNUT STAIR: ENGLISH UNITS

Floor-to-Floor Height (ft-in.)	Number of Risers	Riser Height (in.)	Tread Depth (in.)	Overall Inside Length of Stair Enclosure (ft-in.)				
				36" Width	44" Width	56" Width	66" Width	88" Width
7-8	14	6.57	11	7-10 × 8-9	9-2 × 10-1	11-2 × 12-1	12-10 × 13-9	16-6 × 17-5
8-0	14	6.86	11	7-10 × 8-9	9-2 × 10-1	11-2 × 12-1	12-10 × 13-9	16-6 × 17-5
8-4	15	6.67	11	8-9 × 8-9	10-1 × 10-1	12-1 × 12-1	13-9 × 13-9	17-5 × 17-5
8-8	15	6.93	11	8-9 × 8-9	10-1 × 10-1	12-1 × 12-1	13-9 × 13-9	17-5 × 17-5
9-0	16	6.75	11	8-9 × 8-9	10-1 × 10-1	12-1 × 12-1	13-9 × 13-9	17-5 × 17-5
9-4	16	7.00	11	8-9 × 8-9	10-1 × 10-1	12-1 × 12-1	13-9 × 13-9	17-5 × 17-5
9-8	17	6.82	11	8-9 × 9-8	10-1 × 11-0	12-1 × 13-0	13-9 × 14-8	17-5 × 18-4
10-0	18	6.67	11	8-9 × 9-8	10-1 × 11-0	12-1 × 13-0	13-9 × 14-8	17-5 × 18-4
10-4	18	6.89	11	8-9 × 9-8	10-1 × 11-0	12-1 × 13-0	13-9 × 14-8	17-5 × 18-4
10-8	19	6.74	11	9-8 × 9-8	11-0 × 11-0	13-0 × 13-0	14-8 × 14-8	18-4 × 18-4
11-0	19	6.95	11	9-8 × 9-8	11-0 × 11-0	13-0 × 13-0	14-8 × 14-8	18-4 × 18-4
11-4	20	6.80	11	9-8 × 9-8	11-0 × 11-0	13-0 × 13-0	14-8 × 14-8	18-4 × 18-4
11-8	20	7.00	11	9-8 × 9-8	11-0 × 11-0	13-0 × 13-0	14-8 × 14-8	18-4 × 18-4
12-0	21	6.86	11	9-8 × 10-7	11-0 × 11-11	13-0 × 13-11	14-8 × 15-7	18-4 × 19-3
12-4	22	6.73	11	9-8 × 10-7	11-0 × 11-11	13-0 × 13-11	14-8 × 15-7	18-4 × 19-3
12-8	22	6.91	11	9-8 × 10-7	11-0 × 11-11	13-0 × 13-11	14-8 × 15-7	18-4 × 19-3
13-0	23	6.78	11	10-7 × 10-7	11-11 × 11-11	13-11 × 13-11	15-7 × 15-7	19-3 × 19-3
13-4	23	6.96	11	10-7 × 10-7	11-11 × 11-11	13-11 × 13-11	15-7 × 15-7	19-3 × 19-3
13-8	24	6.83	11	10-7 × 10-7	11-11 × 11-11	13-11 × 13-11	15-7 × 15-7	19-3 × 19-3
14-0	24	7.00	11	10-7 × 10-7	11-11 × 11-11	13-11 × 13-11	15-7 × 15-7	19-3 × 19-3
14-4	25	6.88	11	10-7 × 11-6	11-11 × 12-10	13-11 × 14-10	15-7 × 16-6	19-3 × 20-2
14-8	26	6.77	11	10-7 × 11-6	11-11 × 12-10	13-11 × 14-10	15-7 × 16-6	19-3 × 20-2
15-0	26	6.92	11	10-7 × 11-6	11-11 × 12-10	13-11 × 14-10	15-7 × 16-6	19-3 × 20-2
16-0	28	6.86	11	11-6 × 11-6	12-10 × 12-10	14-10 × 14-10	16-6 × 16-6	20-2 × 20-2
17-0	30	6.80	11	11-6 × 12-5	12-10 × 13-9	14-10 × 15-9	16-6 × 17-5	20-2 × 21-1
18-0	31	6.97	11	12-5 × 12-5	13-9 × 13-9	15-9 × 15-9	17-5 × 17-5	21-1 × 21-1
19-0	33	6.91	11	12-5 × 13-4	13-9 × 14-8	15-9 × 16-8	17-5 × 18-4	21-1 × 22-0
20-0	35	6.86	11	13-4 × 13-4	14-8 × 14-8	16-8 × 16-8	18-4 × 18-4	22-0 × 22-0
21-0	36	7.00	11	13-4 × 13-4	14-8 × 14-8	16-8 × 16-8	18-4 × 18-4	22-0 × 22-0
22-0	38	6.95	11	13-4 × 14-3	14-8 × 15-7	16-8 × 17-7	18-4 × 19-3	22-0 × 22-11
23-0	40	6.90	11	14-3 × 14-3	15-7 × 15-7	17-7 × 17-7	19-3 × 19-3	22-11 × 22-11
24-0	42	6.86	11	14-3 × 15-2	15-7 × 16-6	17-7 × 18-6	19-3 × 20-2	22-11 × 23-10

Stairway widths may be determined rapidly by using the tables and graphs on pages 286–287 and 292–293.

EXIT STAIRWAY DESIGN TABLES

DOUGHNUT STAIR: METRIC UNITS (280-MM TREAD, 180-MM RISER)

Floor-to-Floor Height (m)	Number of Risers	Riser Height (mm)	Tread Depth (mm)	Overall Inside Length of Stair Enclosure (m)				
				900-mm Width	1100-mm Width	1400-mm Width	1650-mm Width	2200-mm Width
2.3	13	177	280	2.36 × 2.64	2.76 × 3.04	3.36 × 3.64	3.86 × 4.14	4.96 × 5.24
2.4	14	172	280	2.36 × 2.64	2.76 × 3.04	3.36 × 3.64	3.86 × 4.14	4.96 × 5.24
2.5	14	179	280	2.36 × 2.64	2.76 × 3.04	3.36 × 3.64	3.86 × 4.14	4.96 × 5.24
2.6	15	174	280	2.64 × 2.64	3.04 × 3.04	3.64 × 3.64	4.14 × 4.14	5.24 × 5.24
2.7	15	180	280	2.64 × 2.64	3.04 × 3.04	3.64 × 3.64	4.14 × 4.14	5.24 × 5.24
2.8	16	175	280	2.64 × 2.64	3.04 × 3.04	3.64 × 3.64	4.14 × 4.14	5.24 × 5.24
2.9	17	171	280	2.64 × 2.92	3.04 × 3.32	3.64 × 3.92	4.14 × 4.42	5.24 × 5.52
3.0	17	177	280	2.64 × 2.92	3.04 × 3.32	3.64 × 3.92	4.14 × 4.42	5.24 × 5.52
3.1	18	173	280	2.64 × 2.92	3.04 × 3.32	3.64 × 3.92	4.14 × 4.42	5.24 × 5.52
3.2	18	178	280	2.64 × 2.92	3.04 × 3.32	3.64 × 3.92	4.14 × 4.42	5.24 × 5.52
3.3	19	174	280	2.92 × 2.92	3.32 × 3.32	3.92 × 3.92	4.42 × 4.42	5.52 × 5.52
3.4	19	179	280	2.92 × 2.92	3.32 × 3.32	3.92 × 3.92	4.42 × 4.42	5.52 × 5.52
3.5	20	175	280	2.92 × 2.92	3.32 × 3.32	3.92 × 3.92	4.42 × 4.42	5.52 × 5.52
3.6	20	180	280	2.92 × 2.92	3.32 × 3.32	3.92 × 3.92	4.42 × 4.42	5.52 × 5.52
3.7	21	177	280	2.92 × 3.20	3.32 × 3.60	3.92 × 4.20	4.42 × 4.70	5.52 × 5.80
3.8	22	173	280	2.92 × 3.20	3.32 × 3.60	3.92 × 4.20	4.42 × 4.70	5.52 × 5.80
3.9	22	178	280	2.92 × 3.20	3.32 × 3.60	3.92 × 4.20	4.42 × 4.70	5.52 × 5.80
4.0	23	174	280	3.20 × 3.20	3.60 × 3.60	4.20 × 4.20	4.70 × 4.70	5.80 × 5.80
4.1	23	179	280	3.20 × 3.20	3.60 × 3.60	4.20 × 4.20	4.70 × 4.70	5.80 × 5.80
4.2	24	175	280	3.20 × 3.20	3.60 × 3.60	4.20 × 4.20	4.70 × 4.70	5.80 × 5.80
4.3	24	180	280	3.20 × 3.20	3.60 × 3.60	4.20 × 4.20	4.70 × 4.70	5.80 × 5.80
4.4	25	176	280	3.20 × 3.48	3.60 × 3.88	4.20 × 4.48	4.70 × 4.98	5.80 × 6.08
4.5	25	180	280	3.20 × 3.48	3.60 × 3.88	4.20 × 4.48	4.70 × 4.98	5.80 × 6.08
4.8	27	178	280	3.48 × 3.48	3.88 × 3.88	4.48 × 4.48	4.98 × 4.98	6.08 × 6.08
5.1	29	176	280	3.48 × 3.76	3.88 × 4.16	4.48 × 4.76	4.98 × 5.26	6.08 × 6.36
5.4	30	180	280	3.48 × 3.76	3.88 × 4.16	4.48 × 4.76	4.98 × 5.26	6.08 × 6.36
5.7	32	179	280	3.76 × 3.76	4.16 × 4.16	4.76 × 4.76	5.26 × 5.26	6.36 × 6.36
6.0	34	177	280	3.76 × 4.04	4.16 × 4.44	4.76 × 5.04	5.26 × 5.54	6.36 × 6.64
6.3	35	180	280	4.04 × 4.04	4.44 × 4.44	5.04 × 5.04	5.54 × 5.54	6.64 × 6.64
6.6	37	179	280	4.04 × 4.32	4.44 × 4.72	5.04 × 5.32	5.54 × 5.82	6.64 × 6.92
6.9	39	177	280	4.32 × 4.32	4.72 × 4.72	5.32 × 5.32	5.82 × 5.82	6.92 × 6.92
7.2	40	180	280	4.32 × 4.32	4.72 × 4.72	5.32 × 5.32	5.82 × 5.82	6.92 × 6.92
7.4	42	177	280	4.32 × 4.60	4.72 × 5.00	5.32 × 5.60	5.82 × 6.10	6.92 × 7.20

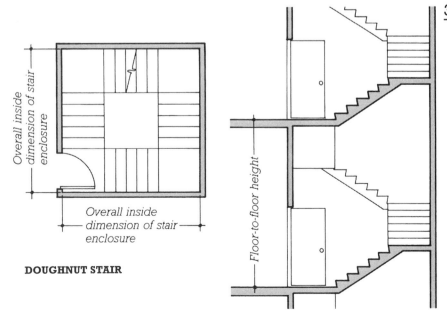

Overall inside dimension of stair enclosure

Overall inside dimension of stair enclosure

Floor-to-floor height

DOUGHNUT STAIR

DESIGNING
FOR PARKING

■■■■■■

1
DESIGN CRITERIA FOR PARKING FACILITIES

This chapter will help you select an appropriate type of parking facility and establish criteria for its capacity, level of amenity, and accessibility. For facilities other than surface parking, it will also assist you in the selection and configuration of a structural system.

PARKING FACILITY TYPES

Surface parking is constructed solely at grade. It is the least expensive form of parking, requiring little more than site preparation, paving, and related improvements. Surface parking is the most land-use intensive of all parking types and also the most common type, comprising more than two-thirds of all parking in the United States.

Structured parking consists of parking contained within enclosed or open buildings. In comparison to surface parking, structured parking consumes less land. However, due to the added construction required, it is also significantly more expensive. Structured parking is normally selected as an option only where land is sufficiently costly or limited in availability that surface parking becomes uneconomic or impractical. Structured parking may also be preferred for very large parking facilities where limits such as the maximum comfortable distance from parking stalls to the facility served become excessive in a surface parking solution.

Structured parking can take a number of forms. *Open parking* refers to structures which are naturally ventilated. Where vehicles are stored within a building, toxic exhaust gasses and flammable vapors that may be released by these vehicles must not be allowed to accumulate to the extent that they can become a health or safety hazard. In structures where parking is located entirely or mostly aboveground, the least expensive means of preventing such accumulations is to provide openings in significant portions of the exterior of the structure such that natural ventilation can be relied upon to remove such hazards. The minimum extent of openings in the exterior walls and other requirements for open garages can be found for each model code on page 329.

Where natural ventilation is not a practical option, parking may be contained in mechanically ventilated structures called *enclosed parking*. Because of the added expense of the mechanical systems and a complete building enclosure, enclosed parking structures are more expensive than open ones. Enclosed parking may be constructed above or below grade. Above-grade structures are designed as enclosed rather than open when natural ventilation is not practical, such as where exterior walls abut other buildings or are too close to permit the extensive openings required for an open garage. Wherever parking is constructed substantially below grade, enclosed parking is the only choice, since natural ventilation is not feasible. Because of the significant added costs associated with excavation and other aspects of subgrade construction, enclosed below-grade parking is the most expensive form of conventional parking facility. On the other hand, from a resource conservation point of view, it also consumes the least land of any conventional type of parking facility.

Automated parking is a specialized type of structured parking in which vehicles are transported within the facility on proprietary lifting and conveying equipment rather than through a conventional system of drivable ramps and parking aisles. The additional expense of the conveying systems in these facilities is offset by their ability to store roughly twice as many vehicles as a conventional facility of equal size. Automated parking facilities may also offer advantages in improved car security, lower staffing costs, and more rapid vehicle delivery than conventional facilities. They are most economically attractive in locations with

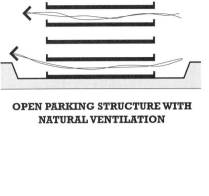

OPEN PARKING STRUCTURE WITH NATURAL VENTILATION

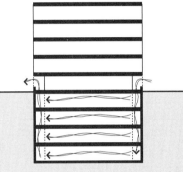

ENCLOSED BELOW-GRADE PARKING STRUCTURE WITH MECHANICAL VENTILATION

very high land costs or on highly constrained sites. This chapter does not provide design guidelines for this type of facility; manufacturers of automated parking facility equipment should be consulted for more information.

In summary, listed in order from least to highest cost, the choice of parking facility type typically proceeds as follows:

- Surface parking
- Open parking structure, above grade
- Enclosed parking structure, above grade
- Enclosed parking structure, below grade
- Automated parking facility

PARKING CAPACITY AND LEVEL OF SERVICE

PARKING CAPACITY

The planned capacity of a parking facility, that is, the number of parking stalls that will be provided, may be dictated by local land-use regulations or other ordinances, or it may be established on the basis of anticipated demand, reflecting the parking needs of the facilities to be served. Ordinances that dictate parking requirements are not addressed in this chapter, as they are unique to each locality. The designer should always seek out such information and verify regulatory requirements for his or her project at the earliest possible stage of design.

Where parking capacity is based on estimates of demand, factors to be considered may include the types of facilities being served, analyses of comparable sites, expected peak and average parking volumes, level of service expectations, anticipated use patterns, the impact of nearby existing or planned parking facilities, area traffic studies, the availability of alternative transportation, and area economic and development projections. Since the combination of such factors is unique to any location, no one set of parking demand figures can be applied universally to all sites. However, where location-specific information is not available or has not yet been developed, the recommended parking ratios provided in the table on this page are suitable for preliminary design purposes.

FACILITY LEVEL OF SERVICE

Parking facility design allows trade-offs between user convenience and comfort, on the one hand, and the economy and compactness of the facility, on the other. For example, the optimal size of a stall in a parking garage built in a dense urban setting, where space is at a premium and users are accustomed to constrained parking conditions, may be significantly smaller than that of a stall in a suburban shopping center, where land costs are lower and user amenity is a higher priority. Similar trade-offs may be made for the width of driving lanes, turning radii, floor-to-ceiling heights, driving and walking distances within the facility, traffic flow capacity, wait times at entrances and exits, and other aspects of the facility's design.

In this chapter, parking facilities are classified according to four *levels of service*, A through D. Level of Service A describes conditions that place the highest priority on user comfort and convenience; Level of Service D describes those placing the greatest emphasis on economy and the efficient utilization of space; and Levels of Service B and C represent intermediate conditions. In choosing a level of service for your project, the most important criteria are the familiarity of the user with the facility (familiar users can comfortably tolerate lower level of service conditions), the rate of parking turnover (with more vehicles moving through a facility at any given time, more generous dimensions should be provided to avoid

Type of Use Served by Parking	Recommended Parking Ratios for Preliminary Design (1000 gross ft^2 = 93 m^2 gross)
Assembly Spaces such as theaters, arenas, cinemas, etc.	0.25 to 0.5 spaces per seat or occupant
Convenience Stores	2–10 per 1000 gross ft^2
Convention Centers	20 per 1000 gross ft^2
Hospitals and Medical Centers	The sum of: 0.1–0.75 per staff, plus 0.3–0.75 per bed, plus 0.2 per daily outpatient Or: 4–10 per 1000 gross ft^2
Hotels	The sum of: 0.2–1.5 spaces per room, plus 10–20 per 1000 gross ft^2 of public space and meeting rooms
Industrial Facilities	0.5–4 per 1000 gross ft^2
Office Buildings	0.5–3 per 1000 gross ft^2
Residential, Single-Family	1–2 spaces per dwelling unit
Residential, Multifamily	0.5–2 spaces per dwelling unit
Restaurants	10–25 per 1000 gross ft^2
Retail	2–4 per 1000 gross ft^2
Schools K-12	The sum of: 1–1.5 per classroom, plus 0.25 per driving age student
Shopping Centers, Malls	4–6 per 1000 gross ft^2
Universities	The sum of: 0.1–0.5 spaces per student, and 0.8 spaces per staff

conflicts or bottlenecks), and the expectations of the user (users accustomed to constrained parking conditions will be more tolerant of lower level of service conditions). Additional factors that may be considered in choosing the level of service for a facility include the following. Consider higher level of service designations for:

■ Parking facilities in which users will frequently be carrying bulky packages or large materials

■ Facilities used by the elderly or infirm

■ Facilities serving family-oriented activities

■ Outdoor parking in cold climate regions, where users wearing bulky clothing may have greater difficulty entering and exiting cars during periods of inclement weather

■ Parking located in rural or suburban locales where drivers are accustomed to readily available, less constrained parking

Lower level of service designations may be appropriate for:

■ All-day or long-term parking

■ Employee parking, residential parking, and other parking for repeat users who will be familiar with a facility

■ Parking located in dense urban areas, where users are accustomed to congested traffic conditions and limited availability of parking

The following table provides recommended level of service ranges for parking serving various types of uses.

Type of Use Served by Parking	Recommended Level of Service (LOS) Range			
	LOS A	LOS B	LOS C	LOS D
Airports, Transportation Centers, all day and long-term		━━━	━━━	━━━
Airports, Transportation Centers, short-term	━━━	━━━		
Assembly Spaces such as theaters, sports arenas, cinemas, etc.	━━━	━━━		
Convention Centers	━━━	━━━		
Hospitals and Medical Centers	━━━	━━━		
Hotels		━━━	━━━	
Industrial Facilities			━━━	━━━
Office Buildings		━━━	━━━	
Residential			━━━	━━━
Retail, Shopping Centers	━━━	━━━		
Schools K-12		━━━	━━━	
Universities		━━━	━━━	━━━

ACCESSIBLE PARKING

INTERNATIONAL BUILDING CODE

The International Building Code requires accessible parking wherever surface or structured parking facilities serve accessible buildings. This includes most building types except detached one- and two-family residences (see pages 266–270 for more information). The table on this page lists the number of accessible spaces required for parking, depending on the building type served.

Where accessible parking spaces are required, one of every six spaces (or a fraction of six spaces) must be an accessible van space. In other words, where anywhere from 1 to 6 accessible spaces are required, at least one must be accessible for vans; where 7 to 12 accessible spaces are required, at least two must be accessible for vans; and so on.

Accessible parking spaces must be located along the shortest accessible route to the building being served. Where there are multiple accessible entrances to a building, accessible parking spaces must be similarly dispersed. However, due to the special vertical clearance requirements of accessible van spaces, these may always be located solely on one level of a multilevel parking facility. Where accessible parking occurs on ramped tiers with slopes greater than 1:20 (5%), accessible routes must meet the requirements of accessible ramps (see pages 266–267 for more information on accessible routes).

Accessible car spaces must be at least 96 in. (2440 mm) wide, and accessible van spaces must be at least 132 in. (3350 mm) wide. Accessible van spaces, and the parking facility aisles and lanes connecting these spaces to public roadways, must provide a minimum vertical clearance of 98 in. (2490 mm).

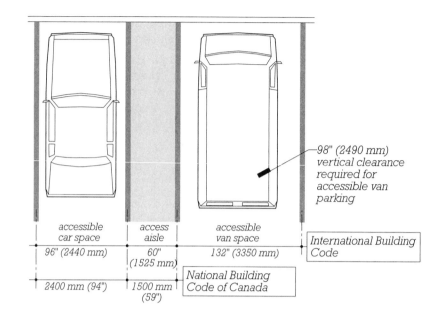

98" (2490 mm) vertical clearance required for accessible van parking

International Building Code

National Building Code of Canada

accessible car space	access aisle	accessible van space
96" (2440 mm)	60" (1525 mm)	132" (3350 mm)
2400 mm (94")	1500 mm (59")	

DIMENSIONS FOR ACCESSIBLE PARKING IN THE INTERNATIONAL BUILDING CODE AND THE NATIONAL BUILDING CODE OF CANADA

Type of Use Served by Parking	Number of Accessible Parking Spaces Required by the International Building Code
Hospital outpatient facilities	10% of visitor and patient parking
Rehabilitation and physical therapy facilities	20% of visitor and patient parking
Occupancy Group R-2 Multifamily Residential and Group R-3 One- and Two-Family Residential buildings, where required to provide Type A or Type B accessible units	2% of all parking, but not less than 1 accessible car space and 1 accessible van space
All other accessible buildings with:	
1–25 total spaces	1 accessible space
26–50 total spaces	2 accessible spaces
51–75 total spaces	3 accessible spaces
76–100 total spaces	4 accessible spaces
101–150 total spaces	5 accessible spaces
151–200 total spaces	6 accessible spaces
201–500 total spaces	6 accessible spaces, plus one per 100 (or fraction of 100) over 200
501–1000 total spaces	2% of the total number of spaces to be accessible
1001 or more spaces	20 accessible spaces, plus one per 100 (or fraction of 100) over 1000

ACCESSIBLE PARKING

All accessible parking spaces must have an access aisle, at least 60 in. (1525 mm) wide on at least one side, extending the full length of the accessible space. One aisle can be shared by two accessible spaces, one on either side. Where accessible van parking spaces are angled, the access aisle must be on the passenger side of the van.

NATIONAL BUILDING CODE OF CANADA

The National Building Code of Canada refers to local jurisdictions for barrier-free parking requirements. In the absence of such requirements, the code provides guidelines recommending that wherever more than 50 surface or structured parking spaces are provided, barrier-free spaces should be provided at the rate of one per every 100 spaces (or fraction of 100 spaces); see the table on this page.

Type of Use Served by Parking	Number of Accessible Parking Spaces Recommended by the National Building Code of Canada
1–50 total spaces	None
51–100 total spaces	1 accessible space
101–200 total spaces	2 accessible spaces
201–300 total spaces	3 accessible spaces
301–400 total spaces	4 accessible spaces
401–500 spaces	5 accessible spaces
501 more total spaces	1 accessible space for every 100 total spaces (or fraction of 100 spaces)

Barrier-free parking spaces must be located close to a barrier-free entrance to the building they serve. Long paths of travel should be avoided. Where accessible parking occurs on ramped tiers with slopes greater than 1:20 (5%), barrier-free routes must meet all the requirements of barrier-free ramps (see pages 270–271 for more information on barrier-free routes).

Barrier-free spaces must be not less than 2400 mm (7'-1") wide and must be provided with an access aisle not less than 1500 mm (4'-11") wide on at least one side. One aisle can be shared by two barrier-free spaces, one on either side.

2
CONFIGURING PARKING FACILITIES

This chapter will aid you in the selection of a circulation scheme for your parking facility, provide guidance in the design of other aspects of the facility, and, in the case of structured parking, offer recommendations for the choice of a structural system.

PARKING CIRCULATION BASICS

ENTRANCES AND EXITS

Parking facility entrances and exits should be located away from street intersections, especially busy ones. Entrances may be located on streets with high volumes of traffic inbound to the facility, making them easy for drivers to find and access. Or, in congested areas, entrances may be located on secondary streets to minimize interference with traffic on more heavily traveled thoroughfares. Entrances should provide one lane for every 300 to 500 stalls of parking. Entrance lanes should be long enough to allow queuing of several vehicles ahead of control points or turns into parking aisles. In structured parking facilities on sloped sites, entrances should be located strategically to minimize ramping within the facility. For example, for below-grade parking, entrances should be located at the lowest point on the site. Where entrances and exits are separate, exits may be located where they discharge onto low-traffic-volume secondary streets, helping to minimize back-ups within the facility or disruption of traffic on main thoroughfares during times of heavy use.

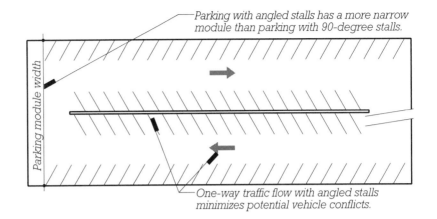

Parking with angled stalls has a more narrow module than parking with 90-degree stalls.

Parking module width

One-way traffic flow with angled stalls minimizes potential vehicle conflicts.

PARKING AISLE WITH ONE-WAY TRAFFIC FLOW AND ANGLED STALLS

PARKING AISLES AND STALLS

Within parking facilities, the designer has a choice of one-way or two-way traffic flow. One-way traffic flow minimizes opportunities for vehicle conflicts or collisions and reduces opportunities for congestion in heavily used facilities. One-way traffic flow is especially advantageous for structured parking facilities where driver site distances tend to be limited and parking dimensions are often more constrained. With one-way traffic flow, parking stalls should be angled. Stalls angled 75 degrees to the flow of traffic result in the highest efficiency, that is, the least area required per stall. Stalls angled at 60 degrees, though less efficient, may provide more comfortable vehicle entry and exit. Stalls angled at 45 degrees are the least efficient but also result in a *parking module* of the least width, that is, in the least combined width of drive aisle and stalls on either side. Intermediate angles may also be used, but stalls should never be angled at less than 45 degrees or more than 75 degrees.

PARKING CIRCULATION BASICS

Two-way traffic flow is most suitable for facilities with generous vehicle clearances, for surface parking with multiple points of access where enforcing one-way flow is impractical, or where the configuration of structured parking requires two-way circulation. Where two-way traffic flow is provided, 90-degree parking stalls are preferred to allow the greatest flexibility in entering and exiting stalls from either direction. However, where a narrower parking module is required, angled stalls also may be used with stalls on opposite sides of aisles angled for flow in opposite directions. When comparing the space efficiency of 90-degree and angled stalls, two-way aisles with 90-degree stalls are typically about as efficient as one-way aisles with 75-degree stalls, as the greater compactness of the 90-degree stalls themselves is offset by the wider aisles required for two-way traffic circulation.

Circulation within a facility should be designed so that entering the facility, locating a stall, entering and exiting the stall, and leaving the facility require the fewest possible distinct vehicle maneuvers such as turns or reversals in direction. Dead-end aisles should be avoided. The arrangements of stalls and aisles should be as consistent as possible from one section or tier of a facility to the next. There should be a logical, continuous route through the facility.

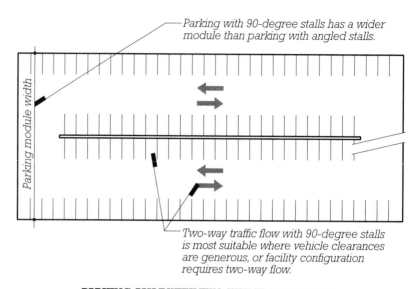

Parking with 90-degree stalls has a wider module than parking with angled stalls.

Parking module width

Two-way traffic flow with 90-degree stalls is most suitable where vehicle clearances are generous, or facility configuration requires two-way flow.

PARKING AISLE WITH TWO-WAY TRAFFIC FLOW AND 90-DEGREE STALLS

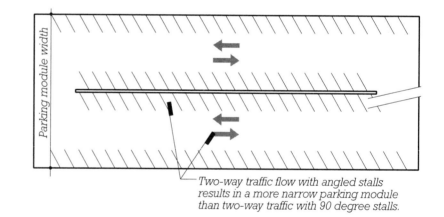

Parking module width

Two-way traffic flow with angled stalls results in a more narrow parking module than two-way traffic with 90 degree stalls.

PARKING AISLE WITH TWO-WAY TRAFFIC FLOW AND ANGLED STALLS

SURFACE PARKING DESIGN

SURFACE PARKING CIRCULATION

In its most common arrangement, surface parking is configured with an access lane located directly in front of the buildings served by the parking and with parking aisles aligned at right angles to the access lane. This arrangement permits passenger pickup and dropoff close to building entrances and allows pedestrian circulation between stalls and building entrances to occur within vehicle aisles. With long, narrow sites, stall efficiency may dictate that aisles be parallel to the longer dimension of the site. In this case, dedicated pedestrian pathways crossing rows of parking stalls may be required. Providing perimeter stalls, as illustrated in the accompanying diagram, increases stall efficiency but may interfere with snow removal in cold climate regions. For the sizing of surface parking facilities, see pages 336–337.

LANDSCAPING

Where the priority is to maximize parking capacity, landscaping with trees and shrubs is customarily confined to areas unusable for parking, such as ends of stall rows, inaccessible corners, and so on. Alternatively, greater extents of landscaping may be incorporated into a facility to meet requirements set by local design ordinances, to enhance the facility's comfort and appearance, or to mitigate its ecological impact. (In such cases, the number of available parking spaces will be reduced from the quantities indicated in the sizing guidelines provided in this chapter.) Where provided, landscaping must not interfere with sight lines. Plants that produce foliage within the range of 3 to 8 ft (0.9 to 2.4 m) above the ground should be avoid-

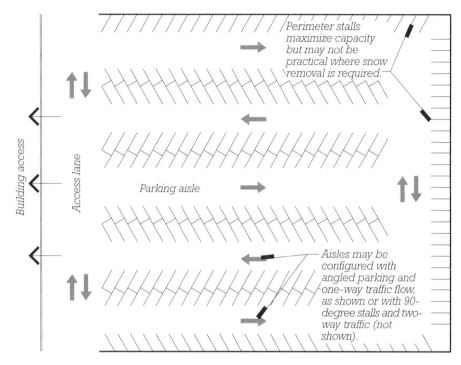

EXAMPLE SURFACE PARKING CIRCULATION PLAN

ed. Plants should also be kept comfortably away from vehicles to prevent damage to vehicle finishes and to avoid interference with users entering and exiting cars.

SURFACE PARKING AND SUSTAINABILITY

Surface parking consumes open land, reduces the quality of water in streams and lakes, and degrades the environment. Consider the following guidelines for minimizing these detrimental effects and designing greener, more sustainable surface parking.

Reduce the Number of Parking Stalls: Reducing the number of parking stalls reduces the area consumed by parking. Where land-use regulations set requirements for parking capacity, design to the minimum permitted. Where capacity is established through analysis of demand, design to projected

average demand rather than peak demand, or work with neighboring facilities to share parking where peak use times differ (e.g., day and evening uses or weekday and weekend uses).

Reduce Impervious Area: Reducing impervious (paved) area reduces the volume and intensity of stormwater runoff, helping to protect streams, lakes, and other water features. Design narrower parking stalls and less generous aisles and lanes; in other words, consider a lower level of service for the facility. Lay out stalls and circulation for maximum efficiency. Use pervious paving materials (ones that permit surface storm water to pass through the paving to the ground beneath) for overflow parking areas. Consider structured parking as an alternative to surface parking.

Increase Planting: Plants and trees reduce stormwater runoff. They hold water in their leaves and on their branches and stems. Plant roots increase the permeability of soil and its capacity to absorb water. Plantings, especially canopy trees, reduce heat island effects. Planted areas also create wildlife habitat and a more aesthetically interesting environment.

Provide Natural Stormwater Retention: By directing stormwater into shallow landscaped swales, stormwater can infiltrate back into the soil or be discharged from the site at a more controlled rate. Such bioretention areas also aid the removal of pollutants in stormwater runoff and can reduce the need for more expensive, traditional stormwater management facilities.

Minimize the Extent of Heat-Absorbing Surfaces: Reducing the area of heat-absorbing paving lowers the air and surface temperatures of a parking facility, thereby improving user comfort, reducing health risks, lowering the temperature of stormwater leaving the site,

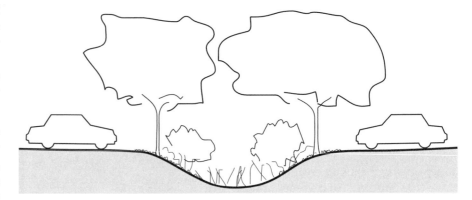

BIORETENTION SWALE

and even lessening energy consumption of nearby buildings. By using shading, lighter-colored or pervious paving, and covered parking to reduce the absorptive area by 50% or more, significant improvements in heat island effects can be achieved.

Avoid Development of Ecologically Valuable Land: Do not develop parking on prime farmland, in floodplains, on land providing habitat for endangered species, close to wetlands or productive bodies of water, or land previously used as public parkland.

STRUCTURED PARKING DESIGN

STRUCTURED PARKING CIRCULATION

This chapter provides design guidelines for four configurations of vertical circulation in structured parking: single-threaded helix, double-threaded helix, split level, and multi-bay. These configurations are suitable for the preliminary design of efficient parking solutions meeting a broad range of requirements for facilities varying in size, use characteristics, and site constraints.

Single-Threaded Helix

The single-threaded helix consists of a single continuously spiraling ramp, a configuration that is intuitive for users to navigate even when unfamiliar with the facility. An important characteristic of the single-threaded helix is that, being a single spiral, it cannot form a complete loop. Users leaving the facility must traverse in the opposite direction the same path used to arrive at their parking stall. Consequently, in its simplest form, single-threaded helix structures must be designed for two-way traffic flow. For the sizing of single-threaded helix structures, see pages 338–339.

Double-Threaded Helix

In a double-threaded helix configuration, two spiral ramps are interlocked so that a continuous loop is formed. Users traveling through such a facility can return to their original point of entry without ever retracing their path. A double-threaded helix structure can therefore be designed for one-way traffic flow, a configuration that minimizes congestion and conflicts between vehicles. This advantage is particularly important in facilities accessed by large numbers of users in relatively short time

frames, where high peak vehicle flows create the greatest potential for traffic conflicts. In addition, users searching an entire facility for an available stall will have to pass each stall only once, since at the end of their search they will arrive back at the facility's entry. This is not the case in a single-threaded helix, where once users have searched all stalls, they arrive at the end of the spiral and must then retrace their path past the same stalls a second time in order to return to the place where they started. Double-threaded helix structures also allow for crossover aisles between adjacent ramps, providing shortcuts to facility exits. However, the double helix structure is also a less intuitive configuration, and one that may be confusing to infrequent users. For the sizing of double-threaded helix parking structures, see pages 340–341.

Split Level

In a split level parking structure, level parking tiers are connected by *speed ramps* at either end. Adjacent tiers are staggered in a manner that creates a vehicle circulation pattern similar to that of a single helix, that is, a closed loop is not possible, and two-way traffic flow is required. In a split level structure, parking areas themselves are level, a benefit for user comfort and a feature that is particularly advantageous on constrained sites where bay lengths are short. As the length of the parking bay decreases in a single- or double-helix structure, ramps become more steeply sloped and increasingly uncomfortable for users. This is not the case for the split level structure, where parking tiers remain level regardless of length. Split level structures also conserve height (or depth in the case of below-grade structures) in comparison to ramped helix struc-

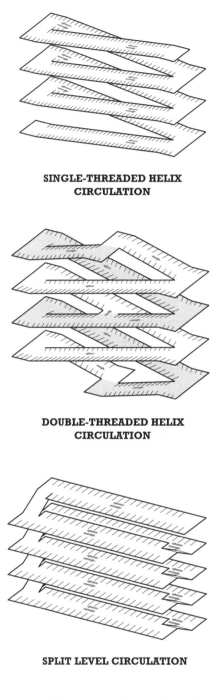

SINGLE-THREADED HELIX CIRCULATION

DOUBLE-THREADED HELIX CIRCULATION

SPLIT LEVEL CIRCULATION

tures. For example, a three-bay split level structure rises only as much as required for two ramps, since the first level is entirely at grade. In comparison, a three-bay single-threaded helix of similar extent and capacity must rise the combined height of three ramps. For the sizing of split level parking structures, see pages 342–343.

CONFIGURING PARKING FACILITIES

Multi-Bay

Multi-bay facilities consist of relatively large-area parking tiers without slope connected by internal ramped parking or external *express ramps*. Facilities of this type offer advantages of high capacity, high user comfort, and the capability to manage high peak flows. For the sizing of multi-bay parking structures, see pages 344–345.

MULTI-BAY CIRCULATION

Other Configurations

Variations on the circulation systems described above are also possible, though beyond the scope of this book to be treated in detail. However, the overall capacity of such structures will not deviate significantly from the capacities derived from the charts in this text when considered on a proportional basis. In other words, for the purposes of preliminary design, an efficiently designed facility twice as wide as one designed using the charts in this book may be assumed to accommodate approximately twice as many vehicles, and so on. Where more detailed information on such configurations is needed, consult the references listed in this book's bibliography.

STRUCTURED PARKING FACILITY DESIGN

The parking facility sizing information provided on pages 335–345 can be used to quickly determine the length, width, and height of a structure sufficient to provide parking for a specified number of vehicles. The dimensions provided by the charts account only for the parking system itself, that is, the ramps and aisles that vehicles use to circulate within the facility and the stalls in which they park. As explained in the text accompanying the charts, in some cases allowance is also made for the placement of structural columns or bearing walls. However, these charts do not account for other features such as stair towers, elevator

GIVE SPECIAL CONSIDERATION TO THE SYSTEMS INDICATED IF YOUR STRUCTURED PARKING FACILITY:	Single-Threaded Helix (Pages 338-339)	Double-Threaded Helix (Pages 340-341)	Split Level (Pages 342-343)	Multi-bay (Pages 344-345)
Is planned primarily for infrequent visitors unfamiliar with the facility	●		●	●
Will be used primarily by regular users familiar with the facility		●		●
Is being constructed on a small, highly constrained site			●	
Will have high peak volume use		●		●
Is intended for large-capacity, high-volume parking				●

STRUCTURED PARKING DESIGN

shafts and lobbies, spaces for mechanical and electrical systems, and other possibly necessary items. In order to complete the preliminary design of a structured parking facility, the following requirements should also be considered, and the necessary spaces and elements incorporated into the design as appropriate to your project's requirements.

Exterior Walls

The parking facility sizing charts provide the length and width of the facility measured to the inside of the exterior walls of the structure. To arrive at overall dimensions, the thickness of exterior walls must be added to these figures. For preliminary purposes, thicknesses ranging from 6 to 12 in. (150 to 300 mm) may be assumed. Or, once you have selected a structural system for your facility, information on specific wall systems can be found on the following pages:

■ Wood stud walls: pages 56–57

■ Brick masonry walls: pages 80–81

■ Concrete masonry walls: pages 88–89

■ Steel stud walls: pages 94–95

■ Sitecast concrete walls: pages 116–117

■ Precast concrete wall panels: pages 134–135

Ventilation

Open parking structures must meet building code requirements for the extent of openings in exterior walls to ensure effective natural ventilation of the facility. If you do not already know which model building code applies to your project, see pages 7–15.

In the International Building Code, each tier of an open parking structure must have exterior wall openings on at least two sides. These openings must be uniformly distributed, and their combined area may not be less than 20% of that tier's total exterior wall area. In addition, where exterior openings are not located on opposite sides of the structure, their aggregate length may not be less than 40% of the total length of the perimeter of the tier. Interior walls in open parking structures must also contain uniformly distributed openings constituting not less than 20% of each wall's total area. The parking of trucks, buses, or other large vehicles, the dispensing of fuel, and the repair of vehicles are all activities that are prohibited in open parking garages under this code.

The National Building Code of Canada requires each tier of an open parking garage to have exterior wall openings with an area totaling not less than 25% of that tier's total exterior wall area. These openings must be located to ensure cross ventilation for the entire tier.

Enclosed garages, which rely on mechanical ventilation to remove hazardous gasses and vapors, must include spaces for air handling equipment and ductwork. Air intakes for the ventilation system must be located safely away from sources of potentially contaminated air (above the uppermost tier or roof level, for example), and exhausts must not discharge toward exterior occupied areas or walkways. In order to minimize ceiling height conflicts, main supply ducts should be routed vertically through the structure and located such that the size and extent of horizontal branch ducts can be minimized. Required ventilation rates for enclosed parking garages are relatively high compared to those of conventionally occupied buildings to ensure adequate air handling capacity and the prevention of toxic gas accumulations. In order to reduce the high costs of continuously moving large quantities of air, many facilities rely on a system of carbon monoxide detectors to control ventilation rates, running the system at its highest capacity only when dangerous gas concentrations rise above specified levels. Cashier booths, offices, and other continuously occupied employee or public-use spaces within the facility should have their own dedicated supplies of conditioned air. For more information, see pages 191–192 for the design of fan rooms and pages 218–219 for the sizing of air handling system components. When using the chart on page 219, read to the far right in the bands labeled for various building types.

Pedestrian Circulation

Pedestrian circulation within a single tier or floor normally occurs along the same aisles used by vehicles to access stalls. However, where the potential for hazardous conflicts between vehicles and pedestrians may occur, dedicated walkways or other safety measures should be provided. Examples of such areas include the top and bottom of ramps (especially steep ones), points where pedestrian or driver vision is limited, facility entrances and exits, where automatic gates control vehicle movement, and so on.

To aid in wayfinding and maximize personal safety, pedestrian pathways should to the greatest extent possible provide a direct line of sight from car stalls to a level's primary entrance/exit, stairway, or elevator. For the same reason, exit stairs, elevator lobbies, and other components of the circulation system should be designed to be as open and transparent as possible. For user comfort, pedestrian routes within a facility should not exceed 350 to 700 ft (100 to 200 m) in total length, although they may be as long as 1200 ft (370 m) long in facilities designed to low level of service standards. Exits must also comply with building code egress requirements. Information on the minimum number of exits, remoteness of exits, maximum travel distance, and other such criteria can be found beginning on page 253.

Facilities with more than two levels should provide elevators for vertical circulation. Elevators should be located prominently and as close as possible to the building or facility being served by the parking. Parking serving retail and office facilities should provide one elevator for approximately every 250 to 450 stalls. Parking serving special-use facilities with high peak demand will require a greater number of elevators, and large-area parking serving uses such as airports or hospitals will require fewer. When elevators are provided, at least one exit stairway should be located nearby to provide alternative vertical circulation when elevators are out of service or wait times are excessive. For more information on the configuration and sizing of elevator systems, see pages 207–209.

OTHER REQUIREMENTS

Other elements that should be considered in the design of a structured parking facility include:

- Structural systems: pages 335–336
- Accessible parking: pages 318-319
- Sprinkler closet for sprinklered buildings: page 206
- Electrical closet: page 199
- Trash room for trash chute serving facilities above: page 194
- Staff offices or workrooms: page 195
- Transformer vault and switch gear vault for primary electrical power service for adjacent facilities: page 188
- Storage rooms
- Bicycle parking

STRUCTURAL SYSTEMS FOR STRUCTURED PARKING

COLUMN LOCATIONS AND STRUCTURAL SPAN

Wherever possible, structural systems should be selected that can span the full width of one parking module, that is, the combined width of one drive aisle and the stalls on either side. For typical parking layouts, this dimension varies from 50 to 65 ft (15 to 20 m). In this arrangement, columns do not intrude between stalls, stall widths are not compromised, and the greatest flexibility in current and future stall layouts is preserved.

Where shorter-span systems are used, columns must be located between parking stalls. In this arrangement, column spacing must be coordinated with stall spacing, and stalls adjacent to columns must be widened to provide clearance for vehicle movement and to allow space for opening doors. The result is less flexibility in the layout of parking stalls and a reduction in the total number of stalls. However, where such configurations are used, span requirements for the structural system may be as low as 15 to 25 ft (5 to 8 m).

MIXED-USE BUILDINGS

In buildings where parking occurs above or below other uses, an important consideration is the coordination of structural elements between the different building parts. Structures that are part of the building's vertical or lateral load-resisting systems must be continuous from their highest point to the building's foundation. Other lines of bearing must usually be vertically continuous to foundations as well, although in some circumstances and at significant cost, transfer structures may be used to shift the locations of these elements between different levels of a struc-

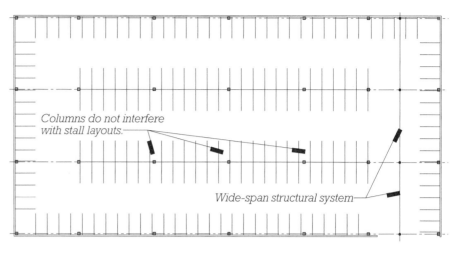

Columns do not interfere with stall layouts.

Wide-span structural system

WIDE-SPAN STRUCTURE COLUMN LOCATIONS

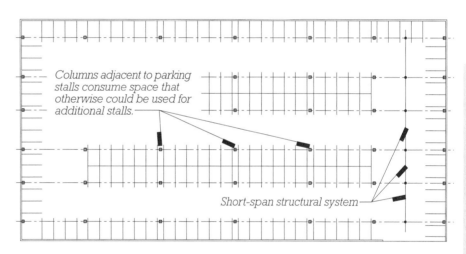

Columns adjacent to parking stalls consume space that otherwise could be used for additional stalls.

Short-span structural system

SHORT-SPAN STRUCTURE COLUMN LOCATIONS

ture. Regardless of the approach taken, careful planning is required to develop structural configurations that are compatible with the requirements of the different parts of the building. In many cases, constraints on the placement of structural elements within the parking portion of the building may be the most restrictive. In such cases, the design of this portion of the building may have a strong influence on the entire structure, even to the spoint of dictating the column grid of the whole building. Due to the significant design and cost implications, the designer should thoroughly investigate the structural configuration of such mixed-use buildings at the earliest possible time. For more information on the configuration of structural systems, see pages 37–51, and for more information on the planning of service cores in buildings, see pages 196–198.

331

STRUCTURAL SYSTEMS FOR STRUCTURED PARKING

SELECTION OF STRUCTURAL SYSTEMS

Structural systems for structured parking facilities should be capable of spanning the required distances for optimum column placement within the facility and, in the case of open parking structures, should be resistant to the effects of weather, road salt, and other exterior conditions. The most commonly used systems are precast concrete, sitecast concrete, and structural steel.

Precast Concrete

Precast concrete is especially economical when used in repetitive configurations such as are common in parking garage construction; it is resistant to the effects of exterior exposure; and it does not require added finishes to attain an acceptable appearance or to be protected from fire. The most common precast concrete spanning system used in structured parking facilities is the double tee. Although single tees are also capable of spanning the required distances, they are less economical and infrequently used. Where span requirements are more modest, hollow core planks may also be used. Guidelines for the design of precast concrete structures can be found on pages 131–141.

Sitecast Concrete

Like precast concrete, sitecast concrete does not require added finishes to attain an acceptable appearance or for protection from fire. Where sitecast concrete will be exposed to the weather, systems with very thin slab sections, such as one-way joist or waffle slab, should be avoided due to their vulnerability to corrosion of reinforcing. A post and beam system with posttensioned one-way or two-way slabs may be a more suitable option in these conditions. Posttensioning, in which reinforcing is prestressed after it has been cast, has several advantages for the construction of sitecast concrete parking structures: It increases spans while minimizing structural depth, and for structures exposed to the weather, it improves the concrete's resistance to salts and corrosion. Guidelines for the design of sitecast concrete systems can be found on pages 113–129.

Structural Steel

Structural steel is also used for the construction of structured parking facilities. Where it is exposed to the weather, it must be protected by high-performance paint-like coatings, galvanizing, or other protective coverings to prevent corrosion. Where required, protection from fire is most economically provided with spray-on insulating materials. (In open parking structures, materials applied for protection from fire, unless naturally weather-resistant, must themselves also be coated or covered to be protected from the weather.) Steel structural systems for structured parking facilities take the form of a steel post and beam with either concrete-topped steel floor decking or precast concrete solid or hollow core slabs. Guidelines for the design of steel structural systems can be found on pages 93–105.

BUILDING CODE HEIGHT AND AREA LIMITS

Choice of a construction system for a structured parking facility is also limited by building code requirements. Information on permitted height and area, and on types of construction, for parking facilities constructed to the requirements of the International Building Code can be found on pages 420–425. Information for such facilities constructed to the requirements of the National Building Code of Canada can be found on pages 428–453. If you do not know what building code applies to your project, see pages 7–15.

3
SIZING PARKING FACILITIES

This chapter will allow you to quickly determine the dimensions of a surface or structured parking facility to accommodate any required number of parking stalls

GENERAL SIZING CRITERIA

The parking facility sizing charts on the following pages allow quick determination of the overall dimensions of a parking configuration and the number of stalls accommodated. On this page, additional sizing information is provided for other aspects of the facility.

Access Lanes: For lanes without parking, a single lane should be 10'-0" to 11'-6" (3.0 to 3.5 m) wide, with an additional clearance to walls or other obstructions of not less than 6" to 2'-0" (0.15 to 0.61 m) on either side. A double lane should be 18'-0" to 21'-0" (5.5 to 6.4 m) wide (for both drive lanes) plus the same side clearances as for a single lane. The outside radius of a turning lane should be 24'-0" to 42'-0" (7.3 to 12.8 m). Turning lanes are generally several feet wider than straight lanes.

Vertical Clearance within Structured Facilities: The International Building Code requires a minimum vertical clearance in parking structures of 7'-0" (2.13 m). The National Building Code of Canada requires a minimum of 2.0 m (6'-7"). Clearances of 7'-4" (2.24 m) or more improve user comfort, and this dimension may be increased to as much as 9'-0" to 9'-8" (2.74 to 2.95 m) in large facilities or those designed to high level of service conditions. Where accessible van parking spaces are provided, the required minimum clearance is 8'-2" (2.49 m). For more information on accessible parking requirements, see pages 318–319.

In determining overall floor-to-floor dimensions, prior to selection of a specific structural system, depth of structure may be estimated at 2'-6" to 3'-0" (0.75 to 0.9 m), assuming wide-span structural systems. For more information on choosing structural systems for structured parking, see pages 331–332.

Ramps: Ramped parking areas (see Single-Threaded Helix, pages 338–339, or Double-Threaded Helix, pages 340–341) should not exceed slopes of 5% wherever possible. More steeply sloped parking areas are less comfortable for users, make car entry and exit more difficult, and must be treated as ramps where accessible routes are required. Where an accessible route is not required, parking ramp sloped up to approximately 7% may be considered for facilities designed to lower level of service standards. In high level of service facilities, ramped parking areas should be minimized or eliminated to the greatest extent possible. See pages 266–267 for information on accessible routes in the International Building Code or pages 270–271 for information on barrier-free routes in the National Building Code of Canada.

Speed ramps (see Split Level, pages 342–343) should normally not exceed slopes of 12.5%. Steeper slopes may be acceptable in locales where drivers are accustomed to steep drives. Express ramps (see Multi-Bay Parking, pages 344–345) should not exceed slopes ranging from 8% to 16%.

Number of Tiers: The number of complete 360-degree revolutions required to reach the farthest stalls in a facility should not exceed six to seven. For facilities designed to a high level of service, the number should be less.

Stall Sizes: The parking facility sizing charts in this text are based on the assumption of uniform stall sizes throughout the facility. This approach is consistent with contemporary parking design guidelines that recommend against routinely providing a percentage of stalls sized for small cars only. This change from earlier practice reflects trends in the North American passenger vehicle population toward a larger percentage of wider vehicles and the lessening of the size difference between small and medium-sized cars. The effect of these trends has been to reduce the need for compact stalls and to blur the definition of what vehicles they are intended for, to the degree that their use has become increasingly problematic. For the preliminary layout of individual standard stalls, a size of 8'-6" $\times$ 18'-0" (2.59 $\times$ 5.49 m) may be used.

Where the use of compact stalls is considered, they should be limited to not more than 10% to 15% of the total spaces in a facility. They may also be used in particular locations within a facility where a standard-sized stall will not fit due to physical constraints. For preliminary design purposes, a compact stall size of 7'-6" $\times$ 15'-0" (2.29 $\times$ 4.57 m) may be used.

PARKING BAY WIDTH

On the charts on the facing page, *Bay width* is the width of one typical double-loaded parking aisle. Bay widths differ for each level of service, and are indicated on the chart for Level of Service A and D conditions. Within any band, widths for intermediate levels of service may be interpolated by adding or subtracting approximately 1 ft (0.3 m) for each single step in level.

When configured with angled stalls, parking bays located at either end of the parking area will be 1 to 3 ft (0.3 to 0.9 m) wider than the inner bays. To determine the overall width of the parking area, multiply the width of one bay by the number of bays and then add 2 to 6 ft (0.6 to 1.8 m) for the wider bays at either end. When configured for 90-degree parking, no special allowance for end bays is required, and parking area width is determined simply by the width of one parking bay multiplied by the number of bays.

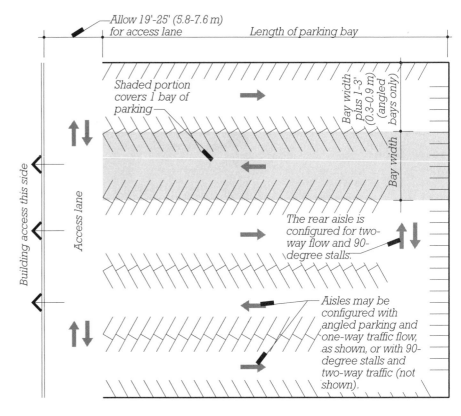

Allow 19'-25' (5.8-7.6 m) for access lane

Length of parking bay

Shaded portion covers 1 bay of parking

Bay width plus 1-3' (0.3-0.9 m) (angled bays only)

Bay width

Building access this side

Access lane

The rear aisle is configured for two-way flow and 90-degree stalls.

Aisles may be configured with angled parking and one-way traffic flow, as shown, or with 90-degree stalls and two-way traffic (not shown).

EXAMPLE USE OF CHARTS

At least 500 stalls of surface parking are required as part of a suburban shopping center. The mall building is set back 450 ft from the main public roadway. Assuming high-turnover parking and users frequently accompanied by children or carrying bulky packages, Level of Service A conditions are proposed.

To provide the most convenient access to the mall building, parking aisles will be oriented perpendicular to the mall itself, as shown on the diagram on this page. To determine the space available for parking, 25 ft is subtracted from the building setback to account for landscape buffering, pedestrian walkways, and miscellaneous site features, and an additional 25 ft is subtracted to provide for the access lane running parallel to the mall entrance. The remaining available distance is 400 ft.

The first option considered is 75-degree angle parking with one-way traffic aisles. Reading from the upper chart on the facing page, we determine that a parking bay 400 ft long with Level of Service A conditions can accommodate 74 stalls in a bay 56'-4" wide. To accommodate the required number of stalls, 7 bays are needed, providing 518 stalls (7 bays * 74 stalls per bay). To determine the overall width of the parking area, the width of one bay is multiplied by the number of bays, and an additional allowance of 3 ft is added to each side to account for wider end bays, as noted above. The result is 400'-3" (7 bays × 56'-4" per bay + 2 * 3' end bay allowance).

As a possible alternative, parking with 90-degree stalls and two-way traffic aisles is also considered. Reading from the lower chart on the facing page, we determine that a parking bay 400 ft long with Level of Service A conditions can accommodate 72 stalls in a bay 61'-6" wide. Again, 7 bays of parking are required, providing 504 stalls total. In this case, since end bays do not need to be widened, the overall width of the parking area is the width of one bay multiplied by the number of bays, or 430'-6" (7 × 61'-6").

We conclude that either option is a viable configuration. If minimizing land area occupied by parking is the higher priority, the angled parking solution may be used. Or, if providing the greatest flexibility in vehicle circulation is desired, the 90-degree parking solution may be chosen.

SIZING SURFACE PARKING

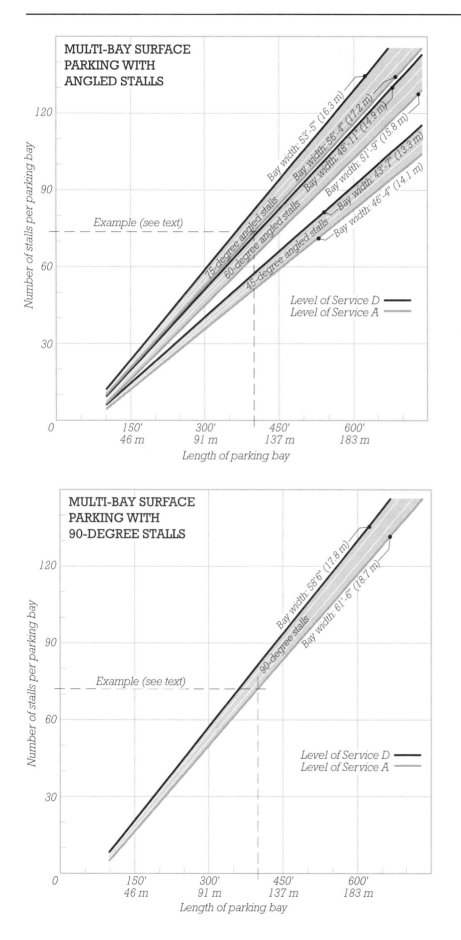

MULTI-BAY SURFACE PARKING WITH ANGLED STALLS

Number of stalls per parking bay

120

90

Example (see text)

60

30

Bay width: 53'-5" (16.3 m)
Bay width: 56'-4" (17.2 m)
Bay width: 48'-11" (14.9 m)
Bay width: 51'-9" (15.8 m)
Bay width: 43'-7" (13.3 m)
Bay width: 46'-4" (14.1 m)

75-degree angled stalls
60-degree angled stalls
45-degree angled stalls

Level of Service D ——
Level of Service A ——

0   150'   300'   450'   600'
      46 m   91 m   137 m   183 m
Length of parking bay

MULTI-BAY SURFACE PARKING WITH 90-DEGREE STALLS

Number of stalls per parking bay

120

90

Example (see text)

60

30

Bay width: 58'6" (17.8 m)
Bay width: 61'-6" (18.7 m)

90-degree stalls

Level of Service D ——
Level of Service A ——

0   150'   300'   450'   600'
      46 m   91 m   137 m   183 m
Length of parking bay

Use the two charts on this page to determine the length and width of a multi-bay surface parking facility as illustrated on the facing page. *Length of parking bay* is the length of one parking aisle and the adjacent perimeter aisle and stalls. *Number of stalls per parking bay* is the number of stalls within one bay (see the shaded area in the diagram).

The top chart is for parking aisles configured primarily with one-way aisles and angled stalls.

■ Read in one of the three indicated bands for parking configured within the one-way aisles as either 75-, 60-, or 45-degree angled stalls. Within each band, read along the bottom for Level of Service A conditions (most generously dimensioned) or along the top for Level of Service D (most constrained). Intermediate Levels of Service B and C are also represented by the thin white lines within each band. See page 316 for more information on selecting the appropriate level of service for your facility.

■ To determine the width of one parking bay, as well as the overall width of the parking facility, see the instructions for Parking Bay Width on the facing page.

The bottom chart is for aisles configured throughout for two-way traffic flow with 90-degree stalls.

■ Read along the bottom of the indicated band for Level of Service A conditions (most generously dimensioned) or along the top for Level of Service D conditions (most constrained). Intermediate Levels of Service B and C are also represented by the white lines within each band.

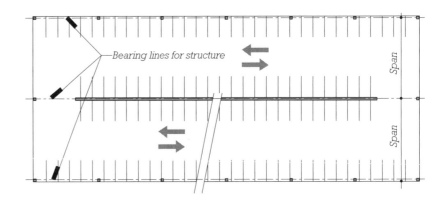

Bearing lines for structure

Span

Span

LOCATION OF COLUMNS AND BEARING WALLS

The dimensions read from the chart on the facing page (as well as those on pages 341 and 343) include allowances for columns and bearing walls located along three lines of bearing, as indicated in the adjacent diagram. Columns located along the perimeter may intrude up to 2 ft (0.6 m) into the ends of parking stalls or into the turning lanes at the ends of the ramps. A 2-ft (0.6-m) allowance is also provided for columns or a wall located along the bearing line between the ramps on either side. In this configuration, a floor system capable of spanning one-half of the total width of the structure is required. Shorter-span systems should be avoided, since when columns fall between stalls, stalls must be widened and the number of stalls per bay must be reduced. See page 331 for more information on selecting structural systems for parking structures.

EXAMPLE USE OF CHART

At least 500 stalls of structured parking are required for a small urban shopping complex. The site available for the parking structure is 420 ft long. Assuming mostly short-term parking and users unfamiliar with the facility, a single-threaded helix configuration is proposed, with two-way traffic, 90-degree parking stalls, and Level of Service B conditions.

To determine the maximum possible length of the parking bays within the structure, 5 ft is subtracted from each end of the site to allow for site features and the thickness of exterior walls, resulting in a length of 410 ft. Referring to the chart on the facing page, we see that one such parking bay, sized for Level of Service B conditions, can accommodate 85 stalls. Six bays of parking will be required, providing 510 stalls total (6 bays × 85 stalls per bay). Interpolating between the bay widths indicated for Levels of Service A and D, we determine that the width of the structure, excluding exterior walls, will be 123'-0".

To determine the height of the structure, we refer to the lower diagram on the facing page and note that each sloped bay of a single-threaded helix structure rises one-half of the structure's floor-to-floor height. Allowing 11 feet floor-to-floor, each bay will rise 5½ ft, and 6 bays of parking will have a total height of 33 ft (6 × 5.5 ft = 33 ft). Assuming that open-air parking is acceptable on the uppermost levels, no additional roof structure is proposed, and the height of the structure from its entrance to its highest parking level, excluding parapets, will be 33 ft. (For more information on floor-to-floor heights in structured parking, see page 335.)

In order not to compromise stall widths, structural systems considered for this building should be capable of spanning one-half of the building's overall width, or approximately 60 to 65 ft. Now that the configuration of the parking system itself has been completed, the next steps in this design process will be the consideration of pedestrian circulation, building systems, and other elements. See page 329 for more information on these subjects.

SIZING SINGLE-THREADED HELIX PARKING STRUCTURES

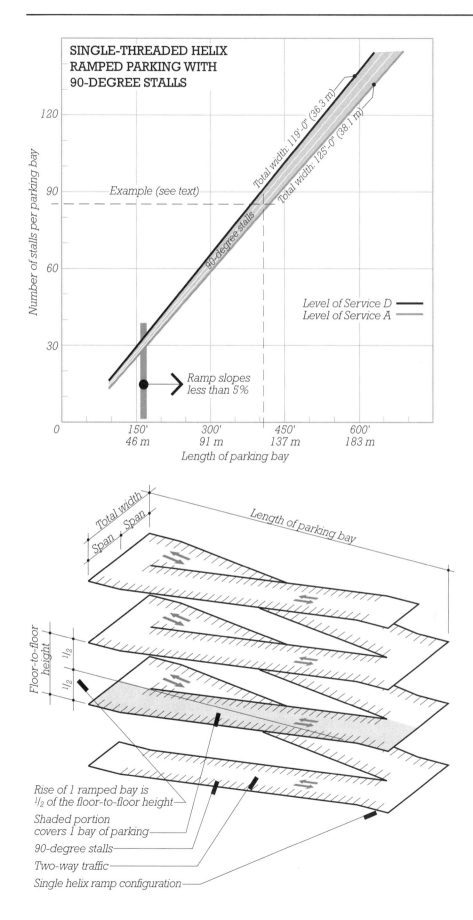

SINGLE-THREADED HELIX RAMPED PARKING WITH 90-DEGREE STALLS

Number of stalls per parking bay

Example (see text)

Total width: 119'-0" (36.3 m)

Total width: 125'-0" (38.1 m)

90-degree stalls

Level of Service D ▬▬▬
Level of Service A ▬▬▬

Ramp slopes less than 5%

| | 150' 46 m | 300' 91 m | 450' 137 m | 600' 183 m |

Length of parking bay

Total width

Span Span

Length of parking bay

Floor-to-floor height

$^1/_2$

$^1/_2$

Rise of 1 ramped bay is $^1/_2$ of the floor-to-floor height

Shaded portion covers 1 bay of parking

90-degree stalls

Two-way traffic

Single helix ramp configuration

Use this chart to determine the length and width of a parking structure configured as a single-threaded helix ramp, with two-way traffic and 90-degree stalls. *Length of parking bay* is the dimension of the structure parallel to the ramps, excluding the thickness of exterior walls. *Number of stalls per parking bay* is the number of stalls within one parking bay (see the shaded area in the diagram below).

■ Read along the bottom of the indicated band for Level of Service A conditions (most generously dimensioned) or along the top for Level of Service D (most constrained). Intermediate Levels of Service B and C are also represented by the white lines within each band. See page 316 for more information on selecting the appropriate Level of Service condition for your facility.

■ *Total width,* which differs with each level of service condition, is the dimension of the structure perpendicular to the ramps, excluding the thickness of exterior walls. Total width is indicated on the chart for Level of Service A and D conditions. Within any band, widths for intermediate levels of service may be interpolated by adding or subtracting approximately 2 ft (0.6 m) for each single step in level.

■ To avoid parking ramps with uncomfortably steep slopes, read to the right of the vertical bar indicated for ramp slopes less than 5%.

■ Guidelines for incorporating pedestrian circulation, building systems, and other elements necessary to complete the design of a structured parking facility are provided on pages 329–330.

339

LOCATION OF COLUMNS AND BEARING WALLS

The chart on the facing page includes allowances for columns and bearing walls for a structural system spanning one-half of the total width of the structure. This structural configuration is discussed in more detail on page 331.

TOTAL WIDTH OF STRUCTURE

To determine the width of the structure, read *Total width* on the chart, which differs with each level of service condition. This dimension is the width of the structure perpendicular to the ramps, excluding the thickness of exterior walls. Figures are provided for Level of Service A and D conditions. Within any band, widths for intermediate levels of service may be interpolated by adding or subtracting 2 ft (0.6 m) for each single step in level.

CROSSOVER AISLES

Figures provided on the chart on the facing page allow for crossover aisles at every other pair of ramps as illustrated in the lower diagram. If crossovers are provided at every crossing, stall totals will be reduced.

RAMP SLOPES

To avoid parking ramps with uncomfortably steep slopes, read only to the right of the vertical bar, as indicated for ramp slopes less than 5%.

EXAMPLE USE OF CHART

At least 255 stalls of structured parking are required as part of an urban office building complex. The site available for the parking structure is 265 ft long. Assuming mostly all-day parking and users familiar with the facility, a double-threaded helix

configuration is proposed, with one-way traffic, 75-degree parking stalls, and Level of Service C conditions.

To determine the maximum possible length of the parking bays within the structure, 2'-6" is subtracted from each end of the site to allow for site features and the thickness of exterior walls, resulting in a length of 260 ft. Referring to the chart on the facing page, we see that one such parking bay with 75-degree angled parking and sized for Level of Service C conditions can provide 53 stalls. To provide the required 255 stalls, slightly more than 5 bays of parking are required. Referring to the diagram below the chart, we note that a double-helix structure must always be configured with an even number of parking bays (pairs of half-bays at the top and bottom, and pairs of full bays in between). In the proposed configuration, a four-bay structure can provide 220 stalls (four bays × 55 stalls per bay), an insufficient number, and a six-bay structure can provide 330 stalls (six bays × 55 stalls per bay), a number significantly in excess of that required. One option to arrive closer to the required number of stalls would be to reduce the structure's length. However, studying the chart, we note that parking bays less than approximately 250 ft in length will have ramps with slopes greater than 5%, an important threshold for user comfort and accessible routes. So, we reject this option. Another option is to adjust the angle of parking stalls to 60 degrees. Although somewhat less space-efficient, 60-degree angled stalls are also more comfortable for parkers. In

this configuration, each parking bay can accommodate 45 stalls, and six bays can provide a total of 270 stalls (six bays × 45 stalls per bay), slightly more than the number required. To determine the width of the structure, with Level of Service C conditions, we interpolate between the figures provided for Levels A and D for 60-degree angled parking and obtain a width of 106'-0".

To determine the height of the structure, we refer to the lower diagram on the facing page and note that each pair of bays of a double-threaded helix structure rises the same distance as the structure's floor-to-floor height. Allowing 10 ft floor-to-floor, each parking bay will also rise that same distance, and three pairs of parking bays will have a total height of 30'-0" (3 × 10'-0"). Assuming that the top bays of parking should be protected from the weather, an additional 10'-0" is added for the roof level, and the overall building height is calculated as 40 ft from its entrance level to the top of the roof. (For more information on floor-to-floor heights in structured parking, see page 335.)

In order not to compromise stall widths, structural systems considered for this building should be capable of spanning one-half of the building's overall width, or approximately 50 to 55 ft. Now that the configuration of the parking system itself has been completed, the next steps in this design process would be the consideration of pedestrian circulation, building systems, and other elements. See page 329 for more information on these subjects.

SIZING DOUBLE-THREADED HELIX PARKING STRUCTURES

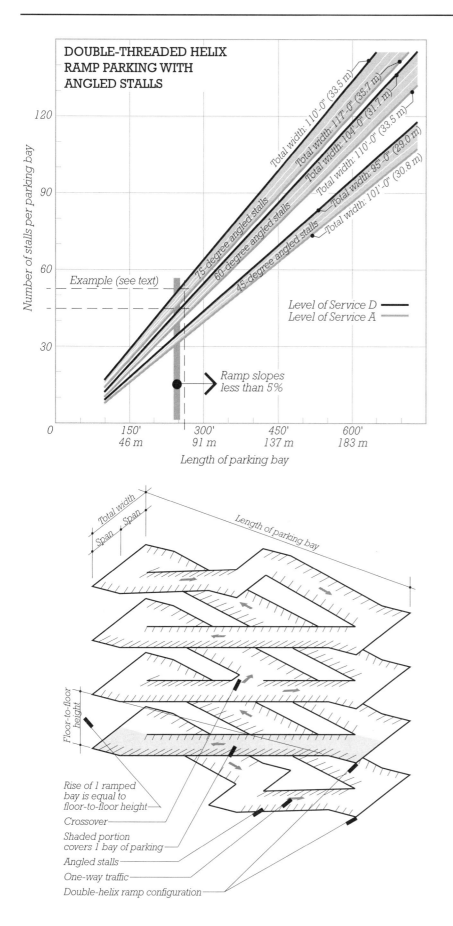

DOUBLE-THREADED HELIX RAMP PARKING WITH ANGLED STALLS

Number of stalls per parking bay

120

90

60

30

0

Example (see text)

Total width: 110'-0" (33.5 m)
Total width: 117'-0" (35.7 m)
Total width: 104'-0" (31.7 m)
Total width: 110'-0" (33.5 m)
Total width: 95'-0" (29.0 m)
Total width: 101'-0" (30.8 m)

75-degree angled stalls
60-degree angled stalls
45-degree angled stalls

Level of Service D ▬▬▬
Level of Service A ▬▬▬

Ramp slopes less than 5%

| 150' | 300' | 450' | 600' |
| 46 m | 91 m | 137 m | 183 m |

Length of parking bay

Total width
Span Span
Length of parking bay

Floor-to-floor height

Rise of 1 ramped bay is equal to floor-to-floor height
Crossover
Shaded portion covers 1 bay of parking
Angled stalls
One-way traffic
Double-helix ramp configuration

Use this chart to determine the length and width of a parking structure configured as a double-threaded helix ramp, with one-way traffic and angled stalls. *Length of parking bay* is the dimension of the structure parallel to the ramps, excluding the thickness of exterior walls. *Number of stalls per parking bay* is the number of stalls within one parking bay (see the shaded area in the diagram below).

■ Read in one of the three indicated bands for parking configured within the one-way aisles as either 75-, 60-, or 45-degree angled stalls. Within each band, read along the bottom for Level of Service A conditions (most generously dimensioned), or along the top for Level of Service D (most constrained). Intermediate Levels of Service B and C are also represented by the thin white lines within each band. See page 316 for more information on selecting the appropriate level of service condition for your facility.

■ In determining the number of bays required, note that double-helix structures must always have an even number of parking bays.

■ See the facing page for instructions on determining the overall width of the structure and further information on crossover aisles and ramp slopes.

■ Guidelines for incorporating pedestrian circulation, building systems, and other elements necessary to complete the design of a structured parking facility are provided on pages 329–330.

SIZING SPLIT LEVEL PARKING STRUCTURES

LOCATION OF COLUMNS AND BEARING WALLS

The chart on the facing page includes allowances for columns and bearing walls for a structural system spanning one-half of the total width of the structure. This plan configuration is discussed in more detail on page 331.

OVERALL WIDTH OF STRUCTURE

To determine the width of the structure, read *Total width* on the chart, which differs with each level of service condition. This dimension is the width of the structure pendicular to the ramps, excluding the thickness of exterior walls. Figures are provided for Level of Service A and D conditions. Within any band, widths for intermediate levels of service may be interpolated by adding or subtracting 2 ft (0.6 m) for each single step in level.

SPEED RAMPS

The slope of the speed ramps in a split level parking structure varies with the elevation difference between adjacent tiers and to a lesser extent, with aisle dimensions derived from the stall angle and level of service condition. For preliminary purposes, elevation differences of greater than 5 ft (1.5 m) between adjacent tiers should be avoided in order to avoid ramps with uncomfortably steep slopes of more than approximately 12.5%.

EXAMPLE USE OF CHART

At least 55 stalls of Level of Service D structured parking are required beneath a condominium building in a dense urban setting. The building site is 130 ft long. Ramped single- and double-threaded helix structures have already been considered and rejected for this relatively small site due to the uncomfortably steep slopes that result within the stall areas.

To determine the maximum possible length of the parking bays within the structure, 2'-6" is subtracted from each end of the site to allow for the thickness of foundation walls and related construction, resulting in a length of 125 ft. Referring to the chart on the facing page, we see that such a parking bay can provide 23 stalls with Level of Service D conditions. Three bays of parking will be required, capable of providing up to 69 stalls. In this case, 55 stalls will be provided and the excess area will be set aside for building service spaces.

From the chart, we can also see that with Level of Service D conditions, the width of the structure within surrounding foundation walls must be at least 119'-0".

Referring to the lower diagram on the facing page, we see that a split level parking structure is similar to a single-threaded helix in that the elevation change from one tier to the next is one-half of the structure's floor-to-floor height. Allowing 10 ft floor-to-floor, each parking bay will descend 5'-0". However, unlike the single-threaded helix, in a split level structure the first bay of parking occurs entirely at the entrance level. In a three-bay structure, the lowest bay is only two tiers below the uppermost. Therefore, the lowest bay of parking will be only 10'-0" (2 × 5'-0") below the entrance.

In order not to compromise stall widths, structural systems considered for this building should be capable of spanning one-half of the building's overall width, or approximately 60 ft. Now that the configuration of the parking system itself has been completed, the next steps in this design process would be the consideration of pedestrian circulation, building systems, and other elements. See page 329 for more information on these subjects.

SIZING SPLIT LEVEL PARKING STRUCTURES

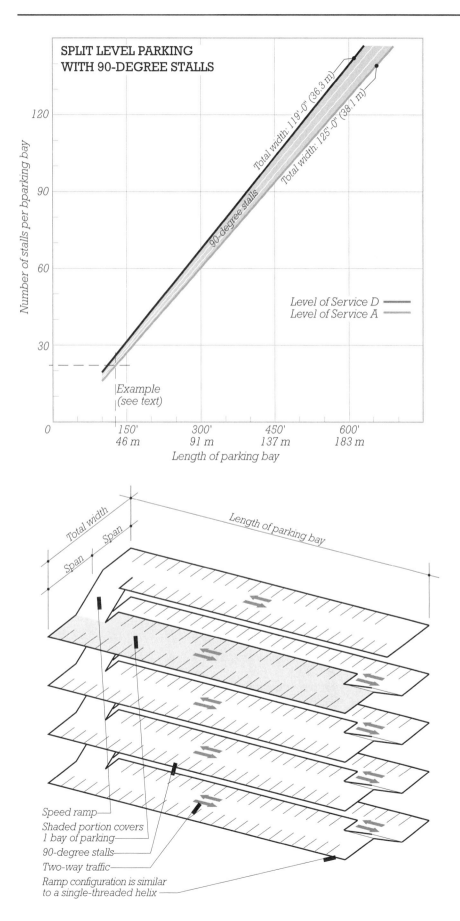

SPLIT LEVEL PARKING WITH 90-DEGREE STALLS

Number of stalls per bparking bay

120

90

60

30

0

Total width: 119'-0" (36.3 m)

Total width: 125'-0" (38.1 m)

90-degree stalls

Level of Service D ━━━
Level of Service A ━━━

Example
(see text)

| 150' | 300' | 450' | 600' |
| 46 m | 91 m | 137 m | 183 m |

Length of parking bay

Total width

Span

Span

Span

Length of parking bay

Speed ramp
Shaded portion covers
1 bay of parking
90-degree stalls
Two-way traffic
Ramp configuration is similar
to a single-threaded helix

Use this chart to determine the length and width of a parking structure configured as split level parking, with two-way traffic and 90-degree stalls. *Length of parking bay* is the dimension of the structure parallel to the parking aisles, excluding the thickness of exterior walls. *Number of stalls per parking bay* is the number of stalls within one parking bay (see the shaded area in the diagram below).

■ Read along the bottom of the indicated band for Level of Service A conditions (most generously dimensioned) or along the top for Level of Service D (most constrained). Intermediate Levels of Service B and C are also represented by the white lines within each band. See page 316 for more information on selecting the appropriate level of service condition for your facility.

■ See the facing page for instructions on determining the overall width of the structure and further information on ramp slopes.

■ Guidelines for incorporating pedestrian circulation, building systems, and other elements necessary to complete the design of a structured parking facility are provided on pages 329–330.

STRUCTURAL SYSTEMS

A structural system should be selected that is capable of spanning the full width of a single parking bay. Shorter-span systems should be avoided, since when columns fall between stalls, stalls must be widened and the number of stalls per bay must be reduced. See page 331 for more information on selecting structural systems for parking structures.

PARKING BAY WIDTH AND WIDTH OF STRUCTURE

On the chart on the facing page, *Bay width* is the width of one typical double-loaded parking aisle. Bay width differs with each level of service condition and is indicated on the chart for Level of Service A and D conditions. Within any band, widths for intermediate levels of service may be interpolated by adding or subtracting approximately 1 ft (0.3 m) for each single step in level. Parking bays located at either end of the parking area will be 1 to 3 ft (0.3 to 0.9 m) wider than inner bays. To determine the overall width of the parking area, multiply the width of one parking bay by the number of bays and then add 2 to 6 ft (0.6 to 1.8 m) for the wider bays at each end.

EXAMPLE USE OF CHART

At least 950 stalls of parking are required for a regional airport facility. The building site is 260 ft in length in the direction parallel to the planned parking aisles within the facility and 490 ft wide in the perpendicular direction. Assuming mostly short-term parking and users unfamiliar with the facility, Level of Service A conditions with

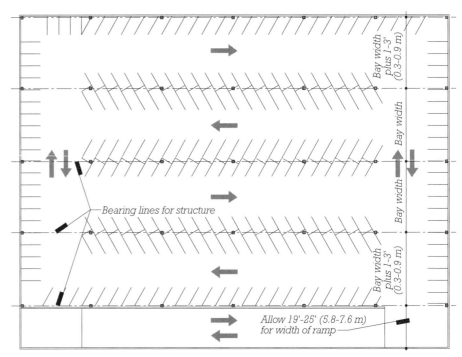

Bay width plus 1-3' (0.3-0.9 m)

Bay width

Bay width

Bay width plus 1-3' (0.3-0.9 m)

—Bearing lines for structure

Allow 19'-25' (5.8-7.6 m) for width of ramp

60-degree angled parking are proposed.

To establish the maximum possible length of the parking bays within the structure, 10 ft is subtracted from each end of the site to allow for site features and the thickness of exterior walls, resulting in a length of 240 ft. Referring to the chart on the facing page, we determine that such a parking bay with 60-degree angled stalls and Level of Service A conditions can provide 38 stalls in a bay 51'-9" wide.

To determine the width available for parking bays, we subtract from the width of the site 10 ft at each end for site conditions and exterior wall thickness, 25 ft at one end for the express ramp, 15 ft at the other end for various vertical circulation and building services, and 3 ft at each end for the wider parking bays required at the sides, as noted above. The resulting width is 424'-0". Eight parking bays with an overall width of 414'-0" (8 × 51'-

9" per bay) and a total of 304 stalls (8 × 38 stalls per bay) can fit within this dimension. As an alternative, we also try a configuration with 75-degree angle stalls. In this case, a bay 56'-4" wide can provide 45 stalls of parking. Only seven bays can fit within the space, but with a total of 315 stalls in an overall width of 394'-4". In this second configuration, we can accommodate 11 more stalls per parking level in a structure roughly 20 ft smaller in width. We select the second option.

Assuming 11'-6" ft floor-to-floor heights and open-air parking at the top level, the top of the structure, not including parapets, will be 34'-6" (3 × 11'-6") above the entrance level. Now that the configuration of the parking system itself has been completed, the next steps in this design process will be the consideration of pedestrian circulation, building systems, and other elements. See page 329 for more information on these subjects.

SIZING MULTI-BAY PARKING STRUCTURES

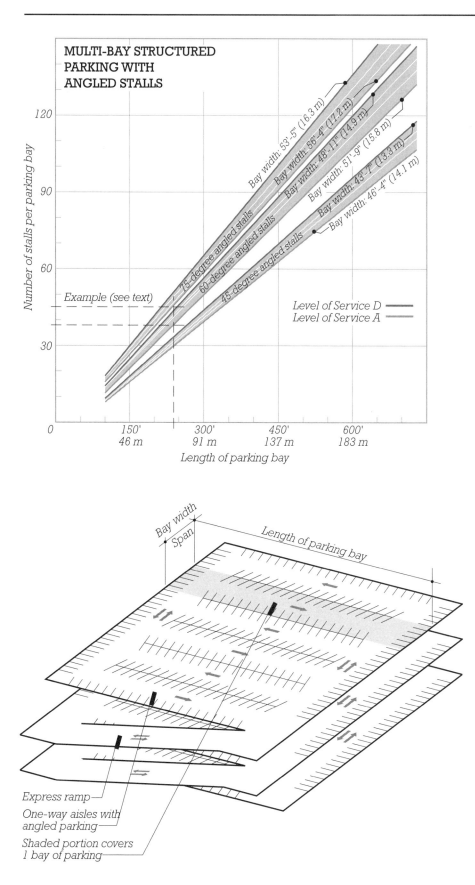

MULTI-BAY STRUCTURED PARKING WITH ANGLED STALLS

Number of stalls per parking bay

120

90

60

30

0

Bay width: 53'-5" (16.3 m)
Bay width: 56'-4" (17.2 m)
Bay width: 48'-11" (14.9 m)
Bay width: 51'-9" (15.8 m)
Bay width: 43'-7" (13.3 m)
Bay width: 46'-4" (14.1 m)

75-degree angled stalls
60-degree angled stalls
45-degree angled stalls

Example (see text)

Level of Service D
Level of Service A

| 150' | 300' | 450' | 600' |
| 46 m | 91 m | 137 m | 183 m |

Length of parking bay

Bay width
Span
Length of parking bay

Express ramp
One-way aisles with angled parking
Shaded portion covers 1 bay of parking

Use this chart to determine the length and width of a large-area multi-bay parking structure configured with express ramps and a combination of one-way and two-way aisles, as shown in the diagram below. *Length of parking bay* is the dimension of the structure parallel to the parking aisles, excluding the thickness of exterior walls. *Number of stalls per parking bay* is the number of stalls within one bay (see the shaded area in the diagram).

■ Read in one of the three indicated bands for parking configured within the one-way aisles as either 75-, 60-, or 45-degree angled stalls. Within each band, read along the bottom for Level of Service A conditions (most generously dimensioned) or along the top for Level of Service D (most constrained). Intermediate Levels of Service B and C are also represented by the thin white lines within each band. See page 316 for more information on selecting the appropriate level of service condition for your facility.

■ Guidelines for incorporating pedestrian circulation, building systems, and other elements necessary to complete the design of a structured parking facility are provided on pages 329–330.

SIZING PARKING FACILITIES

SECTION

7

DESIGNING WITH HEIGHT AND AREA LIMITATIONS

HEIGHT
AND AREA
LIMITATIONS

This chapter will help you determine which Construction Types are legally permitted for a building of a given height and area under the model building codes.

HEIGHT AND AREA LIMITATIONS

The model codes place limitations on building heights and areas in relation to the type of construction employed and the uses to which the building will be put. This is done in order to ensure a minimum standard of fire safety for the occupants of the building as well as for surrounding buildings. Height and area limitations, because they dictate the types of construction from which the designer may choose, have the largest impact on building design of any building code provisions. It is not uncommon during early design stages for consideration of these limits to lead to significant changes in building program requirements or massing simply to enable the use of the most economical construction systems possible.

Though similar in their approaches to limiting building height and area, the model codes differ in detail. To the maximum extent possible, these differences have been minimized in the following height and area tables by presenting the data from the codes in a consistent format, so that the designer may work as readily with one code as with the other. The authors have adopted the names "3-Hour," "2-Hour," and so on, for the Construction Types. These names are based on the required fire resistance ratings of the structural loadbearing frame in each Type and are used to overcome inconsistencies in nomenclature between the codes. In addition, the adjustments permitted in each code for allowable area and height due to the number of stories, use of sprinklers, and other particulars have been precalculated for instant reference.

One difference between the codes that was not possible to resolve relates to the determination of allowable area. For the International Building Code, the tabulated values are for the *total area for all floors of the building combined.* For the National Building Code of Canada, the tabulated values are for the *area of any single floor.* When working with these tables, be sure to apply the indicated values appropriately.

INTERNATIONAL BUILDING CODE

Use these indexes to find the height and area limitations table for the building code and use group you are working with.

See pages 7-12 for more information on Occupancy Groups in the International Building Code.

Each code has seemingly endless exceptions to its own basic height and area limitations. The most important exceptions deal with height and area increases permitted in exchange for approved automatic sprinkler systems and excess street frontage. The increases for sprinklered buildings have been incorporated fully into the tables, while the frontage increases are tabulated prominently in the accompanying notes. Other important exceptions have been noted in the text accompanying each table. A few exceptions are so complex that they could not reasonably be digested into these pages; for these you are directed to the code itself by notes accompanying the appropriate tables. Some exceptions were deemed by the authors to be so minor as not to warrant their inclusion here. For this reason, you must carry out a thorough investigation of the building code itself as a building design progresses to its developmental stage.

The following pages provide information on a number of topics closely related to determining the height and area of a building. Pages 352–355 explain how the model codes address a building with more than one type of occupancy. Pages 356-357 discusses guidelines for the incorporation of mezzanines and floor openings or atriums into the height and area calculations of a building. Pages 358-359 discuss the construction and fire-resistance requirements of fire walls, exterior walls, and a concept unique to the International Building Code, fire areas. Descriptions of the requirements for Construction Types for both model codes, and listings of typical construction systems that meet these requirements, are presented on pages 360–368.

NATIONAL BUILDING CODE OF CANADA

Occupancy Group	Page
A-1: Assembly, Theaters	428-429
A-2: Assembly, Miscellaneous	430-431
A-3: Assembly, Arenas	432-433
A-4: Assembly, Open-Air	434-435
B-1: Care or Detention, Restrained	436-437
B-2: Care or Detention, Unrestrained	438-439
C: Residential	440-441
D: Business and Personal Services	442-443
E: Mercantile	444-445
F-1: Industrial, High-Hazard	446-447
F-2: Industrial, Medium-Hazard	448-449
F-3: Industrial, Low-Hazard	450-451
F-3: Open-Air Garages	452-453

See pages 13-15 for more information about Occupancy Groups in the National Building Code of Canada.

Single buildings often accommodate more than one type of occupancy, for example retail space on the ground floor of an office building, restaurants, bars, and meeting rooms in a hotel, or parking garages beneath commercial or residential occupancies. Use the following guidelines for preliminary design of such mixed-use structures.

INTERNATIONAL BUILDING CODE

When two or more Occupancy Groups are combined in one building, the International Building Code allows these mixed uses to be treated as either *Nonseparated* or *Separated Occupancies*.

Nonseparated Occupancies

When occupancies are Nonseparated, there are no requirements for fire separation between them, and the allowable building height and area are determined for the whole structure by applying the requirements of the most restrictive occupancy throughout. Within each occupancy area, occupant load calculations, egress configuration, and other such requirements are applied according to the code restrictions for that particular occupancy.

Separated Occupancies

Separated Occupancies are segregated from one another by fire separations, which may consist of fire-resistant walls, fire doors and other rated openings, and fire-resistant floor/ceiling assemblies. The degree of fire resistance required for such separations may vary from 1 to 4 hours, depending on the occupancies involved and whether the building is sprinklered. For preliminary purposes, a 2-hour

rated separation for nonsprinklered buildings and a 1-hour separation for sprinklered buildings may be assumed. Some High-Hazard occupancies may not be mixed with other occupancies under any circumstances. In general, building code requirements for Separated Occupancy buildings result in higher construction costs and greater restriction on space planning in comparison to Nonseparated Buildings. However, under most circumstances, Separated Occupancy Buildings may be built to a larger area and greater height as well.

In a Separated Occupancy building, each occupancy area is required to conform to its own height limitations, both in number of stories and in feet (or meters) above grade. For example, in a four-story Separated Occupancy building, where one of the occupancy's height limitations restricts it to no more than two stories, that occupancy may only be located on the first or second floor of the building. Some other occupancy, with height limits permitting four stories, may be located on any floor.

Considering building area limits, where an entire building floor contains only one type of occupancy, the area of that floor is limited by the restrictions for that particular occupancy. Where a floor shares two or more separated occupancies, the allowable area determination for that floor is based on a proportional calculation as follows:

1. For each occupancy, divide its proposed area on the floor by the maximum area permitted by the code to get a decimal fraction.

2. Add the fractional results for each occupancy on the floor.

3. The sum total must not exceed 1.

For example, consider a four-story university building, sprin-

klered, of Type II-A construction. The proposed footprint of the building is 85,000 sq ft. On the first floor are three 5000-sq-ft auditoriums classified as Group A-3 Assembly and 70,000 sq ft of classroom space classified as Group B Business. In the height and area limit tables on pages 376 and 382, the allowable single floor areas in multifloor buildings for these two Occupancy Groups are 46,500 sq ft for the Assembly Occupancy and 112,500 sq ft for the Business Occupancy (these figures are read from the bottom row of the height and area limit tables). To check the floor area, first divide the proposed area by the allowable area for each occupancy:

Group A-3, area on floor 1:
$$\frac{3 \times 5000 \text{ sq ft } proposed}{46,500 \text{ sq ft } allowed} = 0.32$$

Group B, area on floor 1:
$$\frac{70,000 \text{ sq ft } proposed}{112,500 \text{ sq ft } allowed} = 0.62$$

Then sum the fractions and compare to 1:

$$0.32 + 0.62 = 0.94 < 1 \text{ OK}$$

In this case, the sum of the fractions is less than 1, and this combination of occupancies is within allowable area limits. In a building with more than one floor, this check must be performed for each floor. (These additional checks are omitted in this example.)

For Separated Occupancy buildings over three stories in height, an additional check must be made to verify area limits for the building as a whole. In this case, a similar proportional calculation is performed, but comparing the proposed area on all floors to the allowable area on all floors. Continuing with the example above, assume that the second through fourth floors of the building each contain 85,000 sq ft of classroom and office space all classified as Group B Business. Consulting again the height and area limit tables on pages 376 and 382, the total allowable area on all floors for these two occupancy groups are 139,500 sq ft for the Assembly Occupancy and 337,500 sq ft for the Business Occupancy (these figures are read from the row corresponding to the proposed story height of the building). First, for each occupancy, divide the proposed area on all floors by its allowable area on all floors:

Group A-3, area on all floors:
$$\frac{3 \times 5000 \text{ sq ft } proposed}{139,500 \text{ sq ft } allowed} = 0.11$$

Group B, area on all floors:
$$\frac{70,000 \text{ sq ft} + 3 \times 85,000 \text{ sq ft } proposed}{337,500 \text{ sq ft } allowed} = 0.96$$

Then sum the fractions and compare to 1:

$$0.11 + 0.96 = 1.07 > 1 \text{ NOT OK}$$

In this case, considering the area on all floors of the building, the sum of the fractions exceeds 1 and the proposed building is not within the code's area limits for the proposed mix of occupancies. To correct this problem, the building must be reduced in size, the mix of occupancies must be adjusted, or a Construction Type with greater allowable area must be selected.

Accessory and Incidental Uses

Some combinations of uses need not fully meet requirements for mixed-use occupancies. For example, certain specific use combinations are not required to be recognized as mixed use at all and may be treated as single occupancies:

■ Assembly areas less than 750 sq ft (70 m²) in area or with an occupant load of less than 50 may be considered part of any other occupancy within which they occur (for example, meeting rooms in a Business occupancy).

■ Assembly areas not exceeding 10% of the floor area of a Group E Educational Occupancy are considered part of the Educational Occupancy (for example auditoriums, lunch rooms, gymnasiums, etc. in K-12 school buildings).

■ In places of worship buildings, classrooms and auditorium spaces less than 100 sq ft (9 m²) in area, that might otherwise be classified as Group E Educational, may be considered part of the main occupancy, usually Group A-3 Assembly.

Other uses may, at the designer's option, be treated as *Accessory* or *Incidental* to the major occupancy within which they occur, rather than according to the Separated or Nonseparated Occupancy provisions discussed above. One or more uses may be considered Accessory when, in total, they occupy no more than 10% of the area of the floor on which they are located. In such cases, no separation is required between uses, and building height, area, and sprinkler requirements are governed by the major occupancy. Occupant load and egress requirements for each occupancy are still applied individually to each area, and accessory areas themselves may not exceed the unsprinklered height and area limits for their particular occupancy type. Certain occupancies, such as High-Hazard, may not be treated as Accessory to another, regardless of size.

Incidental Uses areas consist of a specific list of uses which may be treated in a manner similar to Accessory spaces. However, because of their higher degree of hazard, additional protection is required in the form of fire-extinguishing systems, fire sprinklers, and/or rated fire separations between the Incidental Use and the major occupancy within which it is located. Except for these protections, all other requirements, such as height and area requirements, are governed by the major occupancy. Examples of Incidental Uses and their protection requirements include the following:

■ Furnace and boiler rooms with equipment over certain size limits, with either a 1-hour rated separation or an automatic fire-extinguishing system and construction capable or resisting the passage of smoke

■ Paint shops in other than Group F Factory Occupancies, with either a 2-hour separation or a 1-hour separation and an automatic fire-extinguishing system

■ Parking garages, with either a 2-hour separation, or a 1-hour separation and an automatic fire-extinguishing system

■ Laboratories or vocational shops within Group E Educational or I-2 Institutional Occupancies, with either a 1-hour rated separation or an automatic fire-extinguishing system and construction capable or resisting the passage of smoke

■ Laundry, storage, waste collection, and linen collection rooms greater than 100 sq ft (9 m²) in area, with either a 1-hour rated separation or an automatic fire-extinguishing system and construction capable or resisting the passage of smoke

■ Incinerator rooms with a 2-hour rated separation and an automatic sprinkler system

For a complete list of Incidental Uses and their requirements, consult the code.

HEIGHT AND AREA LIMITATIONS

353

Parking Garages and Mixed-Use Occupancies

The International Building Code recognizes unique circumstances where parking of one Construction Type is located above or beneath other occupancies of other Construction Types, as summarized below. See the code for details.

Open or Enclosed Parking Below Group A, B, M, R, or S Occupancies: In this configuration, the upper and lower portions of the structure may be treated as separate buildings for the purpose of determining each portion's limitations in area, number of stories, height (measured in feet or meters), continuity of fire walls, and type of construction for each. The following requirements must also be met:

■ The parking garage is located in a basement and/or not more than in the first story above grade.

■ The garage is used solely for the storage of private motor vehicles, except for entry lobbies, equipments rooms, and other spaces incidental to its operation.

■ The garage is constructed of Type IA construction only.

■ There is a 3-hour rated horizontal assembly between the parking and the occupancy above.

■ No single Group A assembly space may have an occupant load in excess of 300.

In addition to motor vehicle parking in the lower portion of the structure, Group B and M occupancies and Group A Occupancies with rooms with an occupant load not exceeding 300 are also permitted, provided that the upper structure is fully sprinklered throughout.

Open Parking Below Group A, I, B, M, or R Occupancies: In this configuration, the height, number of floors, and area of the garage may comply with the requirements of the table on pages 422–423, based on the Construction Type of that part of the structure. The height and area requirements of the upper portion of the structure may be based on its own occupancy and Construction Type requirements. However, both height (in feet or meters) and number of stories above grade for the upper-occupancy portion of the structure must be taken from grade, including the lower (parking) portions of the structure. The following requirements must also be met:

■ There is a horizontal separation between the garage and the occupancy above, with a fire-resistance rating of not less than that required by the code for the separated occupancies (typically 2 hours).

■ If the Construction Type requirements of the upper portion of the structure exceed those for the parking below, the structural members of the lower portion have fire protection meeting the requirements of the upper portion.

Open Parking with Group B or M Occupancies Below: In this configuration, the height and area of the upper portion of the structure may comply with the requirements of the table on pages 420–421, with the building height and number of stories measured from grade (including the occupancies below). The height and area of the lower portion of the structure must comply with the requirements for the occupancies in that portion of the structure. The following requirements must also be met:

■ There is a horizontal separation between the garage and the occupancy below, with a fire-resistance rating of not less than that required by the code for the separated occupancies (typically 2 hours).

■ The lower portion of the structure is constructed of Type I or Type II construction, but not less than that required for the open parking above.

■ Exits from the parking must discharge directly to public ways and must be separated by 2-hour rated enclosures from the lower occupancies.

Single-Story Enclosed or Open Parking Below Group R Occupancy: In this configuration, the height and area of the upper portion of the structure may be determined based on the Group R Occupancy and its Construction Type requirements, with the number of stories measured from the first floor above the parking structure. Building height (in feet or meters) must be measured from grade. The following requirements must also be met:

■ The garage is single-story, located on grade.

■ The garage is of Type I or Type IV (open garage only) construction.

■ There is a horizontal separation between the garage and the occupancy above with a fire-resistance rating of not less than that required for floors in the lower garage and not less than that required by the code for separation of the two occupancies (typically 2 hours).

Enclosed Parking Below Open Parking: In this configuration, the Construction Type, height, and number of floors of the upper, open garage may comply with the requirements of the table on pages 420–421. The total area of both structures combined is limited as explained previously in this section for Separated, mixed-occupancy buildings—that is, the ratio of the total floor area of the lower garage divided by its maximum permitted area plus the ratio of the total floor area of the upper garage divided by its maximum permitted area may not exceed 1. The following requirements must also be met:

■ The lower garage is located in a basement and/or first story above grade.

■ The lower garage is of Type I or Type II construction or, if the garage above is of Type I construction, then the lower garage is of Type I construction only.

■ There is a horizontal separation between the garages, with a fire-resistance rating of not less than that required for a floor assembly in the lower garage.

■ The lower garage is used solely for the storage of private motor vehicles, except for equipment rooms incidental to the operation of the garage, and up to 1000 sq ft (93 m^2) of office, waiting room, and toilet room areas.

NATIONAL BUILDING CODE OF CANADA

The National Building Code of Canada treats mixed occupancies as separated uses. They must be segregated from one another by fire separations including fire-resistant walls, fire doors and other rated openings, and fire-resistant floor/ceiling assemblies. The degree of fire resistance required varies from 1 to 3 hours, with 1 to 2 hours required for the most common occupancy types. Some High-Hazard Industrial occupancies may not be mixed with other occupancies at all.

In most mixed-use buildings, height and area requirements of the most restrictive occupancy type are applied to the whole building. In cases where one occupancy type occurs fully above or below another, the code provides an alternative treatment in which each portion of the structure may meet the Construction Type requirements for that portion's particular occupancy, while the more restrictive height and area requirements of either occupancy are applied to the building as a whole. This option allows the possibility of a single building of multiple Construction Types, for example, combustible residential units above a noncombustible commercial first story. Accessory uses are also recognized, in which the area of one or more occupancies does not exceed 10% of the total area on a floor. Accessory uses are not required to be separated from the major occupancy and are not considered in the determination of height and area limits for the building. High- and Medium-Hazard Industrial occupancies may not be treated as accessory to other occupancies. As a related consideration, whenever mixed occupancies or other varied requirements result in a condition where only part of a structure is required to be sprinklered, all portions of a building beneath the portion required to be sprinklered must be sprinklered as well.

Parking Garages and Mixed-Use Occupancies

When a basement is used primarily as a parking garage, exclusive of servicing or fueling of vehicles, it may be considered as a separate building, provided that the separation between the garage and the occupancies above, as well as the portions of the garage walls above grade, are constructed of masonry or concrete with a 2-hour fire-resistance rating. In this case, the structure above the garage is subject to its own Construction Type, height, and area requirements. In some cases, the garage may also require sprinklers. See the code for details.

MEZZANINES

A mezzanine is an intermediate platform located between the floor and ceiling of a room. Under both model building codes, a mezzanine is not counted toward the number of floors or area limits of a building. However, the area of the mezzanine is considered when calculating occupant loads and egress requirements.

International Building Code

In the International Building Code, the area of a mezzanine usually may not exceed one-third of the open area of the room in which it is located (enclosed portions of the room are not included in this calculation). The mezzanine itself is also required to remain open. However, portions of a mezzanine with an occupant load of 10 or less or that do not exceed 10% of the mezzanine area may be enclosed, and mezzanines with two means of egress, at least one of which leads directly to an exit, may be fully enclosed. A mezzanine has the same Construction Type requirements as the floor on which it is located. The number of means of egress required is determined as for any other room or space within a building, considering, for example, the number of occupants, occupancy type, common path of travel requirements, travel distance, and so on; see the Exit Access, beginning on page 254, for more information. Mezzanines in buildings of Noncom-bustible Construction may be up to one-half of the open area of the room in which they are located when the building is protected throughout with sprinklers and an emergency alarm and communication system. Mezzanines of increased area are also permitted in noncombustible buildings housing certain large-scale industrial occupancies; see the code for details.

National Building Code of Canada

In the National Building Code of Canada, the area of a mezzanine usually may not exceed 40% of the open area of the room in which it is located (enclosed portions of the room are not included in this calculation). A mezzanine is required to remain open to the room, except that portions of the mezzanine not exceeding 10% of the open area of the room below may be enclosed. In some cases, a mezzanine may be constructed to a lesser fire-resistance than the floor on which it is located; see pages 362–363 for more information. The number of means of egress from a mezzanine is generally determined as for any other floor area, except that depending on occupancy type, some mezzanines of limited area and travel distance to an exit may have lesser requirements; see the code for details. In some cases, mezzanines must also meet the requirements for *interconnected floor spaces;* see the following section, Floor Openings, for more information.

FLOOR OPENINGS

In both model codes, openings that create atmospheric connections between floors within a building, other than enclosed vertical structures for exit stairways, elevator hoistways, shafts, and other such elements, are subject to special restrictions intended to protect occupants against the rapid spread of smoke or fire between floors in the event of a building fire.

International Building Code

In the International Building Code, openings between floors are termed *atriums* and must comply with the following:

■ Activities on the floor level of the atrium itself are restricted to those with a low fire hazard, unless that area is protected by sprinklers.

■ Buildings containing atriums must be sprinklered throughout, except that areas adjacent to or above the atrium need not be sprinklered when separated from the atrium by 2-hour rated assemblies. Additionally, ceilings of atriums more than 55 ft (17 m) above the atrium floor need not be sprinklered.

■ Atriums connecting more than two floors must be provided with a mechanical smoke control system designed to protect occupants from smoke and toxic gasses during a fire emergency.

■ An atrium must be separated from adjacent spaces by 1-hour rated walls, except that up to three floors may be open to the atrium as long as the smoke control system design accounts for the volume of such connected areas. Additionally, walls separating the atrium from adjacent spaces may include glass when the glass areas are protected with a specially designed sprinkler system that will completely wet the glass surface when activated, or they may be constructed of glass block with not less than a ?-hour fire-resistance rating.

■ Except at its lowest level, portions of exit access travel within the atrium space may not exceed 200 ft (61 m).

Floor openings meeting the following requirements are not subject to atrium requirements:

■ Openings between a floor and its mezzanine spaces

■ Openings within individual dwelling units not more than four stories in height

■ In fully sprinklered buildings, openings of limited area for escalators or stairs not part of the means of egress

■ In other than Group I-2 or I-3 Occupancies, openings connecting not more than two floors

■ Openings connecting not more than two floors as permitted for unenclosed exit stairs (see page 260 for more information)

■ In mall buildings, openings not more than three stories in height

■ Automobile ramps in parking garages and open exit stairways in open garages

National Building Code of Canada

In the National Building Code of Canada, openings between floors are referred to as *interconnected floor spaces*. Floor openings treated as interconnected floor spaces must conform to the following requirements:

■ Buildings with interconnected floor spaces must be sprinklered throughout and must be of either Noncombustible or Heavy Timber Construction.

■ Exit access ways must be separated from interconnected floor spaces by fire separations with a fire-resistance rating not less than the required rating for floor assemblies.

■ Exits opening into interconnected floor spaces must be protected by vestibules. Elevator shafts that open into interconnected floor spaces as well as spaces on higher floors must be protected by vestibules either on all interconnected floor space floors or all floors above.

■ A mechanical smoke exhaust system serving the interconnected floor spaces is required.

■ The quantity of combustible contents located in interconnected floor spaces is limited.

■ Sleeping rooms in Group B-2 Care or Detention Occupancies may not be located within interconnected floor spaces.

All openings between floors, including openings for mezzanines, are subject to the requirements for interconnected floor spaces, except as follows:

■ Openings for mezzanines within Group A-1 Occupancies, Group A-3 Occupancies in buildings not more than two stories in height, or for mezzanines not more than 500 m^2 (5380 sq ft) in area in Group A, C, D, E, or F Occupancies

■ Openings connecting only first floors of a building and one floor above or below, used for stairways, escalators, or moving walks, in Group A-1, A-2, A-3, D, E, F-2, and F-3 Occupancies, in buildings not exceeding one-half of their permitted area according to the height and area tables beginning on page 372

■ Openings connecting only two floors in Group B-1 Occupancy buildings

■ Floor openings of limited area for escalators in sprinklered buildings of Group A-1, A-2, A-3, D, and E Occupancies

■ Floor openings for vehicular ramps in parking garages

■ Openings in special industrial buildings necessary for the flow of materials for the manufacturing processes taking place within the building

FIRE WALLS

Fire walls are used to divide structures into two or more parts such that each distinct part may then be considered a separate building for the purposes of determining its allowable height and area. In this way, a building of virtually any horizontal extent can be built, so long as it is subdivided by fire walls into self-contained parts that individually comply with code height and area limitations, and Construction Type requirements, for the types of occupancies involved.

Fire walls require a fire-resistance rating of 2 to 4 hours, depending on the occupancies being separated. They must be constructed either as two separate walls, each independently supported by structure on opposite sides, or as one wall that can remain standing in the event of a structural collapse on either side. They must extend continuously from one exterior wall of the structure to another and from the building foundation to the roof. The International Building Code requires fire walls to be of Noncombustible Construction, unless separating solely Type V Wood Light Frame structures on both sides. The National Building Code of Canada in some cases restricts fire walls to concrete and masonry construction. Depending on the fire resistance of the building exterior construction, fire walls may be required to project beyond exterior walls and/or roofs a distance ranging from 6 to 36 in. (150 to 900 mm) to limit the chance for fire to jump from one side of the wall to the other. Where exterior walls and roofs have sufficient fire resistance themselves, fire walls may be permitted to terminate at these boundaries without projecting beyond. For the same reason, openings in exterior walls or roofs within certain distances of the fire wall may be restricted as well. Within the fire walls themselves, openings, most commonly for doors, must be fire rated. Each opening must meet specified size limits, and the area of all openings taken together must not exceed 25% of the wall's total area. Where fire walls coincide with property lines (also known as *party walls*), the International Building Code does not permit openings of any type. Fire walls may be vertical structures only. That is, horizontal floor/ceiling assemblies may not be part of fire wall structures.

FIRE-RESISTANCE REQUIREMENTS FOR EXTERIOR WALLS

Exterior walls must be constructed to resist fires originating from within the building itself as well as from nearby structures. In cases where buildings are particularly close to property lines or other structures, the risk of exposure to fire from adjacent buildings may create a more stringent requirement for the fire resistance of the exterior walls of a building than would otherwise be required for its Construction Type. Specific requirements vary with the type of construction, the occupancies within the building, and the distance between buildings. In the International Building Code, excluding High-Hazard Occupancy groups, fire-resistance rating requirements for exterior walls of buildings less than 60 ft (18 m) apart range from 0 to 1 hour, and for buildings separated by less than 20 ft (6 m) from 1 to 2 hours. Exterior wall fire-resistance rating requirements in the National Building Code of Canada range from 45 minutes to 2 hours at distances ranging from 10 m to as much as 140 m (33 to 460 ft) between buildings, and may also include additional restrictions on the combustibility of the wall construction and its exterior cladding. Similarly, as the distance between buildings decreases, the extent of windows, doors, and other unprotected openings permitted in opposing exterior walls also declines. Consult the code for details.

FIRE AREAS

In the International Building Code, fire-rated walls and floor/ceiling assemblies may be used to subdivide portions of a building into so-called *fire areas,* most frequently as a means of avoiding sprinkler requirements. In its simplest form, a fire area is the total area for any single occupancy classification within a building, including the area on all floors and mezzanines allocated to that occupancy type, where these areas are not separated by fire-resistance rated assemblies. For example, where a 1000-sq-ft meeting room classified as Group A-3 Assembly occurs on a building floor that otherwise contains Group B occupancy space, the Assembly fire area is 1000-sq-ft. If there are three such rooms on the floor, without fire-rated separations between them, the Assembly fire area becomes 3000 sq ft (3×1000 sq ft = 3000 sq ft). If an additional three such rooms are located on an adjacent floor and the floor/ceiling construction between the floors is not a fire-rated separation, the Assembly fire area then becomes 6000 sq ft. If, on the other hand, the floor/ceiling construction does meet requirements for a fire-rated separation, this last example would instead be treated as two separate 3000-sq-ft fire areas.

To give an example of how fire area is applied in relation to sprinkler requirements, consider a one-story building classified as a Group F-1 Factory Occupancy, with a total area of 20,000 sq ft. According to the sprinkler requirements listed at the top of page 386, such a building, having a fire area exceeding 12,000 sq ft, must be sprinklered throughout. Therefore, if the factory floor remains entirely open, the building must be sprinklered.

However, if the floor is divided in half by a fire-rated wall into two separate fire areas each 10,000 sq ft in area, this sprinkler requirement is avoided.

Fire-resistance rating requirements for separations between fire areas range from 1 to 4 hours, depending on the type of occupancy involved. For preliminary purposes, a 2-hour rating may be assumed for occupancies other than High-Hazard, and Moderate Hazard Storage or Factory.

CONSTRUCTION TYPES

INTERNATIONAL BUILDING CODE

This section summarizes the fire-resistance rating and construction requirements for Construction Types in the International Building Code. Once you have determined an appropriate Construction Type for a project, based on the height and area tables on pages 372–425, use this section to relate this information to systems of construction. The table on these two facing pages consolidates and simplifies fire-resistance requirements for each Construction Type. The pages following this chart define each Construction Type in terms of specific structural systems, materials, and minimum thicknesses of components necessary to meet the required minimum fire-resistance rating. The values in the table below may be modified as follows:

■ **Reduction in 1-Hour Rated Construction:** Where building height and area are read from the Unsprinklered column of the Height and Area tables in this book, and a sprinkler system is not otherwise a code requirement, the use of sprinklers may be applied toward a reduction in the protection requirements for buildings of any 1-Hour Construction Type. In such a case, height and area requirements for the building are determined by reading from the Height and Area tables for either Type II-A, III-A, or V-A construction (unsprinklered), but the fire-resistance requirements for the building structure are based on the unprotected versions of these Construction Types, either Type II-B, III-B, or V-B, respectively. Exterior bearing wall fire-resistance requirements are not reduced.

■ **Exterior Bearing Walls:** In addition to the requirements indicated in the table on these two facing pages, see also Fire-Resistance Requirements for Exterior Walls, page 358, for information regarding protection of exterior walls when in close proximity to other buildings.

■ **Structure Supporting Roofs Only:** Interior bearing walls, columns, girders, trusses, and other members of the structural frame supporting roofs only may be 1-hour rated maximum for any

INTERNATIONAL BUILDING CODE

	Noncombustible			
CONSTRUCTION TYPE **INTERNATIONAL BUILDING CODE NOMENCLATURE**	3-Hour (page 364) Type I-A	2-Hour (page 364) Type I-B	1-Hour (page 365) Type II-A	Unprotected (page 366) Type II-B
STRUCTURAL FRAME INCLUDING COLUMNS, GIRDERS, TRUSSES	3	2	1	0
EXTERIOR BEARING WALLS	3	2	1	0
INTERIOR BEARING WALLS	3	2	1	0
FLOOR CONSTRUCTION	2	2	1	0
ROOF CONSTRUCTION	1½	1	1	0
PARTY WALLS AND FIRE WALLS	2–4	2–4	2–4	2–4
ENCLOSURES OF EXITS, EXIT HALLWAYS, EXIT STAIRWAYS, SHAFTS	2	2	2 hours connecting 4 stories or more, 1 hour connecting fewer than 4 stories	
EXIT ACCESS CORRIDORS	0–1	0–1	0–1	0–1
TENANT SPACE SEPARATIONS	1	1	1	1
DWELLING UNIT AND GUEST ROOM SEPARATIONS	1	1	1	1
OTHER NONBEARING PARTITIONS	Noncombustible			

CONSTRUCTION TYPES

Construction Type. Exterior bearing wall fire-resistance requirements are not reduced.

■ **Roof Construction:** Roof structures 20 ft (6 m) or more above the floor below may be unprotected in all occupancies except F-1, H, M, and S-1. Type IV-HT Heavy Timber Construction is permitted wherever a Noncombustible or Combustible roof structure with a fire-resistance rating of 1 hour or less is permitted.

■ **Enclosures for Corridors and Exits:** For more information on corridor enclosure requirements, see page 257, and for exit enclosures, page 260.

■ **Dwelling Unit Separations:** Dwelling unit and guest room sep-arations may be reduced to ½-hour rated in any Unprotected Construction Type, provided that the building is sprinklered.

■ **Tall Buildings:** Most buildings with occupied floors more than 75 ft (23 m) above grade must be fully sprinklered. For such buildings with a roof height not exceeding 420 ft (128 m), Construction Type and rated assembly requirements may be adjusted as follows:

Buildings of Type I-B construction may be built to the height and area limits of Type I-A construction, except that columns supporting floors must be built to the requirements of Type I-A construction. In other than Group F-1, M, and S-1 Occupancies, buildings of Type II-A construction may be built to the height and area limits of Type I-B construction. Shafts for other than exits and elevators may be enclosed with 1-hour fire-resistance rated assemblies when the interiors of the shafts themselves are protected with an automatic sprinkler system.

These provisions do not apply to open parking garages, airport traffic control towers, outdoor sports arenas, and some unusually tall Low- and Medium-hazard industrial buildings. For special egress system and smoke control requirements in tall buildings, see High-rise and Underground Buildings, page 277.

CONSTRUCTION TYPE / INTERNATIONAL BUILDING CODE NOMENCLATURE	Combustible				
	Ordinary		Mill	Wood Light Frame	
	1-Hour (page 368)	Unprotected (page 368)	(page 366)	1-Hour (page 368)	Unprotected (page 368)
	Type III-A	Type III-B	Type IV-HT	Type V-A	Type V-B
STRUCTURAL FRAME INCLUDING COLUMNS, GIRDERS, TRUSSES	1	0	Heavy Timber	1	0
EXTERIOR BEARING WALLS	2 Noncombustible	2 Noncombustible	2 Noncombustible	1	0
INTERIOR BEARING WALLS	1	0	1 or Heavy Timber	1	0
FLOOR CONSTRUCTION	1	0	Heavy Timber	1	0
ROOF CONSTRUCTION	1	0	Heavy Timber	1	0
PARTY WALLS AND FIRE WALLS	2–4	2–4	2–4	2–4	2–4
	2 hours connecting 4 stories or more, 1 hour connecting fewer than 4 stories				
ENCLOSURES OF EXITS, EXIT HALLWAYS, EXIT STAIRWAYS, SHAFTS	0–1	0–1	0–1	0–1	0–1
EXIT ACCESS CORRIDORS	1	1	1	1	1
TENANT SPACE SEPARATIONS	1	1	1	1	1
DWELLING UNIT AND GUEST ROOM SEPARATIONS					
OTHER NONBEARING PARTITIONS	0	0	0	0	0

HEIGHT AND AREA LIMITATIONS

361

CONSTRUCTION TYPES

NATIONAL BUILDING CODE OF CANADA

This section summarizes the fire-resistance rating and construction requirements for Construction Types in the National Building Code of Canada. Once you have determined an appropriate Construction Type for a project, based on the Height and Area Tables on pages 428–453, use this section to relate this information to systems of construction. The table on these two facing pages consolidates and simplifies fire-resistance requirements for each Construction Type. The pages following this chart define each Construction Type in terms of specific structural systems, materials, and minimum thicknesses of components necessary to meet the required minimum fire-resistance rating. The values in the table below may be modified as follows:

■ **Exterior Bearing Walls:** In addition to the requirements indicated in the table on these two facing pages, see also Fire-Resistance Requirements for Exterior Walls, page 358, for information regarding protection of exterior walls when in close proximity to other buildings.

■ **Heavy Timber Construction:** Heavy Timber construction is an acceptable substitute for any building where ¾-Hour or Unprotected Noncombustible Construction is permitted.

NATIONAL BUILDING CODE OF CANADA

CONSTRUCTION TYPE	Noncombustible			
	2-Hour (page 364)	1-Hour (page 365)	¾-Hour (page 365)	Unprotected (page 366)
LOADBEARING COLUMNS, WALLS AND ARCHES	2	1	¾	0
FLOOR CONSTRUCTION	2	1	¾	0
MEZZANINES	1	1	0	0
ROOF CONSTRUCTION	0–1	0–1	0–¾	0
PARTY WALLS AND FIRE WALLS	2–4	2–4	2–4	2–4
ENCLOSURES OF EXITS, EXIT HALLWAYS, EXIT STAIRWAYS	2	1	¾	¾
EXIT ACCESS CORRIDORS	1¾	1¾	¾	¾
SUITE SEPARATIONS	1	1	¾	¾
DWELLING UNIT AND GUEST ROOM SEPARATIONS	1	1	¾	¾
OTHER NONBEARING PARTITIONS	Noncombustible			

CONSTRUCTION TYPES

■ Structure Supporting Roofs Only: Walls, columns, girders, trusses, and other members of the structural frame supporting roofs only may be constructed to the fire-resistance rating as required for the roof itself.

■ Roof Construction: Where roofs support any occupancy, they must be constructed to the fire-resistance rating requirements for a floor assembly. Long-span roofs over arenas, swimming pools, gymnasiums, and other similar types of space may be of Unprotected Construction when supporting roof loads only and not less than 6 m (20 ft) above the floor. Roofs for fully sprinklered one- and two-story buildings of any occupancy and any construction type may be of Heavy Timber Construction.

■ Corridor Enclosures: For more information on corridor enclosure requirements, see page 257.

Combustible				CONSTRUCTION TYPE
1-Hour (page 368)	**Heavy Timber** (page 366)	**3/4-Hour** (page 368)	**Unprotected** (page 368)	
1	Heavy Timber	$\frac{3}{4}$	0	**LOADBEARING COLUMNS, WALLS AND ARCHES**
1	Heavy Timber	$\frac{3}{4}$	0	**FLOOR CONSTRUCTION**
1	Heavy Timber	$0-\frac{3}{4}$	0	**MEZZANINES**
0–1	Heavy Timber	$0-\frac{3}{4}$	0	**ROOF CONSTRUCTION**
2–4	2–4	2–4	2–4	**PARTY WALLS AND FIRE WALLS**
1	$\frac{3}{4}$	$\frac{3}{4}$	$\frac{3}{4}$	**ENCLOSURES OF EXITS, EXIT HALLWAYS, EXIT STAIRWAYS**
1	$\frac{3}{4}$	$\frac{3}{4}$	$\frac{3}{4}$	**EXIT ACCESS CORRIDORS**
1	$\frac{3}{4}$	$\frac{3}{4}$	$\frac{3}{4}$	**SUITE SEPARATIONS**
1	$\frac{3}{4}$	$\frac{3}{4}$	$\frac{3}{4}$	**DWELLING UNIT AND GUEST ROOM SEPARATIONS**
0	0	0	0	**OTHER NONBEARING PARTITIONS**

HEIGHT AND AREA LIMITATIONS

363

3-HOUR NONCOMBUSTIBLE CONSTRUCTION

3-Hour Noncombustible Construction requires a fire-resistance rating of 3 hours for columns and bearing walls and 2 hours for floor construction.

■ **Structural Steel** columns, beams, joists, and decking must be protected to these values with applied fireproofing materials or an appropriately fire-resistive ceiling of plaster, gypsum board, or fibrous panels (see pages 98–111).

■ **Reinforced Concrete** columns must be at least 12 in. (300 mm) in dimension, and loadbearing walls must be at least 6 in. (150 mm) thick. Floor slabs must be at least 5 in. (125 mm) thick. Concrete one-way and two-way joist systems (ribbed slabs and waffle slabs) with slabs thinner than 5 in. (125 mm) between joists require protection with applied fireproofing materials or an appropriately fire-resistive ceiling of plaster, gypsum board, or fibrous panels (see pages 113–129).

■ **Posttensioned Concrete** floor slabs must be at least 5 in. (125 mm) thick (see pages 120–129).

■ **Precast Concrete** columns must be at least 12 in. (300 mm) in dimension, and beams at least 7 in. (175 mm) wide. Loadbearing wall panels must be at least 6 (150 mm) thick. Solid slabs may not be less than 5 in. (125 mm) thick. Hollow core slabs must be at least 8 in. (200 mm) deep and may be used without a topping. Double and single tees require applied fireproofing materials or an appropriately fire-resistive ceiling of plaster, gypsum board, or fibrous panels, unless a concrete topping 3.25 in. (85 mm) is poured (see pages 131–141).

■ **Brick Masonry** loadbearing walls must be at least 6 in. (150 mm) thick. Vaults and domes must be at least 8 in. (200 mm) deep with a rise not less than one-twelfth the span (see pages 80–81).

■ **Concrete Masonry** Columns must be at least 12 in. (300 mm) in dimension, and loadbearing walls must be at least 8 in. (200 mm) thick. Depending on the composition and design of the masonry unit, applied plaster or stucco facings may also be required (see pages 86–89).

Fire-resistive requirements for non-loadbearing walls and partitions are summarized on pages 360–363.

2-HOUR NONCOMBUSTIBLE CONSTRUCTION

2-Hour Noncombustible Construction requires a fire-resistance rating of 2 hours for floor construction, columns, and bearing walls.

■ **Structural Steel** columns, beams, joists, and decking must be protected to these values with applied fireproofing materials or an appropriately fire-resistive ceiling of plaster, gypsum board, or fibrous panels (see pages 98–111).

■ **Reinforced Concrete** columns must be at least 10 in. (250 mm) in dimension, and loadbearing walls must be at least 5 in. (125 mm) thick. Floor slabs must be at least 5 in. (125 mm) thick. Concrete one-way and two-way joist systems (ribbed slabs and waffle slabs) with slabs thinner than 5 in. (125 mm) between joists require protection with applied fireproofing materials or an appropriately fire-resistive ceiling of plaster, gypsum board, or fibrous panels (see pages 113–129).

■ **Posttensioned Concrete** floor slabs must be at least 5 in. (125 mm) thick (see pages 120–129).

■ **Precast Concrete** columns must be at least 10 in. (250 mm) in dimension, and beams at least 7 in. (175 mm) wide. Loadbearing wall panels must be at least 5 in. (120 mm) thick. Solid slabs may not be less than 5 in. (120 mm) thick. Hollow core slabs must be at least 8 in. (200 mm) deep and may be used without a topping. Double and single tees require applied fireproofing materials or an appropriately fire-resistive ceiling of plaster, gypsum board, or fibrous panels, unless a concrete topping 3.25 in. (85 mm) thick is poured (see pages 131–141).

■ **Brick Masonry** loadbearing columns must be at least 12 in. (300 mm) in dimension, and walls must be at least 6 in. (150 mm) thick. Vaults and domes must be at least 8 in. (200 mm) deep with a rise not less than one-twelfth the span (see pages 78–81).

■ **Concrete Masonry** columns must be at least 10 in. (250 mm) in dimension, and loadbearing walls must be at least 8 in. (200 mm) thick. Depending on the composition and design of the masonry unit, applied plaster or stucco facings may also be required (see pages 86–89).

Fire-resistive requirements for non-loadbearing walls and partitions are summarized on pages 360–363.

CONSTRUCTION TYPES

1-HOUR NONCOMBUSTIBLE CONSTRUCTION

1-Hour Noncombustible Construction requires a fire-resistance rating of 1 hour for floor construction, columns, and bearing walls.

■ **Structural Steel** columns, beams, joists, and decking must be protected to these values with applied fireproofing materials or an appropriately fire-resistive ceiling of plaster, gypsum board, or fibrous panels (see pages 98–111).

■ **Light Gauge Steel** framing fire protection requirements vary with factors such as size and weight of the steel framing and the presence of other materials, such as acoustical insulation or resilient attachment channels, within the assembly. For preliminary design purposes, you may assume that a 1-hour fire-resistance rating can be achieved for both floor and wall framing with two layers of ½-in. (13-mm) Type X gypsum wallboard or other equivalent material applied to the fire-exposed sides of the framing (see pages 94–97).

■ **Reinforced Concrete** columns must be at least 8 in. (200 mm) in dimension, and loadbearing walls must be at least 4 in. (100 mm) thick. Floor slabs must be at least 3.5 in. (90 mm) thick. Concrete one-way and two-way joist systems (ribbed slabs, skip-joist slabs, and waffle slabs) require protection with applied fireproofing materials or an appropriately fire-resistive ceiling of plaster, gypsum board, or acoustical panels unless the slab thickness is at least 3.5 in. (90 mm) between joists (see pages 113–129).

■ **Posttensioned Concrete** floor slabs must be at least 3.5 in. (90 mm) thick (see pages 120–129).

■ **Precast Concrete** columns must be at least 10 in. (250 mm) in dimension, and beams at least 4 in. (100 mm) wide. Loadbearing wall panels must be at least 3.5 (90 mm) thick. Solid slabs may not be less than 3.5 in. (90 mm) thick. Hollow core slabs must be at least 8 in. (200 mm) deep and may be used without a topping. Double and single tees require applied fireproofing materials or an appropriately fire-resistive ceiling of plaster, gypsum board, or acoustical panels unless a concrete topping 1.75 in. (45 mm) thick is poured (see pages 131–141).

■ **Brick Masonry** columns must be at least 8 in. (200 mm) in dimension, and loadbearing walls must be at least 6 in. (150 mm) thick. Vaults and domes must be at least 4 in. (100 mm) deep with a rise not less than one-twelfth the span (see pages 78–81).

■ **Concrete Masonry** columns must be at least 8 in. (200 mm) in dimension, and loadbearing walls must be at least 8 in. (200 mm) thick. Depending on the composition and design of the masonry unit, applied plaster or stucco facings may also be required (see pages 86–89).

Fire-resistive requirements for non-loadbearing walls and partitions are summarized on pages 360–363.

¾-HOUR NONCOMBUSTIBLE CONSTRUCTION

¾-Hour Noncombustible Construction requires a fire-resistance rating of 45 minutes for floors, columns, and bearing walls. This Construction Type, unique to the National Building Code of Canada, may include any noncombustible construction materials meeting the requirements listed on pages 362–363. In practice, it is most commonly applied to light gauge steel framing systems. For preliminary purposes, the information provided on this page for 1-Hour Noncombustible Construction may be used to achieve this system's required levels of fire resistance.

UNPROTECTED NONCOMBUSTIBLE CONSTRUCTION

Unprotected Noncombustible Construction has no fire-resistive requirements for floor construction, columns, or bearing walls, except that they must be constructed of noncombustible materials.

■ **Structural Steel** columns, beams, joists, and decking may be used without applied fireproofing materials or fire-resistive ceilings (see pages 98–111).

■ **Light Gauge Steel Framing** may be used with minimum facings of gypsum board or its equivalent to brace the studs and joists against buckling (see pages 94–97).

■ **Reinforced Concrete** structures of all types may be designed to the minimum dimensions dictated by structural considerations, without need for applied fireproofing materials (see pages 114–129).

■ **Posttensioned Concrete** structures of all types may be designed to the minimum dimensions dictated by structural considerations, without need for applied fireproofing materials (see pages 120–129).

■ **Precast Concrete** structures of all types may be designed to the minimum dimensions dictated by structural considerations, without need for applied fireproofing materials (see pages 132–141).

■ **Masonry** structures of all types may be designed to the minimum dimensions dictated by structural considerations, without need for applied fireproofing materials (see pages 78-91).

Fire-resistive requirements for nonloadbearing walls and partitions are summarized on pages 360–363.

HEAVY TIMBER CONSTRUCTION AND MILL CONSTRUCTION

Heavy Timber and Mill Construction depend for their fire-resistant properties on wood framing members and decking of sufficient thickness such that they are slow to catch fire and burn. Either solid wood or glue laminated members may be used.

International Building Code

In the International Building Code, where Heavy Timber Construction is permitted, exterior walls must be of not less than 2-hour fire-resistance rated Noncombustible Construction. In this text, this combination of heavy timber interior structure and rated noncombustible exterior walls is referred to as *Mill Construction*, a name reflecting its origins in early industrial era fire-resistant brick masonry and heavy timber building systems. In this model code, Heavy Timber Construction is also an acceptable substitute for roof structures and their supporting members where any 1-Hour or less, Combustible or Noncombustible Construction system is permitted.

National Building Code of Canada

In the National Building Code of Canada, buildings of Heavy Timber Construction must meet the minimum size requirements for wood members, but there are no special combustibility limitations on the exterior walls of such buildings. In this model code, Heavy Timber Construction is also an acceptable substitute for any building where ?-Hour Combustible Construction is permitted.

Minimum Dimensions for Wood Members

Use the following minimum dimensions for wood members for the preliminary design of both Heavy Timber Construction and Mill Construction buildings in either code:

■ **Solid Wood Columns:** In both model codes, solid wood columns supporting floor loads must be at least 8×8 nominal dimensions ($7\frac{1}{2} \times 7\frac{1}{2}$ in. or 191×191 mm actual size). Columns supporting roof loads only must be not less than nominal 6×8 ($5\frac{1}{2} \times 7\frac{1}{2}$ in. or 140×191 mm).

■ **Glue Laminated Wood Columns:** In the International Building Code, glue laminated wood columns supporting floor loads must be at least $6\frac{3}{4} \times 8\frac{1}{4}$ in. (171×210 mm) actual size, and supporting roof loads only, at least $5 \times 8\frac{1}{4}$ in. (127×210 mm). In the National Building Code of Canada, such columns supporting floors and roofs must be at least 175×190 mm ($6\frac{7}{8} \times 7\frac{1}{2}$ in.) actual size, and supporting roofs only, at least 130×190 mm ($5\frac{1}{8} \times 7\frac{1}{2}$ in.).

■ **Solid Wood Beams and Girders:** In both model codes, solid wood beams and girders supporting floor loads must be at least 6×10 nominal dimensions ($5\frac{1}{2} \times 9\frac{1}{2}$ in. or 140×241 mm actual size), and supporting roof loads only, at least nominal 4×6 ($3\frac{1}{2} \times 5\frac{1}{2}$ in. or 89×140 mm). The National Building Code of Canada also permits solid wood beams and girders supporting floors and roofs to have a minimum actual size of 191×191 mm ($7\frac{1}{2} \times 7\frac{1}{2}$ in.). In some circumstances, the International Building Code permits solid wood members supporting roof loads only to be as small as nominal 3 in. ($2\frac{1}{2}$ in. or 64 mm actual size) wide; see the code for details.

CONSTRUCTION TYPES

■ **Glue Laminated Wood Beams and Girders:** In the International Building Code, glue laminated wood beams and girders supporting floor loads must be at least 5 × 10½ in. (127 × 267 mm) actual size, and supporting roof loads only, at least 3 × 6⅞ in. (76 × 175 mm). In the National Building Code of Canada, such beams and girders supporting floors and roofs must be not less than 130 × 228 mm (5⅛ × 9 in.) or 175 × 190 mm (6⅞ × 7½ in.) actual size, and supporting roofs only, at least 80 × 152 mm (3⅛ × 6 in.).

■ **Trusses Made of Solid Wood Members:** In the International Building Code, trusses supporting floor loads must be made of solid wood members no smaller than 8 x 8 nominal dimensions (7½ × 7½ in. or 191 × 191 mm actual size). Roof trusses must be made of members no smaller than nominal 4 x 6 (3½ × 5½ in. or 89 × 140 mm). When trusses are composed of paired solid wood members and the space between members is blocked or covered, individual members may be as little as nominal 3 in. (2½ in. or 64 mm actual size) wide. In the National Building Code of Canada, minimum sizes for truss members made of solid wood are the same as required in that code for solid wood beams and girders.

■ **Trusses Made of Glue Laminated Wood Members:** In the International Building Code, trusses supporting floor loads must be made of glue laminated wood members no smaller than 6¾ × 8¼ in. (171 × 210 mm) actual size. Roof trusses must be made of glue laminated wood members no smaller than 3 × 6⅞ in. (76 × 175 mm). In the National Building Code of Canada, minimum sizes for truss members made of glue laminated wood are the same as required in that code for glue laminated wood beams and girders.

■ **Glue Laminated Wood Arches:** In the International Building Code, glue laminated wood arches supporting floor loads must be no smaller than 6¾ × 8¼ in. (171 ×210 mm) actual size. Arches supporting roof loads only and springing from the floor level must be no smaller than 5 × 8¼ in. (127 × 210 mm) for the lower half and no smaller than 5 × 6 in. (127 ×152 mm) for the upper half. Arches supporting roof loads only and springing from the tops of walls must be not less than 3 × 6⅞ in. (76 × 175 mm). In the National Building Code of Canada, minimum sizes for glue laminated arches supporting floor loads are the same as required in that code for glue laminated wood beams and girders. Arches supporting roof loads only

and springing from the floor level must be no smaller than 130 × 152 mm (5⅛ × 6 in.) actual size, and when springing from the tops of walls, no smaller than 80 × 152 mm (3⅛ × 6 in.).

■ **Floors and Roof Decks:** In both model codes, wood floors must consist of not less than 3 in. nominal dimension (2½ in. or 64 mm actual size) solid or glue laminated wood structural decking. The decking must also be overlaid with either finish wood flooring not less than nominal 1-in. (½ in. or 64 mm) thick or wood panels (plywood or other) not less than ½ in. (12.5 mm) thick. Wood roofs must consist of solid or glue laminated wood structural decking not less than nominal 2 in. (1½ in. or 38 mm actual size), or of 1⅛-in. (28 mm) plywood structural panels.

See pages 64–75 for structural information on the wood members in Heavy Timber and Mill Construction. Information on Noncombustible wall systems for Mill Construction may be found on the following pages: 80–81 for brick masonry, 88–89 for concrete masonry, 94–95 for steel lightweight studs, 98–101 for structural steel columns, 114–117 for sitecast concrete, and 132–135 for precast concrete.

CONSTRUCTION TYPES

ORDINARY CONSTRUCTION

Ordinary Construction, like Mill Construction, is a system with historical roots in early industrial era fire-resistant buildings. It consists of noncombustible exterior walls and interior structure that is usually wood light framing but may also be of concrete or steel.

■ **Exterior Walls** must be noncombustible, with a fire-resistance rating of not less than 2 hours.

■ **Interior Framing** members of wood must meet the requirements listed on this page for Wood Light Frame Construction. For 1-Hour Ordinary Construction, use the requirements for 1-Hour Wood Light Frame; for Unprotected Ordinary Construction, use the requirements for Unprotected Wood Light Frame.

Information on noncombustible wall systems for Ordinary Construction may be found on the following pages: 80–81 for brick masonry, 88–89 for concrete masonry, 94–95 for steel lightweight studs, 98–101 for structural steel columns, 114–117 for sitecast concrete, and 132–135 for precast concrete.

¾-HOUR COMBUSTIBLE CONSTRUCTION

¾-Hour Combustible Construction requires a fire-resistance rating of 45 minutes for floors, columns, and bearing walls. This construction classification, unique to the National Building Code of Canada, permits both combustible and noncombustible materials. In practice, it is most commonly applied to Light Wood Frame systems. For preliminary purposes, the information provided on this page for 1-Hour Wood Light Frame Construction may be used to achieve this system's required levels of fire resistance. In this model code, Heavy Timber Construction (page 366) is also permitted as a substitute wherever ¾-Hour Combustible Construction is permitted.

WOOD LIGHT FRAME/ COMBUSTIBLE CONSTRUCTION

Floors, walls, and roofs of Wood Light Frame/Combustible Construction are framed with wood members not less than 2 in. in nominal thickness (actually 1.5 in., or 38 mm). These members are usually spaced at center-to-center distances of ei-ther 16 or 24 in. (400 or 600 mm) and covered with any of a very wide range of sheathing and finish materials.

■ **Unprotected Wood Light Frame/ Combustible Construction** allows the structure of the building to remain exposed or to be finished with materials that do not have a suficient fire-resistance rating to satisfy a higher classification of construction, such as wood paneling or thin gypsum board.

■ **1-Hour Wood Light Frame/ Combustible Construction** requires that loadbearing walls and floors have 1-hour fire-resistance ratings. A 1-hour wall may be constructed of wood studs by applying ⅝-in. (16-mm) Type X gypsum board or its equivalent to each face of the studs. A floor with 1-in, nominal subflooring and finish flooring (actual dimensions ¾ in., or 19 mm) has a 1-hour fire-resistance rating if it is finished below with a ceiling of ⅝-in. (16-mm) Type X gypsum board or its equivalent.

For structural information on Wood Light Frame/Combustible Construction, see pages 56–63. Fire-resistive requirements for nonloadbearing walls and partitions are summarized on pages 360–363.

This chapter provides simplified tables for determining the allowable building height and area for each Occupancy Group and model code.

HOW TO USE THE TABLES OF HEIGHT AND AREA LIMITATIONS FOR THE INTERNATIONAL BUILDING CODE

1. Be sure you are consulting the tables for the proper building code. If you are not sure which code you are working under, see pages 7, 13.

2. The Occupancy Group is given at the upper left-hand corner of the table. If you are not sure about the Occupancy Group into which your building falls, consult the indexes on pages 7–15.

3. Noncombustible Construction Types are tabulated on the left-hand page, Combustible Construction Types on the right-hand page.

4. Each pair of columns represents one Construction Type. For specific information on the different materials and modes of construction that conform to that Construction Type, follow the page reference given here.

5. The paired columns tabulate height and area information for both sprinklered and unsprinklered buildings of each Construction Type.

6. The significance of the floor area numbers in the chart, which varies from one model code to another, is explained at the lower left-hand corner.

INTERNATIONAL BUILDING CODE

OCCUPANCY GROUP B: BUSINESS

Sprinklers

In addition to the requirements indicated in the table on these two facing pages, a sprinkler system is required for any stories or basements exceeding 1500 sq ft (139 m²) in area without openings to the exterior, in underground portions of most buildings with occupancy more than 30 ft (9 m) below the lowest level of exit discharge, and throughout any building containing floors 55 ft (17 m) or more above grade with an occupant load of 30 or more.

Unlimited Area Buildings

One- and two-story Occupancy B buildings, fully sprinklered, may be of unlimited area when surrounded on all sides by public ways or yards not less than 60 ft (18 m) in width. In such one-story buildings, Group A-1 and A-2 occupancies are permitted, so long as these occupancies are treated as mixed-use Separated Occupancies, such areas each comply with their own code height and area limits, and all required exits from these areas discharge directly to the exterior. In some circumstances, reductions in the required width of open space around these

building types are permitted; see the code for details.

Fire Walls

For multiplication of the allowable area by subdividing the building with fire walls, see page 358.

Basements

Basements are not included in area calculations provided their area does not exceed the area permitted for a one-story building.

Excess Frontage

If more than 25% of the building perimeter fronts on a street or open space at least 20 ft (6.1 m) wide that is accessible to firefighting vehi-

OCCUPANCY GROUP B: BUSINESS

		Noncombustible							
CONSTRUCTION TYPE		3-Hour (page 364)		2-Hour (page 364)		1-Hour (page 365)		Unprotected (page 366)	
IBC NOMENCLATURE		Type I-A		Type I-B		Type II-A		Type II-B	
MAXIMUM HEIGHT IN FEET		Spr	Unspr	Spr	Unspr	Spr	Unspr	Spr	Unspr
		UH	75'	180'	75'	85' b	65'	75'	65'
	UH	UA	UA						
	12			UA					
	11				UA				
	10								
	9								
HEIGHT IN STORIES ABOVE GRADE AND MAXIMUM AREA IN SQ FT ALL FLOORS a	8								
	7								
	6					337,500	c		
	5					337,500	112,500	207,000	
	4					337,500	112,500	207,000	69,000
	3					337,500	112,500	207,000	69,000
	2					225,000	75,000	138,000	46,000
	1					150,000	37,500	92,000	23,000
MAXIMUM AREA IN SQ FT FOR ANY SINGLE FLOOR OF A MULTISTORY BUILDING	UA	UA	UA	UA	UA	112,500	37,500	69,000	23,000

Each number in the table represents the maximum total area in square feet for all floors for a building of the indicated story height.

382

7. As an example of the use of this chart, a sprinklered building of Occupancy Group B, 1-Hour Non-combustible Construction, under the International Building Code, may be no more than

a. six stories, or

b. 85 ft tall, whichever is less,

c. with a total floor area (on all floors) no larger than 337,500 sq ft.

8. As another example, if we wish to construct a five-story unsprinklered building with 22,000 sq ft per floor, or 110,000 sq ft total area, we must use 1-Hour Noncombustible Construction as a minimum. Looking to the right along the same row of the chart, we see that the addition of sprinklers would allow us to use Unprotected, Ordinary, or Mill Construction. We also note that by slightly reducing the total building area to 108,000 sq ft, unsprinklered Mill Construction would be permitted. By following the page references at the heads of these columns, we can determine exactly what each of these Construction Types is and proceed to preliminary configuration and sizing of the structural system we select.

The reference tables appearing on pages 372–475 are for preliminary purposes only. They represent the authors' interpretation of certain major provisions of the International Building Code. No official interpretation has been sought from or granted by the International Code Council. For design development work and final preparation of building plans, you must consult the building codes and regulations in effect in you project's locale.

INTERNATIONAL BUILDING CODE

cles, the tabulated area limitations below may be increased according to the adjacent table. For example, for a building with half of its perimeter accessible to firefighting equipment via a space not less than 24 ft (7.3 m) wide, the allowable area increase is:

0.80 increase × 25% excess frontage = 20% total area increase

Measurements

Height is measured from the average finished ground level adjoining the building to the average level of the highest roof. Floor area is measured within exterior walls or exterior walls and fire walls, exclusive of vent shafts and courtyards.

Width of Frontage[a]	Percent Area Increase for Each 1% of Frontage[a] in Excess of 25%
20' (6.1 m)	0.67
22' (6.7 m)	0.73
24' (7.3 m)	0.80
26' (7.9 m)	0.87
28' (8.5 m)	0.93
30' (9.1 m) or wider	1.00

[a]Intermediate values may be interpolated.

Further Information

For information on Occupancy Group classifications, see page 17. For information on mixed-used buildings, see page 352. For information on which code to consult, see pages 7, 13.

Unit Conversions

1 ft = 304.8 mm, 1 sq ft = 0.0929 m².

	Combustible										CONSTRUCTION TYPE	
	Ordinary				Wood Light Frame							
	1-Hour (page 368)		Unprotected (page 368)		Mill (page 366)		1-Hour (page 368)		Unprotected (page 368)			
	Type III-A		Type III-B		Type IV-HT		Type V-A		Type V-B		IBC NOMENCLATURE	
	Spr	Unspr	Spr	Unspr	Spr	Unspr	Spr	Unspr	Spr	Unspr		
	85'	65'	75'	55'	85'	65'	70'	50'	60'	40'	MAXIMUM HEIGHT IN FEET	
UH												
12												
11												
10												
9												
8												HEIGHT IN STORIES ABOVE GRADE AND MAXIMUM AREA IN SQ FT ALL FLOORS
7												
6	256,500				324,000							
5	256,500	85,500	171,000		324,000	108,000						
4	256,500	85,500	171,000	57,000	324,000	108,000	162,000					
3	256,500	85,500	171,000	57,000	324,000	108,000	162,000	54,000	81,000			
2	171,000	57,000	114,000	38,000	216,000	72,000	108,000	36,000	54,000	18,000	MAXIMUM AREA IN SQ FT FOR ANY SINGLE FLOOR OF A MULTISTORY BUILDING
1	114,000	28,500	76,000	19,000	144,000	36,000	72,000	18,000	36,000	9,000	
	85,500	28,500	57,000	19,000	108,000	36,000	54,000	18,000	27,000	9,000	

This table was compiled from information contained in the International Building Code 2006. It does not represent an official interpretation by the organization that issues this code.

Key to Abbreviations

| UA | Unlimited area | Spr | With approved sprinkler system | NP | Not permitted |
| UH | Unlimited height | Unspr | Without approved sprinkler system | | |

383

HEIGHT AND AREA TABLES

OCCUPANCY GROUP A-1: ASSEMBLY, THEATERS

Sprinklers

In addition to the requirements indicated in the table on these two facing pages, a sprinkler system is required for Group A-1 Occupancy fire areas meeting any of the following conditions:

■ When located on a floor other than the level of exit discharge

■ With an area exceeding 12,000 sq ft (1115 m²)

■ With an occupant load of 300 or more

■ Containing multitheater complexes

For an explanation of fire areas, see page 358. A sprinkler system is also required for any stories or basements exceeding 1500 sq ft (139 m²) in area without openings to the exterior, in underground portions of most buildings with occupancy more than 30 ft (9 m) below the lowest level of exit discharge, and throughout any building containing floors 55 ft (17 m) or more above grade with an occupant load of 30 or more.

Unlimited Area Buildings

One-story motion picture theater buildings constructed of any Noncombustible Construction Type and fully sprinklered may be of unlimited area when surrounded on all sides by public ways or yards not less than 60 ft (18 m) in width. Buildings one story in height, fully sprinklered, of other than Wood Light Frame Construction, surrounded on all sides by public ways or yards at least 60 ft (18.3 m) in width, and containing multiple Group A-1 and A-2 occupancy areas, may be of unlimited area, provided that assembly areas are treated as Separated Uses (see page 352), each such area, complies with the area limits for that occupancy, and all exits discharge directly to the exterior. In some circumstances, reductions in the required width of open space around these building types are permitted; see the code for details.

Basements

Basements are not included in area calculations, provided that their

OCCUPANCY GROUP A-1: ASSEMBLY, THEATERS

CONSTRUCTION TYPE	Noncombustible							
	3-Hour (page 364)		2-Hour (page 364)		1-Hour (page 365)		Unprotected (page 366)	
IBC NOMENCLATURE	Type I-A		Type I-B		Type II-A		Type II-B	
	Spr	Unspr	Spr	Unspr	Spr	Unspr	Spr	Unspr
MAXIMUM HEIGHT IN FEET	UH	75'	180'	75'	85'	65'	75'	55'
UH	UA	UA						
12								
11								
10								
9								
8								
7								
6			UA					
5				UA^a				
4					139,500			
3					139,500	49,500^a	76,500	
2					93,000	31,000^a	51,000	17,000^a
1					62,000	15,500	34,000	8,500
MAXIMUM AREA IN SQ FT FOR ANY SINGLE FLOOR OF A MULTISTORY BUILDING	UA	UA	UA	UA	46,500	15,500	25,500	8,500

HEIGHT IN STORIES ABOVE GRADE AND MAXIMUM AREA IN SQ FT ALL FLOORS

Each number in the table represents the maximum total area in square feet for all floors for a building of the indicated story height.

^aUnsprinklered areas are only permitted at grade level, normally limiting unsprinklered occupancies to only one or a few stories in height.

area does not exceed the area permitted for a one-story building.

Excess Frontage

If more than 25% of the building perimeter fronts on a street or open space at least 20 ft (6.1 m) wide that is accessible to firefighting vehicles, the tabulated area limitations below may be increased according to the adjacent table. For example, for a building with half of its perimeter accessible to firefighting equipment via a space not less than 24 ft (7.3 m) wide, the allowable area increase is:

0.80 increase × 25% excess frontage = 20% total area increase

Measurements

Height is measured from the average finished ground level adjoin-

Width of Frontage[a]	Percent Area Increase for Each 1% of Frontage in Excess of 25%
20' (6.1 m)	0.67
22' (6.7 m)	0.73
24' (7.3 m)	0.80
26' (7.9 m)	0.87
28' (8.5 m)	0.93
30' (9.1 m) or wider	1.00

[a]Intermediate values may be interpolated.

ing the building to the average level of the highest roof. Floor area is measured within exterior walls or exterior walls and fire walls, exclusive of courtyards.

Further Information

For information on Occupancy Group classifications, see page 7. For information on mixed-use buildings, see page 352. For infor-

mation on which code to consult, see pages 7, 13.

Unit Conversions

1 ft = 304.8 mm, 1 sq ft = 0.0929 m²

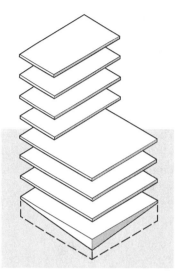

Combustible											
Ordinary				Mill (page 366)		Wood Light Frame					**CONSTRUCTION TYPE**
1-Hour (page 368)		Unprotected (page 368)				1-Hour (page 368)		Unprotected (page 368)			
Type III-A		Type III-B		Type IV-HT		Type V-A		Type V-B			**IBC NOMENCLATURE**
Spr	Unspr	Spr	Unspr	Spr	Unspr	Spr	Unspr	Spr	Unspr		
85'	65'	75'	55'	85'	65'	70'	50'	60'	40'		**MAXIMUM HEIGHT IN FEET**
										UH	
										12	
										11	
										10	
										9	
										8	**HEIGHT IN STORIES ABOVE GRADE AND**
										7	**MAXIMUM AREA IN**
										6	**SQ FT ALL FLOORS**
										5	
126,000				135,000						4	
126,000	42,000[a]	76,500		135,000	45,000[a]	103,500				3	
84,000	28,000[a]	51,000	17,000[a]	90,000	30,000[a]	69,000	23,000[a]	33,000		2	
56,000	14,000	34,000	8,500	60,000	15,000	46,000	11,500	22,000	5,500	1	**MAXIMUM AREA IN SQ FT FOR ANY SINGLE FLOOR OF A MULTISTORY BUILDING**
42,000	14,000	25,500	8,500	45,000	15,000	34,500	11,500	16,500			

This table was compiled from information contained in the International Building Code 2006. It does not represent an official interpretation by the organization that issues this code.

Key to Abbreviations

UA	Unlimited area	Spr	With approved sprinkler system
UH	Unlimited height	Unspr	Without approved sprinkler system
NP	Not permitted		

INTERNATIONAL BUILDING CODE

OCCUPANCY GROUP A-2: ASSEMBLY, FOOD AND DRINK ESTABLISHMENTS

Sprinklers

In addition to the requirements indicated in the table on these two facing pages, a sprinkler system is required for Group A-2 Occupancy fire areas meeting any of the following conditions:

■ When located on a floor other than the level of exit discharge

■ With an area exceeding 5000 sq ft (465 m²)

■ With an occupant load of 100 or more

For an explanation of fire areas, see page 358. A sprinkler system is also required for any stories or basements exceeding 1500 sq ft (139 m²) in area without openings to the exterior, in underground portions of most buildings with occupancy more than 30 ft (9 m) below the lowest level of exit discharge, and throughout any building containing floors 55 ft (17 m) or more above grade with an occupant load of 30 or more.

Unlimited Area Buildings

Buildings one story in height, fully sprinklered, of other than Wood Light Frame Construction, surrounded on all sides by public ways or yards at least 60 ft (18.3 m) in width, and containing multiple Group A-1 and A-2 occupancy areas, may be of unlimited area provided that assembly areas are treated as Separated Uses (see page 352), each such area complies with the area limits for that occupancy, and all exits discharge directly to the exterior. In some circumstances, reductions in the required width of open space around these building types are permitted; see the code for details.

Fire Walls

For multiplication of the allowable area by subdividing the building with fire walls, see page 358.

Basements

Basements are not included in area calculations, provided their area does not exceed the area permitted for a one-story building.

OCCUPANCY GROUP A-2: ASSEMBLY, FOOD AND DRINK ESTABLISHMENTS

	Noncombustible							
CONSTRUCTION TYPE	**3-Hour** (page 364)		**2-Hour** (page 364)		**1-Hour** (page 365)		**Unprotected** (page 366)	
IBC NOMENCLATURE	Type I-A		Type I-B		Type II-A		Type II-B	
	Spr	Unspr	Spr	Unspr	Spr	Unspr	Spr	Unspr
MAXIMUM HEIGHT IN FEET	UH	75'	180'	75'	85'	65'	75'	55'
UH	UA	UAª						
12			UA					
11				UAª				
10								
9								
8								
7								
6								
5								
4					139,500			
3					139,500	46,500ª	85,500	
2					93,000	31,000ª	57,000	10,000ª
1					62,000	15,500	38,000	9,500
MAXIMUM AREA IN SQ FT FOR ANY SINGLE FLOOR OF A MULTISTORY BUILDING	UA	UA	UA	UA	46,500	15,500	28,500	9,500

Left labels: MAXIMUM HEIGHT IN FEET; HEIGHT IN STORIES ABOVE GRADE AND MAXIMUM AREA IN SQ FT ALL FLOORS

Each number in the table represents the maximum total area in square feet for all floors for a building of the indicated story height.

ªUnsprinklered areas are only permitted at grade level, normally limiting unsprinklered occupancies to only one or a few stories in height.

374

Excess Frontage

If more than 25% of the building perimeter fronts on a street or open space at least 20 ft (6.1 m) wide that is accessible to firefighting vehicles, the tabulated area limitations below may be increased according to the adjacent table. For example, for a building with half of its perimeter accessible to firefighting equipment via a space not less than 24 ft (7.3 m) wide, the allowable area increase is:

0.80 increase × 25% excess frontage = 20% total area increase

Measurements

Height is measured from the average finished ground level adjoining the building to the average level of the highest roof. Floor area

Width of Frontage[a]	Percent Area Increase for Each 1% of Frontage[a] in Excess of 25%
20' (6.1 m)	0.67
22' (6.7 m)	0.73
24' (7.3 m)	0.80
26' (7.9 m)	0.87
28' (8.5 m)	0.93
30' (9.1 m) or wider	1.00

[a]Intermediate values may be interpolated.

is measured within exterior walls or exterior walls and fire walls, exclusive of vent shafts and courtyards.

Further Information

For information on Occupancy Group classifications, see page 7. For information on mixed-use buildings, see page 352. For information on which code to consult, see pages 7, 13.

Unit Conversions

1 ft 304.8 mm, 1 sq ft = 0.0929 m^2

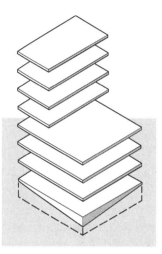

	Combustible											CONSTRUCTION TYPE
	Ordinary						Wood Light Frame					
	1-Hour (page 368)		Unprotected (page 368)		Mill (page 366)		1-Hour (page 368)		Unprotected (page 368)			IBC NOMENCLATURE
	Type III-A		Type III-B		Type IV-HT		Type V-A		Type V-B			
	Spr	Unspr	Spr	Unspr	Spr	Unspr	Spr	Unspr	Spr	Unspr		
	85'	65'	75'	55'	85'	65'	70'	50'	60'	40'		MAXIMUM HEIGHT IN FEET
UH												
12												
11												
10												
9												
8												HEIGHT IN STORIES
7												ABOVE GRADE AND
6												MAXIMUM AREA IN SQ FT ALL FLOORS
5												
4	126,000				135,000							
3	126,000	42,000[a]	85,500		135,000	45,000[a]	103,500					
2	84,000	28,000[a]	57,000	19,000[a]	90,000	30,000[a]	69,000	23,000[a]	36,000			
1	56,000	14,000	38,000	9,500	60,000	15,000	46,000	11,500	24,000	6,000		MAXIMUM AREA IN SQ FT FOR ANY SINGLE FLOOR OF A MULTISTORY BUILDING
	42,000	14,000	28,500	9,500	45,000	15,000	34,500	11,500	18,000			

This table was compiled from information contained in the International Building Code 2006. It does not represent an official interpretation by the organization that issues this code.

Key to Abbreviations

UA	Unlimited area	Spr	With approved sprinkler system
UH	Unlimited height	Unspr	Without approved sprinkler system
NP	Not permitted		

HEIGHT AND AREA TABLES

OCCUPANCY GROUP A-3: ASSEMBLY, MISCELLANEOUS

Sprinklers

In addition to the requirements indicated in the table on these two facing pages, a sprinkler system is required for Group A-3 Occupancy fire areas meeting any of the following conditions:

■ When located on a floor other than the level of exit discharge

■ With an area exceeding 12,000 sq ft (1115 m^2)

■ With an occupant load of 300 or more

For an explanation of fire areas, see page 358. A sprinkler system is also required for any stories or basements exceeding 1500 sq ft (139 m^2) in area without openings to the exterior, in underground portions of most buildings with occupancy more than 30 ft (9 m) below the lowest level of exit discharge, and throughout any building containing floors 55 ft (17 m) or more above grade with an occupant load of 30 or more.

Unlimited Area Buildings

Places of worship with auditoriums, community halls, dance halls, exhibition halls, gymnasiums, lecture halls, indoor swimming pools, indoor tennis courts, and similar facilities without stages or platforms, not more than one story in height, and of any Noncombustible Construction Type may be of unlimited area when all of the following conditions are met:

■ The building is fully sprinklered.

■ The assembly floor is within 21 in. (533 mm) of grade, and only ramps, but no stairs, connect exits to grade.

■ The building is surrounded on all sides by public ways or yards at least 60 ft (18.3 m) in width.

In some circumstances, reductions in the required width of open space around these building types are permitted; see the code for details.

Fire Walls

For multiplication of the allowable area by subdividing the building with fire walls, see page 358.

Basements

A single-story basement is not included in area calculations, provided that the basement area does

OCCUPANCY GROUP A-3: ASSEMBLY, MISCELLANEOUS

	Noncombustible							
CONSTRUCTION TYPE	**3-Hour** (page 364)		**2-Hour** (page 364)		**1-Hour** (page 365)		**Unprotected** (page 366)	
IBC NOMENCLATURE	Type I-A		Type I-B		Type II-A		Type II-B	
	Spr	Unspr	Spr	Unspr	Spr	Unspr	Spr	Unspr
MAXIMUM HEIGHT IN FEET	UH	75'	180'	75'	85'	65'	75'	55'
UH	UA	UA^a						
12			UA					
11				UA^a				
10								
9								
8								
7								
6								
5								
4					139,500			
3					139,500	46,500^a	85,500	
2					93,000	31,000^a	57,000	19,000^a
1					62,000	15,500	38,000	9,500
MAXIMUM AREA IN SQ FT FOR ANY SINGLE FLOOR OF A MULTISTORY BUILDING	UA	UA	UA	UA	49,500	15,500	28,500	9,500

HEIGHT IN STORIES ABOVE GRADE AND MAXIMUM AREA IN SQ FT ALL FLOORS

Each number in the table represents the maximum total area in square feet for all floors for a building of the indicated story height.

^{a}Unsprinklered areas are only permitted at grade level, normally limiting unsprinklered occupancies to only one or a few stories in height.

376

not exceed the area permitted for a one-story building.

Excess Frontage

If more than 25% of the building perimeter fronts on a street or open space at least 20 ft (6.1 m) wide that is accessible to firefighting vehicles, the tabulated area limitations below may be increased according to the adjacent table. For example, for a building with half of its perimeter accessible to fire-fighting equipment via a space not less than 24 ft (7.3 m) wide, the allowable area increase is:

0.80 increase x 25% excess frontage = 20% total area increase

Measurements

Height is measured from the average finished ground level adjoining the building to the average

Width of Frontage[a]	Percent Area Increase for Each 1% of Frontage[a] in Excess of 25%
20' (6.1 m)	0.67
22' (6.7 m)	0.73
24' (7.3 m)	0.80
26' (7.9 m)	0.87
28' (8.5 m)	0.93
30' (9.1 m) or wider	1.00

[a]Intermediate values may be interpolated.

level of the highest roof. Floor area is measured within exterior walls or exterior walls and fire walls, exclusive of vent shafts and court-yards.

Further Information

For information on Occupancy Group classifications, see page 7. For information on mixed-use buildings, see page 352. For information on which code to consult, see pages 7, 13.

Unit Conversions

1 ft = 304.8 mm, 1 sq ft = 0.0929 m²

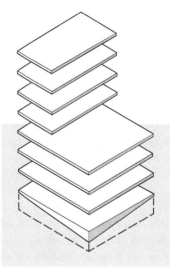

	Combustible										CONSTRUCTION TYPE
Ordinary						Wood Light Frame					
1-Hour (page 368)		Unprotected (page 368)		Mill (page 366)		1-Hour (page 368)		Unprotected (page 368)			IBC NOMENCLATURE
Type III-A		Type III-B		Type IV-HT		Type V-A		Type V-B			
Spr	Unspr	Spr	Unspr	Spr	Unspr	Spr	Unspr	Spr	Unspr		
85'	65'	75'	55'	85'	65'	70'	50'	60'	40'		MAXIMUM HEIGHT IN FEET

										UH	
										12	
										11	
										10	
										9	
										8	HEIGHT IN STORIES ABOVE GRADE AND MAXIMUM AREA IN SQ FT ALL FLOORS
										7	
										6	
										5	
126,000				135,000						4	
126,000	42,000[a]	85,500		135,000	45,000[a]	103,500				3	
84,000	28,000[a]	57,000	19,000[a]	90,000	30,000[a]	69,000	23,000[a]	36,000		2	
56,000	14,000	38,000	9,500	60,000	15,000	46,000	11,500	24,000	6,000	1	MAXIMUM AREA IN SQ FT FOR ANY SINGLE FLOOR OF A MULTISTORY BUILDING
42,000	14,000	28,500	9,500	45,000	16,000	34,500	11,500	18,000			

This table was compiled from information contained in the International Building Code 2006. It does not represent an official interpretation by the organization that issues this code.

Key to Abbreviations

UA	Unlimited area	Spr	With approved sprinkler system	NP	Not permitted
UH	Unlimited height	Unspr	Without approved sprinkler system		

HEIGHT AND AREA TABLES

OCCUPANCY GROUP A-4: ASSEMBLY, INDOOR ARENAS

Sprinklers

In addition to the requirements indicated in the table on these two facing pages, a sprinkler system is required for Group A-4 Occupancy fire areas meeting any of the following conditions:

- When located on a floor other than the level of exit discharge
- With an area exceeding 12,000 sq ft (1115 m^2)
- With an occupant load of 300 or more

For an explanation of fire areas, see page 358. A sprinkler system is not required for participant sports facilities when such facilities are located on the level of exit discharge, regardless of floor area and occupant load. A sprinkler system is required for any stories or basements exceeding 1500 sq ft (139 m^2) in area without openings to the exterior, in underground portions of most buildings with occupancy more than 30 ft (9 m) below the lowest level of exit discharge, and throughout any building containing floors 55 ft (17 m) or more above grade with an occupant load of 30 or more.

Unlimited Area Buildings

A one-story Occupancy A-4 building, fully sprinklered, and of any Construction Type other than Type V Wood Light Frame, may be of unlimited area, provided that it is surrounded on all sides by public ways or yards at least 60 ft (18.3 m) in width. A sprinkler system is not required for parts of such buildings used for participant sport activities, such as tennis, skating, swimming, and equestrian sports, provided that these areas' exits discharge directly to the exterior and the facility is equipped with a manual fire alarm system. In such buildings, Group A-1 and A-2 Occupancies are also permitted, so long as these occupancies are treated as mixed-use Separated Occupancies (see page 352), such areas each comply with their own code height and area limits, and all required exits from these areas discharge directly to the exterior. In some circumstances, reductions in the

OCCUPANCY GROUP A-4: ASSEMBLY, INDOOR ARENAS

		Noncombustible							
CONSTRUCTION TYPE		3-Hour (page 364)		2-Hour (page 364)		1-Hour (page 365)		Unprotected (page 366)	
IBC NOMENCLATURE		Type I-A		Type I-B		Type II-A		Type II-B	
		Spr	Unspr	Spr	Unspr	Spr	Unspr	Spr	Unspr
MAXIMUM HEIGHT IN FEET		UH	75'	180'	75'	85'	65'	75'	55'
HEIGHT IN STORIES ABOVE GRADE AND MAXIMUM AREA IN SQ FT ALL FLOORS	UH	UA	UA[a]						
	12			UA					
	11				UA[a]				
	10								
	9								
	8								
	7								
	6								
	5								
	4					139,500			
	3					139,500	46,500[a]	85,500	
	2					93,000	31,000[a]	57,000	19,000[a]
	1					62,000	15,500	38,000	9,500
MAXIMUM AREA IN SQ FT FOR ANY SINGLE FLOOR OF A MULTISTORY BUILDING		UA	UA	UA	UA	45,500	15,500	28,500	9,500

Each number in the table represents the maximum total area in square feet for all floors for a building of the indicated story height.

[a]Unsprinklered areas are only permitted at grade level, normally limiting unsprinklered occupancies to only one or a few stories in height.

required width of open space around these building types are permitted; see the code for details.

Fire Walls

For multiplication of the allowable area by subdividing the building with fire walls, see page 358.

Basements

Basements are not included in area calculations, provided that their area does not exceed the area permitted for a one-story building.

Excess Frontage

If more than 25% of the building perimeter fronts on a street or open space at least 20 ft (6.1 m) wide that is accessible to firefighting vehicles, the tabulated area limitations below may be increased according to the adjacent table. For example, for a building with half of its perimeter accessible to firefighting equipment via a space not less than 24 ft (7.3 m) wide, the allowable area increase is:

$$0.80 \text{ increase} \times 25\% \text{ excess frontage} = 20\% \text{ total area increase}$$

Further Information

For information on Occupancy Group classifications, see page 7. For information on mixed-use buildings, see page 352. For information on which code to consult, see pages 7, 13.

Unit Conversions

1 ft = 304.8 mm, 1 sq ft = 0.0929 m².

Width of Frontage[a]	Percent Area Increase for Each 1% of Frontage[a] in Excess of 25%
20' (6.1 m)	0.67
22' (6.7 m)	0.73
24' (7.3 m)	0.80
26' (7.9 m)	0.87
28' (8.5 m)	0.93
30' (9.1 m) or wider	1.00

[a]Intermediate values may be interpolated.

Combustible											
Ordinary				Mill		Wood Light Frame					
1-Hour (page 368)		Unprotected (page 368)		Mill (page 366)		1-Hour (page 368)		Unprotected (page 368)			
Type III-A		Type III-B		Type IV-HT		Type V-A		Type V-B			CONSTRUCTION TYPE / IBC NOMENCLATURE
Spr	Unspr	Spr	Unspr	Spr	Unspr	Spr	Unspr	Spr	Unspr		
85'	65'	75'	55'	85'	65'	70'	50'	60'	40'		MAXIMUM HEIGHT IN FEET
										UH	
										12	
										11	
										10	
										9	
										8	HEIGHT IN STORIES ABOVE GRADE AND MAXIMUM AREA IN SQ FT ALL FLOORS
										7	
										6	
										5	
126,000				135,000						4	
126,000	42,000[a]	85,500		135,000	45,000[a]	103,500				3	
84,000	28,000[a]	57,000	19,000[a]	90,000	30,000[a]	69,000	23,000[a]	36,000		2	
56,000	14,000	38,000	9,500	60,000	15,000	46,000	11,500	24,000	6,000	1	MAXIMUM AREA IN SQ FT FOR ANY SINGLE FLOOR OF A MULTISTORY BUILDING
42,000	14,000	28,500	9,500	45,000	15,000	34,500	11,500	18,000			

This table was compiled from information contained in the International Building Code 2006. It does not represent an official interpretation by the organization that issues this code.

Key to Abbreviations

UA	Unlimited area	Spr	With approved sprinkler system	NP	Not permitted
UH	Unlimited height	Unspr	Without approved sprinkler system		

HEIGHT AND AREA TABLES

OCCUPANCY GROUP A-5: ASSEMBLY, OUTDOOR ARENAS

Sprinklers

In Occupancy A-5 buildings, a sprinkler system is required for concession stands, retail areas, press boxes, and other such accessory facilities greater than 1000 sq ft (93 m²) in floor area. A sprinkler system is also required in stories or basements exceeding 1500 sq ft (139 m²) in area without openings to the exterior and underground portions of most buildings with occupancy more than 30 ft (9 m) below the lowest level of exit discharge.

Measurements

Height is measured from the average finished ground level adjoining the building to the average level of the highest roof. Floor area is measured within exterior walls or exterior walls and fire walls, exclusive of vent shafts and courtyards.

Further Information

For information on Occupancy Group classifications, see page 7. For information on mixed-used buildings, see page 352. For information on which code to consult, see pages 7, 13.

Unit Conversions

1 ft = 304.8 mm, 1 sq ft = 0.0929 m².

OCCUPANCY GROUP A-5: ASSEMBLY, OUTDOOR ARENAS

	Noncombustible							
CONSTRUCTION TYPE	**3-Hour** (page 364)		**2-Hour** (page 364)		**1-Hour** (page 365)		**Unprotected** (page 366)	
IBC NOMENCLATURE	Type I-A		Type I-B		Type II-A		Type II-B	
	Spr	Unspr	Spr	Unspr	Spr	Unspr	Spr	Unspr
MAXIMUM HEIGHT IN FEET	UH	UH	180'	160'	85'	65'	75'	55'
UH	UA	UA	UA	UA	UA	UA	UA	UA
12								
11								
10								
9								
HEIGHT IN STORIES ABOVE GRADE AND MAXIMUM AREA IN SQ FT ALL FLOORS 8								
7								
6								
5								
4								
3								
2								
MAXIMUM AREA IN SQ FT FOR ANY SINGLE FLOOR OF A MULTISTORY BUILDING 1	UA	UA	UA	UA	UA	UA	UA	UA

Each number in the table represents the maximum total area in square feet for all floors for a building of the indicated story height.

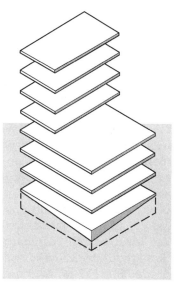

Combustible											
Ordinary				Mill (page 366)		Wood Light Frame					**CONSTRUCTION TYPE**
1-Hour (page 368)		Unprotected (page 368)				1-Hour (page 368)		Unprotected (page 368)			
Type III-A		Type III-B		Type IV-HT		Type V-A		Type V-B			**IBC NOMENCLATURE**
Spr	Unspr	Spr	Unspr	Spr	Unspr	Spr	Unspr	Spr	Unspr		
85'	65'	75'	55'	85'	65'	70'	50'	60'	40'		**MAXIMUM HEIGHT IN FEET**
UA	UA	UA	UA	UA	UA	UA	UA	UA	UA	UH	
										12	
										11	
										10	
										9	
										8	**HEIGHT IN STORIES**
										7	**ABOVE GRADE AND**
										6	**MAXIMUM AREA IN SQ FT ALL FLOORS**
										5	
										4	
										3	
										2	
										1	**MAXIMUM AREA**
UA	UA	UA	UA	UA	UA	UA	UA	UA	UA		**IN SQ FT FOR ANY SINGLE FLOOR OF A MULTISTORY BUILDING**

This table was compiled from information contained in the International Building Code 2006. It does not represent an official interpretation by the organization that issues this code.

Key to Abbreviations

UA	Unlimited area	Spr	With approved sprinkler system	NP	Not permitted
UH	Unlimited height	Unspr	Without approved sprinkler system		

HEIGHT AND AREA TABLES

381

INTERNATIONAL BUILDING CODE

OCCUPANCY GROUP B: BUSINESS

Sprinklers

In addition to the requirements indicated in the table on these two facing pages, a sprinkler system is required for any stories or basements exceeding 1500 sq ft (139 m²) in area without openings to the exterior, in underground portions of most buildings with occupancy more than 30 ft (9 m) below the lowest level of exit discharge, and throughout any building containing floors 55 ft (17 m) or more above grade with an occupant load of 30 or more.

Unlimited Area Buildings

One- and two-story Occupancy B buildings, fully sprinklered, may be of unlimited area when surrounded on all sides by public ways or yards not less than 60 ft (18 m) in width. In such one-story buildings, Group A-1 and A-2 occupancies are permitted, so long as these occupancies are treated as mixed-use Separated Occupancies, such areas each comply with their own code height and area limits, and all required exits from these areas discharge directly to the exterior. In some circumstances, reductions in the required width of open space around these building types are permitted; see the code for details.

Fire Walls

For multiplication of the allowable area by subdividing the building with fire walls, see page 358.

Basements

Basements are not included in area calculations provided their area does not exceed the area permitted for a one-story building.

Excess Frontage

If more than 25% of the building perimeter fronts on a street or open space at least 20 ft (6.1 m) wide that is accessible to firefighting vehi-

OCCUPANCY GROUP B: BUSINESS

CONSTRUCTION TYPE	Noncombustible							
	3-Hour (page 364)		2-Hour (page 364)		1-Hour (page 365)		Unprotected (page 366)	
IBC NOMENCLATURE	Type I-A		Type I-B		Type II-A		Type II-B	
	Spr	Unspr	Spr	Unspr	Spr	Unspr	Spr	Unspr
MAXIMUM HEIGHT IN FEET	UH	75'	180'	75'	85'	65'	75'	55'
UH	UA	UA						
12			UA					
11				UA				
10								
9								
8								
7								
6					337,500			
5					337,500	112,500	207,000	
4					337,500	112,500	207,000	69,000
3					337,500	112,500	207,000	69,000
2					225,000	75,000	138,000	46,000
1					150,000	37,500	92,000	23,000
UA	UA	UA	UA	UA	112,500	37,500	69,000	23,000

HEIGHT IN STORIES ABOVE GRADE AND MAXIMUM AREA IN SQ FT ALL FLOORS

382 MAXIMUM AREA IN SQ FT FOR ANY SINGLE FLOOR OF A MULTISTORY BUILDING

Each number in the table represents the maximum total area in square feet for all floors for a building of the indicated story height.

cles, the tabulated area limitations below may be increased according to the adjacent table. For example, for a building with half of its perimeter accessible to firefighting equipment via a space not less than 24 ft (7.3 m) wide, the allowable area increase is:

0.80 increase × 25% excess frontage = 20% total area increase

Measurements

Height is measured from the average finished ground level adjoining the building to the average level of the highest roof. Floor area is measured within exterior walls or exterior walls and fire walls, exclusive of vent shafts and courtyards.

Width of Frontage[a]	Percent Area Increase for Each 1% of Frontage[a] in Excess of 25%
20' (6.1 m)	0.67
22' (6.7 m)	0.73
24' (7.3 m)	0.80
26' (7.9 m)	0.87
28' (8.5 m)	0.93
30' (9.1 m) or wider	1.00

[a]Intermediate values may be interpolated.

Further Information

For information on Occupancy Group classifications, see page 7. For information on mixed-used buildings, see page 352. For information on which code to consult, see pages 7, 13.

Unit Conversions

1 ft = 304.8 mm, 1 sq ft = 0.0929 m^2.

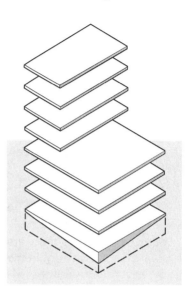

Combustible											
Ordinary				Mill (page 366)		Wood Light Frame					CONSTRUCTION TYPE
1-Hour (page 368)		Unprotected (page 368)				1-Hour (page 368)		Unprotected (page 368)			IBC NOMENCLATURE
Type III-A		Type III-B		Type IV-HT		Type V-A		Type V-B			
Spr	Unspr	Spr	Unspr	Spr	Unspr	Spr	Unspr	Spr	Unspr		MAXIMUM HEIGHT IN FEET
85'	65'	75'	55'	85'	65'	70'	50'	60'	40'		
										UH	
										12	
										11	
										10	
										9	
										8	HEIGHT IN STORIES ABOVE GRADE AND MAXIMUM AREA IN SQ FT ALL FLOORS
										7	
256,500				324,000						6	
256,500	85,500	171,000		324,000	108,000					5	
256,500	85,500	171,000	57,000	324,000	108,000	162,000				4	
256,500	85,500	171,000	57,000	324,000	108,000	162,000	54,000	81,000		3	
171,000	57,000	114,000	38,000	216,000	72,000	108,000	36,000	54,000	18,000	2	
114,000	28,500	76,000	19,000	144,000	36,000	72,000	18,000	36,000	9,000	1	MAXIMUM AREA IN SQ FT FOR ANY SINGLE FLOOR OF A MULTISTORY BUILDING
85,500	28,500	57,000	19,000	108,000	36,000	54,000	18,000	27,000	9,000		

HEIGHT AND AREA TABLES

This table was compiled from information contained in the International Building Code 2006. It does not represent an official interpretation by the organization that issues this code.

Key to Abbreviations

UA	Unlimited area	Spr	With approved sprinkler system	NP	Not permitted
UH	Unlimited height	Unspr	Without approved sprinkler system		

OCCUPANCY GROUP E: EDUCATIONAL

Sprinklers

In addition to the requirements indicated in the table on these two facing pages, a sprinkler system is required for Group E Occupancies meeting either of the following conditions:

■ Throughout fire areas exceeding 20,000 sq ft (1858 m2) in area

■ Throughout all portions of a building below the level of exit discharge

For an explanation of fire areas, see page 358. These requirements do not apply to buildings where every classroom throughout the building has at least one exit door opening directly to the exterior. A sprinkler system is also required for any stories or basements exceeding 1500 sq ft (139 m^2) in area without openings to the exterior, in underground portions of most buildings with occupancy more than 30 ft (9 m) below the lowest level of exit discharge, and throughout any building containing floors 55 ft (17 m) or more above grade with an occupant load of 30 or more.

Unlimited Area Buildings

A one-story Occupancy E building, fully sprinklered, of Noncombustible construction, 1-Hour Ordinary Construction, or Mill Construction may be of unlimited area, provided that the building is surrounded on all sides by public ways or yards at least 60 ft (18.3 m) in width, and each classroom in the building has two means of egress, at least one of which opens directly to the outside.

Fire Walls

For multiplication of the allowable area by subdividing the building with fire walls, see page 358.

Basements

Basements are not included in area calculations, provided that their area does not exceed the area permitted for a one-story building.

Excess Frontage

If more than 25% of the building perimeter fronts on a street or open space at least 20 ft (6.1 m) wide that

OCCUPANCY GROUP E: EDUCATIONAL

		Noncombustible						
CONSTRUCTION TYPE		3-Hour (page 364)		2-Hour (page 364)		1-Hour (page 365)		Unprotected (page 366)	
IBC NOMENCLATURE		Type I-A		Type I-B		Type II-A		Type II-B	
		Spr	Unspr	Spr	Unspr	Spr	Unspr	Spr	Unspr
MAXIMUM HEIGHT IN FEET		UH	75'	180'	75'	85'	65'	75'	55'
HEIGHT IN STORIES ABOVE GRADE AND MAXIMUM AREA IN SQ FT ALL FLOORS	UH	UA	UA						
	12								
	11								
	10								
	9								
	8								
	7								
	6			UA					
	5				UA				
	4					238,500			
	3					238,500	79,500	130,500	
	2					159,000	53,000	87,000	29,000
	1					106,000	26,500	58,000	14,500
MAXIMUM AREA IN SQ FT FOR ANY SINGLE FLOOR OF A MULTISTORY BUILDING		UA	UA	UA	UA	79,500	26,500	43,500	14,500

Each number in the table represents the maximum total area in square feet for all floors for a building of the indicated story height.

Key to Abbreviations

UA	Unlimited area	Spr	With approved sprinkler system	NP	Not permitted
UH	Unlimited height	Unspr	Without approved sprinkler system		

is accessible to firefighting vehicles, the tabulated area limitations below may be increased according to the adjacent table. For example, for a building with half of its perimeter accessible to firefighting equipment via a space not less than 24 ft (7.3 m) wide, the allowable area increase is:

0.80 increase × 25% excess frontage = 20% total area increase

Measurements

Height is measured from the average finished ground level adjoining the building to the average level of the highest roof. Floor area is measured within exterior walls or exterior walls and fire walls, exclusive of vent shafts and courtyards.

Width of Frontage[a]	Percent Area Increase for Each 1% of Frontage[a] in Excess of 25%
20' (6.1 m)	0.67
22' (6.7 m)	0.73
24' (7.3 m)	0.80
26' (7.9 m)	0.87
28' (8.5 m)	0.93
30' (9.1 m) or wider	1.00

[a]Intermediate values may be interpolated.

Further Information

For information on Occupancy Group classifications, see page 7. For information on mixed-use buildings, see page 352. For information on which code to consult, see pages 7, 13.

Unit Conversions

1 ft = 304.8 mm, 1 sq ft = 0.0929 m².

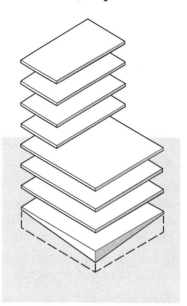

Combustible									
Ordinary				**Mill** (page 366)		**Wood Light Frame**			
1-Hour (page 368)		**Unprotected** (page 368)				**1-Hour** (page 368)		**Unprotected** (page 368)	
Type III-A		**Type III-B**		**Type IV-HT**		**Type V-A**		**Type V-B**	
Spr	Unspr	Spr	Unspr	Spr	Unspr	Spr	Unspr	Spr	Unspr
85'	65'	75'	55'	85'	65'	70'	50'	60'	40'
211,500				229,500					
211,500	70,500	130,500		229,500	76,500				
141,000	47,000	87,000	29,000	153,000	51,000	111,000		57,000	
94,000	23,500	58,000	14,500	102,000	25,500	74,000	18,500	38,000	9,500
70,500	23,500	43,500	14,500	76,500	25,500	55,500		28,500	

Right-side legend:
- CONSTRUCTION TYPE
- IBC NOMENCLATURE
- MAXIMUM HEIGHT IN FEET
- UH, 12, 11, 10, 9, 8, 7, 6, 5, 4, 3, 2, 1 — HEIGHT IN STORIES ABOVE GRADE AND MAXIMUM AREA IN SQ FT ALL FLOORS
- MAXIMUM AREA IN SQ FT FOR ANY SINGLE FLOOR OF A MULTISTORY BUILDING

HEIGHT AND AREA TABLES

385

This table was compiled from information contained in the International Building Code 2006. It does not represent an official interpretation by the organization that issues this code.

OCCUPANCY GROUP F-1: FACTORY, MODERATE HAZARD

Sprinklers

In addition to the requirements indicated in the table on these two facing pages, a sprinkler system is required throughout buildings containing, in whole or in part, a Group F-1 Occupancy meeting any of the following conditions:

■ Any single F-1 fire area exceeds 12,000 sq ft (1115 m²) or the area of all F-1 fire areas combined exceeds 24,000 sq ft (2230 m²)

■ An F-1 fire area is located more than three stories above grade

A sprinkler system is required throughout F-1 Occupancy fire areas (but not necessarily through-out the building) which include sanding or other woodworking operations that generate or utilize finely divided combustible materials and exceed 2500 sq ft (232 m²) in area. For an explanation of fire areas, see page 358. A sprinkler system is also required for any stories or basements exceeding 1500 sq ft (139 m²) in area without openings to the exterior, in underground portions of most buildings with occupancy more than 30 ft (9 m) below the lowest level of exit discharge, and throughout any building containing floors 55 ft (17 m) or more above grade with an occupant load of 30 or more.

Unlimited Height and Area Buildings

A one- or two-story Occupancy F-1 building, fully sprinklered, may be of unlimited area provided that it is surrounded on all sides by public ways or yards at least 60 ft (18.3 m) in width. In such one-story buildings, Group A-1 and A-2 Occupancies are permitted, so long as these occupancies are treated as mixed-use Separated Occupancies, such areas each comply with their own code height and area limits, and all required exits from these areas discharge directly to the exterior. Some Group H-2, H-3, and H-4 Occupancies may also be permitted. In some circumstances, reductions in the required width of open space around the building are permitted. See the code for details.

Industrial facilities that require large areas or unusual heights to accommodate special processes or equipment, such as rolling mills, foundries, fabrication shops, and power generation facilities, may

OCCUPANCY GROUP F-1: FACTORY, MODERATE HAZARD

	Noncombustible							
CONSTRUCTION TYPE	**3-Hour** (page 364)		**2-Hour** (page 364)		**1-Hour** (page 365)		**Unprotected** (page 366)	
IBC NOMENCLATURE	**Type I-A**		**Type I-B**		**Type II-A**		**Type II-B**	
	Spr	Unspr	Spr	Unspr	Spr	Unspr	Spr	Unspr
MAXIMUM HEIGHT IN FEET	UH	75'	180'	75'	85'	65'	75'	55'
UH	UA							
12			UA					
11								
10								
9								
8								
7								
6								
5					229,500			
4					229,500			
3		24,000		24,000	229,500	24,000	139,500	
2		24,000		24,000	153,000	24,000	93,000	24,000
1		24,000		24,000	102,000	24,000	62,000	15,500
MAXIMUM AREA IN SQ FT FOR ANY SINGLE FLOOR OF A MULTISTORY BUILDING	UA	24,000	UA	24,000	76,500	24,000	46,500	15,500

CONSTRUCTION TYPE, **IBC NOMENCLATURE**, **MAXIMUM HEIGHT IN FEET**, **HEIGHT IN STORIES ABOVE GRADE AND MAXIMUM AREA IN SQ FT ALL FLOORS**

Each number in the table represents the maximum total area in square feet for all floors for a building of the indicated story height.

Key to Abbreviations

UA	Unlimited area	Spr	With approved sprinkler system	NP	Not permitted	
UH	Unlimited height	Unspr	Without approved sprinkler system			

also be exempt from the code's usual height and area limits.

Fire Walls

For multiplication of the allowable area by subdividing the building with fire walls, see page 358.

Basements

Basements are not included in area calculations, provided that their area does not exceed the area permitted for a one-story building.

Excess Frontage

If more than 25% of the building perimeter fronts on a street or open space at least 20 ft (6.1 m) wide that is accessible to firefighting vehicles, the tabulated area limitations below may be increased according to the following table. For example, for a building with half of its perimeter accessible to firefighting equipment via a space not less than 24 ft (7.3 m) wide, the allowable area increase is:

0.80 increase × 25% excess frontage = 20% total area increase

Width of Frontage[a]	Percent Area Increase for Each 1% of Frontage[a] in Excess of 25%
20' (6.1 m)	0.67
22' (6.7 m)	0.73
24' (7.3 m)	0.80
26' (7.9 m)	0.87
28' (8.5 m)	0.93
30' (9.1 m) or wider	1.00

[a]Intermediate values may be interpolated.

Measurements

Height is measured from the average finished ground level adjoining the building to the average level of the highest roof. Floor area is measured within exterior walls or exterior walls and fire walls, exclusive of vent shafts and courtyards.

Further Information

For information on Occupancy Group classifications, see page 7. For information on mixed-used buildings, see page 352. For information on which code to consult, see pages 7, 13.

Unit Conversions

1 ft = 304.8 mm, 1 sq ft = 0.0929 m².

	Combustible											
	Ordinary						Wood Light Frame					
	1-Hour (page 368)		Unprotected (page 368)		Mill (page 366)		1-Hour (page 368)		Unprotected (page 368)			CONSTRUCTION TYPE
	Type III-A		Type III-B		Type IV-HT		Type V-A		Type V-B			IBC NOMENCLATURE
	Spr	Unspr	Spr	Unspr	Spr	Unspr	Spr	Unspr	Spr	Unspr		
	85'	65'	75'	55'	85'	65'	70'	50'	60'	40'		MAXIMUM HEIGHT IN FEET
UH												
12												
11												
10												
9												
8												HEIGHT IN STORIES ABOVE GRADE AND MAXIMUM AREA IN SQ FT ALL FLOORS
7												
6												
5					301,500							
4	171,000				301,500							
3	171,000	24,000	108,000		301,500	24,000	126,000					
2	114,000	24,000	72,000	24,000	201,000	24,000	84,000	24,000	51,000			
1	76,000	19,000	48,000	12,000	134,000	24,000	56,000	14,000	34,000	8,500		
	57,000	19,000	36,000	12,000	100,500	24,000	42,000	14,000	25,500			MAXIMUM AREA IN SQ FT FOR ANY SINGLE FLOOR OF A MULTISTORY BUILDING

HEIGHT AND AREA TABLES

387

This table was compiled from information contained in the International Building Code 2006. It does not represent an official interpretation by the organization that issues this code.

OCCUPANCY GROUP F-2: FACTORY, LOW HAZARD

Sprinklers

In addition to the requirements indicated in the table on these two facing pages, a sprinkler system is required for any stories or basements exceeding 1500 sq ft (139 m^2) in area without openings to the exterior, in underground portions of most buildings with occupancy more than 30 ft (9 m) below the lowest level of exit discharge, and throughout any building containing floors 55 ft (17 m) or more above grade with an occupant load of 30 or more.

Unlimited Height and Area Buildings

An Occupancy F-2 building, one story tall, with or without sprinklers, or two stories tall and fully sprinklered, may be of unlimited area provided that it is surrounded on all sides by public ways or yards at least 60 ft (18.3 m) in width. In such one-story buildings, sprinklered Group A-1 and A-2 Occupancies are permitted, so long as these occupancies are treated as mixed-use Separated Occupancies, such areas each comply with their own code height and area limits, and all required exits from these areas discharge directly to the exterior. Some Group H-2, H-3, and H-4 Occupancies may also be permitted. In some circum-stances, reductions in the required width of open space around the building may be permitted. See the code for details.

Certain types of nonpublic unlimited area rack storage facilities, of Noncombustible Construction, may be of unlimited height. Industrial facilities that require large areas or unusual heights to accommodate special processes or equipment, such as rolling mills, foundries, fabrication shops, and power generation facilities, also may be exempt from the code's usual height and area limits.

Fire Walls

For multiplication of the allowable area by subdividing the building with fire walls, see page 358.

OCCUPANCY GROUP F-2: FACTORY, LOW-HAZARD

	Noncombustible							
CONSTRUCTION TYPE	**3-Hour (page 364)**		**2-Hour (page 364)**		**1-Hour (page 365)**		**Unprotected (page 366)**	
IBC NOMENCLATURE	**Type I-A**		**Type I-B**		**Type II-A**		**Type II-B**	
	Spr	Unspr	Spr	Unspr	Spr	Unspr	Spr	Unspr
MAXIMUM HEIGHT IN FEET	UH	75'	180'	75'	85'	65'	75'	55'
UH	UA	UA						
12			UA					
11				UA				
10								
9								
8								
7								
6					337,500			
5					337,500	112,500		
4					337,500	112,500	207,000	
3					337,500	112,500	207,000	69,000
2					225,000	75,000	138,000	46,000
1					150,000	37,500	92,000	23,000
MAXIMUM AREA IN SQ FT FOR ANY SINGLE FLOOR OF A MULTISTORY BUILDING	UA	UA	UA	UA	112,500	37,500	69,000	23,000

HEIGHT IN STORIES ABOVE GRADE AND MAXIMUM AREA IN SQ FT ALL FLOORS

Each number in the table represents the maximum total area in square feet for all floors for a building of the indicated story height.

Key to Abbreviations

UA	Unlimited area	Spr	With approved sprinkler system	NP	Not permitted
UH	Unlimited height	Unspr	Without approved sprinkler system		

INTERNATIONAL BUILDING CODE

Basements

Basements are not included in area calculations, provided that their area does not exceed the area permitted for a one-story building.

Excess Frontage

If more than 25% of the building perimeter fronts on a street or open space at least 20 ft (6.1 m) wide that is accessible to firefighting vehicles, the tabulated area limitations below may be increased according to the following table. For example, for a building with half of its perimeter accessible to firefighting equipment via a space not less than 24 ft (7.3 m) wide, the allowable area increase is:

0.80 increase × 25% excess frontage = 20% total area increase

Width of Frontage[a]	Percent Area Increase for Each 1% of Frontage[a] in Excess of 25%
20' (6.1 m)	0.67
22' (6.7 m)	0.73
24' (7.3 m)	0.80
26' (7.9 m)	0.87
28' (8.5 m)	0.93
30' (9.1 m) or wider	1.00

[a]Intermediate values may be interpolated.

Measurements

Height is measured from the average finished ground level adjoining the building to the average level of the highest roof. Floor area is measured within exterior walls or exterior walls and fire walls, exclusive of vent shafts and courtyards.

Further Information

For information on Occupancy Group classifications, see page 7. For information on mixed-used buildings, see page 352. For information on which code to consult, see pages 7, 13.

Unit Conversions

1 ft = 304.8 mm, 1 sq ft = 0.0929 m².

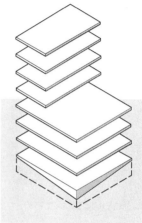

	Combustible										
	Ordinary						Wood Light Frame				
	1-Hour (page 368)		Unprotected (page 368)		Mill (page 366)		1-Hour (page 368)		Unprotected (page 368)		
	Type III-A		Type III-B		Type IV-HT		Type V-A		Type V-B			CONSTRUCTION TYPE
	Spr	Unspr	Spr	Unspr	Spr	Unspr	Spr	Unspr	Spr	Unspr		IBC NOMENCLATURE
	85'	65'	75'	55'	85'	65'	70'	50'	60'	40'		MAXIMUM HEIGHT IN FEET

Type III-A Spr	Type III-A Unspr	Type III-B Spr	Type III-B Unspr	Type IV-HT Spr	Type IV-HT Unspr	Type V-A Spr	Type V-A Unspr	Type V-B Spr	Type V-B Unspr	Story
										UH
										12
										11
										10
										9
										8
										7
				454,500						6
256,500				454,500	151,500					5
256,500	85,500	162,000		454,500	151,500	189,000				4
256,500	85,500	162,000	54,000	454,500	151,500	189,000	63,000	117,000		3
171,000	57,000	108,000	36,000	303,000	101,000	126,000	42,000	78,000	26,000	2
114,000	28,500	72,000	18,000	202,000	50,500	84,000	21,000	52,000	13,000	1
86,500	28,500	54,000	18,000	151,500	50,500	63,000	21,000	39,000	13,000	

HEIGHT IN STORIES ABOVE GRADE AND MAXIMUM AREA IN SQ FT ALL FLOORS

MAXIMUM AREA IN SQ FT FOR ANY SINGLE FLOOR OF A MULTISTORY BUILDING

HEIGHT AND AREA TABLES

389

This table was compiled from information contained in the International Building Code 2006. It does not represent an official interpretation by the organization that issues this code.

OCCUPANCY GROUP H-1: HIGH-HAZARD, DETONATION HAZARD

Special Requirements

All Group H-1 Occupancy buildings must be used solely for the H-1 use, must be sprinklered, may not exceed one story in height, may not include basements, crawlspaces, or other underfloor areas, and must be set back at least 75 ft (23 m) from adjacent lots. See the code for additional requirements.

Excess Frontage

If more than 25% of the building perimeter fronts on a street or open space at least 20 ft (6.1 m) wide that is accessible to firefighting vehicles, the tabulated area limitations below may be increased according to the following table. For example, for a building with half of its perimeter accessible to firefighting equipment via a space not less than 24 ft (7.3 m) wide, the allowable area increase is:

0.80 increase × 25% excess
frontage = 20 total area increase

Width of Frontage[a]	Percent Area Increase for Each 1% of Frontage[a] in Excess of 25%
20' (6.1 m)	0.67
22' (6.7 m)	0.73
24' (7.3 m)	0.80
26' (7.9 m)	0.87
28' (8.5 m)	0.93
30' (9.1 m) or wider	1.00

[a]Intermediate values may be interpolated.

OCCUPANCY GROUP H-1: HIGH-HAZARD, DETONATION HAZARD

	Noncombustible							
CONSTRUCTION TYPE	3-Hour (page 364)		2-Hour (page 364)		1-Hour (page 365)		Unprotected (page 366)	
IBC NOMENCLATURE	Type I-A		Type I-B		Type II-A		Type II-B	
	Spr	Unspr	Spr	Unspr	Spr	Unspr	Spr	Unspr
MAXIMUM HEIGHT IN FEET	UH		160'		65'		55'	

HEIGHT IN STORIES ABOVE GRADE AND MAXIMUM AREA IN SQ FT ALL FLOORS: UH, 12, 11, 10, 9, 8, 7, 6, 5, 4, 3, 2

MAXIMUM AREA IN SQ FT FOR ANY SINGLE FLOOR OF A MULTISTORY BUILDING	Spr	Unspr	Spr	Unspr	Spr	Unspr	Spr	Unspr
1	21,000	NP	16,500	NP	11,000	NP	7,000	NP

Each number in the table represents the maximum total area in square feet for all floors for a building of the indicated story height.

Key to Abbreviations

UA	Unlimited area	Spr	With approved sprinkler system	NP	Not permitted
UH	Unlimited height	Unspr	Without approved sprinkler system		

INTERNATIONAL BUILDING CODE

Measurements

Height is measured from the average finished ground level adjoining the building to the average level of the highest roof. Floor area is measured within exterior walls or exterior walls and fire walls, exclusive of vent shafts and courtyards.

Further Information

For information on Occupancy Group classifications, see page 7. For information on mixed-used buildings, see page 352. For information on which code to consult, see pages 7, 13.

Unit Conversions

1 ft = 304.8 mm, 1 sq ft = 0.0929 m².

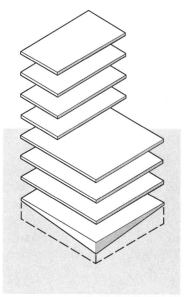

Combustible										
Ordinary				Mill (page 366)		Wood Light Frame				
1-Hour (page 368)		Unprotected (page 368)				1-Hour (page 368)		Unprotected (page 368)		CONSTRUCTION TYPE
Type III-A		Type III-B		Type IV-HT		Type V-A		Type V-B		IBC NOMENCLATURE
Spr	Unspr	Spr	Unspr	Spr	Unspr	Spr	Unspr	Spr	Unspr	
65'		55'		65'		50'				MAXIMUM HEIGHT IN FEET
										UH
										12
										11
										10
										9
										8 — HEIGHT IN STORIES
										7 — ABOVE GRADE AND
										6 — MAXIMUM AREA IN SQ FT ALL FLOORS
										5
										4
										3
										2
9,500	NP	7,000	NP	10,500	NP	7,500	NP	NP	NP	1 — MAXIMUM AREA IN SQ FT FOR ANY SINGLE FLOOR OF A MULTISTORY BUILDING

This table was compiled from information contained in the International Building Code 2006. It does not represent an official interpretation by the organization that issues this code.

HEIGHT AND AREA TABLES

OCCUPANCY GROUP H-2: HIGH-HAZARD, ACCELERATED BURNING HAZARD

Special Requirements

A sprinkler system is required for all Group H-2 Occupancy areas. When part of a mixed-use building, at least 25% of the perimeter of the H-2 Occupancy area must be along an exterior wall to facilitate firefighter access. Other restrictions vary with the quantities and types of hazardous materials stored. For example:

- H-2 Occupancies greater than 1000 sq ft (93 m²) in area must be

set back at least 30 ft (7 m) from adjacent properties.

- Some H-2 Occupancies must be detached from other uses and housed in structures set back at least 50 ft (15 m) from adjacent properties.

- Some H-2 Occupancy buildings may be restricted solely to H-2 use, may not exceed one story in height, and may not include basements, crawlspaces, or other underfloor areas.

- In some cases, H-2 Occupancies of limited area may be permitted within an unlimited area building of F or S Occupancy.

See the code for additional requirements.

Fire Walls

For multiplication of the allowable area by subdividing the building with fire walls, see page 358.

Basements

Basements are not included in area calculations, provided that their area does not exceed the area permitted for a one-story building.

Excess Frontage

If more than 25% of the building perimeter fronts on a street or open space at least 20 ft (6.1 m) wide that is accessible to firefighting vehicles, the tabulated area limitations below may be increased according to the following table. For example, for a

OCCUPANCY GROUP H-2: HIGH-HAZARD, ACCELERATED BURNING HAZARD

	Noncombustible							
CONSTRUCTION TYPE	3-Hour (page 364)		2-Hour (page 364)		1-Hour (page 365)		Unprotected (page 366)	
IBC NOMENCLATURE	Type I-A		Type I-B		Type II-A		Type II-B	
	Spr	Unspr	Spr	Unspr	Spr	Unspr	Spr	Unspr
MAXIMUM HEIGHT IN FEET	UH		160'		65'		55'	
UH	63,000							
12	63,000							
11	63,000							
10	63,000							
9	63,000							
8	63,000							
7	63,000							
6	63,000							
5	63,000							
4	63,000							
3	63,000		49,500					
2	42,000		33,000		22,000			
1	21,000	NP	16,500	NP	11,000	NP	7,000	NP
MAXIMUM AREA IN SQ FT FOR ANY SINGLE FLOOR OF A MULTISTORY BUILDING	21,000		16,500		11,000			

HEIGHT IN STORIES ABOVE GRADE AND MAXIMUM AREA IN SQ FT ALL FLOORS

392

Each number in the table represents the maximum total area in square feet for all floors for a building of the indicated story height.

Key to Abbreviations

UA	Unlimited area	Spr	With approved sprinkler system	NP	Not permitted
UH	Unlimited height	Unspr	Without approved sprinkler system		

building with half of its perimeter accessible to firefighting equipment via a space not less than 24 ft (7.3 m) wide, the allowable area increase is:

0.80 increase × 25% excess frontage = 20% total area increase

Width of Frontage[a]	Percent Area Increase for Each 1% of Frontage[a] in Excess of 25%
20' (6.1 m)	0.67%
22' (6.7 m)	0.73%
24' (7.3 m)	0.80%
26' (7.9 m)	0.87%
28' (8.5 m)	0.93%
30' (9.1 m) or wider	1.00%

[a]Intermediate values may be interpolated.

Measurements

Height is measured from the average finished ground level adjoining the building to the average level of the highest roof. Floor area is measured within exterior walls or exterior walls and fire walls, exclusive of vent shafts and courtyards.

Further Information

For information on Occupancy Group classifications, see page 7. For information on mixed-used buildings, see page 352. For information on which code to consult, see pages 7, 13.

Unit Conversions

1 ft = 304.8 mm, 1 sq ft = 0.0929 m².

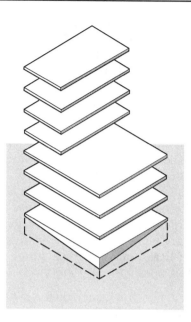

Combustible										
Ordinary						Wood Light Frame				
1-Hour (page 368)		Unprotected (page 368)		Mill (page 366)		1-Hour (page 368)		Unprotected (page 368)		CONSTRUCTION TYPE
Type III-A		Type III-B		Type IV-HT		Type V-A		Type V-B		IBC NOMENCLATURE
Spr	Unspr	Spr	Unspr	Spr	Unspr	Spr	Unspr	Spr	Unspr	
65'		55'		65'		50'		40'		MAXIMUM HEIGHT IN FEET

										Stories
										UH
										12
										11
										10
										9
										8
										7
										6
										5
										4
										3
19,000				21,000						2
9,500	NP	7,000	NP	10,500	NP	7,500	NP	3,000	NP	1
9,500				10,500						

HEIGHT IN STORIES ABOVE GRADE AND MAXIMUM AREA IN SQ FT ALL FLOORS

MAXIMUM AREA IN SQ FT FOR ANY SINGLE FLOOR OF A MULTISTORY BUILDING

This table was compiled from information contained in the International Building Code 2006. It does not represent an official interpretation by the organization that issues this code.

HEIGHT AND AREA TABLES

393

OCCUPANCY GROUP H-3: HIGH HAZARD, COMBUSTIBLES

Special Requirements

A sprinkler system is required for all Group H-3 Occupancy areas. When part of a mixed-use building, at least 25% of the perimeter of an H-3 occupancy area must be along an exterior wall to facilitate firefighter access. Other restrictions vary with the quantities and types of hazardous materials stored. For example:

■ Some H-3 Occupancies must be detached from other uses and housed in structures set back at least 50 ft (15 m) from adjacent properties.

■ Some H-3 Occupancy buildings may be restricted solely to the H-3 use, may not exceed one story in height, and may not include basements, crawlspaces, or other underfloor areas.

■ In some cases, an H-3 Occupancy of limited area may be permitted within an unlimited area building of F or S Occupancy.

See the code for additional details.

Fire Walls

For multiplication of the allowable area by subdividing the building with fire walls, see page 358.

Basements

Basements are not included in area calculations, provided that their area does not exceed the area permitted for a one-story building.

Excess Frontage

If more than 25% of the building perimeter fronts on a street or open space at least 20 ft (6.1 m) wide that is accessible to firefighting vehicles, the tabulated area limitations below may be increased according to the following table. For example, for a building with half of its perimeter accessible to firefighting equipment via a space not less than 24 ft (7.3 m) wide, the allowable area increase is:

OCCUPANCY GROUP H-3: HIGH-HAZARD, COMBUSTIBLES

CONSTRUCTION TYPE	Noncombustible							
	3-Hour (page 364)		2-Hour (page 364)		1-Hour (page 365)		Unprotected (page 366)	
IBC NOMENCLATURE	Type I-A		Type I-B		Type II-A		Type II-B	
	Spr	Unspr	Spr	Unspr	Spr	Unspr	Spr	Unspr
MAXIMUM HEIGHT IN FEET	UH		160'		65'		55'	
UH	UA							
12								
11								
10								
9								
8 HEIGHT IN STORIES ABOVE GRADE AND MAXIMUM AREA IN SQ FT ALL FLOORS								
7								
6			180,000					
5			180,000					
4			180,000		79,500			
3			180,000		79,500			
2			120,000		53,000		28,000	
1		NP	60,000	NP	26,500	NP	14,000	NP
MAXIMUM AREA IN SQ FT FOR ANY SINGLE FLOOR OF A MULTISTORY BUILDING	UA		60,000		26,500		14,000	

Each number in the table represents the maximum total area in square feet for all floors for a building of the indicated story height.

Key to Abbreviations

UA	Unlimited area	Spr	With approved sprinkler system	NP	Not permitted
UH	Unlimited height	Unspr	Without approved sprinkler system		

INTERNATIONAL BUILDING CODE

0.80 increase × 25% excess frontage = 20% total area increase

Width of Frontage[a]	Area Increase for Each 1% of Frontage[a] in Excess of 25
20' (6.1 m)	0.67
22' (6.7 m)	0.73
24' (7.3 m)	0.80
26' (7.9 m)	0.87
28' (8.5 m)	0.93
30' (9.1 m) or wider	1.00

[a]Intermediate values may be interpolated.

Measurements

Height is measured from the average finished ground level adjoining the building to the average level of the highest roof. Floor area is measured within exterior walls or exterior walls and fire walls, exclusive of vent shafts and courtyards.

Further Information

For information on Occupancy Group classifications, see page 7. For information on mixed-use buildings, see page 352. For information on which code to consult, see pages 7, 13.

Unit Conversions

1 ft = 304.8 mm, 1 sq ft = 0.0929 m^2.

	Combustible										CONSTRUCTION TYPE
	Ordinary					Wood Light Frame					
	1-Hour (page 368)		Unprotected (page 368)		Mill (page 366)		1-Hour (page 368)		Unprotected (page 368)		
	Type III-A		Type III-B		Type IV-HT		Type V-A		Type V-B		IBC NOMENCLATURE
	Spr	Unspr	Spr	Unspr	Spr	Unspr	Spr	Unspr	Spr	Unspr	
	65'		55'		65'		50'		40'		MAXIMUM HEIGHT IN FEET
UH											
12											
11											
10											
9											
8											HEIGHT IN STORIES ABOVE GRADE AND MAXIMUM AREA IN SQ FT ALL FLOORS
7											
6											
5											
4	52,500				76,500						
3	52,500				76,500						
2	35,000		26,000		51,000		20,000				
1	17,500	NP	13,000	NP	25,500	NP	10,000	NP	5,000	NP	MAXIMUM AREA IN SQ FT FOR ANY SINGLE FLOOR OF A MULTISTORY BUILDING
	17,500		13,000		25,500		10,000				

HEIGHT AND AREA TABLES

395

This table was compiled from information contained in the International Building Code 2006. It does not represent an official interpretation by the organization that issues this code.

OCCUPANCY GROUP H-4: HIGH-HAZARD, CORROSIVES AND TOXICS

Special Requirements

A sprinkler system is required for all Group H-4 Occupancy areas. In some cases, a Group H-4 Occupancy of limited area may be permitted within an unlimited area building of F or S Occupancy. See the code for additional requirements.

Fire Walls

For multiplication of the allowable area by subdividing the building with fire walls, see page 358.

Basements

Basements are not included in area calculations, provided that their area does not exceed the area permitted for a one-story building.

Excess Frontage

If more than 25% of the building perimeter fronts on a street or open space at least 20 ft (6.1 m) wide that is accessible to firefighting vehicles, the tabulated area limitations below may be increased according to the adjacent table. For example, for a building with half of its perimeter accessible to firefighting equipment via a space not less than 24 ft (7.3 m) wide, the allowable area increase is:

0.80 increase $\times$ 25% excess frontage = 20% total area increase

Width of Frontage[a]	Percent Area Increase for Each 1% of Frontage[a] in Excess of 25%
20' (6.1 m)	0.67
22' (6.7 m)	0.73
24' (7.3 m)	0.80
26' (7.9 m)	0.87
28' (8.5 m)	0.93
30' (9.1 m) or wider	1.00

[a]Intermediate values may be interpolated.

Measurements

Height is measured from the aver-

OCCUPANCY GROUP H-4: HIGH-HAZARD, CORROSIVES AND TOXICS

	Noncombustible							
CONSTRUCTION TYPE	**3-Hour (page 364)**		**2-Hour (page 364)**		**1-Hour (page 365)**		**Unprotected (page 366)**	
IBC NOMENCLATURE	**Type I-A**		**Type I-B**		**Type II-A**		**Type II-B**	
	Spr	Unspr	Spr	Unspr	Spr	Unspr	Spr	Unspr
MAXIMUM HEIGHT IN FEET	UH		180'		85'		75'	
UH	UA							
12								
11								
10								
9								
8			UA					
7								
6					337,500			
5					337,500			
4					337,500		157,500	
3					337,500		157,500	
2					225,000		105,000	
1		NP		NP	150,000	NP	70,000	NP
MAXIMUM AREA IN SQ FT FOR ANY SINGLE FLOOR OF A MULTISTORY BUILDING	UA		UA		112,500		52,500	

Each number in the table represents the maximum total area in square feet for all floors for a building of the indicated story height.

Labels in left margin: CONSTRUCTION TYPE / IBC NOMENCLATURE / MAXIMUM HEIGHT IN FEET / HEIGHT IN STORIES ABOVE GRADE AND MAXIMUM AREA IN SQ FT ALL FLOORS / MAXIMUM AREA IN SQ FT FOR ANY SINGLE FLOOR OF A MULTISTORY BUILDING

INTERNATIONAL BUILDING CODE

age finished ground level adjoining the building to the average level of the highest roof. Floor area is measured within exterior walls or exterior walls and fire walls, exclusive of vent shafts and courtyards.

Further Information

For information on Occupancy Group classifications, see page 7. For information on mixed-use buildings, see page 352. For information on which code to consult, see pages 7, 13.

Unit Conversions

1 ft = 304.8 mm, 1 sq ft = 0.0929 m².

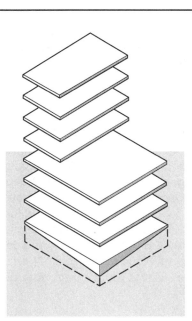

Combustible											
Ordinary						**Wood Light Frame**					**CONSTRUCTION TYPE**
1-Hour (page 368)		Unprotected (page 368)		Mill (page 366)		1-Hour (page 368)		Unprotected (page 368)			**IBC NOMENCLATURE**
Type III-A		Type III-B		Type IV-HT		Type V-A		Type V-B			
Spr	Unspr	Spr	Unspr	Spr	Unspr	Spr	Unspr	Spr	Unspr		
85'		75'		85'		70'		60'			**MAXIMUM HEIGHT IN FEET**
										UH	
										12	
										11	
										10	
										9	
										8	**HEIGHT IN STORIES ABOVE GRADE AND MAXIMUM AREA IN SQ FT ALL FLOORS**
										7	
				324,000						6	
256,500				324,000						5	
256,500		157,500		324,000		162,000				4	
256,500		157,500		324,000		162,000		58,500		3	
171,000		105,000		216,000		108,000		39,000		2	
114,000	NP	70,000	NP	144,000	NP	72,000	NP	26,000	NP	1	**MAXIMUM AREA IN SQ FT FOR ANY SINGLE FLOOR OF A MULTISTORY BUILDING**
85,500		52,500		108,000		54,000		19,500			

This table was compiled from information contained in the International Building Code 2006. It does not represent an official interpretation by the organization that issues this code.

Key to Abbreviations

UA	Unlimited area	Spr	With approved sprinkler system	NP	Not permitted
UH	Unlimited height	Unspr	Without approved sprinkler system		

HEIGHT AND AREA TABLES

397

OCCUPANCY GROUP H-5: HIGH-HAZARD, HAZARDOUS PRODUCTION FACILITIES

Special Requirements

A sprinkler system is required throughout any building containing, in whole or in part, a Group H-5 Occupancy. Occupied portions of H-5 Occupancies may not be located below grade. Floor structures within H-5 fabrication areas must be of Noncombustible Construction. Areas containing hazardous production materials must have at least one exterior wall not less than 30 ft (9.1 m) from property lines. See the code for additional requirements.

Fire Walls

For multiplication of the allowable area by subdividing the building with fire walls, see page 358.

Basements

Basements are not included in area calculations, provided that their area does not exceed the area permitted for a one-story building.

Excess Frontage

If more than 25% of the building perimeter fronts on a street or open space at least 20 ft (6.1 m) wide that is accessible to firefighting vehicles, the tabulated area limitations below may be increased according to the following table. For example, for a building with half of its perimeter accessible to firefighting equipment via a space not less than 24 ft (7.3 m) wide, the allowable area increase is:

0.80 increase 3 25% excess frontage = 20% total area increase

OCCUPANCY GROUP H-5: HIGH-HAZARD, HAZARDOUS PRODUCTION FACILITIES

CONSTRUCTION TYPE	Noncombustible							
	3-Hour (page 364)		2-Hour (page 364)		1-Hour (page 365)		Unprotected (page 366)	
IBC NOMENCLATURE	Type I-A		Type I-B		Type II-A		Type II-B	
	Spr	Unspr	Spr	Unspr	Spr	Unspr	Spr	Unspr
MAXIMUM HEIGHT IN FEET	UH		160'		65'		55'	
UH								
12								
11								
10								
9								
8								
7								
6								
5								
4	UA		UA					
3					337,500		207,000	
2					225,000		138,000	
1		NP		NP	150,000	NP	92,000	NP
MAXIMUM AREA IN SQ FT FOR ANY SINGLE FLOOR OF A MULTISTORY BUILDING	UA		UA		112,500		69,000	

(HEIGHT IN STORIES ABOVE GRADE AND MAXIMUM AREA IN SQ FT ALL FLOORS)

Each number in the table represents the maximum total area in square feet for all floors for a building of the indicated story height.

[a]Floor structures within fabrication areas must be Noncombustible Construction.

Width of Frontage[a]	Percent Area Increase for Each 1% of Frontage[a] in Excess of 25%
20' (6.1 m)	0.67%
22' (6.7 m)	0.73%
24' (7.3 m)	0.80%
26' (7.9 m)	0.87%
28' (8.5 m)	0.93%
30' (9.1 m) or wider	1.00%

[a]Intermediate values may be interpolated.

Measurements

Height is measured from the average finished ground level adjoining the building to the average level of the highest roof. Floor area is measured within exterior walls or exterior walls and fire walls, exclusive of vent shafts and courtyards.

Further Information

For information on Occupancy Group classifications, see page 7. For information on mixed-use buildings, see page 352. For information on which code to consult, see pages 7, 13.

Unit Conversions

1 ft = 304.8 mm, 1 sq ft = 0.0929 m^2.

Combustible											CONSTRUCTION TYPE
Ordinary				Mill		Wood Light Frame					
[a]1-Hour (page 368)		[a]Unprotected (page 368)		[a]Mill (page 366)		[a]1-Hour (page 368)		[a]Unprotected (page 368)			IBC NOMENCLATURE
Type III-A		Type III-B		Type IV-HT		Type V-A		Type V-B			
Spr	Unspr	Spr	Unspr	Spr	Unspr	Spr	Unspr	Spr	Unspr		
65'		55'		65'		50'		40'			MAXIMUM HEIGHT IN FEET
										UH 12 11 10 9 8 7 6 5 4	HEIGHT IN STORIES ABOVE GRADE AND MAXIMUM AREA IN SQ FT ALL FLOORS
256,500		171,000		324,000		162,000				3	
171,000		114,000		216,000		108,000		54,000		2	
114,000	NP	76,000	NP	144,000	NP	72,000	NP	36,000	NP	1	MAXIMUM AREA IN SQ FT FOR ANY SINGLE FLOOR OF A MULTISTORY BUILDING
85,500		57,000		108,000		54,000		27,000			

This table was compiled from information contained in the International Building Code 2006. It does not represent an official interpretation by the organization that issues this code.

Key to Abbreviations

UA	Unlimited area	Spr	With approved sprinkler system	NP	Not permitted
UH	Unlimited height	Unspr	Without approved sprinkler system		

HEIGHT AND AREA TABLES

OCCUPANCY GROUP I-1: INSTITUTIONAL, RESIDENTIAL CARE

Sprinklers

A sprinkler system is required throughout buildings containing, in whole or in part, a Group I-1 Occupancy. Residential class (NFPA 13R) sprinkler systems are permitted as an option for Group I-1 Occupancy areas. In this case, read from the columns labeled "Residential Spr" in the table on these two facing pages.

Fire Walls

For multiplication of the allowable area by subdividing the building with fire walls, see page 358.

Basements

Basements are not included in area calculations, provided that their area does not exceed the area permitted for a one-story building.

Excess Frontage

If more than 25% of the building perimeter fronts on a street or open space at least 20 ft (6.1 m) wide that is accessible to firefighting vehicles, the tabulated area limitations below may be increased according to the following table. For example, for a building with half of its perimeter accessible to firefighting equipment via a space not less than 24 ft (7.3 m) wide, the allowable area increase is:

0.80 increase × 25% excess frontage = 20% total area increase

Width of Frontage[a]	Percent Area Increase for Each 1% of Frontage[a] in Excess of 25%
20' (6.1 m)	0.67%
22' (6.7 m)	0.73%
24' (7.3 m)	0.80%
26' (7.9 m)	0.87%
28' (8.5 m)	0.93%
30' (9.1 m) or wider	1.00%

[a]Intermediate values may be interpolated.

Measurements

Height is measured from the average finished ground level adjoin-

OCCUPANCY GROUP I-1: INSTITUTIONAL, RESIDENTIAL CARE

	Noncombustible							
CONSTRUCTION TYPE	3-Hour (page 364)		2-Hour (page 364)		1-Hour (page 365)		Unprotected (page 366)	
IBC NOMENCLATURE	Type I-A		Type I-B		Type II-A		Type II-B	
	Spr	[a]Residential Spr	Spr	[a]Residential Spr	Spr	[a]Residential Spr	Spr	[a]Residential Spr
MAXIMUM HEIGHT IN FEET	UH	60'	180'	60'	85'	60'	75'	55'
UH	UA							
12								
11								
10			495,000					
9			495,000					
8			495,000					
7			495,000					
6			495,000					
5			495,000		171,000			
4		UA	495,000	165,000	171,000	57,000	90,000	
3			495,000	165,000	171,000	57,000	90,000	30,000
2			330,000	110,000	114,000	38,000	60,000	20,000
1			220,000	55,000	76,000	19,000	40,000	10,000
MAXIMUM AREA IN SQ FT FOR ANY SINGLE FLOOR OF A MULTISTORY BUILDING	UA	UA	165,000	55,000	57,000	19,000	30,000	10,000

HEIGHT IN STORIES ABOVE GRADE AND MAXIMUM AREA IN SQ FT ALL FLOORS

Each number in the table represents the maximum total area in square feet for all floors for a building of the indicated story height.

[a]Residential class sprinkler system NFPA 13R.

INTERNATIONAL BUILDING CODE

ing the building to the average level of the highest roof. Floor area is measured within exterior walls or exterior walls and fire walls, exclusive of vent shafts and courtyards.

Further Information

For information on Occupancy Group classifications, see page 7. For information on mixed-use buildings, see page 352. For information on which code to consult, see pages 7, 13.

Unit Conversions

1 ft = 304.8 mm, 1 sq ft = 0.0929 m².

Combustible											
Ordinary				Mill (page 366)		Wood Light Frame					CONSTRUCTION TYPE
1-Hour (page 368)		Unprotected (page 368)				1-Hour (page 368)		Unprotected (page 368)			
Type III-A		Type III-B		Type IV-HT		Type V-A		Type V-B			IBC NOMENCLATURE
Spr	aResidential Spr	Spr	aResidential Spr	Spr	aResidential Spr	Spr	aResidential Spr	Spr	aResidential Spr		
85'	60'	75'	55'	85'	60'	70'	50'	60'	40'		MAXIMUM HEIGHT IN FEET

										UH
										12
										11
										10
										9
										8 HEIGHT IN STORIES ABOVE GRADE AND MAXIMUM AREA IN SQ FT ALL FLOORS
										7
										6
148,500				162,000						5
148,500	49,500	90,000		162,000	54,000	94,500				4
148,500	49,500	90,000	30,000	162,000	54,000	94,500	31,500	40,500		3
99,000	33,000	60,000	20,000	108,000	36,000	63,000	21,000	27,000	9,000	2
66,000	16,500	40,000	10,000	72,000	18,000	42,000	10,500	18,000	4,500	1 MAXIMUM AREA IN SQ FT FOR ANY SINGLE FLOOR OF A MULTISTORY BUILDING
49,500	16,500	30,000	10,000	54,000	18,000	31,500	10,500	18,000	4,500	

This table was compiled from information contained in the International Building Code 2006. It does not represent an official interpretation by the organization that issues this code.

Key to Abbreviations

UA	Unlimited area	Spr	With approved sprinkler system	NP	Not permitted		
UH	Unlimited height	Unspr	Without approved sprinkler system				

HEIGHT AND AREA TABLES

401

OCCUPANCY GROUP I-2: INSTITUTIONAL, MEDICAL AND CUSTODIAL CARE

Special Requirements

A sprinkler system is required throughout buildings containing, in whole or in part, a Group I-2 Occupancy. In addition, floors with an occupant load greater than 50, and all floors used by patients for sleeping or treatment, must be subdivided by a smoke barrier into at least two separate areas with independent means of egress. See the code for additional requirements.

Fire Walls

For multiplication of the allowable area by subdividing the building with fire walls, see page 358.

Basements

Basements are not included in area calculations, provided that their area does not exceed the area permitted for a one-story building.

Excess Frontage

If more than 25% of the building perimeter fronts on a street or open space at least 20 ft (6.1 m) wide that is accessible to firefighting vehicles, the tabulated area limitations below may be increased according to the following table. For example, for a building with half of its perimeter accessible to firefighting equipment via a space not less than 24 ft (7.3 m) wide, the allowable area increase is:

OCCUPANCY GROUP I-2: INSTITUTIONAL, MEDICAL AND CUSTODIAL CARE

	Noncombustible							
CONSTRUCTION TYPE	**3-Hour** (page 364)		**2-Hour** (page 364)		**1-Hour** (page 365)		**Unprotected** (page 366)	
IBC NOMENCLATURE	Type I-A		Type I-B		Type II-A		Type II-B	
	Spr	Unspr	Spr	Unspr	Spr	Unspr	Spr	Unspr
MAXIMUM HEIGHT IN FEET	UH		180'		85'		75'	
UH	UA							
12								
11								
10								
9								
8								
7								
6								
5			UA					
4								
3					135,000			
2					90,000			
1		NP		NP	60,000	NP	44,000	NP
MAXIMUM AREA	UA		UA		45,000			

HEIGHT IN STORIES ABOVE GRADE AND MAXIMUM AREA IN SQ FT ALL FLOORS

MAXIMUM AREA IN SQ FT FOR ANY SINGLE FLOOR OF A MULTISTORY BUILDING

Each number in the table represents the maximum total area in square feet for all floors for a building of the indicated story height.

Key to Abbreviations

UA	Unlimited area	Spr	With approved sprinkler system	NP	Not permitted
UH	Unlimited height	Unspr	Without approved sprinkler system		

0.80 increase × 25% excess frontage = 20% total area increase

Width of Frontage[a]	Percent Area Increase for Each 1% of Frontage[a] in Excess of 25%
20' (6.1 m)	0.67
22' (6.7 m)	0.73
24' (7.3 m)	0.80
26' (7.9 m)	0.87
28' (8.5 m)	0.93
30' (9.1 m) or wider	1.00

[a]Intermediate values may be interpolated.

Measurements

Height is measured from the average finished ground level adjoining the building to the average level of the highest roof. Floor area is measured within exterior walls or exterior walls and fire walls, exclusive of vent shafts and courtyards.

Further Information

For information on Occupancy Group classifications, see page 7. For information on mixed-use buildings, see page 352. For information on which code to consult, see pages 7, 13.

Unit Conversions

1 ft = 304.8 mm, 1 sq ft = 0.0929 m^2.

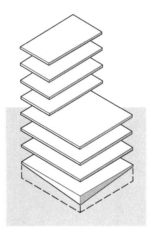

Combustible											
Ordinary				Mill (page 366)		Wood Light Frame				CONSTRUCTION TYPE	
1-Hour (page 368)		Unprotected (page 368)				1-Hour (page 368)		Unprotected (page 368)			
Type III-A		Type III-B		Type IV-HT		Type V-A		Type V-B		IBC NOMENCLATURE	
Spr	Unspr	Spr	Unspr	Spr	Unspr	Spr	Unspr	Spr	Unspr		
85'				85'		70'			'	MAXIMUM HEIGHT IN FEET	
										UH	
										12	
										11	
										10	
										9	
										8	HEIGHT IN STORIES
										7	ABOVE GRADE AND
										6	MAXIMUM AREA IN
										5	SQ FT ALL FLOORS
										4	
										3	
										2	
48,000	NP	NP	NP	48,000	NP	38,000	NP	NP	NP	1	MAXIMUM AREA IN SQ FT FOR ANY SINGLE FLOOR OF A MULTISTORY BUILDING

This table was compiled from information contained in the International Building Code 2006. It does not represent an official interpretation by the organization that issues this code.

HEIGHT AND AREA TABLES

OCCUPANCY GROUP I-3: INSTITUTIONAL, DETENTION AND SECURITY

Special Requirements

A sprinkler system is required throughout buildings containing, in whole or in part, a Group I-3 Occupancy. In addition, floors with an occupant load greater than 50, and all floors used by patients for sleeping or treatment, must be subdivided by a smoke barrier into at least two separate areas with independent means of egress. Alterna-tively, residents must have direct exit access to a public way, separate building, or secured yard or court. See the code for additional requirements.

Fire Walls

For multiplication of the allowable area by subdividing the building with fire walls, see page 358.

Basements

Basements are not included in area calculations, provided that their area does not exceed the area permitted for a one-story building.

Excess Frontage

If more than 25% of the building perimeter fronts on a street or open space at least 20 ft (6.1 m) wide that is accessible to firefighting vehicles, the tabulated area limitations below may be increased according to the following table. For example, for a building with half of its perimeter accessible to firefighting equipment via a space not less than 24 ft (7.3 m) wide, the allowable area increase is:

0.80 increase $\times$ 25% excess frontage = 20% total area increase

OCCUPANCY GROUP I-3: INSTITUTIONAL, DETENTION AND SECURITY

	Noncombustible							
CONSTRUCTION TYPE	3-Hour (page 364)		2-Hour (page 364)		1-Hour (page 365)		Unprotected (page 366)	
IBC NOMENCLATURE	Type I-A		Type I-B		Type II-A		Type II-B	
	Spr	Unspr	Spr	Unspr	Spr	Unspr	Spr	Unspr
MAXIMUM HEIGHT IN FEET	UH		180'		85'		75'	

HEIGHT IN STORIES ABOVE GRADE AND MAXIMUM AREA IN SQ FT ALL FLOORS

Stories	Type I-A Spr	Type I-A Unspr	Type I-B Spr	Type I-B Unspr	Type II-A Spr	Type II-A Unspr	Type II-B Spr	Type II-B Unspr
UH	UA							
12								
11								
10								
9								
8								
7								
6								
5			UA					
4								
3					135,000			
2					90,000		60,000	
1		NP		NP	60,000	NP	44,000	NP

MAXIMUM AREA IN SQ FT FOR ANY SINGLE FLOOR OF A MULTISTORY BUILDING

Type I-A		Type I-B		Type II-A		Type II-B	
UA		UA	NP	45,000		33,000	

Each number in the table represents the maximum total area in square feet for all floors for a building of the indicated story height.

Key to Abbreviations

UA	Unlimited area	Spr	With approved sprinkler system	NP	Not permitted
UH	Unlimited height	Unspr	Without approved sprinkler system		

Width of Frontage[a]	Area Increase for Each 1% of Frontage[a] in Excess of 25%
20' (6.1 m)	0.67
22' (6.7 m)	0.73
24' (7.3 m)	0.80
26' (7.9 m)	0.87
28' (8.5 m)	0.93
30' (9.1 m) or wider	1.00

*Intermediate values may be interpolated.

Measurements

Height is measured from the average finished ground level adjoining the building to the average level of the highest roof. Floor area is measured within exterior walls or exterior walls and fire walls, exclusive of vent shafts and courtyards.

Further Information

For information on Occupancy Group classifications, see page 7. For information on mixed-use buildings, see page 352. For information on which code to consult, see pages 7, 13.

Unit Conversions

1 ft = 304.8 mm, 1 sq ft = 0.0929 m².

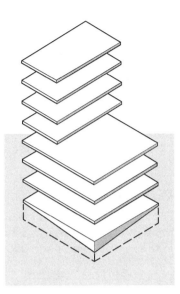

	Combustible											CONSTRUCTION TYPE
	Ordinary						Wood Light Frame					
	1-Hour (page 368)		Unprotected (page 368)		Mill (page 366)		1-Hour (page 368)		Unprotected (page 368)			
	Type III-A		Type III-B		Type IV-HT		Type V-A		Type V-B			IBC NOMENCLATURE
	Spr	Unspr	Spr	Unspr	Spr	Unspr	Spr	Unspr	Spr	Unspr		
	85'		75'		85'		70'		60'			MAXIMUM HEIGHT IN FEET
UH												
12												
11												
10												
9												
8												HEIGHT IN STORIES
7												ABOVE GRADE AND
6												MAXIMUM AREA IN SQ FT ALL FLOORS
5												
4												
3	94,500				108,000		67,500					
2	63,000		45,000		72,000		45,000		30,000			
1	42,000	NP	30,000	NP	48,000	NP	30,000	NP	20,000	NP		MAXIMUM AREA IN SQ FT FOR ANY SINGLE FLOOR OF A MULTISTORY BUILDING
	31,500		22,500		36,000		22,500		15,000			

HEIGHT AND AREA TABLES

This table was compiled from information contained in the International Building Code 2006. It does not represent an official interpretation by the organization that issues this code.

OCCUPANCY GROUP I-4: INSTITUTIONAL, DAY CARE

Sprinklers

A sprinkler system is required throughout buildings containing, in whole or in part, a Group I-4 Occupancy.

Fire Walls

For multiplication of the allowable area by subdividing the building with fire walls, see page 358.

Basements

Basements are not included in area calculations, provided that their area does not exceed the area permitted for a one-story building.

Excess Frontage

If more than 25% of the building perimeter fronts on a street or open space at least 20 ft (6.1 m) wide that is accessible to firefighting vehicles, the tabulated area limitations below may be increased according to the following table. For example, for a building with half of its perimeter accessible to firefighting equipment via a space not less than 24 ft (7.3 m) wide, the allowable area increase is:

0.80 increase × 25% excess frontage = 20% total area increase

Width of Frontage[a]	Percent Area Increase for Each 1% of Frontage[a] in Excess of 25%
20' (6.1 m)	0.67%
22' (6.7 m)	0.73%
24' (7.3 m)	0.80%
26' (7.9 m)	0.87%
28' (8.5 m)	0.93%
30' (9.1 m) or wider	1.00%

[a]Intermediate values may be interpolated

OCCUPANCY GROUP I-4: INSTITUTIONAL, DAY CARE

	Noncombustible							
CONSTRUCTION TYPE	**3-Hour (page 364)**		**2-Hour (page 364)**		**1-Hour (page 365)**		**Unprotected (page 366)**	
IBC NOMENCLATURE	**Type I-A**		**Type I-B**		**Type II-A**		**Type II-B**	
	Spr	Unspr	Spr	Unspr	Spr	Unspr	Spr	Unspr
MAXIMUM HEIGHT IN FEET	UH		180'		85'		75'	
UH	UA							
12								
11								
10								
9								
8								
7								
6			544,500					
5			544,500					
4			544,500		238,500			
3			544,500		238,500		117,000	
2			363,000		159,000		78,000	
1		NP	242,000	NP	106,000	NP	52,000	NP
	UA		181,500		79,500		39,000	

CONSTRUCTION TYPE

IBC NOMENCLATURE

MAXIMUM HEIGHT IN FEET

HEIGHT IN STORIES ABOVE GRADE AND MAXIMUM AREA IN SQ FT ALL FLOORS

MAXIMUM AREA IN SQ FT FOR ANY SINGLE FLOOR OF A MULTISTORY BUILDING

Each number in the table represents the maximum total area in square feet for all floors for a building of the indicated story height.

Key to Abbreviations

UA	Unlimited area	Spr	With approved sprinkler system	NP	Not permitted
UH	Unlimited height	Unspr	Without approved sprinkler system		

INTERNATIONAL BUILDING CODE

Measurements

Height is measured from the average finished ground level adjoining the building to the average level of the highest roof. Floor area is measured within exterior walls or exterior walls and fire walls, exclusive of vent shafts and courtyards.

Further Information

For information on Occupancy Group classifications, see page 7. For information on mixed-use buildings, see page 352. For information on which code to consult, see pages 7, 13.

Unit Conversions

1 ft = 304.8 mm, 1 sq ft = 0.0929 m^2.

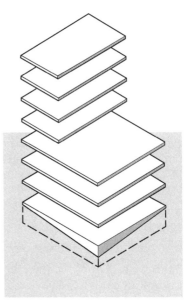

				Combustible							
	Ordinary						Wood Light Frame				
1-Hour (page 368)		Unprotected (page 368)		Mill (page 366)		1-Hour (page 368)		Unprotected (page 368)			CONSTRUCTION TYPE
Type III-A		Type III-B		Type IV-HT		Type V-A		Type V-B			IBC NOMENCLATURE
Spr	Unspr	Spr	Unspr	Spr	Unspr	Spr	Unspr	Spr	Unspr		
85'		75'		85'		70'		60'			MAXIMUM HEIGHT IN FEET
										UH	
										12	
										11	
										10	
										9	
										8	HEIGHT IN STORIES ABOVE GRADE AND MAXIMUM AREA IN SQ FT ALL FLOORS
										7	
										6	
										5	
211,500				229,500						4	
211,500		117,000		229,500						3	
141,000		78,000		153,000		111,000		54,000		2	
94,000	NP	52,000	NP	102,000	NP	74,000	NP	36,000	NP	1	MAXIMUM AREA IN SQ FT FOR ANY SINGLE FLOOR OF A MULTISTORY BUILDING
70,500		39,000		76,500		55,500		27,000			

This table was compiled from information contained in the International Building Code 2006. It does not represent an official interpretation by the organization that issues this code.

HEIGHT AND AREA TABLES

407

OCCUPANCY GROUP M: MERCANTILE

Sprinklers

In addition to the requirements indicated in the table on these two facing pages, a sprinkler system is required throughout buildings containing, in whole or in part, a Group M Occupancy meeting any of the following conditions:

■ With a fire area exceeding 12,000 sq ft (1115 m²)

■ Where merchandise is stored in high-piled or rack storage arrays

For an explanation of fire areas, see page 358. A sprinkler system is also required for any stories or basements exceeding 1500 sq ft (139 m²) in area without openings to the exterior, in any underground portions of a building with occupancy more than 30 ft (9 m) below the lowest level of exit discharge, and throughout any building containing floors 55 ft (17 m) or more above grade with an occupant load of 30 or more.

Unlimited Area Buildings

One- and two-story Occupancy M buildings, fully sprinklered, may be of unlimited area when surrounded on all sides by public ways or yards not less than 60 ft (18 m) in width. In such one-story buildings, Group A-1 and A-2 Occupancies are permitted, so long as these occupancies are treated as mixed-use Separated Occupancies, such areas each comply with their own code height and area limits, and all required exits from these areas discharge directly to the exterior. In some circumstances, reductions in the required width of open space around these building types are permitted; see the code for details.

Covered Mall Buildings

Covered mall buildings, consisting of single buildings enclosing multiple retail, entertainment, and related facilities, are permitted to be of unlimited area, provided that they are fully sprinklered, no more than three stories in height, of any Construction Type except Wood Light Frame, and surrounded on all sides by public ways or yards at least 60 ft (18.3 m) in width. See the code for additional requirements.

Fire Walls

For multiplication of the allowable area by subdividing the building with fire walls, see page 358.

OCCUPANCY GROUP M: MERCANTILE

CONSTRUCTION TYPE	Noncombustible							
	3-Hour (page 364)		2-Hour (page 364)		1-Hour (page 365)		Unprotected (page 366)	
IBC NOMENCLATURE	Type I-A		Type I-B		Type II-A		Type II-B	
	Spr	Unspr	Spr	Unspr	Spr	Unspr	Spr	Unspr
MAXIMUM HEIGHT IN FEET	UH	75'	180'	75'	85'	65'	75'	55'
UH	UA							
12			UA					
11								
10								
9								
8								
7								
6								
5					193,500		112,500	
4					193,500		112,500	
3		24,000		24,000	193,500	24,000	112,500	24,000
2		24,000		24,000	129,000	24,000	75,000	24,000
1		24,000		24,000	86,000	21,500	50,000	12,500
MAXIMUM AREA IN SQ FT FOR ANY SINGLE FLOOR OF A MULTISTORY BUILDING	UA	24,000	UA	24,000	64,500	21,500	37,500	12,500

(Row labels on left: HEIGHT IN STORIES ABOVE GRADE AND MAXIMUM AREA IN SQ FT ALL FLOORS)

Each number in the table represents the maximum total area in square feet for all floors for a building of the indicated story height.

Key to Abbreviations

UA	Unlimited area	Spr	With approved sprinkler system	NP	Not permitted
UH	Unlimited height	Unspr	Without approved sprinkler system		

Basements

Basements are not included in area calculations, provided that their area does not exceed the area permitted for a one-story building.

Excess Frontage

If more than 25% of the building perimeter fronts on a street or open space at least 20 ft (6.1 m) wide that is accessible to firefighting vehicles, the tabulated area limitations below may be increased according to the following table. For example, for a building with half of its perimeter accessible to firefighting equipment via a space not less than 24 ft (7.3 m) wide, the allowable area increase is:

0.80 increase × 25% excess frontage = 20% total area increase

Width of Frontage[a]	Percent Area Increase for Each 1% of Frontage[*] in Excess of 25%
20' (6.1 m)	0.67
22' (6.7 m)	0.73
24' (7.3 m)	0.80
26' (7.9 m)	0.87
28' (8.5 m)	0.93
30' (9.1 m) or wider	1.00

[*]Intermediate values may be interpolated.

Measurements

Height is measured from the average finished ground level adjoining the building to the average level of the highest roof. Floor area is measured within exterior walls or exterior walls and fire walls, exclusive of vent shafts and courtyards.

Further Information

For information on Occupancy Group classifications, see page 7. For information on mixed-use buildings, see page 352. For information on which code to consult, see pages 7, 13.

Unit Conversions

1 ft = 304.8 mm, 1 sq ft = 0.0929 m^2.

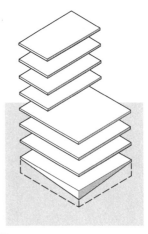

	Ordinary			Combustible		Wood Light Frame					
	1-Hour (page 368)		Unprotected (page 368)		Mill (page 366)		1-Hour (page 368)		Unprotected (page 368)		
	Type III-A		Type III-B		Type IV-HT		Type V-A		Type V-B		
	Spr	Unspr	Spr	Unspr	Spr	Unspr	Spr	Unspr	Spr	Unspr	
	85'	65'	75'	55'	85'	65'	70'	50'	60'	40'	
UH											
12											
11											
10											
9											
8											
7											
6											
5	166,500		112,500		184,500						
4	166,500		112,500		184,500		126,000				
3	166,500	24,000	112,500	24,000	184,500	24,000	126,000	24,000			
2	111,000	24,000	75,000	24,000	123,000	24,000	84,000	24,000	54,000		
1	74,000	18,500	50,000	12,500	82,000	20,500	56,000	14,000	36,000	9,000	
	55,500	18,500	37,500	12,500	82,000	20,500	42,000	14,000	27,000		

CONSTRUCTION TYPE

IBC NOMENCLATURE

MAXIMUM HEIGHT IN FEET

HEIGHT IN STORIES ABOVE GRADE AND MAXIMUM AREA IN SQ FT ALL FLOORS

MAXIMUM AREA IN SQ FT FOR ANY SINGLE FLOOR OF A MULTISTORY BUILDING

HEIGHT AND AREA TABLES

This table was compiled from information contained in the International Building Code 2006. It does not represent an official interpretation by the organization that issues this code.

OCCUPANCY GROUP R-1: RESIDENTIAL, HOTELS AND MOTELS

Sprinklers

A sprinkler system is required throughout buildings containing, in whole or in part, a Group R-1 Occupancy. Residential class (NFPA 13R) sprinkler systems are permitted as an option for Group R-1 Occupancy areas. In this case, read from the columns labeled "Residential Spr" in the table on these two facing pages.

Fire Walls

For multiplication of the allowable area by subdividing the building with fire walls, see page 358.

Basements

Basements are not included in area calculations, provided that their area does not exceed the area permitted for a one-story building.

Excess Frontage

If more than 25% of the building perimeter fronts on a street or open space at least 20 ft (6.1 m) wide that is accessible to firefighting vehicles, the tabulated area limitations below may be increased according to the following table. For example, for a building with half of its perimeter accessible to firefighting equipment via a space not less than 24 ft (7.3 m) wide, the allowable area increase is:

0.80 increase × 25% excess frontage = 20% total area increase

OCCUPANCY GROUP R-1: RESIDENTIAL, HOTELS AND MOTELS

	Noncombustible							
CONSTRUCTION TYPE	**3-Hour** (page 364)		**2-Hour** (page 364)		**1-Hour** (page 365)		**Unprotected** (page 366)	
IBC NOMENCLATURE	Type I-A		Type I-B		Type II-A		Type II-B	
	Spr	[a]Residential Spr	Spr	[a]Residential Spr	Spr	[a]Residential Spr	Spr	[a]Residential Spr
MAXIMUM HEIGHT IN FEET	UH	60'	180'	60'	85'	60'	75'	55'
UH	UA							
12			UA					
11								
10								
9								
8								
7								
6								
5					216,000		144,000	
4		UA		UA	216,000	72,000	144,000	48,000
3					216,000	72,000	144,000	48,000
2					144,000	48,000	96,000	32,000
1					96,000	24,000	64,000	16,000
MAXIMUM AREA IN SQ FT FOR ANY SINGLE FLOOR OF A MULTISTORY BUILDING	UA	UA	UA	UA	72,000	24,000	48,000	16,000

HEIGHT IN STORIES ABOVE GRADE AND MAXIMUM AREA IN SQ FT ALL FLOORS

Each number in the table represents the maximum total area in square feet for all floors for a building of the indicated story height.

[a]Residential class sprinkler system NFPA 13R.

Width of Frontage[a]	Percent Area Increase for Each 1% of Frontage[a] in Excess of 25%
20' (6.1 m)	0.67
22' (6.7 m)	0.73
24' (7.3 m)	0.80
26' (7.9 m)	0.87
28' (8.5 m)	0.93
30' (9.1 m) or wider	1.00

[a]Intermediate values may be interpolated.

Measurements

Height is measured from the average finished ground level adjoining the building to the average level of the highest roof. Floor area is measured within exterior walls or exterior walls and fire walls, exclusive of vent shafts and courtyards.

Further Information

For information on Occupancy Group classifications, see page 7. For information on mixed-use buildings, see page 352. For information on which code to consult, see pages 7, 13.

Unit Conversions

1 ft = 304.8 mm, 1 sq ft = 0.0929 m².

	Combustible											CONSTRUCTION TYPE
	Ordinary						Wood Light Frame					
	1-Hour (page 368)		Unprotected (page 368)		Mill (page 366)		1-Hour (page 368)		Unprotected (page 368)			
	Type III-A		Type III-B		Type IV-HT		Type V-A		Type V-B			IBC NOMENCLATURE
	Spr	[a]Residential Spr	Spr	[a]Residential Spr	Spr	[a]Residential Spr	Spr	[a]Residential Spr	Spr	[a]Residential Spr		
	85'	60'	75'	55'	85'	60'	70'	50'	50'	40'		MAXIMUM HEIGHT IN FEET
UH												
12												
11												
10												
9												
8												HEIGHT IN STORIES ABOVE GRADE AND MAXIMUM AREA IN SQ FT ALL FLOORS
7												
6												
5	216,000		144,000		184,500							
4	216,000	72,000	144,000	48,000	184,500	61,500	108,000	36,000				
3	216000	72,000	144,000	48,000	184,500	61,500	108,000	36,000	63,000	21,000		
2	144,000	48,000	96,000	32,000	123,000	41,000	72,000	24,000	42,000	14,000		
1	96,000	24,000	64,000	16,000	82,000	20,500	48,000	12,000	28,000	7,000		MAXIMUM AREA IN SQ FT FOR ANY SINGLE FLOOR OF A MULTISTORY BUILDING
	72,000	24,000	48,000	16,000	61,500	20,500	36,000	12,000	21,000	7,000		

HEIGHT AND AREA TABLES

This table was compiled from information contained in the International Building Code 2006. It does not represent an official interpretation by the organization that issues this code.

Key to Abbreviations

UA	Unlimited area	Spr	With approved sprinkler system	NP	Not permitted
UH	Unlimited height	Unspr	Without approved sprinkler system		

OCCUPANCY GROUP R-2: RESIDENTIAL, MULTIFAMILY

Special Requirements

A sprinkler system is required throughout buildings containing, in whole or in part, a Group R-2 Occupancy. Residential class (NFPA 13R) sprinkler systems are permitted as an option for the Group R-2 Occupancy Areas. In this case, read from the columns labeled "Residential Spr" in the table on these two facing pages.

In addition to the limits indicated in the table on these two facing pages, R-2 Occupancy buildings may be constructed to greater heights as follows: When of 1-Hour Ordinary Construction (or a more fire-resistive Construction Type), building height may be increased to six stories and 75 ft (23 m) where the floor construction above the basement has a fire-resistance rating of not less than 3 hours and all occupant floors are subdivided by 2-hour rated walls into areas not larger than 3000 sq ft (279 m^2). When of 1-Hour Noncombustible Construction (or a more fire-resistive Construction Type), building height may be increased to nine stories and 100 ft (30 m) where floor construction above the basement has a fire-resistance rating of 1½ hours, the building is separated by not less than 50 ft (15 m) from other buildings and property lines, and exits are protected by 2-hour rated enclosures.

Fire Walls

For multiplication of the allowable area by subdividing the building with fire walls, see page 358.

Basements

Basements are not included in area calculations, provided that their area does not exceed the area permitted for a one-story building.

Excess Frontage

If more than 25% of the building perimeter fronts on a street or open space at least 20 ft (6.1 m) wide that is accessible to firefighting vehicles,

OCCUPANCY GROUP R-2: RESIDENTIAL, MULTIFAMILY

	Noncombustible							
CONSTRUCTION TYPE	3-Hour (page 364)		2-Hour (page 364)		1-Hour (page 365)		Unprotected (page 366)	
IBC NOMENCLATURE	Type I-A		Type I-B		Type II-A		Type II-B	
	Spr	[a]Residential Spr	Spr	[a]Residential Spr	Spr	[a]Residential Spr	Spr	[a]Residential Spr
MAXIMUM HEIGHT IN FEET	UH	60'	180'	60'	85'	60'	75'	55'
HEIGHT IN STORIES ABOVE GRADE AND MAXIMUM AREA IN SQ FT ALL FLOORS								
UH	UA							
12			UA					
11								
10								
9								
8								
7								
6								
5					216,000		144,000	
4		UA		UA	216,000	72,000	144,000	48,000
3					216,000	72,000	144,000	48,000
2					144,000	48,000	96,000	32,000
1					96,000	24,000	64,000	16,000
MAXIMUM AREA IN SQ FT FOR ANY SINGLE FLOOR OF A MULTISTORY BUILDING	UA	UA	UA	UA	72,000	24,000	48,000	16,000

Each number in the table represents the maximum total area in square feet for all floors for a building of the indicated story height.

[a]Residential class sprinkler system NFPA 13R.

the tabulated area limitations below may be increased according to the following table. For example, for a building with half of its perimeter accessible to firefighting equipment via a space not less than 24 ft (7.3 m) wide, the allowable area increase is:

0.80 increase × 25% excess

Width of Frontage[a]	Area Increase for Each 1% of Frontage[a] in Excess of 25%
20' (6.1 m)	0.67
22' (6.7 m)	0.73
24' (7.3 m)	0.80
26' (7.9 m)7	0.87
28' (8.5 m)	0.93
30' (9.1 m) or wider	1.00

*Intermediate values may be interpolated.

Measurements

Height is measured from the average finished ground level adjoining the building to the average level of the highest roof. Floor area is measured within exterior walls or exterior walls and fire walls, exclusive of vent shafts and courtyards.

Further Information

For information on Occupancy Group classifications, see page 7. For information on mixed-use build- ings, see page 352. For information on which code to consult, see pages 7, 13.

Unit Conversions

1 ft = 304.8 mm, 1 sq ft = 0.0929 m².

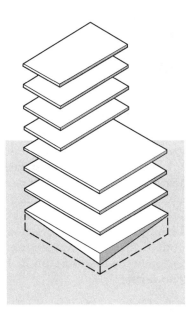

Combustible											
Ordinary					Mill (page 366)		Wood Light Frame				
1-Hour (page 368)		Unprotected (page 368)					1-Hour (page 368)		Unprotected (page 368)		
Type III-A		Type III-B			Type IV-HT		Type V-A		Type V-B		CONSTRUCTION TYPE
											IBC NOMENCLATURE
Spr	[a]Residential Spr	Spr	[a]Residential Spr		Spr	[a]Residential Spr	Spr	[a]Residential Spr	Spr	[a]Residential Spr	
85'	60'	75'	55'		85'	60'	70'	50'	60'	40'	MAXIMUM HEIGHT IN FEET
											UH
											12
											11
											10
											9
											8 HEIGHT IN STORIES
											7 ABOVE GRADE AND
											6 MAXIMUM AREA IN SQ FT ALL FLOORS
216,000		144,000			184,500						5
216,000	72,000	144,000	48,000		184,500	61,500	108,000	36,000			4
216,000	72,000	144,000	48,000		184,500	61,500	108,000	36,000	63,000	21,000	3
144,000	48,000	96,000	32,000		123,000	41,000	72,000	24,000	42,000	14,000	2
96,000	24,000	64,000	16,000		82,000	20,500	48,000	12,000	28,000	7,000	1
72,000	24,000	48,000	16,000		61,500	20,500	36,000	12,000	21,000	7,000	MAXIMUM AREA IN SQ FT FOR ANY SINGLE FLOOR OF A MULTISTORY BUILDING

HEIGHT AND AREA TABLES

413

This table was compiled from information contained in the International Building Code 2006. It does not represent an official interpretation by the organization that issues this code.

Key to Abbreviations

UA	Unlimited area	Spr	With approved sprinkler system	NP	Not permitted
UH	Unlimited height	Unspr	Without approved sprinkler system		

OCCUPANCY GROUP R-3: RESIDENTIAL, ONE- AND TWO-FAMILY

International Residential Code

Detached residential one- and two-family dwellings and townhouses not more than three stories in height are governed by the requirements of the *International Residential Code*, a separate model code developed by the International Code Council. For buildings of this type, use the following preliminary guidelines:

■ Building height is limited to three stories.

■ Building area is unlimited.

■ Each dwelling unit must have its own separate means of egress.

■ Every habitable basement and every sleeping room must have at least one emergency window or door to the exterior. See page 277 for more information.

■ Buildings may be of any construction type.

■ Abutting dwelling units in two-family buildings must be separated by 1-hour rated wall and floor/ceiling assemblies.

■ Exterior walls of separate buildings facing within 3 ft (0.9 m) of each other must be 1-hour rated and free of openings.

■ Common walls separating adjoining townhouses may consist either of two independent 1-hour walls or a single 2-hour rated wall kept free of plumbing and mechanical services.

■ Local regulations should be consulted for possible sprinkler requirements and other special provisions.

International Building Code

Occupancy Group R-3 of the International Building Code governs one- and two-family buildings that exceed the limitations of the Residential Code. These include buildings taller than three stories, buildings where separate dwelling units share means of egress, townhouses without open space on at

OCCUPANCY GROUP R-3: RESIDENTIAL, ONE- AND TWO-FAMILY

	Noncombustible							
CONSTRUCTION TYPE	3-Hour (page 364)		2-Hour (page 364)		1-Hour (page 365)		Unprotected (page 365)	
IBC NOMENCLATURE	Type I-A		Type I-B		Type II-A		Type II-B	
	Spr	ªResidential Spr	Spr	ªResidential Spr	Spr	ªResidential Spr	Spr	ªResidential Spr
MAXIMUM HEIGHT IN FEET	UH	60'	180'	60'	85'	60'	75'	55'

HEIGHT IN STORIES ABOVE GRADE AND MAXIMUM AREA IN SQ FT ALL FLOORS

Chart (vertical axis: UH, 12, 11, 10, 9, 8, 7, 6, 5, 4, 3, 2, 1):

Column	UA location
Type I-A, Spr	UA (UH)
Type I-A, ªResidential Spr	UA (story 4)
Type I-B, Spr	UA (story 12)
Type I-B, ªResidential Spr	UA (story 4)
Type II-A, Spr	UA (story 5)
Type II-A, ªResidential Spr	UA (story 4)
Type II-B, Spr	UA (story 5)
Type II-B, ªResidential Spr	UA (story 4)

MAXIMUM AREA IN SQ FT FOR ANY SINGLE FLOOR OF A MULTISTORY BUILDING (story 1):

UA	UA	UA	UA	UA	UA	UA	UA

Each number in the table represents the maximum total area in square feet for all floors for a building of the indicated story height.

ªResidential class sprinkler system NFPA 13R.

least two sides, or mixed-use buildings that include other occupancies in addition to R-3. For all such buildings, use the table on these two facing pages to determine building height and area limitations.

A sprinkler system is required throughout buildings containing, in whole or in part, a Group R-3 Occupancy. Residential class (NFPA 13R and 13D) sprinkler systems are permitted as an option for the Group R-3 Occupancy areas. Where NFPA 13R systems are used, read from the columns labeled "Residential Spr" in the table on these two facing pages. For applicability of NFPA 13D systems, consult the code for more information.

For separation requirements between dwelling units or adjacent buildings, use the following preliminary guidelines:

■ Adjacent dwelling units must be separated by 1-hour rated assemblies.

■ Common walls separating adjoining townhouses must be 2-hour rated.

Basements

Basements are not included in area calculations.

Measurements

Height is measured from the average finished ground level adjoining the building to the average level of the highest roof. Floor area is measured within exterior walls or exterior walls and fire walls, exclusive of vent shafts and courtyards.

Further Information

For information on Occupancy Group classifications, see page 7. For information on mixed-use buildings, see page 352. For information on which code to consult, see pages 7, 13.

Unit Conversions

1 ft = 304.8 mm, 1 sq ft = 0.0929 m^2.

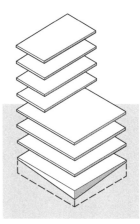

Combustible											
Ordinary						Wood Light Frame					
1-Hour (page 368)		Unprotected (page 368)		Mill (page 366)		1-Hour (page 368)		Unprotected (page 368)			
Type III-A		Type III-B		Type IV-HT		Type V-A		Type V-B			
Spr	[a]Residential Spr	Spr	[a]Residential Spr	Spr	[a]Residential Spr	Spr	[a]Residential Spr	Spr	[a]Residential Spr		CONSTRUCTION TYPE
											IBC NOMENCLATURE
55'	60'	75'	55'	85'	60'	70'	50'	60'	40'		MAXIMUM HEIGHT IN FEET
										UH	
										12	
										11	
										10	
										9	
										8	HEIGHT IN STORIES ABOVE GRADE AND MAXIMUM AREA IN SQ FT ALL FLOORS
										7	
										6	
UA		UA		UA						5	
	UA		UA		UA	UA	UA	UA	UA	4	
										3	
										2	
										1	MAXIMUM AREA IN SQ FT FOR ANY SINGLE FLOOR OF A MULTISTORY BUILDING
UA	UA	UA	UA	UA	UA	UA	UA	UA	UA		

This table was compiled from information contained in the International Building Code 2006. It does not represent an official interpretation by the organization that issues this code.

Key to Abbreviations

UA	Unlimited area	Spr	With approved sprinkler system	NP	Not permitted
UH	Unlimited height	Unspr	Without approved sprinkler system		

HEIGHT AND AREA TABLES

OCCUPANCY GROUP R-4: RESIDENTIAL, ASSISTED LIVING

Sprinklers

A sprinkler system is required throughout buildings containing, in whole or in part, a Group R-4 Occupancy. Residential class (NFPA 13R) sprinkler systems are permitted as an option for the Group R-4 Occupancy areas. In this case, read from the columns labeled "Residential Spr" in the table on these two facing pages.

Fire Walls

For multiplication of the allowable area by subdividing the building with fire walls, see page 358.

Basements

Basements are not included in area calculations, provided that their area does not exceed the area permitted for a one-story building.

Excess Frontage

If more than 25% of the building perimeter fronts on a street or open space at least 20 ft (6.1 m) wide that is accessible to firefighting vehicles, the tabulated area limitations below may be increased according to the following table. For example, for a building with half of its perimeter accessible to firefighting equipment via a space not less than 24 ft (7.3 m) wide, the allowable area increase is:

0.80 increase × 25% excess frontage = 20% total area increase

OCCUPANCY GROUP R-4: RESIDENTIAL, ASSISTED LIVING

CONSTRUCTION TYPE	Noncombustible							
	3-Hour (page 364)		2-Hour (page 364)		1-Hour (page 365)		Unprotected (page 366)	
IBC NOMENCLATURE	Type I-A		Type I-B		Type II-A		Type II-B	
	Spr	[a]Residential Spr	Spr	[a]Residential Spr	Spr	[a]Residential Spr	Spr	[a]Residential Spr
MAXIMUM HEIGHT IN FEET	UH	60'	180'	60'	85'	60'	75'	55'
UH	UA							
12			UA					
11								
10								
9								
8								
7								
6								
5					216,000		144,000	
4		UA		UA	216,000	72,000	144,000	48,000
3					216,000	72,000	144,000	48,000
2					144,000	48,000	96,000	32,000
1					96,000	24,000	64,000	16,000
MAXIMUM AREA IN SQ FT FOR ANY SINGLE FLOOR OF A MULTISTORY BUILDING	UA	UA	UA	UA	72,000	24,000	48,000	16,000

HEIGHT IN STORIES ABOVE GRADE AND MAXIMUM AREA IN SQ FT ALL FLOORS

Each number in the table represents the maximum total area in square feet for all floors for a building of the indicated story height.

[a]Residential class sprinkler system NFPA 13R.

Width of Frontage[a]	Percent Area Increase for Each 1% of Frontage[a] in Excess of 25%
20' (6.1 m)	0.67
22' (6.7 m)	0.70
24' (7.3 m)	0.80
26' (7.9 m)	0.87
28' (8.5 m)	0.93
30' (9.1 m) or wider	1.00

*Intermediate values may be interpolated.

Measurements

Height is measured from the average finished ground level adjoining the building to the average level of the highest roof. Floor area is measured within exterior walls or exterior walls and fire walls, exclusive of vent shafts and courtyards.

Further Information

For information on Occupancy Group classifications, see page 7. For information on mixed-use buildings, see page 352. For information on which code to consult, see pages 7, 13.

Unit Conversions

1 ft = 304.8 mm, 1 sq ft = 0.0929 m^2.

Combustible											
Ordinary				Mill (page 366)		Wood Light Frame					
1-Hour (page 368)		Unprotected (page 368)				1-Hour (page 368)		Unprotected (page 368)			CONSTRUCTION TYPE
Type III-A		Type III-B		Type IV-HT		Type V-A		Type V-B			IBC NOMENCLATURE
Spr	[a]Residential Spr	Spr	[a]Residential Spr	Spr	[a]Residential Spr	Spr	[a]Residential Spr	Spr	[a]Residential Spr		
85'	60'	75'	55'	85'	60'	70'	50'	60'	40'		MAXIMUM HEIGHT IN FEET
										UH	
										12	
										11	
										10	
										9	
										8	HEIGHT IN STORIES ABOVE GRADE AND MAXIMUM AREA IN SQ FT ALL FLOORS
										7	
										6	
216,000		144,000		184,500						5	
216,000	72,000	144,000	48,000	184,500	61,500	108,000	36,000			4	
216,000	72,000	144,000	48,000	184,500	61,500	108,000	36,000	63,000	21,000	3	
144,000	48,000	96,000	32,000	123,000	41,000	72,000	24,000	42,000	14,000	2	
96,000	24,000	64,000	16,000	82,000	20,500	48,000	12,000	28,000	7,000	1	MAXIMUM AREA IN SQ FT FOR ANY SINGLE FLOOR OF A MULTISTORY BUILDING
72,000	24,000	48,000	16,000	61,500	20,500	36,000	12,000	21,000	7,000		

This table was compiled from information contained in the International Building Code 2006. It does not represent an official interpretation by the organization that issues this code.

Key to Abbreviations

UA	Unlimited area	Spr	With approved sprinkler system	NP	Not permitted
UH	Unlimited height	Unspr	Without approved sprinkler system		

HEIGHT AND AREA TABLES

417

OCCUPANCY GROUP S-1: STORAGE, MODERATE HAZARD

Sprinklers

In addition to the requirements indicated in the table on these two facing pages, a sprinkler system is required throughout buildings containing, in whole or in part, a Group S-1 Occupancy meeting any of the following conditions:

■ Any single S-1 Occupancy fire area exceeds 12,000 sq ft (1115 m²) or the area of all S-1 fire areas combined exceeds 24,000 sq ft (2230 m²).

■ An S-1 fire area is located more than three stories above grade.

For an explanation of fire areas, see page 358. A sprinkler system is also required throughout buildings containing motor vehicle repair garages meeting any of the following conditions:

■ Buildings two or more stories in height, including basement levels, where the vehicle repair floor or fire area exceeds 10,000 sq ft (929 m²)

■ One-story buildings with a floor or fire area exceeding 12,000 sq ft (1115 m²)

■ Buildings including basement storage for serviced vehicles

A sprinkler system is required for any stories or basements exceeding 1500 sq ft (139 m²) in area without openings to the exterior, in underground portions of most buildings with occupancy more than 30 ft (9 m) below the lowest level of exit discharge, and throughout any building containing floors 55 ft (17 m) or more above grade with an occupant load of 30 or more.

Unlimited Area Buildings

One- and two-story Occupancy S-1 buildings, fully sprinklered, may be of unlimited area when surrounded on all sides by public ways or yards not less than 60 ft (18 m) in width. In such one-story buildings, Group A-1 and A-2 Occupancies are permitted, so long as these occupancies are treated as mixed-use Separated Occupancies, such areas each comply with their own code height and area limits, and all required exits from these areas discharge directly to the exterior. Some Group H-2, H-3, and H-4 Occupancies may also be permitted. In some circumstances, reductions in the required width of open space around the building are

OCCUPANCY GROUP S-1: STORAGE, MODERATE HAZARD

		Noncombustible						
CONSTRUCTION TYPE		3-Hour (page 364)		2-Hour (page 364)		1-Hour (page 365)		Unprotected (page 366)	
IBC NOMENCLATURE		Type I-A		Type I-B		Type II-A		Type II-B	
		Spr	Unspr	Spr	Unspr	Spr	Unspr	Spr	Unspr
MAXIMUM HEIGHT IN FEET		UH	75'	180'	160'	85'	65'	75'	55'
HEIGHT IN STORIES ABOVE GRADE AND MAXIMUM AREA IN SQ FT ALL FLOORS	UH	UA							
	12			432,000					
	11			432,000					
	10			432,000					
	9			432,000					
	8			432,000					
	7			432,000					
	6			432,000					
	5			432,000		234,000			
	4			432,000		234,000		157,500	
	3		24,000	432,000	24,000	234,000	24,000	157,500	24,000
	2		24,000	288,000	24,000	156,000	24,000	105,000	24,000
	1		24,000	192,000	24,000	104,000	24,000	70,000	17,500
MAXIMUM AREA IN SQ FT FOR ANY SINGLE FLOOR OF A MULTISTORY BUILDING		UA	UA	144,000	48,000	78,000	26,000	52,500	17,500

Each number in the table represents the maximum total area in square feet for all floors for a building of the indicated story height.

Key to Abbreviations

UA	Unlimited area	Spr	With approved sprinkler system	NP	Not permitted
UH	Unlimited height	Unspr	Without approved sprinkler system		

permitted. Certain types of non-public unlimited area rack storage facilities may be of unlimited height. See the code for details.

Fire Walls

For multiplication of the allowable area by subdividing the building with fire walls, see page 358.

Basements

A single-story basement is not included in area calculations, provided that the basement area does not exceed the area permitted for a one-story building.

Excess Frontage

If more than 25% of the building perimeter fronts on a street or open space at least 20 ft (6.1 m) wide that is accessible to firefighting vehicles, the tabulated area limitations below may be increased according to the following table. For example, for a building with half of its perimeter accessible to firefighting equipment via a space not less than 24 ft (7.3 m) wide, the allowable area increase is:

0.80 increase × 25% excess frontage = 20% total area increase

Width of Frontage[a]	Percent Area Increase for Each 1% of Frontage* in Excess of 25%
20' (6.1 m)	0.67
22' (6.7 m)	0.73
24' (7.3 m)	0.80
26' (7.9 m)	0.87
28' (8.5 m)	0.93
30' (9.1 m) or wider	1.00

[a]Intermediate values may be interpolated.

Measurements

Height is measured from the average finished ground level adjoining the building to the average level of the highest roof. Floor area is measured within exterior walls or exterior walls and fire walls, exclusive of shafts and courtyards.

Further Information

For information on Occupancy Group classifications, see page 7. For information on mixed-use buildings, see page 352. For information on which code to consult, see pages 7, 13.

Unit Conversions

1 ft = 304.8 mm, 1 sq ft = 0.0929 m².

	Combustible										
	Ordinary				Mill		Wood Light Frame				
	1-Hour (page 368)		Unprotected (page 368)		(page 366)		1-Hour (page 368)		Unprotected (page 368)		
	Type III-A		Type III-B		Type IV-HT		Type V-A		Type V-B		
	Spr	Unspr	Spr	Unspr	Spr	Unspr	Spr	Unspr	Spr	Unspr	
	85'	65'	75'	55'	85'	65'	70'	50'	60'	40'	
UH											
12											
11											
10											
9											
8											
7											
6											
5					229,500						
4	234,000		157,500		229,500		126,000				
3	234,000	24,000	157,500	24,000	229,500	24,000	126,000	24,000			
2	156,000	24,000	105,000	24,000	153,000	24,000	84,000	24,000	54,000		
1	104,000	24,000	70,000	17,500	102,000	24,000	56,000	14,000	36,000	9,000	
	78,000	26,000	52,500	17,500	76,500	25,500	42,000	14,000	27,000		

CONSTRUCTION TYPE

IBC NOMENCLATURE

MAXIMUM HEIGHT IN FEET

HEIGHT IN STORIES ABOVE GRADE AND MAXIMUM AREA IN SQ FT ALL FLOORS

MAXIMUM AREA IN SQ FT FOR ANY SINGLE FLOOR OF A MULTISTORY BUILDING

HEIGHT AND AREA TABLES

419

This table was compiled from information contained in the International Building Code 2006. It does not represent an official interpretation by the organization that issues this code.

OCCUPANCY GROUP S-2: STORAGE, LOW-HAZARD

Sprinklers

In addition to the requirements indicated in the table on these two facing pages, a sprinkler system is required throughout buildings containing enclosed parking (except when located below Group R-3 Occupancies) or containing storage of commercial trucks or buses with a fire area exceeding 5000 sq ft (464 m²). For an explanation of fire areas, see page 358. A sprinkler system is required for any stories or basements exceeding 1500 sq ft (139 m²) in area without openings to the exterior, in underground portions of most buildings with occupancy more than 30 ft (9 m) below the lowest level of exit discharge, and throughout any

building containing floors 55 ft (17 m) or more above grade with an occupant load of 30 or more.

Vehicle Parking Garages

For enclosed parking garages, which rely on mechanical ventilation to prevent the accumulation of exhaust gasses, and for naturally ventilated open parking garages when combined with other occupancies, use the height and area table on these two facing pages. For buildings containing solely open parking, see Occupancy S-2: Open Parking, on pages 422–423. For private garages and carports, see Occupancy Group U: Utility, on pages 424–425. For information on height and area requirements for parking garages part of mixed-use occupancies, see pages 354–355.

The minimum clear height within parking garage tiers is 7 ft (2.1 m). For more information on the design of parking facilities, see Design for Parking, beginning on page 311.

Unlimited Area Buildings

An Occupancy S-2 building, one story tall, with or without sprinklers, or two stories tall and fully sprinklered, may be of unlimited area, provided that it is surrounded on all sides by public ways or yards at least 60 ft (18.3 m) in width. In such one-story buildings, sprinklered, Group A-1 and A-2 Occupancies are permitted, so long as these occupancies are treated as mixed-use Separated Occupancies, such areas each comply with their own code height and area limits, and all required exits from these areas discharge directly to the exterior. Some Group H-2, H-3, and H-4 Occupan-

OCCUPANCY GROUP S-2: STORAGE, LOW-HAZARD

		Noncombustible						
CONSTRUCTION TYPE		3-Hour (page 364)		2-Hour (page 364)		1-Hour (page 365)		Unprotected (page 366)	
IBC NOMENCLATURE		Type I-A		Type I-B		Type II-A		Type II-B	
		Spr	Unspr	Spr	Unspr	Spr	Unspr	Spr	Unspr
MAXIMUM HEIGHT IN FEET		UH	75'	180'	160'	85'	65'	75'	55'
	UH	UA	UA						
	12			711,000					
	11			711,000	237,000				
	10			711,000	237,000				
	9			711,000	237,000				
HEIGHT IN STORIES ABOVE GRADE AND MAXIMUM AREA IN SQ FT ALL FLOORS	8			711,000	237,000				
	7			711,000	237,000				
	6			711,000	237,000	351,000			
	5			711,000	237,000	351,000	117,000	234,000	
	4			711,000	237,000	351,000	117,000	234,000	78,000
	3			711,000	237,000	351,000	117,000	234,000	78,000
	2			474,000	158,000	234,000	78,000	156,000	52,000
	1			316,000	79,000	156,000	39,000	104,000	26,000
MAXIMUM AREA IN SQ FT FOR ANY SINGLE FLOOR OF A MULTISTORY BUILDING		UA	UA	237,000	79,000	117,000	39,000	78,000	26,000

Each number in the table represents the maximum total area in square feet for all floors for a building of the indicated story height.

Key to Abbreviations

UA	Unlimited area	Spr	With approved sprinkler system	NP	Not permitted
UH	Unlimited height	Unspr	Without approved sprinkler system		

cies may also be permitted. In some circumstances, reductions in the required width of open space around the building may be permitted. Certain types of nonpublic unlimited area rack storage facilities may be of unlimited height. See the code for details.

Fire Walls

For multiplication of the allowable area by subdividing the building with fire walls, see page 358.

Basements

Basements are not included in area calculations, provided that their area does not exceed the area permitted for a one-story building.

Excess Frontage

If more than 25% of the building perimeter fronts on a street or open space at least 20 ft (6.1 m) wide that is accessible to firefighting vehicles, the tabulated area limitations below may be increased according to the following table. For example, for a building with half of its perimeter accessible to firefighting equipment via a space not less than 24 ft (7.3 m) wide, the allowable area increase is:

0.80 increase × 25% excess frontage = 20% total area increase.

Measurements

Height is measured from the average finished ground level adjoining the building to the average level of the highest roof. Floor area is measured within exterior walls or exterior walls and fire walls, exclusive of courtyards.

Width of Frontage[a]	Percent Area Increase for Each 1% of Frontage[a] in Excess of 25%
20' (6.1 m)	0.67
22' (6.7 m)	0.73
24' (7.3 m)	0.80
26' (7.9 m)	0.87
28' (8.5 m)	0.93
30' (9.1 m) or wider	1.00

[a]Intermediate values may be interpolated.

Further Information

For information on Occupancy Group classifications, see page 7. For information on mixed-use buildings, see page 352. For information on which code to consult, see pages 7, 13.

Unit Conversions

1 ft = 304.8 mm, 1 sq ft = 0.0929 m².

	Combustible											
	Ordinary						Wood Light Frame					
	1-Hour (page 368)		Unprotected (page 368)		Mill (page 366)		1-Hour (page 368)		Unprotected (page 368)			CONSTRUCTION TYPE
	Type III-A		Type III-B		Type IV-HT		Type V-A		Type V-B			IBC NOMENCLATURE
	Spr	Unspr	Spr	Unspr	Spr	Unspr	Spr	Unspr	Spr	Unspr		
	85'	65'	75'	55'	85'	65'	70'	50'	60'	40'		MAXIMUM HEIGHT IN FEET
UH												
12												
11												
10												
9												
8												HEIGHT IN STORIES ABOVE GRADE AND MAXIMUM AREA IN SQ FT ALL FLOORS
7												
6					346,500							
5	351,000		234,000		346,500	115,500	189,000					
4	351,000	117,000	234,000	78,000	346,500	115,500	189,000	63,000				
3	351,000	117,000	234,000	78,000	346,500	115,500	189,000	63,000	121,500			
2	234,000	78,000	156,000	52,000	231,000	77,000	126,000	42,000	81,000	27,000		
1	156,000	39,000	104,000	26,000	154,000	38,500	84,000	21,000	54,000	13,500		
	117,000	39,000	78,000	26,000	115,500	38,500	63,000	21,000	40,500	13,500		MAXIMUM AREA IN SQ FT FOR ANY SINGLE FLOOR OF A MULTISTORY BUILDING

HEIGHT AND AREA TABLES

421

This table was compiled from information contained in the International Building Code 2006. It does not represent an official interpretation by the organization that issues this code.

OCCUPANCY GROUP S-2: OPEN PARKING GARAGES

Use the information on these two facing pages for structures containing only single-use, open parking garages. To qualify, two or more sides of the structure must be substantially open to the passage of air, the garage must be used for the parking or storage of private motor vehicles only, excluding commercial trucks and buses, and mixed occupancies are not permitted, except that no more than 1000 sq ft (93 m²) of office space, toilet facilities, and waiting area may be included on the ground level. For all other parking structures, see

Occupancy S-2: Storage, Low-Hazard, pages 420–421. For private garages and carports, see Occupancy Group U: Utility, pages 424–425.

Special Requirements

The minimum vertical clear height within parking garage tiers is 7 ft (2.1 m). Rooftops may be used as parking. Minimum requirements for open area in exterior and interior walls of an open parking garage can be found on page 329.

Garages open on three sides are permitted to increase the tabulated limits on these two facing pages by 25% in area and one floor in height. Garages open on four

sides are permitted to increase the tabulated limits by 50% in area and one floor in height. For garages of the maximum tabulated area but less than the maximum allowable height, at least three sides must be open, no point on a parking tier may be located more than 200 ft (61 m) from an open wall, and standpipes for firefighting must be provided. Garages of Type II Noncombustible Construction may be of unlimited area if no higher than 75 ft (23 m), open on all four sides, and having no point on a parking tier more than 200 ft (61 m) from an open wall.

In some circumstances, the tabulated heights may be increased

OCCUPANCY GROUP S-2: OPEN PARKING GARAGES

	Noncombustible							
CONSTRUCTION TYPE	3-Hour (page 364)		2-Hour (page 364)		1-Hour (page 365)		Unprotected (page 366)	
IBC NOMENCLATURE	Type I-A		Type I-B		Type II-A		Type II-B	
	Spr	Unspr	Spr	Unspr	Spr	Unspr	Spr	Unspr
MAXIMUM HEIGHT IN FEET	UH	75	180'	160'	85'	65'	75'	55'
UH	UA	UA						
12			UA	UA				
11								
10					500,000	500,000		
9					500,000	500,000		
8					500,000	500,000	400,000	400,000
7					500,000	500,000	400,000	400,000
6					500,000	500,000	400,000	400,000
5					500,000	500,000	400,000	400,000
4					500,000	500,000	400,000	400,000
3					500,000	500,000	400,000	400,000
2					500,000	500,000	400,000	400,000
1					500,000	500,000	400,000	400,000
MAXIMUM AREA IN SQ FT FOR ANY SINGLE FLOOR OF A MULTISTORY BUILDING	UA	UA	UA	UA	500,000	500,000	400,000	400,000

Row labels at left of data: **HEIGHT IN STORIES ABOVE GRADE AND MAXIMUM AREA IN SQ FT ALL FLOORS**

Each number in the table represents the maximum total area in square feet for all floors for a building of the indicated story height.

Key to Abbreviations

UA	Unlimited area	Spr	With approved sprinkler system	NP	Not permitted
UH	Unlimited height	Unspr	Without approved sprinkler system		

for garages that are fully sprinklered, that use lifts or other mechanical devices to move vehicles to and from the street level, and that have limited public access; see the code for details.

For more information on the design of parking facilities, see Designing for Parking, beginning on page 311.

Fire Walls

For multiplication of the allowable area by subdividing the building with fire walls, see page 358.

Measurements

Height is measured from the average finished ground level adjoining the building to the average level of the highest roof. Floor area is measured within exterior walls or exterior walls and fire walls, exclusive of courtyards.

Further Information

For information on Occupancy Group classifications, see page 7. For information on mixed-use buildings, see page 352. For information on which code to consult, see pages 7, 13.

Unit Conversions

1 ft = 304.8 mm, 1 sq ft = 0.0929 m^2.

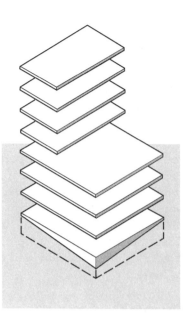

Combustible											
Ordinary				Mill (page 366)		Wood Light Frame					
1-Hour (page 368)		Unprotected (page 368)				1-Hour (page 368)		Unprotected (page 368)		CONSTRUCTION TYPE	
Type III-A		Type III-B		Type IV-HT		Type V-A		Type V-B		IBC NOMENCLATURE	
Spr	Unspr	Spr	Unspr	Spr	Unspr	Spr	Unspr	Spr	Unspr		
				85'	65'					MAXIMUM HEIGHT IN FEET	
										UH	
										12	
										11	
										10	
										9	
										8	HEIGHT IN STORIES ABOVE GRADE AND MAXIMUM AREA IN SQ FT ALL FLOORS
										7	
										6	
										5	
				200,000	200,000					4	
				200,000	200,000					3	
				200,000	200,000					2	
NP	NP	NP	NP	200,000	200,000	NP	NP	NP	NP	1	MAXIMUM AREA IN SQ FT FOR ANY SINGLE FLOOR OF A MULTISTORY BUILDING
				200,000	200,000						

HEIGHT AND AREA TABLES

This table was compiled from information contained in the International Building Code 2006. It does not represent an official interpretation by the organization that issues this code.

OCCUPANCY GROUP U: UTILITY

Sprinklers

In addition to the requirements indicated in the table on these two facing pages, a sprinkler system is required for underground portions of most buildings with occupancy more than 30 ft (9 m) below the lowest level of exit discharge and throughout any building containing floors 55 ft (17 m) or more above grade with an occupant load of 30 or more.

Private Garages and Carports

Private garages attached to residences must be separated from adjacent living areas by construction protected with at least ½-in. (12.5-mm) gypsum wallboard, or where living space is located above the garage, with construction protected with at least ⅝-inch (16-mm) Type X (fire-rated) gypsum wallboard. Doors separating living space from private garages must be self-closing, self-latching, and not less than 1⅜-in. (35 mm) thick, made of solid wood or hollow metal, or may be of other types with at least a 20-minute fire rating. Windows, doors, or other openings between garages and sleeping areas are not permitted. Carports open on at least two sides are not subject to these separation requirements, except that where living space is located above the carport, the floor/ceiling construction must be protected with at least ⅝-in. (16-mm) Type X gypsum wallboard.

The floor surface of all private garages and carports must be noncombustible.

When regulated by the International Residential Code, there are no area limitations on private garages or carports (see page 414 for the building types that apply). When regulated by the International Building Code, Occupancy Group U private garages and carports are limited to 1000 sq ft (93 m²) in area and one story in height. When used for vehicle storage only, excluding vehicle repair or dispensing of fuel, they may be up to 3000 sq ft (279 m²) in area when the exterior walls are constructed to meet the fire-resistance requirements for the building's primary occupancy. Private garages within mixed-use buildings are considered accessory to the main use, and

OCCUPANCY GROUP U: UTILITY

CONSTRUCTION TYPE	Noncombustible							
	3-Hour (page 364)		2-Hour (page 364)		1-Hour (page 365)		Unprotected (page 366)	
IBC NOMENCLATURE	Type I-A		Type I-B		Type II-A		Type II-B	
	Spr	Unspr	Spr	Unspr	Spr	Unspr	Spr	Unspr
MAXIMUM HEIGHT IN FEET	UH	75'	180'	160'	85'	65'	75'	55'
UH	UA	UA						
12								
11								
10								
9								
8								
7								
6			319,500					
5			319,500	106,500	171,000			
4			319,500	106,500	171,000	57,000		
3			319,500	106,500	171,000	57,000	76,500	
2			213,000	71,000	114,000	38,000	51,000	17,000
1			142,000	35,500	76,000	19,000	34,000	8,500
MAXIMUM AREA IN SQ FT FOR ANY SINGLE FLOOR OF A MULTISTORY BUILDING	UA	UA	106,500	35,500	57,000	19,000	25,500	8,500

HEIGHT IN STORIES ABOVE GRADE AND MAXIMUM AREA IN SQ FT ALL FLOORS

Each number in the table represents the maximum total area in square feet for all floors for a building of the indicated story height.

Key to Abbreviations

UA	Unlimited area	Spr	With approved sprinkler system	NP	Not permitted
UH	Unlimited height	Unspr	Without approved sprinkler system		

height and area limitations for building should be determined according to the requirements of the major occupancy.

Private garages exceeding Occupancy Group U area limitations must be classified as Occupancy Group S-2, or, 1-hour rated walls may be used to divide the garage area into multiple separated garages complying with Group U limits.

Fire Walls

For multiplication of the allowable area by subdividing the building with fire walls, see page 358.

Basements

Basements are not included in area calculations, provided that their area does not exceed the area permitted for a one-story building.

Excess Frontage

If more than 25% of the building perimeter fronts on a street or open space at least 20 ft (6.1 m) wide that is accessible to firefighting vehicles, the tabulated area limitations below may be increased according to the adjacent table. For example, for a building with half of its perimeter accessible to firefighting equipment via a space not less than 24 ft (7.3 m) wide, the allowable area increase is:

0.80 increase × 25% excess frontage = 20% total area increase

Measurements

Height is measured from the average finished ground level adjoining the building to the average level of the highest roof. Floor area is measured within exterior walls or exterior walls and fire walls, exclusive of vent shafts and courtyards.

Width of Frontage[a]	Percent Area Increase for Each 1% of Frontage[a] in Excess of 25%
20' (6.1 m)	0.67
22' (6.7 m)	0.73
24' (7.3 m)	0.80
26' (7.9 m)	0.87
28' (8.5 m)	0.93
30' (9.1 m) or wider	1.00

[a]Intermediate values may be interpolated.

Further Information

For information on Occupancy Group classifications, see page 7. For information on mixed-use buildings, see page 352. For information on which code to consult, see pages 7, 13.

Unit Conversions

1 ft = 304.8 mm, 1 sq ft = 0.0929 m²

Combustible											
Ordinary						Wood Light Frame					CONSTRUCTION TYPE
1-Hour (page 368)		Unprotected (page 368)		Mill (page 366)		1-Hour (page 368)		Unprotected (page 368)			IBC NOMENCLATURE
Type III-A		Type III-B		Type IV-HT		Type V-A		Type V-B			
Spr	Unspr	Spr	Unspr	Spr	Unspr	Spr	Unspr	Spr	Unspr		
85'	65'	75'	55'	85'	65'	70'	50'	60'	40'		MAXIMUM HEIGHT IN FEET
										UH	
										12	
										11	
										10	
										9	
										8	HEIGHT IN STORIES ABOVE GRADE AND MAXIMUM AREA IN SQ FT ALL FLOORS
										7	
										6	
				162,000						5	
126,000				162,000	54,000					4	
126,000	42,000	76,500		162,000	54,000	81,000				3	
84,000	28,000	51,000	17,000	108,000	36,000	54,000	18,000	33,000		2	
56,000	14,000	34,000	8,500	72,000	18,000	36,000	9,000	22,000	5,500	1	MAXIMUM AREA IN SQ FT FOR ANY SINGLE FLOOR OF A MULTISTORY BUILDING
42,000	14,000	25,500	8,500	54,000	18,000	27,000	9,000	16,500			

This table was compiled from information contained in the International Building Code 2006. It does not represent an official interpretation by the organization that issues this code.

HEIGHT AND AREA TABLES

425

HOW TO USE THE TABLES OF HEIGHT AND AREA LIMITATIONS FOR THE NATIONAL BUILDING CODE OF CANADA

1. Be sure you are consulting the tables for the proper building code. If you are not sure which code you are working under, see pages 7, 13.

2. The Occupancy Group is given at the upper left-hand corner of the table. If you are not sure about the Occupancy Group into which your building falls, consult the indexes on pages 7–15.

3. Noncombustible Construction Types are tabulated on the left-hand page, and Combustible Construction Types are tabulated on the right-hand page.

4. Each pair of columns represents one Construction Type. For specific information on the different materials and modes of construction that conform to that Construction Type, follow the page reference given here.

5. The paired columns tabulate height and area information for both sprinklered and unsprinklered buildings of each Construction Type.

6. The significance of the floor area numbers in the chart, which varies from one model code to another, is explained at the lower left-hand corner.

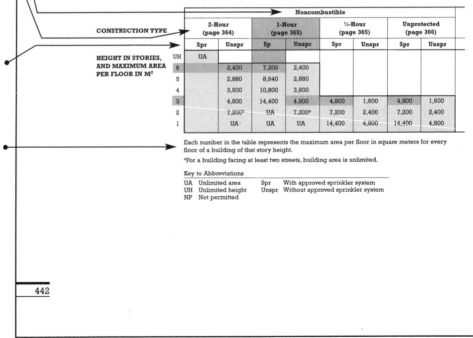

NATIONAL BUILDING CODE OF CANADA

OCCUPANCY GROUP D: BUSINESS AND PERSONAL USES

Basements
Basements must be fully sprinklered or subdivided by fire separations into areas not more than 600 m² (6460 sq ft). A fire separation is also required between a basement and the floor above, and if there is more than one story below grade, between every below-grade story.

Excess Frontage
For unsprinklered buildings, except as noted in the table, the tabulated areas shown below may be increased by 25% if the building faces at least two streets, and by 50% if facing at least three.

Fire Walls
For multiplication of the allowable area by subdividing the building with fire walls, see page 358.

Measurements
Area is measured as the greatest horizontal area of a building above grade within the outside surfaces of the exterior walls, or between the outside surfaces of the exterior walls and the center line of a fire wall.

Further Information
For information on Occupancy Group classifications, see page 15. For information on mixed-use buildings, see page 355. Formation on which code to consult, see pages 7, 13.

Unit Conversion
1 m² = 10.76 sq ft.

OCCUPANCY GROUP D: BUSINESS AND PERSONAL SERVICES

CONSTRUCTION TYPE		Noncombustible							
		2-Hour (page 364)		1-Hour (page 365)		¾-Hour (page 365)		Unprotected (page 366)	
		Spr	Unspr	Sp	Unspr	Spr	Unspr	Spr	Unspr
HEIGHT IN STORIES, AND MAXIMUM AREA PER FLOOR IN M²	UH	UA							
	6		2,400	7,200	2,400				
	5		2,880	8,640	2,880				
	4		3,600	10,800	3,600				
	3		4,800	14,400	4,800	4,800	1,600	4,800	1,600
	2		7,200ᵃ	UA	7,200ᵃ	7,200	2,400	7,200	2,400
	1		UA	UA	UA	14,400	4,800	14,400	4,800

Each number in the table represents the maximum area per floor in square meters for every floor of a building of that story height.

ᵃFor a building facing at least two streets, building area is unlimited.

Key to Abbreviations
UA	Unlimited area	Spr	With approved sprinkler system
UH	Unlimited height	Unspr	Without approved sprinkler system
NP	Not permitted		

442

7. As an example of the use of this chart, a sprinklered building of Occupancy Group D, 1-Hour Noncombustible Construction, under the National Building Code of Canada, may be no more than six stories tall, with no floor larger in area than 7200 m².

8. As another example, if we wish to construct a three-story unsprinklered building with 3150 m² per floor, we must use 1-Hour Noncombustible Construction as a minimum. Looking to the right along the same row of the chart, we see that the addition of sprinklers would allow us to use ¾-Hour or Unprotected Noncombustible Construction, Heavy Timber Construction, or 1 or ¾-Hour Combustible Construction. By following the page references at the heads of these columns, we can determine exactly what each of these Construction Types is, and proceed to preliminary configuration and sizing of the structural system we select.

NATIONAL BUILDING CODE OF CANADA

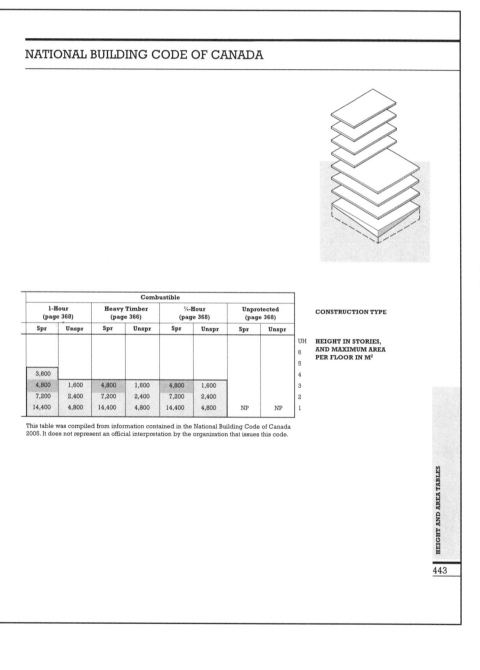

CONSTRUCTION TYPE

Combustible									HEIGHT IN STORIES, AND MAXIMUM AREA PER FLOOR IN M²
1-Hour (page 368)		Heavy Timber (page 366)		¾-Hour (page 368)		Unprotected (page 368)			
Spr	Unspr	Spr	Unspr	Spr	Unspr	Spr	Unspr		
								UH	
								6	
								5	
3,600								4	
4,800	1,600	4,800	1,600	4,800	1,600			3	
7,200	2,400	7,200	2,400	7,200	2,400			2	
14,400	4,800	14,400	4,800	14,400	4,800	NP	NP	1	

This table was compiled from information contained in the National Building Code of Canada 2005. It does not represent an official interpretation by the organization that issues this code.

The reference tables appearing on pages 428–453 are for preliminary purposes only. They represent the authors' interpretation of certain major provisions of the National Building Code of Canada. No official interpretation has been sought from or granted by the National Research Council of Canada. For design development work and final preparation of building plans, you must consult the building codes and regulations in effect in your project's locale.

HEIGHT AND AREA TABLES

HEIGHT AND AREA TABLES

OCCUPANCY GROUP A-1: ASSEMBLY, THEATERS

Unlimited Area Buildings

Group A-1 Occupancy one-story buildings, fully sprinklered, with an auditorium occupant load not greater than 300 may be of unlimited area when of any Noncombustible Construction Type, Heavy Timber Construction, or at least ¾-Hour Combustible Construction.

Basements

Basements must be fully sprinklered or subdivided by fire-separations into areas of not more than 600 m² (6460 sq ft). A fire separation is also required between a basement and the floor above, and if there is more than one story below grade, between every below-grade story.

Fire Walls

For multiplication of the allowable area by subdividing the building with fire walls, see page 358.

Measurements

Area is measured as the greatest horizontal area of a building above grade within the outside surfaces of the exterior walls, or between the outside surfaces of the exterior walls and the center line of a fire wall.

Further Information

For information on Occupancy Group classifications, see page 15. For information on mixed-use buildings, see page 355. For information on which code to consult, see pages 7, 13.

Unit Conversion

1 m² = 10.76 sq ft.

OCCUPANCY GROUP A-1: ASSEMBLY, THEATERS

CONSTRUCTION TYPE		Noncombustible							
		2-Hour (page 364)		1-Hour (page 365)		¾-Hour (page 365)		Unprotected (page 366)	
		Spr	Unspr	Spr	Unspr	Spr	Unspr	Spr	Unspr
HEIGHT IN STORIES, AND MAXIMUM AREA PER FLOOR IN M²	UH	UA							
	6								
	5								
	4								
	3								
	2			600ª		600ª			
	1		NP	600ª	NP	600ª	NP	NP	NP

Each number in the table represents the maximum area per floor in square meters for every floor of a building of the indicated story height.

ªBuilding occupant load may not exceed 600. In two-story buildings, the area of the second story may not exceed 40% of the area of the first story and the second story may contain only nonpublic uses.

Key to Abbreviations

UA	Unlimited area	Spr	With approved sprinkler system
UH	Unlimited height	Unspr	Without approved sprinkler system
NP	Not permitted		

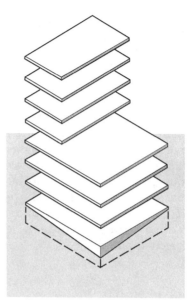

Combustible								
1-Hour (page 368)		Heavy Timber (page 366)		¾-Hour (page 368)		Unprotected (page 368)		CONSTRUCTION TYPE
Spr	Unspr	Spr	Unspr	Spr	Unspr	Spr	Unspr	
								UH
								6
								5
								4
								3
		600ᵃ						2
NP	NP	600ᵃ	NP	NP	NP	NP	NP	1

CONSTRUCTION TYPE

UH · **HEIGHT IN STORIES, AND MAXIMUM AREA PER FLOOR IN M²**
6
5
4
3
2
1

This table was compiled from information contained in the National Building Code of Canada 2005. It does not represent an official interpretation by the organization that issues this code.

OCCUPANCY GROUP A-2: ASSEMBLY, MISCELLANEOUS

Basements

Basements must be fully sprinklered or subdivided by fire separations into areas of not more than 600 m² (6460 sq ft). A fire separation is also required between a basement and the floor above, and if there is more than one story below grade, between every below-grade story.

Excess Frontage

For unsprinklered buildings, the tabulated areas shown below may be increased by 25% if the building faces at least two streets, and by 50% if facing at least three.

Fire Walls

For multiplication of the allowable area by subdividing the building with fire walls, see page 358.

Measurements

Area is measured as the greatest horizontal area of a building above grade within the outside surfaces of the exterior walls, or between the outside surfaces of the exterior walls and the center line of a fire wall.

Further Information

For information on Occupancy Group classifications, see page 15. For information on mixed-use buildings, see page 355. For information on which code to consult, see pages 7, 13.

Unit Conversion

1 m² = 10.76 sq ft.

OCCUPANCY GROUP A-2: ASSEMBLY, MISCELLANEOUS

CONSTRUCTION TYPE		Noncombustible							
		2-Hour (page 364)		1-Hour (page 365)		¾-Hour (page 365)		Unprotected (page 366)	
		Spr	Unspr	Spr	Unspr	Spr	Unspr	Spr	Unspr
HEIGHT IN STORIES, AND MAXIMUM AREA PER FLOOR IN M²	UH	UA							
	6			UA					
	5								
	4								
	3								
	2		800		800	2,400	800	2,400	800
	1		1,600		1,600	4,800	1,600	4,800	1,600

Each number in the table represents the maximum area per floor in square meters for every floor of a building of that story height.

ªOne-story buildings with no basement may be 2400 m² in area.

Key to Abbreviations

UA	Unlimited area	Spr	With approved sprinkler system
UH	Unlimited height	Unspr	Without approved sprinkler system
NP	Not permitted		

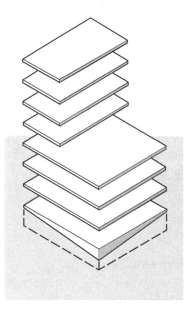

Combustible								CONSTRUCTION TYPE
1-Hour (page 368)		Heavy Timber (page 366)		¾-Hour (page 368)		Unprotected (page 368)		
Spr	Unspr	Spr	Unspr	Spr	Unspr	Spr	Unspr	
								UH HEIGHT IN STORIES, AND MAXIMUM AREA PER FLOOR IN M²
								6
								5
								4
								3
2,400	800	2,400	800	2,400	800	600		2
4,800	1,600	4,800	1,600	4,800	1,600	ª1200	400	1

This table was compiled from information contained in the National Building Code of Canada 2005. It does not represent an official interpretation by the organization that issues this code.

OCCUPANCY GROUP A-3: ASSEMBLY, ARENAS

Basements

Basements must be fully sprinklered or subdivided by fire separations into areas of not more than 600 m² (6460 sq ft). A fire separation is also required between a basement and the floor above, and if there is more than one story below grade, between every below-grade story.

Excess Frontage

For unsprinklered buildings, the tabulated areas shown below may be increased by 25% if the building faces at least two streets, and by 50% if facing at least three.

Fire Walls

For multiplication of the allowable area by subdividing the building with fire walls, see page 358.

Measurements

Area is measured as the greatest horizontal area of a building above grade within the outside surfaces of the exterior walls, or between the outside surfaces of the exterior walls and the center line of a fire wall.

Further Information

For information on Occupancy Group classifications, see page 15. For information on mixed-use buildings, see page 355. For information on which code to consult, see pages 7, 13.

Unit Conversion

1 m² = 10.76 sq ft.

OCCUPANCY GROUP A-3: ASSEMBLY, ARENAS

CONSTRUCTION TYPE		Noncombustible							
		2-Hour (page 364)		1-Hour (page 365)		¾-Hour (page 365)		Unprotected (page 366)	
		Spr	Unspr	Spr	Unspr	Spr	Unspr	Spr	Unspr
HEIGHT IN STORIES, AND MAXIMUM AREA PER FLOOR IN M²	UH	UA							
	6								
	5								
	4								
	3								
	2		2,000	6,000	2,000				
	1		4,000	12,000	4,000	7,200	2,400	7,200	2,400

Each number in the table represents the maximum area per floor in square meters for every floor of a building of the indicated story height.

Key to Abbreviations

UA	Unlimited area	Spr	With approved sprinkler system
UH	Unlimited height	Unspr	Without approved sprinkler system
NP	Not permitted		

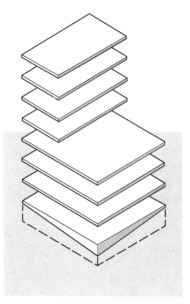

Combustible									
1-Hour (page 368)		Heavy Timber (page 366)		¾-Hour (page 368)		Unprotected (page 368)			
Spr	Unspr	Spr	Unspr	Spr	Unspr	Spr	Unspr		
								UH	
								6	
								5	
								4	
								3	
								2	
7,200	2,400	7,200	2,400	7,200	2,400	7,200	1,000	1	

CONSTRUCTION TYPE

HEIGHT IN STORIES, AND MAXIMUM AREA PER FLOOR IN M²

This table was compiled from information contained in the National Building Code of Canada 2005. It does not represent an official interpretation by the organization that issues this code.

OCCUPANCY GROUP A-4: ASSEMBLY, OPEN-AIR

Special Conditions

Group A-4 Occupancy buildings may have roof assemblies of Heavy Timber Construction. All occupied spaces below seating tiers must be sprinklered. Buildings of Combustible Construction are limited to less than 1500 occupants, and exposed building faces must be at least 6 m (20 ft) from adjacent property lines or buildings.

Basements

Basements must be fully sprinklered or subdivided by fire sepa-rations into areas of not more than 600 m^2 (6460 sq ft). A fire separation is also required between a basement and the floor above, and if there is more than one story below grade, between every below-grade story.

Fire Walls

For multiplication of the allowable area by subdividing the building with fire walls, see page 358.

Measurements

Area is measured as the greatest horizontal area of a building above grade within the outside surfaces of the exterior walls, or between the outside surfaces of the exterior walls and the center line of a fire wall.

Further Information

For information on Occupancy Group classifications, see page 15. For information on mixed-use buildings, see page 355. For information on which code to consult, see pages 7, 13.

Unit Conversion

1 m^2 = 10.76 sq ft.

OCCUPANCY GROUP A-4: ASSEMBLY, OPEN-AIR

CONSTRUCTION TYPE	Noncombustible							
	2-Hour (page 364)		1-Hour (page 365)		¾-Hour (page 365)		Unprotected (page 366)	
	Spr	Unspr	Spr	Unspr	Spr	Unspr	Spr	Unspr
HEIGHT IN STORIES, AND MAXIMUM AREA PER FLOOR IN M² — UH	UA		UA		UA		UA	
6								
5								
4								
3								
2								
1		NP		NP		NP		NP

Each number in the table represents the maximum area per floor in square meters for every floor of the indicated story height.

[a]Building occupant load may not exceed 1500. Exposed building faces must be at least 6m from adjacent property.

Key to Abbreviations

UA	Unlimited area	Spr	With approved sprinkler system
UH	Unlimited height	Unspr	Without approved sprinkler system
NP	Not permitted		

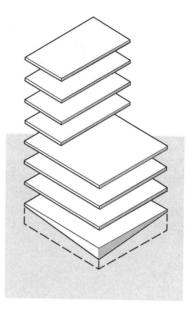

CONSTRUCTION TYPE

Combustible								
1-Hour (page 368)		Heavy Timber (page 366)		¾-Hour (page 368)		Unprotected (page 368)		
Spr	Unspr	Spr	Unspr	Spr	Unspr	Spr	Unspr	
UA[a]		UA[a]		UA[a]		UA[a]		UH
								6
								5
								4
								3
								2
	NP		NP		NP		NP	1

HEIGHT IN STORIES, AND MAXIMUM AREA PER FLOOR IN M²

This table was compiled from information contained in the National Building Code of Canada 2005. It does not represent an official interpretation by the organization that issues this code.

OCCUPANCY GROUP B-1: CARE OR DETENTION, RESTRAINED

Basements

Basements must be fully sprinklered or subdivided by fire separations into areas of not more than 600 m² (6460 sq ft). A fire separation is also required between a basement and the floor above, and if there is more than one story below grade, between every below-grade story.

Fire Walls

For multiplication of the allowable area by subdividing the building with fire walls, see page 358.

Measurements

Area is measured as the greatest horizontal area of a building above grade within the outside surfaces of the exterior walls, or between the outside surfaces of the exterior walls and the center line of a fire wall.

Further Information

For information on Occupancy Group classifications, see page 15. For information on mixed-use buildings, see page 355. For information on which code to consult, see pages 7, 13.

Unit Conversion

1 m² = 10.76 sq ft.

OCCUPANCY GROUP B-1: CARE OR DETENTION, RESTRAINED

CONSTRUCTION TYPE		Noncombustible							
		2-Hour (page 364)		1-Hour (page 365)		¾-Hour (page 365)		Unprotected (page 366)	
		Spr	Unspr	Spr	Unspr	Spr	Unspr	Spr	Unspr
HEIGHT IN STORIES, AND MAXIMUM AREA PER FLOOR IN M²	UH	UA							
	6								
	5								
	4								
	3			8,000					
	2			12,000					
	1		NP	UA	NP	NP	NP	NP	NP

Each number in the table represents the maximum area per floor in square meters for every floor of a building of that story height.

Key to Abbreviations

UA	Unlimited area	Spr	With approved sprinkler system
UH	Unlimited height	Unspr	Without approved sprinkler system
NP	Not permitted		

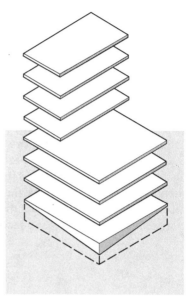

Combustible								
1-Hour (page 368)		Heavy Timber (page 366)		¾-Hour (page 368)		Unprotected (page 368)		
Spr	Unspr	Spr	Unspr	Spr	Unspr	Spr	Unspr	
								UH
								6
								5
								4
								3
								2
NP	NP	NP	NP	NP	NP	NP	NP	1

CONSTRUCTION TYPE

HEIGHT IN STORIES, AND MAXIMUM AREA PER FLOOR IN M²

This table was compiled from information contained in the National Building Code of Canada 2005. It does not represent an official interpretation by the organization that issues this code.

OCCUPANCY GROUP B-2: CARE OR DETENTION, UNRESTRAINED

Basements

Basements must be fully sprinklered or subdivided by fire separations into areas of not more than 600 m² (6460 sq ft). A fire separation is also required between a basement and floor above, and if there is more than one story below grade, between every below-grade story.

Fire Walls

For multiplication of the allowable area by subdividing the building with fire walls, see page 358.

Measurements

Area is measured as the greatest horizontal area of a building above grade within the outside surfaces of the exterior walls, or between the outside surfaces of the exterior walls and the center line of a fire wall.

Further Information

For information on Occupancy Group classifications, see page 15. For information on mixed-use buildings, see page 355. For information on which code to consult, see pages 7, 13.

Unit Conversion

1 m² = 10.76 sq ft.

OCCUPANCY GROUP B-2: CARE OR DETENTION, UNRESTRAINED

CONSTRUCTION TYPE	Noncombustible							
	2-Hour (page 364)		1-Hour (page 365)		¾-Hour (page 365)		Unprotected (page 366)	
	Spr	Unspr	Spr	Unspr	Spr	Unspr	Spr	Unspr
HEIGHT IN STORIES, AND MAXIMUM AREA PER FLOOR IN M² UH	UA							
6								
5								
4								
3			8,000					
2			12,000		1,600			
1		NP	UA	NP	2,400	NP	500	NP

Each number in the table represents the maximum area per floor in square meters for every floor of a building of that story height.

Key to Abbreviations

UA	Unlimited area	Spr	With approved sprinkler system
UH	Unlimited height	Unspr	Without approved sprinkler system
NP	Not permitted		

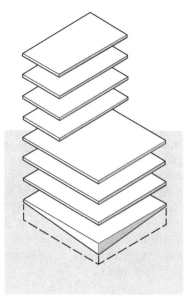

CONSTRUCTION TYPE

HEIGHT IN STORIES, AND MAXIMUM AREA PER FLOOR IN M²

Combustible									
1-Hour (page 368)		Heavy Timber (page 366)		¾-Hour (page 368)		Unprotected (page 368)			
Spr	Unspr	Spr	Unspr	Spr	Unspr	Spr	Unspr		
								UH	
								6	
								5	
								4	
								3	
1,600		1,600		1,600				2	
2,400	NP	2,400	NP	2,400	NP	500	NP	1	

This table was compiled from information contained in the National Building Code of Canada 2005. It does not represent an official interpretation by the organization that issues this code.

HEIGHT AND AREA TABLES

OCCUPANCY GROUP C: RESIDENTIAL

Basements

In residential occupancies that are not otherwise required to be sprinklered, basements containing only residential occupancies and providing at least one access door or window for each 15 m (49 ft) of wall in at least one wall facing a street are not required to be sprinklered. Other basements must be fully sprinklered, or subdivided by fire separations into areas of not more than 600 m² (6460 sq ft).

Dwelling Unit Construction Requirements

Within individual dwelling units with uppermost floors not more than 6 m (20 ft) above the ground floor level, fire-resistance rating requirements for floor assemblies may be reduced from the requirements tabulated in the table on these two facing pages as follows:

■ Dwelling unit floors in a building of 2-Hour Construction may be 1-Hour fire-resistance rated.

■ Dwelling unit floors in buildings of 2-Hour or 1-Hour Construction, where the building is fully sprinklered and not more than three stories in height, may be 45-minute fire-resistance rated.

A 1½-hour fire-resistance rated separation is required between dwelling units and private garages except as follows. No fire separation is required between a dwelling unit and a garage serving that dwelling unit only, provided that the construction and openings between the dwelling unit and the garage provide effective barriers to the passage of gas and exhaust fumes, and doors from the garage do not open into rooms intended for sleeping. A separation between dwelling units and a shared garage containing not more than five vehi-

OCCUPANCY GROUP C: RESIDENTIAL

CONSTRUCTION TYPE		Noncombustible							
		2-Hour (page 364)		1-Hour (page 365)		¾-Hour (page 365)		Unprotected (page 366)	
		Spr	Unspr	Spr	Unspr	Spr	Unspr	Spr	Unspr
HEIGHT IN STORIES, AND MAXIMUM AREA PER FLOOR IN M²	UH	UA							
	6			6,000					
	5			7,200					
	4			9,000					
	3		4,000	12,000	4,000	1,800	600	600[b]	600[b]
	2		6,000[a]	UA	6,000[a]	2,700	900	600[b]	600[b]
	1		UA	UA	UA	5,400	1,800	600[b]	600[b]

Each number in the table represents the maximum area per floor in square meters for every floor of a building of that story height.

[a]For a building facing at least two streets, building area is unlimited.

[b]Dwelling units only, when one unit does not occur above or below another unit or other occupancy. No area increases permitted for excess frontage.

Key to Abbreviations

UA	Unlimited area	Spr	With approved sprinkler system
UH	Unlimited height	Unspr	Without approved sprinkler system
NP	Not permitted		

cles may be unrated, provided that the requirements in the previous sentence are met, and, additionally, the dwelling units and garage are sprinklered.

For fire separation requirements between dwelling units, and between dwelling units and other occupancies, see pages 362–363.

Excess Frontage

For unsprinklered buildings, except as noted in the table, the tabulated areas shown below may be increased by 25% if the building faces at least two streets, and by 50% if facing at least three.

Fire Walls

For multiplication of the allowable area by subdividing the building with fire walls, see page 358.

Measurements

Area is measured as the greatest horizontal area of a building above grade within the outside surfaces of the exterior walls, or between the outside surfaces of the exterior walls and the center line of a fire wall.

Further Information

For information on Occupancy Group classifications, see page 15. For information on mixed-use buildings, see page 355. For information on which code to consult, see pages 7, 13.

Unit Conversion

$1 \ m^2 = 10.76$ sq ft.

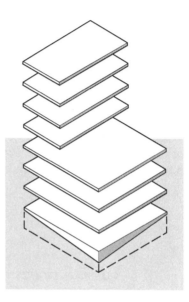

CONSTRUCTION TYPE

			Combustible							
1-Hour (page 368)		**Heavy Timber** (page 366)		**¾-Hour** (page 368)		**Unprotected** (page 368)				
Spr	Unspr	Spr	Unspr	Spr	Unspr	Spr	Unspr			
								UH		**HEIGHT IN STORIES,**
								6		**AND MAXIMUM AREA**
								5		**PER FLOOR IN M²**
1,800								4		
2,400	800	1,800	600	1,800	600	600[b]	600[b]	3		
3,600	1,200	2,700	900	2,700	900	600[b]	600[b]	2		
7,200	2,400	5,400	1,800	5,400	1,800	600[b]	600[b]	1		

This table was compiled from information contained in the National Building Code of Canada 2005. It does not represent an official interpretation by the organization that issues this code.

OCCUPANCY GROUP D: BUSINESS AND PERSONAL USES

Basements

Basements must be fully sprinklered or subdivided by fire separations into areas not more than 600 m² (6460 sq ft). A fire separation is also required between a basement and the floor above, and if there is more than one story below grade, between every below-grade story.

Excess Frontage

For unsprinklered buildings, except as noted in the table, the tabulated areas shown below may be increased by 25% if the building faces at least two streets, and by 50% if facing at least three.

Fire Walls

For multiplication of the allowable area by subdividing the building with fire walls, see page 358.

Measurements

Area is measured as the greatest horizontal area of a building above grade within the outside surfaces of the exterior walls, or between the outside surfaces of the exterior walls and the center line of a fire wall.

Further Information

For information on Occupancy Group classifications, see page 15. For information on mixed-use buildings, see page 355. For information on which code to consult, see pages 7, 13.

Unit Conversion

1 m² = 10.76 sq ft.

OCCUPANCY GROUP D: BUSINESS AND PERSONAL SERVICES

CONSTRUCTION TYPE		Noncombustible							
		2-Hour (page 364)		1-Hour (page 365)		¾-Hour (page 365)		Unprotected (page 366)	
		Spr	Unspr	Spr	Unspr	Spr	Unspr	Spr	Unspr
HEIGHT IN STORIES, AND MAXIMUM AREA PER FLOOR IN M²	UH	UA							
	6		2,400	7,200	2,400				
	5		2,880	8,640	2,880				
	4		3,600	10,800	3,600				
	3		4,800	14,400	4,800	4,800	1,600	4,800	1,600
	2		7,200ª	UA	7,200ª	7,200	2,400	7,200	2,400
	1		UA	UA	UA	14,400	4,800	14,400	4,800

Each number in the table represents the maximum area per floor in square meters for every floor of a building of that story height.

ªFor a building facing at least two streets, building area is unlimited.

Key to Abbreviations

UA	Unlimited area	Spr	With approved sprinkler system
UH	Unlimited height	Unspr	Without approved sprinkler system
NP	Not permitted		

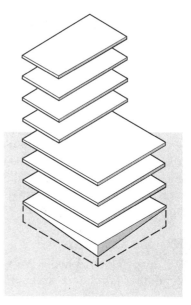

| Combustible | | | | | | | |
| 1-Hour (page 368) | | Heavy Timber (page 366) | | ¾-Hour (page 368) | | Unprotected (page 368) | |
Spr	Unspr	Spr	Unspr	Spr	Unspr	Spr	Unspr
3,600							
4,800	1,600	4,800	1,600	4,800	1,600		
7,200	2,400	7,200	2,400	7,200	2,400		
14,400	4,800	14,400	4,800	14,400	4,800	NP	NP

CONSTRUCTION TYPE

UH
6
5
4
3
2
1

HEIGHT IN STORIES, AND MAXIMUM AREA PER FLOOR IN M²

This table was compiled from information contained in the National Building Code of Canada 2005. It does not represent an official interpretation by the organization that issues this code.

HEIGHT AND AREA TABLES

443

OCCUPANCY GROUP E: MERCANTILE

Basements

Basements must be fully sprinklered or subdivided by fire separations into areas not more than 600 m^2 (6460 sq ft). A fire separation is also required between a basement and the floor above, and if there is more than one story below grade, between every below-grade story.

Excess Frontage

For unsprinklered two-story buildings, the tabulated areas shown below may be increased by 25% if the building faces at least two streets. For unsprinklered three-story buildings, the tabulated areas may be increased by 25% if the building faces at least two streets, and by 50% if facing at least three.

Fire Walls

For multiplication of the allowable area by subdividing the building with fire walls, see page 358.

Measurements

Area is measured as the greatest horizontal area of a building above grade within the outside surfaces of the exterior walls, or between the outside surfaces of the exterior walls and the center line of a fire wall.

Further Information

For information on Occupancy Group classifications, see page 15. For information on mixed-use buildings, see page 355. For information on which code to consult, see pages 7, 13.

Unit Conversion

1 m^2 = 10.76 sq ft.

OCCUPANCY GROUP E: MERCANTILE

CONSTRUCTION TYPE		Noncombustible							
		2-Hour (page 364)		1-Hour (page 365)		¾-Hour (page 365)		Unprotected (page 366)	
		Spr	Unspr	Spr	Unspr	Spr	Unspr	Spr	Unspr
HEIGHT IN STORIES, AND MAXIMUM AREA PER FLOOR IN M^2	UH	UA							
	6								
	5								
	4			1,800					
	3		800	1,800	800	2,400	800		
	2		1,200	1,800	1,200	3,600	1,200		
	1		1,500	1,800	1,500	7,200	1,500		

Each number in the table represents the maximum area per floor in square meters for every floor of a building of that story height.

Key to Abbreviations

UA	Unlimited area	Spr	With approved sprinkler system
UH	Unlimited height	Unspr	Without approved sprinkler system
NP	Not permitted		

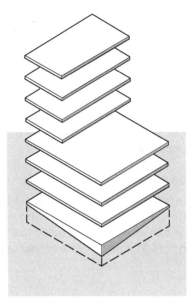

Combustible							
1-Hour **(page 368)**		**Heavy Timber** **(page 366)**		**¾-Hour** **(page 368)**		**Unprotected** **(page 368)**	
Spr	**Unspr**	**Spr**	**Unspr**	**Spr**	**Unspr**	**Spr**	**Unspr**
1,800							
1,800	800	2,400	800	2,400	800		
1,800	1,200	3,600	1,200	3,600	1,200		
1,800	1,500	7,200	1,500	7,200	1,500		

CONSTRUCTION TYPE

UH
6
5
4
3
2
1

HEIGHT IN STORIES, AND MAXIMUM AREA PER FLOOR IN M²

This table was compiled from information contained in the National Building Code of Canada 2005. It does not represent an official interpretation by the organization that issues this code.

HEIGHT AND AREA TABLES

445

OCCUPANCY GROUP F-1: INDUSTRIAL, HIGH HAZARD

Sprinklers

Provincial or local laws may require sprinklering of buildings in this Occupancy Group.

Basements

Basements must be fully sprinklered or subdivided by fire separations into areas not more than 600 m² (6460 sq ft). A fire separation is also required between a basement and the floor above, and if there is more than one story below grade, between every below-grade story.

Fire Walls

For multiplication of the allowable area by subdividing the building with fire walls, see page 358.

Measurements

Area is measured as the greatest horizontal area of a building above grade within the outside surfaces of the exterior walls, or between the outside surfaces of the exterior walls and the center line of a fire wall.

Further Information

For information on Occupancy Group classifications, see page 15. For information on mixed-use buildings, see page 355. For information on which code to consult, see pages 7, 13.

Unit Conversion

1 m² = 10.76 sq ft.

OCCUPANCY GROUP F-1: INDUSTRIAL, HIGH HAZARD

CONSTRUCTION TYPE	Noncombustible							
	2-Hour (page 364)		1-Hour (page 365)		¾-Hour (page 365)		Unprotected (page 366)	
HEIGHT IN STORIES, AND MAXIMUM AREA PER FLOOR IN M²	Spr	Unspr	Spr	Unspr	Spr	Unspr	Spr	Unspr
UH								
6								
5								
4	2,250							
3	3,000		1,200		1,200			
2	4,500		1,800		1,800		1,200	
1	9,000	800	3,600	800	3,600	800	2,400	800

Each number in the table represents the maximum area per floor in square meters for every floor of a building of that story height.

Key to Abbreviations

UA	Unlimited area	Spr	With approved sprinkler system
UH	Unlimited height	Unspr	Without approved sprinkler system
NP	Not permitted		

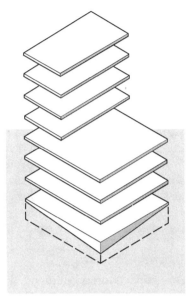

Combustible								
1-Hour (page 368)		**Heavy Timber** (page 366)		**¾-Hour** (page 368)		**Unprotected** (page 368)		
Spr	Unspr	Spr	Unspr	Spr	Unspr	Spr	Unspr	
								UH
								6
								5
								4
		1,200						3
		1,800		1,200				2
800	800	3,600	800	2,400	800	800	800	1

CONSTRUCTION TYPE

HEIGHT IN STORIES, AND MAXIMUM AREA PER FLOOR IN M²

This table was compiled from information contained in the National Building Code of Canada 2005. It does not represent an official interpretation by the organization that issues this code.

OCCUPANCY GROUP F-2: INDUSTRIAL, MEDIUM HAZARD

Basements

Basements must be fully sprinklered or subdivided by fire separations into areas not more than 600 m² (6460 sq ft). A fire separation is also required between a basement and the floor above, and if there is more than one story below grade, between every below-grade story.

Excess Frontage

For unsprinklered buildings of Noncombustible Unprotected Construction only, the tabulated areas shown below may be increased by 25% if the building faces at least two streets, and 50% if facing at least three. For all other unsprinklered Construction Types, excess frontage area increases are permitted for three-story buildings only, where when facing at least two streets, the area per floor may be increased to 1340 m² (14,424 sq ft), and when facing at least three streets, the area per floor may be increased to 1500 m² (16,146 sq ft).

Fire Walls

For multiplication of the allowable area by subdividing the building with fire walls, see page 358.

Measurements

Area is measured as the greatest horizontal area of a building above grade within the outside surfaces of the exterior walls, or between the outside surfaces of the exterior walls and the center line of a fire wall.

Further Information

For information on Occupancy Group classifications, see page 15. For information on mixed-use buildings, see page 355. For information on which code to consult, see pages 7, 13.

Unit Conversion

1 m² = 10.76 sq ft.

OCCUPANCY GROUP F-2: INDUSTRIAL, MEDIUM-HAZARD

CONSTRUCTION TYPE		Noncombustible							
		2-Hour (page 364)		1-Hour (page 365)		¾-Hour (page 365)		Unprotected (page 366)	
		Spr	Unspr	Spr	Unspr	Spr	Unspr	Spr	Unspr
HEIGHT IN STORIES, AND MAXIMUM AREA PER FLOOR IN M²	UH	UA							
	6								
	5								
	4			4,500		2,400			
	3		1,070	6,000	1,070	3,200	1,070		
	2		1,500	9,000	1,500	4,800	1,500	1,800	600
	1		1,500	18,000	1,500	9,600	1,500	4,500	1,000

Each number in the table represents the maximum area per floor in square meters for every floor of a building of that story height.

Key to Abbreviations

UA	Unlimited area	Spr	With approved sprinkler system
UH	Unlimited height	Unspr	Without approved sprinkler system
NP	Not permitted		

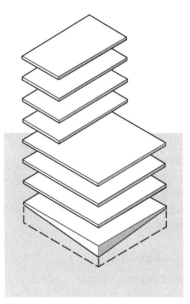

Combustible										
1-Hour **(page 368)**		**Heavy Timber** **(page 366)**		**¾-Hour** **(page 368)**		**Unprotected** **(page 368)**			**CONSTRUCTION TYPE**
Spr	Unspr	Spr	Unspr	Spr	Unspr	Spr	Unspr		
								UH	**HEIGHT IN STORIES,**
								6	**AND MAXIMUM AREA**
								5	**PER FLOOR IN M²**
2,400		2,400		2,400				4	
3,200	1,070	3,200	1,070	3,200	1,070			3	
4,800	1,500	4,800	1,500	4,800	1,500			2	
9,600	1,500	9,600	1,500	9,600	1,500	NP	NP	1	

This table was compiled from information contained in the National Building Code of Canada 2005. It does not represent an official interpretation by the organization that issues this code.

OCCUPANCY GROUP F-3: INDUSTRIAL, LOW HAZARD

Unlimited Area Buildings

Occupancy Group F-3 buildings, one story in height, of Noncombustible Construction, and used solely for low fire load occupancies such as power generating plants or the manufacture of noncombustible materials, may be unlimited in area.

Basements

Basements must be fully sprinklered or subdivided by fire separations into areas not more than 600 m^2 (6460 sq ft). A fire separation is also required between a basement and the floor above, and if there is more than one story below grade, between every below-grade story.

Vehicle Parking Garages

For enclosed parking garages, which rely on mechanical ventilation to prevent the accumulation of exhaust gasses, and for naturally ventilated open parking garages with other occupancies above, use the height and area tables on these two facing pages.

For open parking garages without other occupancy above, see Occupancy F-3: Open-Air Garages, pages 452–453. For private garages attached to Group C Occupancy dwelling units, see pages 440–451. For special height and area provisions for mixed-use, below-grade parking with other occupancies above, see page 355.

The minimum clear height within parking garage tiers is 2 m (6'-7"). Every story of a below-grade garage must be sprinklered, except where the story is open-air. For more information on the design of parking facilities, see Designing for Parking, beginning on page 311.

Excess Frontage

For unsprinklered buildings, the tabulated areas shown below may be increased by 25% if the building faces at least two streets, and by 50% if facing at least three.

Fire Walls

For multiplication of the allowable area by subdividing the building with fire walls, see page 358.

OCCUPANCY GROUP F-3: INDUSTRIAL, LOW HAZARD

CONSTRUCTION TYPE		Noncombustible							
		2-Hour (page 364)		1-Hour (page 365)		¾-Hour (page 365)		Unprotected (page 366)	
		Spr	Unspr	Spr	Unspr	Spr	Unspr	Spr	Unspr
HEIGHT IN STORIES, AND MAXIMUM AREA PER FLOOR IN M^2	UH	UA							
	6		2,400	7,200	2,400				
	5		2,880	8,640	2,880				
	4		3,660	10,800	3,660	3,600	1,200	3,600	1,200
	3		4,800	14,400	4,800	4,800	1,600	4,800	1,600
	2		7,200	21,600	7,200	7,200	2,400	7,200	2,400
	1		UA	UA	UA	14,400	4,800	14,400	4,800

Each number in the table represents the maximum area per floor in square meters for every floor of a building of that story height.

Key to Abbreviations

UA	Unlimited area	Spr	With approved sprinkler system
UH	Unlimited height	Unspr	Without approved sprinkler system
NP	Not permitted		

Measurements

Area is measured as the greatest horizontal area of a building above grade within the outside surfaces of the exterior walls, or between the outside surfaces of the exterior walls and the center line of a fire wall.

Further Information

For information on Occupancy Group classifications, see page 15. For information on mixed-use buildings, see page 355. For information on which code to consult, see pages 7, 13.

Unit Conversion

$1 \text{ m}^2 = 10.76$ sq ft.

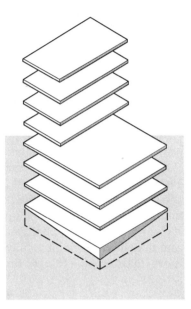

| Combustible | | | | | | | | | | CONSTRUCTION TYPE |
| 1-Hour (page 368) | | Heavy Timber (page 366) | | ¾-Hour (page 368) | | Unprotected (page 368) | | | | |
Spr	Unspr	Spr	Unspr	Spr	Unspr	Spr	Unspr			
								UH		HEIGHT IN STORIES, AND MAXIMUM AREA PER FLOOR IN M²
								6		
								5		
3,600	1,200	3,600	1,200	3,600	1,200			4		
4,800	1,600	4,800	1,600	4,800	1,600			3		
7,200	2,400	7,200	2,400	7,200	2,400			2		
14,400	4,800	14,400	4,800	14,400	4,800	16,800	5,600	1		

This table was compiled from information contained in the National Building Code of Canada 2005. It does not represent an official interpretation by the organization that issues this code.

HEIGHT AND AREA TABLES

OCCUPANCY GROUP F-3: OPEN-AIR GARAGES

Special Requirements

Garages as shown in the table below must have at least 25% of their perimeter open in a manner that provides cross ventilation to the entirety of each floor, may not be more than 22 m (72 ft) high, measured from grade to the underside of the top-level ceiling, may have no other occupancy above, and may have no point on any floor more than 60 m (197 ft) from an exterior wall opening. For garages not meeting these criteria, see the height and area requirements for Occupancy F-3, Industrial, Low Hazard, pages 450–451.

The minimum vertical clear height within parking garage tiers is 2 m (6'-7"). For more information on the design of parking facilities, see Designing for Parking, beginning on page 311.

Fire Walls

For multiplication of the allowable area by subdividing the building with fire walls, see page 358.

Measurements

Area is measured as the greatest horizontal area of a building above grade within the outside surfaces of the exterior walls, or between the outside surfaces of the exterior walls and the center line of a fire wall.

Further Information

For information on Occupancy Group classifications, see page 15. For information on mixed-use buildings, see page 355. For information on which code to consult, see pages 7, 13.

OCCUPANCY GROUP F-3: OPEN-AIR GARAGES

CONSTRUCTION TYPE		Noncombustible							
		2-Hour (page 364)		1-Hour (page 365)		¾-Hour (page 365)		Unprotected (page 366)	
		Spr	Unspr	Spr	Unspr	Spr	Unspr	Spr	Unspr
HEIGHT IN STORIES, AND MAXIMUM AREA PER FLOOR IN M²	UH	10,000	10,000	10,000	10,000	10,000	10,000	10,000	10,000
	6	10,000	10,000	10,000	10,000	10,000	10,000	10,000	10,000
	5	10,000	10,000	10,000	10,000	10,000	10,000	10,000	10,000
	4	10,000	10,000	10,000	10,000	10,000	10,000	10,000	10,000
	3	10,000	10,000	10,000	10,000	10,000	10,000	10,000	10,000
	2	10,000	10,000	10,000	10,000	10,000	10,000	10,000	10,000
	1	10,000	10,000	10,000	10,000	10,000	10,000	10,000	10,000

Each number in the table represents the maximum area per floor in square meters for every floor of a building of that story height.

Key to Abbreviations

UA	Unlimited area	Spr	With approved sprinkler system
UH	Unlimited height	Unspr	Without approved sprinkler system
NP	Not permitted		

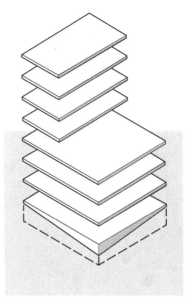

Combustible									
1-Hour (page 368)		Heavy Timber (page 366)		¾-Hour (page 368)		Unprotected (page 368)			CONSTRUCTION TYPE
Spr	Unspr	Spr	Unspr	Spr	Unspr	Spr	Unspr		
								UH	HEIGHT IN STORIES, AND MAXIMUM AREA PER FLOOR IN M²
								6	
								5	
								4	
								3	
								2	
NP	NP	NP	NP	NP	NP	NP	NP	1	

This table was compiled from information contained in the National Building Code of Canada 2005. It does not represent an official interpretation by the organization that issues this code.

HEIGHT AND AREA TABLES

APPENDIX A
EXAMPLE USE OF THIS BOOK

The following example illustrates the use of this book to complete the preliminary design of a building's technical systems. For a more brief explanation of approaches to using this text, see How to Use This Book, page ix.

THE PROBLEM

You are beginning the design of a suburban office building on a large site. Preliminary design assumptions are:

- A three-story structure
- Building area of 86,000 sq ft per floor
- Structural column bays 30 ft × 34 ft, to work well with office furniture system modules
- A floor to ceiling height of about 9'-6"
- A fully sprinklered building.

BUILDING CODE AND OCCUPANCY

We refer first to Designing with Building Codes. On page 7, we determine that our building should be designed to the requirements of the International Building Code. Referring to the Index of Occupancies on page 10, we see that Business Offices are classified as Occupancy Group B, Business. To learn more about this Occupancy Group, we also review its description on page 7 and verify that this Occupancy Group is the appropriate choice for our project.

BUILDING HEIGHT AND AREA LIMITS

Next, we refer to the introductory material on building code height and area limitations on page 350. Reading from the table on that page, we note that requirements for International Building Code Occupancy Group B buildings can be found on pages 382–383. Turning to these pages, we note that the area figures provided in the table are for all floors of a building. The total area of our proposed building is 258,000 sq ft (86,000 sq ft per floor × 3 floors).

Reading from the table, we determine that our building must use at least Type II-A 1-Hour Construction. Noting that the fire walls may be used to subdivide the building and allow use of a less expensive Construction Type, we turn to page 358 to learn more about this possibility. We present this option to our client, but they do not want to divide the building with a fire wall, so we proceed with Type II-A as the required Construction Type.

CONSTRUCTION TYPE

Following the page references in the height and area table for Type II-A Construction, we turn to page 365 and determine that we can use any of the following construction methods:

- Structural steel with 1 hour of fire protection
- Sitecast concrete or precast concrete, with minimum sizes of components as noted in the text

- Light-gauge steel
- Masonry

SELECTING A STRUCTURAL SYSTEM

We turn to pages 21–33 for advice on selecting a structural system. Light gauge steel and masonry are rejected because of the long spans required for our design. Other factors that seem most important for this project are minimizing erection time during construction and providing concealed spaces for mechanical and electrical services, which will be large and complex in this building. We decide to proceed with structural steel, which satisfies these requirements and tends to be economical in the location where we are building. Turning to page 29, we verify that structural steel can easily span the 30 × 34 ft dimensions assumed for our standard structural bay.

CONFIGURING THE STRUCTURAL SYSTEM

Reviewing pages 37–45, we determine that our structure should be a column and beam system. Economical options for achieving lateral stability include shear wall, braced frame, or a system using semirigid joints in combination with one of the former. With these options, we are satisfied that we will be able to include the necessary elements to achieve lateral stability in our structure without difficulty.

SIZING THE STRUCTURAL SYSTEM

Columns

The page references at the top of the chart on pages 26–27 refer us to pages 93 and 98–107 for information on sizing steel structures. After reviewing the introductory information on page 93, we turn to pages 98-99 for the sizing of structural steel columns. A ground floor column is the most critical, as it supports a total tributary area of two floors plus one roof times the size of a column bay, or 3,060 sq ft (3 levels × 30 ft × 34 ft).

The normal-height column chart on page 99 indicates that a W8 or W10 column is required. For preliminary purposes, we will assume a W10 column and note its dimensions as 10 in. by 8 in. On upper floors, we will also use a lighter-weight version of the W10 shape. Maintaining the same nominal size will simplify connections between column sections. (Alternatively, our fabricator and erector may opt to use a single piece, three stories high, for each column.)

Decking

Next, we turn to pages 102–103 for steel floor and roof decking, and determine that decking spans in the range of 6 to 9 ft are most practical. We will return to these pages to determine the final floor slab thickness after we investigate further the framing of beams and girders.

Bay Framing and Floor Slab

Turning to page 104, we look at a beam and girder framing and note the recommendation to span girders the short direction of the structural bay, or, in our case, in the 30-ft direction. For beam spacing, first we consider placing beams at third points along the girder. This results in a beam spacing of 10 ft, somewhat

outside the optimal span for floor decking established in the previous step. Next, we try placing beams at quarter points of the girder span, resulting in a beam spacing of 7.5 ft, a distance comfortably within the span range of floor decking recommended earlier. Returning to page 103, we see that we will need 2-in. metal decking and a total slab depth of about 5 in. including the concrete topping. Roof decking will be about 1½ in. deep.

Sizing of Beams and Girders

Next, we turn to pages 104-105 for the sizing of beams and girders. Reading from the chart, we see that beams spanning 34 ft will need to be 18 or 21 in. deep. Alternatively, with composite construction, this depth could be reduced to approximately 16 in. We decide on an 18-in.-deep beam. Girders spanning 30 ft need to be at least 18 in. deep. We will increase this to a lighter-weight section 21 in. deep to facilitate the connection with the 18-in.-deep beams.

TO SUMMARIZE:

- Structural bay: 30 ft × 34 ft
- Girders: 21-in.-deep, span 30 ft
- Beams: 18 in. deep, span 34 ft, spacing 7.5 ft
- Decking: 2 in. deep, 5-in.-deep total floor slab
- Columns: 10 in. × 8 in.

DAYLIGHTING

We wish to investigate how the use of daylighting may affect the shape of our building. Using the tabs on the page edges, we find the Daylighting chapter. On page 149, we determine that our site is open and does not have any significant obstructions to daylight. On page 151, we note that an elongated plan

that puts work areas within approximately 30 ft of windows is recommended. This is further explained on pages 152–153. Considering our building, if it were two bays at 30 ft wide each, or 60 ft wide total, it would be 1400 ft long, over a quarter of a mile. Alternatively, we could build to four or five stories, or we could arrange the plan of the building with many branches, as illustrated in the plan diagrams.

On a more detailed level, we note that light shelves could help to control light distribution (page 157), and that we should try to keep window heads as high as possible (page 159). On the uppermost floor, toplighting may be a good option to consider.

In conclusion, we will explore building designs as long and slender as practical, in order to place the highest number of workers within daylit distance of outside walls. We will also keep window heads as high as possible. After the building design has progressed further and basic floor plans and sections have been prepared, we will return to this section to carry the daylighting design farther.

MECHANICAL AND ELECTRICAL EQUIPMENT

HVAC Systems

We turn to page 166 to begin the design of our mechanical and electrical systems. Typical choices of HVAC systems are given on pages 170–171. For office buildings, VAV, VAV induction, multizone, and hydronic convectors are listed as recommended options. We will have plenty of space for ductwork, which rules out the need for VAV induction. Multizone is too complex for this simple, economical building. Hydronic convectors are an auxiliary system that we may wish to use in conjunction with VAV. We select VAV.

Pages 174–175 describe a VAV system and its variants and list the major components of the system for which we must find space. VAV box dimensions are given here, but the sizes of the rest of the components will be found elsewhere in this section.

Can we use a packaged system? Suppose that we want to restrict duct runs to 120 ft for economy of operation. This means that each fan room or packaged unit can service an area 240 ft long (ducts run in two opposite directions). For a building 1400 ft long, we would need six zones, each with its own fan room or packaged unit. Each zone would contain 43,000 sq ft on three floors (258,000 sq ft / six zones). Consulting the sizing chart on page 216, to which we are referred by the note on page 175, we discover that these zones are too large for the largest single-packaged unit.

Proceeding with a fan room solution, we turn to the chart on page 218 to determine the sizes of major components of the air handling system. We assume one fan room per zone, serving all three floors in that zone. We read from this chart that for a floor area of 43,000 sf, 50,000 cfm of air is required for cooling. Main supply and return ducts will total about 30 sq ft each. If on each floor two main supply ducts are used, each duct will have to be about 5 sq ft (30 sq ft / three floors / two ducts per floor) in area. At a depth of 18 in., each duct will be about 3½ ft wide. Branch ducts will total about 50 sq ft in area for all three floors.

Reading further down on the same chart, each fan room will occupy about 1500 sq ft of floor area, and will need about 130 sf of fresh air louver and about 100 sf of exhaust air louver. To minimize ductwork for these items, we will try to locate fan rooms as close as possible to outside wall locations.

Pages 190–191 give additional information on fan rooms and ductwork arrangements.

Returning to the chart on page 216, we determine that each zone requires 130 tons of cooling and a mechanical room for the boiler and chiller 1000 sq ft in area. On page 186 is a more detailed description of this facility. Note the need for a chimney. In addition, 200 sq ft of the roof will be occupied by a cooling tower, as shown and described on page 187.

PLENUM SPACE AND FLOOR-TO-FLOOR HEIGHT

Assuming that most horizontal distribution of services will be above the ceiling, we need to determine the depth of the plenum. Page 214 tells us that we need 20 in. of plenum height beneath the girders. We have previously determined that the girders will be 21 in. deep and the floor slab and decking 5 in. deep, for a total of 26 in. Adding the depths of structure and plenum, we arrive at a total depth of 46 in., or 3'-10".

A ceiling height of about 9'-6" is desired. Adding the 3'-10" plenum to this, we arrive at a floor-to-floor height of about 13'-4".

BUILDING EGRESS AND CIRCULATION

Again starting with the page-edge index marks, we go to pages 253–265 for general definitions and advice on egress layout.

Occupant Load

To size the egress components, we need to know the occupant load of the building. This is found using page 283. For a business use, an occupant load of 100 sq ft per occupant is specified. Thus, the egress system on each floor must be

designed to accommodate 860 occupants (86,000 sq ft per floor / 100 sq ft per occupant).

Egress System

On page 259, we find that we must provide a minimum of three exits from each floor. If the building is 1400 ft long, three exits will give a maximum travel distance of 350 ft. On page 284, we see that the maximum distance to the nearest exit is 300 ft in a sprinklered Business Occupancy building. Therefore, we must provide at least four exits. We decide that for convenience and safety, we will provide six exits.

With six exits, the occupant load per exit is 143 (860 occupants per floor / six exits per floor). Referring to page 286, we see that we must provide 0.15 in. of width per occupant for doors, corridors, and ramps and 0.2 in. per occupant for stairs. We can either work this out arithmetically or use the chart on page 287. For example, for exit stairs, the required width based on the number of occupants is 28.6 in. (143 occupants x 0.2 in. per occupant). But page 285 tells us that the stair may not be less than 44 in. when serving more than 50 occupants. We will use 44-in. stairs.

Exit Stairway Design

Now we can determine how big each stair tower is. We go to the Two-Flight Exit Stairway Design Table on page 302. Earlier, we calculated our floor-to-floor height to be 11'-4". The table tells us that we will have 20 risers at 6.80 in., with treads at 11 in. The inside length of the stairway will be 15'-7". The width will be twice 44 in. plus a center space or wall if we wish it; we assume a 6-in. center wall to arrive at a width of 94 in., or 7'-10". If we assume 8-in. walls around the stair, the outside dimensions of the stairway will be 16'-11" by 9'-2".

Elevators

Page 207 tells us that we need one elevator for every 35,000 sq ft served. Our building has 258,000 sq ft of floor area, but the ground floor does not need to be considered as a served floor. So the served area is 172,000 sq ft ($\frac{2}{3}$ × 258,000 sq ft). Dividing 172,000 sq ft by 35,000 sq ft yields 4.9, which we round up to five elevators required. We may want to distribute these in banks of two elevators each to minimize waiting times, which would require six elevators as a minimum.

If we use 3000-lb elevators, we see from the table on the same page that each shaft must have at least 8'-4" by 7'-5" inside clear dimensions. If we add to this shaft walls 4 in. thick, the overall shaft dimensions are 9'-0" by 8'-1".

Further advice on elevators and elevator lobbies is offered on the following pages.

Accessible Routes

Information on accessibility is provided on pages 266-268. We note that accessibility requirements do apply to our building and that at least 60% of its entrances must be accessible. Accessible egress will be provided by elevators and stairways, with adjacent areas of refuge. As our design develops, we will also be sure to meet the requirements for minimum widths of accessible routes, latchside door clearances, and so on.

ANCILLARY SPACES

Transformers and Switchgear Rooms

We will need one or more large transformers to reduce high transmission voltages to lower voltages for use in our building. Pages 188-189 indicate that these may be either mounted on concrete pads at ground level or placed in transformer vaults underground. The sizes required for underground vaults are large, and we realize that pad mounting will be more economical. The largest floor area listed per transformer pad is 180,000 sq ft, which can serve more than half the floor area of our building. We will look for good locations for at least two transformer pads just outside the walls of the building.

The diagrams on page 189 indicate that each pad will require a switchgear room. If we use two transformers and switchgear rooms, each will serve 129,000 sq ft. The accompanying table says that a 100,000 sq ft building needs a room 30 ft by 20 ft in plan dimension by 11 ft tall. We may need a room somewhat larger than this, say 30 ft by 30 ft. As noted in the text on this page, each switchgear room should be on an outside wall to facilitate ventilation.

Electrical Closets

Electrical closets are described on page 199; no point on any floor should be more than 125 ft from a closet. We will look at our floor plans with this in mind. Additionally, one telecommunication closet is needed for every 10,000 sq ft of floor area, meaning that we will need to provide about 25 of them distributed around the building. These should be aligned above one another on the three floors. Thus, we note that we will need about eight closets per floor, each about 10 ft by 12 ft in area. Given the rapid changes in telecommunications services, this assumption should be reviewed at an early date by technical personnel familiar with the industry.

Toilets

Toilet facilities may be sized and planned with the aid of the charts on pages 201-203.

PARKING

If provision for parking is required, information on the preliminary design of parking facilities can be found on pages 313–354.

WHERE THIS BRINGS US

In an hour or two, with this book as our consultant, we have made preliminary decisions in every technical area that impacts the configuration of the building we are about to design:

■ We have selected a structural system and assigned approximate sizes to its members.

■ We are aware of the requirements for daylighting the building.

■ We have made a tentative choice of an HVAC system and know the sizes and locations of its major components.

■ We know the requirements for egress from the building, including the sizes of the stair enclosures.

■ We know the number and size of elevators and have determined requirements for accessibility.

■ We have determined the floor-to-floor height and the depth of the ceiling plenum space.

■ We know the required components of the electrical and telecommunications systems, their locations, and their sizes.

■ We have sized the toilet facilities and, if needed, allocated space for parking.

Thus, we are ready to launch the process of finding a good form for the building, knowing that we will make adequate provisions for all of its major systems.

APPENDIX B
UNITS OF CONVERSION

ENGLISH (U.S. Customary Units)	METRIC	METRIC	ENGLISH (U.S. Customary Units)
1 in.	25.4 mm	1 mm	0.0394 in.
1 ft	304.8 mm	1 m	39.37 in.
1 ft	0.3048 m	1 m	3.2808 ft
1 lb	0.454 kg	1 kg	2.205 lb
1 ft^2	0.0929 m^2	1 m^2	10.76 ft^2
1 psi	6.89 kPa	1 kPa	0.145 psi
1 lb/ft^2	4.884 kg/m^2	1 kg/m^2	0.205 lb/ft^2
1 lb/ft^3	16.019 kg/m^3	1 kg/m^3	0.0624 lb/ft^3
1 ft/min	0.0051 m/sec	1 m/sec	196.85 ft/min
1 cfm	0.0005 m^3/sec	1 m^3/sec	2119 cfm
1 BTU	1.055 kJ	1 kJ	0.9479 BTU
1 BTU	3.9683 kcal	1 kcal	0.252 BTU
1 BTUH	0.2928 W	1 W	3.412 BTUH

$$1 \text{ Pa} = 0.102 \text{ kg/m}^2$$
$$1 \text{ kg/m}^2 = 9.80 \text{ Pa}$$

BIBLIOGRAPHY

The following references are recommended as starting points for additional information. Website addresses are provided for organizations that offer additional resources.

DESIGNING THE STRUCTURE

For a comprehensive treatment of structural design and analysis: Daniel L. Schodeck. *Structures* (5th ed.). Upper Saddle River, New Jersey, Pearson Prentice Hall, 2004.

For a comprehensive treatment of construction materials and methods: Allen, Edward and Joseph Iano. *Fundamentals of Building Construction* (4th ed.). Hoboken, New Jersey, John Wiley & Sons, Inc., 2004.

For wood construction: American Wood Council. *Allowable Stress Design Manual for Engineered Wood Construction (2001)*. American Wood Council, division of the American Forest & Paper Association, 2001 (Website: http:// www.awc.org); Emmanuel Desurvire. *Timber Construction Manual* (5th ed.). Hoboken, New Jersey, John Wiley & Sons, Inc., 2004. Also highly recommended is the literature published by APA–The Engineered Wood Association (Website: http://www.apawood.org).

For brick and concrete masonry construction: Brick Industry Association. *Technical Notes on Brick Construction*. Reston, Virginia, various dates (Website: http:// www.bia.org); James E. Amrhein. *Reinforced Masonry Engineering Handbook*. Torrance, California, Masonry Institute of America, 1998 (Website: http://www.masonryinstitute.org); National Concrete Masonry Association. *TEK Manual— Concrete Masonry Design and Construction*. Herndon, Virginia, various dates (Website: http://www.ncma .org); American Concrete Institute. *Building Code Requirements for Masonry Structures (ACI 530-05)*. Farmington Hills, Minnesota, American Concrete Institute, 2005.

For steel construction: American Institute of Steel Construction. *Steel Construction Manual* (13th ed.). Chicago, Illinois, American Institute of Steel Construction, 2006 (Web site: http://www.aisc.org/); The American Iron and Steel Institute provides numerous technical resources for the design of light gauge steel framing (Website: http://www.steel.org).

Iyad M. Alsamsam and Mahmoud E. Kamara. *Simplified Design, Reinforced Concrete Buildings of Moderate Size and Height* (3rd ed.). Skokie, Illinois, Portland Cement Association, 2004 (Website: http:// www.cement.org); Precast Concrete Institute. *PCI Design Handbook—Precast and Prestressed Concrete,* (6th ed.). Chicago, Illinois, Precast Concrete Institute, 2004; for concrete construction: American Concrete Institute. *ACI Manual of Concrete Practice 2006*. Farmington Hills, Minnesota, American Concrete Institute, 2006 (Website: http:// www.concrete.org).

DESIGNING FOR DAYLIGHTING

N. Baker, and K. Steemers. *Daylight Design of Buildings, A Handbook for Architects and Engineers*. London, Earthscan Publications, 2001; G. Ander, *Daylighting Performance and Design*. Hoboken, New Jersey, John Wiley & Sons, Inc., 2003.

DESIGNING SPACES FOR MECHANICAL AND ELECTRICAL SYSTEMS

S. Kavanaugh. *HVAC Simplified*. Atlanta, Georgia, American Society of Heating, Refrigerating and Air Conditioning, 2006; B. J. S. Stein, W. T. Reynolds, Grondzik, and A. G. Kwok. *Mechanical and Electrical Equipment for Buildings* (10th ed.). Hoboken, New Jersey, John Wiley & Sons, Inc., 2006.

DESIGNING FOR EGRESS AND ACCESSIBILITY

Francis D. K. Ching and Steven R. Winkel. *Building Codes Illustrated*. Hoboken, New Jersey, John Wiley & Sons, Inc., 2007; International Code Council. *Accessible and Usable Buildings and Facilities 2003 (ICC/ANSI A117.1-2003)*. Country Club Hills, Illinois, International Code Council, Inc., 2003; National Fire Protection Association. *NFPA 101 Life Safety Code 2006*. Quincy, Massachusetts, National Fire Protection Association, 2006.

BIBLIOGRAPHY

DESIGN FOR PARKING

ULI-Urban Land Institute and NPA-National Parking Association. *The Dimensions of Parking* (4th ed.). Washington, D.C., ULI-Urban Land Institute, 2000; A. P. Chrest, M. S. Smith, S. Bhuyan, D. R. Monahan, and M. Iqbal. *Parking Structures* (3rd ed.). Norwell, Massachusetts, Kluwer Academic Publishers, 2004.

BUILDING CODES

National Research Council of Canada. *National Building Code of Canada, 2005*. Ottawa, National Research Council of Canada, 2005; International Code Council. *International Building Code 2006*. Country Club Hills, Illinois, International Code Council, Inc., 2006.

INDEX

INDEX

INDEX

INDEX

INDEX

INDEX